POLITICS AND GOVERNMENT IN THE UNITED STATES

Emmette S. Redford
University of Texas

David B. Truman
Columbia University

Alan F. Westin
Columbia University

Robert C. Wood
Massachusetts Institute of Technology

Alan F. Westin   COORDINATING EDITOR

Politics
and
Government
in
the
United
States

SECOND EDITION

National Edition

HARCOURT, BRACE & WORLD, INC.
New York / *Chicago* / *San Francisco* / *Atlanta*

PHOTO CREDITS

COVER		Blueprint of the Capitol, showing the House Chamber at the top, the Rotunda in the middle, and the Senate Chamber at the bottom.
PART	I	Henri Cartier-Bresson from Magnum
	II	Cornell Capa from Magnum
	III	White House
	IV	Bruce Davidson from Magnum
	V	Wide World

ACKNOWLEDGMENTS

W. H. ALLEN & COMPANY—For excerpt from Richard M. Nixon, *Six Crises*, reprinted by permission.

ASHLEY FAMOUS AGENCY, INC.—For excerpts from Ray C. Bliss, "The Role of the State Chairman," and John F. Kennedy, "Why Go Into Politics?" in James M. Cannon, ed., *Politics U.S.A.* Reprinted by permission of Ashley Famous Agency, Inc. Copyright © 1960 by James M. Cannon. All rights reserved.

BEACON PRESS—For excerpt from Ben H. Bagdikian, *In the Midst of Plenty*, reprinted by permission of the Beacon Press, copyright © 1964 by Ben H. Bagdikian.

THE CHRISTIAN SCIENCE MONITOR—For excerpt from Josephine Ripley, "Children's Bureau Shift Fought," reprinted by permission from *The Christian Science Monitor.* © 1967 The Christian Science Publishing Society. All rights reserved.

ACKNOWLEDGMENTS continue on p. 798.

PREFACE

As the preface to the first edition of *Politics and Government in the United States* explained, we believe that the rise of television in recent years, coupled with the improvement of high school social studies courses, has greatly increased the exposure of college freshmen and sophomores to political events—nominating conventions, State of the Union messages, presidential press conferences, and election-night analyses.

We have tried to respond to this new level of student sophistication by reproducing in textbook form the reality of daily political analysis—the sort of discourse that occurs among public officials in weighing policy alternatives or among political scientists in evaluating government decisions. We believe that the complexity of the American political system can best be conveyed through an integrated treatment of its three main aspects: the *process* of politics, the *structure* of government institutions, and the substantive *policies* that emerge from the interaction between institutions and politics.

The second edition continues the integrated treatment of process, structure, and policies, but it differs from the first edition in three other respects. First, we have made the text narrative roughly one-third shorter by simplifying language and by curtailing details and minor observations not directly relevant to the main points.

This method of streamlining has put stronger emphasis on the basic analytical themes of each chapter, while subordinating secondary points. Key concepts are further highlighted by a brief introduction at the beginning of each chapter and a point-by-point summary at the end.

Second, as the new part introductions suggest, we have adopted a political-systems framework to integrate the second edition. Chapter 1, consisting largely of new material, begins with a case study and discussion of the systems approach to politics. The student is offered three suggested guides for judging his own political system as he studies its operations. The rest of Part I explores the basic determinants of the American political system: our political culture and socioeconomic milieu, our Constitution and political institutions, and our characteristic responses to the pressures of social change since the founding of the Republic.

Part II, consisting wholly of new material, shows the effect of these basic determinants on the American political process: the development of interest groups and political parties as connecting links between the people and government; the organization, properties, and functions of interest groups and parties in a federal, constitutional system; and the distinctive patterns of American voting behavior.

Parts III and IV show how the basic features of our system influence the politics of our institutional arenas: the Presidency, the executive branch, Congress, and the courts.

The last two chapters of Part IV and all of Part V deal with the substantive policies produced by our system: the rights and benefits that American government has come to offer its citizens in response to demands made by individuals, groups, and the environment. Part V has been heavily revised to emphasize the "how" and "why" of the politics of government action.

Part VI (in the national, state, and local edition) applies the basic concepts of Parts I and II to the state and local political systems.

Third, the format of *Politics and Government* has been redesigned to provide a more leisurely, more readable page, and the cartoon program has been revised and updated. The balance between conservative and liberal cartoons has been paralleled by a new program of boxed quotations from primary sources, designed to expose students to a wide spectrum of political views and to illustrate the political process in action.

We believe that our approach to the second edition has allowed us to improve significantly our answers to three central questions of American government and politics: How does the American political system really work? *Why* does it work this way? And what changes in the system are likely in the coming years?

As for the division of responsibility among the authors in this edition, Part I is the work of Robert Wood (Chapter 1), Emmette Redford (Chapter 2), and Alan Westin (Chapter 3); Part II the work of Alan Westin (Chapters 4, 6, and 7) and Emmette Redford (Chapters 5 and 8); Part III of David Truman; Part IV of Alan Westin; Part V of Emmette Redford (except for Chapter 20, written by Robert Wood); and Part VI (national, state, and local edition) of Robert Wood.

Finally, we are grateful to Professors Hugh Douglas Price of Harvard University and Fred M. Greenstein of Wesleyan University for their detailed comments on the drafts of Part II, as well as to Professor Mark Kesselman of Columbia University for his reading of Chapter 2. We also warmly thank Nan Senior Robinson, who began as collaborator for Part VI of the national, state, and local edition, but whose insights, judgment, and style ultimately graced many parts of the book; Professor Caren Goretsky Dubnoff for her work on the boxed-insert program; Professor Richard E. Morgan of Columbia University for aid in Part II and in the revised bibliography; Mary O'Melveny for assistance with Chapter 3 and Part IV; and Donald Haider for assistance on Part III.

In addition, we are pleased to acknowledge the very helpful suggestions made by the following instructors based on their classroom experience with the first edition: Professors Rodney A. Bell and Orion White, Jr., at the University of Texas; Wilbourn E. Benton at Texas A&M University; Louellyn Cohan at the University of California (Davis); and John B. Palmer at Cerritos College.

EMMETTE S. REDFORD
DAVID B. TRUMAN
ALAN F. WESTIN
ROBERT C. WOOD

CONTENTS

I

**DEMOCRACY
AND THE
AMERICAN
WAY**

Part I introduces the framework of the book by showing how the concept of "political system" may be applied to the study of American government and politics. In this part we examine in detail the basic determinants, or components, of our political system. Chapter 1, which begins with a case study on passage of the model cities bill, discusses the systems approach and then goes on to examine the distinctive characteristics of our political system, our political culture, and our socioeconomic milieu. Chapter 2 explores another determinant of the system: our institutional framework, expressed primarily through the Constitution. Finally, Chapter 3 examines the instruments within the American political system for responding to technological and social pressures, and it explores the influence of our federal structure on our politics.

AMERICAN GOVERNMENT

System

and

Environment

1

What is "political" activity? This introductory
chapter examines the meaning of this term
and suggests that a useful way to study
American politics today is by "systems analysis."
What are the components of a political
system? How do systems interact with their
environments? The chapter then explores the
distinctive characteristics of the American
political system and our political culture.
How have the distinctive traits of our
society helped to stabilize our political
system? What impact have domestic and
international changes had on our political system
over the past two centuries? And, finally,
what dilemmas in the American style have
resulted from the interaction of system,
environment, and change?

MODEL CITIES: A CASE STUDY IN
POLITICAL PROCESS

On October 17, 1966, President Lyndon Johnson and his key foreign-policy advisers embarked on a seventeen-day trip to the Far East to consult with Asian allies on the Vietnam war.[1] The President left Washington with the belief that the bill he had termed "one of the most important pieces of legislation for the good of all mankind," the Demonstration Cities Act,[2] would receive final congressional approval within a matter of days. This bill incorporated several major urban-development measures recommended by the President at the opening of the 1966 congressional session. It authorized $24 million for planning grants in 1967 and 1968, to be followed by $900 million in 1968 and 1969 to set up programs for rebuilding slum neighborhoods and developing model neighborhoods in cities with heavy urban blight. The bill also authorized FHA mortgage insurance for developers of "new towns" or "new communities," set up $250 million of additional urban-renewal funds, and initiated "incentive" planning grants to encourage comprehensive urban planning throughout the country.

Like most pieces of major legislation, the bill for model cities depended for its success on complex interactions among the President and his executive agencies, legislative leaders, political parties, and interest groups. White House spokesmen, officials of the Department of Housing and Urban Development, key congressmen, and various business, labor, civic, religious, and urban leaders had worked closely together to mold the bill for passage by the Eighty-ninth Congress.

But hardly had the wheels of Air Force One left the ground when a series of frantic telephone calls began to circulate through Washington. The bill's sponsors suddenly faced the prospect of failure in the last round. Months of painstaking work, careful planning, artful compromise, and political pressure had suddenly come unglued over a procedural technicality. What had happened to threaten this bill at the last minute?

The Eighty-ninth Congress was one of the most liberal and reform minded in many decades; in addition to passing far-reaching welfare and civil-rights legislation (Medicare and voting rights, for example), this

---

[1] Material for this case study was drawn primarily from Robert B. Semple, Jr., "Signing of Model Cities Bill Ends A Long Struggle To Keep It Alive," New York Times, November 4, 1966. Other sources include: Business Week, October 29, 1966; Commonweal, March 11, 1966; Newsweek, October 24, 1966; Congressional Quarterly Almanac, 1966, Washington, D.C., 1967; Congress and the Nation, 1945–1964, Washington, D.C., 1965; Congressional Record, 89th Congress, 2nd Session, October 14, 17, 18, 20, 1966, Washington, D.C., 1966.

[2] Soon after passage this act was rechristened as "model cities," the name by which present activities and appropriations are designated.

Congress had already enacted two major pieces of housing legislation in 1965. The first was an omnibus bill that authorized federal aid for new construction and urban development, featuring a bold new program of rent supplements to low-income families who could not otherwise obtain adequate housing. The second bill had established a new cabinet agency, the Department of Housing and Urban Development, after years of defeat for similar proposals. Both measures had been passed by heavy Democratic majorities over the customary opposition of conservative Republicans, Southern Democrats, real-estate interests, and conservative business groups. By mid-1966 battle-weary congressmen, many facing reelection campaigns in which "white backlash" over civil rights would be a major issue, were reluctant to act on new housing proposals.

Ordinarily, a major presidential measure is aided by pressure on congressmen from powerful interest groups. Past housing legislation had received the support of such groups as the National Housing Conference, the United States Conference of Mayors, the National League of Cities, the National Association of Housing and Redevelopment Officials, and various labor and veterans' groups. But these traditional sources had given only tentative or ambivalent support to the Demonstration Cities Bill. In part, resistance was due to the bill's provisions of aid to large cities but not to smaller urban areas, suburbs, and rural communities. In part, traditionally supportive groups, such as builders, found the bill less financially beneficial to their interests than previous housing measures had been. In his original request, President Johnson had asked Congress for $2.3 billion over a developmental period of six years. Sixty to seventy participating cities were to be selected, using strict federal standards, to receive supplementary grants of up to 80 percent of the local share of all federal urban aid. These funds were to be spent on local programs to rehabilitate slum neighborhoods. The bill also provided that federal liaison personnel were to coordinate local efforts with federal agency programing guidelines. Provisions like these drew fire from ordinarily friendly groups like the mayors and the National Association of Home Builders.

Hearings were held from March to June of 1966 by the Housing Subcommittee of the House Committee on Banking and Currency. The new chairman of the subcommittee was Representative William Barrett, an "organization" Democrat from Philadelphia. Barrett faced strong Republican opposition to the bill in the subcommittee. Fearing that the President's original measure would never pass the House in a year when spending in Vietnam occupied the spotlight, and believing that the bill was not regarded as crucial by the President, Barrett accepted a revision of the bill reducing the Demonstration Cities program to a $12 million authorization for project-planning only. The appearance of this revised bill, supported by an informal majority in the subcommittee, precipitated a meeting on June 1 of government sponsors and congressional leaders in the office of Presidential Assistant Joseph Califano.

HUD Secretary Robert Weaver, the first Negro to serve in the Cabinet, came to this White House meeting determined to fight for the Demonstration Cities Bill. But others at the meeting were less convinced or less optimistic and said so. At this point, Postmaster General Lawrence O'Brien, congressional liaison for both the Johnson and Kennedy Administrations, delivered an impassioned speech on the issue. " I reminded them," O'Brien later told a reporter, "that this was a major piece of legislation and this just wasn't the way we operated around here. . . . I . . . had never before presided over the premature burial of one of the President's bills and . . . I wasn't about to begin. Everybody seemed to be looking around for the nearest hole to toss it in and I was just plain exasperated." O'Brien's fiery speech won over the group. They decided, first, to try to convince a majority of Barrett's subcommittee to support the original version of the bill; second, to enlist allies for the measure in the Senate; and, third, to establish a broad coalition of interest groups for grassroots support.

Secretary Weaver flew to Dallas on June 12 to address the annual meeting of the United States Conference of Mayors, whose mixed reactions to the bill had been partially prompted by fears that the funds required for "model neighborhoods" would cut into badly needed urban-renewal money. Weaver told the mayors that "For decades, important urban problems were dumped into the attic of the nation's conscience . . . [but now] the whole thrust of the Demonstration Cities Bill goes right to the heart of those most pressing needs. It is our best real chance for meeting those needs, and we must fight for it together, against those who would shortchange our cities in the name of bogus patriotism." Weaver strongly hinted that endorsement of Demonstration Cities by the mayors might produce White House support for additional urban-renewal funds. The mayors responded with a resolution urging strong support for both the objectives of the bill and the funds to carry them out. Other HUD officials engaged in intensive contacts with old friends as well as with potential new allies—homebuilders; mortgage bankers; representatives of the urban poor; health and welfare groups; and labor, business, religious, and civil-rights leaders—building "a new urban alliance" to contact congressmen in support of the bill.

Lawrence O'Brien also went to work. First, he sought the aid of Vice-President Hubert Humphrey, a veteran of many years in Congress and an experienced liberal legislator. Humphrey called Chairman Barrett to tell him that the Administration was very anxious to see the watered-down bill dropped. As a result of the Vice-President's call, Barrett postponed the hearings until June 21, giving Administration forces three crucial weeks to go to work. The new unity of the urban coalition, the shift of interest by the Conference of Mayors, and the demonstration of strong White House interest in the original bill produced a subcommittee majority, including Chairman Barrett, in favor of the Administration bill. On June 22, the subcommittee reported out a bill embodying almost all the President's original recommendations.

Knowing that a controversial measure would be unlikely to reach the floor of the House unless the Senate acted positively on it, the Administration sought a suitable manager to steer the bill through committee and floor debate in the Senate. O'Brien and Califano settled on Senator Edmund Muskie, a Democrat from Maine, an articulate speaker and an able parliamentarian, as well as a past victor with difficult legislation. Muskie had reservations about the bill; but, after the Administration forces changed it to allow smaller towns and cities to qualify for support, Muskie agreed on July 5 to accept responsibility for the Senate battle.

Republican efforts in the Senate against the bill were well coordinated and effective. The Senate subcommittee was divided, and the swing vote rested with a conservative Democrat, Thomas J. McIntyre of New Hampshire. Anticipating opposition to the bill, Muskie had drafted an amendment that would reduce authorized funds from $2.3 billion over six years to $900 million for two years. The Administration forces reluctantly agreed to this amendment: first, they recognized that even the original bill would have allocated only $900 million for the first two years; and, second, they realized that the bill would die in committee unless McIntyre could be persuaded to vote for the measure. Muskie's aide presented the amendment to Senator McIntyre, asking if he would consider offering it and noting that "the Administration says it's within the ballpark." McIntyre's acceptance was the compromise that kept the bill moving and allowed it to reach the floor. On August 19, the Senate passed the bill 53–22.

Two very different bills now existed in the House and Senate. Because the Senate version was more restrictive, the House committee reconvened to consider it, and on September 1, 1966, the full committee approved the Senate bill with a few minor changes. The two bills differed in five technical respects, on such matters as graduate fellowships, historic preservation, seasonal homes, and inserting the name of HUD in old housing laws. These differences were later to spark a crisis.

At this point, a decision was made that almost cost the bill its life. Although the Administration was anxious to take the House version to the floor immediately, Speaker John McCormack believed that since at least forty House votes were "doubtful," a delay would be helpful in marshaling additional grassroots support. But the delay created unanticipated problems. A rise in the price index and accompanying fears of inflation, plus the uncomfortable specter of "white backlash," caused some strong backers of the bill to become shaky. Meanwhile, a bitter fight on the bill was mounted by conservative Republican Paul Fino of the Bronx. Calling the bill a disguised civil-rights measure, he contended that sections of the bill would be used to justify "busing" children into integrated schools and federal rewriting of school boundaries. As support for the bill seemed to fade, majority whip Senator Hale Boggs of Louisiana suggested that the measure be postponed until the next session; Administration forces realized that they were again in trouble.

On October 6, 1966, another crisis meeting was held at the White House between congressional leaders and agency sponsors of the bill. Chairman of the House Banking and Currency Committee, Democrat Wright Patman of Texas suggested that perhaps another demonstration of strong presidential support was needed. Califano, designated to call Johnson, came back from the telephone with a smile and reported that the President had just responded to a question at a news conference by saying: "I believe there is no domestic problem that is more critical than the problem of rebuilding our cities and giving our people who live in the cities the opportunities to develop as healthy, educated, productive citizens of our society—citizens who have the ability to get and to hold jobs, and to take pride in the place in which they live." Favorable congressional action was also encouraged by the White House behind the closed doors of Speaker McCormack's office. There, reported *Newsweek* magazine, "a number of doubtful Democrats were asked what they needed in their districts. 'It isn't the kind of thing you talk about,' said one observer, 'but you wouldn't be wrong if you guessed that a lot of post offices, sewers, highways and other construction projects which had been hanging fire were promised.'" Another important demonstration of support came from the business world. On October 10, twenty-two leading corporate executives, including Henry Ford and David Rockefeller, issued a strong endorsement of the legislation.

During the harsh floor debate, Representative Fino's battle created such pressure that Administration forces accepted an amendment stipulating that the bill could not be used to improve racial balance in school districts. After defeating several attempts to kill the bill completely, the House finally approved the measure late on the evening of October 14, by a vote of 178–141.

The remaining obstacle seemed to be a matter of minor surgery—the meeting of a conference committee, composed of representatives from the House and Senate, to resolve the differences between the two bills. Breathing eased, victory smiles began to appear, and President Johnson went off on his Asian tour. However, the seasonal-homes provision, which had been inserted by the Senate and later dropped by the House, was reinstituted by the conference committee. Due to a procedural quirk, restoration of this provision in the conference version would require a fresh vote in the House on the conference report if the opponents of the bill requested it, and there was no doubt that they would do so. Since the session was almost over, this would have resulted in the death of the bill for that session. Yet, certain senators insisted that the seasonal-homes provision be included. Dismayed at the prospect of seeing ten months of intensive legislative work killed,

Administration forces once again took to the phones. As they talked, they tried to avoid the need to contact the President aboard his plane. They knew that he would be less than pleased to discover that his legislation was once again in difficulty, only a few short hours after his departure from the scene. Fortunately, HUD officials were able to persuade the Senate conferees to reconvene and drop the seasonal-homes provision. Leading Democrats on the housing subcommittee aided the Administration forces by assuring key senators that hearings would be held on the seasonal-homes plan early in 1967. On October 18, the Senate approved the conference version by a 38–22 roll-call vote, and the House followed suit on October 20, 142–126. The measure was then sent to the President for his signature.

On November 3, 1966, in the White House East Room, President Johnson signed the "Demonstration Cities Act of 1966" into law. The array of executive, legislative, and interest-group representatives assembled there shared responsibility for the success of a measure that, in the words of the President, provided "the tools to reach out into our environment and shape it to our will."

The sequence of events that led to the passage of the Demonstration Cities Act illustrates not only the complexity of the legislative process but the whole range of activities we refer to as "political." That is, they involve people engaged in influencing or directing actions of other people. The objectives and motivations of those wanting a particular outcome, the steps they take to assure it, the impact of these steps on other people, and *their* reactions in turn are all part of the political process.

STUDYING POLITICS

The key concept we use to explain political events is *power*. It specifies the kinds of relationships and acts involved, and it serves political science as the concept of "price" serves economics or "status" serves sociology. The economist uses the idea of price to explain how scarce material resources are allocated, and the sociologist relies on the notion of status to group people according to who they believe is superior to them and who is inferior. In the same way the political scientist asks who holds power in order to predict how a public crisis will be resolved.

Political scientists ask five key questions about political activity:

1. *Who is able to determine the actions of whom?* Who rules, and in what form: one man (a dictatorship), a class (an aristocracy), a group (an oligarchy), or a majority of the population (a democracy)?

2. *When?* Is political activity rare, periodic, or continual? Is it an avocation or a profession?

3. *How?* Does the government operate by means of physical superiority, persuasion, cajolery, deception, reason, or other resources?

4. *Through which characteristic channels of communication and contact?* Do government and public communicate primarily through riots, elections, legislative debates, or executive committees?

5. *With what characteristic outcomes?* What results from political activity—wars, treaties, legislative programs, administrative spending?

Politics, then, is a continuing association among people in which the central concern is the relative allocation of power, the tactics and skills needed to influence that allocation, and the purposes and outcomes of that allocation. This association goes forward under conditions of conflict and interdependency that shape the roles of the participants. The associations can be stable or unstable, the roles vary, and the relationships change frequently. But the central focus in these associations is always on the allocation of power.

Almost every association among people has a political dimension. There are family politics (Who wins when brother and sister make competing appeals to the parents?), office politics (Who gets the next promotion?), club politics (Why did the lady in the flowered hat become president of the Garden Club again?). But the focus of political science is larger: it involves the interaction of sizable numbers of people *within a specific geographical domain*. The individuals or groups involved may have different motivations and may represent divergent economic or social interests, but the consequences of political acts are territorial—that is, they apply to people within a specific jurisdiction.

Since political science focuses on "real" political acts that proceed in close sequence and involve many actors in complex relationships, the predominant way we study politics today is by systems analysis. That is, we examine the *relation* of concrete political events to other events over time. Hence, rather than study in detail the particular characteristics of a politician, a political institution, or a government, the political scientist focuses on a "system."

A *system* is composed of (1) *components*, with properties or characteristics capable of precise description, (2) *so related* that changes in the behavior of one component leads to changes in the behavior of others, operating within (3) *discrete* (though somewhat arbitrary) *boundaries*, that is, within a field or arena of action. In those ways, it resembles the systems and subsystems of the human body—circulatory, nervous, and digestive—and the gears, levers, and bands of a machine.

Thus, for example, Congress represents a political system consisting of 535 members, whose actions involve one another and whose principal concern is prescribed as legislative activity. Our federal structure of government also includes judicial, executive, state, local, and administrative systems. These are all *subsystems* of the American government system, which in turn can be considered a subsystem (though a very powerful one) of international politics.

There is still no complete agreement in political science as to the most appropriate names, categories, and classifications of political systems. Some political scientists emphasize the functions of particular structures, others the evolution of the political process over time; some concentrate on decision-making, others on the characteristics of the decision makers. In this book we view the essentials of a political system as scope, participants, objectives, roles, rules, and instruments.

The *scope* (boundaries) of the system refers to the activities with which the system is principally concerned—those its decisions govern and direct. Scope distinguishes the activities included within the jurisdiction of a system from those outside it, and scope defines the system's authority in relation to other political systems. Public education, public welfare, public highways define particular political boundaries.

The *participants* (components) in a system are those who seek to influence or direct its activities. Every political system has its specified elective officials—congressmen, governors, aldermen—its appointed administrators and permanent personnel, and its party officers and workers. In addition there are a host of other actors who try, formally or informally, to influence the system's decisions and activities: newspaper editors, veterans' organizations, chambers of commerce, labor unions, women's clubs, students. The smaller the area a government encompasses, the more likely it is that a relatively small number of participants are consistently influential.

The *objectives* (prime properties) the participants seek are conditioned by the character of the decisions involved, the traditions of the system, and the goals and relative influence of the other participants. A group's objectives often change with the passage of time: the goals of the labor movement in the 1960's, for example, are quite different from its goals in the 1930's. Similarly, a group's objectives change after it has achieved partial success: after the civil-rights movement secured Negro access to public facilities during the mid-1960's, it turned to voting rights and employment.

Finally, a political system is distinguished by the roles its participants assume, the rules under which the political game is played, and the instruments used to settle conflicts and to achieve compromise. In the American system the roles of political participants are defined, for example, by the predisposition of national and state governments for bicameral legislatures, independently elected executives, and separate judiciaries. The basic rules, or framework, of our system derive in large part from English common law. Some of the instruments of our system are devices such as primaries, recalls, and referendums, institutions such as party organizations and judicial actions.

It is not enough, however, to analyze the internal components of a political system or even its relationship with other systems. Systems operate within larger frameworks generally identified as *environments:* the conditioners and determinants of system behavior. The environment of a *political* system consists of the cultural and educational conditions that help determine who will join the political system, who will work for particular programs, and how the results of the system will be accepted. The environment can be thought of as providing the *inputs* and receiving the *outputs* of a system that is nothing more than a "black box"—a mysterious mechanism—to students of sociology or economics, but whose workings are critical to the political scientist.

Looking at political systems and subsystems within the framework of an economic or cultural or anthropological environment places emphasis on how things actually seem to work. This approach thus differs from political philosophy, which has historically been concerned with the development of abstract and ideal political patterns and the justification or advocacy of particular forms of government. Systems analysis seeks mainly to discover generalizations about contemporary political phenomena; it does not make normative judgments. Thus the goal of this book is to identify the principal characteristics of the American political *system* and to understand its operations within the distinctive American *environment*. On the other hand, the lines between empirical analysis and philosophical speculation are not clear cut, and commitments to particular political systems—democratic rule via persuasion in peaceful elections, for example—are evident in this book. Evident too is our preference for emphasizing the policy results of particular political processes, for inquiring about the consequences of particular political decisions for the populations involved.

THE AMERICAN POLITICAL SYSTEM

The American political system is characterized formally by explicit divisions of government authority according to function and territory. So we customarily speak of our system as based on a separation of powers among our legislative, executive, and judicial branches, on a federal plan for shared powers between national and state governments, and on a written constitution.

There are other distinctive characteristics of our politics: our preference for a two-party system as the vehicle for courting public opinion, our requirement of fixed periodic elections, our guarantee of free expression and communication of political opinion, and so forth.

Usually, however, five properties are singled out as distinctive to the American political system.

Popular Government

There is no question that our government is rooted in the consent of the governed. Deviations from this principle have persisted throughout our history in the special privileges accorded property owners and in the long-time exclusion of women, Negroes, and some others from the polls. But the political history of the United States can be read as an inexorable reduction of these barriers and a continuing expansion of the rights of political participation. Moreover, even the most cynical of politicians is intensely concerned with capturing the attention and affection of the voter.

This does not mean that all Americans are actively involved in politics or that minority rule does not occur. Machines, bosses, élites, courthouse rings are parts of our history, and in this country, unlike other free nations, the number of political activists is relatively small. Our voting turnout, for example, is among the lowest of the democracies in the world today. Our parties cannot manage to recruit more than a small fraction of the citizen body to work in campaigns, and even interest groups rely more on salaried lobbyists than on their members at the grassroots. But despite the distress it causes democratic idealists, this apathy may be a good sign: it may indicate that Americans are fundamentally content with the way they are being governed. This explanation is borne out by the fact that totalitarian movements have never been more than fringe groups in America, and extreme political positions are continually being modified to become acceptable to the moderate groups of the public.

Limited Government

While we are a democratic people, we are by no means prepared to let democratic government assume responsibility for the majority of social and economic functions. Alongside our commitment to a popular polity is our conviction that the public sphere should be a fundamentally limited one—excluded from many collective as well as private endeavors. This conviction stems not only from our colonial experience and from seventeenth-century philosophy but also from our success in achieving affluence through private efforts and organizations. Capitalism, property rights, and individualism combine to maintain our large and flourishing realm of private activity. Moreover, there is a general American skepticism about public action—arising in part from fear of political power *per se*.

Relatively few Americans are interested in assuming public office, and most parents would be upset were their children to embark on political careers. Americans commonly assume that corruption, personal ambition, and compromise of principle mark political life. The American attitude toward government is a reflection of a more general attitude toward human nature that has changed little over our nation's lifetime:

The suspicion of power and government is based on a suspicion of human nature. The popular view of human nature has reflected the Calvinist doctrine of original sin, and Americans have sought or anticipated evidence of human frailty and weakness in politics. Much of our politics has been based on the assumption that human nature is base nature and that the political man embodies human nature writ large.[3]

In modern circumstances, the reluctance to rely on public action places special constraints on the conduct of government and possibly even on the effective functioning of the entire economy. The expenditures of individuals and private businesses are regarded as legitimate; those made by government agencies are looked upon with distrust. Economist John Kenneth Galbraith has suggested that in the American view there is a "certain mystique attributed to the satisfaction of privately supplied wants" that is lacking in the satisfaction of "public desires which must be paid for by taxation."[4]

Political Innocence

Americans are quite prepared to talk politics, but often their talk is unrealistic and illogical. The attitude of the uninformed American to political matters is often tinged with a disillusionment that is close to a feeling of alienation.

Thus, Americans have frequently been prone to accept the "devil theory" of political crisis and disaster. Whenever a depression occurs, Wall Street is to blame. If a foreign country falls into the hands of left-wing elements, a small group of diplomats has sold out. If a new state tax is voted, legislators have been bought. If the nation is second best in defense or in space exploits, spies have been at work.

By contrast, Americans in positions of power—elected officials, political officials, community leaders, heads of associations, and so forth—are usually more moderate, more tolerant of opposition, and more sensitive to the complexities of modern life. Thus, the American political culture breeds a sizable gap between political sophisticates and ordinary citizens in understanding what the actual problems faced by a political system are and what real solutions are possible. Bridging this gap presents a crucial and difficult task of leadership for public officials, thus increasing the burdens and difficulties of those who are accountable to the public. Executives, legislators, and judges must frequently oppose popular conceptions if they are to fulfill the duties of their offices. On such matters as school prayers, trading with communist nations, or public finances, the Supreme Court,

[3] Arnold Rogow and Harold Lasswell, *Power, Corruption, and Rectitude* (Englewood Cliffs, N.J.: Prentice-Hall, 1963), p. 30.
[4] John Kenneth Galbraith, *The Affluent Society* (Boston: Houghton Mifflin, 1958), p. 267.

the President, and the Senate all have taken actions from time to time that the majority of the citizens neither understand nor approve.

The Distinction Between Nation and Government

The naiveté and lack of information about politics that many Americans display fosters another political trait—the sharp distinction we often draw between our nation and our government. As W. W. Rostow has pointed out, this distinction results partly from the problem of "American rhetoric." [5] Since the Revolution, we have adopted a set of idealized, vaguely expressed, and highly moral national goals, filled with implicit philosophical ambiguities.

These high purposes have served to unify a diverse and divided society and have provided an umbrella of symbols under which practical compromise and adjustment could occur. But they have also compounded the disillusionment of the public as it observed specific deviations from the norms. "Americanism" has become a deep and abiding faith in the rhetoric of our timeless purposes rather than a confidence in the specific policies of particular politicians at a given moment.

This distinction between nation and government is made in many cultures, of course. But Americans, professing greater loyalty to their nation, seem to emphasize the distinction more than members of older societies do. This difference is a consequence of the mobility and swift tempo that have characterized the American experience.

> The United States is a country which has undergone rapid changes; it is loose in its attachment to most traditions except those of individual freedom and reverence for the Constitution. Americans are relatively unbound by professional and occupational ties and by local loyalties. When men's loyalties are loosely anchored to particular places and institutions, they sometimes feel the need to be loyal to their nation more urgently than do those persons and societies which are firmly established in traditional loyalties. The very looseness of local loyalties, which on the one hand is a condition of freedom, makes on the other hand for more sensitivity about national loyalty.[6]

An Emphasis on Process

The major features of the American political culture sketched so far may seem inadequate and unsatisfactory for the world's most powerful nation: our unshakable commitment to democracy is coupled with a disinclination to permit democratic government to fulfill the demands placed upon it; and the public whose consent is essential appears uninterested, uninformed,

---

[5] W. W. Rostow, *The United States in the World Arena: An Essay in Recent History* (New York: Harper & Row, 1960), p. 480.
[6] Edward Shils, *The Torment of Secrecy* (Glencoe, Ill.: Free Press, 1956), p. 78.

and often unskilled in its role. It reserves its admiration and loyalty for symbolic and ritualistic articulation of moral purposes and not for the officials and machinery assigned the task of realizing the national destiny.

Yet one crucial component of our political culture is at work to make our system operative: the American attention to *process*—the extraordinary weight we place on the *means* for working out our unarticulated compromises while continuing our grander rhetoric. As we shall see in later chapters, this emphasis on process is institutionalized in a complex set of checks, balances, procedures, and rules that help to ensure the protection of minority rights and that make compromise and bargaining prerequisites for political action, no matter how popular a cause may be. It is this commitment that underlies the American reliance on legal solutions for complex policy issues as well as our search for boundary lines in the use of power and for restraints on arbitrary action by public or individual centers of power.

Finally, and perhaps most fundamentally, the American commitment to process is a substitute for the bonds of family, class, and station that stabilize more traditional cultures. Precisely because we view society as atomistic rather than corporate, and because our goals are so vague and our rhetoric so general, respect for ways and means is the only foundation we have for broad agreement. Consensus on the process of ordering our mutual relations is almost a minimal condition for orderly community existence.

It is this commitment to explicit process that in general sets democracy apart from other types of political system and in particular often marks the difference between our system and other democracies. This commitment is also the prerequisite for the successful operation of the world's largest freely constituted government. Our political philosophy offers few real guidelines on policy matters of the day. Our diverse groups have no great public program in common. Our belief in individualism and self-assertiveness precludes total commitment to an overarching set of aspirations. We have tamed the give-and-take of continuing struggle by means of explicit rules of the game. An emphasis on process, coupled with a leadership skilled in making it work and a public disposed to accept the decisions that emerge, is a prerequisite of our system's stability.

THE AMERICAN POLITICAL ENVIRONMENT

Systems are never explicable solely in terms of their internal characteristics. Political institutions and processes do not spring full blown from the minds of philosophers; still less are they the products of pure reason. They arise out of a society's total environment and are fully understandable only in terms of other patterns of national behavior.

That environment can itself be subdivided into the methods a society uses for various purposes: to produce and consume material resources (its economic structure), to establish households and raise children (its family life), to deal with other individuals and groups in the immediate geographical area (its pattern of community), and to maintain contact and share experiences with other Americans across the continent and beyond (the society). These behavior patterns represent the nonbiological conditions of human life, and they reflect the distinctive beliefs, customs, values, and skills children learn early in life from their experiences with others.

So habits of courtship, marriage, education of the young, burial of the dead, use of leisure time, and choice of leaders and definition of their proper duties may vary greatly from continent to continent, from nation to nation, and even from region to region. They represent different responses, developed and transmitted across generations, to the common requirements for sustaining human life—eating, sleeping, loving, working, and playing. These response patterns affect behavior in the political system.

Our shorthand terms for summarizing the distinctive life patterns of particular groups in particular places are "culture," "style," and "character." Individuals acquire traits through a gradual process of *socialization*—the conditioning of the infant or child to adjust his personality structure to the patterns of the larger group. Political culture and political socialization are *slices* of the larger human environment—they consist of the particular beliefs and practices that determine which activities are carried out in common and the ways in which public power is obtained and applied.

Elusive as the notions of culture and socialization are, most observers since colonial times have been convinced that there is a unique American character. Our early physical isolation from other cultures, our rich endowment of natural resources, our pattern of immigration, the conditions under which our first organized communities were established, and the role of our frontier have all been cited as special variables contributing to our special culture.

Among the distinctive characteristics of American society most frequently singled out over the years, five in particular have contributed to the building of our remarkably stable society: (1) our *de novo establishment* —the break with tradition that American settlers made when, possessing advanced techniques of social organization and economic production, they ventured into a continental wilderness and consequently became committed to equality rather than class or status; (2) our *affluence*—the rich bounty that nature provided this continent with and our skill in utilizing that bounty; (3) our *mobility*—the readiness of Americans to advance in status and their readiness to pull up stakes and move on to greener pastures; (4) our *pragmatism*—the national disposition to try to find specific solutions to immediate problems of the day, rather than to seek general philosophical answers for all time; and (5) our *pluralism*—the accommodation of diverse national, ethnic, and religious groups.

America as the First "Developing Nation"

The initial impetus to a distinctive American character was the fact that our early settlers "began again." In the words of Louis Hartz, the American nation was "born free," unfettered by an *ancien régime* and by feudal notions of class and status.[7] So its early institutions had the stamp of genuine originality. The American innovation of federalism, for instance, was a unique response to unique circumstances.

Perhaps the most striking characteristic derived from this abrupt break with the past is the American emphasis on equality. Alexis de Tocqueville, the famous young French aristocrat who set down his impressions of this country in the 1830's, singled out this atmosphere of egalitarianism. "Amongst the novel objects that attracted my attention during my stay in the United States," he wrote, "nothing struck me more forcibly than the general equality of condition among the people."[8]

[7] Louis Hartz, *The Liberal Tradition in America* (New York: Harcourt, Brace & World, 1955), Ch. 1.
[8] Alexis de Tocqueville, *Democracy in America* (New York: Knopf, 1945).

Drawing by Erikson © 1961 by the New York Times Co. Reprinted with permission

"What are we reading these days?"

The American tradition of egalitarianism encourages social and intellectual conformity.

In most countries of Europe and in many other parts of the world, people tend to accept their allotted station in life and do not question the rights or privileges of those standing above them on the social scale. Americans, in contrast, are suspicious of those who claim to possess superior capacities or competence. A glance at the letters-to-the-editor column of any American newspaper will show that the judgment and even the credentials of educators, economists, scientists, foreign-affairs specialists, and other supposed experts are constantly being questioned by laymen. A television repairman in Omaha sees nothing untoward in matching his own theories about the proper role of the Supreme Court against those of an Ivy League law-school professor.

Equality carries other connotations as well: conformity, commonness in tastes, and suspicion of the unusual opinion. De Tocqueville noted this when he wrote that the "manly and lawful passion for equality tends to elevate the humble to the rank of the great. But there exists also in the human heart a depraved taste for equality, which impels the weak to attempt to lower the powerful to their own level. . . ." [9] Contemporary analysts such as David Riesman see this aspect of our colonial endowment increasing in significance today. Formerly "inner-directed" in his striving for personal success, the modern American now seems to Riesman "other-directed," an organization man with built-in radar constantly seeking out and adjusting to the opinions of others. [10]

But, whether the "passion for equality" liberates or suffocates the individual, this predisposition seems to be a pervasive national trait that is applicable to our family life and our business dealings as well as to our politics.

The Affluent Society

The great majority of Americans not only are comfortable but possess luxuries that are the envy of the world. In the 1960's, over three-quarters of American families had washing machines and dryers, over four-fifths had at least one car, and over nine-tenths had television sets. The median family income for 1965 was almost $6,900.

American affluence can be measured in social terms as well. The proportion of white-collar jobs has been steadily rising: since 1955 more people have been employed in office, sales, and service work than in the actual processes of production. If American social classes are arranged in a pyramid, it is misshapen indeed: the middle class now far outnumbers the working class, and the moderately prosperous are far more numerous than the poor.

[9] *Ibid.*
[10] David Riesman, *The Lonely Crowd* (New Haven, Conn.: Yale University Press, 1950).

I BELIEVE
IN THE SUPREMACY OF
THE INDIVIDUAL OVER
THE STATE
IN FREEDOM OF INITIATIVE,
WHICH HAS GIVEN US
THE HIGHEST LIVING
STANDARD IN HISTORY
IN THE INVIOLABILITY
OF PRIVATE PROPERTY
IN PRIVATE ENTERPRISE
GUIDED BUT NOT
HAMSTRUNG BY GOV'T.
IN THE STRENGTH AND
VIABILITY OF OUR
FREE ECONOMY

In America, virtually all groups invoke the language and ideology of free enterprise and capitalism.

Drawing by Lorenz
© 1965 The New Yorker Magazine, Inc.

From this affluence has flowed a series of behavior patterns so powerful that they lead distinguished scholars such as David Potter to conclude that our material abundance decisively influences our lives from cradle to grave. To him, the manner in which we feed and train our babies, build and heat our houses, and make our clothes is basically dependent on our wealth. So are the average age at which we marry, our divorce rate, and our choice of neighbors and jobs.

The American emphasis on material well-being was already noticeable at the time of De Tocqueville's visit: "When the distinctions of rank are confounded together and privileges are destroyed; when hereditary property is subdivided, and education and freedom widely diffused; the desire of acquiring the comforts of the world haunts the imagination." [11]

So materialism helps provide the American with a sense of identity that in traditional societies is supplied by family, birthplace, and occupation. The very ownership of goods—an automobile, a boat, a workshop, a swimming pool—gives status and definition to the individual personality.

In pursuing their goal of material well-being, Americans have shown a remarkably stable commitment to capitalism—the free-enterprise system—for organizing and managing the economy. The ideas of eighteenth-century economists and the worldly philosophy of Adam Smith found fertile ground in the young United States, and even today our faith in private ownership is still firmly embedded in our ideology. There has never been a major socialist movement in the United States, and even in the depths of the depression of the 1930's there was little support for radical changes in the country's economic system.

[11] De Tocqueville, *op. cit.*, Vol. II.

Social Mobility: The Success Ethic

The first time I saw him he couldn't have been much more than sixteen years old, a little ferret of a kid, sharp and quick. Sammy Glick. Used to run copy for me. Always ran. Always looked thirsty.

"Good morning, Mr. Manheim," he said to me the first time we met, "I'm the new office boy, but I ain't going to be an office boy long."

"Don't say ain't," I said, "or you'll be an office boy forever."

"Thanks, Mr. Manheim," he said, "that's why I took this job, so I can be around writers and learn all about grammar and how to act right."

Nine out ten times I wouldn't have even looked up, but there was something about the kid's voice that got me. It must have been charged with a couple of thousand volts....

The boss told me Sammy was getting a three-week tryout. But Sammy did more running around that office in those three weeks than Paavo Nurmi did in his whole career. Every time I handed him a page of copy, he ran off with it as if his life depended on it. I can still see Sammy racing between the desks, his tie flying, wild-eyed, desperate....

"Hey, kid, take it easy."

That was like cautioning Niagara to fall more slowly.

"You said rush, Mr. Manheim."

"I didn't ask you to drop dead on us."

"I don't drop dead very easy, Mr. Manheim."

"Like your job, Sammy?"

"It's a damn good job—this year."

"What do you mean—this year?"

"If I still have it next year, it'll stink."...

From Budd Schulberg, *What Makes Sammy Run?*, 1941.

So far as political values are concerned, the American emphasis on private property makes the protection of property rights a fundamental goal of the political system (although there is sometimes tension between these rights and the execution of government duties). Americans regard the ownership of property as a safeguard of their freedom, because it provides a realm in which they can act as they please with only minimal public restrictions. So the home owner takes pleasure in practices seldom allowed the tenant, hammering picture hooks in the plaster, changing wall colors, removing shrubs. Similarly, owning one's business appeals strongly to Americans as an escape from the role of employee. The path to independence is property ownership—a home, a retail store, a manufacturing concern, a service establishment.

This view of society persists even though the economic system has now become vastly more complex. In an industrialized, job-dependent society, man's realization of affluence is more contingent on what wages will buy than it is upon independent ownership of shops or farms. His financial protection depends upon social security and public benefit payments as well as on his savings. New developments in science and industry depend upon the billions of dollars in research money contributed annually by the federal government and large industrial concerns. Yet, despite these changes, the American still defends the basic freedoms of the capitalist system—to choose his employment, invest his money, and organize his own business for maximum profit—and the basic assumptions that affluence rests on a vigorous private economy and that liberty is inseparable from individual initiative.

The Upward-and-Outward American

Reinforcing our national qualities of newness and equality, of affluence and capitalism is the fact that Americans seem forever in motion. They

Geographic Mobility: The Cosmopolitan American

Intimately connected with the pride of country which generally distinguishes the Americans is the feeling which they cherish toward their institutions. Indeed, when the national feeling of an American is alluded to, something very different is implied from that which is generally understood by the term. In Europe ... the love of country resolves itself into a reverence for locality irrespective of all other considerations.... But the American exhibits little or none of the local attachments which distinguish the European. His feelings are more centered upon his institutions than his mere country. He looks upon himself more in the light of a republican than in that of a native of a particular territory. His affections have more to do with the social and political system with which he is connected than with the soil which he inhabits. The national feelings which he and a European cherish being thus different in their origin and their object are also different in their results. The man whose attachments converge upon a particular spot of earth is miserable if removed from it, no matter how greatly his circumstances otherwise may have been improved by his removal; but give the American his institutions and he cares but little where you place him. In some parts of the Union the local feeling may be comparatively strong, such as in New England; but it is astonishing how readily even there an American makes up his mind to try his fortunes elsewhere, particularly if he contemplates removal merely to another part of the Union, no matter how remote or how different in climate and other circumstances from what he has been accustomed to, provided the flag of his country waves over it and republican institutions accompany him in his wanderings.

From Alexander Mackay, *The Western World*, 1847.

are on the move both geographically and socially—toward the frontier and toward success.

The willingness of Americans to migrate has been manifested at every stage of our history: in the westward expansion and in the population shifts from small towns and rural areas to the cities, from the older cities to the suburbs, and from the nation's Midwestern heartland to its metropolitan rims. While not all Americans are nomads, the transient spirit affects many of us. Young people are prepared to move a thousand miles away to take up an interesting job or simply to carry on with their education.

One consequence of this mobility has been the weakening of family ties. Whereas once all generations of a family would reside in one community, now first the children and then the grandchildren strike out for new communities and lives of their own. Typical of mobile America are the mushrooming suburbs, where everyone is a newcomer. In many ways the busy social life of the suburbs is an attempt by uprooted individuals to create a community and a sense of belonging for themselves. So the modern premium on adjustment, on an easy tolerance in group relations, reenforces the tradition of equality.

Social mobility is the process through which individuals enter new occupations and achieve higher status in the course of their life. The number of Americans who actually go from rags to riches is not very great, but tens of millions have made modest progressions beyond the homes and surroundings in which they were raised. Men whose fathers were unskilled laborers are now salesmen and office workers; men whose fathers were small shopkeepers are now doctors, lawyers, and executives. While social barriers continue to exist in the United States, they have never been rigid. In particular, public education—free and almost universally available in America, unlike most other countries—is the key to advancement.

Both kinds of mobility—geographically horizontal and occupationally vertical—have their political implications. Geographical migration disfranchises literally millions of citizens in the short run and inhibits their inclination for political activity in the long run. For political power in community, state, and national party affairs tends to remain with the stay-at-homes while transients are often alienated from participation. An interesting example of this trend occurs in the growing suburbs, where it is typically the *noncommuters*—professionals and businessmen who work in the area and intend to stay there—who control party organizations.

Vertical mobility tends to complicate political preferences and loyalties. Voters who are socially "on the way up" are subject to strong cross-pressures. Do they stay with the party of their working-class parents? Do they continue to identify themselves with the ethnic group and church of their childhood? Or do they adopt the preferences of their fellows in the professional or occupational group to which they now belong? These conflicts help account for the large number of independents or switch voters in our elections, as well as for many who simply avoid political affairs.

The Pragmatic Passion

No account of the United States is complete without underscoring our special penchant for concentrating on matters of the moment and our preference for using technology to solve human and social problems. "Does it work?" is the critical test for almost every national proposal, and the exponents of this experimental approach to life—William James and John Dewey—are the most notable American philosophers. As W. W. Rostow has written:

> At his best the American came to be knowledgeable and wise about the nature of the physical world and about how life was really conducted: but he remained close to the facts and processes with which he lived. As an intellectual, the American was an empiricist: as a philosopher, he was a rather liberal pragmatist, loosely generalizing the situations and experiences his round of life made real. . . . [He] tended to elevate "life, experience, process, growth, function" over "logic, abstraction, deduction, mathematics and mechanics." [12]

Moreover, our national pragmatism is distinctive in its heavy reliance on technology as a means for finding *ad hoc* solutions to problems. Until the Second World War, American science was never first rate, but American engineering was. Eli Whitney, Samuel Morse, Alexander Bell, Thomas Edison, Henry Ford gained fame by means of inventions, not discoveries. Yankee ingenuity—but not Yankee wisdom—was heralded early around the world. As tinkerers, gadget makers, masters of production and the assembly line, we practiced both rural and urban pragmatism, mechanizing first the farm and later the city. It was through technological skills that Americans were able to convert natural abundance into economic affluence.

In politics, pragmatism and inventiveness—applying moderately radical innovation to essentially familiar problems, as Rostow puts it—have been evident throughout our history. Ever since the Declaration of Independence and the Constitution established our national goals in broad idealistic terms, we have been ingenious in our interpretation and reinterpretation of the intentions of the Founding Fathers. Under the cover of lofty moral pronouncements, sometimes irritating to foreign observers, we have approached public issues on a piecemeal, experimental basis. The stubborn fact and the concrete situation, not well-rounded theoretical arguments, have been the catalyst for major public programs in the United States.

[12] W. W. Rostow, *op. cit.*, p. 14.

The Melting Pot: The Goal

Not like the brazen giant of Greek fame,
With conquering limbs astride from land to land;
Here at our sea-washed, sunset gates shall stand
A mighty woman with a torch, whose flame
Is the imprisoned lightning, and her name
Mother of Exiles. From her beacon-hand
Glows world-wide welcome; her mild eyes command
The air-bridged harbor that twin cities frame.
"Keep, ancient lands, your storied pomp!" cries she
With silent lips. "Give me your tired, your poor,
Your huddled masses yearning to breathe free,
The wretched refuse of your teeming shore.
Send these, the homeless, tempest-tost to me,
I lift my lamp beside the golden door!"

Emma Lazarus, "The New Colossus," 1883.

The United States as Melting Pot

Any interpretation of the American style must take into account the special mix of our population. The continent was settled by a disparate agglomeration of nationalities and classes. Until well into the nineteenth century, immigration was predominantly Anglo-Saxon in character. Thereafter, as the tide of immigration reached flood proportions, Irish, Germans, Italians, Scandinavians, and Eastern Europeans came in increasing numbers, while English and Scottish immigration declined.

The new arrivals did not overrun the institutions, customs, and life styles established earlier. The children of the great waves of immigrants adjusted themselves to the main currents of American life, which were shaped primarily by the "Anglo-Saxon" pattern of the past. In other words, the immigrants had less impact on America than America had on them. This is the first major characteristic of American pluralism.

There were reasons for this. One was that the Anglo-Saxons, having arrived first, controlled many of the dominant institutions of the society: the citadels of finance and higher education, the higher reaches of business and the national government. Any immigrant who wished to succeed in his adopted country had to adapt himself to the standards and rules already laid down. Moreover, the immigrants never actually outnumbered the old Americans. And even as successive waves arrived, immigrants from earlier waves were beginning to identify with the prevailing patterns. Thus German-Americans, already well established by 1900, looked on the Eastern

European arrivals who came between 1900 and 1910 in much the same way that those of British stock did. The most important factor making for assimilation, however, was the sharp drop in immigration after 1920. After that time the melting pot was able to set to work amalgamating whatever undigested elements were left.

By 1960, of a total population of 180 million, only 9.7 million people were born outside this country. In other words, about 170 million of us—approximately 95 percent—are native-born Americans. More than 80 percent of us also have parents who were born here.

Nonetheless, the security of immigrant neighborhoods in a strange country has permitted and encouraged the continuation of subcultures in

The Melting Pot: The Obstacles

It was only eight years after the founding of the Republic when a member of the House of Representatives took the floor to complain about the riff-raff flooding the big cities. Unrestricted immigration might have been satisfactory when the country was new and unsettled, he declared; but now that the United States had reached maturity and was fully populated, the nation's well-being required an end to immigration.

The congressman was not the first to voice these sentiments. Concern over the flood of foreign riff-raff had been growing throughout the eighteenth century; it was to remain a recurrent theme down to our own day. As early as 1718, "proper" Bostonians worried that "these confounded Irishmen will eat us all up"; and in 1729, a mob prevented the docking of several ships bringing immigrants from Belfast and Londonderry. Pennsylvanians were equally outraged by the flood of German immigrants into their territory: in the middle of the century, the great Benjamin Franklin delivered a number of attacks on "the Palatine Boors," i.e., the Germans, migrating to Pennsylvania. Jefferson, too, opposed mass immigration, fearing that it would expose the new nation to the corrupting influence of a decadent Europe. And the first Congress heard a plea to bar admission of "the common class of vagrants, paupers, and other outcasts of Europe."

Thirty years later, things seemed to be going from bad to worse. "This inlet of pauperism threatens us with the most overwhelming consequences," the Managers of the Society for the Prevention of Pauperism in the City of New York reported in 1819. The immigrants, they added, "are frequently found destitute in our streets; they seek employment at our doors; they are found in our almshouses, and in our hospitals; they are found at the bar of our criminal tribunals, in our bridewell, our penitentiary, and our state prison. And we lament to say that they are too often led by want, by vice, and by habit to form a phalanx of plunder and depredation rendering our city more liable to the increase of crimes, and our houses of correction more crowded with convicts and felons."

From Charles E. Silberman, *Crisis in Black and White*, 1964.

both city neighborhoods and rural settlements. Pockets of distinctive living styles remain—in Jewish apartment houses, on Italian streets, on Amish farms.

To the pluralism of nationality has been added the pluralism of a specialized industrial society covering a large territory. This pluralism is expressed in the extraordinary number and variety of organizations and associations throughout the United States, each representing one of the varied roles in life that most Americans play. These groups range from the National Association of Manufacturers to the Little League, from the Congress on Racial Equality to the Women's Christian Temperance Union, from the Teamsters' Union to the National Education Association. Millions of Americans join at least one group, and many have memberships in several. They join because they have interests to protect and promote, information to share, and activities of mutual enjoyment and concern to conduct. Except for a few occupational groups, these organizations are voluntary. And it is the voluntary character of American associational life that makes it distinctive.

All societies, of course—traditional and modern, democratic and totalitarian—are "pluralistic" in the sense that they contain groups. In traditional societies, however, such groups are organic units—guilds, estates, and established churches—with deep roots and long histories. And in totalitarian societies groups are firmly attached to the state apparatus and must act as arms of official policy.

In the United States, by contrast, group life is shifting and transitory. Associations are formed and dissolved every year, and members come and go as their interest rises and declines. While most American associations have little to do with politics directly, all of them have a political impact. In adhering to a variety of associations Americans develop a plurality of loyalties. These plural loyalties are in an important sense symptomatic of personal freedom. For they signify a society's willingness to allow each citizen to pursue his own interests, and they encourage individuals to limit the actions of government.

An appreciation both of this country's pluralism of nationality and of our specialization in role and function is essential to a proper understanding of the workings of American government. Lingering ethnic loyalties come to the surface in politics. A third-generation American of European background is pleased to have one of his "own kind" in the Senate or in the Cabinet as a demonstration that people of immigrant origin have been accepted in the higher councils of the nation's life. In addition to such symbolic representation, local and state political slates have long been the object of "ticket-balancing"—that is, efforts to represent each of the important ethnic groups in the party's constituency.

Today there are signs that ticket-balancing is being framed more on religious than on national lines. Neighborhood Roman Catholic churches, for example, used to be "Irish" or "Italian" or "Polish" or "German," depending on the complexion of their parishes. Now, as their parishioners move up and out to other parts of the city, to the suburbs, or across the country, they join a new church that has no ethnic designation. Similarly, the classic divisions among Spanish, German, and Russian Jews are disappearing.

By contrast, voluntary groups—economic, social, and fraternal associations—appear to be more stable. Not only are they prepared to apply pressure to government agencies, but those agencies regard such intervention as entirely legitimate. For the political activities of groups are an important part of the representative process. A physician, for example, casts his ballot in a congressional election along with his fellow citizens. But, after his congressman has gone to Washington, that doctor continues to be concerned over legislation that affects the practice of medicine. The American Medical Association, speaking on behalf of its members, will be in constant contact with various congressmen, and it will make certain that the doctors' views on impending laws are heard. Representation in American politics, then, is not achieved simply by electing public officials through a majority vote. It is a continuous process that goes on between elections, and organized groups play a particularly vital role in ensuring that the opinions of interested citizens are transmitted to the various agencies of government.

OUR CHANGING SYSTEM, OUR CHANGING ENVIRONMENT

The two preceding sections have discussed the more or less constant aspects of the American political system and the environment in which it operates. But our system has also been shaped by certain immense changes in its internal structure and in the American and world environments. Changes in our material resource base, and in our technology for dealing with that base, in the size and mixture of the American population, and in the relation of the United States to the international community— these are principal transformations. Their profound effect becomes highly visible when we examine the changes in each, even during the short period of recent history, and then see what changes they have wrought in our political system.

The Expansion of Knowledge

Man's knowledge of himself and his environment has increased more rapidly over the course of American history than in any previous period. Today this expansion of knowledge continues to accelerate. The harnessing of atomic energy, revolutions in weaponry, and the exploration of outer space attest to new knowledge in physics, metallurgy, electronics, and many related fields. Developments in biology promise to unlock the secrets of heredity; information theory and computer technology have reduced the labor requirements in many manufacturing and office processes to a fraction of their previous level. The sophistication of our present knowledge about illness—especially the relation of microorganisms to disease—underlies most of contemporary public-health practice and many of the accomplishments of modern surgery. Increased knowledge of man's social arrangements has extended to a manipulation of the conditions controlling economic growth and levels of productivity.

The national government stands at the center of this great expansion of knowledge. It initiates and supports research and development on a scale unheard of even thirty years ago. In 1967 the federal government spent $16 billion, two-thirds more than its total prewar annual budget, for research and development. Much of this sum is spent on specific defense and space technology through the Department of Defense, the Atomic Energy Commission, and the National Aeronautics and Space Administration. Nevertheless, the National Science Foundation, the National Institutes of Health, and many other government agencies are supporting broader research—some with very large sums of money.

The government puts much of this expanded knowledge to direct use. For example, the military and space programs, the Federal Aviation Agency's program of air-traffic control, and the uses of automated devices in administrative operations (essential to the effective conduct of such large programs as social security, tax collection, and national defense) are some obvious products of applied research.

The political effect of this expansion of knowledge has been to change the expectations of the American people (as well as those of other nations). The knowledge that large-scale preventive medicine is technically possible generates public expectations that money for research and medical services will be made available, if not by private effort, then by government action. The same is true of developing supersonic airplanes, miniaturizing circuitry for communication, or collecting statistics on seasonal unemployment.

Important also is the sudden change in the political role of the country's scientists. Barely three decades ago they were primarily university specimens. Today the scientific aspects of weapons development and of rivalry in outer space—and hence of government expenditure decisions—are so significant and so complex that the country's most competent scientists must play an important part in the making of government policy. (See Chapter 20 for a discussion of the new issues generated by government involvement in research management.)

The Development of Production Technology

Expansion in knowledge begets innovation in its practical application, with consequent political repercussions. When technological change occurs very rapidly, as it has in the field of agriculture, it can create vast manpower dislocations even as it increases the material well-being of society. In 1860 an American farm worker could supply fewer than 5 people. It took eighty years for production power to double—reaching a capacity of 10.69 people for each farm worker by 1940. But by 1966 a single farm worker could supply 34 people. This threefold increase in productive power in twenty-six years is the result of exponential growth in knowledge about soils, products, and agricultural methods and the application of this knowledge and machinery to farm production. Farms are becoming factories; today 30 percent of them account for 83 percent of all farm cash receipts.

The revolutionary effects of technology—in both stimulating and reducing employment—are apparent in other industries as well. The automobile has produced employment for millions of workers in iron, steel, and manufacturing industries, in oil production, and in gas stations, motels, and other local businesses. In the bituminous-coal industry, on the other hand, new mechanical methods put 200,000 men out of work between 1940 and 1955, and coal consumption itself declined with increased use of new fuels. West Virginia, the chief producer of bituminous coal, was the only state in the country with a net decline in population between 1950 and 1965. But many of the displaced workers, with skills that were useful only in the coal industry, did not want to leave the state. The question of what to do about this stranded, poor, and increasingly embittered population became a serious government problem for the state, and, given limited state resources, for Washington as well.

Technological changes have also caused subtler changes in other occupations. Technological developments in medicine, for example, have led to increasing specialization by doctors and to group practice. New uses for television may reduce manpower needs in education. Still another effect of technological change is that very few Americans are still self-employed; $5 out of every $6 of income in this country are from wages and salaries. Workers are thus directly dependent on the state of the economy for their incomes, and they have increasingly come to expect government to follow policies that support maximum employment and economic growth. Significant differences of opinion exist, however, over what kinds of policy will yield these results (for example, should the budget be balanced or unbalanced?), and out of these differences arise political issues. But, from the "full dinner pail" campaign of the Republicans in 1896 to the present, our government has been increasingly involved in the problems created by individual dependence on the condition of the economy.

Jensen in the Chicago *Daily News*

"Relax."

Americans love the machine for its contributions to the "good life," but they
have always been uncomfortable about
technology's threat to freedom.

Still another by-product of technological change has been the growth
of large-scale corporate enterprises. Currently four manufacturing companies in each of the following fields account for 50 to 80 percent
of the nation's total production: motor vehicles and parts, steel works
and rolling mills, aircraft engines, organic chemicals, cigarettes, tin
cans and other tinware, synthetic fibers, and tractors. Large corporate
enterprises are also characteristic of insurance, banking, transportation,
utilities, and, more recently, retailing. They operate nationally, without
respect to state boundaries. Giant national labor unions have arisen to negotiate with giant national corporate enterprises on an equal footing. At present about one-third of all nonagricultural employees belong to unions.
In 1967 three unions had over 1 million members, three had 500,000 to
1 million, and fifteen had 200,000 to 500,000.

Yet even these figures fail to reveal fully the power of corporate and
union leaders. The corporate community's interests are reflected in the
United States Chamber of Commerce, the National Association of Manufacturers, national trade associations, and other business organizations;
similarly, most large unions are federated in the AFL-CIO. Such organizations are potent both in the economy and in politics. Moreover, these interests exert vast power through decisions made by corporate boards of industries and those reached in union-management negotiations. A strategic decision on wages or on price increases in one industry—for example, in steel- or

automobile-manufacturing—may set a pattern for wage or price increases throughout the economy. In fact, such decisions may have more impact on the economy than those made by Congress, the President, or the Federal Reserve Board.

During the nineteenth century, Congress left economic regulation largely to the states, except for the institution of banking regulation in 1863. The President intervened in a labor dispute for the first time in 1894. Today, by contrast, we have a large volume of statutes dealing with antitrust, collective bargaining, the transportation and communications industries, banking, the power and gas utilities, and food-processing and drug production. The states have also passed regulations in most of these fields. Still, questions of how much national or state governments should intervene in questions of economic policy, such as pricing decisions or wage controversies, and what methods should be used continue to divide both the American public and the experts who must work on the problems. (See Chapter 19 for a further discussion of these issues.)

Patterns of Population Change

Technological change has not only caused substantial changes in our economic structure, but it has led to sweeping changes in the composition and distribution of the American people—changes that in turn have had a tremendous effect on the functions of local, state, and national government.

In essence, technology has interacted with our permanent penchant for mobility to produce striking patterns of population redistribution across the country. Three types of population shifts are particularly significant.

Perhaps the most far-reaching trend has been the rise of urbanism. Historians date the disappearance of the "frontier" at 1890, but not until 1920 was a majority of the American population "urban"—that is, living in places with 2,500 or more inhabitants. Even as late as 1940, 1 out of every 5 persons was employed in agriculture. But in 1966 only 1 out of 18 was so employed, and over 70 percent of the population was urban. Even more striking, however, is the fact that urbanization has become metropolitanization. In 1960 nearly two-thirds (64 percent) of the population lived in 202 large metropolitan areas—that is, in areas with more than 100,000 population —in comparison with a mere 15 percent in 28 metropolitan centers in 1890 and with only 29 percent in 106 centers as late as 1950.

The consequences of these changes are important, and they receive attention in many chapters of this book. Metropolitan government has become big government. Transportation, utility service, recreation, housing, crime, and other problems have far more extensive and complex dimensions in metropolitan than in rural or small urban areas. Moreover, as cities have found it difficult to finance their many functions, they have turned first to the states and then to the national government for financial help. Other problems are created by the existence within the same metropolitan area of several governments that need to cooperate but are often in conflict with one another and by the inability of central cities to enlist the interest and collect the taxes of those who work there but live in the suburbs.

The impact of urbanization on politics is obscured by the persistence of rural attitudes and the underrepresentation of urban populations in state legislatures. Because Congress has been more responsive to urban populations than have many state legislatures, metropolitan government leaders have turned to Washington for aid. The 1964 reapportionment decisions of the Supreme Court are beginning to give the urban population a greater influence, particularly in state legislatures. Urbanism also tends to increase the nationalization of politics. The classic cleavages in American politics have traditionally been sectional—the Atlantic seaboard versus the trans-Allegheny West, the North against the South, and the trans-Mississippi West against the East. Today, although these differences have not disappeared, the politically significant cleavages are increasingly those within urban areas—retired taxpayers versus the parents of school children, employers versus employees, commuters versus full-time residents, and so forth. Although the massive impact of urbanization and industrialization has not yet been fully felt, the diminishing of the sectionalism that characterized rural politics has been noticeable in presidential elections.

Second, the redeployment and redistribution of population across the continent is an important change factor. Both the sheer volume and constant movement have had a political impact over the years. Such shifts weaken local and sectional loyalties and encourage the tendency to seek national solutions for problems. The man who is born in Massachusetts, gets a college degree in Michigan, serves in the armed forces in South Carolina, and takes a job first in Colorado, then in Texas, and then in California is likely to be more interested in national than in local or state politics, and he is not likely to be much concerned over the preservation of local self-government or states' rights.

Certain shifts in population have had specific political consequences. One important example is the emigration of Negroes from the South. As recently as 1920, more than 85 percent of the Negro population of the country lived in the region the Bureau of the Census defines as the South (the eleven states of the Confederacy, five border states, and the District of Columbia). In 1960 this proportion had dropped sharply to 59 percent.

A host of political problems have stemmed from this massive Negro migration. First, Negroes are moving primarily to cities in the North. Except for a language problem, these newcomers encounter all the difficulties of adjustment experienced by the previous waves of immigrants, who came from European farms to American cities—including the problems associated with inadequate education in the places from which they have come. These difficulties have been compounded by city segregation patterns: large numbers of whites have moved out of the cities to the suburbs, and Negroes have filled up the "old core" of the metropolis. Thus, almost all the most difficult problems facing city governments—housing, urban renewal, education, retention of a skilled labor supply, relations with state governments—are inevitably involved with the issue of racial discrimination. Since Negroes have free access to the ballot in the North, they can make their demands felt in local, state, and national elections. It is not an accident that the advocacy of civil rights by Northern members of Congress has increased as Negroes have settled in Northern cities or that recent Presidents and presidential candidates of both parties have given support to the claims of Negroes. Nor is it accidental that "white backlash"—attitudes hitherto characteristic of the South—should appear throughout the North as Negroes have migrated from the South in large numbers. The spread of intolerant attitudes toward Negroes further demonstrates how the redistribution of population, along with urbanization and industrialization, is reducing the sectional differences in the country and producing a national politics in which voters divide along the same lines, though not in the same proportions, in all parts of the country.

Third, technological change—particularly medical advances—has been chiefly responsible for the significant changes in the age structure of the American population. During the last thirty years or so, substantial increases have occurred in the proportion of the aged and children in the total population. Aged people increased from 3 percent of the population in 1890 to almost 7 percent in 1940 and to over 9 percent in 1966. A population explosion after the Second World War enlarged the percentage of persons under nineteen from 30 percent in 1940 to 40 percent in 1966.

These changes are reflected in increased costs of government for support of the aged and for education of children and adolescents. Technological change, which has simultaneously increased the life span and decreased the employment opportunities of older persons, has forced most people to rely on some kind of support other than earnings for five, ten, twenty, or more years after they retire. The increased number of children, coupled with technological changes, has led to low employment opportunities for youth and to a need for longer periods of education. These trends have brought an amazingly large growth in the costs of education—not merely for children but for young adults who want college and professional education.

Changes in the age distribution of the population bring new issues to politics. The growth of the aged population during the first quarter of this century eventually made social-security payments an issue during the 1930's, and, similarly, medical care for the aged has been a controversial issue of the 1960's. Also creating tension is the issue of federal aid for education. Traditionally, education has been a local function. Yet the increasingly uneven distribution of financial resources among localities, the burden of local real-estate taxes, and the desire to provide good educational opportunities for all have led to state support for education; and now the same unevenness of state resources, the difficulties of raising ample state taxes, and burgeoning consciousness of the need for education have led to pressures for national support. The Elementary and Secondary Education Act of 1965 came closer to providing general school aid than had any previous national legislation.

The Changing International Environment

In the gradual evolution of the American political system, few changes are more striking than those of the international environment, particularly during the twentieth century. Changes in weapons, transportation, and communications; shifts in the relative power of different nations; the emergence of new states; and the rising expectations of peoples around the globe have all affected American government in our age.

Throughout the nineteenth century, protected from foreign aggression by two oceans and the British Navy, the United States was left in relative isolation; we were thus free to concentrate on domestic matters, and we had only a rudimentary foreign policy, almost no military establishment, and no strategic policy. Then in 1898 we suddenly acquired an empire—Cuba, Puerto Rico, the Philippines, Hawaii. But neither the Spanish-American War nor the First World War materially changed the American conception that the destiny of the United States was to be shaped by its domestic conditions and institutions. It was victory in the Second World War and our growing technological resources that suddenly gave the United States a dominant position over half the globe. Our dominance is one of influence and responsibility rather than political subjugation; it is greater and at the same time more fragile than that of an empire created by military conquest. Domestic support for an empire that was not sought but cannot be abandoned has had to be created after the responsibilities of world leadership were acquired. In the space of less than half an average American's lifetime, the country has had to move from a position of security behind two ocean barriers to the role of being the military and diplomatic anchor of Western civilization.

One way to understand the impact of this shift is to recognize that the actions of the national government have an impact on hundreds of millions of people outside the country's boundaries. These people also exert direct influence on our policies by their decisions. They or their leaders make choices that affect the fortunes of the United States as deeply as those made by American voters, corporations, labor unions, and other groups of citizens. The threat of hostilities between India and Pakistan, among the Middle Eastern countries, or within Saigon, Cyprus, or the Congo would concern the security and well-being of the

United States as clearly, if not as directly, as the state of our own economy. The instruments available to the United States in conducting negotiations with other sovereign nations are different from those used to handle domestic issues, but the need to reconcile conflicting interests is basically the same.

Conflicts also occur between these groups abroad and groups in the American citizenry. Other countries may attempt to increase their exports by supplying goods—textiles, for example—to the United States at prices that undercut those in the American market. The domestic industries concerned promptly demand tariff protection or a system of import quotas. They are backed by local unions and members of Congress. The government must weigh their needs against the possibility that the country involved will restrict American imports or take its trade to America's enemies.

Such conflicts, whether indirect or overt, are almost as much a part of American politics as a dispute over public or private ownership of an electric-power plant on the Columbia River. In this sense, politics—the politics of international leadership—does not stop at the water's edge. It cannot, for the American government in its new role is compelled to contest for the loyalties of the foreign populations within its orbit, while maintaining the allegiance of its own citizens and attempting to bring American attitudes into closer conformity with our country's international requirements.

The recent changes in the American world position accentuate certain purely domestic problems. Thus government concern with the decisions of large business and labor organizations—with all the controversy that such concern invites—is reinforced by an awareness that the growth and stability of the American economy have become an essential element of American power and prestige in the contemporary world. Other centralizing tendencies are also reinforced. The decision of federal officials to attempt with increased vigor to eliminate racial segregation in the North and South and to enforce constitutionally guaranteed political rights is related to the question of our international "image" as well as to our domestic concerns. And the power and prestige of different groups in our society—scientists and soldiers, for example—rise as our international commitments grow.

DILEMMAS OF THE AMERICAN STYLE

The properties of the American political system, the characteristics of its culture, and the changes in both environment and system over time do not necessarily mesh neatly. Sometimes properties and characteristics contradict one another. Sometimes they change unevenly over the years. In either event, certain contradictions and discrepancies have resulted in persistent

"The delinquency problem must be faced—we've got to build more jails."

This liberal cartoon stresses the need for long-run economic and social measures to undercut the roots of crime.

From *Straight Herblock*, Simon & Schuster, 1964

tensions in our national life, and it is inaccurate to assume that our government achieves stability automatically.

Central to these tensions is the American commitment to equality, born of our fresh beginning. As Louis Hartz has emphasized,[13] outside the antebellum South, the United States has never had a political aristocracy. Hence, it has never produced a genuine, successful conservative movement, intent on preserving the established order. Instead two strands of liberalism—committed in varying degrees to individuality, equality, and change—have vied with one another throughout our history. Hartz traces the tortuous paths of these national "impulses"—one toward democracy and the other toward capitalism—in American political and intellectual history. Theoretically, the impulses can be brought together in the notion of *democratic capitalism*. In practice, the desire to applaud and encourage Horatio Alger's characters in their climb to success sometimes contradicts the desire to assist the more unfortunate who are left behind, especially in public policy. So the slogans "human rights" and "property rights" remain persuasive, but often contradictory, guides to national action.

The "capitalist impulse" emphasizes individual responsibility in explaining differences in social and economic status. The presumption is that the unemployed could find work if they wanted to instead of expecting a handout; that those who do not like living in slums should better themselves so that they can afford the move to a nicer neighborhood; that the indigent

[13] Hartz, *op. cit.*

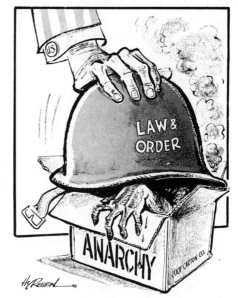

The Lid

This conservative cartoon emphasizes the need for immediate military and police measures to solve the problem of crime in the streets.

Rosen in the Albany *Times-Union*
Ben Roth Agency

aged should have put aside savings for their retirement or, if not, that their children should accept the responsibility of caring for them.

The "democratic impulse" takes a different tack, holding that in a complex industrial society, the luckless individual may be an innocent victim of impersonal forces—automation, the business cycle, structural unemployment —rather than personally incompetent or lazy. Over the years, spurred on by economic crises, advocates of this view have been responsible for our nation's social-security and unemployment-compensation programs, as well as its low-cost housing, welfare, and Medicare services.

Whatever the line of reasoning employed, one of the most persistent problems of the American creed is how to account for poverty. Despite the national rise in living standards, almost one-fifth of Americans today live in poverty. They are the aged who have no savings and live on minimal pensions or old-age-assistance payments. They are the unskilled laundry, restaurant, and farm workers who have jobs paying only $40 or $50 per week; they are members of the fatherless households with young children. They are the families of former coal miners and of assembly workers displaced by automation. Twenty-two percent of the American poor are Negroes—twice the proportion of Negroes in the population. But the great majority of the poor are white. Neither the capitalist doctrine of "opportunity for all" nor the democratic doctrine of public support seems entirely satisfactory.

The second national paradox that arises from our simultaneous emphasis

on equality and individuality is sociopolitical rather than economic. Tolerance, the necessary corollary of the individuality that an open society promotes, is always threatened by the pressures for conformity that the impulse
of equality has set loose. De Tocqueville's observation, made in the first
part of the nineteenth century, indicates that this dilemma is not new:

> As the conditions of men become equal amongst a people, individuals seem
> of less and society of greater importance. Or rather, every citizen, being
> assimilated to all the rest, is lost in the crowd, and nothing stands conspicuous
> but the great and imposing image of the people at large. This naturally gives
> the men of democratic periods a lofty opinion of the privileges of society,
> and a very humble notion of the rights of individuals. . . . The public has
> a singular power. It does not persuade to certain opinions, but it enforces
> them and infuses them into the intellect by a sort of enormous pressure of
> the minds of all upon the reason of each.[14]

So alongside our cherished value of individuality is our frequent preference
for group endeavors, committees, and team operations, our search for
harmony, and our distrust for the deviant and the dissenter.

The problem of tolerance is especially complex in the United States.
Each wave of immigrants has struggled for acceptability, and frequently
the second-generation immigrants have been the most hostile to the latest
arrivals. The difficulties created by a heritage of many nationalities is compounded by our legacy of slavery. The Civil War compelled white Americans to grant equal ideological status to all races, but legal, social, and
political equality have been slow in coming and difficult to achieve. For
example, church-burnings, beatings, and shotgun attacks marked the progress
of the civil-rights movement across the Deep South in the middle 1960's.
In some places even giving food or shelter to a civil-rights worker was
considered grounds for violence.

The position of the dissenter in America is recurrently perilous. Individuals who wish to discourse on what they think to be the merits of
communism, atheism, apartheid, or Black Power discover that many Americans prefer that such utterances not be made. The right of such individuals
to express their ideas is juxtaposed against the security of the nation, the
moral development of our youth, or, more commonly, our society's way
of life. And with such juxtapositions it is usually suggested that the individual give way to the greater good that will ensue from his silence.

According to recent opinion polls, the majority of our citizens believe
"radical" books should be removed from public libraries, atheists should be
barred from teaching, and communists should be prevented from speaking
or holding a job. The Know-Nothing party of the nineteenth century and
the "red scares" of the twentieth exemplify the temptation to define patriotism in narrow and parochial terms—what has been called "our inveterate

---

[14] De Tocqueville, *op. cit.*, pp. 307, 311.

tending to judge others by the extent to which they contrive to be like ourselves." [15]

The problem of tolerance, then, is partly political and partly social. It is political in that government agencies—especially state legislatures—are often quite zealous in establishing rules that penalize those who deviate from established patterns. Yet the problem is largely social in the sense that popular feeling is frequently antagonistic to individuals and ideas that appear to run counter to custom. Even if there were no political disabilities for dissenters, society would still make life difficult for them.

AMERICAN POLITICAL ACCOMPLISHMENTS

Not all is tension and contradiction in the American political system, however. More impressive by far are the solid achievements of our system. Over the years, against a backdrop of great environmental change, American political behavior has moved increasingly toward (1) *nonviolent means* of responding to and reconciling demands, (2) an *open system* that provides increasingly free access to all, and (3) *political responses* to the felt needs of the people in bestowing both *rights* and *benefits*.

The approach of this book is predicated on the belief that these tendencies—toward the rule of law, popular government, and reliance on the political process—are both enduring and desirable. They are not, however, inevitable: many aspects of the present environment challenge these trends, and many people feel they are invalid or inadequate for the needs of a mass society faced with the necessity for social change.

A fourth element in the American experience might well be survival itself. Many deep national conflicts—over the extension of slavery, the rights of labor, free silver, internationalism versus isolationism—have threatened to destroy our basic consensus and reduce our political system to a chaos of centrifugal forces. The ability of that system to contain and ultimately to resolve conflict has continually been tested. And the system itself has been changed in the process. Thus the final question facing a student of American government today is simply this: Will the system break up or will it continue to hold together?

The stresses have never been more severe. Sheer numbers present an unprecedented challenge. From a nation of 4 million persons, we have become a nation of 190 million, three-fourths of whom live in cities or metropolitan areas. By the year 2000, there will be almost 312 million Americans, with 187 million living in the nation's 14 major urban regions. The implications

[15] George Kennan, *American Diplomacy, 1900–1950* (Chicago: University of Chicago Press, 1951), p. 135.

of this growth for educational, residential, political, and economic patterns can scarcely be imagined.

Demands for an active decision-making role by groups that were formerly politically dispossessed—students, ghetto residents, tenant farmers—are calling into question many of the cherished compromises and processes by which our disparate society has been held together. Is a real realignment of power under way? If so, will it happen without violence? Will the alienation of the young and the poor find expression within the system or outside it?

The resort to "direct action" techniques—sit-ins, strikes, boycotts, picketing—for the achievement of political ends is an accepted part of the civil-rights movement and, increasingly, of poverty politics as well. This threat to the nation's consensus on procedure could become a throwback to vigilantism. On the other hand, these techniques are part of a new political instrument that is more immediately responsive than elections and referendums. Will it acquire a legitimacy of its own?

A final source of pressure is external rather than internal. As our democratic society struggles to reconcile the many dilemmas posed by its past, its hopes, and its weaknesses, it must also cope with threats from the outside. The legacy of the Cold War has been the realization that peace is the precarious product of accommodation, hard work, courage, and good fortune. The "long twilight struggle," as President Kennedy described it, puts strains on American society that world war never did.

THE WORK AHEAD

The chapters that follow examine the operation of the systems and subsystems that make up our political life. The rest of Part I continues with the ground rules of American government—our constitutional framework, the major instruments for fleshing it out, and the evolution of federalism. Part II considers the American political process—the history, functions, and organization of our parties, as well as interest groups and voting behavior. Parts III and IV examine our major government institutions—the Presidency, Congress, the executive bureaucracy, and the judiciary—while Part V examines what government actually does and how its decisions are arrived at. Part VI (in the national, state, and local edition) discusses state and local political systems as important components—and in some ways microcosms—of our federal system.

As you thus survey the political landscape, you will be able to identify the scope, participants, objectives, and rules of the several systems and the respective influence of actors, resources, and environment in determining the outcome of particular events and decisions. You will also see the American political and social characteristics that we have described at work in shaping both our history and our institutions.

SUMMARY

"Politics," we have seen, is a continuing association among people in which the main focus is on how to influence the allocation of power. One useful way to explore political activity is through systems analysis. A *system* consists of definable components, operating within a discrete arena of action, whose behavior affect one another. Each system has boundaries that define the scope of its activities, participants who try to influence those activities in order to achieve certain objectives, rules of the political game, and instruments for resolving conflicts and reflecting demands.

The American political system has five distinctive characteristics. First, despite sporadic deviations, our country has from its founding been based on the principle of consent of the governed. Second, our traditional suspicion about politics and politicians has led us to believe that the government sphere should be a limited one, with important powers and activities left to the private sphere. Third, Americans are often naive and even unrealistic about politics—a tendency that sometimes creates a gap between the expectations of laymen and the outlook of political leaders who understand political realities better. Fourth, Americans have tended to distinguish sharply between their loyalty to the nation and their loyalty to their government. This distinction has often led us to commit ourselves to idealized and vague goals rather than to specific policies. It is the fifth characteristic of the American system that allows us to work out compromises within our grand rhetoric: our emphasis on process, reflected in our institutions of checks and balances, our procedures for ensuring minority rights, and our reliance on legal solutions for policy disputes.

The American political system, like all systems, is significantly influenced by its social and cultural environment. Several characteristics make up the distinctive American culture: first, our emphasis on equality, which resulted largely from the absence of a feudal past; second, our social and economic affluence and our persistent commitment to the capitalist system and private property; third, our marked penchant for geographic mobility and social mobility—both of which affect political activity and voting behavior; fourth, our pragmatic solutions to policy issues and our faith in technology to solve problems; and, finally, our "melting pot" tradition of amalgamating vastly disparate immigrant groups into our dominant Anglo-Saxon culture.

The characteristics of the American political system and its cultural environment have been relatively stable since the founding of the Republic. But technological and social change have also helped to shape our system. Our scientific and technological knowledge has expanded enormously over the last century, and national government agencies now play a leading role in initiating and underwriting research-and-development projects. Technological advances have had revolutionary effects on agriculture and industry, causing manpower surpluses in some fields, opening up new jobs in others, and giving rise to giant corporations and greater government regulation of the economy.

Technology has combined with our traditional mobility to produce three types of population shifts: the rise of urbanism; the increased velocity of mobility, exemplified by the emigration of Negroes from the South; and the increasing proportion of children and aged people in the total population.

Finally, the American political system has been significantly affected by our evolution from an isolated, insignificant nation to a superpower, leader of half the globe. This enormous change in status has forced us to try to reconcile interests beyond our borders, to settle conflicts between American groups and competitors abroad, and to consider the effect of domestic policies on our international image.

The interaction of our political system and our cultural environment with social and technological change has produced several "dilemmas." Two of these arise from our simultaneous commitment to equality and individuality. The first is the tension between the "capitalist impulse," which emphasizes that each person is responsible for achieving his own social and economic status, and the "democratic impulse," which argues that in an urban industrial society, economic and technological forces may overwhelm innocent victims and that the government should thus step in to help them.

The second tension is sociopolitical: our penchant for individuality leads to a belief in tolerance, but our emphasis on equality creates pressures for conformity; as a result the dissenter has often been on shaky political and social ground in America.

Despite these tensions, however, the American political system has many impressive achievements, and we have evolved in the direction of nonviolent means for responding to demands and settling conflicts, increasingly free access to the system for everyone, and political responses in bestowing rights and benefits.

BUILDING THE POLITICAL FOUNDATIONS OF A NATION

2

We have identified two major influences on the American political system: our political culture and our national social character. This chapter examines another determinant of any political system: its basic institutional framework. The chapter begins by examining the ways in which our institutions reflect our English heritage. What was the significance of the American Revolution? How did the early state constitutions and the Articles of Confederation contribute to our basic institutions? The final section discusses the drawing up and ratifying of our Constitution. How did the Constitution differ from the Articles? What basic governmental features did it establish? And, finally, what political gaps did the Constitution leave unfilled?

The United States has been called "the first new nation." [1] Like the new nations of the twentieth century, it broke from an established metropolitan system and sought for itself national unity, economic development, and a viable political system. It established the foundations for these objectives in a period of conscious *institution-building* from 1776 to 1787, beginning with the writing of the state constitutions and ending with a grand and enduring plan for union. This was the most constructive short period in the history of modern political institutions and the first example of conscious nation-building in modern times.

The institution makers of this period were able to draw on a heritage of political wisdom and experience obtained from the mother country and from 180 years of political development between the founding of the Virginia colony and the Constitutional Convention of 1787. It has been said that the American experience is unique in "the continuity of its political and constitutional aspects with the experience and institutions of the past." [2] Providing this continuity were the concepts of *rule of law* and *self-government*, which formed the core of the American consensus and the foundation for our political development.

The foremost task was to consolidate the union and thus to ensure the survival of the United States and, with it, the rule of law and self-government. Rare creativeness is exhibited in the plan of union that joined the political wisdom of the past with the requirements for a durable union.

The continuities and the creativeness in the political development of the new nation are shown in the account that follows.

THE ENGLISH CONTRIBUTION

English thinkers and writers and English traditions are responsible for many, if not most, of what we like to think of as early American innovations. These contributions were made in four major areas: philosophy, institutional structure, law, and rights.

Philosophy

In 1690, in the second of his *Two Treatises on Government*, John Locke synthesized the doctrines of *natural right* and *social contract* that had developed in Western Europe. His philosophy, which was to become the foundation for the declaration of American principles in 1776, stated that

[1] Seymour Lipset, *The First New Nation: The United States in Historical and Comparative Perspective* (New York: Basic Books, 1963).
[2] Benjamin Fletcher Wright, "Consensus and Continuity, 1776-1787," *Boston University Law Review*, Vol. XXXVIII (Winter 1958), pp. 1, 50.

man's rights came to him from nature and included life, liberty, and property. Man needed government because he needed a legislature to define these rights and an executive to enforce them, and so he entered into a contract with his fellows to establish government. The basic premise of this concept was that government rested on the consent of men, not upon the divine ordination of kings. Moreover, said Locke, whenever government acted arbitrarily or abused its trust, it was legally dissolved, and the people were free to establish a new government.

Locke also declared that government should act through known, general rules. Another Englishman, James Harrington—whose *Commonwealth of Oceana* (1656) was also read in America, argued for an "empire of laws and not of men." This idea, too, was to influence Americans as they sought to safeguard liberty through constitutional law.

Locke also gave to America the concept of *limited government*—limited by its purpose and its methods. He differed from other seventeenth- and eighteenth-century philosophers—Hobbes, for example, who argued for the absolute power of kings, or Rousseau, who argued for placing absolute power in the will of the people. Locke presented a conservative liberalism, combining the liberal philosophy of rights and contract with the British tradition of rule of law.

Institutional Structure

It has been said that the Constitution of the United States is descended from the British Constitution as it was in 1701. At that time English laws were made by the "king in Parliament," which meant by the assent of the House of Commons, representing those who had voting rights, the House of Lords, representing the aristocracy, and the king. The king had the power of veto and the power to execute the laws. The Act of Settlement in 1701 confirmed the independence of the judiciary by decreeing that the Crown could not remove judges. This structure is quite similar to that adopted for the United States in 1787.

Explanations of the British system were given to Americans primarily by two men—John Locke and the Baron de Montesquieu. Locke, in his second treatise, said that the British system was one of separation of powers. He saw three powers: the *legislative*, vested in the Commons, the Lords, and the king; the *executive*, vested in the king and consisting mainly of maintaining domestic peace and fulfilling judicial functions; and the *federative*, vested in the king and encompassing relations with other states.

Montesquieu, writing in 1748, modified Locke's listing of powers. He was first in the modern world to define the chief powers of government as *legislative, executive,* and *judicial.* In addition, he pointed to the need for *separation of powers,* claiming that there could be no liberty if any two of the three powers were united in the same persons or body of magistrates.

Furthermore, he argued for *checks and balances* within government, praising the British example: "The legislative body being composed of two parts, they check one another by the privilege of rejecting." [3] He claimed that the legislature would become despotic if it were not checked by a veto power in the executive; that the executive could moderate the dangers in the judiciary by mitigating sentences; and that the legislature could restrain the executive and the judicial through the power of impeachment.

Ironically, Montesquieu's interpretation of the British Constitution as instituting separation of powers and checks and balances was not accurate at the time he offered it, but it had great influence on the Founding Fathers in America.

Law

From England also came a system of law that has remained the basis for the American legal system.[4] The core of this system is the *common law*—an accumulation of judicial precedents that have been evolving since the eleventh century. Common law defines the rights and obligations of men with respect to contracts, damages to persons and property, and other everyday matters. It also defines relations of citizens to government, as in the rule that officers of government are answerable to the citizens for damages caused by illegal government actions. Supplementing the common law is judge-made law called *equity*, which contains additional remedies for rights—such as the writ of injunction, by which a court orders a party to do or to refrain from doing specified acts. Also embodied in the law of England were some great procedural protections of freedom, such as the right of habeas corpus and the right to trial by jury.

Lawyers in America learned their law first from Sir Edward Coke's *Institutes* and then from Sir William Blackstone's four-volume *Commentaries on the Laws of England* (1765–69), the bible of American lawyers for generations. While Locke's second treatise provided a philosophy to justify a revolution, Blackstone's *Commentaries* supplied continuity between the common law in England and the legal thinking of Americans.

Rights

Finally, the British gave to America a heritage of rights developed over the centuries through its laws and great documents. Magna Carta (1215) declared that a man's rights should be determined by the law of the land and the judgment of his peers; the Confirmation of Charters (1295) declared that no new taxes should be levied without the consent of the people; the

---

[3] Baron de Montesquieu, *The Spirit of the Laws* (New York: Hafner, 1949), Book II, Ch. 6, p. 160.

[4] Except in the state courts of Louisiana, where the origins of the legal system are French.

Habeas Corpus Act (1678) set up more effective procedures to protect the fundamental guarantee against imprisonment without legal basis; and the Bill of Rights (1689) affirmed such liberties as the right of petition, the right to bear arms for defense, and the right of the members of Parliament to freedom of debate. Many of these rights became embedded in the procedural and substantive safeguards of the common law. Americans were to differ with the British over some claims of right, but upon achieving their independence they were to retain the most valuable bundle of civil rights ever possessed by a people to that date. The American Revolution itself was a struggle of Americans for what they considered their rights as Englishmen.

COLONIAL INSTITUTIONAL DEVELOPMENT

Anchored off the coast of New England in 1620, the Pilgrim Fathers subscribed their names to the Mayflower Compact, declaring that we "doe by these presents solemnly and mutually in the presence of God, and one of another, covenant and combine our selves togeather into a civill body politick . . . ." Although they had just acknowledged loyalty to King James, "by the grace of God" their king, they were asserting in the compact that government is formed by a social contract—that is, that political power stems from the consent of the governed. This idea that men could forge their own institutions was to be basic in the New World and was ultimately to shatter the traditions of the Old.

One year earlier, at Jamestown, Virginia, another group of colonists had met in the first representative assembly in America. Representative government already existed in the parliaments of Europe, but the meeting at Jamestown was nonetheless a symbol that man was using a method of building government by consent.

Nineteen years after the Mayflower Compact a group of emigrants from Massachusetts settled in Connecticut and there framed and decreed the Fundamental Orders of Connecticut. This document, which established the institutions of government for the new colony, was the first written constitution in the modern world. While governments in the Old World had evolved over a period of time, Americans began the practice of establishing them by positive acts of people assembled in conventions.

Three years later the legislative assembly (General Court) of Massachusetts enacted the Massachusetts Body of Liberties. They declared an intention "to collect and expresse . . . freedomes" and "to ratify them with our solemn consent." The idea of declaring rights, embodied in the great English documents, was being nurtured until the day that such declarations would become formal "bills of rights" in constitutions.

These more-or-less isolated episodes foretold the trends in American political thought and experience: popular sovereignty, representative government, fundamental law embodied in a written constitution, freedoms solemnly declared and guaranteed. Of these only the idea of a written constitution was novel, but the combination of these ideas in the American setting was to produce a political system distinct from any that had existed in the Old World.

Other solid foundations for political practice were developed in the institutions of the colonies. By the eighteenth century there was much uniformity in the major features of their governments. In each colony a charter set forth the main elements of structure. These documents, along with the compacts of the colonists and the guarantees of rights in English law, came to be regarded as basic law. This idea of a fundamental law was strengthened by the right of appeal from the highest court of a colony to the Judicial Committee of the Privy Council in England, which could set aside legislation of the colonies that contravened the charters or English law. However, the colonists in fact tended to appeal politically to their charters, rather than legally to the Privy Council, in their struggles with their British governors, and this tendency was probably the strongest factor in developing the colonial idea that the charters contained the higher, controlling law.

The structure of colonial governments came to bear close resemblance to English government structure as it had been in 1701. Each colony had a governor, who usually had prerogatives similar to those of the king: appointment of executive and judicial officials, command of the armed forces, summoning and proroguing the assembly, and an absolute veto over legislation. In each colony there was an elected assembly, which gained the right to raise taxes, to appropriate money, and to initiate and vote on legislation. In all colonies except Pennsylvania there was a second house, which, in addition to its legislative function, was ordinarily an advisory cabinet for the governor and a court of appeal (as was the House of Lords in England). Normally, the king or the proprietor appointed persons recommended by the governor to be members of the second house—usually higher administrative and judicial officials and some of the wealthier colonists. Judges were generally appointed by the governor, but in the eighteenth century the courts came to be independent in practice from executive control. Though there was much confusion of powers, especially in the second house, this system embodied a separation of powers similar to that in England.[5] Moreover, there was a working system of checks and balances between the governor, who had executive powers, and the assemblies, which had the power of the purse.

These systems were not democratic in the modern sense, for ownership of property was a prerequisite for voting, and in most colonies the require-

[5] See Benjamin Fletcher Wright, "The Origins of the Separation of Powers in America," *Economica*, Vol. VIII (May 1933), pp. 169–85.

ment could only be met by ownership of real property. Even higher qualifications were common for officeholding. Recent historical studies indicate, however, that the diffusion of property was sufficient in some parts of the country to allow a majority—in some places, even most—of the male citizens to vote. In any event, as Clinton Rossiter has shown, this was the "seedtime" for constitutionalism and popular government, when regard for constitutions and the rights of men under law fixed the spirit of constitutionalism in the colonial mind.[6] In addition, local governments throughout the colonies operated with substantial autonomy and popular control. Except for the South, where local government was appointive and aristocratic, these governments served as excellent training grounds for self-government, particularly in New England, where the town meeting and unpaid public officers prevailed. Moreover, all the colonies had a more democratic social structure than existed in the Old World, for there was no titled aristocracy, and there was freehold ownership of property as well as greater opportunity to acquire land or to move up the social scale than in the older, more developed countries.

THE EFFECTS OF THE AMERICAN REVOLUTION

Although continuity with the English tradition was not severed, the revolution in America was a moment of monumental change in the history of the world. The Revolution did much more than break connections with a mother country; it had profound additional economic, social, and political effects.

Economic Independence

One consequence of modern revolutions against colonial status is to free new nations from economic dependence and provide them with the opportunity for autonomous economic development. The American Revolution gave this opportunity to the people of "the first new nation." They were freed from taxation and commercial regulations imposed by interests dominant in the mother country and were permitted to devise, through legislatures familiar with American conditions and interests, institutions and policies to stimulate the development of American resources and to promote domestic and foreign commerce.

As colonists, Americans had had no opportunity to influence the economic policies of the mother country, because they were not represented in the House of Commons. By 1774 they were demanding complete auton-

[6] Clinton Rossiter, *Seedtime of the Republic: The Origin of the American Tradition of Political Liberty* (New York: Harcourt, Brace & World, 1953).

New York Public Library Picture Collection

Poor Old England

This eighteenth-century cartoon shows Father England having trouble restraining his American children.

omy on "taxation and internal policy," but they assented to regulations of "external commerce."[7] For American interests to have been protected by such regulations, a federal arrangement, with American representation in an imperial parliament, would have been necessary. This was, as Edmund Burke noted, rendered impossible by the ocean alone; but there were the additional difficulties of differences in economic interests between Britain and the colonies and a general lack of knowledge about federal systems of government. Samuel Adams suggested a more radical solution: full political and economic independence for the colonies, with symbolic allegiance to the monarch. This solution, similar to the twentieth-century British Commonwealth of Nations, was far too drastic for the eighteenth century. Consequently, only complete severance of ties with the mother country would permit economic development in response to the interests of the people of America.

The Dominance of Lockean Philosophy

The second effect of the Revolution was that the philosophical doctrines of Locke came out of the library, taking precedence over the rival contentions

[7] *Declaration of Rights and Resolves of the First Continental Congress.*

of other philosophers, and were adopted by the common man. Henceforth, the "natural rights of men" and "popular consent" were to be familiar themes in the political doctrine of this nation.

The Declaration of Independence would summarize these themes in 1776, but its way had been prepared by fifteen years of discussion beginning in 1761 with James Otis' speech in Boston against the writs of assistance.[8] "Then and there," said John Adams, "the child independence was born." Until 1774 Americans rested their case primarily on their legal rights as English citizens. The writs, said Otis, were an infringement of an Englishman's right of "House." A few years later others would assert that "taxation without representation" was a violation of the English Constitution. Americans also believed in a higher moral law: Otis, for example, referred to "natural equity" in 1761. The belief, however, was consonant with the rights of English citizens, because the English Constitution was presumed to embody natural equity. In 1765 the House of Representatives of Massachusetts asserted both a legal and a moral claim: it resolved that "there are certain essential rights of the British Constitution of government, which are founded in the law of God and nature, and are the common rights of mankind . . . ." [9]

By 1774, however, the colonists were prepared to separate these legal and moral claims. In the Declaration and Resolves of the First Continental Congress, they declared that they had rights "by the immutable laws of nature, the principles of the English constitution, and the several charters or compacts." Finally, by 1776 they were ready to make that ultimate appeal to a higher law of morality men make when they decide that their condition is no longer tolerable.

Tom Paine was the man who stirred Americans to this step. In a pamphlet called *Common Sense*, printed in January 1776, he assailed monarchy: "Of more worth is one honest man to society, and in the sight of God, than all the crowned ruffians that ever lived." He attacked the English Constitution as being "so exceedingly complex, that the nation may suffer for years together without being able to discover in which part the fault lies." And he appealed for independence: "Oh ye that love mankind! Ye that dare oppose, not only the tyranny, but the tyrant, stand forth!" This cry had mass appeal, and the pamphlet got mass distribution. Its significance was that it "rallied the undecided and the wavering, and proved a trumpet call to the radicals." [10] On June 7, the congress resolved that "these united colonies are and of right ought to be free and independent states" and appointed a com-

---

[8] *Writs of assistance* were general search warrants allowing officers to search homes and other premises at will. For a fuller summary of the events see Andrew C. McLaughlin, *A Constitutional History of the United States* (New York: Appleton-Century-Crofts, 1935), Chs. 1–9.

[9] Quoted in *ibid.*, p. 42.

[10] Samuel Eliot Morison and Henry Steele Commager, *The Growth of the American Republic*, 4th ed. (New York: Oxford University Press, 1950), Vol. I, p. 194.

The Natural Rights of Man: John Locke

Whenever the legislators endeavor to take away and destroy the property of the people, or to reduce them to slavery under arbitrary power, they put themselves into a state of war with the people, who are thereupon absolved from any further obedience, and are left to the common refuge which God hath provided for all men against force and violence. Whensoever, therefore, the legislative shall transgress this fundamental rule of society, and either by ambition, fear, folly, or corruption, endeavor to grasp themselves or put into the hands of any other an absolute power over the lives, liberties, and estates of the people, by this breach of trust they forfeit the power the people had put into their hands, for quite contrary ends, and it devolves to the people, who have a right to resume their original liberty, and by the establishment of the new legislative (such as they shall think fit) provide for their own safety and security, which is the end for which they are in society. What I have said here concerning the legislative in general, holds true also concerning the supreme executor, who having a double trust put in him, both to have a part in the legislative and the supreme execution of the law, acts against both when he goes about to set up his own arbitrary will as the law of the society.

From the second treatise in John Locke, *Two Treatises of Government*, 1690.

mittee with Jefferson as chairman to draft a document proclaiming the revolution.

The Declaration of Independence has two parts. The second states the grievances of the colonies and imputes to the king a long list of abuses and violations of rights. The first part is a statement of principles. In 110 words Jefferson captures Lockean philosophy in phrases so well known that their conciseness, beauty, import, and force are easily overlooked. The opening is confident: "We hold these truths to be self-evident."

1. "That all men are created equal." The meaning of this phrase is ambiguous, but the ambiguity gives new force in new situations. Jefferson made this assertion as a moral fact and as a test of government. The statement seems to mean that all men must be equal in rights; but the more specific connotations of the phrase, as with those of "equal protection of the law" in the Fourteenth Amendment, are left for the moral conscience of succeeding generations.

2. "That they are endowed by their Creator with certain unalienable Rights, that among these are Life, Liberty and the pursuit of Happiness." The Declaration gives divine sanction to natural rights—that is, rights which man has by virtue of his existence; not even his own acts can alienate these rights. This statement assumes that there is a moral law higher than civil law.

3. "That to secure these rights, Governments are instituted among Men."

This statement, which assumes a single purpose for government, represents pure Lockean doctrine. It overlooks the fact that some rights may have to be compromised to accommodate other men's claims of right as well as the fact that the objective of some men in instituting government is to obtain power over others.

4. "[Governments] deriving their just Powers from the consent of the governed." This is the principle of popular sovereignty and is opposed to claims of either divine or prescriptive right. The Declaration is silent on the possibility of conflict between popular sovereignty and natural right—that is, on actions of the people that infringe "unalienable" rights. It is silent too about how the "consent of the governed" should be provided in the organization and process of government and particularly on how divisions among the governed, arising because of their various interests and ideas, should be mediated. These were to be the central problems for the constitution makers.

The Natural Rights of Man: Samuel Adams

A Common Wealth or state is a body politick or civil society of men, united together to promote their mutual safety and prosperity, by means of their union.

The *absolute Rights* of Englishmen, and all freemen in or out of Civil society, are principally, *personal security, personal liberty* and *private property.*

All Persons born in the British American Colonies are by the laws of God and nature, and by the Common law of England, *exclusive of all charters from the Crown,* well Entitled, and by the Acts of the British Parliament are declared to be entitled to all the natural essential, inherent & inseparable Rights Liberties and Privileges of Subjects born in Great Britain, or within the Realm. Among those Rights are the following; which no men or body of men, consistently with their own rights as men and citizens or members of society, can for themselves give up, or take away from others.

First, "The first fundamental positive law of all Commonwealths or States, is the establishing the legislative power; as the first fundamental *natural* law also, which is to govern even the legislative power itself, is the preservation of the Society."

Secondly, The Legislative has no right to absolute arbitrary power over the lives and fortunes of the people: Nor can mortals assume a prerogative, not only too high for men, but for Angels; and therefore reserved for the exercise of the *Deity* alone....

Thirdly, The Supreme power cannot Justly take from any man, any part of his property without his consent, in person or by his Representative.

From Samuel Adams, "The Rights of the Colonists," in Harry Alonzo Cushing, ed., *The Writings of Samuel Adams,* 1906.

5. "That, whenever any form of Government becomes destructive of these ends, it is the Right of the People to alter or to abolish it." This too is pure Lockean doctrine. However, the Declaration immediately adds a note of caution: "Prudence, indeed, will dictate that Governments long established should not be changed for light and transient causes."

It must be made clear, however, that the equalitarianism announced in the first clause and implied in those that follow did not herald a full-scale social revolution. The temper of the Revolution can be understood only by examining the balance between social change and continuity that characterized the period.

Change and Continuity

A third consequence of the Revolution was the beginning of a period of economic, social, and religious change. The power of the aristocratic elements in society was diminished by the exodus of the Tories, the confiscation of much of their property, and the destruction of the colonial governments through which their power had been exerted. New groups of men who were not as committed to tradition rose to positions of influence. Land ownership broadened as royal limitations on free settlement were swept away, as confiscated properties were distributed, and as entails and primogeniture, which had the effect of preserving landed estates, were generally abolished. Laws were passed for the benefit of debtors—the Revolution being the first period of debtor ascendancy in the politics of America. There was a trend toward disestablishing churches and extending religious freedom. In some states slavery was abolished, or the slave trade was prohibited. And legal systems were reformed to reduce the severity of the criminal law.

Yet the striking fact about these changes, in view of their revolutionary context, is their moderation. The laws in favor of debtors are an exception, but this tendency in legislation was to be corrected by restrictions on the states in the Constitution in 1787. Some historians have found a great difference between the "spirit of 1776," which they characterize as a period of populism, and the "spirit of 1787," called a period of reaction. Any consideration of this difference between the two, however, must begin with a recognition of the overall moderation of both the social changes that followed 1776 and the work of the Framers in 1787.

This relative moderation becomes evident when the American Revolution is compared with the French Revolution of 1789 or with the Russian Revolution of 1917. The French sought the elimination of their feudal inheritance and proclaimed rights that lacked foundation in a precedent constitution or tradition. The Americans, as Louis Hartz has said, skipped the feudal stage of history and hence had no economic and social inheritance to liquidate; in the main, they sought preservation of their existing institutions. The Russians—who, according to Hartz, skipped the liberal stage of history—tore up the roots of society in a complete social revolution; the Americans sought principally *political* rather than social change.

In fact, Hartz argues that throughout American history the lack of a feudal past to be liquidated has militated against socialist doctrine; thus, the gap between the political "right" and the political "left" in America has been narrower and conflicts less intense than in Europe, where broader social antagonisms existed.[11] He refers us to a thesis of Alexis de Tocqueville: "The great advantage of the Americans is, that they have arrived at a state of democracy without having to endure a democratic revolution; and that they are born equal, instead of becoming so." [12]

The First State Governments

The fourth consequence of the Revolution was the formation of state governments. In 1775, as fighting occurred and royal governors and other officials fled, governments began to pass into the hands of revolutionary assemblies. Following the Declaration of Independence there was a period of constitution-making, in which men freed of old governments but familiar with history and doctrine were given the opportunity to create new forms of government to implement the doctrines of rule of law and popular consent.

The framing of constitutions

The first step was to base state governments on written constitutions. These constitutions repeated the principles of the Declaration of Independence, but at the same time they limited majority rule by establishing a fundamental law, by instituting separation of powers and checks and balances, and by continuing the limitations on suffrage. Also, despite their emphasis on democratic principles, these constitutions were drafted and put into effect in ways that would seem somewhat undemocratic today. In Connecticut and Rhode Island the old charters were simply used as the state constitutions without a vote of the people. In some states constitutions were framed by revolutionary assemblies and put into operation without any approval by voters. But there was some protest: Jefferson said that the Virginia convention had usurped the "natural right" of the people, and a Massachusetts constitution was rejected by voters in 1778 mainly on the ground that a legislature had no right to draft a constitution. There was special authorization by the electorate in some states and informal submission in some others. Finally, in 1780, Massachusetts developed a procedure to implement the

---

[11] Louis Hartz, *The Liberal Tradition in America* (New York: Harcourt, Brace & World, 1955), Ch. 1.

[12] Alexis de Tocqueville, *Democracy in America* (New York: Knopf, 1945), Vol. II, p. 108.

principles of popular sovereignty and fundamental law. First, the legislature submitted to the people the question of whether they wanted to elect delegates to a constitutional convention. Second, after their affirmative vote, the people elected delegates to a convention. And, third, the constitution that emerged was ratified by popular vote. This procedure was to become typical of American practice.

Prominent in some of these constitutions were bills of rights. The rights enumerated were mainly those of the English common law, such as trial by jury, or those of the great English documents. Yet some constitutions went beyond these rights; the Virginia bill of rights (1776), for example, included a precedent-setting provision guaranteeing religious freedom. Mixed with the guarantees of rights were statements of principle, one of which was the rule of law—"to the end it may be a government of laws and not of men," as the Massachusetts constitution of 1780 declared.

That constitution also affirmed separation of powers in government as the means of obtaining a government of law. This principle was stated in many of the constitutions. For instance, the Maryland constitution declared that "the legislative, executive and judicial powers of government ought to be forever separate and distinct from each other."

Nevertheless, the first state governments showed a marked concentration of powers in the legislature. Reacting against the colonial experience of strong executives, the framers of state constitutions established legislative supremacy in two ways. First, most of the states provided that the legislature elect the governor, and it usually selected the judges as well. Accompanying provisions set short terms and limitations on reelection of governors. Second, the constitutions failed to provide for checks on the legislature. Thus, in Rhode Island and Connecticut, where the governor was elected by the people, he possessed no veto power over legislation. Yet legislative supremacy, like adoption of constitutions, encountered protest. Jefferson, noting that the Virginia constitution of 1776 provided no checks on the legislature, declared that "one hundred and seventy-three despots would surely be as oppressive as one." The New York constitution of 1777 was the first to point toward the independence of the three departments and the combination of separation of powers and checks and balances that was to prevail in American governments.

It was the Massachusetts constitution of 1780, however, that set the real pattern for the future. It joined the principles of popular sovereignty and of fundamental law limiting government to a written constitution emanating from the people, and, similarly, it joined the twin principles of separation of powers and checks and balances with the idea of liberty under law. This constitution provided for a two-house legislature, as did all but three state constitutions. The legislature could appoint some executive officers, and the lower house could bring impeachment charges for trial in the upper house. The governor was elected by the people. He could appoint most executive and all judicial officers with the consent of a council predominantly legislative in composition; he could veto legislation (subject to repassage by two-thirds vote of both houses of the legislature); and he could pardon criminal offenses with the consent of the council. Judges would hold office during good behavior (except for removal by the governor with the consent of the council upon request of the legislature), and their salaries could not be diminished during their terms of office. Judges of the supreme court could give advisory opinions to the legislature (and still can in Massachusetts). Here then was a distribution of powers in which some legislative power was vested in the executive and the judiciary, some judicial power in the legislature and the governor, and some executive power in the legislature. The Massachusetts constitution embodied separation of powers, qualified and thus made effective by checks and balances.

Another development that was to increase the checks and balances in the system of government was the rise of *judicial review*. The state courts soon began to assert that they had the power to hold acts of the legislature unconstitutional and thus assumed what was to become the primary role of the judiciary in the system of checks and balances.

Men and property

How were these institutional arrangements for government related to the social composition of society? Who among the people could participate in government? The qualifications for voting varied widely. In Virginia, according to Jefferson, less than half the taxpayers could vote, while, according to a recent study, most adult men in Massachusetts could vote.[13] And in some states, where the only requirement was that one be a taxpayer, there was virtual white manhood suffrage. Yet the movement for extension of the suffrage was irregular and not always successful.[14]

A larger amount of property was required in some states for voting for the upper house than for the lower one, and substantial property ownership was required in some states for holding elective office. The prerequisites for voting and holding office in the several states indicate that those who possessed power believed that it should be retained in the hands of those who had some stake in society and that ownership of property was the safest proof of such a stake. Yet the possession of property was so widespread, and the qualifications for voting often so easy to meet, that the popular base for government was quite broad in many parts of the country.

[13] See Robert E. Brown, *Middle-Class Democracy and the Revolution in Massachusetts, 1691–1780* (Ithaca, N.Y.: Cornell University Press, 1955).
[14] See Elisha P. Douglass, *Rebels and Democrats: The Struggle for Equal Political Rights and Majority Rule during the American Revolution* (Chapel Hill, N.C.: University of North Carolina Press, 1955).

The United States of America and the Articles of Confederation

The fifth result of the War of Independence was the creation of the United States of America. Union had been discussed on earlier occasions, but its real beginnings lay in the cooperation that developed among the colonies during the conflict with England. Local committees of correspondence arose to keep in touch with one another throughout the colonies, and in 1774 representatives of extralegal groups met in the First Continental Congress. In 1775 the Second Continental Congress met, and for the next six years it was the extralegal central government. It declared independence, selected a commander in chief, conducted negotiations with friendly nations, and sought support for Washington's armies.

When the resolution for independence was introduced in the Continental Congress on June 7, 1776, it was accompanied by a resolution outlining steps to be taken to form a confederation. The Continental Congress selected a committee to draft a constitution, and the committee drew up the Articles of Confederation. The Congress debated it, approved it, and submitted it to the states. Ratification of the document was delayed until a conflict between the states that owned Western lands and those that did not was settled. The Articles, the first constitution of the United States, went into effect on March 1, 1781.

The first article officially created the name "The United States of America." The union thus born was a confederation—that is, a union of states rather than of people, similar to the United Nations today. The Articles declared that "Each state retains its sovereignty, freedom, and independence," and every power not "expressly delegated" to the national government was reserved to the states. The powers given to the confederation were vested in a congress in which each state had one vote.

The lasting contributions of the Articles to the solution of the problems of federal union have generally been overlooked. First, the Articles enumerated several "sole and exclusive" powers of Congress to: negotiate peace and declare war, enter into treaties and alliances, regulate the value of coins, fix standards of weights and measures, regulate trade with the Indians, establish post offices, build and equip a navy, and borrow money on its own authority. Second, it established some basic rules of interstate comity and cooperation: (1) "The free inhabitants of each of these states . . . shall be entitled to all privileges and immunities of free citizens in the several states." This declaration was accompanied by a statement of the specific rights of free ingress and egress to and from every state and of trade and commerce on the same conditions with inhabitants of the state. (2) Each state was required to return fugitives from justice to the state from which they had escaped. (3) "Full faith and credit shall be given in each of these states to the records, acts and judicial proceedings of the courts and magistrates in every other state."

There were, nevertheless, fundamental defects in the Articles of Confederation. First, the national government lacked two important powers—to tax and to regulate commerce. Second, no provision was made for an executive, other than committees of Congress, or for a judiciary, except such courts as Congress might establish for trial of piracy and felony on the high seas and for hearing appeals in all cases of prize capture. Third, no important decisions could be made without the concurrence of nine states. Fourth, in the absence of power to tax, Congress had to requisition the states for funds, and to raise an army it had to requisition each state for its quota of troops. Fifth, the new government had no enforcement power over individuals through executive officials or judges. Finally, the Articles could be strengthened only through amendments proposed by Congress and ratified by the legislature of every state. The defect of this procedure was revealed by the failure of two amendments proposed by Congress because only twelve of the thirteen states ratified them.

Foremost among the practical difficulties of the confederation was the failure of the states to honor requisitions upon them and to abide by treaty obligations. The provision in the Articles that "every state shall abide by the determinations of the united states in Congress assembled" on questions within its province proved to be admonition only.

Added difficulties arose from the states' encroachments upon one another's commerce and from the inability of Congress to make treaty arrangements concerning commerce. Another problem, Madison noted, was the "multiplicity," "mutability," and "injustice" of the laws of the states. The states not only engaged in commercial competition with one another, but each issued its own paper money and loosened the obligations of contract by allowing payment of debts in depreciated currency. These conditions naturally led to dissatisfaction among financial and commercial groups. The activities of the business community were seriously impaired by the lack of a single monetary system, the multiple regulations of the states on commerce, the inability of Congress to conclude and enforce trade treaties, and its lack of power to levy duties to protect infant manufactures.

Some statesmen attributed the failure of the Articles to weak and evil human nature; but others saw its problems as institutional and as early as 1780 made proposals for a stronger central government for the Union. In succeeding years Congress proposed amendments, state legislatures suggested changes, and leading figures corresponded about government reform. Many proposals related to commerce, indicating the truth of Madison's statement that "most of our political evils can be traced to our commercial ones."

A dispute between Virginia and Maryland over commerce on the Potomac precipitated the series of events leading to a new constitution. In 1786 Virginia invited all the states to send commissioners to a meeting to consider the trade of the United States. Commissioners from five states met at Annapolis in September. This group decided that discussion should be extended to other subjects and suggested that the states send delegates to Philadelphia "to devise such further provisions as shall appear to them necessary to render the constitution of the federal government adequate to the exigencies of the union." On February 21, 1787, Congress issued its own call for the meeting in Philadelphia "for the sole and express purpose of revising the Articles of Confederation." The convention met in Philadelphia in May 1787.

A CONSTITUTION FOR THE UNION

Challenge and Response

The task of constructing political institutions for a nation in 1787 was among the most complex ever faced by institution builders.[15] The dominant objective that held the delegates together through months of division and tension was the establishment of a durable union. Complicating this task was the problem of providing protective and expansionist opportunities to commercial and financial interests, who were hampered by the existing system of state sovereignty. Moreover, the delegates had to solve issues of structural arrangements similar to those that had confronted the framers of state constitutions.

The convention that faced this task brought into focus all the major conflicts of interest and opinion in the nation: large versus small states, North versus South, East versus West, nationalists versus states'-righters, popular-government advocates versus élitists. These conflicts made decisions difficult, but the confrontation of interests ensured that solutions arrived at would bridge the diversities within the nation.

It has been customary to attribute the success of the convention to a spirit of give and take and to call the Constitution a "bundle of compromises." There were indeed many compromises, well illustrated by those between the North and the South. The differences between an agricultural, exporting, slave-holding South and a manufacturing, commercial, free-labor North deeply affected many aspects of the Constitution. Madison said that "the great danger to our general government is the great southern and northern interests of the continent, being opposed to each other." In one compromise, the Southern delegates accepted the regulation of commerce desired by the Northern commercial interests with the proviso that exports would not be taxed; in another, South and North agreed on a three-fifths ratio for counting slaves in determining representation in the national House of Representatives. In still another, the South obtained a guarantee

[15] The material in this section was drawn substantially from Max Farrand, *The Framing of the Constitution* (New Haven, Conn.: Yale University Press, 1913), Ch. 2.

that no limitations would be imposed on the importation of slaves before 1808.

Yet the convention's success was due also to concurrence—indeed unanimity—of opinion on many matters. The delegates were agreed on the evils of the existing system, and they all sought a viable republican government—one in which, as Madison was to say later, the government "derives all its powers directly or indirectly from the great body of the people." [16] They were agreed that the government should embody separation of powers and checks and balances, that the Constitution of the Union should be "the supreme law," and that state restrictions on commerce and invasions of property rights should be restrained.[17]

A third factor contributing to the Convention's success was the persistence and seriousness of the delegates in groping for workable solutions—their problem-solving attitude. This was reflected in a willingness to deliberate. Difficult problems or those on which there was division were postponed, brought up for reconsideration, and then patiently reanalyzed in the light of decisions taken in the interim.

The men who made the momentous decisions were the type one would expect to be sent to a convention of this kind—lawyers and judges, businessmen, a few doctors, college presidents, college professors, and gentlemen of leisure—men of education and of experience in public affairs. Of the fifty-five delegates who attended, thirty-one had college educations, thirty-nine had been members of Congress, seven had been state governors, and eight had served in constitutional conventions.[18] Farrand has said that they "took their work seriously." [19] Indeed, some of them would have agreed with Madison's statement to the convention that they "were now to decide for ever the fate of republican government."

The member who made the greatest contribution to the success of the convention was James Madison, who has been called "the Father of the Constitution." Thirty-six years old, experienced in state government and in Congress, he—in the words of a fellow delegate—blended "together the profound politician with the scholar" and was "a most agreeable, eloquent and convincing speaker." [20] He had made a thorough study of man's experience with confederations, had corresponded with others about the problems of union, and was apparently regarded as the leader of the faction in the convention that favored a strong national government.

[16] *The Federalist*, No. 39.

[17] For fuller discussion, see Carl J. Friedrich and Robert G. McCloskey, *From the Declaration of Independence to the Constitution: The Roots of American Constitutionalism* (New York: Liberal Arts Press, 1954), pp. xlvi–liv.

[18] Charles Warren, *The Making of the Constitution* (Boston: Little, Brown and Company, 1928), Vol. I, pp. 55–56.

[19] Farrand, *op. cit.*, p. 61.

[20] Quoted from Notes of Major William Pierce (Georgia) in the Federal Convention of 1787, in *Documents Illustrative of the Formation of the Union of the American States* (Washington: 1927).

A few others played key roles in the drafting of the Constitution. One was James Wilson of Pennsylvania, forty-five, an immigrant from Scotland, an able lawyer, a signer of the Declaration of Independence, and several times a member of Congress. As draftsman in the committee of detail, he had an unusual opportunity to influence the content of the Constitution. George Washington's influence on the members must have been great, and it was given in support of the plan for a strong national government. Gouverneur Morris, brilliant member of the Pennsylvania delegation, also supported a strong government and, as a member of the committee on style and arrangement, did much to shape the final form and language of the Constitution. Alexander Hamilton, only thirty years of age, was one of the convention's ablest members, but his views favoring a strong government were more extreme than those of his colleagues, and he left early, returning only to sign the finished document.

The convention selected Washington as president and resolved to meet in secret and to allow each state one vote in the proceedings. Ultimately, all states except Rhode Island were represented at the convention, which was in almost continuous session from May 25 until September 17. Late in the sessions the convention referred the resolutions it had passed to a committee of detail composed of five members and finally to a committee on style and arrangement. A full record of the convention's deliberations and votes is preserved for us in Madison's notes.

Let us examine the four most significant achievements of the convention: its establishment of a national government; its provision of economic opportunities for commercial and financial interests; its plan for electing a President; and its accommodation of conflicting viewpoints on the issues of property and popular government.

A National Government

The most important decision of the convention was made on the first day of its deliberations, when it adopted a resolution by Governor Randolph of Virginia, seconded by Gouverneur Morris, "that a *national* government ought to be established consisting of a *supreme* legislative, executive, and judiciary." [21] The delegates understood the purport of this momentous resolution: Morris said that a "national, supreme government" would be a "*compulsive* operation." Mason added that a government was needed that "could operate directly on individuals." General Pinkney, moreover, expressed doubt as to whether the delegates' instructions from their states allowed them to go this far, for technically they had been assembled to amend the Articles of Confederation, which was a confederation of states, rather than to create a national government whose authority applied directly to individuals. The resolution passed, with six ayes, New York divided, Connecticut opposed.

[21] The emphases appear in Madison's notes.

This was a bold decision, and it took genius to adapt the concept of a national government to the coexistence of thirteen states of varying size. The genius was collective, born out of debate, conflict, compromise, and consciousness of realities. The product was something theretofore unknown— a federal system of government, different both from a confederation of states and from a consolidation of powers in a single government. To produce the blueprint for this new type of union the convention had to solve several problems.

Division of powers

First, how much power should be delegated to the national government, and how should this be done? The Virginia Plan, which was no doubt primarily the work of Madison, proposed that the national legislature should have, in addition to the powers vested in the Congress of the Confederation, the power "to legislate in all cases to which the separate states are incompetent, or in which the harmony of the United States may be interrupted by the exercise of individual legislation." This general statement on the scope of national powers was adopted but was later followed by an enumeration of national powers. The national government was to be one with delegated powers of two types. First, it was granted express powers, stated at various points in the Constitution but primarily in seventeen grants of power in Article I, Section 8. They include authority over matters of war and foreign affairs, such as the power to declare war, raise armies, equip navies, establish uniform rules of naturalization, and so on. Other powers relate to the regulation and service of the economy, such as the powers to coin money and regulate its value and to regulate interstate and foreign commerce. The national power to tax was granted in broad terms: to pay the debts and provide for the "common defense" and "general welfare" of the United States. Miscellaneous powers included authority to grant patents and copyrights, establish post offices and post roads, and make laws on bankruptcy. Second, the government was granted specifically what might have been implicit—the power to carry out its express powers. The provision making this grant was subsequently to be called the *implied-powers clause:* "To make all laws which shall be necessary and proper for carrying into execution the foregoing powers, and all other powers vested by this Constitution in the government of the United States, or in any department or officer thereof."

Conspicuously absent from the Constitution was the provision of the Articles of Confederation that every power not "expressly delegated" to the Union was reserved to the states. Such a clause would of course have been inconsistent with the implied-powers clause. The blueprint of the Framers was to be affirmed, not altered, by the Tenth Amendment to the Constitution, passed in 1791: "The powers not delegated to the United States by the Constitution, nor prohibited by it to the States, are reserved to the States respectively, or to the people." The amendment does not say "expressly delegated," and thus it acknowledges that the national government has implied as well as express powers.

This delegation of powers left the states substantial independent authority with respect to many matters, such as regulation of the ownership, use, and transmission of property; definition of offenses against persons and property (criminal law and torts); rules for marriage and divorce; regulation of local business, trades, and professions; provisions for education, welfare, and correctional activities; construction of roads, canals, and other public works; taxation for these and other purposes; and the organization of local governments.

Although both national and state governments were to have some exclusive powers, the Constitution allowed both to exercise authority over the same affairs. Under these concurrent powers, both could tax, spend money for the general welfare, and pass overlapping or complementary laws on many matters.

The blueprint of the Framers also included certain prohibitions on the national and state governments. A few of these, such as the prohibitions against *ex post facto* laws (making an act a criminal offense retroactively) and bills of attainder (punishing a person or group without giving them a judicial trial), protected persons against both governments. Some, like the prohibition against taxes by the national government on exports, were compromises necessary to get agreement on the Constitution. Most prohibitions, however, applied to the states and were designed either to safeguard the national unity sought by the Constitution, or to protect commercial and financial interests, or both. Some powers were absolutely denied to the states—such as authority to coin money, to enter into treaties with foreign powers, or to interfere with the obligations of contract. Other powers were denied to the states unless Congress gave its consent—such as laying of duties on imports or exports, entering into compacts with other states, or keeping troops and warships in peacetime.

The enforcement of national supremacy

A second problem has been referred to as "the problem of coercion." How could the national government enforce its policies? The Virginia Plan proposed that the national legislature have the power "to negative all laws passed by the several states, contravening in the opinion of the national legislature the articles of union" and the further power "to call forth the force of the union" against states failing to fulfill their duties. It is fortunate that these solutions were not adopted, for the first would have brought direct conflict between national and state governments, and the second would have created civil war between the Union and resisting states.

The convention devised a four-part solution for the problem. First, the

Constitution, following the basic recommendation of the Virginia Plan, established a national government operating through executive and judicial organs on *people* rather than on states. The second and third parts come from a plan submitted by the New Jersey delegation. The Constitution declares: "This Constitution, the laws of the United States which shall be made in pursuance thereof, and all treaties made or which shall be made, under the authority of the United States, shall be *the supreme law of the land*." (Italics added.) This supreme-law-of-the-land clause embodies the principle of national supremacy—that is, the principle that the Constitution and national actions taken in accord with it take precedence over state constitutions and state actions. The Constitution continues: "And the judges in every state shall be bound thereby, anything in the constitution or laws of any state to the contrary notwithstanding." Thus, the judges of the states were made the instrument for enforcing national supremacy.

This method of enforcement would have been a feeble answer to the problem of coercion had it not been supplemented by a fourth provision. The Constitution defined the "judicial power of the United States" to apply to all cases arising under the Constitution, laws, or treaties of the United States. In accordance with this provision the First Congress passed the Judiciary Act of 1789, providing that a case could be appealed from the highest *state* court to the Supreme Court of the United States if it involved a claim made under the Constitution or laws of the United States and denied by the state court.

The basic answers, therefore, to the problem of national-state conflict were: (1) enforcement of national law on *individuals*, not states; (2) a declaration of the supremacy of the Constitution, constitutional laws, and treaties of the United States; (3) resolution of issues of national and state power in the courts as these are presented by *individuals;* and (4) the right of *individuals* to appeal issues to the Supreme Court. This set of solutions for the crucial issue in the plan of union accorded with the ideal of the rule of law, basic to the thinking of the Framers. It solved the problem of state coercion by avoiding its necessity. Only in the Civil War and in the struggles over desegregation has "the force of the union" been used against the states.

Representation

The third problem in forming a national union was that of representation. This is always a difficult problem in forming a union of unequal states. The large-state–small-state cleavage actually threatened to wreck the convention. Feelings were so intense on one occasion that Franklin suggested prayer, to which Hamilton—the first American isolationist—is reported to have replied that the convention had no need of "foreign aid." The Virginia Plan proposed that the national legislature consist of two houses, with rep-

The Case for Equal Representation

[WILLIAM PATERSON of New Jersey] considered the proposition for a proportional representation as striking at the existence of the lesser states.... The idea of a national government, as contradistinguished from a federal one, never entered into the mind of any of [the states]; and to the public mind we must accommodate ourselves. We have no power to go beyond the federal scheme; and if we had, the people are not ripe for any other. We must follow the people; the people will not follow us. The *proposition* could not be maintained, whether considered in reference to us as a nation or as a confederacy. A confederacy supposes sovereignty in the members composing it and sovereignty supposes equality. If we are to be considered as a nation, all state distinctions must be abolished, the whole must be thrown into hotchpot, and when an equal division is made, then there may be fairly an equality of representation....

Give the large states an influence in proportion to their magnitude, and what will be the consequences? Their ambition will be proportionally increased, and the small states will have everything to fear....

He alluded to the hint thrown out by Mr. Wilson, of the necessity to which the large states might be reduced, of confederating among themselves by a refusal of the others to concur. Let them unite if they please, but let them remember that they have no authority to compel the others to unite. New Jersey will never confederate on the plan before the Committee. She would be swallowed up. He had rather submit to a monarch, to a despot, than to such a fate.

From James Madison, *Journal of the Constitutional Convention of 1787*, ed. 1819.

resentation in both apportioned among the states on the basis of "quotas of contribution" or of number of free inhabitants. A fight ensued, and the large states won a temporary victory. But New Jersey brought forth an alternative plan, and both plans were referred to the committee of the whole for consideration. The New Jersey Plan proposed a revision of the Articles—retaining a one-house congress with equal state representation but granting it additional powers, such as the powers to levy import duties and to regulate commerce, and providing for an executive and a judiciary. This plan would have continued the need to requisition funds from the states. After debate the convention confirmed the important decision made earlier to base its deliberations on the Virginia Plan. But it was now brought perilously close to adjournment without agreement on the crucial issue of representation. The Great Compromise, which solved the problem, was itself a narrow decision, made by 5 yeas and 4 nays (Massachusetts divided, New York delegates absent). It is probably the most significant single-vote majority in American history. A few men of compromise saved the convention. The heart of the solution was equal representation in the Senate and proportional representation in the House of Representatives. Other features were the counting of each slave as three-fifths of a person in the enumeration of population, the apportionment of direct taxes on the same basis as representation in the House of Representatives, and the requirement that revenue bills originate in the House.

The compromise on representation in Congress was accompanied by another adjustment between the representation of people and the representation of states: the method of amending the Constitution preserves state participation through the role of the Senate and through the requirement that amendments be ratified by three-fourths of the states.

Intergovernmental relations

Creating the blueprint of a federal union required arrangements concerning the relation of the states to each other. These problems were not difficult for the convention, largely because the Articles of Confederation had already solved many of them. Each state was required to respect and enforce

The Case for Proportional Representation

[JAMES WILSON of Pennsylvania] entered elaborately into the defense of a proportional representation, stating for his first position, that, as all authority was derived from the people, equal numbers of people ought to have an equal number of representatives, and different numbers of people, different numbers of representatives. This principle had been improperly violated in the Confederation, owing to the urgent circumstances of the time....

Are not the citizens of Pennsylvania equal to those of New Jersey? Does it require one hundred and fifty of the former to balance fifty of the latter? Representatives of different districts ought clearly to hold the same proportion to each other as their respective constituents hold to each other. If the small states will not confederate on this plan, Pennsylvania, and he presumed some other states, would not confederate on any other. We have been told that each state being sovereign, all are equal. So each man is naturally a sovereign over himself, and all men are therefore naturally equal. Can he retain this equality when he becomes a member of civil government? He cannot. As little can a sovereign state, when it becomes a member of a federal government. If New Jersey will not part with her sovereignty, it is vain to talk of government. A new partition of the states is desirable, but evidently and totally impracticable.

From James Madison, *Journal of the Constitutional Convention of 1787*, ed. 1819.

in the courts the laws and judicial decisions "of every other state" (the full-faith-and-credit clause); to give citizens of other states all the privileges and immunities given to its own citizens; and to "deliver up" at the request of state executive authorities persons charged with crime in another state. The states could, with the consent of Congress, enter into agreements or compacts with each other. New states were to be admitted to the Union by Congress, but no state could be created within the boundaries of an existing state or from parts of several states without the consent of their state legislatures. In addition, the national government was charged with the obligation to guarantee every state a "republican form of government," protect states against invasion, and control "domestic violence" when invited into the state by its legislature (or executive when the legislature "cannot be convened").

The result of the solution to these problems—delegation, coercion, representation, intergovernmental relations—was a system of government unique in two ways. First, it established a constitution for two governments, each possessing substantial powers and independence and both having power over the same individuals. Second, the system combined the characteristic feature of a confederacy (that is, participation of sovereign states) with the characteristic feature of a national, or unitary, system (namely, representation of people). This system, called *federalism*, accommodates the conflicting desires for unity and separateness.

Economic Opportunities

The second major problem confronting the Framers was the one that had brought the convention into existence—the need to provide economic opportunity and security for the commercial and financial interests of the nation. The convention solved this problem in several constitutional provisions. First, the Framers retained from the Articles of Confederation the privileges-and-immunities section, which provided every citizen with *free access* to the resources of the entire nation. Another constitutional clause provided for national regulation of interstate and foreign commerce—a provision won by Northern business interests by granting Southerners a proviso that exports would not be taxed. The commerce provision, later broadly interpreted by the Supreme Court, made the United States *one large common market*. Third, the convention expressed its general consensus on security for the entrepreneur by giving Congress the power to coin money and regulate its value and by prohibiting the states from coining money, issuing paper money, or impairing the obligation of contracts. Fourth, the Framers made treaties—including, of course, trade treaties—supreme law of the land. And, finally, they provided the national government with sufficient strength to preserve tranquility, protect commerce, and aid in the development of Western territory.

The Choice of the Executive

The third major problem solved by the Framers—which perhaps best exemplifies their persistence in seeking answers to difficult questions—was that of deciding on a method for selecting the President. Said Wilson, "It is in truth the most difficult [problem] we have had to decide." Both the Virginia and the New Jersey Plans provided for election by the national legislature, and five times the delegates voted for this method.[22] Yet objections were repeatedly raised against this solution: the President's election would be the subject of intrigues in the legislature; the Presidency would be weakened by its dependence on the legislature; and "usurpation and tyranny on the part of the legislature will be the consequence." Madison argued that it was "a fundamental principle of free government" that the three powers of government should be "independently exercised." Wilson and Gouverneur Morris preferred election by the people, and Madison agreed that this was "the fittest in itself." But Wilson and a majority of the delegates doubted the practicality of a popular election over such a large area. Madison noted too that the great variations in suffrage qualifications among the states created a problem for a system of popular election. Proposals for selection of the executive by the state legislatures or governors were rejected because they would weaken the national government. Selection of the President by electors chosen by the people in local districts was proposed early by Wilson, when he was asked to "digest" the method of election by the people into "form." The final decision to choose the President by state electors was a result of the common desire to avoid the defects of all the other suggested methods.

Property and Men

The fourth major problem successfully dealt with by the Framers was the need to resolve the conflicting desires for popular government and for special protection for property rights. In interpreting the work of the convention, many writers have stressed the fact that it reflected a conservative reaction against the populism of the Revolutionary period. Although this interpretation is substantially accurate, it should not overshadow the recognition of other elements in a complex matrix.

Many members did indeed express fear and distrust of the people, and some undoubtedly agreed with Gerry (who did not sign the Constitution) that "the evils we experience flow from the excess of democracy." Others, however, would not have agreed. Thus, when Madison predicted that in the future the majority of the people would have no property and argued that "the freeholders of society would be the safest depositories of republican

[22] Clinton Rossiter, *The American Presidency*, 2nd ed. (New York: Harcourt, Brace & World, 1960), p. 77.

liberty," Franklin responded "that we should not depress the virtue and public spirit of our common people."

The views of three convention leaders exemplify the major lines of opinion among the delegates. At one extreme was the simple national democracy of James Wilson. He desired a strong national government, and to achieve this he argued for a government based on the people rather than on the states. He favored popular election of both houses of Congress and of the President and annual election of members of the lower house. He believed that the "majority of people wherever found ought in all questions to govern the minority." The President should be a "man of the people."

In contrast was the more complex political thought of Gouverneur Morris—scornful of democracy but nonetheless showing some strains of democratic thought. He asserted that men "unite in society for the protection of property," and he fought vigorously for a freehold qualification for suffrage, fearing that people who have no property would sell their votes "to the rich who will be able to buy them." Yet he favored election of the President by the people, arguing first that "if the people should elect, they will never fail to prefer some man of distinguished character, or services" and second that the President "should be the guardian of the people, even of the lower classes, against legislative tyranny, against the great and the wealthy who in the course of things will necessarily compose the legislative body."

Between the two was the qualified democracy of James Madison. Government, he said, "ought to secure the permanent interests [i.e., of property] of the country against innovation." He feared that majorities "might under sudden impulses be tempted to commit injustice on the minority." To avoid this he recommended dividing "the trust between different bodies of men, who might watch and check each other"; "refining the popular appointments" through indirect election of senators, President, and judges; and, in particular, making the Senate a check on democracy by providing long terms for senators.

There were many provisions in the Constitution to protect property rights. The Senate, for example, was intended to represent state legislatures, which were presumed to be more favorable to property rights than the people. There were also the prohibitions against states' coining money, issuing paper money, or impairing the obligation of contracts. There were compromises to protect sectional economic interests—East versus West, North versus South. And there was even acceptance of the right of one man to hold another as his property.

Yet on certain issues of vast importance the convention left the door open for democratic developments. For example, it left the determination of voting rights to the states; and, though it was doubtless impracticable to do anything else because of the differences among the states in suffrage requirements, the delegates could see that liberal suffrage provisions would prevail. Similarly, the delegates left to Congress the right to admit new states with the same rules of representation as the original states had. Thus, although the delegates could foresee the democratic tendencies of the Western frontier, they did not place barriers against equality for the people of the West.

When time brought veneration to the convention, historians attributed to its members lofty moral motivations. Then, in direct contrast, Charles A. Beard in 1913 wrote *An Economic Interpretation of the Constitution*. Beard argued that the convention was called because certain economic interests were adversely affected by existing conditions. These interests included people who held depreciated government bonds and desired a government that would pay their face value; those engaged in manufacturing and commerce, who wanted a protective tariff and relief from state interference with commerce; those who wanted a government that could protect their investments in Western lands; and those with money to invest, who wanted to be rid of state paper money and laws impairing contracts. According to Beard, the members of the convention framed a Constitution to protect their own interests. These conclusions have aroused heated discussions about the motivations of the Framers.[23]

Undoubtedly the Framers recognized the adverse effects of the confederation system on important economic interests and sought to correct the causes, for they were realistic men with knowledge of the problems of their day. It is no reflection on human nature to recognize that men seek to protect their economic interests through the use of government, for there is an economic foundation to human welfare. But were the self-interests of the Framers so dominant that they prevented the establishment of a government in which the interests of all classes and groups of men were protected? Beard himself did not intend to draw this conclusion. For it is clear that statesmanship of an unusually high quality ruled the deliberations of the convention. The result was a system of government under which, save only for the Civil War, there could be peaceful processes of struggle, compromise, and consensus among widely disparate interests and opinions within a large and growing nation.

RATIFICATION

The convention resolved to submit the new Constitution to conventions in the separate states for ratification and to provide that it go into effect when nine states had approved it. There were several reasons for submitting the

[23] Among these discussions, reference may be made to Robert E. Brown, *Charles Beard and the Constitution: A Critical Analysis of "An Economic Interpretation of the Constitution"* (Princeton, N.J.: Princeton University Press, 1956), and Forrest McDonald, *We the People: The Economic Origins of the Constitution* (Chicago: University of Chicago Press, 1958).

The Ninth PILLAR erected !

" The Ratification of the Conventions of nine States, shall be sufficient for the establishment of this Constitution, between the States so ratifying the same." *Art.* vii.

INCIPIENT MAGNI PROCEDERE MENSES.

This 1787 cartoon illustrates the significance of Virginia's ratification of the Constitution: as the ninth state to ratify, she put the new government into effect; and, as one of the most powerful states, her support was essential to its success.

Constitution to state conventions rather than to the state legislatures. First, as Rufus King said, the state legislatures, "being [about] to lose power, will be most likely to raise objections." Second, as Madison put it, a national constitution ought to be a source of authority "paramount to the respective constitutions of the states," which would not be true if it rested on the sanction of the state legislatures only. Third, again in Madison's words, "the new constitution should be ratified in the most unexceptional form, and by the supreme authority of the people themselves."

Legal or Political Act?

The convention began by violating its instructions to revise the Articles; it closed by submitting a Constitution for ratification by a method that violated the amendment clause of the Articles in two ways: the Constitution was to be ratified in state conventions rather than state legislatures, and it was to go into effect on approval of nine states rather than all thirteen. Thus, the framing and ratification of the Constitution—following in the tradition of the Declaration of Independence, the framing of the state constitutions, and the adoption of the Articles—represented not a legal act but a *political* act of establishing a new government. This act, however, like the Massachusetts constitution, was grounded on popular approval, which, according to the theory of popular sovereignty, is the only sound basis for a supreme political act.

A Contest and Its Aftermath

The battle over ratification was a bitter one, and the Constitution squeezed through by a narrow margin. Rumors about the content of the Constitution spread, and suspicion arose that popular liberties were being threatened. Hostility developed among diverse economic groups: small farmers who feared domination by financial and commercial interests; men of property who were concerned about the government's new taxing powers; and sectional groups who thought too much had been granted to other sections. Patrick Henry and George Mason in Virginia, Governor George Clinton in New York, and Elbridge Gerry in Massachusetts fought vigorously, sometimes viciously, against ratification. The deciding factor, however, was superior leadership among the forces seeking ratification. Men held in high esteem by their fellows used influence, strategy, argument, and persuasion to win narrow victories in four pivotal states. In Pennsylvania they dragged in a quorum from the inns and steamrollered a resolution through the legislature authorizing a convention to be held only five weeks later, thus preventing the organization of effective opposition. In Massachusetts they beguiled John Hancock into support and won over Samuel Adams by promising amendments to the Constitution; these powerful men helped to achieve ratification by a vote of 187 to 168. In Virginia the first step was to win over the influential Governor Randolph, who at the Philadelphia convention had refused to sign the Constitution; the second was to align a list of great speakers—Randolph, Edmund Pendleton, George Wythe, "Light-Horse Harry" Lee, John Marshall, Madison, and others; and the third was to agree to submit to Congress amendments containing guarantees of rights. In New York the strategy included writing *The Federalist* in exposition of the Constitution. When these four big states and seven others had ratified the Constitution, the proponents of ratification worked to arrange that it be put into effect. Two states—North Carolina and Rhode Island—ratified it only after the new government was established.

Three aspects of the struggle over ratification are worthy of special note. First, Patrick Henry's pointed question early in the debates in the Virginia ratifying convention as to why the Framers started the preamble to the Constitution with "We, the people" instead of "We, the states" not only reflected the objection to a strong national union among the opponents of ratification but presaged a continuing political conflict. Within a few years the advocates of states' rights joined with populists and farmers in a political movement under Jefferson's leadership.[24] From then on, the struggle between nationalism and states' rights, which had been so violent in the ratification contest, would continue to be reflected in differing interpretations of the Constitution.

Second, the opponents of ratification themselves made an important positive contribution to the Constitution: a bill of rights. A bill of rights was regarded as crucial by Mason, author of the Virginia bill of rights, who refused to sign the Constitution and opposed its ratification. He voiced the

---

[24] See Friedrich and McCloskey, *op. cit.*, p. lvii.

Ratification of the Constitution: The Opposition

Here is a resolution as radical as that which separated us from Great Britain. It is radical in this transition; our rights and privileges are endangered, and the sovereignty of the states will be relinquished: and cannot we plainly see that this is actually the case? The rights of conscience, trial by jury, liberty of the press, all your immunities and franchises, all pretensions to human rights and privileges, are rendered insecure, if not lost, by this change, so loudly talked of by some, and inconsiderately by others....

This Constitution is said to have beautiful features; but when I come to examine these features, sir, they appear to me horribly frightful. Among other deformities, it has an awful squinting; it squints towards monarchy; and does not this raise indignation in the breast of every true American?

Your President may easily become king. Your Senate is so imperfectly constructed that your dearest rights may be sacrificed by what may be a small minority; and a very small minority may continue forever unchangeably this government, although horridly defective. Where are your checks in this government? Your strongholds will be in the hands of your enemies. It is on a supposition that your American governors shall be honest, that all the good qualities of this government are founded; but its defective and imperfect construction puts it in their power to perpetrate the worst of mischiefs, should they be bad men; and, sir, would not all the world, from the eastern to the western hemisphere, blame our distracted folly in resting our rights upon the contingency of our rulers being good or bad? Show me that age and country where the rights and liberties of the people were placed on the sole chance of their rulers being good men, without a consequent loss of liberty!

From Patrick Henry, debate in the Virginia Ratifying Convention, 1788.

fears of many who opposed ratification. The proponents of ratification answered that there was no need for a bill of rights in a government that had only delegated powers. This reply did not satisfy the opponents, and the use and expansion of national powers has proved them right. The agreement of the ratification forces to propose amendments was kept promptly, and the Bill of Rights was added as the first ten amendments.

Third, the struggle for ratification in New York led to the writing of *The Federalist*. This group of eighty-five articles constituted a forceful argument for ratification of the Constitution, an able exposition of that document's principles, and a notable treatise on political science. They were written by Hamilton, Madison, and Jay (who wrote only five of them) under the pen name "Publius." The essays were printed in New York newspapers at the rate of three or four a week during the struggle for ratification in New York. What effect these profound, precise analyses had on the members of the New York convention is uncertain, but they have been a great repository of constitutional exposition and political wisdom for succeeding generations.

THE CONSTITUTION'S INFLUENCES ON THE FUTURE

The constitutional convention of 1787 has been followed by 180 years of political developments that have fleshed out the framework it established. Later chapters will discuss these developments in detail, but they cannot be properly understood without recognizing that the Constitution shaped the destiny of the nation and its political system in several major ways:

Ratification of the Constitution: The Sponsors

The great and radical vice in the construction of the existing Confederation is in the principle of LEGISLATION *for* STATES *or* GOVERNMENTS, *in their* CORPORATE *or* COLLECTIVE CAPACITIES, as contradistinguished from the INDIVIDUALS of which they consist.... The consequence of this is that, though in theory [government resolutions] are laws constitutionally binding on the members of the Union, yet in practice they are mere recommendations which the States observe or disregard at their option....

Government implies the power of making laws. It is essential to the idea of a law that it be attended with a sanction; or, in other words, a penalty or punishment for disobedience. If there be no penalty annexed to disobedience, the resolutions or commands which pretend to be laws will, in fact, amount to nothing more than advice or recommendation. This penalty, whatever it may be, can only be inflicted in two ways: by the agency of the courts and ministers of justice, or by military force; by the COERCION of the magistracy, or by the COERCION of arms. The first kind can evidently apply only to men; the last kind must, of necessity, be employed against bodies politic, or communities, or States. It is evident that there is no process of a court by which the observance of the laws can, in the last resort, be enforced. Sentences may be denounced against them for violations of their duty; but these sentences can only be carried into execution by the sword. In an association where the general authority is confined to the collective bodies of the communities that compose it, every breach of the laws must involve a state of war; and military execution must become the only instrument of civil obedience. Such a state of things can certainly not deserve the name of government, nor would any prudent man choose to commit his happiness to it.

From Alexander Hamilton, *The Federalist*, No. 15, 1787.

First, the Constitution laid the basis for the achievement of two objectives in modern state-building—national unity and economic development. The sinews of national strength were provided by a government with ample powers, its own sources of revenue, and its own executive and judiciary. It had the powers necessary for national survival and for representation of American interests in world commerce. Internally, the great contribution of the Constitution was that it laid the basis for a national economic system—thus uniting the country and promoting prosperity—by providing for a common market, free access for all citizens to the resources of the entire nation, and economic security for entrepreneurs. It is not too much to say that the Constitution is the greatest political contribution in history to economic development and material benefits for the people of a nation and that it offers an example to other nations of the value of a political unit large enough to encompass a viable aggregation of economic resources.

Second, the Constitution dispersed political power, creating a system of shared powers—shared both between nation and states and among national institutions. This resulted in opportunities for policy initiatives at many power centers; it also enabled diverse interests to deploy these centers against one another and to appeal to constitutional doctrines to support their positions. It resulted, moreover, in a dispersion of political influence, because groups and parties have been forced to direct their pressures to the many forums where public policies are made. The Constitution, by scattering powers among institutions in a nation of diversified interests, produced decentralized and fragmented party politics. Unknowingly, however, the Framers made their most significant contribution to the politics of the nation in their decision on how to elect the President, for (as Chapters 5 and 8 will show) this arrangement alone has provided a centripetal force in American politics.

Third, the Constitution, because it dealt only with institutions, left critical political gaps. It defined a set of offices without setting up the political means for recruiting people to fill them. It provided a set of institutions to prevent dominance over government by one set of interests, but it did not provide for the articulation of group interests, the reconciliation of conflicts among these interests, or the organization of legitimate opposition to ruling groups. It provided for shared powers among branches of government but not for coordination among the branches or for political leadership within them. Nor did it provide a means of political socialization through which the people would become attached to the Union and the political system. As Part II will show, these gaps were to be filled through a long process of political development that included the rise of organized interest groups and political parties.

Finally, the Constitution in many respects allowed opportunities for flexible future development. The distribution of legal powers between nation and states and among the branches of government was stipulated in general phrases that permitted adaptation to the changing demands of people on government. The distribution of political power was left open by the absence of national suffrage requirements, the procedures for admission of new states, and the political gaps described above. Thus the Constitution has significantly influenced the future by leaving open certain political questions, as well as by establishing an institutional framework.

SUMMARY

In the great epoch of institution-building (1776–87), Americans tried to embody in constitutions the political concepts they had acquired from their British and colonial heritage. From John Locke came the concept of natural law—that man had rights that were derived from a higher source than government—and the concept of a government based on popular consent. From Montesquieu came the concepts of separation of powers and checks and balances to establish internal curbs on government.

From the early experience of the colonies in drawing up compacts and charters came four principles: popular sovereignty—that governments derive their just powers from the consent of the governed; republicanism—that the people's will could be expressed only through representation in government; constitutionalism—that the proper foundation of government is a written constitution, which is paramount law and must emanate directly from the people; freedom—that governments' powers were limited both in scope and procedure. Of these concepts, only the idea of a written constitution as the basis for popular government under law was novel.

Though the American Revolution did not destroy the continuity of our political development with our British heritage, it did produce important economic, social, and political changes. First, it freed the American states to establish institutions and policies that reflected our best economic interests, allowing us to develop our natural resources and stimulate commerce. Second, the Revolution gave predominance to the doctrines of John Locke— principally those of natural rights and popular consent. Third, the Revolution brought moderate democratization of land ownership, extension of religious freedom, and in some states abolition of slavery. Fourth, the Revolution led to the formation of state governments based on written constitutions. These documents were to set significant precedents for our national constitution: many contained bills of rights, and those of New York and Massachusetts provided for separation of powers and checks and balances among the branches of government.

Fifth, the Revolution led to the creation of the United States of America under its first constitution, the Articles of Confederation. The Articles made several imporant contributions to a viable pattern of federal union: it designated certain powers as the sole province of Congress, and it established some basic rules of interstate cooperation. But it had several major defects, the most important of which was the national government's lack of power to tax or to regulate commerce. The states often failed to abide by their obligations, they engaged in commercial competition with one another, and they issued their own money.

The Constitutional Convention grew out of the desire of financial and commercial groups to establish national protection of their business interests. The convention, however, went beyond its original goal of revising the Articles and instead drew up a new constitution. Four achievements of the convention were particularly significant:

First, it created a national government, consisting of a legislature, an executive, and a judiciary. This government was equipped with both express and implied powers and institutions. Significantly, it operated directly on the American people, rather than on the states, and the Constitution was declared to be the "supreme law of the land." The judges in the states were responsible for upholding national supremacy, but cases could be appealed to the Supreme Court of the United States. The convention in effect created a new kind of system called "federalism," which allowed the national and state governments each to maintain substantial powers and independence. The federal pattern made it more palatable for the states to accept a stronger union and helped to reconcile conflicting claims between large and small states.

The second achievement of the convention was that it laid the basis for one national market, thus providing every citizen with free access to the entire nation's resources and giving Congress the power to regulate commerce and foreign trade.

Third, the convention established a system of electing the President independently of the legislature through electors chosen by the people. And finally, the convention established a compromise between those who wanted security for property and those who wanted a strong popular basis for government.

The Constitution shaped the future in several ways. First, it ensured stability and unity by granting the national government ample powers, its own sources of revenues, and separate executive and judicial branches. Second, its establishment of a national economic system was to encourage unprecedented economic development. Third, it left political gaps to be filled by interest groups and party politics, as Chapters 4 and 5 will show.

THE EVOLUTION OF THE AMERICAN POLITICAL SYSTEM

3

During the past 180 years, our political system has undergone significant changes in response to the pressures of rapid technological and social advances. This chapter begins by examining the formal and informal political instruments through which changes in our system have occurred. How have our political culture, our national character, and our constitutional structure influenced the means of adaptation we have chosen? And how have formal and informal political processes fleshed out our constitutional framework? The second half of the chapter examines the evolution of our system of federalism—a case study in political adaptation. Has our federal system kept pace with technological and social demands? Which instruments have helped to shape this system?

In the century and three-quarters since the Republic was launched, the United States has passed through three major phases of national development. Between 1789 and 1860, we grew from a country of 4 million persons in thirteen states huddled along the Atlantic seaboard to a continental republic of thirty-four states, whose 32 million people developed a flourishing economy and acquired through aggressive expansion a territory stretching south to Texas and west to Oregon. Between 1861 and 1913, we fought a civil war to preserve an indissoluble union, formally emancipated our slave population, moved into large-scale industrialization and urbanization, grew to a population of 100 million, and became a major nation in the international balance of power. Finally, between 1913 and the present, we expanded to 200 million people, fought two world wars, became one of the world's two nuclear superpowers, and developed an advanced technological system with widespread affluence, broad social-welfare guarantees, and a serious racial crisis.

Despite these sweeping changes in our national life, the United States is governed today by the same national constitution that was adopted in 1789—the oldest written constitution in use by any major nation. Only twenty-five amendments have been added to it in more than a century and three-quarters. In addition to this formal framework, a reader who compared the leading American newspapers of 1850, 1900, and today would find that most patterns of American government and politics have remained remarkably stable in their essentials. Press coverage of the political scene would reveal presidential concern over congressional appropriations for important executive programs; debate over Supreme Court rulings holding legislative acts unconstitutional; factional and sectional rivalries within our political parties; economic and social groups seeking government action to promote their interests; conflicts over race relations, civil liberties, and public order; federal-state tensions alongside federal-state cooperation; conflicts over which should be private functions in our society and which public. The institutions and policy debates of our political system today would certainly be more familiar to the well-informed American of 1850 or 1900 than would our contemporary physical environment or our technology.

Yet fundamental changes *have* occurred in our political system, even though they have generally come about gradually and peacefully. During the life of our republic, four basic shifts have taken place in the priorities of government and in the allocations of functions in our political system:

1. Foreign- and defense-policy matters have increased greatly in importance over domestic affairs.

2. The President has taken on broad powers at the expense of traditional congressional authority.

3. The federal government has assumed responsibility for vast areas of regulation that once lay under the jurisdiction of state and local governments.

4. National, state, and local governments as a whole have assumed responsibility for social, economic, and civic concerns that were once conducted by individuals and private groups.

To see how these changes took place, we must examine the two main types of instrument through which the American political system has adapted to new conditions: (1) our formal government processes, such as constitutional amendment, judicial interpretation, and the legislative process; and (2) our informal political processes, such as our party system and interest-group activity. Though several of these topics will be treated in detail in later chapters, each deserves a brief analysis here as an instrument of political change.

FORMAL GOVERNMENT PROCESSES

Constitutional Amendment

When the Framers completed their draft of the Constitution in 1787, they provided in Article V a two-step process for amending the document. First, amendments must be proposed by either a two-thirds majority of both houses of Congress or a national convention called by Congress on the petition of two-thirds of the states. Second, proposed amendments must be ratified either by the legislatures of three-fourths of the states or at ratification conventions held in three-fourths of the states. Unless Congress chooses to set a time limit, there is no legal cutoff date for state ratification. Since the 1920's, however, it has been congressional practice to include for each new proposal a clause providing that valid ratification must be accomplished within seven years of presentation to the states.

Since 1787, twenty-five amendments have been added to the Constitution (Table 3–1)—all proposed by Congress. For twenty-four of these, ratification was by state legislatures; only once, in 1933, when Prohibition was repealed, was ratification carried out by state conventions. The provision for proposing amendments through a national convention called on petition of the states has never been used.

Three main periods of constitutional reform can be clearly identified. The first, 1789–1804, was an era in which the Constitution was brought into line with the power realities and the ideological consensus of the new republic. The period produced twelve amendments, but the first ten, proposed in 1789 and promulgated in 1791, can really be regarded as part of the Constitution itself, for they were the price that the anti-Federalists demanded for ratification. The Eleventh Amendment (1798) prevented states from being sued in federal courts by citizens of another state; the action responded to powerful states'-rights protests against a Supreme Court de-

Table 3-1 Amendments to the Federal Constitution, 1789–1967

Amendment number	Year promulgated	Subject treated	Stimulus	Date proposed	Date ratified	Time elapsed Yrs.	Mos.
1–10	1791	Bill of Rights	Failure to include civil-liberty guarantees in Constitution	Sept., 1789	Dec., 1791	2	3
11	1798	Immunity of state from suit in federal courts by citizen of another state	Supreme Court decision, *Chisholm v. Georgia* (1793)	Mar., 1794	Feb., 1798	3	11
12	1804	Separate election of President and Vice-President	Tie vote for President and Vice-President in 1800 election	Dec., 1803	July, 1804	0	7
13	1865	Outlawing of slavery	Civil War; slavery issue	Feb., 1865	Dec., 1865	0	10
14	1868	Federal citizenship, privileges and immunities for former slaves; limit on state interference with equal protection and due process; and other provisions	Civil War; Supreme Court decision in *Dred Scott* case (1857)	June, 1866	July, 1868	2	1
15	1870	Right to vote regardless of race, color, or prior slavery	Civil War; Reconstruction conditions	Feb., 1869	Feb., 1870	1	0
16	1913	Federal power to tax individual incomes	Supreme Court decision, *Pollock v. Farmer's Loan* (1895)	July, 1909	Feb., 1913	3	7
17	1913	Direct election of U.S. senators	"Popular election" movement; government reform	May, 1912	Apr., 1913	0	11
18	1919	Prohibition of liquor	Prohibition movement	Dec., 1917	Jan., 1919	1	1
19	1920	Women's suffrage	Women's suffrage movement; Supreme Court decision, *Minor v. Happersett* (1875)	June, 1919	Aug., 1920	1	2
20	1933	Elimination of "lame duck" session of Congress	Government reform; Progressive movement	Mar., 1932	Jan., 1933	0	10
21	1933	Repeal of Prohibition	Failure of Prohibition; "wet" movement	Feb., 1933	Dec., 1933	0	10
22	1951	Two-term limit on presidential tenure	Anti-Roosevelt sentiment following fourth term; Republican party pressure	Mar., 1947	Feb., 1951	3	11
23	1961	Right to vote in presidential elections for District of Columbia residents	General public support for D.C. voters; Democratic party pressure	June, 1960	Mar., 1961	0	9
24	1964	Ban on poll tax for voting in federal elections	Civil-rights movement	Aug., 1962	Feb., 1964	1	6
25	1967	Presidential succession and disability	Increasing public concern over presidential succession after Kennedy assassination	Jan., 1965	Feb., 1967	2	1

cision that had held otherwise. The last amendment in this period, the Twelfth (1804) was adopted because of the unforeseen rise of political parties. The Framers had expected the best man to receive a majority of state electoral votes and thus become President, while the runner-up would be Vice-President. But in 1800, because the electors voted along party lines, the two Republican nominees, Jefferson and Burr, each received the same number of electoral votes, and a choice between them had to be made in the House of Representatives. The Twelfth Amendment solved this breakdown of the system by requiring state electors to vote separately for President and Vice-President.

The second period, 1865–70, saw the addition of three amendments designed to incorporate the practical results of the Civil War into the formal Constitution and to define the new relationships created by emancipation of the slaves. The Thirteenth Amendment (1865) freed all slaves and forbade slavery; the Fourteenth Amendment (1868) extended federal citizenship to former slaves and forbade states to deny persons equal protection of the laws or due process of law; and the Fifteenth Amendment (1870) forbade states to deny the right to vote on the basis of race, color, or previous condition of servitude.

The third period, from 1913 to the present, has brought ten constitutional amendments. Four of them were intended to democratize national government processes: the Seventeenth Amendment (1913) provided for direct election of senators, and the Nineteenth (1920) for women's suffrage; the Twenty-third (1961) allowed District of Columbia residents to vote in presidential elections; and the Twenty-fourth (1964) banned the poll tax as a prerequisite for voting in federal elections. The six remaining amendments apply to assorted areas. The Sixteenth Amendment (1913) instituted the federal income tax. The prohibition of liquor by the Eighteenth Amendment (1919) culminated a half-century crusade against the "evils of drink," but the Twenty-first Amendment (1933) repealed Prohibition after its failure had become apparent. The Twentieth Amendment (1933) eliminated the "lame duck" congressional session by providing that the inauguration of the President and the convening of Congress both begin in January after the presidential election. The Twenty-second Amendment (1951) limited presidential tenure to two terms; it was sponsored by conservatives who wished to prevent a recurrence of Roosevelt's unprecedented four terms in office. The Twenty-fifth Amendment (1967) created procedures to deal with presidential disability, following public concern over the continuity of government after the assassination of President Kennedy as well as during the prior illnesses in office of President Eisenhower.

Many other changes in the Constitution have been urged vigorously in sustained campaigns since 1789 but have never been adopted by Congress. Among the serious contenders have been proposals to change the Electoral College, to lengthen the congressman's term to four years, to require a

Hammond in the Wichita *Eagle*

A 1918 cartoon showed John Barleycorn "seeing stars" as state after state ratified the Eighteenth Amendment, forbidding the sale of alcoholic beverages.

popular referendum before declaring war, to limit the Supreme Court's power to declare acts of Congress unconstitutional, and to require Senate approval of executive agreements with foreign nations.

The record of successful and unsuccessful amendment efforts prompts four main observations about the amendment process:

First, most of the amendments have played a major role in the adaptation of American government institutions to social change. The income-tax amendment fundamentally altered the fiscal balance of power between the national and state governments. The amendments that democratized government brought the aristocratic features of the eighteenth-century Constitution into harmony with twentieth-century ideas about popular government. The Fourteenth Amendment became the basic instrument for federal intervention in order to protect the rights of corporations, unions, and religious and racial minorities against infringement by the states.

Second, Congress—not the states—has been the critical battleground for proposed amendments. Since 1789, some 4,500 resolutions calling for amendments have been introduced in Congress by the members of the two houses. Of these, only 30 were adopted and sent to the states. And in only 3 dozen instances did one house pass the resolution and the other fail to approve. Thus, while senators and congressmen please constituents and register their own political convictions by filing amendment resolutions on every conceivable subject, congressional committees have seen to it that only a tiny fraction of these resolutions ever reaches the floor for debate. Once Congress adopts a proposed amendment, however, ratification has followed in 25 of the 30 instances. Approval by the states has been prompt, with an average of 18 months between congressional submission to the states and ratification.

Third, there has been a close connection between leading Supreme Court decisions and the amendment process. Three amendments were directly prompted by Supreme Court rulings: the Eleventh Amendment took away a federal jurisdiction approved by the justices, and the Fourteenth and Sixteenth Amendments gave Congress powers it had been denied by judicial decisions. Equally significant is the fact that quite a few unsuccessful campaigns for amendments have been set in motion by assertive Supreme Court decisions, such as restrictive rulings on congressional power over labor relations, child labor, and trusts; rulings expanding presidential authority in foreign affairs and military power; and rulings limiting the authority of the states in areas such as internal security, censorship, police practices, labor relations, and segregation. The primary reason for the small number of such reversals (there has been none since 1913) is that when the pressure for amendment begins to reflect a dominant consensus in the nation, changes in the Court's personnel or its majority philosophy have often led to modification of its positions. Such was the case, for example, in the 1930's; if the Court had not reversed its original opposition to New Deal legislation, constitutional amendments would very likely have been adopted to overturn the restrictive judicial rulings.

Fourth, the amendment process has been basically responsive to popular will and changing national needs. During the nineteenth and early twentieth centuries, political scientists deplored the total inertia at the congressional-proposal stage of the amendment process. The fact that, apart from the three post-Civil War amendments, the Constitution had been left unamended for more than a century (1804–1913) was cited by critics as proof that formal amendment seemed impossible as a matter of political practice. The addition of four major amendments between 1913 and 1920, however, and the ratification of six more since then has led critics to soften or abandon the charge of total freeze and to focus instead on whether the pace of amendment is dangerously slow or merely properly careful.

Debates over the ratification process have followed a different path of argument. Modern critics note that in theory the fourteen smallest states, with only 2 percent of the national population, could defeat ratification. Similarly, the thirty-seven least-populous states, with only about 50 percent of the national population, could ratify an amendment opposed by the thirteen largest states. In fact, however, such a split is highly unlikely, and the record of previous ratification fights shows that there has never been a division of states according to population size.

Probably the most pertinent answer to the debate over flexibility versus rigidity is that the amendment process is only one of several means for constitutional change in our system. Because we rely more on these other means, particularly judicial interpretation, our amendment process has really been an extraordinary remedy reserved for special occasions.

Judicial Interpretation

Whenever a litigant in state or federal court properly raises the claim that the government has violated the federal Constitution in dealing with him, the judges hearing that case must construe the meaning of the constitutional provision at issue. If the government's action was something faced squarely by the Framers, on which they adopted a clear policy expressed in un-equivocal language, the judge usually has a relatively easy task. Thus, if federal agents slipped in through a basement window to search a man's home for counterfeit money without first obtaining a search warrant from a judge, and if there were no special circumstances to justify the failure to get a warrant, a federal judge would have little trouble in ruling that this was an "unreasonable search" forbidden by the Fourth Amendment to the Constitution. (That amendment provides that "the right of the people to be secure in their persons, houses, papers, and effects, against unreasonable searches and seizures, shall not be violated . . . .")

However, even where the Framers expressed a clear constitutional policy on a given issue, such as searches and seizures, sometimes the development of new technology, new socioeconomic forces, new patterns of government operations, or changes in the nation's social values require courts to reinter-pret the constitutional provision. Does government use of electronic equip-ment to tap telephone or room conversations from outside the home of a suspected person violate the Fourth Amendment if done without a judicial warrant? Indeed, is it so "unreasonable" and unlimited a search (since it picks up the conversations of all those who happen to talk on the tapped line or in the room) that it should be held invalid *even if* a warrant has been secured?

In 1928, when the Supreme Court first faced this question in *Olmstead v. United States*, it held that telephone-tapping was not barred by the Fourth Amendment at all.[1] In this case the police had not entered the home of the citizen (a suspected liquor bootlegger); the Court ruled that nothing "tangible" had been seized and that the suspect had chosen to "project" his voice by telephone to others outside the house with the knowledge that his conversations might be overheard. During the next four decades, this ruling was heavily criticized. By 1967, the Supreme Court had decided a series of "hidden mike" cases[2] that seriously undercut the 1928 ruling. No longer

[1] *Olmstead* v. *United States*, 277 U.S. 438 (1928).
[2] *Silverman* v. *United States*, 365 U.S. 505 (1961); *Clinton* v. *Virginia*, 377 U.S. 158 (1964); *Lopez* v. *United States*, 373 U.S. 427 (1963); *Berger* v. *New York*, 388 U.S. 41 (1967).

was an "entry" necessary to constitute an infringement of privacy; listening from outside the property was enough. Eavesdropping on private conversation was held to be a seizure of something quite tangible and valuable in constitutional terms. Moreover, the Court ruled that when a person spoke on the telephone or in a room the risk of being overheard could not be expected to include the risk of systematic surveillance by government agents. Though by the end of 1967 the Supreme Court had not ruled that all government telephone-tapping and room-microphoning was unconstitutional, it had redefined the meaning of the Fourth Amendment so that a great many practices in electronic surveillance were declared illegal. The Fourth Amendment had not been changed between 1928 and 1967. What had changed, however, were the nature of the search-and-seizure problems and public attitudes on the developing threat to privacy brought about by government use of new instruments of surveillance.

In hundreds of other cases the Supreme Court has adapted constitutional provisions to new conditions. The constitutional power of Congress to regulate interstate commerce, for example, has been held to authorize Congress to regulate railroads, television, and airplanes; to punish interstate automobile theft; to set standards of purity for food and drugs; to forbid racial segregation on interstate buses or at interstate terminals; and to set up collective-bargaining machinery for labor and management in order to avoid strikes that would hamper interstate commerce.

Although American practice has in fact been to reserve the amendment process for extraordinary occasions and to rely heavily on judicial interpretation for lesser questions, an issue still vigorously debated today is *which* issues should be left for amendment, and which should be settled by judicial interpretation?

The *strict-constructionist* view is that constitutional amendment should be used for all basic changes in constitutional policy. Chief Justice Roger Taney said for the Court in 1856: "Any other rule of construction would abrogate the judicial character of this court, and make it the mere reflex of the popular opinion or passion of the day." [3]

Strict-constructionist positions have been advanced to support both conservative and liberal economic and political doctrines. For example, conservative Justice George Sutherland protested in the late 1930's against Supreme Court rulings that interpreted the commerce clause as sustaining congressional power over labor-management relations, agriculture, and industrial conditions. The proper role of the judiciary, he said, "does not include the power of amendment under the guise of interpretation." On other occasions, however, strict construction has been invoked by liberals to oppose judicial doctrines that were believed to be "interpreting away" the "precious safeguards of civil liberty." Justice Hugo Black, for example,

[3] *Dred Scott* v. *Sanford,* 19 How. 393 (1857).

The Case for Strict Construction

Some people regard the prohibitions of the Constitution, even its most unequivocal commands, as mere admonitions which Congress need not always observe....

I cannot accept this approach to the Bill of Rights. It is my belief that there are "absolutes" in our Bill of Rights, and that they were put there on purpose by men who knew what words meant, and meant their prohibitions to be "absolutes."... The historical and practical purposes of a Bill of Rights, the very use of a written constitution, indigenous to America, the language the Framers used, the kind of three-department government they took pains to set up, all point to the creation of a government which was denied all power to do some things under any and all circumstances, and all power to do other things except precisely in the manner prescribed.... I am primarily discussing here whether liberties admittedly covered by the Bill of Rights can nevertheless be abridged on the ground that a superior public interest justifies the abridgment. I think the Bill of Rights made its safeguards superior....

To my way of thinking, at least, the history and language of the Constitution and the Bill of Rights ... make it plain that one of the primary purposes of the Constitution with its amendments was to withdraw from the Government all power to act in certain areas—whatever the scope of those areas may be. If I am right in this then there is, at least in those areas, no justification whatever for "balancing" a particular right against some expressly granted power of Congress. If the Constitution withdraws from Government all power over subject matter in an area, such as religion, speech, press, assembly, and petition, there is nothing over which authority may be exerted.

From Justice Hugo L. Black, "The Bill of Rights," New York University *Law Review*, April 1960.

has argued that the provisions of the First Amendment are "absolutes," not subject to flexible relaxation or suspension by the Court in the belief that we live "in times of emergency and stress."

The competing approach, *flexible construction*, usually starts by invoking Chief Justice John Marshall's famous remark that "We must never forget that it is a constitution we are expounding . . . a constitution intended to endure for ages to come and, consequently, to be adapted to the various crises of human affairs." [4] Flexible constructionists recognize the growth of some constitutional principles and the contraction of others through changing conditions, government experience, and social values. They point out that if the Supreme Court does not register the changing weights of consti-

[4] *McCulloch* v. *Maryland*, 4 Wheat. 316 (1819).

tutional provisions, dozens, even hundreds, of constitutional amendments might be necessary each generation.

The flexible approach has also been used by both conservative and liberal spokesmen. Liberals have supported expanded interpretations of clauses dealing with the commerce and taxing powers of Congress or with the President's authority as Chief Executive in order to uphold federal regulation of the economy, welfare laws, and internationalist measures. Conservatives have also spoken of the need for flexibility: for example, they favored the expansion of property guarantees under the due-process clauses of the Constitution during the nineteenth and early twentieth centuries, and they have urged limitations on the broad language of the First Amendment in order to support internal-security measures and congressional investigation of subversive activities in today's Cold War era. Since many important and heavily debated parts of the Constitution are ambiguous, the self-conscious judge, as Justice Robert Jackson once remarked frankly, is forced to interpret

The Case for Flexible Construction

[The] search for a static security—in the law or elsewhere—is misguided. The fact is that security can only be achieved through constant change, through the wise discarding of old ideas that have outlived their usefulness, and through the adapting of others to current facts. There is only an illusion of safety in a Maginot Line. Social forces like armies can sweep around a fixed position and make it untenable. A position that can be shifted to meet such forces and at least partly absorb them alone gives hope of security....

There are usually plenty of precedents to go around; and with the accumulation of decisions, it is no great problem for the lawyer to find legal authority for most propositions. The difficulty is to estimate what effect a slightly different shade of facts will have and to predict the speed of the current in a changing stream of the law. The predictions and prophecies that lawyers make are indeed appraisals of a host of imponderables. The decisions of yesterday or of the last century are only the starting points....

A judge looking at a constitutional decision may have compulsions to revere past history and accept what was once written. But he remembers above all else that it is the Constitution which he swore to support and defend, not the gloss which his predecessors may have put on it. So he comes to formulate his own views, rejecting some earlier ones as false and embracing others. He cannot do otherwise unless he lets men long dead and unaware of the problems of the age in which he lives do his thinking for him.

From Justice William O. Douglas, "Stare Decisis," *The Record* of the Association of the Bar of the City of New York, April 1949.

the Constitution "from materials almost as enigmatic as the dreams Joseph was called upon to interpret for Pharaoh." [5]

For this reason, despite protests from segments of the population adversely affected by such judicial rulings, public opinion in America from John Marshall's day to the present has supported a consciously adaptive and creative style of Supreme Court judicial review.

Such a role for the American judiciary initially grew out of the needs for legal protection of minority groups in a heterogeneous population, the ideas of higher law and limited government that lay deep in our political culture, and the problems of resolving conflicts under a written constitution that deliberately divided and shared powers among the three branches of the national government and between the nation and the states. These factors have made our federal and state court systems a central instrument of change down to the present.

The Legislative Process

The generality and ambiguity of the Constitution—as well as its vast gaps—have encouraged its fleshing out not only through judicial interpretation but through congressional legislation as well. Statutes do more than create specific programs in response to immediate needs. In at least two ways, they have created and expanded basic features of the American political system.

First, the Constitution set up a framework for the national government but did not specify its operating structure; congressional statutes have been a major instrument for filling this gap. For example, statutes have established the organization and jurisdiction of the federal court system. All federal courts other than the Supreme Court are creatures of the Judiciary Act of 1789. Congressional statutes also determine the number of judges in all federal courts (including the Supreme Court), fix the jurisdiction of all courts (except for the "original jurisdiction" of the Supreme Court), determine what cases arising under federal law will be heard in state courts, and determine the rights of appeal within the system.

Statutes have also developed the structure of the executive branch. For example, it is through legislation that the federal independent regulatory agencies—such as the Federal Trade Commission and the Federal Communications Commission—have been created. These agencies combine legislative, judicial, and executive functions and thus modify strict separation-of-powers doctrines. In addition, Congress must pass on any changes or reorganizations in both executive departments and regulatory agencies; congressional approval here is far from automatic, especially when political or ideological conflicts are present.

The Constitution also left unspecified the relationship between the Presi-

[5] *Youngstown Sheet and Tube Co. v. Sawyer,* 343 U.S. 579, 634-5 (1952).

dent and Congress in directing and supervising departments, bureaus, and commissions. It gave the President certain powers, such as the appointment of "officers" of the United States and the power "to take care that the laws shall be faithfully executed." On the other hand, it gave Congress the power to make all laws "necessary and proper" to carrying out the powers delegated to the national government. Congress has construed broadly its own powers to direct administration through legislation and has regulated in detail the powers and procedures of offices within the executive branch. Such legislation, combined with supervision over administration through congressional committees, has produced a system unusual among governments of the world—joint executive-legislative direction of administration.

Legislation has also co-opted states into the administration of national laws, especially through federal grant-in-aid programs. Such legislation, to be discussed later in connection with federalism, has created cooperative federal-state administration of public functions.

The second fundamental way in which legislation has contributed to the evolution of our political system has been in setting the boundaries between the public and private sectors. Because we began as a rural society with heavy reliance on private effort, this boundary-setting process has consisted almost entirely of expanding government responsibilities as new technological, environmental, or international situations created social needs that the private sector was unable to fulfill. The passage of federal legislation to provide social security, financial aid to the poor, and medical care for the aged illustrates this trend.

It is important to note that this establishment of socioeconomic rights and benefits is a distinctive feature of the American legislative process. In most other nations with written constitutions, such rights and benefits are stipulated explicitly in those documents. In France, Italy, Israel, and India, for example, constitutions guarantee the right to work, a decent standard of living, security in old age, and the right of labor to bargain freely and to strike. By contrast, the American Bill of Rights, ratified in 1791 and reflecting eighteenth-century concerns, restrains government action. Thus, socioeconomic guarantees reflecting twentieth-century concerns had to be fought for and won through the legislative process. Congressional acts providing unemployment payments, minimum wages, social security, collective bargaining, and the like were initiated largely in the New Deal years and have been expanded in recent decades to fields such as medical care for the aged and federal aid to education. They represent what could be called "semiconstitutional" legislation. Legally any of the statutes could be repealed tomorrow, but politically they are untouchable. Furthermore, their basic operative clauses resemble constitutional provisions in the broadness of their statements of public policy and in their tendency to pass along to administrative agencies and courts the discretion to apply these general policy definitions to concrete situations.

INFORMAL POLITICAL PROCESSES

If an observer were to look only at our formal government processes, he would find himself unable to explain some of the most profound changes in the American political system since 1790. These have come about through the operations of institutions outside our government structure. The two most important examples of these informal institutions are political interest groups and political parties.

Political interest groups—collections of individuals united to further some common stake or idea by political action—were not mentioned in the Constitution; indeed, they were viewed by men like Madison as semiconspiratorial "factions" dangerous to a republic. But the proliferation of political interest groups of all types—economic, religious, civic, cultural, educational, and so on—have been a characteristic of American society, and their role in the process of social change has been to give a legal and legitimate voice in the political system to new immigrant groups and new socioeconomic interests developed by the changes in the American economy. The ease of interest-group formation has been one reason that the United States has had few underground and revolutionary movements, and this has affected the way our entire political system has related to the tensions of socioeconomic change.

Political parties, also unknown at the time the Constitution was written, have played similar roles—those of receiving new groups into the political system, offering broad new political policies to deal with new issues as they gained major support in the nation, and carrying these issues from party programs to government policy responses.

It is important to note that some of the major trends in American socioeconomic and political development in the past 170 years have been accomplished by a complex *blend* of formal and informal processes. For example, the steady democratization of American government has taken place through constitutional amendments (extending the vote to Negroes and women, electing U.S. senators directly, forbidding the poll tax in federal elections); court decisions (outlawing racial discrimination in voting or jury service); legislation (establishing federal and state standards in voting); the political parties (which have championed the entry of new groups into the electorate in the hope of gaining new supporters); and interest groups (which have lobbied for increased suffrage and for referendum and recall measures and have developed "direct-action" techniques, such as picketing and demonstrating, to call attention to issues that may otherwise be ignored). As this brief sketch suggests, it took all our formal and informal processes to transform our system from an eighteenth-century republic, with some rather aristocratic institutional remnants, to a more democratic political system for a mass industrial society.

AMERICAN FEDERALISM:
A CASE STUDY IN POLITICAL CHANGE

How significant are the changes in our political system that have been wrought by our formal and informal processes? To get some idea of the ingenuity and scope of these changes, let us examine the evolution of American federalism—the carefully balanced union between nation and states created by the Framers—during the past century and three quarters.

As Chapter 2 has discussed, the federal union designed by the Framers in the Constitution had three primary characteristics: (1) Major government functions were allotted to two separate and independent authorities —the nation and the states—each of which was to be supreme in its own jurisdiction. (2) Both the nation and the states were allowed to enforce their laws, which operated directly on individuals, through their own officials and courts. And (3) the Supreme Court of the United States was installed (consciously or by fairly strong implication) as general umpire of federal-state conflicts, so that neither Congress nor any state or group of states could determine conclusively for itself whose authority was legitimate in a disputed area.

The blueprint of the federal union set out to balance national and state authorities in four primary ways: by specifying what functions and authority were given to the national government (*delegated powers*), by listing what functions and powers were denied to the national government or to the states (*prohibited powers*), by assuming that some powers (such as taxation) would be exercised by both the national and state governments (*concurrent powers*), and by stating the standard for settlement of national-state conflicts (*national supremacy*).

Conventions can write constitutions, but the meaning of their provisions must be tested in practical application and political conflict. These tests of the federal design emerged in the three major periods of sociopolitical change mentioned at the beginning of this chapter: 1790–1861, 1861–1913, and 1913 to the present.

Developing the Ground Rules of American Federalism, 1790–1861

A persistent American myth is the belief that "in the good old days" national and state governments operated in two entirely separate compartments. But, in fact, a study of American federalism shows that since the earliest days of our republic the nation and states have always been mutually active in each other's sphere of authority—sometimes in cooperation and sometimes in direct conflict.[6]

[6] See Daniel J. Elazar, *American Federalism: A View from the States* (New York: Crowell, 1966).

Although the national government ran its postal system, maintained a navy, conducted wars, and had its own court system, it began early to assist the states and seek their cooperation. It set aside land in the Western territories for education—the first grant-in-aid by the national government. It relied for its federal land forces on the state militia, which the Constitution had provided should be maintained by the states, subject to regulations of Congress and the right of the national government to call forth the militia.

In addition, practical guidelines were developed for accommodating local and national exercise of concurrent powers. When Pennsylvania set up an elaborate system of control over pilots in the port of Philadelphia, a ship owner holding a federal coastal license claimed that the state's regulations were illegal when applied to ships operating in interstate or foreign commerce. In the famous case of *Cooley* v. *Board of Wardens*,[7] the Supreme Court asserted that when a matter was local, when Congress had not acted directly on it, and when state action did not burden or interfere with commerce, state law could stand even though it was incidentally a regulation of interstate or foreign commerce. Thus, under the "Cooley doctrine" states were later allowed to exclude aliens with communicable diseases, regulate headlights on interstate trains, and set interstate shipping rates.

This period also saw the rise of the political tradition of using the "states' rights" slogan to serve the concrete interests of economic groups and political movements. Groups and parties cried "states' rights" when this served their immediate uses and reversed their position to defend national authority when that position advanced their claims more effectively. For example, the Northern mercantile interests, the backbone of the Federalist party, supported national power against the states'-rights position of the agrarian Southwestern Republicans in the 1790's—they bitterly condemned the Virginia and Kentucky resolutions of 1798, which were based on the claim that states had the power to disobey the national sedition laws. But when President Madison's conduct of the War of 1812 with Britain badly hurt Northern commercial interests, the Federalists rushed to endorse a principle of "lawful resistance" to national action.

Still another basic element of federalism developed in this first period was the "rule of public demand." That is, when the American people want something done for them by government, if the local governments fail to do it, state or national governments will enter the field with public approval and provide the services. In this period, however, most of these demands were met by state governments. Thus, when the broad internal-improvement plans of Gallatin, Secretary of the Treasury under Jefferson, were put aside by Presidents Madison and Monroe because of their narrow constitutional interpretation of national powers, the states came to the assistance of roads, canals, and, later, railroads. The states spent some $300 million and

[7] 12 How. 299 (1851).

Lithograph published in 1833 by Endicott and Swett

Despotism—Anarchy—Disunion

This 1832 cartoon depicts the dangers of Nullification, a doctrine introduced by states'-rights advocates against President Jackson's tariffs of 1828 and 1832. Jackson is shown at the far right trying to stop John C. Calhoun (top) and other spokesmen of states' rights.

local governments over $125 million on internal improvements before the Civil War, while the national government spent only $7 million. The states also chartered banks to provide the services to commerce that Hamilton had wanted the national government to supply. And they began to assist education, chartered corporations, and initiated regulation of insurance, banking, and railroad transportation. In an era when state and local governments could respond effectively to the demands for assistance in commercial development and for regulation of abuses to protect the public, the national government made small use of its vast powers.

Finally, the years from 1790 to 1861 saw the establishment of the Supreme Court's role as umpire of the federal system and referee of nation-state conflicts. During the long period that Chief Justice John Marshall presided over the Supreme Court (1801–35), spanning the terms of five Presidents and giving rise to major political and economic changes, the basic constitutional rules of American federalism were given their classic statement by the Court.

First, the implied-powers clause of the Constitution gave Congress the power "to make all laws necessary and proper for carrying into execution" the powers of the national government, and the Marshall Court made this the most significant grant of power to Congress. Congress had established a United States Bank in 1791 to serve as a depository for national money and to facilitate federal borrowing. The bank's constitutionality was vigorously debated at that time. Alexander Hamilton argued that the bank was a proper means of exercising the fiscal powers expressly delegated to the national government, while Thomas Jefferson contended that Congress could not establish a bank because the legislature could use only those means that were "indispensably necessary" to carry out its delegated functions. Hamilton's was a liberal construction of the implied-powers clause, Jefferson's a strict one.

When Maryland levied a tax on the United States Bank and the bank refused to pay it, the issue of the bank's constitutionality came before the Supreme Court. "Let the end be legitimate," Marshall wrote in *McCulloch* v. *Maryland*, "let it be within the scope of the Constitution, and all means which are appropriate, which are plainly adapted to that end, which are not prohibited, but consist with the letter and the spirit of the Constitution, are constitutional." Thus, the implied-powers clause was held to give Congress the right to choose any appropriate means for carrying out the powers of the national government. Through its choice of means, Congress has been able to adopt new measures and new techniques when confronted with new situations, and hence the implied-powers clause has come to be called the "elastic" clause.

Second, the Marshall Court made clear the crucial importance of the national-supremacy clause in the American federal system. In the McCulloch case, the Court established the principle that when a state law interferes with a national activity being carried out "in pursuance of the Constitution," the state law will be declared unconstitutional by the federal courts. From Marshall's time to the present, the national-supremacy clause has been both a valuable tool and a source of controversy for the federal union. In contemporary times, it has been the basis of rulings striking down state taxes on interstate business, state registration systems for aliens, and many other state regulations or programs that conflict with the programs and authority of the national government.

Third, the Marshall Court emphasized in a series of leading cases that the federal union is a compact of all the people of the United States, not one of the individual states as sovereigns. The Court declared that this union was permanent, that no state could withdraw from it, and that no state could refuse to obey valid national measures. This principle was easier to declare in judicial decisions than to enforce against resisting states, but it was eventually to become a fundamental tenet of the federal system.

The constitutional battlegrounds of this era—the commerce clause, the national-supremacy clause, the taxing power, the necessary-and-proper clause, and the Tenth Amendment—have remained the major terrain of federalism disputes ever since. But the basic patterns of national programs, federal-state interconnection, and the judiciary's role as umpire were set for the century to come.

Civil War and the Rise of the Organic Union, 1861–1913

The "irrepressible conflict" of 1861–65 settled the basic question of the federal system: Could a state oppose national law to the point of secession from the Union? When the cannons were silenced in 1865, war had established that the answer was "no," that ours was, as the Supreme Court was to say two years later, "an indestructible union, composed of indestructible states." [8] This indestructible Union, preserved by war, was cemented first by developments in the economy and then by the new national loyalties of late nineteenth- and twentieth-century Americans. Two years after Appomattox, the union of East and West was symbolized by the completion of the first transcontinental railway. The expansion of large corporate empires created nationwide industries. It also bound the economy of the nation to the steel mills of Pittsburgh, the meat-packaging plants of Chicago, and the financial centers of the East. The period 1861–1913 began with war industries and ended with Sears and Roebuck catalogues—national mass marketing of the products of mammoth industrial complexes. The entrepreneurs of the nation were now taking advantage of their free access to a national pool of resources and a great national market, which the Framers in their foresight had provided for. Reinforcing these economic developments was the Spanish-American War of 1898, in which Americans of North and South fought under the same banner, gained new national territories, and deepened their national pride in the strength and progress of the American nation.

In this period, the national government began to make fuller use of its resources and powers to assist in the nation's economic development; for example, it gave land grants to the railroads and passed the Morrill Act of 1862, which awarded large land tracts to the states to establish agricultural and mechanical colleges. The national government also began to respond to demands for political controls over the national economy. In 1863 the national banking system was initiated. In 1887 statutes to regulate the railroads were passed. In 1890 the Sherman Antitrust Act was passed. In 1894 the Pullman strike was broken by use of national troops. And in 1906 laws requiring federal meat inspection and setting standards for food and drugs were passed.

The Supreme Court, however, failed to perceive the need for the American political system to adjust to the new economic realities. The

[8] *Texas* v. *White*, 7 Wall 700 (1869).

Constitution had laid the foundation for a national economy, and the corporate revolution was bringing about its actual development; but equally necessary was the systematic national regulation of this economic system. Responding to the arguments of business interests seeking immunity from national regulation, the Supreme Court interpreted national powers narrowly just when the United States was becoming an organic nation. In 1895–96 it declared the national income-tax law unconstitutional and severely limited the Sherman Antitrust Act of 1890 because it did not regard the commerce power of the national government as sufficient grounds for upholding action against the national sugar trust. Yet the Court, hostile to unionism, had no difficulty in using this same commerce clause to uphold national action in breaking up the Pullman strike of 1894. In this period the Court also construed the due-process clause of the Fourteenth Amendment broadly enough to enable it to judge the wisdom of economic legislation being passed by the states. Many state laws on labor, utilities, and trusts were struck down under restrictive due-process rules. On the other hand, the prohibitions against racial discrimination in the Fourteenth and Fifteenth Amendments were construed so narrowly by the Court that states were able to flout them and create a totally segregated and discriminatory racial system in the South and in many non-Southern states. By the same token, Court rulings drastically limited the power of Congress to enforce the rights guaranteed in those amendments through positive legislation. The Court's philosophy reflected many currents of popular thought in the United States in this period: high respect for business, low prestige of government, Darwinian theories of "survival of the fittest," and widespread antiforeign, antiminority, and antilabor sentiment among the white middle class.

In sum, though some aspects of the federal system responded well to the needs of society during our development into an industrial power, many of the actions that would have softened the harsher effects of industrialization on American society were blocked by a combination of business influence in the economy, political corruption, and narrow judicial rulings. In the opinion of most historians and political scientists, the formal division of authority between nation and state and the creation of a no man's land of unregulated corporate power between their authorities contributed considerably to this condition.

The New Federalism, 1913 to the Present: National Supremacy and National Crisis

Many commentators choose the date 1913, when the Sixteenth Amendment gave the national government the power to tax incomes directly, as the symbol of the beginning of a new era of national supremacy in the federal system. This amendment was to shift the financial balance of power from the states to Washington. Under its aegis the Wilson Administration initiated federal grants-in-aid to the states for highway construction and loan programs for agriculture in 1916 and successfully financed a war in 1917–18. The shift to Washington was accentuated when government credit institutions were vastly expanded under both Hoover and Roosevelt. During the New Deal, grants-in-aid were greatly increased through the Social Security Act, housing acts, and other social-welfare programs. The ability of the government to finance the Second World War and maintain its present-day defense establishment without new constitutional amendments shows how broad and significant the development of new national instruments has been.

Another change accompanying the new balance of power was the establishment of extensive national controls over the economy, subject to the ultimate confirmation of the Supreme Court. Beginning in 1913, the regulatory powers of the federal government spanned a wide range of activities: authority over the monetary system was exercised by the national government in the passage of the Federal Reserve Act in 1913; antitrust legislation was strengthened in 1914 and later; the growth of industrialization and freedom for trade across state lines created an economy of interstate businesses, which in turn led to federal regulations on agriculture, labor, and many industries operating in interstate commerce, such as stockyards, interstate power utilities, airlines, and securities exchanges. During the early part of this period, the Supreme Court placed obstacles in the way of national regulation, thus creating a crisis in American federalism. In 1918, in a 5–4 decision holding that Congress could not prohibit child labor in manufacturing establishments, the Court said in effect that production of goods—agriculture, manufacturing, and labor—was outside the reach of the national government, except for antitrust laws. Again, in the Schechter decision in 1935,[9] in which it held unconstitutional the New Deal program of industrial and labor codes created by the National Industrial Recovery Act, and in the Butler decision in 1936,[10] in which it held unconstitutional the government's agricultural-controls program, the Supreme Court seemed to be saying that the national government's commerce and taxing powers could not be applied to the production of goods. The problem was that the Supreme Court's rulings had created a no man's land in which no government had effective powers. The national government lacked the constitutional power to regulate the production of goods, and the states lacked the actual power, since, acting separately, they were unable to deal effectively with the complex interstate issues presented. Moreover, the Court's denial of national power was out of harmony with rising public demands that government soften the harsh side-effects of industrialization and protect the minimum health, safety, and welfare of its citizens.

Ultimately, the Court yielded. It recognized the right of state governments to regulate the production of goods in such decisions as those uphold-

[9] *Schechter Poultry Co.* v. *United States*, 295 U.S. 495 (1935).
[10] *United States* v. *Butler*, 297 U.S. 62 (1936).

ing state power to set prices and fix minimum wages. The Court also ratified the extensive powers of the national government over production, agriculture, and labor relations whenever these affected interstate commerce. Between 1937, when the National Labor Relations Act was upheld, and 1941, when a national law was upheld setting maximum hours and minimum wages and forbidding child labor, the Supreme Court fully confirmed congressional power to regulate all interstate aspects of the economy. Reserved to the states for economic regulation were those areas that Congress chose not to regulate itself.

Yet the tension between national and state authority has remained as new issues have arisen. Today, debates occur over "federal preemption"— whether Congress intended its legislation in a particular field to preclude the states from exercising concurrent powers over this subject. For example, when Congress gives the National Labor Relations Board jurisdiction over labor disputes affecting interstate commerce, can state labor boards exercise control over labor disputes that have interstate aspects as long as the NLRB has not specifically ruled on such cases? After some conflicting court rulings, Congress stated clearly that they could. Can states pass their own laws to make aliens living in their jurisdiction register with state authorities? The Supreme Court has said "no"; this is a matter in which congressional alien-registration laws preempt the field. In these controversies, the Supreme Court must determine whether the subject matter is essentially national in character, whether the state regulation interferes with the federal policy enacted, and whether the silence of Congress on the subject of parallel state action implies consent or hostility to such action in the particular instance. The Supreme Court has used the "federal preemption" doctrine to strike down more than a dozen major types of state law in the fields of internal security, taxation, and economic regulation since 1945. As a result, some conservatives have sponsored legislation to require the federal courts to assume that Congress intended to allow states to legislate in areas of concurrent jurisdiction *unless* the congressional act expressly declares that the states may not do so. These proposals have been defeated throughout the late 1950's and 1960's by those who argue that they would upset the existing balances between federal and state authority and would limit the creative role of the courts in adjusting the borderlines between Congress and the states when concurrent powers exist.

In addition, the tremendous rise in the importance of our foreign policy has had its impact on the theory and practice of the federal system in these decades. From the explosion of the First World War through the Second World War, the Korean War, and Vietnam, the federal government has had to spend vast sums of money for national defense and to apply sweeping regulatory programs to support war and defense efforts. Recognizing these demanding international conditions, the Supreme Court has upheld broad national powers in the field of foreign affairs, often over the complaints of states'-rights protesters.

Court support has taken two main forms. First, the Supreme Court has upheld national legislation enacted to carry out treaty obligations of the United States, even though these laws would not have been within national power except for the treaty.

Second, the Supreme Court has ruled that the national government has inherent powers in foreign relations that do "not depend upon the affirmative grants of the Constitution." [11] This doctrine of inherent powers validated such exercises of national power as the acquisition of territory by discovery and occupation, the expulsion of undesirable aliens, and "executive agreements" made by the President—all powers not specifically delegated to the federal government in the Constitution. Executive agreements, for example, do not require the Senate's approval, and thus the states are unable to exercise political control over them through their representation in the Senate. Conservatives in the late 1950's tried to pass the so-called Bricker Amendment, which would have required Senate approval of executive agreements and would have prevented treaties from enlarging presidential power. These efforts were defeated, however, when the Eisenhower Administration stressed the need for presidential freedom of action and pointed out that the requirement of Senate approval of treaties protected the public from infringement of their constitutional guarantees.

Of course, all the forces that had begun in the second period—the rise of giant industry, economic inflations and depressions, foreign-policy and war pressures—were accelerated from the First World War to the present. Moreover, public demands for welfare services pulled the national government into areas that were once primarily local and state responsibilities. During Lyndon Johnson's Administration, rising public concern for better services and the weakness of Republican conservatives in Congress after the Goldwater defeat in 1964 led to passage of large federal programs rejected by Congresses in previous decades—measures such as Medicare, the antipoverty program, and new federal aid to education.

In this third period, national regulation of the economy and national provision for basic social-welfare programs became part of our court-accepted and politically approved pattern. Yet the national-state-local mixture of functions was retained, not scrapped in favor of a national monopoly.

The Instruments of the New Federalism

Sketching the overall shift in power from the states to the national government does not do justice to several important factors: the political controls

---

[11] *United States* v. *Curtiss-Wright Export Corporation*, 299 U.S. 304 (1936).

"You see, sir, my federal anti-poverty grant is now contingent on my ability to raise matching funds in the private sector. . . ."

Drawing by Ed Fisher in the *Saturday Review*

Government programs dealing with socioeconomic problems today rely on a mixture of federal, state, local, and private efforts.

that still limit national authority; the national-state cooperation involved in much national action; and the continued vitality of state and local governments.

The image of the national government as an unlimited autocrat would cause most federal officials either to laugh wildly in disbelief or to cry in remembered frustration. The national government itself still lies under strong state controls. Some controls stem from our election system, which distributes presidential electoral votes by states, guarantees each state two senators, and apportions representatives by election districts within states. Senators and representatives, though federal legislators, defend and advance local and state interests against any threats, real or imagined, from "Washington bureaucrats." States also exert controls through the weapon of Senate confirmation of presidential appointees and through the practice of "senatorial courtesy," [12] which in effect gives state and local officials veto power over many "federal" appointments. Still other state controls flow from the party system, which has its strongest roots in the state and local party organizations, and from the influence that locally based interest groups can exert on national policy-making through various forms of lobbying.

The fact that our federalist development is not simply a steady shift from state to national power is well illustrated by Washington's tendency to enter an area but allow it to be administered by the states. Examples of this basic tendency are the federal grant-in-aid programs. Beginning on a large scale with the grants for highway construction in 1916, these programs have provided the states with funds to do a wide variety of things—build

[12] See Ch. 11, pp. 362–64, for further discussion.

hospitals and health centers, pay old-age pensions, institute vocational-education programs, provide maternal care and child-health service, renew urban areas, and so on. Direct federal grants-in-aid were estimated at about $17 billion per year in the late 1960's. The federal government chooses the program to support, dangles the inviting cash before the state governments to win their "voluntary" participation, and sets certain standards of administration (such as that employees in public-welfare programs be selected through civil-service procedures or that standardized accounting methods be used for highway-fund disposals). But the states do the actual administering, contribute from 10 to 50 percent of the funds themselves, and have important leeway in shaping the real policy impact of these programs on local residents.

Actually, although grants-in-aid are the most conspicuous examples of cooperative federalism, other instances are numerous. When a person steals a car or kidnaps a baby and moves it across state lines, both state and national laws are violated, and the governments cooperate in the search for the guilty party; in addition, state and local police officers are often trained in national police schools. In economic matters, national and state regulatory agencies have worked out common requirements for the accounting data to be kept by utility corporations; state banks are offered the opportunity to become members of the Federal Reserve and the Federal Deposit Insurance systems; and cooperative arrangements have been established between the national and state authorities that approve sales of securities. In conservation of resources, food and drug regulation, protection of health, and wars on poverty or river pollution, national and state agencies are in constant contact with each other. Cooperation and adjustment of responsibilities are the day-to-day characteristics of modern federalism.

In addition, there has been an important growth in direct relationships between the federal government and local communities—towns, cities, and counties—often bypassing state controls. The federal government now subsidizes the building of municipal and county airports, awards large sums for local housing and slum clearance under federal urban-renewal programs, gives poverty-program grants to cities, and awards billions of dollars in defense contracts to shipyards or factories that spell jobs and prosperity for local areas. This leads mayors, city planning boards, local chambers of commerce, and union leaders into direct negotiations with federal agencies charged with awarding funds under the applicable national program, often with congressmen from the locality or the state's United States senators serving as key intermediaries.

In addition, political scientists have noted that a pattern of informal but important information-sharing and administrative cooperation has developed among the specialized local, state, and federal bureaucracies dealing with a particular function. For example, city boards of education, state education departments, and the United States Office of Education are in frequent

The Dangers of Increased Federal Power

"What have you given us?" a woman asked Ben Franklin toward the close of the Constitutional Convention. "A Republic," he said, "*if you can keep it!*"

We have not kept it.... The system of restraints has fallen into disrepair. The federal government has moved into every field in which it believes its services are needed. The state governments are either excluded from their rightful functions by federal preemption, or they are allowed to act at the sufferance of the federal government. Inside the federal government both the executive and judicial branches have roamed far outside their constitutional boundary lines. And all of these things have come to pass without regard to the amendment procedures prescribed by Article V. The result is a Leviathan, a vast national authority out of touch with the people, and out of their control. This monolith of power is bounded only by the will of those who sit in high places....

How did it happen? How did our national government grow from a servant with sharply limited powers into a master with virtually unlimited power?

In part we were swindled. There are occasions when we have elevated men and political parties to power that promised to restore limited government and then proceeded, after their election, to expand the activities of government. But let us be honest with ourselves. Broken promises are not the major causes of our trouble. *Kept* promises are. All too often we have put men in office who have suggested spending a little more on this, a little more on that, who have proposed a new welfare program, who have thought of another variety of "security." We have taken the bait, preferring to put off to another day the recapture of freedom and the restoration of our constitutional system.

From Senator Barry Goldwater of Arizona, *The Conscience of a Conservative*, 1960.

contact and collaboration. The same is true of health, welfare, police, and other specialized agencies.

The continued vitality of the states and the vast scope of the demands upon their attention are frequently overlooked in discussing the consolidation of national power. Anyone who looks at the statutes passed in regular sessions of state legislatures will see a wider span of domestic problems dealt with than in the legislation of Congress during the same period. State measures deal with far-reaching issues of labor, education, public utilities, and agriculture; and they are still the centers of licensing and other forms of regulation for the professions and service trades. Furthermore, while the national government sets standards when it grants money, the states retain much discretion in legislation concerning health, welfare, roads, and other matters for which federal money is received.

Another example of the continued vitality of the states is the development of new forms and institutions by which states and localities can cope themselves with the spillage of issues over formal government boundaries. One such device is the interstate compact, in which two or more states, with the permission of Congress, enter into an agreement to govern jointly or share something of common interest. There are now over four hundred interstate compacts in existence, governing river development, conservation, ports and bridges, civil defense, and other subjects. Some of these, like the Delaware River Basin compact, provide for federal representation on the governing authority, making the venture a federal-state as well as multi-state enterprise.

Another new local institution is metropolitan government, which consolidates a cluster of separate city, town, suburban, and sometimes county

---

The Need for Increased Federal Power

The reality of increased federal power is undeniable. The events and circumstances which have created it are more tangled and ambiguous. Most obvious is the necessity for federal leadership in the conduct of foreign affairs, accepted by even the most conservative. Thus, as America became a global power with swiftly spreading burdens and ambitions, government waxed. Our relations with other countries, deeply and even mortally consequential in themselves, inevitably seep into a hundred areas of national life, shaping the structure of our industrial system, setting priorities for education and scholarship, pushing us toward technology and away from other pursuits.

Through this indirect effect on other institutions, and through the immediate impact of particular decisions and acts, the conduct of foreign affairs pervades the attitudes of the nation, contributing to a national mood of enthusiasm or resignation, anger or despair, which unavoidably carries over into a wide range of unrelated public problems and private sensibilities. The war in Vietnam has crippled and drained the drive behind civil rights. The presence and potential of nuclear power has entered into our art, and probably into the psychological structure of every citizen. Yet this towering power is for the most part in the hands of a single man and his employees. Even the normal checks on public dissent are partially sterilized by ignorance, central control over information, and the fact that immediate self-interest is usually not involved, thus depriving protest of the passion which comes from simple personal engagement. It is part of the naivete of the conservative position to believe that foreign affairs can be compartmentalized—that enormous power can be granted in the world arena while being withdrawn from domestic affairs. The truth is that authority over foreign affairs carries with it a new, wholly modern, ability to alter the nature and direction of our society.

From Richard N. Goodwin, former special assistant to Presidents Kennedy and Johnson, "The Shape of American Politics," *Commentary*, June 1967.

governments into a single metropolitan authority for providing services such as police, water, sewers, or recreation. The participating governments retain their local powers on other matters but join in one paramount governing agency to cope effectively with matters that require large-area programs. "Metro" government in Dade County, Florida—the greater Miami area—is a leading instance of such action.

A Balance Sheet of the New Federalism

An issue of continuing debate today is whether the United States should move toward still stronger national power or restore greater local authority. National-power advocates cite the need for overall national planning and programs to deal with urban blight, transportation decay, civil rights, and similar critical issues. State actions in these areas are often fiscally inadequate, planned piecemeal, and highly inefficient because of the lower levels of skill available in state governments as a whole. The national government, which is much more responsive to the will of the national majority, can act forcefully where public needs and demands are clear and can better arrange compromises among warring minority groups. Moreover, when funds for domestic problems such as civil rights, educational facilities, and scientific development depend on how much goes to national defense and foreign policy, central guidance is more vital than ever. Finally, the national-power advocate dismisses the idea that local control is *necessarily* a greater protection of the citizen's freedom than national responsibility. The Negroes and whites in Little Rock who wanted peaceful high-school integration were coerced into continued segregation by the state of Arkansas; similarly, the person convicted of a crime on the basis of a confession obtained through the use of force by the local police will usually find the national Supreme Court his most reliable defender.

Those who advocate restoring state authority, on the other hand, question whether the national public really wants Washington to take on more and more programs in education, labor, civil rights, and the like. They argue that such matters need the diverse programs and approaches of local jurisdictions in order to reflect faithfully the great diversity in local conditions and local attitudes toward these issues. Furthermore, states and local communities are portrayed as being closer to the people—and closer to the voters—so programs at these levels respond quickly to public will. Finally, states are described as little laboratories in which different laws and programs can be experimented with, to the overall benefit of other states and even of the national government.

This debate has been central to our national politics for the past several decades. The most significant point to note, however, is that every effort in recent decades to decentralize the government through congressional legislation has come to naught. The two Hoover Commissions in the 1940's on reorganization of the federal government and the President's Federal-State Action Committee during the 1950's were unable to come up with any proposals for major decentralization that proved acceptable to Congress. This is because national programs and policies satisfy three basic criteria that ensure their maintenance: (1) They meet strongly felt public needs and expectations. (2) They activate interest groups and local elements that strongly support their continuation. And (3) the states offer no viable alternative solutions.

The basic truth about the federal system, then, is that it is a nondoctrinaire, pragmatic arrangement, responsive to political and constitutional limits and opportunities. Speaking in Ann Arbor, Michigan, in 1964, President Johnson recognized this fact and called for a policy of "Creative Federalism" for the 1960's as the only way to work effectively on massive problems such as urban living, poverty, civil rights, and education. What he referred to was a deliberate pooling of resources, agencies, and supporting groups at all levels of American government in cooperative association, with the particular mixture of rules, operating procedures, and review authorities adapted to the problem involved.

Formulating this goal, of course, does not automatically solve all the political problems involved. For example, mayors have applauded the federal antipoverty program but have been leery of letting local branches of the federal antipoverty agency distribute the funds, since this minimizes the gratitude of recipients to city hall. Poverty officials, on the other hand, have wanted to avoid the city welfare and political bureaucracies and build indigenous neighborhood organizations to design and administer local programs. Similarly, the United States Office of Education wants to give grants for educational-innovation programs directly to local school districts that present imaginative proposals, while many state officials and the National Education Association have insisted such funds should go primarily to the states for distribution. Despite such problems, however, Creative Federalism is an idea that reflects the realities of our political tradition, constitutional structure, and party system and is clearly the direction of our policy in the future.

SUMMARY

Through its formal and informal processes of change, the American political system has managed to respond gradually and relatively successfully to the pressures of rapid social change during the past century and three-quarters. There have been periods of high political stress on the system, as with sectional rivalries in the pre-Civil War period; struggles among farmers, laborers, and corporations during our early industrialization; and racial tension today. Yet only once in the past—when the Civil War divided the nation into two warring camps—did the system fail to resolve conflict by gradualism.

Each of our interlocking mechanisms for accomplishing gradual change has had its distinctive characteristics. The amending process, while it has been used rarely, has been of major importance in democratizing our government processes and institutions. The availability of a "continuing constitutional convention"—our judicial process—has enabled amendments to be used infrequently, and the political determinants of our system have led the Supreme Court throughout our history to play an active role in adapting our classic rules to new situations. The legislative process has also played a major role here, particularly in shaping the structure of our executive, administrative, and judicial institutions and in creating public programs where responsibility was once legally and politically in private hands.

Informal political processes have also been instruments of our system's gradual adaptation to new conditions. Our party system has institutionalized loyal opposition, helped adjust conflicts between local, state, and national interests, and brought new groups into the political system. Interest groups have also played a key role, providing the connective circuits between party and government and providing an essential mechanism for voicing and responding to new claims in times of social change.

The impact of our varied instruments of change has been illustrated by our discussion of federalism. The basic ground rules of cooperative contacts, political debate, and judicial umpiring of most disputes were laid in the 1789–1861 period. To be sure, our techniques of flexible federalism broke down with the Civil War, and the nation's response to industrialization between 1880 and 1913 was far from adequate. From 1913 on, however, the federal system has been rapidly modernized to provide the increased national responsibility demanded by domestic and international trends, while still maintaining the political and administrative relevance of state and local governments.

But the dilemma of our times is whether our processes of change and our federal system are swift and flexible enough to solve the problems of running a continental industrial nation with world commitments in an age of clashing empires and weapons of total destruction.

Is separation of powers a valid system for running a national government that must act speedily and decisively in labor disputes, defense policies, or civil rights? Is our system of elections one that really captures the attention of the citizenry, brings the best men into competition for office, and provides national leaders with the mandate to govern firmly? Is Congress organized to function properly as a representative body? Do we need new intergovernmental agencies to replace the "formalistic" boundaries of city, county, and state?

The chapters that follow will present full discussions of the institutions, processes, personalities, and functions of the American governmental system. With this background, students will be able to weigh intelligently the issues of maintenance, reform, or fundamental change, and, in a real sense, these issues are what will be at the heart of each student's civic participation as voter and citizen in the years to come.

II

**THE
POLITICAL
PROCESS**

*Part II explores the effect of our
system's basic determinants—its
political culture, its constitutional
framework, and its changing socioeconomic milieu—on the American
political process. Chapters 4, 5, and
6 explore the distinctive evolution,
functions, and organization of interest
groups and parties in a political
system with a Constitution that left
certain political questions unanswered,
with a culture that encourages
pluralism and group formation, in a
society lacking profound economic,
social, or political cleavages. Chapter
7 examines the distinctive patterns of
voting behavior in this political
system, while Chapter 8 discusses the
quadrennial competition for the
supreme prize of the system—the
American Presidency.*

INTERESTS, OPINIONS, AND GROUPS

4

A distinctive feature of the American political system is the multiplicity of interests that arise in our society and the ease with which groups form to advance these interests in the political arena. We begin by exploring the social, economic, and political factors shaping the pattern of interests in the United States. We then explore the types of groups in our society, the characteristics of group members, and the role of the "active minority" in groups. Finally, we examine the techniques of interest groups in the major political arenas of our system. Which groups tend to be favored by the structure and rules of each arena? How much power do groups really wield over the outcomes of elections? How democratic is the group basis of our system?

INTERESTS AND THE POLITICAL SYSTEM

The United States surpasses all other nations in the number of groups in its society organized to pursue private and public purposes. Pick up any American newspaper, and note the groups listed in the news. For example, we chose to examine the New York *Times* for a typical Friday.[1] On that day, the United Federation of Teachers announced they would strike the New York City schools; their action drew comments from the Public Education Association, the United Parents Association, the Afro-American Teachers Association, and the Congress of Puerto Rican Hometowns. An item from Milwaukee described a violent sit-in conducted by seventy-five commandos of the Milwaukee NAACP Youth Council in the mayor's anteroom to protest housing discrimination. The Nixon-for-President Committee issued a statement questioning the political abilities of Republican presidential candidate George Romney. In Washington, the National Association of State Universities and Land Grant Colleges announced its opposition to a proposed forty-year-loan plan to students for college costs. Also in Washington, a representative of the Association to Repeal Abortion Laws urged relaxation of state prohibitions in this area. In the New York suburb of New Rochelle, a dozen women belonging to a local church antigambling committee collected evidence on a $7-million bookmaking operation, resulting in the indictment of its ringleaders. Among other groups mentioned in the *Times* for that day were the American Nazi party, the Junior League, the Association of Investment Bankers, the Boy Scout Councils of Greater New York, the American Civil Liberties Union, the Friends of Prospect Park, the Bronx Council Against Poverty, and the United States Lawn Tennis Association.

Any viable political system must either respond to the pattern of interests existing within the society or develop authoritarian techniques for the containment and "management" of those interests. The democratic systems that have enjoyed the greatest stability and a gradualist response to social change over time (the British, American, Swiss, and Scandinavian systems—and to a lesser extent the French) are those in which the political system most closely reflects the social and cultural configurations of the nation. A political system with a small, homogeneous population (especially if it enjoys relative prosperity) faces few interest groups articulating demands; it can operate with tightly organized and program-oriented political parties, and its formal structure of government requires few safeguards for minority rights. But, if a large, heterogeneous nation were to attempt to manage with the same political system, intense conflicts would quickly develop and lead to civil conflict.

[1] September 8, 1967.

Much of the grief and confusion that surround the breakdowns of Western parliamentary forms in the new nations of Asia, Africa, and Latin America results from a failure to recognize that writing a constitution and setting up a parliament do not create a parliamentary system of government. The parliamentary system has certain social and cultural prerequisites —a government structure may function effectively in one social setting and quite badly in another. As the shrewd British Labourite Sir Stafford Cripps once remarked, "Political systems are not for export." Thus, an analysis of the American political system is best begun by examining its basic determinants.

Factors Shaping the American Pattern of Interests

Three main factors have shaped the American pattern of interests: our socioeconomic structure, our political culture, and our institutional development.

The American economic and social structure

As we saw in Chapters 1 and 2, American society in its colonial and early national periods was fragmented by various religious, ethnic, regional, and economic differences arising out of our patterns of settlement, immigration, and self-government. During the nineteenth century, these trends were continued through new immigration and internal migration, the founding of new states, and the physical variations in the American continent. As the nation moved from agriculture to industry, our economic structure became more specialized, increasing the number of industries and the competition within industries and giving rise to a heterogeneous labor force. These socioeconomic factors produced a diversified society, and in such a society a broad range of interests sought expression in the political system.

The history of the American labor movement shows clearly how changing economic arrangements create new interests and give rise to new groups. In the early decades of this century, there was rapid growth in such industries as automobiles, rubber, chemicals, electrical manufacturing, and metals. With this growth came new technological developments, including mass production and the elimination of many old crafts, which had previously been the bases for unionization. The number of organizable workers increased greatly, but their interests were new and did not correspond to the old organizational lines. During the 1920's, the number and diversity of these interests increased, but the relative prosperity of the country reduced the need for organization. The coming of the Great Depression, however, saw an unprecedented spurt of unionization along *industrial* rather than craft lines, with such powerful new unions as the United Auto Workers, the

United Steel Workers, and the United Rubber Workers entering the political arena.

Even for the farmers (in many ways the group least affected by industrialization), it was the rapid decline in agriculture coupled with the rapid growth of industry in the latter decades of the nineteenth century that spawned formation of what remain to this day the most powerful farm organizations: the Grange, the Farmers Union, and the American Farm Bureau Federation. These groups were formed in direct response to the needs for protection against the railroads and banks and for dissemination of new agricultural techniques to sustain the competitive capacity of farmers faced by an increasingly inhospitable market situation.

The proliferation of interest groups has been accentuated by the fact that our government has traditionally been a distributor of economic benefits—from protective tariffs for "infant industries" and free land for farmers and railroad companies in our early years to Medicare payments for senior citizens today. A distributive government naturally stimulates the formation of interest groups and competition among them for their share of government-sponsored benefits.

The American political culture

A diversified economy and a heterogeneous population may well give rise to interests and to interest groups, but this process will be significantly affected by whether citizens tend to view group formation and interest-group activity as legitimate and useful political phenomena or as an impediment to the system.

As we noted in Chapter 1, the American political culture puts a high value on the formation of private groups to accomplish social objectives usually provided for in other nations by government or privileged classes. This American attitude has been formalized in the constitutional protections we give to the right of association, to incorporated bodies, and to the right of individuals and groups to petition the government for "redress of grievances." Our political ideals also reflect a desire to safeguard minority rights (particularly those of economic, religious, and social minorities), and our absence of class ideology leads us to view the expression of self-interest and group claims as the proper way to balance interests in the political community. Our stress on localism—from our town-meeting ideal and our reliance on informal intergroup resolution of local conflicts to our experiments with neighborhood antipoverty programs—encourages the articulation of interests through groups organized at the grassroots rather than pushing citizens toward national arenas and national parties. Finally, our view of government as servant rather than master and our lack of deference to its authority strengthen the trend toward framing group demands on government to encourage its responsiveness to private interests.

Interest Groups: A Nuisance to the Republic

By a faction, I understand a number of citizens, whether amounting to a majority or a minority of the whole, who are united and actuated by some common impulse of passion, or of interest, adverse to the rights of other citizens, or to the permanent and aggregate interests of the community....

The latent causes of faction are ... sown in the nature of man.... A zeal for different opinions concerning religion, concerning government, and many other points, as well of speculation as of practice; an attachment to different leaders ambitiously contending for pre-eminence and power; or to persons of other descriptions whose fortunes have been interesting to the human passions, have, in turn, divided mankind into parties, inflamed them with mutual animosity, and rendered them much more disposed to vex and oppress each other, than to co-operate for their common good. So strong is this propensity of mankind to fall into mutual animosities, that where no substantial occasion presents itself, the most frivolous and fanciful distinctions have been sufficient to kindle their unfriendly passions and excite their most violent conflicts. But the most common and durable source of factions has been the various and unequal distribution of property. Those who hold and those who are without property have ever formed distinct interests in society. Those who are creditors, and those who are debtors, fall under a like discrimination. A landed interest, a manufacturing interest, a mercantile interest, a moneyed interest, with many lesser interests, grow up of necessity in civilized nations, and divide them into different classes, actuated by different sentiments and views. The regulation of these various and interfering interests forms the principal task of modern legislation.

From James Madison, *The Federalist*, No. 10, 1787.

American government institutions and the party system

The nature of the American party system and the way our formal government power is constitutionally arranged also have a major impact on the way interests are expressed and on the rate of group formation. As later chapters will show, power in the American political system is widely fragmented and diffused. Our constitutional provisions for separation of powers and for checks and balances among the branches of government have created a number of separate political arenas, all producing public-policy decisions, and a multitude of access points into these arenas. Moreover, wide powers of discretion are lodged with individual officeholders. This diffusion of policy-making stimulates the formation of interest groups, which inevitably seek to influence decisions wherever power is exercised.

Our party system, for example, is a decentralized confederation of state and local parties, in which political ideology does not play a significant role and in which the rewards and punishments available to national party leaders are much less significant than those in countries with highly disciplined, ideological, and national parties. Moreover, our federal system divides power between the national government and the fifty states; the states in turn share power with local authorities (counties, cities, towns, etc.). In addition, we have created semi-independent authorities, such as the Port Authority of New York and New Jersey or the federal Tennessee Valley Authority, that govern activities encompassing several states. Finally, within each level of government—federal, state, and local—power is divided among the legislative, executive, and judicial branches; in addition, the creation of semi-independent regulatory agencies at each level adds what some have called a "fourth branch" of government.

The result is that our political institutions offer multiple access points

Interest Groups: A Bulwark Against Tyranny

In no country in the world has the principle of association been more successfully used, or more unsparingly applied to a multitude of different objects, than in America....

The right of association was imported from England, and it has always existed in America; so that the exercise of this privilege is now amalgamated with the manners and customs of the people. At the present time the liberty of association is become a necessary guarantee against the tyranny of the majority. In the United States, as soon as a party is become preponderant, all public authority passes under its control; its private supporters occupy all the places, and have all the force of the administration at their disposal. As the most distinguished partisans of the other side of the question are unable to surmount the obstacles which exclude them from power, they require some means of establishing themselves upon their own basis, and of opposing the moral authority of the minority to the physical power which domineers over it....

Americans of all ages, all conditions, and all dispositions, constantly form associations. They have not only commercial and manufacturing companies, in which all take part, but associations of a thousand other kinds—religious, moral, serious, futile, extensive or restricted, enormous or diminutive. The Americans make associations to give entertainments, to found establishments for education, to build inns, to construct churches, to diffuse books, to send missionaries to the antipodes; and in this manner they found hospitals, prisons, and schools. If it be proposed to advance some truth, or to foster some feeling by the encouragement of a great example, they form a society. Wherever, at the head of some new undertaking, you see the Government in France, or a man of rank in England, in the United States you will be sure to find an association.

From Alexis de Tocqueville, *Democracy in America*, Vols. 1 and 2, 1835 and 1840.

for outside groups, because government decisions are made by men enjoying considerable freedom from either strict party controls or tight supervision by higher authorities.

From Interests to Interest Groups

In viewing the phenomenon of group activity, political scientists concentrate on the *interest group*, which they define as a collection of individuals who share some common attitude, seek recognition or advancement of their position in society, and engage in repeated and patterned activity to advance the group's claims on others in the society.[2]

This definition excludes several types of group. First, it excludes *aggregates*—that is, categories of people who share one or more characteristics (for example, redheaded Texans or left-handed college students) but do not share a common attitude. Second, it excludes groups who may share a common attitude (say, male divorcés) but do not seek measures, such as lower alimony rates, to improve their position. And, third, our definition excludes groups who do share an attitude and do make a claim on society or the government—for example, Negroes who gather on the street corner to protest an act of alleged police brutality—but do not gather regularly enough to achieve cohesion, produce leaders, and take organized group actions, such as sending delegations to city hall.

Two other types of group, while not included in our definition, often modify the behavior of interest groups because they exert profound influence on the attitudes of interest-group members. The *primary group* is a small, face-to-face unit, such as the family, an office clique, or a luncheon club. The *reference group* is one with which a person identifies because of some shared interest, though he has not joined any of the formal organizations that claim to speak for that interest. Neither type of group presses claims through the political system, but because of their psychological importance to members both are likely to influence their economic, social, and political attitudes.

Groups that perceive politics as salient to their claims on society and become active in the political arena become *political interest groups*. Though this term immediately brings to mind economic, racial, religious, or ideological groups that are continuously active in the political process, almost any interest group may become a political interest group at some time for some particular purpose. For example, stamp collectors may become involved in negotiations with the Post Office, cultural groups may seek

[2] We will avoid using the term "pressure group," because it is pejorative, carrying overtones of unfair influence on public policy. "Interest group" is a more neutral term that suggests the legitimate role such groups play in our political system. Our definition is adapted from David B. Truman, *The Governmental Process* (New York: Knopf, 1951), p. 33.

government aid to the arts, and sports associations may lobby for exemption from the antitrust laws.

Political interest groups need not have formal organizations—constitutions, officers, headquarters, letterheads, and so on—to be successful in our political system. In fact, in American politics, organizations are not always more effective than certain informal political interest groups or temporary loose alliances. However, a formal organization provides a group with "a more systematic means for uniting money and effort behind the special functions of leadership." [3] And, more important, it creates an easily identifiable entity from which government officials, parties, and other groups can solicit support and engage in negotiations. For these reasons, most political interest groups are formal organizations.

One of the subtleties of the American political system is that interests may influence its operation even when an interest *group* has not been formed to defend them. Such unprotected interests are called *potential groups*—that is, groups sharing an attitude but lacking patterned, systematic interaction among their members. In the absence of a catalyst (perhaps a dramatic event that would move people to action), this diffuse attitude might never culminate in the formation of an interest group. Yet it may still be politically significant precisely because those in power, and those representing other groups, wish to discourage the formation of a new, competing group. The reactions of the undefended are thus often anticipated, and their interest taken somewhat into account. Needless to say, this is an imperfect process. The established élites in a given city may decide not to economize on welfare funds for fear of bringing articulate and persistent groups into existence within their Negro community—but this is far from saying that Negroes are adequately protected in that municipality's politics.

CHARACTERISTICS OF GROUP MEMBERSHIP IN AMERICA

It has been estimated that there are well over 100,000 voluntary organizations in the United States. Though there has been no definitive national study of how many Americans belong to organizations, sample studies at the national and local levels indicate that between 55 and 65 percent of the population belong to at least one organization.[4] Of the 57 percent who were found to be joiners in one survey, 32 percent belonged to more than one

[3] Abraham Holtzman, *Interest Groups and Lobbying* (New York: Macmillan, 1966), p. 4.
[4] See Gabriel A. Almond and Sidney Verba, *The Civic Culture* (Boston: Little, Brown, 1965), Ch. X. See also the studies cited in Arnold M. Rose, *The Power Structure* (New York: Oxford University Press, 1967), and V. O. Key, Jr., *Public Opinion and American Democracy* (New York: Knopf, 1961).

Table 4–1 Types and Relative Popularity of Organizations in the United States

Organizations	Percentage of joiners belonging to each *
Religious †	19
Trade Unions	14
Social	13
Fraternal	13
Civic-Political	11
Cooperative	6
Veterans	6
Business	4
Professional	4
Farm	3
Charitable	3
Other	6

* A joiner could list his membership in more than one organization.
† Church-related organizations, not religious affiliation itself.
SOURCE: Gabriel A. Almond and Sidney Verba, *The Civic Culture: Political Attitudes and Democracy in Five Nations* (Princeton, N.J., Princeton University Press, 1963), p. 302.

organization (14 percent to 2, 9 percent to 3, and 9 percent to 4 or more).[5] Table 4–1 shows how this survey classified the types of organization people belonged to.

Who joins organizations? The studies show definite patterns of membership. More men than women join groups, more Protestants and Jews than Catholics, more married persons than single, and twice as many homeowners as renters. "The better-off and better-educated in almost any category of potential members are more likely to be members than those not so well off or those with less education. The prosperous, the alert, the informed, and the educated join together in organizations to promote their concerns."[6] The higher the status of individuals in their work, the more likely they are to be group members and the more groups they join. The findings of a 1952 survey are shown in Table 4–2.

How does membership in groups correlate with political participation? Studies show that group joiners have higher levels of political participation than nonjoiners. They are more likely to vote, and they are likely to vote

[5] Almond and Verba, *op. cit.*, p. 264. Americans were found to join twice as many organizations as citizens in the second-ranking country in this five-nation survey of the United States, Great Britain, Germany, Italy, and Mexico.
[6] Key, *op. cit.*, p. 504.

Table 4–2   The Relationship Between Occupation and Group Membership

Occupation of head of household	Percentage belonging to 3 or more groups	Percentage belonging to no groups
Professional	53	19
Business	24	25
Farmer	15	41
Clerical	14	32
Skilled Labor	11	35
Unskilled Labor	5	43

SOURCE: Angus Campbell, Gerald Gurin, and Warren E. Miller, *The Voter Decides* (New York, Harper & Row, 1954), Table 4–2, p. 224.

more frequently than nonjoiners; they engage in more political activity, have a greater willingness to express their political opinions, and have a greater belief in the value of political action to improve their condition or protect their interests. For example, one study asked its sample whether they felt that their actions could influence the government. Only 54 percent of the nonjoiners said they felt they could do so, while 70 percent of the members of nonpolitical organizations and 79 percent of those belonging to political organizations answered in the affirmative.[7]

GROUP LEADERSHIP: THE ACTIVE MINORITY

We have indicated that an interest group comes into existence when interaction takes place among members, based on a shared attitude and a claim on the behavior of others. This basic definition needs further amplification if it is to be applied to large and powerful organizations as well as to small, informal ones. Even in the small, informal group, such as a neighborhood club, members can be characterized as leaders (those who are very active in the group and on its behalf) or followers (those whose activity is less frequent and for whom the group and its goals are often less important). In the large, formal organization, this leader-follower distinction is usually codified, with constitutional provisions stipulating how to choose and change leaders, outlining the duties of full-time functionaries, and guaranteeing some control and direction of this active minority by the less active membership. In the sense that their internal organization is based on this structure of rules, the vast majority of organized political interest groups in America can be regarded as "democratic."

[7] Almond and Verba, *op. cit.*, p. 253.

Vertigo

Peb in the Philadelphia *Inquirer*

When interest-group leaders take stands on issues other than those of immediate concern to their members—such as the civil-rights cause of the Negroes—they are likely to split their following and cause conflicts among organizations representing that sector of the population.

To what extent, however, do the lightly involved members control the behavior of the active minority? Are the leaders delegates and servants of the membership, as they often claim? Or do they constitute élites that make most decisions independently and carry their memberships along by controlling the flow of information within the group and manipulating the symbols revered by the group. While some memberships exercise more control than others, most group leaderships come closer to the élitist model than to the servant model.

The reasons for such élitist patterns are clear. The mere fact of formal organization creates a hierarchy of roles, which implies varying degrees of involvement. Decisions often have to be made quickly, foreclosing the possibility of lengthy meetings or protracted consultations. Since the leaders give more time to the group's business (if the group is large enough, they will be full-time professionals), they possess skills and information that the membership lacks. The internal channels of group communication are managed by the élite (newsletters, conventions, etc.), and they earn the gratitude and deference of the rank and file precisely *because* they are willing to do the work of running the organization.

The danger, however, lies in hurrying to the conclusion that the advantages of inside position, skills, and information enable élites to perpetuate their power and manipulate the group's strength as they please. In fact, three factors act as safeguards on élite power: competing loyalties, the need for the élite to anticipate the reactions of members in certain crucial matters, and what has been called the "rules of the game."

Competing Loyalties

America has very few total institutions. Apart from members of monasteries or inmates in mental institutions,

> no individual is wholly absorbed in any group to which he belongs. Only a fraction of his attitudes is expressed through any one such affiliation . . . an individual generally belongs to several groups—a family, a church, an economic institution, and frequently a very large number of associations . . . .[8]

In other words, individuals possess bundles of loyalties, some of which are at least potentially in conflict. Voluntary organizations tend to supplement, reinforce, or activate basic attitudes held by their members largely as a result of primary group or party loyalties. But when positions adopted by the leadership of a voluntary organization come into conflict with these basic attitudes of members, the organization is likely to come off second best. For example, labor-union leaders in the South have adhered to segregationist views despite national-union pressures; farmers standing to profit from the sale of oleomargarine deserted the American Farm Bureau when it tried to support restrictions of oleo sales; and aged citizens belonging to the Townsend movement for old-age security did not follow Mr. Townsend when he endorsed left-winger Henry Wallace for the Presidency in 1948.[9]

When an interest-group leader makes claims that collide with those of other groups with which his members identify, the conflict is likely to diminish seriously the cohesion and morale of his group, and members may drop out or temporarily withdraw. This trend, in turn, directly affects the leader's potential for future action, for he faces declining numbers, perhaps open disaffection, and certainly declining contributions from the no-longer-so-faithful. The leader who seeks staying power will therefore develop great sensitivity to the nuances of overlapping membership and identification within his "constituency," and he will temper his decisions accordingly. He will not do combat without careful consideration of whom he is likely to offend. For this reason, overlapping membership has a softening effect on political conflict in America.

Anticipating Member Reactions

A leader's behavior is restricted by the concepts his members have of the proper nature and goals of the group. There are certain symbols a leader must venerate, certain postures he must strike, certain conventions he must maintain, and a certain pace he cannot exceed. Otherwise he risks making the members think he is not showing the proper respect for the organization's identity. When this happens, his personal position may be jeopardized,

[8] Truman, *op. cit.*, p. 157.
[9] Holtzman, *op. cit.*, pp. 33–35.

the cohesion of the group adversely affected, and its competitive position weakened. An example of such internal rebellion and its costs to a leader was the 1949 resolution of the House of Delegates of the American Medical Association restricting the freedom of Dr. Morris Fishbein, editor of the association's *Journal*, to act as public spokesman for the organization. The editor had been exceedingly bitter in his attacks on public health insurance and had consistently embarrassed the more moderate elements within the AMA. He had, in short, misjudged the extent to which the whole body could be carried into an all-out attack on socialized medicine. Rather than split the membership, other members of the active minority agreed to "muzzle" Dr. Fishbein.

As long as the leader seems neither too flexible nor too extreme, he is likely to have little trouble securing perfunctory membership approval for what is essentially his own policy line. Because he wishes to preclude unrest and challenges from below, the leader accepts the boundaries set by the expectations of the members and avoids those actions that will precipitate adverse responses from them.

Anticipating membership views is especially important because (as studies in the past two decades have documented) an "attitude gap" frequently exists between the leaders of large organizations and their members. Sometimes, for example, leaders take a more militant stand than their membership will support. For example, an independent survey of union members' attitudes conducted in 1967 showed that only 54 percent supported the AFL-CIO's stand against state right-to-work laws and only 43 percent agreed with its position in favor of open housing. On the other hand, between 67 and 94 percent of the members did support the AFL-CIO's position on seven other contemporary public issues.[10] Studies have found that in a variety of groups—business, labor, veterans', women's, and civic— the "attitude gap" stems from the tendency of organization leaders to believe more strongly than do their members in tolerance for competing viewpoints, in civil liberties and civil rights, and in the political rules of the game.[11] These beliefs of organization leaders make it easier for them to negotiate with one another and manage the "group system," but they pose continuing problems for leaders who diverge too much from their memberships.

The Rules of the Group Game

Americans expect that political struggles will be carried on within certain broad limits of civility and decency. As our political culture has become more refined, we have become increasingly critical of once-common techniques such as bribery, defamation, and violence. The rules of the game of

[10] New York *Times*, July 16, 1967. See also Holtzman, *op. cit.*, p. 31.
[11] Rose, *op. cit.*, pp. 173–74; Samuel Stouffer, *Communism, Conformity and Civil Liberties* (New York: Wiley, 1965).

group politics in the United States are neither codified nor precise, and they are not evenly accepted or understood throughout the society. But they *are* powerful. The group leader, like the elected politician, violates this body of expectations and norms at his peril. Overlapping membership and the need for anticipating reactions are *intragroup* controls on élites, but the rules of the game are enforced from both within and without. If the leader sails close to the wind of "dirty fighting," he may precipitate a crisis of cohesion, and he may also alienate political allies and friendly office-holders. The costs of misbehavior in American politics are high.

In the spring of 1962, Roger Blough, chairman of the board of the United States Steel Corporation, made a hurried appointment with President Kennedy and informed him that a substantial price rise, which the rest of the steel industry would very probably follow, would be announced later that day. Within the week, a panoply of pressures forced Blough and U.S. Steel to rescind the increase. One disadvantage under which Big Steel labored in trying to hold out against an angry and politically skillful President was a broadly shared feeling that Blough had unfairly sprung his company's decision on Kennedy despite a prior understanding—worked out among the Administration, the United Steel Workers, and the industry—that there would be no price hike in the immediate future. Kennedy, in a press conference and in White House press releases, emphasized this violation of the rules of the game, and this factor helped to defeat U.S. Steel.

GOVERNMENT ARENAS FOR INTEREST–GROUP ACTIVITY

Interest-group power is ultimately the group's capacity to achieve access to political decision makers and to produce a more favorable decision than would otherwise have been made by the governmental agency. The kind of access a group has varies with the issue in question or the particular agency being approached. But political scientists have identified certain general factors that affect group access to some degree in all policy-making arenas of government and in regard to most issues:

1. The *number of members* a group has and the number of nonmembers that identify themselves with the group's interests.

2. The *economic and social resources* a group has. First, how much money does it have to spend on campaigns of persuasion? Second, how high are the social prestige of those who belong to the group and the social acceptability of the aims the group is pursuing?

3. The *membership's degree of involvement* with the group and the extent of their willingness to work for the organization's goals.

4. The *quality of a group's leadership*. Good leadership may come about by accident or by group design. That is, some groups are successful because

they happen to produce talented leaders who are able not only to mobilize the group's members but to make a persuasive appeal for sympathy to the general public. Other groups have the financial resources to hire experienced lobbyists who know how to gain access to key public officials and are adept at engineering popular support for the group's goals.

5. The relative *conservatism of a group's goals.* The American political system, like all viable systems, favors groups trying to maintain the status quo in a given area. In particular, our intricate system of procedural hurdles and checks and balances, designed to protect minority interests and prevent hasty action, gives added leverage to the group taking defensive action—to block proposed legislation or evade the decisions of courts or administrative agencies.

Groups possess these resources in varying combinations. Numbers, for example, do not tell the whole story. The AFL-CIO has a fluctuating membership currently estimated at 14.1 million. Its membership is about sixty times that of the American Medical Association, which has only 211,000 physicians on its rolls. But the AFL-CIO is clearly not sixty times as powerful as the AMA; indeed, some observers would say that organized medicine is more powerful than organized labor—chiefly because the AMA makes up in economic and social resources what it lacks in numbers. Doctors contribute more money to further their association's political projects than trade-union members do. Moreover, doctors have high social prestige in the community and are therefore able to enlist wide public sympathy for their point of view. The AMA was particularly successful in the 1940's and 1950's in influencing the public to identify with its values on such issues as opposition to government medical care for the aged. Unions, by contrast, often find it difficult to recruit support outside their own membership. In addition, doctors show greater cohesion and involvement with their association than do trade unionists—partly because physicians are better educated and have a better-developed sense of how power is exercised in society. Finally, the AMA has tended to favor maintenance of the status quo, particularly with regard to private medical practice.

Other groups with fairly modest memberships and minimal economic and social resources still manage to achieve impressive political victories because of the unrelenting energy of their supporters. Often the members of such groups are highly committed and are willing to sacrifice their time and careers for a cause they think important. They will talk, write letters, attend meetings, picket, and even go to jail in an effort to secure ends in which they believe. Such groups have worked for votes for women, Prohibition, civil rights, and nuclear disarmament. Sometimes such groups can rouse popular sympathy for their objectives; sometimes they alienate large sectors of the public. But they do attract legislative and administrative attention, and not infrequently a small but highly involved group can effectively influence government decisions.

Finally, an interest group's access to the arenas of power and its success in achieving its objectives vary according to the special structures, rules, and roles of government institutions and officeholders. This section will examine the distinctive characteristics of three major policy-making arenas: the legislative branch, the executive and regulatory agencies, and the courts. It will then examine the techniques of interest groups for persuading public opinion, which in turn influences decision makers in all three arenas.

Groups in the Legislative Process

In 1965, spokesmen for 304 groups registered as lobbyists seeking to influence decisions in Congress. The *Congressional Quarterly* news service classified the groups they represented as follows: business, 154; citizens, 64; labor and employee, 31; farm, 25; professional, 23; and military and veterans, 7. These 304 groups reported spending a total of $5,485,000 in congressional lobbying activities during 1965.

What kinds of activity did these interest groups pursue? Let us examine the 1966 legislative activities of a representative group in each of the six categories noted above:

1. *The Chamber of Commerce of the United States*, representing 2,800 state and local chambers, opposed a consumer-oriented bill to require "truth in packaging," opposed changes in the existing federal-state unemployment-

From *Puck,* January 23, 1889. Courtesy Roger Butterfield.

This 1889 cartoon criticizes the dominant access to Congress and state legislatures that business groups had in the late nineteenth century.

The Role of the Lobbyist: A Congressman's View

We may define lobbying as the total of all communicated influences upon legislators with respect to legislation.... After thirty-six years as a target of such messages, I still regard them as the bloodstream of the democratic process and a *sine qua non* of effective legislation. It is true that these messages come to us in a Babel of tongues.... But fundamentally, I believe, we all recognize that the touchstone of "good" lobbying and "bad" lobbying is not whether the objectives of persuasion are selfish or altruistic, liberal or conservative, prolabor or probusiness, but solely and simply whether the message conveyed is intelligible, accurate, and informative, or cryptic, deceptive, and obscure.... The task of the Congressman is arduous enough without being complicated by apocryphal or spurious messages....

A number of the modern lobbies operating in Washington are of the highest quality. With plenty of money to spend, they spend it on qualified analysts and advocates and provide Congressional committees with lucid briefs and technical documentation in support of their positions. Nothing is more informative and helpful to a legislative committee than to hear the views of competent well-matched advocates on the opposite sides of a legislative issue.

From Representative Emanuel Celler of Brooklyn, "Pressure Groups in Congress," *The Annals*, September 1958.

compensation system, opposed the Demonstration Cities bill, and opposed repeal of the federal statute allowing states to pass right-to-work laws. The chamber supported a bill to limit state power to tax out-of-state businesses and one to increase tax deductions for self-employed persons, and it supported an Electoral College reform bill that would have reduced the influence of urban majorities in presidential elections.

2. *Americans for Democratic Action*, with 60,000 members, supported civil-rights legislation, increasing the minimum wage, the Demonstration Cities bill, expansion of the antipoverty program, the truth-in-packaging bill, repeal of the right-to-work statute, and home rule for the District of Columbia. The ADA opposed new restrictions on the issuance of passports, contempt citations for Ku Klux Klan witnesses who refused to testify before the House Committee on Un-American Activities, and a proposed amendment to overturn a Supreme Court decision and authorize religious prayers in public schools.

3. *The United Mine Workers of America*, representing 450,000 members, supported a mine work-safety act and joined a labor-union coalition seeking to repeal the right-to-work statute. The UMW opposed a provision in the military-construction bill that would convert an Alaskan base from coal to gas heating and opposed expanded use of atomic energy to supply electric power to federal installations.

4. *The National Council of Farm Cooperatives*, speaking in behalf of 130 regional cooperative associations, opposed a minimum-wage bill for agricultural workers and the truth-in-packaging bill. The Cooperatives Council supported a federal program to buy food and send it overseas as a "peace" effort as well as a bill to prohibit discrimination against farm producers joining a cooperative.

5. *The American Dental Association*, representing 100,000 dentists and dental students, supported a federal grant program to improve the training of health personnel and a bill to relax interstate controls on shipping animals for research purposes. The group opposed bills to provide federal loans to finance group practice of medicine and dentistry.

6. *The Veterans of Foreign Wars*, with 1.3 million members, supported a "Cold War G.I. Bill," veterans'-pension increases, and more national military cemeteries. The VFW opposed a bill to put all American personnel working overseas under the Foreign Service system, since this would weaken existing veterans'-preference rules.

As this sample indicates, some of the efforts by groups in the legislature

---

The Role of the Lobbyist: The Lobbyists' View

We cannot get anything done against the interests of the people on the Hill. We can seldom talk anybody out of one position and into another. A member of Congress is not going to do anything that is contrary to the interests of his constituents; at least not for us. Our job is to keep him informed of the interests we have in common with him and his constituents.

I never initiate anything or assert myself in any way. We operate on the principle that if we produce a good product, the members of Congress will learn to depend on us. We operate on the same code as the doctor and the lawyer, we do not advertise and we do not solicit. I am a fanatic on accuracy and truthfulness of whatever we supply to the people in Congress. The mills of the gods grind slowly, but they grind exceedingly fine. I never take a momentary advantage to win a momentary prize. I avoid all kinds of slick tricks and similar subterfuge that might, in the long run, spoil my effectiveness. Congress has no place for people who try to pull slick tricks. I have watched persons who operate that way come and go; it eventually boomerangs on all of them.

The people in Congress have confidence in our proposals. They feel they are carefully studied, thoroughly prepared, and backed by sound legislative history. I try very hard to develop this confidence in the association. It does not come from going up there and demanding, and it does not come from getting into political issues; rather we go up there and present only our own case.

Lobbyists quoted anonymously in Lester Milbrath, *Washington Lobbyists*, 1963.

are defensive, to protect their existing position against undesired changes; other actions seek federal laws to alter the private, state, or federal status quo in their favor. Some groups tend to concentrate on specific "bread and butter" interests, while other groups, at times or as a general rule, are active on broad public-policy issues that do not directly affect their specific interests.

It is obvious from the time and money spent on such efforts that political interest groups in America consider legislative lobbying vital to their interests. Several characteristics of the legislative structure and process encourage interest groups to seek access to this arena and make it easy for them to do so. The most salient characteristic of Congress is that it lacks the tight party discipline that characterizes other political systems—the British, for example. American senators and congressmen enjoy more discretion than their counterparts in other systems—that is, they are *partially* free agents when they cast their votes and use their influence in Congress for or against proposed legislation. The national parties in Congress do not take official stands on all pending legislation, and many of the stands they do take are not regarded as binding on the party's legislators. Even when the parties do consider votes on a particular measure to be crucial to the party interest, the rewards and punishments available to our party leaders are more limited than those of the British system; and an American legislator may well decide that he risks being defeated in the next election more by defying a powerful group in his district than by defying the national party leaders or even the President, if he is from the same party. If congressional parties had binding legislative programs and could impose strict party discipline, much legislative lobbying would shift to the national headquarters of the parties.

Another aspect of legislative structure that encourages interest-group activity is its particular representational basis. The fact that the United States Senate has two members from each state, chosen by statewide election, gives a degree of influence and representation to nationally small groups, such as sheep growers in Montana, that would not be available if senators were elected at large across the country or by major regions of the country, such as North, Midwest, or South. The 435 relatively small districts into which the House of Representatives is divided provide even greater opportunity for economic, ethnic, and other interest groups, because it is relatively easy for a group to muster significant numbers of well-organized supporters in one small district or in a bloc of districts.

Then, too, the internal structure of the legislature provides a series of access points to groups. The size of legislatures and the complexity of issues has led national and state legislatures to lodge extensive authority in legislative committees (and especially in their chairmen). The committee can consider or ignore bills and exercise substantial influence on their disposition by the full legislative body. Groups seek to cultivate committee chairmen and in this manner can sometimes exert a "veto" effect on measures that could not be sustained if bills went directly to the floor or if it were easier to force them out of a committee.

Finally, the practical needs of legislators enhance group access to the legislature. First, to perform effectively in Congress and help their re-election, legislators need information—both technical information about leading public-policy issues and political information about the reactions of groups and public opinion to pending legislation. The growing information-collecting power of the executive branch, with its departments and staffs and widespread interest-group contacts, makes it especially important that legislators have *independent* sources of information if they are to criticize executive proposals and operations effectively. As one congressman remarked in 1967, in discussing the proposal for a computerized federal data center, "The Executive already knows too much for the safety of the government; Congressmen need the data and the expert analysis if we are to perform our legislative role." Interest-group communications—both directly to legislators and through legislative hearings—help to provide these data.

Second, interest groups help legislators work out ways to resolve the conflicting demands involved in controversial legislation. For, in fact, group-legislator relations are reciprocal: groups seek to influence legislators, and vice versa. And it is often the compromises that legislative leaders are able to negotiate with key interest-group leaders that make passage of contro-versial bills possible. For example, a recent study in four states—California, New Jersey, Ohio, and Tennessee—found that most state legislators con-sidered interest groups highly useful to the fulfillment of their role in the legislature.[12]

The techniques used by groups in the legislative arena have developed well-defined patterns. Direct efforts with individual legislators include personal visits, providing research studies, and drafting bills. Groups also operate directly by giving testimony before legislative committees. Indirect group efforts to influence legislators include organizing activity among con-stituents back home, such as mounting letter-writing campaigns and ar-ranging for influential constituents or personal friends of the legislator to speak to him about an important issue. When the National Council of Churches of Christ conducted a successful campaign in 1952 to defeat Senate confirmation of General Mark Clark as United States ambassador to the Vatican, they organized a delegation to contact each Protestant senator. These delegations were made up of the senator's local minister from back home, the head of his local council of churches (Protestant), and a top national layman and cleric from the particular Protestant denomination to which he belonged.

In addition, many groups in recent years have become convinced that

[12] John C. Wahlke, Heinz Eulau, William Buchanan, and LeRoy E. Ferguson, *The Leg-islative System* (New York: Wiley, 1962).

effective public-relations campaigns in the local and national press are at least as important as direct contacts with legislators. However, though large sums of money have been spent for advertising, planting favorable stories or interviews in the mass media, and winning public endorsements from influential scientific, professional, or academic groups, political scientists have been somewhat skeptical of the efficacy of such campaigns.

Although a wide variety of direct and indirect techniques is available to interest groups in the legislative arena, students of legislative lobbying have identified, through interviews with both legislators and lobbyists, several techniques that are clearly outside the rules of the game. For effective group representation, the most important prerequisites are that the group's representative avoid direct threats to legislators (especially since few groups are so all powerful in a legislative district that they could carry out the threat to defeat a legislator who opposed them), avoid bribes or other corrupt offers, and demonstrate trustworthiness by keeping his word and representing accurately the views of the group.

What sort of group is favored by the structure and process of the legislative arena? Contrary to the popular myth, rich groups are not automatically successful. Very little is up for sale on Capitol Hill in the crude sense of lobbyists' paying hard cash for specific votes. Indeed, some legislators have been successful in attacking interest groups for their great wealth and in winning public support for regulation of their power. But money *does* matter more in legislative lobbying than in the judicial or administrative arenas. For legislators have heavy campaign expenses and often feel that political effectiveness requires them to live in an expensive style costing more than their official salaries. They also want to ensure future financial security for their families, and few legislators can save on their salaries. The groups that can make large campaign contributions, offer lucrative fees for speaking engagements, throw legal business to law firms in which legislators retain a financial interest, and so forth earn at least the chance to have their interests thoughtfully considered by legislators. Few rules have governed this flow of aid to legislators. The Senate's 1967 censure of Senator Thomas Dodd of Connecticut for applying large sums raised at "testimonial dinners" to his personal expenses rather than his campaign costs represented a rare case of defining ethical practices.

By and large, the legislative system favors four types of interest group: those seeking to defend the status quo, those with high prestige and social status, those with the money to mount effective (and expensive) lobbying campaigns, and those with large memberships and bands of fellow travelers who can be mobilized in letter-writing and other direct-contact efforts. Large, busy, established institutions such as American legislatures operate relatively smoothly because of political adjustments worked out over the years; this fact tends to favor groups seeking to defend what is rather than to alter existing arrangements.

Groups with high prestige or large memberships are favored because a legislator who views himself as representing his constituency is really thinking primarily of the powerful and vocal groups within the constituency, along with certain "potential groups" he would rather not disturb. The congressional committee system, especially its seniority principle, reinforces institutional conservatism by elevating as committee chairmen men from the most socially stable and politically noncompetitive states and districts.

These tendencies, however, are not ironbound determinants. A legislator may make himself available to other types of groups because of his own group affiliations, his ambitions for political advancement beyond the legislature, or his conception of his role within the legislature. Committee specialization and the search for an issue to attract publicity also lead some legislators to work with interest groups other than those mentioned above. Furthermore, groups with moral leverage can sometimes exert influence beyond their numbers. During the early 1960's, civil-rights groups were able to confront white Americans effectively with the gap between their professions of equality and the realities of Negro deprivation. The legislative fruits of this confrontation were the Civil Rights Act of 1964 and the Voting Rights Act of 1965. However, when a combination of white resistance to real equality for Negroes and white fears of racial violence and Black Power movements dissolved this moral advantage, the basic power relations reasserted themselves, and the civil-rights bills of 1966 and 1967 were defeated.

The key issue of group activity in the legislative arena is *how much* influence interest groups actually exert on the legislative process. Political scientists who have studied the effects of lobbying have frequently concluded that lobbyists exert far less influence than the layman assumes. Of course, interest-group influence varies with the type of issue involved. Narrow, specialized legislative issues, such as exemption provisions in tax laws or the inclusion of specific activities in omnibus grant-in-aid programs, often directly reflect the influence of a particular group. But the evidence indicates that the influence of groups on the large, public-policy bills is in fact only one of several interacting forces—including the influence of political parties, the interests of the legislator's constituency, and intra-legislative influence.

Groups in the Administrative Process

A bill that passes Congress and is signed into law by the President is only beginning its life. It must be given continuing application by the "permanent government"—executive departments, such as Labor or Commerce, and administrative agencies, such as the Federal Communications Commission and the Interstate Commerce Commission. Government administrators have considerable discretion in this power of application, and, because such discretion will help or hinder groups affected by goverment programs, groups seek to protect themselves by maintaining close communication with executive and administrative agencies.

Conversely, the agency often finds that it needs for political support the very groups it regulates, and these groups become its "clientele." As Marver Bernstein has put it,[13] regulatory agencies tend to pass through a "life cycle" that begins when a broad coalition of reformist groups carries a regulatory scheme through Congress. The newly created agency, however, is rapidly deserted by the reform coalition, many elements of which have only a tangential continuing interest in the particular field being regulated. In such circumstances, the specific regulated interests (which may have been defeated on Capitol Hill) quickly reassert themselves. The agency, which must work with these specialized groups year in and year out sooner or later makes peace with these persistent clients.[14] The result is that the "regulated" interests frequently make their regulators semicaptives.

Groups seek to influence agencies in a variety of ways: by lobbying in Congress (and with the executive) for appointments of "favorable" agency members; by helping or hindering the bureaucrats in the congressional appropriations process; by supporting or discouraging other congressional actions (such as investigations or reorganizations) that might strengthen or harm the agency; by working within party organizations to encourage support or opposition for the agency; and by conducting propaganda campaigns aimed at shaping future consensus in the agency on topics of particular interest. For example, the Federal Power Commission has for years been the target of propaganda from private power interests, which have attacked the fact that government both produces power itself (through TVA, etc.) and regulates the power industry. This campaign aims to prevent further federal power production and perhaps to make the FPC more cautious in its regulatory initiatives.

The intensity of conflict that can develop between a new agency and its immediate clientele is reflected in an article by Elwood Quesada discussing his experiences as the first administrator of the Federal Aviation Agency.[15] The boom in the aircraft industry during the early 1950's and the prospect of more and faster air travel ahead made it clear that policing the skies in this era would become a major federal task. Until 1957 responsibility for regulating air traffic and safety was divided among three federal agencies—the Civil Aeronautics Administration, the Civil Aeronautics Board, and the Department of Defense. Military flying was strictly super-

[13] Marver H. Bernstein, *Regulating Business by Independent Commission* (Princeton, N.J.: Princeton University Press, 1955).

[14] For further discussion see Harmon Zeigler, *Interest Groups in American Society* (Englewood Cliffs, N.J.: Prentice-Hall, 1965), pp. 278–82.

[15] E. R. Quesada, "The Pressures Against Air Safety," *Harper's Magazine*, Vol. CCXXII (January 1961), pp. 58–64. The following quotations are from this article.

"A thousand apologies, gentlemen. He's a new man."

The close ties between clientele groups and regulatory agencies are rarely disturbed by congressional investigating committees.

From *Herblock's Special for Today,*
Simon & Schuster, 1958

vised by the service establishments, but civilian aviation enjoyed great latitude in its operations. The aviation industry participated in all decision-making by the CAA (which was responsible for air safety) and the end product almost invariably bore the industry's stamp of approval. Although the CAB (which was responsible for the commercial aspects of aviation) had managed to maintain more independence, the regulated were becoming the regulators even here.

In 1957 a presidential commission made a series of recommendations to President Eisenhower that were then written into a bill submitted to Congress by the Administration. Congress acted swiftly, and the new Federal Aviation Act was on the books before the end of the year. Under this statute, the CAB retained some of its former authority, but the old CAA was eliminated. In its place, Congress created the FAA, with a more powerful statutory grant of authority, and Elwood Quesada, a distinguished aviator, was named by Eisenhower as head of the agency.

Trouble began almost at once. As Quesada recalled:

From my first day in office the irresponsible pressure asserted itself. The agency was still an embryo when Max Karant, Vice President of the Aircraft Owners and Pilots Association (AOPA)—which purports to represent the fliers of private planes—bitterly warned his members of "increasing military domination of the FAA." [Quesada was a retired Air Force general.] Not long afterward, I was visited by the same organization's President, Joseph Hartranft. His purpose was to protest against our new medical requirements for pilot's licenses. . . . I listened to him attentively and then told him our decision would stand. "This means war," he answered, his face flushed.

Quesada's constituency troubles were not restricted to the pilots of private planes. The Air Line Pilots Association (ALPA) was also restive and suspicious of FAA regulations. Quesada recalled:

> One pilot sent us anonymously what we call the ALPA "Do-It-Yourself Kit." This is a collection of mimeographed material designed to teach pilots how to write to congressmen in protest against the FAA. It includes lists of key committee members, helpful hints on style, outlines, a collection of "suggested tidbits," and miscellaneous advice on how to give letters the ring of originality. Many of the communications from pilots which congressmen refer to our agency have obviously been inspired in this way.

Quesada concluded that even in an area as sensitive as aviation, where human lives literally hang in the balance, more than a few of the forty interest groups affected "have managed to put stumbling blocks in our way. The agency's new devotion to duty—it appears—came as a great shock to them."

In cases where client groups were responsible for the creation of the agency in the first place, this pattern asserts itself even more rapidly, particularly since the client interests are apt to have strong continuing influence with the legislature. In exchange for their access to agencies, client groups may offer the agency intellectual, research, and other resources valuable to its effective operation. Even more important, client groups with whom an agency has established an effective process of bargaining and strong long-term relationships can use their political power, their money, and their prestige to influence favorably the elected officials who oversee the agencies. The support of a group constituency for an agency's new program or controversial stand represents a powerful asset. Friendly defense manufacturers, for instance, are vital allies of the Pentagon in its battles with Congress, other executive agencies, and the President.

The group characteristics that favor success in the administrative process are often the same as those needed for success in the legislative arena. One contrast, however, is that in the administrative field the staying power of a group—its continuing, careful, quiet activity over time—often brings the highest payoff. Even when such groups are jostled by opponents more powerful in Congress, their established relations with the agency may help them to escape or soften their defeat when administrative rules are actually applied.

Because groups with staying power are often able to exercise such influence over administrative agencies, competing groups and reform groups seeking stricter regulation often try to shift control over the area of activity to another agency or to an executive department that will be more accessible to broad political influence. Groups with established client ties to an agency vigorously oppose any reorganization schemes that would subject "their" agency to competing interests as well. In 1966, for example, the bill to create a new Department of Transportation to coordinate the regulation of road, rail, and water transportation was so heavily opposed by the American Waterway Operators, Committee of American Steamship Lines, and AFL-CIO Maritime Committee that Congress had to agree to exempt the Federal Maritime Commission from the Department's control before the bill could be passed.

A point to be noted here is that, more and more, interest-group pressure is being made part of the internal executive and administrative process rather than merely being an outside source of influence. Government officials in many areas of our social-welfare politics, for example, develop programs themselves (or in collaboration with academic advisors) and then try to create a group constituency for their programs, appealing to established interest groups that have not yet been pressing for such programs as well as to potential groups that the agency hopes to activate by its new measures. Such a description would come closer to explaining the origins of the antipoverty program, for example, than would the classic theory of administrative reaction to external group pressures.

Groups in the Judicial Process

Judges in the American legal system have substantial political power because they can overturn acts of legislators and executives as unconstitutional and because they can modify the scope, impact, and timing of legislation through their power of statutory interpretation. Judges enjoy broad discretion in their use of this power because our constitutions, laws, and administrative orders contain broad clauses that must be applied to constantly changing situations and redefined in the context of changing public norms.

Since American judges have such political power and discretion, interest groups have been active in the judicial arena from the earliest days of the Republic. In 1810, for example, a group of investors who had been unsuccessful in getting the aid of Congress or of Presidents Jefferson and Madison in a land-claim dispute with the state of Georgia set up a "friendly" test case, known as *Fletcher* v. *Peck*,[16] and got the issue before the United States Supreme Court. Though the justices realized this was a contrived case to win a ruling on the validity of the land titles, the Court accepted jurisdiction because of the important constitutional issue involved and found for the investors. A history of interest-group activity in American courts since that time would show every major type of group represented—business, labor, professional, farm, religious, racial, and ideological. During

---

[16] 6 Cranch 87 (1810).

the 1965–66 term of the United States Supreme Court, for example, the groups directly involved as parties to litigation included the American Trucking Association, the Pacific Coast Society of Orthodontists, the NAACP, the Scenic Hudson Preservation Conference, and the California Democratic Council.

The Fletcher case illustrates several continuing aspects of interest-group activity in the judicial arena. For groups unsuccessful in the legislative and executive arenas or at the polls in elections, the courts offer one more chance to advance or defend their interests. Powerful groups defeated by more powerful rivals often take their case to the courts, as do small, weak, minority interest groups, whose lack of funds and small memberships are less of a disadvantage in the judicial arena, where they can rely on legal and "public policy" arguments instead. At the same time, the courts are special institutions whose structure and rules of procedure require distinctive styles of interest-group activity. For example, many techniques of legislative activity are clearly inapplicable or forbidden in courts. Group representatives cannot visit judges in their chambers to press claims personally or contribute to "travel" or "research" funds for a judge. Even when judges are elected, as they are in many states, if a group representative with a case pending before a judge were to threaten that group members would vote against the judge for reelection unless his verdict were favorable, the group leader could be punished for contempt of court. In recent years, even group-picketing outside courtrooms has been put under tight controls to prevent "undue influence" on judge and jury.

There are three major ways in which interest groups try to achieve their goals through the judicial process: (1) by gaining favorable judicial decisions on litigation; (2) by using litigation as a tactical lever with the legislative and executive branches of government; and (3) by modifying the composition, organization, or prestige of the courts themselves.

Winning favorable court decisions on litigation

The most significant strategy of interest groups for achieving their goals through litigation is to initiate a test case in court. On the whole, American courts have provided broad access to groups for test-case purposes.[17] Thousands of group test cases are filed annually in state and federal courts, much as thousands of group-drafted bills are thrown into the legislative hoppers. When several Southern states tried to harass or prosecute the NAACP for arranging test cases of segregation laws during the late 1950's, the Supreme Court struck down such actions, stating that litigation "may well be the sole practicable avenue open to a minority to petition for a redress of grievances." [18]

---

[17] See Ch. 14 for a detailed discussion of the basic rules for bringing a case to court in this country.
[18] *NAACP* v. *Button*, 371 U.S. 417 (1963).

In general, interest groups have easier access to state courts than to federal courts, because most states allow "taxpayers' suits" and special proceedings for challenging official actions, whereas the rules of the federal courts are more restrictive. Hence, although state courts may be hostile to an interest group's position, litigants from the group often start their cases in these courts in the hope that they can later get the state decisions reviewed by the United States Supreme Court, which hears cases on appeal from the state supreme courts.

Arranging test cases in hopes of getting the court to uphold broad constitutional doctrines that an interest group desires is, however, a tactic that requires great skills of judgment and carries with it serious risks to the initiating group. A group may secure a judicial decision on a test case only to find that the government action it hoped to reverse has in fact had its scope *extended* against the group's interest. The famous Dred Scott [19] case in 1857 was engineered by antislavery groups to win a precedent for freedom, but it wound up instead as a great victory for the slavery forces. The American Jewish Congress brought a case in New York in 1950 hoping to get the practice of allowing pupils in the public schools to leave early for religious education declared invalid; instead their efforts produced a broad ruling by the justices that approved the New York practice and helped it to spread to other states.[20] Whether to bring a case, when to bring it, who the complaining parties should be, and how to frame the legal issues are key elements for groups using this tactic. In most cases, rather than appearing as parties themselves, groups provide lawyers for individuals in what become test cases. In at least a dozen cases decided by the Supreme Court in 1965–66, though private parties were named, the lawyers handling the briefs and oral arguments were staff counsel of organizations such as the NAACP, the ACLU, and the American Jewish Congress.

A second way that groups attempt to gain favorable judicial decisions in litigation is through the *amicus curiae* ("friend of the court") *brief*, in which the group states that it has interests that would be affected by the decision and therefore seeks to present legal views that supplement those of one of the parties to the litigation. Though the consent of the parties is usually required, the courts can override such refusal at their discretion and have done so. During the 1965–66 term of the Supreme Court, 60 groups filed amicus briefs in 75 cases decided during that term. Of these groups, 25 were business, 14 professional, 10 citizens', 6 labor, and 5 corporate. Only 10 of the 60 groups could be called "minority" groups or spokesmen for unpopular causes.

Whether amicus briefs have any effect on the courts is a matter of dispute. In a few cases, courts have used arguments from these briefs in their judicial opinions when such points were not contained in the briefs of the parties. Sometimes, however, judges have expressed resentment at

[19] *Dred Scott* v. *Sanford*, 19 How. 393 (1857).
[20] *Zorach* v. *Clausen*, 343 U.S. 306 (1952).

amicus briefs, which they felt constituted "pressure" rather than efforts to contribute additional legal arguments. In a 1947 Supreme Court case involving a contempt-of-court prosecution of a local editor for publishing attacks on a judge during a trial, Justice Robert Jackson's opinion noted that the amicus brief of the American Newspaper Publishers Association cited no additional facts or authorities, except to say that the association represented seven hundred newspapers. Jackson concluded, "This might be a good occasion to demonstrate the fortitude of the 'judiciary.' " [21]

It is worth noting that bringing test cases and filing briefs can be valuable for an interest group even if it is ultimately unsuccessful in court. For such steps give concrete evidence of activity by the staff and group leaders, often build litigation alliances with other groups, and may enhance the prestige of one organization in relation to its competitors within a larger group community (as has been the case with the NAACP in the Negro community).

Groups can also try to influence the outcome of specific cases by publishing articles supporting their views in leading law journals that are read by judges, their law clerks, and the lawyers preparing cases. This technique has been used successfully, for example, by racial groups, business organizations, civil-liberties groups, and bar associations. In an even more indirect but still significant way, interest groups can lead public debates to shape the views held on basic constitutional issues by editors, group leaders, and the American public in general. Judges do not respond directly to every twist and turn of public opinion, but some key principles of American constitutional law (such as due process and equal protection of the law) depend for their application on what judges see as the standards of fairness and rules of decency held by the American people in a given era.

Exerting indirect pressure on the political branches

The second major group technique in the judicial arena is the use of litigation to exert pressure on the political branches of government. In a law suit, a group can ask that records of executive-agency proceedings be produced that would otherwise be unavailable to that group or to the public. In Newark, New Jersey, for example, the local NAACP chapter tried unsuccessfully for several years to get the school board or the mayor to undo segregated "neighborhood school districts." Both the board and the mayor's office denied that race had been a factor in drawing up the school districts and refused to meet with the NAACP to draw up a new plan. When the NAACP filed suit in federal court, claiming *de facto* segregation, federal rules of evidence required the school board to produce its minutes for the preceding twenty-five years—records containing evidence

[21] *Craig* v. *Harney*, 331 U.S. 367 (1947).

that racial considerations had in fact been used in drawing district boundaries. Within days after the suit was filed, the school board agreed to sit down with the NAACP and negotiate new boundaries, and the suit was dropped before the records had to be disclosed. The threat of public visibility acted as a powerful lever here.

Modifying the power of the courts

The third major technique of groups in the judicial arena is to try to affect the composition, organization, or prestige of the courts. Groups exert influence on Presidents, governors, and mayors with regard to judicial appointments in order to be "represented" on a court, to advance nominees who hold legal views favorable to the group's interest, or to veto nominees who might be unfavorable to the group's interests. President Johnson's nomination of Thurgood Marshall to the Supreme Court in 1967, though based on Marshall's well-demonstrated talents as a lawyer, a federal judge, and Solicitor General of the United States, as well as on his political service to a Democratic President, also reflected the steady efforts of civil-rights groups to have a Negro appointed to the nation's highest court. Interest groups are active, in addition, in the continual legislative reorganizations of court structure, as when social-welfare groups support special courts for juvenile offenders in order to institute more flexible approaches to dealing with young delinquents.

Attempts to modify the prestige of the Supreme Court are a constant aspect of group activity; groups that lose their cases try to have constitutional amendments passed to overturn the Court's actions or try to get the legislature to "curb" the statutory powers of the judiciary. Not surprisingly, groups being aided by the Court's rulings, such as business groups in the 1920's and civil-rights and liberal groups in the 1950's, defend the Court in these campaigns.

Ultimately, which interests the courts will favor depends on the dominant American values of each era as they are reflected by judges and shaped by the legal process. During the present era, the most significant trend is that the Supreme Court—as demonstrated by its rulings on legislative apportionment, racial segregation, and school prayers—has tended to be far more responsive to liberal and minority groups seeking to overturn the status quo than have the other political arenas.

Groups in the "Single Arena" of Government

So far, we have stressed the distinctive characteristics of legislatures, administrative agencies, and courts that favor different styles of group action in each sphere. Yet it would be inaccurate to see interest-group activity as sealed in a series of closed circuits. While there are some interest groups that concentrate their efforts in only one arena, most groups at the national and state levels must work simultaneously or successively in multiple arenas to protect their interests effectively.

The need for groups to work on several fronts to achieve their goals is illustrated by the issue of federal aid to education during 1966–67. The savage battles and legislative stalemates of the Kennedy era had already ended; basic legislation providing federal aid had been enacted by the Johnson Administration in 1965 with its heavy Democratic majority in Congress. But each year new appropriations had to be voted, and specific programs, old and new, came up for review, first within the Administration, then before Congress. The questions that these continuing reviews raised in 1966–67 were how much aid would be appropriated for whom, in what types of program, and under whose control?

A very broad assembly of interest groups—religious, racial, professional, business, labor, farm, veterans', and so on—were active on this issue. Such groups began by communicating with the White House staff and presidential advisors to exert influence on the Administration's setting of priorities in the bill it would send to Congress. These priorities would affect a wide range of issues, from the basic question of how much could be spent on education during the Vietnam war to specific questions such as whether Title III experimental funds should be given to the states through a general grant or on a specific project basis and what denials of aid would be made to segregated schools. Each group also had to reach the political party leaders outside Congress and the Administration to secure as favorable a "party position" as possible. Groups had to continue their efforts in Congress as well, working on key party leaders, committee chairmen, sectional groupings, and individual legislators. At the same time, executive departments such as Health, Education, and Welfare, Defense, and the Office of Economic Opportunity had to be contacted to protect the group's interests in intraexecutive debates and the public testimony given at hearings.

Meanwhile, those groups that had lost the 1965–66 battle in Congress to exclude parochial schools in such programs as Project Head Start and school construction were raising constitutional challenges to the 1965 legislation in the courts during 1966–67. In this period the 1965 losers also tried to affect the discretionary choices of administrators such as the Commissioner of Education in the Department of Health, Education, and Welfare in the distribution of aid to church institutions and in setting desegregation guidelines. Finally, many groups that had been defeated in 1965 were active at the state level, both to exert influence on national officials from their state and local bases and to influence the discretion of state government officials in deciding how federal aid to education should be used locally.

Thus, many groups find they must work in all the government arenas, sometimes to defend a victory, sometimes to challenge a defeat suffered elsewhere. Such conduct grows out of the decentralization and overlapping powers of our political institutions. This diffusion of interest-group struggles also contributes to the broad consensus on public-policy issues that has marked American society; interest-group fights for changes in policy are so prolonged and so widely distributed that the action finally taken is widely regarded as legitimate when it survives its gladiatorial ordeal in all the separate arenas. This legitimacy will not comfort reform groups in any era, but it reinforces the American belief in the purifying value of divided power that has been an integral part of our philosophy since 1787.

Groups and Public Opinion

Not all interest-group access to government officials is direct, and not all group activity occurs within the government arenas. A major *indirect* means for improving access to government arenas is to influence public opinion. Interest groups have found that they can deal more favorably with legislators, administrators, and party leaders if the group's public reputation is high. They want people to think well of them; but, more important, they want decision makers to *think* that people think well of them, and a vast amount of time and money is dedicated to this effort.

Public opinion has been defined as those attitudes and expectations of people that rulers find it prudent to take into account. How public opinion actually influences and is communicated to government and how government influences public opinion are complex questions. There are formal moments of communication, such as elections, and informal communications between citizens and government officials, such as when a congressman talks to his constituents back home during the July 4th recess. In addition, the professionally conducted public-opinion poll or opinion survey has come to be used increasingly by government officials in the past several decades to obtain clues as to public opinion both on specific issues ("Do you approve of President Johnson's use of bombing raids in the Vietnam war?") and on general trends ("Do you believe that American society is doing enough, too much, or not enough to help Negroes achieve fair treatment?"). Summing up the relation between public opinion and government in American society, V. O. Key has concluded:

> The generality of public preferences, the low intensity of the opinions of many people, the low level of political animosities of substantial sectors of the public, the torturousness of the process of translation of disapproval of specific policies into electoral reprisal, and many other factors point to the existence of a wide latitude for the exercise of creative leadership.[22]

Thus, public opinion in America is another factor contributing to the wide discretion of officeholders and in turn to the proliferation of interest

[22] Key, *op. cit.*, p. 55.

Shaping Public Opinion: The Railroads' Campaign Against the Truckers

The public is only a collective name for countless groups of people, many of whom have bonds of common interest. In terms of our objectives, our subsidiary goals include informing, organizing and activating as many legitimate, strong and politically aggressive groups as already exist or that can be brought into existence for their own self-interest.

The public and its separate parts must be informed by a purposeful barrage of continuing publicity. Our men in the field must organize the individual groups. Together, the publicity given the subject and the actions of the groups must be directed toward the legislators so that they will act in accordance with the demands of the voters.

As we see it, the whole program must have a basic appeal so broad that it will enlist the active support not only of the direct friends of the railroads, but, for example, a group of motorists conscious of the shocking hazards prevailing on our now inadequate and damaged highways, or taxpayers' organizations up and down the several states, or a group of tax authorities interested in improving state revenues, or the state grange and all others who can be shown where their own self-interests parallel those of the railroads.

In other words, the railroads are simply identifying themselves with a program in the public interest.

We must write all publicity in terms of the self-interest of certain groups. This publicity must be aimed at Motor Groups, Real Estate Boards and individual owners, Economy Groups, Service Clubs, Safety Groups, City and County Officials, Rural Road Improvement Groups, and all others *who have something to gain if the burden of financing the highways can be transferred from the individual citizen and the individual motorist to those who alone profit by it—the heavy trucks.*

From memorandums of the public-relations firm of Carl Byoir & Associates, exhibited in *Noerr Motor Freight* v. *Eastern Railroad Presidents Conference*, 1957.

groups and their activities. But the relation between public opinion and interest groups is reciprocal: for interest groups form one of the two major connectives in our system between government and public opinion. (The other link, political parties, will be discussed in Chapters 5 and 6.)

The leading study of American public opinion has concluded that the most important and most elusive way in which groups link public opinion to government is through their "opinion élites" [23]—that is, the leadership

[23] *Ibid.*, pp. 552–55.

29TH YEAR   *The*
Reader's Digest
JUNE 1950

An article a day of enduring significance, in condensed permanent booklet form

*Overloaded trucks are breaking up our highways faster than we can
find the money to replace them*

THE RAPE OF OUR ROADS

Condensed from Buffalo Evening News   Frederick G. Brownell

AMERICA FACES a transportation crisis of the first magnitude. Under the relentless battering of outsize and overloaded trucks, the three million miles of roads that comprise this nation's arteries are going to pieces faster than we can find the money to replace them.

Of the 37,800 miles of interstate trunk highway in the country, 35,500 miles need immediate improvement at a cost of 11 billion dollars. It would cost another 49 billion dollars to bring *all* our roads up to traffic requirements. Even the famed Pennsylvania Turnpike is,

Reprinted from the June 1950 *Reader's Digest*

This story in the June 1950 *Reader's Digest* was part of the campaign by the railroads to impress the public with the harmful effects of trucks on the road system.

of the groups. These political activists shape mass opinion in several significant ways. First, they help to build the "dikes of opinion" within which mass public opinion tends to flow. These dikes define what is to be considered at all and what proposals merit *serious* consideration; thus, they set the agenda of public discussion on both substance and procedure. Group leaders also have a central role in modifying opinions. As Key put it, in a political system moving through time, "the power of mass opinion makes itself manifest in its interactions with democratic leadership—chiefly in its rejection of leadership factions whose outlook lags notably behind or strikes out markedly ahead of the moving average of opinion." [24] Deviants from this consensus are important in a democratic society to encourage changes in belief and policy, but it is the consensus of the leadership that mass public opinion ratifies and makes politically "practical."

Discussing group techniques for shaping public opinion requires that we separate what careful studies have shown from the mythology of "propaganda," "advertising," and "public relations." The assumption that a purposeful group with enough money could "sell" any article, idea, or individual to the public has been proved false time and again. Propagandists do not write upon a blank page; they must thread their way carefully through elaborate structures of existing attitudes, some quite tenaciously held. These opinions are not always systematically arranged or sharply articulated, but they are very real. Successful efforts to shape public opinion must *build* on these existing attitudes and employ accepted ideas and language to lend legitimacy to what is being "sold." People accept what their experiences and beliefs predispose them to accept; their ideas and attitudes can be changed, but only through a process of reorientation and new experiences that is quite slow in our gradualist democracy.

Several factors tend to make some groups more effective in influencing public opinion than others. First, it is obvious that the techniques of influence favor groups with money. Direct mailing is expensive, and costs skyrocket when the media of mass circulation (press, radio, and TV) are used. Second, some élites (such as those of businessmen's and veterans' organizations) are better able to manipulate the venerated symbols of American society (individual enterprise, duty, freedom, etc.) than are other élites (such as those of organizations representing migrant workers, the urban poor, etc.) One analyst has observed:

> The groups and individuals that enjoy most prestige in a society are those that are given major credit for the most highly valued achievements of the society; their status is high. In the United States for more than a century the greatest of these achievements has been the settling of the continent and the revolutionizing of the techniques of production. Because of their close association with these developments, the groups that can be subsumed under the loose heading "business" have in varying degrees throughout our history occupied a status of the highest order . . . [and their] differential propaganda advantage is not hard to verify when a President of the United States could proclaim: "The man who builds a factory builds a temple." [25]

The prestige of business has had its ups and down, of course, but its staying power at the top of the American group hierarchy has been notable.

Third, group propaganda is apt to be more effective when the event being characterized for the public is somewhat ambiguous. For example,

[24] *Ibid.*, p. 554.
[25] Truman, *op. cit.*, p. 246. The President quoted is Calvin Coolidge.

business groups supporting laws to control labor unions in the late 1950's were able to portray these laws to the public as necessary to "union democracy" rather than as "union-busting" by business, because the exposures of considerable union racketeering and malpractice during this period had made the issue sufficiently ambiguous.

Groups go to the public in two ways: in crash campaigns aimed at getting a desired response immediately and in long-term educational programs designed to affect the direction of public opinion years and even decades hence. In the short-run drive, the objective is to mobilize existing attitudes favorable to the group's position and to make this sentiment manifest in some way, such as through a barrage of letters and telegrams to Capitol Hill offices. In such a campaign, the group strategist is completely dependent on *existing* opinion. He cannot hope to remold attitudes in a quick campaign; if he cannot count on immediate sympathetic public attention, as well as on his group's skilled leadership and its membership commitment, he will fail. The efforts of Jewish groups to win support by President Johnson and Congress for Israel's position in the Arab-Israeli conflict of 1967 illustrates strong group commitment, effective building on already favorable public attitudes, and successful mobilization of those attitudes.

In the long-range educational drive, the propagandist's objective is to create public sensitivity to the issues of concern to his group. He knows he cannot hope to reverse established attitudes or to alter the characterization of events already perceived by the public in a highly structured way. So the shrewd educational campaigns are directed at the *gaps* in the existing body of public opinion. The technique of mobilizing unarticulated and unorganized public sentiment was very effectively used, for example, by the public-relations firm hired by the railroads to conduct a campaign against the truckers in Pennsylvania.[26]

One of the most knowledgeable students of American politics, groups, and public opinion—the late V. O. Key—discounted the capacity of interest groups to mold *general* public opinion and to use this to "soften up" government officials.[27] He cited several types of evidence for his conclusion: actions taken by government or by political party leaders that are contrary to the interests of groups spending fortunes in general advertising; the failures of mass-membership groups to shape opinions of their own members on many occasions; the fact that some groups have actually been harmed by exposure of the lavishness of their public campaigns; and the fact that a great segment of the general public is quite ignorant of the issues taken up in propaganda campaigns or even of the campaigns themselves.

[26] See Robert Bendiner, "The Engineering of Consent: A Case Study," *The Reporter* (August 11, 1955), p. 20.
[27] Key, *op. cit.*, pp. 514–18.

Most groups and political activists remain committed to long-range educational efforts despite such disappointing analyses. But they do so more to enhance their general prestige with the public than to exert direct influence on government action. For established groups in society are eager to keep their favored images and general policies before the public in order to counteract the inevitable attacks on them by newcomer groups and social critics. Such established-group efforts may prevent the development of an adverse climate of opinion that could lead to hostile government action. Such action also responds to the American belief in education about public affairs and the duty of groups to "put their case before the people" as well as before the government.

Interest Groups in the Electoral Arena

Still another indirect technique used by interest groups to improve their access to government decision makers is to try to influence the voting behavior of their members.[28] In popular myth, large and powerful interest groups achieve many of their objectives by two methods: they threaten political party leaders with a switch in the partisan allegiance of their group members, and they threaten particular officeholders with reprisals at the polls by group members and fellow travelers. Among political scientists, however, interest groups who make such threats are seen as "usually pointing an unloaded gun" at the party or the legislator.[29]

First, many Americans do not consider it legitimate for the interest groups to which they belong to try to influence their vote. This belief rests partly on the assumption that such political activity will compromise the effectiveness of the group in its primary economic, social, religious, or other role. A poll of farm-household members in 1956 showed that only 58 percent felt that it was "all right" for farm organizations to try "to help certain candidates get elected." Only 49 percent of respondents in union households thought union activity in support of candidates was "all right."[30]

Second, group efforts to change the voting decisions of their members are obstructed by the fact that party identification is the single most important factor in shaping the voting choices of Americans. "In the short run, at least," Key has written,

> group leaders can move only a few of their followers away from their customary partisan attachment. If the president of the Chamber of Commerce of the United States, unhappy about the effectiveness and fidelity of a Republican Administration in the fulfillment of its commitments to business, were to issue a clarion call to American businessmen to vote Democratic, he would not be followed by an impressive proportion of his members.

[28] See Chapter 7 for further discussion of group identification and voting behavior.
[29] Key, *op. cit.*, p. 522.
[30] *Ibid.*, p. 520.

Even so great a union leader as John L. Lewis discovered that his miners remained in the Democratic fold when he sought to bring them to the support of Wendell Willkie [the Republican presidential nominee in 1940].[31]

Third, the major partisan shifts of groups in the electorate—for example, the shift of Negro voters from the Republican party to the Democratic party in the twentieth century, the shift of Catholics from heavily Democratic voting patterns to increased Republican voting, or the increasing number of Southern voters casting Republican ballots in presidential elections—reflect deep socioeconomic and political currents that interest groups may ratify or even exploit but cannot easily reverse for a particular election.

Finally, as we have already discussed, many members of large interest groups have a weak commitment to the organization's goals; the means of communicating the group's electoral recommendations are often ineffective; and an individual's overlapping group memberships may subject him to cross-pressures in deciding how to vote. In addition, political leaders and the parties are adroit at adopting broad and ambiguous positions on issues important to interest groups, and this ambiguity tends to weaken even more a group's declaration that its members should oppose Senator X.

This is *not* to say, however, that groups never affect the votes of their members. The stronger the identification of its members with the policies and leadership of the group and the clearer the group's position in the election campaign, the more likely it is that some members' votes will be affected.[32] But the data show that interest groups are unlikely to sway large percentages of members against their deeper partisan identification.

Nonetheless, the popular myth of group power does operate frequently as a *psychological* force on election candidates. At times, as Key has said, "the sliver of votes delivered by a pressure organization may appear to have turned the tide [of an election]. More often it may seem in prospect that the group can turn the tide." [33] Because candidates in American elections face many uncertainties and amorphous situations, they may be led to make commitments to groups that are not really warranted by what Key calls the "electoral necessities." Yet the candidate does not defy the group—and thus expose its real weakness—for many of the same reasons that experienced poker players who come out ahead at the end of the evening find it prudent not to call every bet in the game. Furthermore, candidates and parties know that the passage of time and changing circumstances will provide many opportunities once they are in office to modify or even sidestep preelection commitments.

How, then, do interest groups function in electoral contests? First, they influence the political parties by promoting the nomination of can-

[31] *Ibid.*, p. 522.
[32] Angus Campbell, Philip E. Converse, Warren E. Miller, and Donald E. Stokes, *The American Voter* (New York: Wiley, 1960), Ch. 12.
[33] Key, *op. cit.*, p. 524.

didates favorable to their interests and by securing favorable planks and declarations in the party platform. Some groups try to achieve their objectives through members who serve as party functionaries. This pattern is illustrated by the participation of labor-union members within the Democratic party. As one student has observed:

> In addition to the influence labor leaders may have on the size of urban majorities, organized labor has gained representation at the Democratic national conventions. Approximately one-eighth of the delegates to the 1960 Democratic National Convention were unionists. It comes as no surprise that the majority of the union delegates were from the big industrial states, although there were a few from southern and western states. Organized labor, obviously, did not control the convention, but its delegates, coupled with the votes of delegates not directly involved in the labor movement but committed to its objectives, gave labor a strong voice in the choice of candidates, and an even stronger voice in the formulation of platform provisions.[34]

Groups may also be active in election campaigns. They contribute to campaign funds, supply campaign workers and experts from their membership, and perform research tasks for candidates. They can "get out the vote" among their own members and fellow travelers, on the assumption that this will probably produce a net majority of favorable votes for the candidates they are supporting. Along with their endorsements, they can supply their own members with information on the voting record and issue positions of the candidates. Group support in election campaigns has grown in importance with the decline of party patronage, and the public's positive response to volunteer campaign organizations makes the group effort especially welcome to candidates and party organizations. Active partisan groups in turn gain credit with party leaders and access to grateful office-holders.

One interesting variant on these electoral activities is the actual sponsorship of elections by some groups through the use of the initiative, referendum, and recall machinery that exists in some states. Business, conservative, and allied groups in California, for example, secured the necessary votes in 1964 to place on the general ballot and carry in the election a proposition to repeal a fair-housing law previously passed by the California legislature. In New York City in 1966 the Patrolmen's Benevolent Association and its allies secured the signatures necessary to place a resolution on the ballot that ultimately overturned a civilian board installed by Mayor Lindsay with power to review police conduct. These campaigns are really "intergroup" election contests. The parties may take stands on the issues involved, but the primary actors tend to be coalitions of interest groups on both sides which dominate the electioneering. Such contests promise to become even more frequent in the 1970's.

[34] Harry R. Mahood, "Pressure Groups in American Politics" (New York: Scribner's, 1966), p. 153.

REFLECTIONS ON THE "GROUP BASIS" OF AMERICAN POLITICS

Does a political system that features such a central role for group conflict and bargaining conform with our notions of a democratic system? One must ultimately judge a political system by the degree to which it responds to the needs and aspirations of its people. Does the group struggle distort the needs and preferences of Americans? Is it a breeding ground for unscrupulous political practices by which the few manipulate the many?

First, whatever its shortcomings, the group-based politics we have described *is the hard reality*. Its shape has been largely determined by the most powerful sort of human and institutional forces: the diversity of our society, our economic and social patterns, our cultural expectations, and a series of historical choices about how our government was to be set up. Asking whether one "approves" of the politics of group bargaining and accommodation in America is a little like asking whether one approves of the Rocky Mountains. Barring cataclysms, both are permanent features of their respective terrains. Important changes and reforms can be effected at the margins of our system, and abusive practices by interest groups can be regulated; but political innovators work within limitations that are historically set. Laws can be torn up and rewritten, but political systems that have grown out of the experiences of a nation demand more respect. Such systems can, of course, be destroyed. But, unless the whole of American civilization is shattered, the basic political patterns will persist, changing only slowly and remaining highly resistant to *ad hoc* tinkering.

Second, the group-based American system has proved remarkably stable and peaceful. A basic fact of politics is that before there can be creative policy output, there must be order. The history of the human race reveals relatively few times and places in which men have managed to conduct community business without breaking one another's heads or submitting to the coercive rule of a tyrant. Just getting things done, year after year, without resort to violence or authoritarianism, is a remarkable achievement. Yet in the heat of debate over how to improve the system—how to get better policy decisions—the importance of stability and order are often discounted.

On the other hand, there *are* injustices built into the interest-group foundation of our political system. We have already noted that the interests of potential groups are inadequately protected by politicians and established group leaders who anticipate the reactions of the unorganized. We have seen that group membership and activity are more common among the upper and middle classes than among the disadvantaged, who need the help of government most. Nor do groups compete on an even footing in our political system. The distinctive structures and rules of our political arenas clearly make it easier for some types of groups to gain access and to achieve ultimate success than for others. And, although poor and unpopular groups can transcend these disadvantages by appealing to the courts, the courts are often unable to grant the benefits that the poor need. Supreme Court justices can make important policy in some areas (such as establishing electoral rules of the game), but they cannot appropriate funds for a job-training program or a public housing project.

In addition, there are many instances in which vigorous competition between groups breaks down, and a few groups achieve something approaching a monopoly of access on a particular issue. Joseph Schumpeter and others have held that democracy is assured by the open combat of groups; thus, democracy is seriously undermined when the system reveals numerous instances in which a narrow set of élites limits conflict, develops close and even inbred relations with official decision makers, and establishes what Douglass Cater has referred to as a "subgovernment." A few interest groups do jockey for position within the subgovernment, of course, but the premium is placed on keeping the bargaining "in the family." Cater offers as an example the way the American sugar market is quietly divided each year between domestic growers and foreign producers in a "closed" bargain controlled by a few American companies and some foreign-government lobbyists. The United States "pegs" the price of sugar well above the world market—in effect providing a subsidy to noncompetitive American producers—and the slices of this attractive pie are doled out by the chairman of the House Agriculture Committee in close consultation with the director of the Sugar Division of the Department of Agriculture and the client sugar-producing groups. On the few occasions when outside interest groups have attempted to intervene in Congress, the chairman has explained that the matter is so complex and technical that it is best left to the "experts." [35] This situation is extreme, but the pattern is not uncommon.

There is no ready solution to these deficiencies, but there is one encouraging trend. Over the years our political system has proven itself remarkably open to new groups and new claims. It is true that the politics of sugar is presently oligarchical, but this subgovernment could be opened up to greater competition if the interest of other groups in doing so were sufficiently strong. The doors to subgovernments can be opened by the determined and the clever. Furthermore, low-status groups that appear quite without resources to compete in the political arena have had a way of establishing themselves in very short historical order. Irishmen, Jews, industrial workers, Roman Catholics, and even farmers—all now influential in the political arena—are aggregates that at some time in the American experience were thought to be hopelessly outside the structure of informal group power. Negroes are presently attempting to enter that structure, and,

[35] Douglass Cater, *Power in Washington* (New York: Random House, 1964), pp. 17–20.

although the obstacles and traumas should not be minimized, some Negro groups are finding it penetrable.

The problem of unfair and even dishonest practices by groups seeking access to government has received a good deal of attention in recent years. Fortunately, it is easier to regulate interest-group malpractices than to remedy the structural inequities of the group system. First, what has been called the "communications revolution" has forced group activity to become more visible than in the past, and this visibility often provides the basis both for identification of group activity and for its regulation when abused.

State and national laws exist against bribery and increasingly against so-called conflicts of interest on the part of legislators and others in positions of public trust. Direct national regulation of interest-group activity began in 1946 with the passage of the Congressional Reorganization Act. Title III of this statute provided that "any person who solicits, collects, or receives money to be used principally to influence federal legislation," is required to register with the clerk of the House and the secretary of the Senate, and to file financial statements along with information as to the group who employed him and its sphere of interest. It is important to note that this law did *not* impose any restrictions on the activities of group representatives but sought simply to regulate through "public visibility"—that is, by making the identity of lobbyists and their expenditures a matter of public record. The flaw of this law was its vagueness: it was difficult to know who had to register, for the law seemed to apply only to lobbyists whose funds were raised *principally* for congressional lobbying. Demands for a more comprehensive statute, which would also cover executive-branch lobbying, have not yet borne fruit.

An alternative approach to formal regulation of interest-group activity has been the strengthening of government institutions to make them less vulnerable to penetration by groups. In Congress, for instance, such measures have included more funds for professional staffs and research aid, as well as help in bill-drafting—all designed to reduce legislators' reliance on interest groups in these matters.

One final question remains: Does the sum of all group interests constitute the "public interest" we speak of so often as the highest good of a democratic society? In fact, there is only rarely a "general interest" of society as a whole that all citizens can discover through the processes of reason and define in operative terms that command universal agreement. Every public policy hurts some people and helps others. Too often, demands that "special privilege" or "minority groups" give way to the "public interest" are really nothing more than the pleas of those well served by existing policies to defend the status quo or the cries of ideologues that society accept on faith visions that are not shared by more pragmatic citizens.

For these reasons, the group basis of American politics remains a fundamental key to understanding the operations of our system and the most likely means for advancing the greatest good for the greatest number, given the social and institutional characteristics of our society. But only the careless political analyst would argue that "groups are all." As we have shown, groups interact with political parties, with public opinion, and with officeholders within political institutions. And this interaction lies at the heart of our political success.

SUMMARY

The multiplicity of interests in American society arises from our complex and diversified socioeconomic structure, the legitimacy our political culture gives to private expression and organization, and the many relatively independent centers of political decision-making created by our federal system. Interests become interest groups when individuals who share some common attitude join together in repeated and patterned activity to seek recognition of their position from others in the society, particularly political decision makers. Though most interest groups are formal organizations, with constitutions, officers, headquarters, and so on, some are *ad hoc* groups that assemble for specific purposes. In addition, the interests of potential groups of unorganized individuals are sometimes taken into account by organized interest groups and government officials. Both *ad hoc* groups and potential groups can significantly affect the political system.

We noted that some 55 to 65 percent of the American population join voluntary organizations in the United States—a considerably higher percentage than in other democracies. Those who join tend to be drawn disproportionately from the better-educated, higher-income, and better-informed segments of the population.

Whatever their formal structure, organizations are led by the active minority of members who are willing to give more time and effort to organizational affairs and who consolidate their positions of influence within the organization by controlling the flow of information to members, the management of meetings, and similar matters. Three factors, however, limit the power of élites over members: the overlapping and sometimes conflicting loyalties of individuals in a heterogeneous, pluralistic society; the opposition generated when élites press beyond the policy positions truly supported by the membership; and the broadly shared American consensus about the rules of proper behavior for groups. Thus, voluntary organizations tend to reinforce and activate basic member attitudes, which are drawn from their primary religious, racial, economic, and other affiliations; when group leaders take positions that diverge from these basic loyalties, the result is usually widespread defection from the organizational position.

We then examined the ways in which groups seek access to various government arenas in order to influence the discretionary choices of office-holders. We noted first that, in general, a group's access to government officials will vary according to a mixture of factors, such as the group's size, its economic resources, the intensity of its membership activity, and the quality of its leadership. We then focused on three main arenas of interest-group activity: the legislature, the executive and administrative agencies, and the courts. We showed that it is the relative freedom of office-holders from strict legal or party control and their capacity to choose among alternative policies that make these arenas attractive to groups. In each arena, the style and techniques of interest-group activity are affected not only by the formal rules the institution adopts to regulate interest-group contact with its officials but by the structure and internal procedures of the institution. Direct personal contact, financial contribution, and the promise of group support at the polls are generally accepted for group relations with legislators and top executive officials, but such activity is forbidden when groups deal with independent regulatory commissioners or judges. Other interest-group techniques, such as the provision of ideas and research, are used in all the government areas, but they vary in form from the drafting of bills for legislators to the supplying of legal arguments in friend-of-the-court briefs filed with the appellate courts. We stressed that most groups must be active in all the government arenas at varying times in order to defend their interests effectively; public-policy making is so diffuse in the American political system that a group which is not active "across the board" could lose in the administrative agencies or the courts much of what it had won in the legislative and executive process, and vice versa.

Interest groups also work to affect government decisions indirectly either by mobilizing public opinion on a particular issue to influence specific responses by elected officeholders or by trying to shape the long-range attitudes of the public, thereby affecting the general political ethos on that issue. Although such campaigns are a significant part of American interest-group activity, the opinions held by individuals and groups on many issues are the result of deeply rooted attitudes and are not easily altered by propaganda or "educational" campaigns, even when well-financed and continuous. The more significant role of interest groups is to link public opinion to the government by setting "opinion dikes" that define the issues the public expects to be seriously debated at a given moment and by shaping a general civic consensus on public-policy issues that guides political actors inside and outside government.

The last aspect of group activity we discussed was group participation in the electoral process. Here, the most significant group contribution consists of the aid groups give to individual candidates for nomination and election and to the party organizations in election campaigns. Group aid consists of financial contributions, research, and, increasingly, of supplying campaign workers from the group's ranks. The popular conception of an interest group's dictating terms to candidates and parties by threatening to "deliver" its members to an opposing party or candidate is largely a myth. Most group members have such definite party identifications and perceptions of candidates that group leaders are not able to deliver votes at will. In addition, many members consider efforts to influence their voting a not-quite-legitimate role of interest groups.

We ended the chapter by asking whether the strong group orientation in our political system was consistent with the assumptions and values of a democratic order. We concluded that although the group process does favor established interests, creating pockets of inequity, the group aspect of American politics nevertheless accurately reflects our basic pattern of interests, has been open to the entry of new groups as they arose, and has served—along with the party system—as a vital connective between our pluralistic society and our deliberately fragmented constitutional system. The group process has thus been a major factor contributing to relative stability through gradual change in our political system throughout our history.

THE NATIONAL PARTIES

Functions, History, and Characteristics

5

American political parties carry out several functions that help produce a viable democratic system: recruiting leaders, reconciling conflicts among interests, and helping to operate the government. This chapter will examine the functions, history, and characteristics of American parties in an effort to answer these basic questions: How have parties been instruments of political stability and popular government? Why do we have a two-party system? Why is our party system decentralized? And why are our parties relatively nonideological?

Any discussion of the functions, political development, and characteristics of the American party system must begin with two fundamental facts: First, American political parties arose in response to needs created by the political gaps in the Constitution. And, second, the lines of party development and their resulting features, though perhaps not in all respects inevitable, were natural responses to specific American conditions—namely, the constitutional requirement that a President be elected nationally, the vast electorate to be mobilized in elections, and the unusual combination of a political consensus and a great diversity of economic interests.

The Framers of the Constitution, engrossed in the establishment of an institutional framework, were not conscious of the vast political gaps left by this document. For, as Chapter 2 has discussed, the Constitution established a set of offices but did not outline a political process by which candidates could compete peacefully to fill these positions. Nor did it provide a political vehicle for reconciling conflicts among different interests or for operating the government machinery. But because the Framers were unaware of these gaps, they did not foresee that parties would be the instrument for bridging them and for creating a viable political system. The Founders simply did not anticipate that people would unite in durable combinations to capture the offices created by the Constitution; their naive expectation that members of the Electoral College would make independent decisions on presidential candidates is particularly indicative of their lack of vision about the constructive role parties were to play.

In fact, the Framers were quite suspicious of parties, because they were unable to distinguish between their useful functions and the harmful effects of factions. Madison, for all his perceptive comments about factions at the convention and in *The Federalist*, Number 10, did not see that parties could be a means of mediating among the factions he feared. And as late as 1797, Washington warned in his Farewell Address against "the baneful effects of the party spirit generally." The Founding Fathers, moreover, did not understand the difference between a loyal party opposition and a genuine threat to the stability of the political system.

This blind spot of the Founders is understandable, for in 1787 there were no parties in the modern sense in this country or elsewhere to serve as a model for the parties that were to originate in the United States during the 1790's. There were clubs, cliques, and juntas that chose candidates in this country, and there were upper-class groupings that competed for office in England, but there were no true political parties—that is, *continuing organizations of leaders mobilizing large numbers of voters for control of offices and policies.*

THE FUNCTIONS OF AMERICAN NATIONAL PARTIES

The American parties have performed three political functions that have made the institutions established by the Constitution viable and have provided a vehicle for popular participation in government. First, the Constitution set up a system of self-government, and parties have implemented this principle by providing an orderly way for rival groups to compete for political office. Second, the Constitution established a union for a people with "various and interfering interests," and parties have stabilized this union by providing for the reconciliation of these interests. Third, the Constitution established a structure of checks and balances, and parties have provided a way to operate the government so that policy can be made despite the limitations of this structure.[1] Let us examine these functions more closely.

Mobilizing the Electorate

The existence of parties in most countries today reflects the almost universal struggle of political leaders for mass support. In dictatorships parties exist to help legitimize and stabilize the regime, because coercion through the military, police, and bureaucracy will not by itself win the people's acceptance. The purpose of such a party is to instill a common idea, to organize cadres of loyal supporters, and to mobilize mass support for the regime. In contrast, democratic political parties are instruments through which rival groups compete for control of the government. In a democratic political system the legitimacy of opposition is accepted, and competition for control of the government occurs through parties, which appeal to enfranchised masses of people, rather than through violence.

In the United States parties have filled two very significant electoral functions: First, they have established an electoral process for recruiting and electing leaders to fill the offices set up by the Constitution. This process consists of two stages—nominating the candidates and choosing the winning candidate. And, second, parties have adapted this electoral process to the participation of the mass constituency as it gradually became enfranchised.

In performing their electoral functions, democratic political parties have developed two elements: The first is the office-oriented segment of the party —officeholders and aspirants for office, who support the party as a means of gaining and maintaining office, and "king-builders" and "coattail" operators, who participate in the inner-party struggle for office and its

[1] For a similar statement of party functions, see Fred I. Greenstein, *The American Party System and the American People* (Englewood Cliffs, N.J.: Prentice-Hall, 1963).

benefits. The second element is "the party in the electorate"—the dependable voters and part-time party workers who adhere to the party from one election to the next. Some of these partisans are issue oriented, seeing in the party a durable instrument for promoting their interests or views on policy. Some are patronage oriented, seeking personal gains through party victory. Some are habitual followers, adhering to the party because of family, class, sectional, or group affiliation, or personal attachment over a period of time.

The linking of these two elements—office seekers and the mass constituency—is what distinguishes the modern democratic party. It provides a vehicle for office seekers to bid for the support of the voters, and it simultaneously simplifies the voter's task by limiting his choice to a small group of candidates.

Reconciling Conflicting Interests

In many nations that have embarked on a democratic course, popular government has been unstable or has collapsed in struggles among sections, classes, or groups seeking to control the government. In this country, by contrast, national parties have been an instrument of *stability*, contributing to the maintenance of the legal order and of nonviolent politics. In Europe, democratic parties have often tended to articulate and represent different interests directly, thus accentuating the differences among these groups. In this country, however, the articulation of diverse interests is left largely to nonparty groups, while the national parties have instead become the instruments for compromise among these disparate interests and for moderation of group conflicts.

Why have American national parties taken on this role of mediator among interests? The answer lies in the givens of the American political and cultural system. To win a presidential election, a party must have a majority of the electoral votes. In a pluralistic society with diverse sectional, class, and functional interests, each party naturally tries to build a majority coalition from two basic elements. First, each party has hard-core groups of supporters who view it as embodying the values they hold dear. To retain and satisfy these loyal party constituents, the party stresses its identification with their values. But, because of the conflicts of interest among its hard-core supporters, the party must define these values in broad terms that stress the compatible aspects of these diverse interests. Second, the party seeks to broaden its support by winning over undecided and independent voters, who determine the result of elections.

Thus, each party tries to win elections by seeking a durable combination of hard-core supporters plus short-term support from those whose habitual attachment to the party is weak or nonexistent. Accomplishing all this is a major feat, involving almost miraculous political tightrope-walking, with commitment that avoids alienation and counterappeal that draws support. Each party searches, with a Madison Avenue touch, for doctrines, symbols, and catch phrases that appeal to the broadly shared attitudes and interests of most Americans. Such appeals to diffuse, unorganized (or weakly organized) values are often vague, but they unite people who hold opposing positions on many controversial, specific issues. The result of accommodating diverse interests and making very broad appeals is that the two parties draw closer to each other in their final electoral positions.

This kind of contest softens the conflict of interests. Thus, the parties have become means for attaining the great hope of the Framers of the Constitution that the violence of faction would be restrained. Moreover, the effort of each party to maximize voting appeal among very diverse elements ensures that a change in government from one party to another will have wide acceptance and that the alterations in government policies will not be so revolutionary as to stimulate the losers to violent attack upon the government. Except for the Civil War, the parties have kept conflict within limits safe for the political system.

Operating the Government Machinery

A third function of parties is to operate the machinery of government.[2] The Framers incorporated into the decision-making system a set of obstacles designed to prevent majority combinations from encroaching on the interests of minorities. That the system has been able to respond to the demands of people for positive government is one of the achievements of parties. First, those who sail together under the flag of the winning party take for themselves the leadership posts of the government. The President, with the approval of the Senate, appoints the chief policy makers in the executive branch, choosing most of them from his own party. The leadership posts in Congress, though formally dependent upon action of the two houses, are actually allocated by the parties, with the key posts, such as the Speakership of the House and the chairmanships of all committees, going to the majority party. In sum, the parties staff the government. The leaders of the majority party, in turn, become the chief decision makers in the government. Collaboration within the executive branch and within the two houses, as well as cooperation across the chasms that separate the houses from each other and from the President, is facilitated when all the leadership posts are held by men who have a common stake in party victory. The system (to be described in detail in later chapters) is a complex one, with much intraparty division and some cooperation among rival party leaders, but its ability to produce decisions is materially dependent on the cooperation that prevails among the leaders and their adherents in the majority party in government.

[2] For a more extensive discussion of this function, see Part III.

Like the electoral contest, this system simultaneously allows and moderates conflicts of interests. The structure of Congress allows minority-party leaders to preserve the continuous opposition that is essential to the open contest for support of the electorate in a democratic system. Yet each member of Congress has his own electoral constituencies and his personal views and stakes of power to promote within the congressional contest. These constituency and personal factors prevent coherence within the parties and discourage the alignment of all members into opposing party blocs on most issues.

The pluralist diversity of interests in our society is pushed upward into the structure of government; and the brokerage of these interests, though maneuvered by the party leaders, is most often achieved through majorities made up of members from both parties. In a party system that has produced Republican senators as diverse in their positions as Javits of New York and Goldwater of Arizona and Democratic senators as diverse as the Kennedy brothers, Morse of Oregon, Russell of Georgia, and Eastland of Mississippi, the conflict between parties is moderated by intraparty divisions and by the President's need to obtain bipartisan support for his policies.

As we have seen, the three major functions of parties—mobilizing the electorate, reconciling conflicts of interest, and helping to operate government machinery—make a vital contribution to the implementation of self-government and to the stability of the political system. But what are the political prices we pay for these benefits? One result of our party system is that issues are often glossed over, and the voter is faced with blurred alternatives. Sharper differences between parties would produce tougher politics, elections with higher stakes, and greater opportunity for revolutionary change. Second, the party exercises only partial control over decision-making in our complex government structure, for neither the President nor members of Congress function strictly as party agents. Consequently, the voter cannot fix responsibility completely on a party for decisions the government makes or fails to make.

Would alterations in our party system to effect clearer partisan divisions on policy issues and stricter party control of government result in more representative government, greater stability of the political system, or greater responsiveness of the system to the demands of groups? That it would is debatable. One's judgment on this issue must depend on an evaluation of the American system's operation as described in subsequent chapters, particularly in Part III. The important point to note here is that the functions of American parties are integral features of the political system that evolved to fill the political gaps in the Constitution. Thus, any realistic proposal for change in the political system would still have to be rooted in the distinctive American conditions—sociocultural, constitutional, and political—that led to the development of this system in the first place.

THE DEVELOPMENT OF THE PARTY SYSTEM, 1787 TO THE PRESENT

Two themes are central to any discussion of American party history: first, how parties developed in response to the constitutional requirements for selection of the President and to the movement toward broader popular participation in government; and, second, how they developed as loose coalitions of diverse interests united for the capture of the Presidency rather than as highly cohesive programatic parties.

Prior to the 1790's, American politics consisted of preparty factionalism characterized by personal rivalries, cliques, and loose aggregations produced primarily by local issues and, in 1787, by the submission of the Constitution for ratification.

Four factors, however, encouraged the development of popularly based *national* parties: (1) As John Jay said, "Providence [has given] this one connected country to one united people—a people descended from the same ancestors, speaking the same language, professing the same religion, attached to the same principles of government, very similar in their manners and customs . . . ."[3] (2) The pre-Revolutionary committees of correspondence had produced extensive communication among the sectional leaders of the nation. These leaders shared a "compatibility of the main values," which was essential for the amalgamation of parties across state and local lines.[4] (3) The new office of the Presidency in a government with substantial powers was a prize of great value, one that could be captured only by cooperation among officeholders, party activists, and a coalition of interests stretching across state lines. And (4) the extension of the suffrage meant that broad campaigns directed at the populace, organized and run by a multitude of party workers, would be required for victory.

One of the by-products of party activity was to make the constitutional unity of the nation a political reality. Modern new nations have often been created under the charismatic leadership of men like Sukarno of Indonesia and Nkrumah of Ghana who symbolized the unity of the nation. Similarly, the American nation had its symbol of unity in President Washington, universally respected and trusted, and it had the added advantage of legitimacy provided by the ratified Constitution. Washington's charismatic leadership gave firmness to the Union in its initial period, but he could provide only a temporary basis for national unity. Paradoxically, it was the nation's competing parties that were to solidify its unity. National parties were to

---

[3] *The Federalist*, No. 2.
[4] See Karl Deutsch, *et al.*, *Political Community and the North Atlantic Area* (Princeton, N.J.: Princeton University Press, 1957), p. 48.

become the instruments for joining sectional interests, operating the government, and educating the people on the rules of political warfare in a popularly based government.[5]

The First Party System, 1793–1824

The first parties arose quickly out of rival positions on major issues.[6] Hamilton had a bold plan for promoting economic development, a strong central government, and national unity by binding the financial and commercial interests to the national government. To achieve this, he proposed a comprehensive national legislative program, including the funding of the national debt at par, assumption by the nation of the war debts of the states, protective tariffs, and establishment of a national bank. Opposition arose immediately, headed initially by Madison, and the capital became the scene of conflict between the two factions.

Hamilton's success was tremendous. He was able to put together a coalition in Congress to enact his legislative program—the first effective management of the process of government by a coordinated group. Hamilton was able to build this faction into the nation's first national party. He and his associates initiated correspondence with their "contacts" throughout the country, founded newspapers to expound the ideology behind the Hamiltonian program, and gained the support of the network of local and state clubs organized as the "Cincinnati." The party ideology was oriented toward the stability of the social order against revolutionary trends and toward a broad interpretation of national powers. Its appeal was primarily to the financial and commercial interests and to the wage earners in shipbuilding and other manufacturing concerns, and its greatest sectional support was from the shipping and shipbuilding interests of New England. By 1793 the Federalist party was a cohesive coalition of office holders, party activists and party supporters throughout the nation.

A rival coalition developed more hesitantly but was ultimately to be more effective. This faction, led by opponents of Hamilton in the capital, was referred to as the Republican party; but, since there was no accepted concept of "legitimate opposition" in this country, this group was somewhat uncomfortable about its role of opposition. Jefferson in particular hesitated to assume the leadership of such a party. Even after his defeat in the presidential contest of 1796 he expressed the hope that he, as the new Vice-President, and the newly elected President could work together. But the Republicans in the meantime had been building a country-wide party

[5] For further discussion of this role of socialization—of educating the people for participation and acceptance of the political system—see Gabriel A. Almond and G. Bingham Powell, Jr., *Comparative Politics: A Developmental Approach* (Boston: Little, Brown, 1966), pp. 120–27.

[6] For full discussion of the first parties, see William Nisbet Chambers, *Political Parties in a New Nation* (New York: Oxford University Press, 1963).

This 1791 Federalist cartoon shows Washington defending his national Administration against the attacks of the Jeffersonians, who are depicted as French Revolutionary "cannibals." Jefferson is shown at the extreme right, trying to stop the Federalists.

similar to that of the Federalists. They had established a communication network among leaders in the states, created newspapers, and formed Democratic or Jacobin clubs. Their appeal was aimed primarily at the agricultural interests; their great strength came initially from the Southern and Middle Atlantic states and from a Virginia-New York alliance that gave the presidential position on the Republican ticket to Virginia and the vice-presidential spot to New York.

The election of 1800 was a highly significant moment in the nation's history. It marked the apex of the nation's first two-party system in several ways:

First, each party for the first time nominated candidates for President and Vice-President in a caucus composed primarily of legislative leaders. And in the actual election, voting on candidates for both offices by the presidential electors for the first time followed strict party lines.

Second, the election gave victory to the party with the more widespread popular appeal. The Republicans began with broader intrinsic appeal in a dominantly agrarian society, and they capitalized on this advantage by creating an organization to mobilize popular support. They campaigned for votes in the two states where the people chose electors directly and for support for legislators committed to their candidate in the states where the legislatures selected electors. Thus, the election of 1800 emphasized the popular foundation of the new nation's government.

The Good Society: The Federalists

The expediency of encouraging manufactures in the United States ... appears at this time to be pretty generally admitted. The embarrassments which have obstructed the progress of our external trade, have led to serious reflections on the necessity of enlarging the sphere of our domestic commerce. The restrictive regulations, which, in foreign markets, abridge the vent of the increasing surplus of our agricultural produce ... beget an earnest desire that a more extensive demand for that surplus may be created at home....

To affirm that the labor of the manufacturer is unproductive, because he consumes as much of the produce of land as he adds value to the raw material which he manufactures, is not better founded than it would be to affirm that the labor of the farmer, which furnishes materials to the manufacturer, is unproductive, because he consumes an equal value of manufactured articles. Each furnishes a certain portion of the produce of his labor to the other, and each destroys a corresponding portion of the produce of the labor of the other. In the meantime, the maintenance of two citizens, instead of one, is going on; the State has two members instead of one; and they, together, consume twice the value of what is produced from the land....

The foregoing considerations seem sufficient to establish, as general propositions, that it is the interest of nations to diversify the industrious pursuits of the individuals who compose them; that the establishment of manufactures is calculated not only to increase the general stock of useful and productive labor, but even to improve the state of agriculture in particular—certainly to advance the interests of those who are engaged in it.

From Alexander Hamilton, *Report on the Subject of Manufactures*, 1791.

Third, the election confirmed the right of an organized opposition to capture the government through ballots rather than revolution. Jefferson's hesitancy about organizing an opposition and the uncertainty of Republicans about their party's role would not recur. Moreover, the Federalists yielded the reins of power, and the Alien and Sedition Acts they had passed to curb opposition in 1798 were quickly repealed. The nation had moved beyond dependence on charismatic leadership "toward the full acceptance of the rational legitimacy of the Constitution, and of elections, decision by majority rule, and the counting of votes." [7]

The election of 1800 inaugurated a period of Republican ascendancy, and the years that followed provided valuable lessons about American politics. At first the united Republican party, like the Hamiltonian faction a decade earlier, was able to establish unity among the branches of government in the operation of the political machinery. The President became the legis-

[7] Chambers, *op. cit.*, pp. 168–69.

lative leader, overcoming the separation of powers, as John Marshall phrased it, by being able "to embody himself with the House" and, as a later commentator described it, by embodying himself also into the Senate, the administration, the capital clubs, and the nation.[8] Under presidential leadership the party was tightly knit within Congress through the party caucus, the committees, the Speaker, and the floor leaders. Prior to 1801 there had been much independent voting in both parties in response to sectional interests, but in the Congress of 1801–03 every member voted with his party on at least two-thirds of the votes. Seldom has a party's dominance provided as much unity in the operation of the government.

It is significant to note that the shift of control over the government from the Federalists to the Republicans did *not* produce the drastic reversal of national trends that was implied in the ideological gulf separating the two parties. Jefferson pursued a moderate course, hoping to detach the commercial interests from the Federalist party. His purchase of the Louisiana Territory was contrary to the strict-constructionist views of his party (the

[8] *Ibid.*, p. 170.

The Good Society: The Republicans

The political economists of Europe have established it as a principle that every state should endeavor to manufacture for itself.... But we have an immensity of land courting the industry of the husbandman. Is it best then that all our citizens should be employed in its improvement, or that one half should be called off from that to exercise manufactures and handicraft arts for the other? Those who labor in the earth are the chosen people of God, if he ever had a chosen people, whose breasts he has made his peculiar deposit for substantial and genuine virtue. It is the focus in which he keeps alive that sacred fire, which otherwise might escape from the face of the earth. Corruption of morals in the mass of cultivators is a phenomenon of which no age nor nation has furnished an example. It is the mark set on those who, not looking up to heaven, to their own soil and industry, as does the husbandmen, for their subsistence, depend for it on the casualties and caprice of customers. Dependence begets subservience and venality, suffocates the germ of virtue, and prepares fit tools for the designs of ambition.... While we have land to labor then, let us never wish to see our citizens occupied at a workbench, or twirling a distaff. Carpenters, masons, smiths, are wanting in husbandry; but, for the general operations of manufacture, let our workshops remain in Europe. It is better to carry provisions and materials to workmen there than bring them to the provisions and materials, and with them their manners and principles. The loss by the transportation of commodities across the Atlantic will be made up in happiness and permanence of government.

From Thomas Jefferson, *Notes on Virginia*, 1784.

Republicans believed in a very narrow interpretation of the powers delegated to the national government in the Constitution), and his action is an
early example of the triumph of national interests over ideology in the policy
choices of the governing party. Moreover, while the Republicans were
emphasizing strict construction, the decisions of the Supreme Court under
John Marshall gave a very broad interpretation to the constitutional powers
of the national government—thus demonstrating that a change in the governing party does not remove all institutional restraints on policy change.
The first changing of the guard showed clearly that party leadership could
be alternated without the destruction of national continuity and stability.

There were, however, strains on the unity of the nation during both the
Federalist and Republican periods, and Robert Dahl has noted the frequent
recurrence of intense conflict.[9] The Alien and Sedition Acts of the Federalist period led to the Kentucky and Virginia resolutions condemning these
acts as an unwarranted use of national authority, and during the War of
1812 New England Federalists issued the Hartford protest against a war
that was harmful to commerce and shipping. Both protests claimed the right
of states to interpose their authority against that of the nation. But repeal of
the Alien and Sedition Acts after the "Revolution of 1800," as Jefferson
called his victory, and the prompt conclusion of the War of 1812 calmed
the tempest in both cases and preserved the benefits of lower-tension politics.

The success of the Republican party was so great in the years following
1800 that the nation had virtually a one-party system, which led in turn to
a multifactional system that destroyed party government. The collapse of
the Federalist party was reflected in the near-unanimous victory of Monroe
in 1820, but the victory cloaked the Republican factionalism that had arisen
with Madison's weak leadership, Monroe's effort to "reign" above partisan
conflict, and the rivalry of ambitious aspirants for power. There was no
Federalist candidate after 1816.

The official Republican caucus chose Crawford in 1824, but there were
in fact four candidates running as Republicans. Since none of them received
a majority of the electoral vote, the House of Representatives chose John
Quincy Adams as President. The first two-party system had been replaced
by personal and multifactional politics.

The Second Party System, 1828–60

America's second party system originated in a social and institutional context very different from that of the 1790's. The popular base of government had been enlarged in a variety of ways. Twenty-three states were in
the Union by 1835, thus increasing the complexity of party combinations

[9] Robert A. Dahl, ed., *Political Oppositions in Western Democracies* (New Haven,
Conn.: Yale University Press, 1966), p. 50.

and lending a frontier spirit to politics. By 1824 the vote had been extended to all adult white males in all but a few states, and new state constitutions had enlarged the participation of voters by providing for popular election of executive officers and judges. By 1840 the delegate convention was the dominant means of nominating candidates, including presidential electors and the presidential candidate himself. The rise of the convention weakened the power of the gentry and increased the number of party activists.

Presidential electors, selected by direct popular vote in only two states in 1800, were by 1832 selected by this method in all states except South Carolina. This change has been called the most important difference between Jeffersonian and Jacksonian politics.

> The general adoption of the popular, state-wide voting procedure gave a popular dimension to the presidential contest, created or enhanced the need for state party machinery, weakened the political authority of legislative caucuses, occasioned the development of national party conventions, and made the presidential election the dramatic focal point of American politics.[10]

The élite leadership of the first party period was replaced by new leaders with broader public followings, such as Jackson and Harrison, or men such as Van Buren who were skilled in party organization. The popular leaders and the multitude of party activists made "folk festivals" of presidential campaigns and gave a dramatic tone to American politics. The new tone, presaged in Jackson's appeal as "Old Hickory" in 1828, was apparent in the Whig campaign of 1840 for "Tippicanoe and Tyler too." The Whigs appealed to frontiersmen by using log cabins, cider barrels, coonskins, and other symbols; to laborers with the slogan "Harrison, two dollars a day, and roast beef"; and to the masses in general by a campaign set to music —winning the Whigs the nickname the "Sing Sing party." [11]

There are several significant aspects of the rise and development of the second party system. While the first party system began at the top with capital factions that broadened into nationwide parties, the second group of parties began at the grassroots as coalitions of state and local leaders and organizations. The diverse factions left in the wake of the first party system combined to form new aggregations that could contest actively in local, state, and national elections. As in the first period, the contest for the Presidency produced the national coalitions and generated organization and spirit among the activists. In 1828 the anti-Adams factions coalesced around Jackson to form the Democratic party; similarly, in 1834 the anti-Jackson factions united to form the Whig party.

In contrast to the first parties, which had pronounced ideological posi-

---

[10] Richard P. McCormick, *The Second American Party System: Party Formation in the Jacksonian Era* (Chapel Hill, N.C.: University of North Carolina Press, 1966), p. 29.
[11] See Wilfred E. Binkley, *American Political Parties: Their Natural History*, 3rd ed. (New York: Knopf, 1959), Ch. 7.

tions, the second pair of parties were pragmatic coalitions of interests without clearly defined ideologies. The Whig party was a loose aggregation consisting of the National Republicans who had supported Adams and Clay, the Southern planters who had backed Calhoun's nullification stand, the anti-Masons, and many dissident groups, The Democrats had a more cohesive coalition of agricultural producers in the West, small planters in the South, workingmen and humble folk in the East.[12] The balance of power between the two parties was determined in the West. Since the parties lacked cohesive ideologies, their orientations on issues fluctuated and lacked the clarity of party positions in the preceding period. This pattern—decentralized parties that are pragmatic coalitions of disparate interests—has remained a dominant fact of American politics ever since.

But this does not mean that parties did not take different stands on issues. Party victories in certain elections clearly made a difference in the policies of the nation. Jackson, like Hamilton and Jefferson before him, put his imprint on the nation through his positions on the major problems of the day, such as national banking and protection of the frontier; and Polk's victory in 1844 was a mandate for the annexation of Texas and for territorial expansion in the Northwest.

The development of a two-party cleavage varied with each section and was materially influenced by the party leadership. Throughout the country, the Whigs arose as the party in opposition to the Democrats, but it did so as a series of local coalitions organized around new leaders. The Whigs brought two-partyism to New England when Henry Clay took the place of John Quincy Adams; to the South when Calhoun moved into their coalition; and to the West when Harrison duplicated for the Whigs the frontier appeal of Jackson and the Democrats. But from 1840 to 1852 a balanced two-party system existed in every section of the nation—a condition that has not been repeated since. In every election of this period the Presidency changed from one party to the other, and both parties won a substantial number of seats in Congress from every section of the country.

Third parties had a substantial impact on the party system. The two large parties absorbed many factional movements, such as the anti-Masons, the Workingmen's party, and the Barnburners in the 1830's and the Know-Nothing party in the 1850's. But the Free-Soilers could not be absorbed. With their double appeal of "Free Soil" and "Free Men" they cast 10 percent of the vote for President in 1848 and over 5 percent in 1852, and they raised the issues that led to the formation of the Republican party and the breakdown of the old party system.

While too much unity had brought the disintegration of the first parties, the divisive issue of slavery destroyed the second parties. The coalitions that

[12] See Arthur N. Holcombe, *The Political Parties of Today: A Study in Republican and Democratic Politics* (New York: Harper & Bros., 1924), Ch. 5.

produced them were too fragile, and the spirit of compromise among the conflicting interest too weak after the Kansas-Nebraska Bill of 1853, to prevent the collapse of party and the appeal to force.

The Third Party System, 1860 to the Present

When one looks at the party system from 1860 to the present he sees the long continuity of the viable political system of this country. The development of the third party system, despite its long-range continuity, is subdivided into three periods by the elections that have marked significant realignments in voting coalitions: 1860, 1896, and 1932.

The realignment of 1860

Following 1860 the Republicans, like the Federalists and the Jacksonians before them, were to stamp their imprint on policy and establish a position of party dominance that would eventually stimulate the Democratic party to form a new and more effective coalition in opposition, thus maintaining the two-party system.

The immediate effect of the Republican party's rise was to demolish the old party alignment. Organized in 1854, the Republicans took the place of the Whigs in the election of 1856, but they did so as a new party rather than as a successor to the Whigs. The Republicans started with Jefferson as a symbol: "The principles of Jefferson are the definitions and axioms of free society," said Lincoln in 1859. They offered free land to those who would "go west" and a slave-free society in the territories. This incentive created a farmer-laborer party, for the laborer of the East could either go west or look for higher wages at home as a result of the exodus westward. Old Whigs and Old Democrats in the North and West flocked to Frémont, the Republican candidate, in 1856. The heart of the Democratic party was reduced to the slavocracy of the South and the conservatives of the North. By 1860 the Republican party became a sectional party, with its area of strong support running south to the Mason-Dixon line and westward along the lines of settlement of Northerners and immigrants. This sectional realignment of parties replaced the balance of parties existing *within* each section from 1840 to 1852.

The Republican party solidified its Northeast-Northwest coalition and governed the nation for the next generation. Coming to power with only 40 percent of the popular vote against three opposing candidates in 1860, lacking a majority in either house of Congress, and losing even its name in 1864, when Lincoln, its candidate, ran on what was called the "Unionist" ticket, the Republicans became the dominant party through the South's withdrawal from national politics and through its subsequent defeat in the

Lack of Party Ideology: The Nineteenth Century

There are now two great and several minor parties in the United States. The great parties are the Republicans and the Democrats. What are their principles, their distinctive tenets, their tendencies? Which of them is for tariff reform, for the further extension of civil service reform, for a spirited foreign policy, for the regulation of railroads and telegraphs by legislation, for changes in the currency?...

Neither party has, as a party, anything definite to say on these issues; neither party has any clean-cut principles, any distinctive tenets. Both have traditions. Both claim to have tendencies. Both have certainly war cries, organizations, interests, enlisted in their support. But those interests are in the main the interests of getting or keeping the patronage of the government. Distinctive tenets and policies, points of political doctrine and points of political practice, have all but vanished. They have not been thrown away, but have been stripped away by Time and the progress of events, fulfilling some policies, blotting out others. All has been lost, except office or the hope of it. . . .

There is still a contrast between the larger and more radical wing of the Democratic party and the older school of Republicans, but the conservative section of the Democrats differ very little from the conservative Republicans; and there are radical Republicans whose views are shared by plenty of Democrats. This approximation seems to indicate that the time for a reconstruction of parties is approaching; but party organizations are strong things, and often interefere with the course of natural evolution.

... An eminent journalist remarked to me in 1908 that the two great parties were like two bottles. Each bore a label denoting the kind of liquor it contained, but each was empty.

From James Bryce, *American Commonwealth*, 1914 ed. (originally written in 1893).

Civil War. As the party of union and emancipation its sentimental appeal was unbeatable. In addition, as Key says, it bound the North and Northwest to it by "loaves and fishes": free land to the farmers of the West by the Homestead Act of 1862, protective tariffs to the manufacturers and laborers of the Northeast, pensions to Union veterans, and land grants to the railroads (enabling them to build the transportation links that joined the commerce of the North and the West).[13]

The Democratic party, on the other hand, was splintered by the South's secession in 1860 and demoralized by the war. It foundered in each election, until in 1872 it entered no candidate. In 1876, however, the Democratic party was resurrected as an effective opposition by the union of the South

[13] V. O. Key, Jr., *Politics, Parties, and Pressure Groups*, 5th ed. (New York: Crowell, 1964), p. 168.

"You sure we should march shoulder to shoulder?"

The major parties of the twentieth century still lack a single ideology, and conflicting factions often develop within them on leading issues of the day. This cartoon shows Republican disagreement over the Vietnam war.

© 1965 Herblock in the Washington *Post*

with the urban, immigrant populations of the North, and the recovery of votes in the southern half of the Western territories. From 1876 to 1896 the parties were as equally balanced throughout the country as a whole as at any time in our history, though they were not balanced within all sections as they had been from 1840 to 1852. The election of 1876 was a very close and hotly disputed contest; the popular majority of the Republicans in 1880 was no more than 10,000 votes out of nearly 9 million votes cast; and the Presidency swung back and forth between the parties at each election between 1884 and 1896. Two parties were again competing equally, and this competition has endured for nearly a hundred years.

The realignment of 1896

The party realignment of 1896 grew out of the economic revolution that had been occurring in the United States since the outbreak of the Civil War. This revolution produced great concentrations of wealth and power in the financial and industrial capitals of the Northeast and Midwest, and it gave rise to a growing urban population fed constantly by immigrants from Ireland and southern Europe. The new monied interests at once gained a foothold in the Republican party, and the Grand Old Party, initially radical, became conservative under their influence.

Gillam in *Judge*

This famous cartoon on McKinley's promise of a "full dinner pail" symbolizes the appeal of the Republican party to the workingman in the late nineteenth and early twentieth centuries.

Discontent and demands for change had been growing for years in the West and among the laboring classes. The protests of farmers were expressed through the Grange, the Greenbackers, the Farmers' Alliance, and ultimately the People's party (the Populists). The Knights of Labor had over 700,000 members by 1896. For years the poor of the nation had been clamoring for "easy money," and their demands had support from the silver-producing states of the Far West. Both parties were threatened when the People's party—demanding public ownership of railroads and utilities, strong action against the trusts, easy money, and heavier taxes on the rich—cast over a million votes for President in 1892, winning twenty-two electoral votes for its candidate, and captured three governorships and hundreds of local offices.

The Democrats of 1896, forsaking the monetary policies of its outgoing President, Grover Cleveland, ran on a platform of free coinage of silver and gold at a ratio of 16 to 1. The Republicans answered with a conservative appeal for the gold standard. The result was a victory that made the conservative Republicans the dominant party until 1932. This dominance is indicated by Figure 5–1, showing when each party controlled the Presidency, the House, and the Senate in the years from 1896 to 1932.

Both parties were coalitions of diverse interests. A one-party system prevailed in the South, forcing differing interests in that section to express themselves through internal competition for control of the Democratic party. The Democrats could win the Presidency only by linking the support

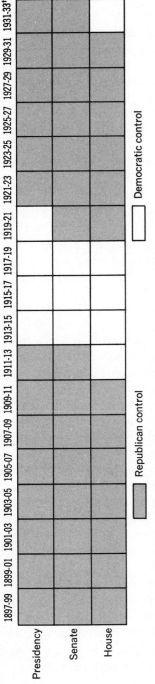

Figure 5–1   Republican Domination of the National Government, 1896 to 1932 *

1897-99   1899-01   1901-03   1903-05   1905-07   1907-09   1909-11   1911-13   1913-15   1915-17   1917-19   1919-21   1921-23   1923-25   1925-27   1927-29   1929-31   1931-33†

Presidency

Senate

House

☐ Republican control   ☐ Democratic control

* In effective political terms, Republican and Democratic domination of the national government was bounded by the dates of the national elections, but power technically changed hands in the year following each election.
† The Republicans had only a plurality in the Senate during this session.

Figure 5–2   Democratic Domination of the National Government, 1932 to 1968

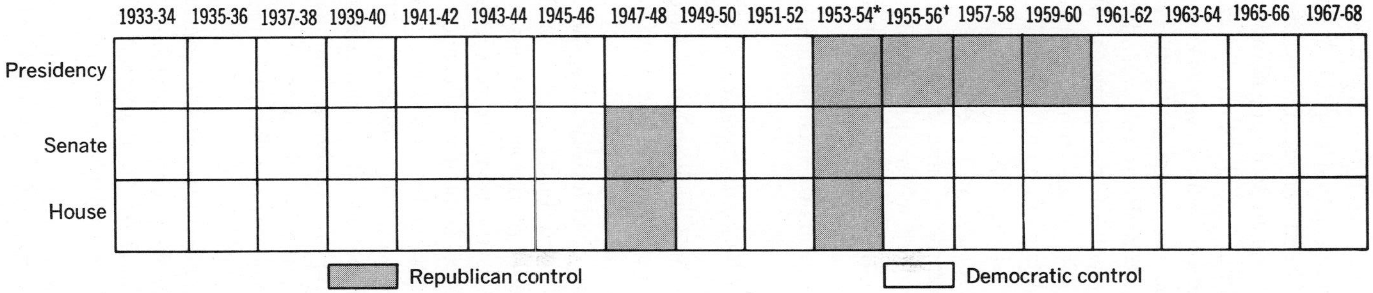

1933-34   1935-36   1937-38   1939-40   1941-42   1943-44   1945-46   1947-48   1949-50   1951-52   1953-54*   1955-56†   1957-58   1959-60   1961-62   1963-64   1965-66   1967-68

Presidency

Senate

House

☐ Republican control   ☐ Democratic control

* The Republicans had only a plurality in the Senate during this session.
† The Democrats had only a plurality in the Senate during this session.

of the Solid South with an approximately equal number of electoral votes from other sections—chiefly the cities of the Middle Atlantic states. The wide diversity in the party was revealed in the victories of ultraconservative forces in nominating Alton Parker in 1904 and John W. Davis in 1924, while the liberal forces prevailed in Bryan's three nominations of 1896, 1900, and 1908 and in Wilson's nomination of 1912. The Republican party after 1896 continued to be a coalition of Eastern business interests, Western grain producers, and city workers who accepted the protective tariff and sound money as boons to them. Only the 1912 split in Republican ranks—when Theodore Roosevelt's candidacy on the Progressive party ticket siphoned off much of its traditional Western support—broke the party's dominance of government from 1896 to 1932.

Again—as when Hamilton, Jefferson, Jackson, Polk, and Lincoln led the controlling coalitions—the choice of one party over the other during this period had real significance for the policies of government. Conservative government, save only for the deviant influence of Theodore Roosevelt, prevailed when the Republicans were in power; and Wilson, with the support of a Democratic majority in Congress, made the platform of his party and his mandate from the people the basis for sweeping legislative enactments on such matters as tariffs, antitrust, banking, and an income tax.

The realignment of 1932

The third realignment of party voters began in 1928, when Al Smith and the Democrats garnered a significant proportion of the urban, industrial, foreign-born, and Catholic voters.[14] But it was not until 1932 that this new Democratic coalition—uniting the South with the urban industrial workers, discontented farmers, and small businessmen in the North and West—was brought to victory. Success was partly due to the initiative of the Democrats and partly to the Great Depression, which—like many depressions of the past—substantially influenced the tides of party in this country.

The Democrats were able to sustain their electoral coalition through their New Deal policies, and the 1932 realignment ushered in a thirty-six-year period of Democratic dominance comparable to the thirty-six-year period of Republican dominance from 1896 to 1932. Figure 5–2 shows that from 1932 to the present the Democrats have held the Presidency during twenty-eight of the years, the Senate and the House of Representatives during thirty-two.

Under Democratic administrations there has been a revolution in the business of government and the allocation of power and influence among the institutions of society. Chapter 18 and Part V of this book will show how the agenda of government—particularly at the national level—encom-

---

[14] See the analysis of New England voting in V. O. Key, Jr., "A Theory of Critical Elections," *The Journal of Politics*, Vol. XVII (February 1955), pp. 3–18.

WELL GOOD NIGHT
THANKS
FOR A PLEASANT
EVENING

This 1932 cartoon shows the Democrats "winning the pot"—including a working-class majority—in the first of the New Deal elections.

Darling in the New York *Herald Tribune*

passes multiple new programs for the regulation and promotion of the economy, education and welfare, national defense and world leadership, promotion of science and technology, and civil rights. The Eisenhower interlude of eight years did not reverse these trends, and the overwhelming defeat of Landon in 1936 and Goldwater in 1964 (whose candidacies implied the substantial overturning of these programs) demonstrated that effective party politics is confined to issues of "more or less" within a broad consensus on policies.

Some changes in alignment have been occurring in recent years, particularly in presidential politics: for the first time since 1852 a balanced two-party system is developing in all parts of the nation. In the presidential election of 1964, five states of the old Confederacy voted Republican, and in five others the percentage of the popular vote for the Democratic candidate was *lower* than the national average. Only two states in the country (Arkansas and North Carolina) have given their electoral vote to the same party in all of the last five elections. Although this tendency toward national two-partyism has been less pronounced in congressional elections, only four states with more than four representatives in Congress have given all their seats to the same party in the last three biennial elections. Among the many causes for the increase of two-partyism are the rise of the civil-rights issue; the breakdown of sectional diversities as industrialization has come to all parts of the country; the general substitution of urban politics for the older, rural, sectional politics; and the importance of certain major issues—such as peace and social security—that cut across sectional lines.

Yet the basic nature of American national parties has remained unchanged. Now, as in the past, major parties are coalitions of disparate interests formed primarily for capture of the Presidency.

FEATURES OF THE AMERICAN PARTY SYSTEM

American political parties have historically revealed three distinctive characteristics: (1) a strong tendency toward the two-party system, (2) decentralization, and (3) lack of ideology. What aspects of the American institutional and sociocultural milieu have made it almost inevitable that American parties would have these features?

Two-Party Politics

It is important for readers to note that there is no inherent tendency toward two-party politics in democratic government. In continental Western Europe, for example, multiparty systems have been characteristic, and in non-European democracies, such as Mexico and India, accommodation of interests has been achieved largely within a single dominant party. In fact, there appears to be something distinctly artificial about a two-party system in a nation of diverse interests.

Why, then, has the United States returned again and again to such a system? First, the United States has not been deeply torn by major sociocultural, political, or economic controversies. European countries have been rent by deep divisions of opinion over their form of government, their economic organization, the relation of church to state, and the status of minority groups wanting to secede from the country in which they were located. Men have believed so deeply in these matters that they have formed separate parties to represent their positions—monarchical versus republican parties, socialist and communist parties versus the parties of the political right, Catholic parties versus anticlerical parties, and nationalistic parties. Americans, on the other hand, have been able to sustain a broad consensus on these basic issues: we started with agreement on republican government. The opportunities here for individual initiative and self-attainment were sufficiently well-distributed to impede the development of radical parties of the left, and the lack of a feudal history meant that we had no *ancien régime* trying to perpetuate itself through reactionary parties. The wide diversity in religious belief made the religious settlement of the First Amendment—guaranteeing freedom to practice any religion and forbidding the establishment of a state church—a practical alternative to religious conflict. Racial parties were inhibited by the subordination of the Negro and by the desire

"Sounds like another party on the line. . . ."

The Republican victories in 1966 demonstrate the tendency of the minority party to pick up strength in the off-year congressional elections and thus continually to renew our two-party system.

Peb in the Philadelphia *Inquirer*

of the European immigrants to become assimilated into American culture. And there have been no frustrations of national objectives in foreign policy sufficient to sustain separatist nationalist parties. Because many potentially divisive issues were smoothed over by the great American consensus, our politics could center on questions of degree that lent themselves to moderate solutions. The exception of the Civil War—the American battle over form of our economy and over the freedom of men versus the rights of property—only reinforces the argument that the moderation of two-party politics can exist only where issues are not deeply divisive.

A second factor contributing to the American two-party system has been described as "the existence of two major complexes of interest in the country." [15] The historical conflict in this country between agricultural interests and financial and commercial interests predated even the adoption of the Constitution and became the basis for the Hamiltonian and Jeffersonian parties. After the Civil War a similar alignment of interests occurred when industrial and financial interests in the Republican party were opposed by the agrarian and populist movements and later by the New Freedom, the New Deal, the New Frontier, and the Great Society of the Democrats. However, this view of natural two-partyism based on economic cleavage does not explain the ability of the Republicans to maintain the support of Western agricultural interests or of the Democrats to hold the Solid South, both for long periods. Nor does this argument explain the ability of the two major parties to prevent the divergent interests from forming splinter parties with more than temporary life. Nevertheless, in combination with

[15] Arthur W. Macmahon, in *Encyclopedia of the Social Sciences* (New York: Macmillan, 1937), Vol. XI, p. 597.

other factors this hypothesis may have some validity in explaining the durability of two-partyism in this country.

A third factor encouraging two-party politics is the ability of established organizations to retain their traditional supporters and gain additional supporters by exploiting new issues as they arise. Parties in a two-party system are like rivers fed by many tributaries. Once the party organization and the coterie of officeholders have fixed the river banks and once the allegiance of interest groups has provided the tributaries, the river system tends to maintain itself, and if new tributaries arise, they tend to feed into the main stream. In other words, once a two-party system is established, the structure of interests behind it will give it an advantage over splinter parties or new aggregations of interests.

A fourth factor contributing to two-party systems in the United States has been referred to as "the dialectic of oppositions." [16] This is the tendency for the dominance of one party in government to stimulate the formation of an opposition coalition. This pattern can be seen in the challenge of the Jeffersonians to the reigning Hamiltonians, of the Whigs to the Jacksonians, and of the revitalized Democratic party to the Radical Republicans after the Civil War.

The last two factors encouraging the two-party system are features of the American electoral system. One is the single-member constituency for election of members of Congress. In systems of proportional representation several members are elected from each district, and seats are allotted to each of several contesting groups on the basis of the percentage of votes cast for their candidates. Thus, for example, in a district electing ten members, a party winning 10 percent of the votes would get one seat, a party with 50 percent of the votes would get five seats, and so on. This system provides an opportunity for a minor party to capture some seats and to build up its support gradually in successive elections from a weak beginning. But in a single-member constituency one winner takes all. This encourages the candidate to align himself with a party that has organization and traditional support, so it can help him obtain the plurality or majority he needs for election. The system also tends to support the politics of moderation, for the party candidate must reconcile a variety of interests in order to form a winning combination. He must be the same kind of political broker within his district that the party is in the nation.

The second electoral factor is the method of electing the President. The President, too, is elected from a single-member constituency, with the usual implication—to win, a candidate must have a combination stronger than any other's. Moreover, the Constitution says that the President must have a majority of the electoral votes. And, finally, under the present practice in all states, the candidate with a plurality of votes within the state gets

[16] M. Donald Hancock, unpublished manuscript on Swedish politics.

all the state's electoral votes. Under this system no minor party could hope to win a plurality in enough states to add up to a national majority. The voters know this, and most of them cast their ballots for a candidate from one of the parties that can hope to win.

Decentralization

"Decentralization is by all odds the most important single characteristic of the American major party," wrote E. E. Schattschneider in his classic discussion of American parties.[17] Yet decentralization, like two-party politics, is not characteristic of democracies. Many parties in other democracies have highly centralized processes for taking stands on issues and for selecting candidates. In fact, Robert Michels, in his study of socialist parties in European democracies, concluded that mass parties had an inexorable tendency toward concentration of power in the leadership at the top of the party hierarchy.

In the American system, by contrast, "the critical action locus of the party structure is at its base," [18] and the national party is in fact dependent on the subsidiary state and local party organizations. This decentralization of party structure is primarily due to the decentralization of the governmental system. The Constitution, Supreme Court interpretations, and historical practice have established a federal system and also self-government at the local level. This system has allocated certain important political functions to state and local governments and has created a hierarchy of officials, independently elected at each level, to carry them out. The offices to be filled are numerous, and the elections are held frequently. The partial autonomy of the state and local governments makes them sources of rewards and benefits for the party that can capture their offices; hence, state and local organizations have formed to carry on party activity and mobilize the electorate wherever these elections occur.

The decentralization of parties is accentuated by factors in the electoral process. The convention system of nominating candidates for President gives state party leaders the controlling voice in selecting the party nominees and gives local party leaders a controlling voice in the state conventions that select delegates to the national convention. The selection of state and local party candidates through primaries further decentralizes the parties, for it weakens control over party nominations from the higher echelons in the party. Indeed, of all the electoral devices in our system, these primaries are the greatest obstacle to control of local parties by national leadership.

Further contributing to decentralization has been the need for national

[17] *Party Government* (New York: Holt, Rinehart and Winston, 1942), p. 129.
[18] Samuel J. Eldersveld, *Political Parties: A Behavioral Analysis* (Chicago: Rand McNally, 1964), pp. 9–10.

parties to adapt to disparate social and economic conditions in a large and diversified nation. In Massachusetts, for example, party struggles in the days of the immigrant influx produced "a Yankee, Protestant, upper social-economic status, rural and suburban Republican party and an Irish, Catholic, lower social-economic status, urban Democratic party." [19] In the South, by contrast, race-class structure produced a dominant Democratic party composed of conservative, professional, and officeholding groups. To win elections the Democrats had to form a coalition out of these very disparate local combinations. Similarly, the Republicans could win only through a coalition of urban financial and commercial interests in the Eastern states and rural agricultural interests in the Midwest and the West.

The single factor operating against party decentralization (and perhaps party disintegration) is the office of the President. To elect a President, a national convention must be held, a national organization developed, a national campaign fund raised, and a national image created for the candidate. The winning party will have a national leader, and each party will equip itself for the next contest.

Nonideological Brokerage Politics

Almost from the beginning—certainly since the defeat of the Federalists in 1800—American parties have tended to submerge ideology in the practical contest for winning combinations of interest. Thus they have emphasized the accommodation of diverse interest rather than programatic purity. This, too, differentiates them from many parties of other democratic nations. In Western Europe parties of both the left and the right have set forth their ideologies and have adopted programs and labels designed to show their allegiance to these ideologies. In new nations the goals of nationality and of economic and political reform become the ideology of programatic parties.

The nonideological nature of American parties and their emphasis on being brokers among diverse interests are due to two of the same factors that have contributed to two-party politics. The first is the American consensus on fundamentals, which made compromise possible in the Convention of 1787, and which has generally confined politics to low-key issues since the adoption of the Constitution. Politics has usually dealt with matters on which bargaining among diverse interests was possible in quadrennial election campaigns.

The other factor is our electoral system, established by the Constitution, congressional legislation, and historical practice. The Constitution established the office of President to be filled by independent election. This office can be obtained only by nationwide coalitions of diverse and conflicting

[19] George Goodwin, Jr., "The Last Hurrahs: George Apley and Frank Skeffington," *The Massachusetts Review,* Vol. I (Spring 1960), p. 466.

interests. Moreover, the single-member electoral district—required by congressional and state legislation for members of the House of Representatives and by the Constitution for senators—forces the same kind of brokerage politics in the election of members of Congress.

In sum, consensus on fundamentals and the brokerage of conflicting interests on issues of lesser significance determines the mood of American politics. The parties contribute to this mood through their search for a winning combination of officeholders, party workers, and party followers—a search that encourages party sensitivity at innumerable points to the demands of a diffuse population. Indeed, their survival depends on this sensitivity. For in order to win absolute majorities in a single-member electoral district or across the state or country, the parties must make a direct appeal to the widely shared ideals of the public. They must sacrifice ideological purity and avoid intransigent positions that strongly espouse particular sectional, class, or functional interests.

This façade of unity in elections does not itself produce a final brokerage of interests; this is achieved only through the intimate grappling with specific policies in the Presidency, Congress, and the bureaucracy—to be described in Part III. But the parties are a ubiquitous influence—at election time and when decisions are made in Washington—in creating the unity that makes possible the resolution of competing demands.

SUMMARY

Our national parties have contributed to the viability of our system by helping to fill the significant political gaps left by the Constitution. First, they have provided an orderly way for competing groups to seek public office by mobilizing voter support. In the United States, as in other modern democracies, parties consist of two elements: first, the officeholders, aspirants for office, and professional party activists and, second, part-time party workers and the traditional party supporters in the electorate.

Second, the parties reconcile conflicting interests by appealing to values that receive broad support in society in order to form nationwide coalitions in a large, pluralistic society. Because our parties strive to maximize their voting appeal among diverse groups, changes of the party in power receive wide acceptance in society, and the stability of the system is maintained.

Third, the parties help to operate the government machinery: the bonds of party affiliation help to overcome the barriers created by separation of powers and checks and balances so that decision-making can be carried on.

The first party system (1793-1824) arose out of the rival policy positions of the Federalists and the Republicans. The Federalists, led by Hamilton, favored a strong central government and promotion of economic development to win the loyalties of financial and commercial interests. The Republicans, led by Jefferson, favored emphasis on agriculture and a weaker central government. Both parties were able to create nationwide networks of state and local party organizations. The election of 1800, a victory for Jefferson, confirmed the legitimacy of peaceful party opposition. The first party system was destroyed, however, by too much unity: the steady Republican successes after 1800 in effect created a one-party system, which then degenerated into multiple factions.

The second party system (1828–60) reflected the greatly expanded suffrage of the period: the leaders in this second period tended to be popular folk heroes or men with organizational skills. Unlike the first parties, which had been formed by small élites to reflect sharp policy differences, the second parties were broad pragmatic coalitions of interests, organized at the grassroots through state and local organizations. Though the parties did sometimes take differing stands, they were not distinguished by major ideological differences. The second party system was wrecked on the issue of slavery.

The third party system (1860 to the present) consisted of the Republicans, who built a farmer-laborer party in the Northeast and Northwest on the axioms of Jefferson, and the Democrats, who were left with the slaveowners of the South and the northern conservatives. From 1860 to 1876 the Republicans governed the nation, while the Democrats were splintered and ineffectual in opposition. By 1876, however, the Democrats found their second wind, and for the next twenty years, the parties competed on a relatively equal basis.

Within the third party system, a significant realignment occurred in 1896: the Republican party became the conservative bastion of Northeastern corporate interests, with support from Western grain producers and urban workers who favored sound-money policies. The Democrats maintained the South, some farmers, and sporadic support from the Middle-Atlantic states. From 1896 to 1932 the Republicans were dominant in capturing both the Presidency and Congress.

In 1932 another realignment of voters took place: the onslaught of the Depression helped the Democratic party to form a successful and stable coalition of the Solid South, discontented farmers, small businessmen, and significant numbers of urban industrial workers and minority-group members. The New Deal policies, followed by the Fair Deal, the New Frontier, and the Great Society, have given the Democrats an effective edge over the Republicans in capturing the Presidency and Congress since 1932.

The evolution of American parties has reflected three tendencies: a preference for two-partyism, decentralized organization, and low levels of ideology.

Several factors encourage a two-party system in this country: our broad consensus on basic issues, which allows parties to form broad coalitions; the historical split between agricultural and financial-commercial interests; the ability of established party organizations to perpetuate themselves; and the constitutional requirements for single-member constituencies in Congress and for nationwide election of the President through a majority of electoral votes.

The decentralization of parties is due mainly to the constitutional provisions for a federal system that allocates significant political power and public offices to the states and localities. The convention system for nominating presidential candidates and the primary system for picking delegates to conventions both weaken national party discipline.

The relative lack of ideology stems from similar factors: the American consensus on basic issues that keeps conflict to a minimum, and the need to form broad nationwide coalitions in order to elect the President.

Nonetheless, changes of the party in power have been reflected in the policies chosen by the government, and in the allocation of benefits among various groups. The party system offers the electorate an opportunity to effect changes in government policy while keeping these changes moderate enough so that the losers accept the results peacefully.

PARTY LEADERSHIP AND ORGANIZATION

6

Chapter 6 explores the American party structure through which national, state, and local politicians operate, the key functions they perform, and the effect of socioeconomic change and public concern on party organization. What discrepancies exist between the organizational structure of our national party system and its actual power bases? How do national, state, and local politics differ from one another? What are the effects of one-party politics at the state and local levels? And, finally, what effect have public attempts to regulate party functions had on party organization and discipline?

We saw in Chapter 5 that American political parties are continuing organizations of professional politicians, supported at key points between elections by party activists and at election time by a large corps of traditional party identifiers. From this perspective, the primary functions of the American party are to recruit and nominate candidates, mount campaigns to elect these nominees, and develop relationships with the elected officeholders that will supply the party organization with the benefits needed to continue its operations. As V. O. Key has noted, the central task of party leadership and organization is thus "arranging collaboration among the political activists." [1]

THE NATIONAL PARTY STRUCTURE:
THE TENSION BETWEEN ORGANIZATION AND POWER

To understand the national structure of the two major American parties, we must look at them twice—first to study their lines of organization and then again to see where power really lies in this subsystem.

The Party Organizational Structure

Organizationally, the national parties both seem to be hierarchies of units closely linked along representational lines and culminating in a unified national authority. The party structure resembles that of a centralized business corporation that has local manufacturing and sales units and regional offices. Figure 6–1 shows the formal organization of the Democratic and Republican parties.

In this figure, the base of the party pyramid is the precinct organization, a relatively small geographic area often corresponding to the local election district set by law. The precinct captain is sometimes appointed by higher party authorities, but more often he is elected in a primary, a party convention, or a party caucus by party members living in the precinct. The precinct is the cell organism of the party: its function is to contact each of the several hundred voters in the district and to "deliver" the maximum number of votes to the party at election time.

On the next rung of the organizational ladder are "the 3,000 or so county chairmen of each party . . . the second lieutenants, or perhaps the noncoms, of the political army. . . . Most commonly the county committee is

[1] V. O. Key, Jr., *Politics, Parties, and Pressure Groups,* 5th ed. (New York: Crowell, 1964), p. 344.

Figure 6–1   The Formal Organizational Structure of the Major Parties

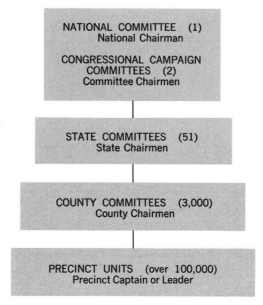

an assemblage of the party's precinct committeemen, township committee-men, or party functionaries from other subdivisions of the county." [2] The county committee focuses primarily on nomination of candidates for county offices and their election campaign.

At the state level, parties generally do not choose their form of organiza-tion; instead a state committee is established by state law. The composition of these committees varies widely from state to state. In some states, mem-bers are chosen in primaries or conventions from electoral districts (state legislative districts, congressional districts, etc.) within the state; in other states the county chairmen (and sometimes the vice-chairmen) automatically become members of the state committee. Headed by a state chairman, state committees range in size from seventy-two members in Alabama to over six hundred in California. The state committees are primarily concerned with the selection and election of candidates at the state level, but they are given other functions by law in some states, such as supervising party pri-mary elections and filling vacancies on the ballot created by the death of party nominees before the election. The state committee is usually a major force in the selection of delegates from that state to the party's national convention, and even where the formal selection is made by direct primary, the state committee frequently plays a key role in that fight.

At the top of the party pyramid are the national party organs: the national committee and its chairman and the congressional campaign com-

[2] *Ibid.*, p. 327.

mittees. The national Democratic committee consists of one man and woman from each state; the Republicans add to this group the state party chairman from those states that (1) have a Republican governor, (2) went Republican at the last presidential election, or (3) have a Republican majority in the state's congressional delegation. The national committee is not created by federal law; it is strictly a party organ, formally chosen by the national convention but, in practice, consisting of either the choices of each state delegation to the convention or the winners of a primary, caucus, or convention within a state. As V. O. Key has noted:

> Since membership on the national committee entails cost in both time and money, national committeemen tend to be men of both substance and stature in their states. Most of them are either lawyers or businessmen; many mix law, business, and politics. . . . The national committeeman may be the real chief of his state party organization or his national power may be rooted in the leadership of a metropolitan center. He may be a lieutenant of the

---

The Role of the State Party Chairman

A state chairman needs the patience of Job, the wisdom of Solomon, and the hide of a rhinoceros—but I have yet to meet anyone who has all these qualities....

Whether his party wins or loses an election, a state chairman should build and maintain an effective year-round organization. If an automobile manufacturer doesn't score a hit with one year's model, he doesn't shut down his plant—he comes along next year with another model. The same philosophy applies to politics. If a party suffers a severe defeat, or if one of its key leaders becomes incapacitated, it should be geared to move ahead. A political organization must be a continuous thing. It must always be an alive, alert, and aggressive operation....

A state chairman needs a reputation for fairness, so that he can mediate differences within his party without aggravating old sore spots or creating new ones. He should be an understanding but firm person who has leadership ability. He must have the desire, the drive, and the energy necessary to inspire and encourage the rank-and-file party worker as well as the candidates. If he fulfills the obligation of his job, he must be both a persuader and a dissuader. He is the common denominator of his party at the state level, and also the link between the national and county committee campaign programs....

A state chairman's efforts should be devoted to building a corps of capable candidates, a compelling party image, and a tightly knit organization, with the ultimate goal of electing the party nominees.

From Ray C. Bliss, Republican State Chairman of Ohio, "The Role of the State Chairman," in James M. Cannon, ed., *Politics U.S.A.*, 1960.

real leader of his state party, or his membership on the national committee may be a recognition by the state organization for financial support or an accolade for an elder statesman.[3]

The national committee has charge of the arrangements for the party's national convention: its decisions on selecting the convention city, recommending a slate of convention officers, and preparing the temporary roll of delegates often have political significance in the battle for presidential nominations and in party factional contests. The national committee aids in the presidential campaign, and meets occasionally between presidential elections to supervise the operations of the national party headquarters, raise funds, and issue party propaganda. Key has called the national committee "a gathering of sovereigns (or their emissaries) to negotiate and treat with each other." [4]

Since the national committees are large, meet only occasionally, and are not viewed by local, state, or national party leaders as a real policy-making body for the party, the major party role at the national level is filled by the party's national chairman. Though formally designated by the party's national committee, the chairman is in practice chosen personally by the party's presidential candidate soon after he himself is selected by the convention. The chairman, whose primary loyalty is thus to the presidential candidate, coordinates the election campaign for the Presidency and helps support all the other nominees running on the party's congressional, state, and local tickets. Between elections, the chairman presides over the permanent staff of some eighty to a hundred persons at the national headquarters.

The other national party organs are the congressional campaign committees, one for the House and one for the Senate. Composed of thirty to forty members of Congress, these committees are relatively independent of the national committee and maintain their own staffs of five to forty persons; they raise funds, distribute them for party candidates for Congress, and issue campaign literature.

The Party Power Structure

The organizational structure of the national parties suggests a hierarchy of command from the national chairman downward to the precinct organization. But where does real power lie? To answer this question we must examine the targets and the tools of power of the party professionals. In any political system, party leaders seek the power to control the nomination of candidates on the party ticket, the raising and distribution of funds, the conduct of the election campaign, and the distribution of patronage and other rewards that come with electing party nominees. In many other nations, it is the national party leadership that has basic control, in varying

[3] *Ibid.*, p. 317.
[4] *Ibid.*, p. 330.

degrees, over these targets and tools. In the United States, control is splintered, but it centers primarily at the state and county levels of the party. The national party leadership does *not* control nominations for governors, congressmen, state senators, mayors, or city councilmen. The national party does *not* raise the funds for these campaigns, control the issues raised or the positions taken by the party nominees, or control the party rewards flowing from these offices once captured. Instead, each layer of party organization performs these functions for the offices at its level, and each gains thereby substantial autonomy from the next higher party unit on the organizational ladder.

The reasons for this decentralization and fragmentation of power in the American party system are quite clear. Our federal system and our separation of legislative and executive offices create hundreds of independent electoral offices, from sheriff to senator and President. Our political culture, which emphasizes the unique problems and needs of each community or state in our diverse society, puts a high value on "local control" over offices at each level. Devices such as the direct popular primary are designed to prevent "outside bosses" from dominating local or state elections.

Moreover, decentralization of power means that the national party lacks control, not only at the state and local levels, but at the national convention as well. Since the delegates to it are chosen at the state level, the national convention (which nominates the presidential candidate) is dominated by

John Ruge in the *Saturday Review*

"He's got to be dumb enough to believe that *we* think he has a chance of winning, but not *so* stupid that the voters'll think we're not serious about the two-party system—and it can't *look* like we're holding back our good guys until 1972."

Though they must keep public sentiment in mind, state party leaders are key actors in picking party nominees for President.

state party chieftains, not by the national chairman or the national committee. The national chairman is a relatively weak figure and the national committee is a weak body because the state and local powers want it that way. Within each state, however, it is the county and city organizations that wield basic power, because of their control over local nominations, funding, and patronage; thus the state party leaders do not exercise nearly as much power downward as they do upward.

If the national party in the United States is such a loose confederation of largely autonomous state and local party units, what holds it together at all? The answer is that the candidates for the higher prizes on each electoral ticket—governor, President, senator, mayor—usually have a powerful effect on the electoral fortunes of the candidates down the line on the ticket. In 1964, for example, the nomination of a weak Republican candidate for President, Barry Goldwater, helped to defeat thousands of Republican candidates in congressional, state, or local elections who would have been elected to office with even a normal Republican showing at the top of the ticket. Thus, the state and local party units have a heavy stake in the choices of candidates for national office and in the success of their campaigns. Furthermore, the top electoral posts on the national and state tickets also carry with them some tangible benefits in patronage and some symbolic rewards that are highly attractive to party professionals at the lower levels. It is these factors that produce the temporary confederative alliances of state and local party units every four years to select and support a party candidate for President; the same process takes place to select the state and city tickets.

NATIONAL PARTY POLITICS

As Chapter 5 has indicated, the United States has had a two-party system at the national level since the early decades of the Republic. Equally important, our national parties have been *competitive* as well. There has been considerable debate among political scientists about which criteria to use for measuring "competitiveness." We will adopt three: (1) a close division of the popular vote in most elections, (2) frequent and serious threats of victory by the opposition, and (3) at least occasional victories by the opposition. Our national parties have met all three criteria. Since 1828, as Allan Sindler has noted, the Republican and Democratic parties together have consistently polled over 90 percent of the total popular vote cast in presidential elections, and the losing party has often obtained between 45 and 49 percent of the two-party total.[5] In the House of Representatives, the

[5] Allan Sindler, *Political Parties in the United States* (New York: St. Martin's, 1966), pp. 15–16.

two major parties have also closely split the national popular vote. Though one party or the other has tended to dominate the White House and Congress for considerable periods of time, it is significant that even during these periods the opposition party has always managed to win a few presidential and congressional victories. Thus, for example, although the period from 1896 to 1932 was one of heavy Republican dominance over both the Presidency and House, the Democrats were still able to capture control of the White House in 1912 and 1916 and the House in four elections from 1910 to 1916.

Control of the House has alternated between the parties more frequently than has the Presidency; moreover, our system of checks and balances ensures power for the opposition in the House even when it cannot gain control of this body. For in fact the minority party has managed to hold on to from one-third to one-half of the House seats even when the Presidency was being won repeatedly and heavily by the majority party. This pattern stems from the strength of local parties in the American system and the fact that all House members must run in off-year elections for Congress (when the Presidency is not being contested).

In Chapter 5 we noted that in our two-party system both parties have customarily tried to gain a nationwide majority by appealing to the widest possible coalition of voters and by muting election issues that would divide party supporters. Despite this tendency, however, our two-party system *does* produce greater competition of issues and program alternatives than do one-party systems—either in the nations of Africa or Asia or in states such as Mississippi or Alabama. For example, the national Republican party's stance in the twentieth century has tended to favor business interests, states' rights, and limited public welfare—thus contrasting noticeably with the Democrats, who have favored labor interests, federal over states' rights, and expanded public welfare. The programs of the two parties in office have reflected these differences, as the contrast between Eisenhower's Administration and those of Truman, Kennedy, and Johnson attest. Even in Congress, as Chapter 11 will show, for all the splintering of party lines on various issues, the voting of the majority of representatives and senators for each party has reflected popularly recognizable differences in policies and programs throughout most of our history.

STATE PARTY POLITICS

The considerable independence of each state government in the American federal system and the absence of tight national control over local party organizations have made the politics of each state highly distinctive. Each state had its special formative period of settlement, and each today has a unique blend of natural resources, population mixture, interest-group structure, political culture, constitutional and legal institutions, and urban-rural-suburban relationships.[6] The state political systems reflect almost as much diversity within a larger cultural framework as one finds in the Latin American nations or the African states.

Despite this diversity, political scientists have identified certain basic types of party systems in the fifty states. One mode of analysis focuses on the degree of election competitiveness among the parties in each state, and the effect of this competition or lack of it on the way parties articulate issues for the public and the way the state government produces programs responding to socioeconomic needs. As we have seen, the national level is characterized by two-party competition and fairly programatic responses to socioeconomic needs by parties once in office. How widely is this pattern reproduced in the states?

Applying the criteria for competitiveness we described earlier, political scientists have developed three measures for state-party competition: (1) the percentage of votes won by each party in elections for statewide offices and the percentage of legislative seats each holds; (2) how long each party has controlled the statewide offices and/or the legislature; and (3) how often control of the executive and legislature has been divided between the parties. Applying these criteria to state elections, Austin Ranney developed an "index of competitiveness" with five major categories: one-party Democratic states, modified one-party Democratic states, two-party states, modified one-party Republican states, and one-party Republican states.

According to his analysis, exactly half the states in this country have two-party systems; seventeen other states have modified one-party systems (nine Democratic and eight Republican); and the eight remaining states have one-party systems (all Democratic). Figure 6–2 shows the geographic distribution of two-party, modified one-party, and one-party states.

Ranney explains that the degree of interparty competition—as well as which party tends to be dominant—is strongly influenced by two basic factors: historical experience and socioeconomic character. In historical terms, the eight one-party Democratic states were all members of the Confederacy. The nine modified one-party Democratic states were Confederate states or border states with strong Southern elements or were settled by Southern emigrants after the Civil War (Arizona, New Mexico, and Oklahoma). The eight modified one-party Republican states were all Union supporters or were settled primarily by Union emigrants (the two Dakotas). These patterns reflect the enduring impact on party identification of such "apocalyptic" events as the Civil War and the Great Depression.[7]

[6] For an excellent treatment of these factors, see Herbert Jacob and Kenneth Vines, eds., *Politics in the American States* (Boston: Little, Brown, 1965).
[7] *Ibid.*, p. 67.

Figure 6-2   The Degree of Interparty Competition in the Fifty States *

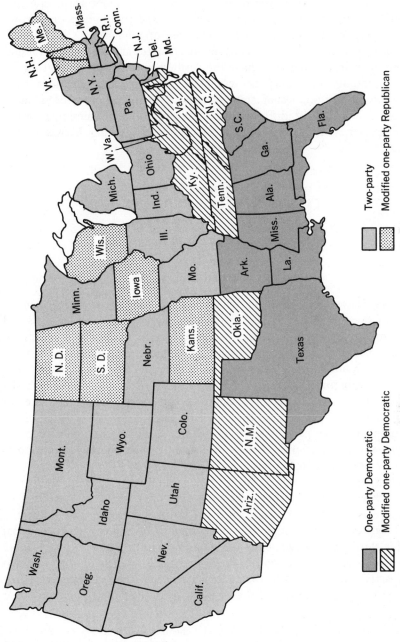

One-party Democratic

Modified one-party Democratic

Two-party

Modified one-party Republican

* Alaska and Hawaii, not included on the map, are both two-party states.

SOURCE: Austin Ranney, "Parties in State Politics," in Herbert Jacob and Kenneth Vines, eds., *Politics in the American States* (Boston: Little, Brown, 1965), p. 66.

In socioeconomic terms, the two-party states are the most urban ones and have "the characteristics usually associated with urbanization: they have the highest median income, the highest percentage of labor force engaged in manufacturing and the lowest in agriculture, and the highest proportion of 'foreign stock' (i.e., immigrants or children of immigrants)."[8] By contrast, the eight modified one-party Republican states are the most rural and the most agricultural, and they have the smallest percentage of Negroes.

These findings on interparty competitiveness in state elections have been supported by studies of state interparty competition in presidential elections. Using slightly different terminology, Joseph Schlesinger found that the 48 states divided as follows in presidential voting between 1872 and 1948:[9]

Two-party states:

Continuously competitive	9
Cyclically competitive	4

One-party states:

Cyclically one-party	16
Predominantly one-party	7
Completely one-party	12

Two-party states were those in which neither party won more than 65 percent of the elections. Of these states, continuously competitive ones had more than 40 percent alternation between parties; cyclically competitive states had between 35 and 40 percent alternation. One-party states were those in which one of the parties won more than 65 percent of the elections. Within this category, cyclically one-party states were those in which the minority party won consecutive elections for short periods of time. In predominantly one-party states the minority party won only isolated victories. Completely one-party states were those in which the majority party won virtually all elections. In these terms, only thirteen states were competitive in presidential elections.

Studies of party competition generally find that lasting multiparty politics (three or more parties contesting elections) is not characteristic of American state politics. Though third parties may sometimes be influential at the local level (for example, the Socialists in Milwaukee), the occasional statewide third-party movements—the Non-Partisan League in North Dakota or the Progressives in Wisconsin—have eventually joined one of the two major parties. In New York, the Liberal party and the Conservative Party wage energetic campaigns, but they cannot elect their own nominees, they

[8] *Ibid.*, pp. 68–69.
[9] Joseph A. Schlesinger, "A Two-Dimensional Scheme for Classifying the States According to Degree of Inter-Party Competition," *American Political Science Review*, Vol. XLIX (December 1955), pp. 1120–29; Sindler, *op. cit.*, pp. 18–19. Alaska and Hawaii were not yet states.

poll less than 10 percent of the votes, and they are really ideological pressure groups on the two major parties in that state.[10] The reasons given in Chapter 5 for the absence of third parties on the national level generally apply at the state and local levels as well; in particular, the prevalence of separation of powers prevents third parties from organizing a whole state government even when their popularity may be strong.

One of the best statements about the general impact of party competition or noncompetition on state political systems was made by Key:[11]

> At the center of the scale the Democratic and Republican parties compete for control of the state government more or less after the fashion of the national parties. As one moves from this central point in one direction, the Democratic party becomes stronger and stronger and the functions of political parties are more and more performed by factions within that party. As one moves in the opposite direction toward the Republican end of the scale, the business of state politics comes to be carried on by factions within the Republican party. Toward the two extremes on the scale parties simply do not function in the sense of providing choices to the electorate between groups of men and sets of policies. In these states elections determine nothing; the essential decisions are made in the nominating processes of the dominant party.

To appreciate this observation, we must study the differences between one-party and two-party politics in operation.

One-Party State Politics

The twenty-five states with one-party politics, like the one-party nations of the Afro-Asian group, are political systems organized around one or two dominant goals, traditions, ideologies, or interests. In the United States the sectional conflict of the Civil War (plus the racial issue) and the predominance of agricultural-rural interests were the two prime bases for our one-party states. Where one-party systems in other nations are sometimes police dictatorships that allow only one faction to operate openly, American one-party states are marked by factions. The two main types of one-party states are two-faction and multifaction systems.[12]

Multifaction states are those in which three or more groups of candidates and their supporters compete in the significant election contests—the party primaries. Most of the Southern states are multifaction states, and Florida and Alabama are often cited as leading examples of this pattern. There is usually no permanent statewide organization behind any of these aspirants.

[10] Sindler, *op. cit.*, pp. 59–66; Frank J. Sorauf, *Political Parties in the American System* (Boston: Little, Brown, 1964), pp. 25–26.
[11] Key, *op. cit.*, p. 290.
[12] This discussion relies on Sorauf, *op. cit.*, pp. 22–26; Sindler, *op. cit.*, pp. 26–44; Key, *op. cit.*, pp. 291–95; and Fred I. Greenstein, *The American Party System and the American People* (Englewood Cliffs, N.J.: Prentice-Hall, 1963), pp. 60–68.

Instead, there is a "free-for-all," "family-friends-and-neighbors" style of politics that is often characterized by flamboyant attempts to capture the attention of the voters by folk-singing, attacking minority groups, refighting the Civil War, and so on. There is usually no clear choice for the voters between liberal and conservative candidates and no coherence in policy issues. The candidate's appeal is based on his personality and his promises of jobs and favors to his friends. This system produces frequently shifting coalitions of politicians and interest groups. After the election, there is less cooperation among state executive officeholders in multifaction states than in two-party systems and more conflict between the governor and legislature.

Two-faction states are those in which two relatively stable cliques of party leaders and supporters develop within the dominant party. The pro- and anti-Long factions in Louisiana, which date from the 1930's, illustrate this situation. The pro-Long faction (named after Huey "Kingfish" Long and his family successors) drew its basic strength from the rural, fundamentalist-Protestant, low-income farmers, with some Negro and labor support added. The anti-Long vote came from the wealthy plantation owners, urban property interests, and the Catholic minority around New Orleans. North Carolina developed similar factions for and against the "Shelby County Dynasty," as did Tennessee for and against the "Boss Crump Machine" of Memphis. Among Republican one-party states, two-factionalism prevailed in North Dakota for some time in recent decades.

The politics of two-faction states resembles two-party competitive states, because there is often a clear liberal-conservative choice for voters, a "ticket" that identifies candidates according to faction, and a bipolar and relatively coherent primary election. The governor also has greater power after election than in multifaction states, and state government is more united than in multifaction states. But two-faction politics differs from two-party government in two ways: First, the levels of voter turnout are lower. And, second, two-faction states do not produce stable ward and precinct organizations, peaceful recruitment and promotion of leaders, or continuing the permanent loyalty of politicians to one faction within the party.

Both types of one-party states, however, share a notable characteristic: their politics favors the well-to-do over the have-nots. Although the primaries are recognized as the decisive elections in one-party states, the fact that they are held at different times from the national elections—which bring national publicity and attention to elections at all levels—has meant that they draw lower turnouts than general elections in two-party states. And it is the poorer, less-educated voters and the racial and ethnic minorities who stay away from the polls. When these groups do vote, they receive fewer cues in one-party states as to the relevant issues and policy directions in state politics; and studies show that the have-nots receive in turn fewer education and welfare services from state government than do lower-income groups in two-party states.[13] In terms of the leading criteria for measuring democracy—coherent election contests, articulation of issues and policy alternatives, and the responsiveness of government to social needs—one-party states perform at significantly poorer levels than two-party states.

Two-Party State Politics

"The fundamental prerequisite" for two-party structures in the states, wrote Key, "is the existence of two complexes of interest with sufficiently divergent objectives to permit them to serve as the foundation for competing parties." [14] These interests may be economic or ethnic or religious. Interests may be organized along "metropolis" versus "countryside" lines, though this division is often another way of expressing a cleavage between urban-wage earners and propertied rural interests or an ethnic division between old settler Protestants and new immigrant Catholics and Jews. Examples of such two-party states are New York (with New York City's Democratic minority-group majority opposing upstate Republicans); Illinois (with Democratic Chicago opposing the downstate Republicans), and Massachusetts (where Boston Democrats oppose the rural Yankee Republicans).

Are there any basic types of two-party state that merit identification? In his recent study of six Midwestern states,[15] John Fenton suggests that there are two main kinds of competitive two-party system: those with "issue-oriented" parties and those with "job-oriented" parties. Fenton identifies three issue-oriented states: Michigan, Wisconsin, and Minnesota, where liberal-labor groups captured the Democratic party after the Second World War and established programatic politics that have defined interparty competition ever since. Let us examine Michigan more closely.

Like Minnesota and Wisconsin, Michigan was Union country during the Civil War. The one-party Republican system that grew out of that heritage lasted until the 1930's, when working-class and new immigrant groups began to shift their allegiance to the Democrats as a result of New Deal economic programs, thus making Michigan a competitive two-party state. A Democrat, Frank Murphy, was elected governor in 1936. However, the Republicans regained state control from 1938 to 1948. The party had a small-town and rural base, coupled with an urban appeal to upper-income voters, professional groups, and the better-educated. Because a strict merit system for hiring state employees (installed in 1941 to restrict party patronage) weakened the interest of job-oriented Republican politicians, issue-oriented leaders from the national automobile corporations located in Detroit were able to take over key positions in the Republican party organization. Their goal was to influence public policy to reduce taxes, hold the

[13] Thomas R. Dye, *Politics, Economics, and the Public* (Chicago: Rand McNally, 1966).
[14] Key, *op. cit.*, p. 295.
[15] John H. Fenton, *Midwest Politics* (New York: Holt, Rinehart and Winston, 1966).

line on public services, attract industry, and offer "better administration" of existing programs.

After the Second World War, the Democratic party organization in Michigan was an "empty shell." There was no large body of Democrats who identified with the party because of its pro-Southern Civil War heritage, and the job-oriented professionals were not attracted to the party because of the 1941 state merit-system law. At this point, a coalition of union leaders from the militantly liberal United Auto Workers joined liberal professional and business people in the state Americans for Democratic Action chapter to take over the Democratic party. The unionists wanted government policies to help the economic interests of unions and workers; the ideological liberals favored egalitarian economic and racial policies. Neither group was interested in government jobs or contracts or in professional party careers.

"The immediate result of the issue-oriented turn of Michigan politics," Fenton notes, "was victory for the Democrats." In 1948, they elected G. Mennen ("Soapy") Williams as governor, and they held the governorship (as well as many federal and local offices) until 1962. Fenton explains that the majority of the Michigan population had become oriented toward the Democrats since the New Deal; what was needed was an effective organization to coalesce that potential vote. Under issue-oriented politics, Michigan's government programs were above average in expenditures for welfare, education, and similar social programs, and the state was a leader in civil-rights measures. In 1962, however, George Romney, formerly president of American Motors and a Republican, was elected governor, and he was reelected in 1964. By this time, a trend toward Republicanism, fiscal economy, and the status quo had begun to grow among the voters in the medium-sized cities, who held the balance of power in the split between urban and rural voters. On this basis, Fenton has predicted that the Republicans will win most of Michigan's competitive elections in the coming decade if they continue to nominate Romney-type, middle-of-the-road candidates.

In Michigan, Wisconsin, and Minnesota, then, issue-oriented competitive politics grew out of factors such as strict civil-service systems that sharply cut state and city patronage, the reduction of one party to an empty shell by repeated defeats at the polls, the existence of well-organized interest groups with the will to take over the moribund party organization, and a division of the electorate between the two major parties along the lines of socioeconomic and political issues.

In Ohio, Indiana, and Illinois, on the other hand, these conditions were not present, and their state politics are what Fenton calls "job-oriented." Let us examine Ohio more closely.

Ohio was a competitive two-party state when the Civil War came, and it has remained so since. Though the state is described as predominantly Republican, it went Democratic in 5 out of 9 presidential elections between 1932 and 1964, and it went Democratic in 5 out of 8 gubernatorial elections between 1946 and 1962. Republicans dominated the state legislature, however, in 7 out of 9 legislative sessions between 1941 and 1963, and Republicans regularly control most of the counties.

The base of the Republican party has been the Union-loyal counties, and its group support has come from farmers, small-town residents, businessmen, Protestants, and some ethnic groups alienated by Woodrow Wilson's policies in World War I, such as the Germans. The Republicans have had a majority in nonindustrial Cincinnati, with its heavy German population and pro-Northern Civil War heritage.

Since the 1930's the Ohio Democrats have been an uneasy mixture of descendants of the pro-Southern elements and the new, post-Depression recruits such as urban liberals, immigrants from eastern Europe, Catholics, and Negroes. Democrats are strong in the northern counties and in industrial cities such as Cleveland, Akron, and Toledo.

The Ohio Republican organization is strong and centrally directed, and the party has substantial ethnic and ideological homogeneity. The concentration of money, jobs, and the heavy Republican vote in Cincinnati gives the party leaders of that city supremacy in the state, but it needs statewide victory to supply the jobs and patronage the party organization depends on heavily. In contrast, the Democratic organization is weak and decentralized. Party leaders have secure patronage bases in the cities, but no one of them is strong enough to dominate the state and they prefer to protect their local positions. The party is highly heterogeneous, containing groups ranging from rural conservatives and Slovenians to low-income urban workers, Negroes, and Jews. While business groups are very powerful in Ohio and support the Republican party generously, labor unions in Ohio are weak in membership and funds, have conservative "old line" leaders who pursue "bread and butter" interests in politics, and have no love for or desire to cooperate with ideological liberals. As a result, professional politicians with a spoils orientation, not an issue-oriented liberal-labor coalition, control the Ohio Democratic party.

Surveys suggest some results of what Fenton calls "issueless politics": many Ohio voters are "bored" by politics, ignorant of state issues, and indifferent to state government. While Ohio business and farm groups identify their interests clearly, working-class and minority groups do not. The Republican party deliberately stresses low-key personality politics to avoid stirring up divisions in the electorate. When Democrats are elected to state office, they are often at least as conservative as the Republicans. An example is Democratic Governor Frank Lausche, who served in 1944–46 and 1948–56. Under these administrations, "job-oriented" politics produces government expenditures for education, welfare, and social services that are below the national average for the states and far below the expenditures of neighboring issue-oriented states. Fenton concluded that job-oriented politics in Ohio produces government programs that reflect the interests of the middle and upper classes, and in this sense such politics resemble the multifaction politics of one-party states. Since Fenton's study there have been signs that changes are under way in states such as Ohio, illustrated by the election of a Negro, Carl Stokes, as mayor of Cleveland in 1967. Nevertheless, the types of party politics in competitive states that Fenton identifies are still useful categories for analysis.

Thus we see that at the state level, the relationship between party systems and socioeconomic factors is reciprocal. The type of party system derives from a state's basic socioeconomic characteristics, but, conversely, the type of party structure influences the expression, growth, and impact of these factors because it produces different election issues, different programs from government, and a different distribution of benefits among interest groups in the state.

LOCAL PARTY POLITICS:
THE TRIUMPH OF ORGANIZATION

Although power in the American party system resides mainly at the state level, it is at the local level—that is, in the counties or cities—that cohesive organization and party discipline are strongest. As Sorauf notes, "the organizational unit of the American party is the county and/or city party. Organizationally the state and national parties are but loose conglomerations of these local parties." [16]

In those counties dominated by a very large city—such as New York—with a huge budget and important political offices that dwarf those of the county, the city organization is the key local unit. But for the great majority of local areas today, the county organization continues to have the political and financial resources to dominate party politics in its territory. The county chairman is much more likely than his state counterpart to control his committee (in terms of choosing and disciplining lower-echelon leaders), and the county organization is likely to speak with a single voice in the councils of the state party.

One source of the cohesion and strength of local parties in the American system is the fact that one-party domination is the rule rather than the exception in most local areas; even when a *state* is competitive, most of its counties may be one-party bastions.

Even in areas of two-party competition, however, local organizations remain strong *so long as* they can win enough elections to carry out their two main functions: first, to provide services and rewards for constituents and party workers and, second, to control the results of the party primaries by capitalizing on the benefits distributed.

[16] Sorauf, *op. cit.*, p. 40.

Party Benefits and Rewards

During the nineteenth and early twentieth centuries, local party organization in the cities was dominated by "machine politics" and the "political boss." In tens of thousands of city precincts, local captains drew their strength from two main groups in the city: native migrants from rural areas and the heavy wave of European immigrants entering the cities during this period. Uprooted from a familiar environment and inexperienced in the complexities of urban life, these groups needed assistance in finding homes and jobs and in coping with the legal and political rules of our system. The machine was able to recruit party workers and aspiring candidates by offering still other tangible incentives—government appointments, government contracts, and nominations for elective office (especially where chances of victory were high).

At the head of the precinct and ward organizations was the city or county boss. Frequently an ethnic-group representative himself, the machine boss might also hold public office (as did Hague of New Jersey, Flynn of the Bronx, and Crump of Memphis). But, even if he did not, he played a key role in nominating candidates and distributing government rewards. The local boss also wielded power in the state and national party organizations because of his ability to mobilize his local organization in statewide and national elections.

Today, party leaders are still active in performing services to recruit voters. A recent survey found that precinct politicians in a New Jersey county performed these tasks for their constituents:

1. Help poorer people get work.
2. Help deserving people get public jobs on a highway crew, in the fire department or police force, or in state positions.
3. Show people how to get their social security benefits, welfare and unemployment compensation.
4. Help citizens with problems like rent gouging, unfair labor practices, zoning, or unfair assessments.
5. Help one's precinct to get a needed traffic light, more parking space, or more policemen.
6. Run clambakes and other get-togethers for interested people even though no political campaign is involved.
7. Help citizens who are in difficulties with the law.
8. Help newcomers to this country to get adjusted and get places to live and work.
9. Work with some of the other party's people to reduce friction and keep the campaign from getting too rough.
10. Help boys with military service problems and advise on the best way to serve.[17]

[17] Richard T. Frost, "Stability and Change in Local Party Politics," *Public Opinion Quarterly*, Vol. XXV (Summer 1961), pp. 231–32.

Modern Services for Constituents

The second major area of the [district] leader's activity is dealing with constituents. Depending upon the area serviced, a leader may have a heavy or light load of constituents *every* Monday and to a lesser extent, Thursday night, fifty-two weeks a year....

A local neighborhood hotspot had repeated trouble with the State Liquor Authority, whose inspectors seemed to be harassing the place looking for a shakedown. Did the leader know anyone at the S.L.A.? He didn't, but he knew a leader who did, the complaint of harassment was made, and the harassment ceased....

A constituent had taken a civil-service exam and passed it, but an ancient matrimonial dispute had led the appointing authority to reject him. Could he get a chance to explain the whole matter in person? He could (though he didn't get the job)....

The residents of a building were going crazy because of excavation for a new apartment house across the street. The racket started at 7:00 A.M. every day, including Saturdays. Could the leader get the contractor to lay off on Saturdays? He could....

A taxi driver had three moving-traffic violations and was about to lose his license. Can we help? Not much....

Once the general counsel of a major oil company (a Republican, by the way, although we never asked anyone their party affiliation—a constituent is a constituent) sought help because a new street light had been put up outside his third-story bedroom window on Beekman Place. It was shining in his eyes all night. Couldn't a shield be placed on the back of the light? It was—and it was carefully adjusted one evening, while the venerable gentleman stuck his head out the window and shouted directions to the man on the ladder.

From Edward N. Costikyan, former district leader in New York County, *Behind Closed Doors*, 1966.

The spread of education, the vastly increased national role in providing welfare, social security, and unemployment benefits, the extension of the civil-service system for government jobs, and the rise in the American standard of living have eliminated many services performed by nineteenth-century machines. But even today, party activists continue to serve as vital intermediaries between a complex government structure and the ordinary citizens who are bewildered by the bureaucratic maze. Party leaders no longer bring baskets of food to hungry families, but they now give expert advice on how to claim welfare, social security, and unemployment benefits. The party may no longer be able to place someone in the fire department on a patronage basis, but it knows when the civil-service examinations are given and where the openings are. While all these services may be legitimately claimed by any individual without party intercession, the fact remains that government agencies often appear unapproachable to the average person.

By contrast, the pool of tangible benefits at the party's disposal to recruit party workers or aspiring candidates has dried up somewhat. In the nineteenth century, party politics was one of the few careers that allowed for rapid upward mobility—particularly for religious and national minorities. Today, there are far more job opportunities in the private sector and more government civil-service and technical positions open on the basis of merit. Thus, the party has fewer jobs to offer and fewer takers for the lower-level posts they do have.

But it is important to note that, despite the decline in their importance, tangible benefits still do play a significant role in both county and city politics. County party organizations, for example, still maintain discipline and power by handing out county road contracts or controlling nominations for such offices as sheriff or county assessor. City parties have had to find new mixtures of tangible rewards to hold their organizations together, and their solutions have ranged from Mayor Daley's highly traditional machine in Chicago to Mayor Lee's more innovative techniques in New Haven. In Chicago, a city that preserves very strong ethnic communities and old-line ethnic leaders, Daley binds these leaders to his party organization by distributing public works and other concrete rewards. The leaders in turn are able to use the playgrounds, hospitals, and municipal pay raises to boost their own prestige and maintain control over their own groups. In New Haven, by contrast, the power of reformist mayor Richard Lee is based largely on his ability to secure substantial federal funds for his programs and then to maneuver key elements within the community into acceptance on the grounds that everyone benefits from comprehensive schemes to solve pressing community problems.[18]

County and city organizations today link the diminished tangible benefits at their disposal with certain *intangible* benefits they offer to a new type of party worker and potential candidate: middle-class and professional groups —particularly among religious and national minorities—who are seeking psychological and social satisfaction in party work. These workers value the chance to be "in politics," to shape the party's ideology, and to influence government policy-making through the electoral process.

The Primary: Test of the Local Organization

What does the county or city organization hope to gain by providing services and benefits for voters and party workers? Its goal is specific and crucial: to deliver the votes for the organization's candidate in the party primaries. It is the precinct, the core unit of both the county and city

[18] Robert A. Dahl, *Who Governs?* (New Haven, Conn.: Yale University Press, 1961).

Getting Out the Vote: Yesterday's Machine

Big Tim's greatest contribution to Tammany power was his organization of "repeaters." He had hundreds of Bowery bums organized in one or two places on election day, and he waited for the reports—"The Fifth District needs two hundred," etc.—and, as each "requirement" came in, Big Tim dispatched a truckload of the required number of bums to the polling place where a henchman went down the line and gave each the name under which he was to vote. The names were usually of those voters who had died between registration day and the election, or of those voters who had not yet voted an hour before the closing of the polls.

Big Tim also had about fifty student barbers working for him on every election day. These barbers performed a great service for Tammany. Here is how it worked. Along about August Big Tim sent word around the Bowery flophouses for the bums to let their beards grow. By election day, Big Tim had at his disposal several hundred Bowery bums, each with a full-grown beard. First, each bum would vote with a full beard under one name. He would then rush to one of the stand-by barbers who immediately clipped off the chin fuzz. So then the bum voted under another name with sideburns, like the Emperor Francis Joseph of the Austro-Hungarian Empire. Then he would rush back to the barber who shaved off the sideburns, and now the bum would vote for the third time with just a moustache; and finally that came off and he would go forth to vote for a fourth time—plain-faced, as Tammany called it.

For this day's work the bum got one dollar, three meals, a pint of whiskey, and, of course, a lesson in civics and good government.

From Harry Golden, *Only in America*, 1958.

organizations, that is primarily responsible for this task, and the stakes of the precinct captain rest almost exclusively on his success in this activity:

> His standing in politics, his place in the organization, and, in most cases, his job at the City Hall or Courthouse, depend upon his ability to carry his precinct in the primaries for the machine candidates. He can afford to lose the precinct in the general election. That will not hurt him much. It may not be his fault. He may be a Democrat in a Republican stronghold and the most he is expected to do is to make a good showing. But there is no excuse for him to lose in the primaries. He must deliver the goods there. If he cannot carry his precinct in the primaries he loses his position as precinct executive, he loses his political pull, and, in all probability, his political place. All hope of promotion in the machine is gone from him.[19]

Though this description was written in 1923, it remains accurate today.

[19] Frank R. Kent, *The Great Game of Politics* (Garden City, N.Y.: Doubleday, 1923), pp. 2–3.

In order to control a predictable number of votes, the precinct captain must know his neighborhood and the people in it; the life of his organization depends on the loyalty of the neighborhood both to him as a person and to the organization. The precinct captain begins with a nucleus of grateful voters who have received party services or rewards. In addition, the precinct leader usually has many personal friends and often many relatives living in the immediate area. He selects the polling place (for which a rental is paid) and several pollwatchers (who get modest fees). Because voting turnouts in primaries are generally so low, even a small number of reliable voters delivered by the precinct captain will generally give victory to the organization's candidate.

The primary is particularly important because party leaders recognize that neither machines nor bosses can be expected to determine the outcome

---

Getting Out the Vote: Today's Organization

Once the polls open, the captain's job is to "pull" the vote. We would make desultory efforts in the afternoon, but I soon found that all that did was tire the workers out. The real push would begin about 3:00 P.M. on a general-election day when the polls close at 7:00 P.M., and at 6:00 P.M. on primary day (when people are just home from work) when the polls close at 10:00 P.M. The runner would go to the poll, compare his copy of the master list with the watcher's list, and cross off the names of those who had voted on his copy.... Then he would hurry back to the command post, cross off these same names on the copy of the list there, so the worker on the phone could get busy calling those who had not yet come in.

This process would be repeated every half hour or so. Meanwhile, another runner or I would head out to climb the stairs in search of those who had no phones, and either remind them in person or leave messages under their doors if they were not at home. While we were at it, we would also leave notes under the doors of those who had not answered their phones. We would keep right on with this operation until about ten minutes before 10:00 on those primary nights when the contest was really hot. As a rule we would all be quite spent by about 9:20. It would become harder to decide who might be worth another prod. We would be deflated, absorbed by our failures—those voters we had not succeeded in "pulling."

It is astonishing how deep is the impact of one irritated lady who answers her phone sharply and says she cannot possibly vote today because she has dinner guests. Of course, we do become as grateful as long-lost puppy dogs to those sleepy voices that say "Oh, I'd forgotten all about it," and then turn up as golden living bodies, sockless and Democratic, five minutes later at the polls.

From Frances H. Costikyan, district captain in Manhattan, "The Captain in the Election District," in Edward N. Costikyan, *Behind Closed Doors*, 1966.

of the general elections in November, where the turnout is much larger than in the primaries (except in one-party states). Although organization support is important to national and statewide candidates, the bloc of votes that professional politicians can count on are but a small fraction of the total electorate in these large elections. Ward and precinct chairmen and committeemen can encompass only a limited number of people in their web of favors and obligations; after that point their control—and influence— diminishes rapidly.

Of course, a precinct captain's standing in the party is enhanced if he can carry his area for the party's candidate in the general election. And the precinct organization is often valuable in the areas of close two-party competition because it can mobilize potential party voters who might ordinarily not vote at all. But no precinct organization can hope to decide general elections solely with its deliverable vote.

The importance of the primary reveals a good deal about the internal structure of the parties. There are, first of all, two kinds of primary contest. In one the voter is asked to choose his party's candidates in the general election to be held in November. This primary, in other words, determines the candidates for *public* office. The other kind of primary contest elects the officials for *party* positions, such as delegates to a state convention or precinct or ward committeemen. Sometimes the two types of contest are related, such as when a particular aspirant for a party post announces his support for a particular individual seeking the nomination for a public position, but there need not be such a connection. The importance of primaries is that they bring to a head the factional and personality conflicts that mark the internal life of the parties.

There are constant struggles for position and power within the ranks of the party. In theory, the precinct leader loyally supports his ward leader, who in turn supports the county leader, who in turn supports the state chairman. In practice there are frequent defections and intraparty contests. The party organization in the Fourth Ward, to use a hypothetical example, is responsible for delivering the necessary votes in the primary to elect county committeemen who will support the county chairman. In return for delivering enough votes to ensure that the organization candidate wins, the leader of the Fourth Ward is allowed to dispense county patronage and related services in his neighborhood.

However, sooner or later a group within the Fourth Ward will become dissatisfied with both the county chairman and the subservient ward leader. This group will put up an "antiorganization" slate in the next primary and run its own candidates for the county committee. The county organization will expect the "regular" ward leader to defeat these insurgents, and he will try his best to do so, since his tenure in party office depends on his controlling the primary vote. The insurgents will make the most of their claim that they are opposing "the machine," and they will try to increase the primary turnout by appealing to party supporters who do not normally vote in the primaries. It is not easy for the opposition group to recruit enough support to overwhelm the loyalists who are prepared to line up behind the regular organization. Nevertheless insurgents often do win, usually because they persuade some precinct leaders to join their camp and bring their followings with them. In 1963, for example, every district leader in New York County was a man who got his position by bolting from the regular organization at one time in his career and running against the prevailing leader. Most insurgents are not "reformers" in the sense that they intend to abolish "machine" politics. What they want, usually, is to displace those ahead of them and become the party organization themselves. But such insurgent victories in the primaries are the exception rather than the rule. The odds favor the regular party organization.

"MACHINES" AND DEMOCRACY: PUBLIC CONTROLS OVER PARTY FUNCTIONS

The basic party functions are performed at both the state and local levels by an élite group of politicians. These activists are headed by a party leader who is usually the local or state organization boss, a national party chieftain, and often an ethnic-group leader as well. This élitist pattern is reflected not only in urban machines but in rural courthouse organizations, suburban county machines, or statewide factions such as the personal organizations of Southern political figures.

Many social scientists and political leaders regard this development as inevitable—power in large organizations naturally gravitates into a few hands. This view has not been accepted by the American public, however, whose distrust of professional politicians and belief in popular control over the electoral process have led it to view the influence of party leaders in this area as a frequent threat to democratic government. On the other hand, the public has been unwilling to establish an official government agency at the national or state level to run all nominating conventions and to conduct elections. The American political tradition has always upheld the private and amateur aspects of party nominations and campaigns, and the public is suspicious of a step that would take power away from the private sphere and might well link political parties more closely to the government. Because of this respect for private organization, the public has also been unsure of precisely how much democracy it should insist on *within* the party organizations.

The result of this public ambivalence has been a series of reform campaigns to regulate alleged abuses of power by party leaders. These regulations have attempted to institute public control over both the nomination of candidates and the campaign and election process. Not surprisingly, party leaders have responded to these challenges by developing new ways to maintain organizational control over these basic party functions. Thus, a hallmark of American politics since soon after the Civil War has been a continuing tension between public efforts to institute democratic controls over party processes and the party ability to use these reforms to improve its own competitive and organizational position. Let us examine the results of this dynamic in the procedures for nominating candidates and for conducting campaigns and elections.

Public Control over the Nominating Process

The first mechanism used in the United States for nominating candidates was the caucus, a gathering of self-elected notables to decide which candidates would be presented to the electorate. As early as 1763, in the preparty era of American colonial life, John Adams wrote in his diary that the Boston Caucus Club "meets at certain times in the garret of Tom Dawes, the Adjutant of the Boston regiment. . . . There they smoke tobacco till you cannot see from one end of the garret to the other. . . . selectmen, assessors, collectors, fire-wards and representatives, are regularly chosen before they are chosen in the town." [20] By 1800 the legislative nominating caucus, composed of all the party's members in the two legislative houses, was the dominant means of nominating candidates for state and federal executive office.

With the expansion of suffrage and the entrance of new groups into the political system during the 1820's, however, the Jackson forces attacked "King Caucus" as an aristocratic and antidemocratic system. They succeeded in replacing it with the nominating convention, which promised to allow masses of party members to participate in local conventions that would select the delegates to the larger county, state, or national conventions.

The nominating convention was supreme in American politics until 1910–12. In the decades following the Civil War, however, the rise of strong party machines at state and local levels resulted in domination of the conventions by the party bosses. Sometimes domination was achieved by tight discipline; and sometimes bribery and "muscle" were added to the process, since this was an era of widespread corruption in American political life. In many areas, one party controlled the state, and mediocre candidates were offered as the voter's only choice. Again, democratic reform movements— this time the Populists and Progressives of the 1890's and early 1900's—rose to champion more democratic nomination procedures. Their efforts led to

[20] Quoted in Greenstein, *op. cit.*, p. 39.

state laws eliminating the convention in all but a few states and replacing it with the direct primary system; this remains our dominant method for nominating candidates today.

The primary system

In the direct primary, a public nominating election is held in which either all party members or all qualified voters (the system varies from state to state) vote on who will be the candidate of that party at the general election.

The direct primary has in several ways democratized the nomination process. First, it has broadened popular participation: the one-fourth to one-third of the electorate who vote in the primaries represent a significantly larger proportion than the number of voters who participated in the convention process. Second, the appeals of rival candidates are now directed at the electorate at large, rather than exclusively to the small élites of party leadership. Third, radio, television, and press coverage of primaries increases the force of public opinion at this stage. And, finally, the primary system is an invitation to those who are outraged over political corruption and inefficiency to try their luck at challenging the organization's candidate. The primary has thus brought the proliferation of amateur reform groups who hope to mobilize public resentment against "the machine" and thus win key primaries. If an energetic reform committee can rouse several thousand normally apathetic voters, it may be able to outvote the handful of party regulars who are loyal to the local organization.

This is precisely what happened, for example, in the Twenty-third Congressional District of the Bronx in 1964. For thirty years the district had been the personal base of Representative Charles A. Buckley, leader of the Bronx organization. While he was occasionally challenged in primary contests, his precinct captains always managed to deliver enough votes for his renomination in that safe Democratic district. Buckley, however, was often not in Washington for roll-call votes in the House of Representatives, and he loaded his congressional payroll with party workers who remained in the Bronx. In the eyes of many New Yorkers he was a highly visible political delinquent. Finally, in 1964 a true reformer arose to contest Buckley's hegemony. Jonathan Bingham hardly looked like a Bronx politician: his background was Anglo-Saxon, his education Ivy League, and his political career had been statewide and national rather than local. Buckley and his followers laughed off this challenger, assuming that ethnic loyalty (in this case, Irish), machine voting, and low turnout would defeat Bingham easily.

Nevertheless Bingham won the June primary. The most interesting lesson of his victory lies in the voting statistics. There were approximately 250,000 adults in the Twenty-third Congressional District, virtually all of them eligible to vote. Yet less than 20 percent customarily bothered to vote in the primary. On this occasion, Buckley's precinct workers brought in about

22,000 voters, ordinarily quite enough to carry the election. However, the amateur reform organization was able, by diligent doorbell-ringing, to rouse 26,000 Democrats to vote for Bingham—citizens who for the most part would ordinarily have sat out a primary contest.

Two factors make regular party organizations vulnerable to insurgent takeover of precinct, ward, and county committees. First, few party leaders conduct a periodic audit to determine whether jobholders who gained their positions through patronage are actually serving the organization with the necessary zeal:

> Ties of friendship, blood, and community militate against the political discipline essential to the administration of patronage. The resulting lax and ineffective use of political jobs, the failure to appoint job-holders and supervise their activities with only the welfare of the party in mind, points to the possibility that one may very well need more of the arts of public administration to run a patronage than a civil service system.[21]

Second, precinct workers in areas undergoing sociological and ethnic change tend to rest on their laurels, assuming that their customary delivery of a hundred or so voters is all that is required. In particular, many are not enthusiastic about canvassing newcomers to their neighborhoods.

> Relatively few precinct workers canvass their areas vigorously or frequently. Once they acquire a patronage job and become a member in good standing of the local political club or ward headquarters, they often concern themselves more with the social and fraternal advantages of membership (getting away from the wife a few nights a week, playing cards with "the boys," and swapping political yarns). . . . Precinct workers canvass principally their friends and a small group of voters who are well known and who can be relied upon. This renders most city machines very vulnerable to demographic changes which break up established contacts and introduce new elements into the neighborhood.[22]

But are reformers willing and able to consolidate their gains after a one-shot victory over the machine? For many well-meaning enthusiasts, a single hard-fought campaign is exhilarating but not the sort of thing they want to repeat every year. Regular-organization workers may be cut down to size by a primary defeat, but are not necessarily out for good; sometimes they can marshal their resources against the reformers a year or two later and resume control of the local party organs. Political amateurs, moreover, may find it difficult to devote the time and energy necessary for serving constituents on a year-round basis. Many of them, for example, work at nine-to-five jobs in another part of the city, and they are not always readily available to intervene on behalf of a voter who has a problem with some public agency. Nevertheless amateurs have shown surprising

[21] Frank J. Sorauf, "Patronage and Party," *Midwest Journal of Political Science*, Vol. III (May 1959), pp. 117–18.
[22] James Q. Wilson, "The Economy of Patronage," *Journal of Political Economy*, Vol. LXIX (August 1961), p. 377*n*.

success in many parts of the country. Most notable are the five thousand clubs in California that comprise the Democratic Council, an organization that enters and endorses candidates in the primaries alongside the regular party hierarchy. California also has an analogous Republican Assembly representing voter sentiments that are not always heard in established party councils. These groups have made headway because many Californians are newcomers to the state and have neither ethnic nor economic ties to the party organizations. Thus, neither the Republicans nor the Democrats have entrenched machines based on long-standing loyalties. Much the same condition prevails in many new suburban communities all over the country—the influx of amateurs into the county has overwhelmed the old court-house professionals. It remains to be seen, however, whether the "amateurization" of politics will develop into a significant national trend.

The preprimary convention

Despite its encouragement of reformers on the political scene, the primary system has been criticized by political scientists as contributing to the decentralization of American politics by lodging effective power over nominations (especially legislative nominations) at the local level. Concomitantly, the primary system undermines the power of state and local party organizations to present to the electorate the candidates they consider best qualified and most representative of the party's interests. As Sorauf has summarized this view:

> By opening the nomination of party standard-bearers to a broad and often undefined party clientele, the direct primary threatens the party in three crucial ways. First, it weakens party control over nominations, with the possible results of candidates disloyal to the party, candidates without good electoral prospects, and the poorly balanced ticket. Often the candidate best able to win in a primary election dominated by small numbers of motivated partisans is not the candidate best calculated to make a broad appeal to the general electorate. Second, since the candidate may pass the independent test of the primary on his own, he may feel and express little debt to the party. Should he be elected, the party may find him uncooperative on patronage matters or unresponsive to party urgings on program and policy. If the legislator can win nomination without party help, or despite its opposition, he has robbed the party of its most powerful sanction over him. Third, the direct primary is the most powerful divisive force within the American parties. Primaries often pit party leader against party leader, party voters against party voters, often opening deep and unhealing party wounds. They also dissipate party financial and personnel resources. Party leadership usually finds that it has no choice but to take sides in a primary battle, the alternative being the possible triumph of the weaker candidate.[23]

In several states—including Massachusetts, Utah, and New Mexico—party leaders have tried to overcome the divisive effects of the primary and

[23] Sorauf, *Political Parties in the American System,* pp. 101–02.

regain organizational control through the *preprimary convention.* This convention, consisting of delegates from various counties, is called before the primary to endorse one candidate for each office as the official party nominee—the one the party feels best represents its statewide interests. Anyone in the state, of course, is allowed to circulate petitions and get his name on the primary ballot, but the party assumes that most registered party voters do want to know who the official candidate is and who the challengers are.

In practice, if the convention is sufficiently united to put forth a candidate who attracts wide support from many sectors of the state party, he is likely to overcome his opposition in the primary easily, and the state party leadership will be strengthened. However, if the state organization is badly split, the preprimary convention only increases intraparty conflict. As Table 6–1 shows, this pattern is illustrated by the effect of the preprimary convention on the Democratic and Republican organizations in Massachusetts. The convention, instituted before the 1952 elections, failed to mend the divisions within the Democratic organization: the number of Democratic

Table 6–1   Contests in Democratic and Republican Primaries for State-wide Offices in Massachusetts, 1950–60

	NUMBER OF DEMOCRATIC CANDIDATES								
	1950 *	1952	1954	1956	1958	1960	1962	1964	1966
Governor	1	1	2	2	1	7	2	4	2
Lt.-Governor	5	6	1	3	1	2	2	1	2
Secretary of State	8	1	1	2	1	3	1	1	1
Treasurer	1	7	3	5	2	6	3	4	1
Auditor	1	1	1	1	1	2	1	6	2
Attorney-General	4	4	1	2	2	1	5	1	3
U.S. Senator	–	1	3	–	1	3	2	1	3
Totals	20	21	12	15	9	24	16	18	14

	NUMBER OF REPUBLICAN CANDIDATES								
	1950 *	1952	1954	1956	1958	1960	1962	1964	1966
Governor	6	1	1	1	3	1	1	1	1
Lt.-Governor	5	1	1	1	1	1	1	1	1
Secretary of State	7	1	1	1	1	1	1	1	1
Treasurer	2	2	1	1	1	2	2	1	1
Auditor	2	1	1	1	1	1	1	1	1
Attorney-General	5	1	1	1	1	1	2	1	1
U.S. Senator	–	1	1	–	1	1	2	1	1
Totals	27	8	7	6	9	8	10	7	7

* The preprimary convention was instituted in both parties just before the 1952 primaries.

candidates running in primaries for each statewide office did *not* decrease after the convention went into effect. The Democrats' inability to achieve unity through the preprimary convention in Massachusetts received national attention in 1962, when Edward McCormack, state attorney general and nephew of House Speaker John McCormack, waged a bitter primary campaign against the choice of the preprimary convention, Edward Kennedy.

On the other hand, the preprimary convention was very successful in strengthening the statewide organization of the less fragmented Republican party: from 1952 on almost all Republican primaries were uncontested.

Public Control over Campaigns and Elections

Popular efforts to control campaigns and elections have produced a network of legal regulations covering the requirements for registering and voting, the form of the ballot, the timing of elections, and party campaign expenditures. Yet it is in this area that party organizations have been most resilient in overcoming challenges to their hegemony, and party leaders have been able to transform some of the regulations instituted as popular controls to advance their own organizational and competitive positions.

Voter registration laws

Studies have shown that the more difficult registration is made (by requiring literacy tests or a long time to establish residence, or by keeping the polls open only for a short period), the lower the voter turnout will be. Idaho, the state with the most lenient registration and voting laws, had an 80.7 percent turnout in the 1960 presidential election. Mississippi, with the most restrictive laws, had a 25.5 percent turnout. Non-Southern states with restrictive laws are also low-turnout states: Alaska, for example, had a turnout of 45 percent and Arizona had 54.5 percent.[24] The disparity among the states in their registration and voting laws reflects the different statewide balances between public control and party strength: party organizations prefer restrictive regulations that keep turnout low and thus increase the relative influence of party activists and partisans; reform or antiorganization movements prefer lenient regulations that introduce into the electorate voters more concerned with issues or with candidate personalities than with party labels.

The form of the ballot

Political scientists have found that the form of the ballot presented to voters at election time can have a significant effect on the outcome of elections.

[24] Lester W. Milbrath, "Political Participation in the States," in Jacob and Vines, *op. cit.*, p. 46.

Figure 6–3   The "Indiana Ballot" (1964)

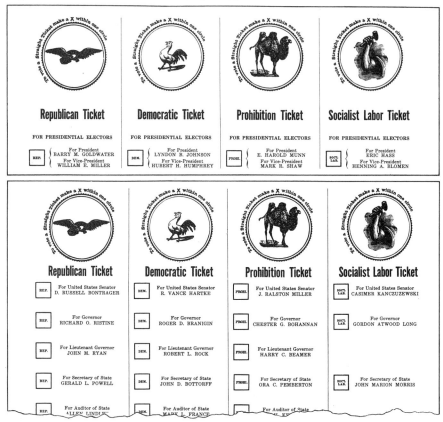

In 42 states, a *long ballot* is specified by law. Instituted by the Jacksonian movement in the 1830's to increase popular influence over elected office-holders, the long ballot places many major state executive offices on the election ballot rather than leaving them to appointment by the governor. The remaining eight states elect only the governor, or the governor and one other executive. The long ballot thus produces a list of anywhere from six to sixteen statewide offices for the voters to fill. The effect of the long ballot has been to increase decentralization of state politics by encouraging each candidate for state executive office to run his own campaign and minimize his allegiance to the party or his fellow candidates, unless an unusually popular candidate heads the ticket. To appreciate the effect of such a system, imagine what would happen if the long-ballot system were used in national elections, and the Secretaries of State, Defense, the Treasury, and other departments were popularly elected. Each would try to develop distinctive appeals to the electorate and would be far less cooperative with the President than under the present appointive system.

Figure 6–4   The "Massachusetts Ballot" (1964)

ELECTORS OF PRESIDENT AND VICE PRESIDENT.	To vote for a Person, mark a Cross X in the Square at the right of the Party Name or Political Designation. X

	GOVERNOR	**Vote for ONE**
	JOHN A. VOLPE – of Winchester~~~~~~Republican	
	JOSEPH D. WARD – of Fitchburg~~~~~~Democratic	
	HENNING A. BLOMEN – of Somerville~~~~~Socialist Labor	
	GUY S. WILLIAMS – of Worcester~~~~~~Prohibition	

To vote for Electors of President and Vice President under any one of the following Party Names or Political Designations, mark a Cross X in the Square at the right of such Party Name or Political Designation. X

Vote for ONE

	LIEUTENANT GOVERNOR	**Vote for ONE**
	EDWARD F. McLAUGHLIN, Jr. – of Boston~~~~~Democratic	
	AUGUSTUS G. MEANS – of Essex~~~~~~Republican	
	THOMAS MARATEA – of Greenfield~~~~~~Prohibition	
	FRANCIS A. VOTANO – of Lynn~~~~~~Socialist Labor	

DECKER and **MUNN**~~~~~~Prohibition

	SECRETARY	**Vote for ONE**
	EDWARD W. BROOKE – of Boston~~~~~~Republican	

HASS and **COZZINI**~~~~~Socialist Labor

	KEVIN H. WHITE – of Boston~~~~~~Democratic	
	FRED M. INGERSOLL – of Lynn~~~~~~Socialist Labor	

KENNEDY and **JOHNSON**~~~~~Democratic

	JULIA B. KOHLER – of Boston~~~~~~Prohibition	

NIXON and **LODGE**~~~~~~Republican

	ATTORNEY GENERAL	**Vote for ONE**
	EDWARD J. McCORMACK, Jr. – of Boston~~~~~Democratic Candidate for Re-election	
	GEORGE MICHAELS – of Newton~~~~~~Republican	
	AUGUST O. JOHNSON – of Medford~~~~~Socialist Labor	
	WILLIAM D. ROSS – of Brookline~~~~~~Prohibition	

To vote for a Person, mark a Cross X in the Square at the right of the Party Name or Political Designation. X

| | | |

SENATOR IN CONGRESS	**Vote for ONE**
LEVERETT SALTONSTALL – of Dover~~Republican Candidate for Re-election	
THOMAS J. O'CONNOR Jr. – of Springfield~~~	

TREASURER	**Vote for ONE**
JOHN THOMAS DRISCOLL – of Boston~~~~~Democratic	
WALTER J. TRYBULSKI – of Chicopee~~~~~Republican	
WARREN C. CARBERG – of ~~~~~~Prohibition	

The arrangement of candidate names on the ballot also influences elections by giving one party an advantage over another and by maximizing or minimizing the local impact of national issues. The chief reason for this is that there are many names on the ballot, and the average voter is usually unfamiliar with all but a few of them. The "Indiana ballot," used in about half the states, arranges all the candidates in vertical party columns. Most states using this form allow the voter to support a "straight ticket" for all offices by simply making a mark or pulling a lever at the top of the party column. Even if a one-for-all vote is not allowed, the "Indiana ballot" nevertheless makes it easy for a voter to run his pencil down a column to vote a straight party ticket. The "Indiana ballot," therefore, encourages party-line voting. It strengthens the dominant party by exploiting the habitual loyalties of a majority of the electorate, and it maximizes the importance of national races because voters tend to decide first on their choices for the national offices at the top of the ticket; in party-line voting a popular national candidate can help pull many other candidates of his party into office with him. Con-

The Case for Greater Party Responsibility

Our system of government is most successful when party responsibility is clearly defined and when political parties are vigorous in their organization, personnel, and policy formulation. Deleting the party square [on the ballot] tends to weaken the internal structure of political parties since it places a premium on individual action by candidates at all levels, regardless of political affiliation. Because of this a political party is in a poor position to offer aid to candidates for the lower positions or to persuade them to work for platform programs. The result is that elections tend to become popularity contests in which issues are submerged and public policy takes a back seat to public relations. Diminishing the importance of political allegiance and philosophy simply strengthens what most people consider an undesirable tendency of modern politics to be "personality-oriented" and, in turn, dominated by publicly invisible special interests.

Leading students of American government contend that we can best improve our state government in America by strengthening party responsibility, rather than by weakening it. In my judgment, a vote based primarily on the political philosophy of a candidate, indicated by his party allegiance, is to be preferred to a vote based solely on personality or ethnic background or social connections.

From Governor Kenneth M. Curtis of Maine, veto message to the Maine Senate and House of Representatives, *Advance Journal and Calendar of the Senate*, April 1967.

versely, a bad showing by the man at the top hurts all the candidates on his party's ticket. Candidates for lower offices like state auditor or children's-court judge may not be widely known, but they can ride in on the party label.

The "Massachusetts ballot" encourages the voter to consider each contest and each set of candidates on their own merits. The candidates running for each office are listed separately, in alphabetical order. If there are five contests, the voter must make five separate decisions. In 1964 in Massachusetts, for example, someone who wanted to vote a straight Republican ticket would have had to mark the fourth line in the list of presidential candidates, the first line in the list for governor, and the second line in the list for lieutenant governor. Such hopping around encourages voters to split their tickets, to consider candidates as individuals rather than as the bearers of party standards, and to consider local races separately from national ones. Candidates of the weaker party, especially if they have strong personalities, naturally prefer the "Massachusetts ballot."

This simple difference in the rules governing the marking of the ballot has a substantial effect on the way the voter casts his vote. We find, in the states which make it relatively easy for the voter to mark a straight ticket, that the number of straight tickets marked is some 20 percent higher than in

"Which booth is for the
Republican party?"

Herbert Goldberg in the *American Magazine*
Ben Roth Agency

those states where the ballot requires a series of separate decisions among
the candidates for each of the various offices.[25]

The timing of elections

The timing of elections also influences party fortunes. The dates for choosing
presidential electors and United States senators and congressmen are fixed
by federal law. Elections to fill federal offices occur every two years, on
the first Tuesday after the first Monday in November. States and localities,
however, are not obliged to elect their officials at these times. In some cases,
to advance local autonomy state and local elections are scheduled for different dates from federal elections dates. Five states have complete separation
of state and federal elections: they choose their governors and their state
legislators in odd-numbered years (national elections, of course, are held in
even-numbered years). Nineteen states choose their governors (but not
their state legislators) in odd-numbered years. Fourteen states have two-
year governorships that alternate between presidential and off-year congressional elections. Finally, twelve states have direct state-federal alignment, electing four-year governors in presidential years.[26] There is no
direct correlation between the degree of party competitiveness in a state and
its choice of election timing.

When state and local elections coincide with national elections, the local
candidate's prospects are inevitably affected by the national races. Popular
candidates for national office can help to increase the votes cast for the
whole party ticket, but local allegiances and issues tend to be submerged.

[25] Angus Campbell, "Recent Developments in Survey Studies of Political Behavior," in
Austin Ranney, ed., *Essays on the Behavioral Study of Politics* (Urbana, Ill.: University of Illinois Press, 1962), pp. 32, 83.

[26] *Ibid.*, pp. 81–82.

The turnout is large because of the interest in national offices; thus local organization leaders have to contend with big, relatively unstable electorates rather than the smaller and more predictable electorates that a purely local election would bring to the polls. Though electoral mechanisms such as these are introduced in the name of honesty, simplicity, voter convenience, and emphasis on local issues, their effect, not surprisingly, is usually to reduce the electoral risks of those responsible for instituting them. Thus, the establishment of off-year elections in Pennsylvania helped the Republican party to achieve state and local victories in the 1930's despite the New Deal Democratic sweep in national voting, and the same system helped the Virginia Democratic party to survive the Eisenhower victories in that state.

Campaign financing

Because candidates have always required sizable sums of money to run their election campaigns, the question of who puts up these funds and what obligations the parties incur by accepting them has been a major issue in the struggle for popular control over American party life. "Good-government" spokesmen would like campaigns to be conducted inexpensively so that parties would not be indebted to special interests such as businessmen, labor unions, or syndicates. On the other hand, the traditional public regard for the private sphere makes it suspicious of the prospect of official government subsidies for election campaigns.

Campaign costs are enormous throughout this country, and they are not significantly lower for primary campaigns in one-party states than they are in the general elections of two-party states. But, although all campaign costs are high, the price of waging a campaign still varies widely from state to state. At one extreme, a statewide election campaign in California in the mid-1950's cost those with the central campaign responsibility between $300,000 and $500,000. With 4 million votes cast, this represented a cost of 8 to 13 cents a vote. At the other extreme, the first and the second statewide primaries in Texas during the same period each cost between $500,000 and $1 million; with 1½ million votes cast, this came to between 33 and 66 cents a vote.[27] More recent estimates are that it costs about $2 million to win a gubernatorial primary in California and $½ million to $1½ million to run for mayor of Chicago. All these costs keep rising as a result of increased television and advertising costs, the increased use of public-relations firms, polls, and surveys, and the increase in independent campaigning by candidates.

It is important to recognize, however, that the effects of financial resources on the outcome of elections is smaller than observers often think. Money does not automatically buy elections. Many other factors—issues,

[27] *Ibid.*, pp. 78–79, drawn primarily from Alexander Heard, *The Costs of Democracy* (Chapel Hill, N.C.: University of North Carolina Press, 1960).

"What are you, some kind of a fresh-air nut?"

This contemporary cartoon criticizes the reliance of both national parties on large contributions from a few "big interests."

From *Straight Herblock,* Simon & Schuster, 1964

group identifications, personalities, the times, and so on—powerfully influence elections. But, if the other factors are evenly balanced, the party that out-spends and out-campaigns the other is likely to win.[28] This is especially true in primaries: John Kennedy, for example, was greatly aided by his superior financial resources in his state-by-state primary battles against Hubert Humphrey in 1960.

On the whole, the Republican party has a national advantage over the Democrats in campaign financing because of the Republicans' close ties with a rich and obliging business community. Moreover, the Republicans can generally secure this money without sacrificing their party control or their electoral independence. The Democrats, on the other hand, must rely on labor unions, wealthy individuals, and similar resources for cash, and they are almost always short of funds in their campaigns.

Both parties, however, rely mainly on large donations from a few contributors rather than a large number of small contributions. In order to prevent the parties from becoming too closely tied to large donors, two federal statutes—the Corrupt Practices Act of 1925 and the Hatch Act of 1940—included rules to regulate financing of campaigns for the House of Representatives, the Senate, and the Presidency. These statutes limit the expenditures that can be made by the candidates themselves, the expenditures and receipts of the Democratic and Republican national committees, and the maximum contributions of private citizens. Moreover, these laws pro-

[28] Ranney, *op. cit.*, p. 80.

hibit corporations and labor unions from making direct contributions to candidates.

Similarly, all but three states have passed legislation to regulate campaign financing for state and local offices. Forty-five states require that public statements of all expenditures be filed with the state. Thirty-three states require public filing of all receipts. Thirty-two states limit the total expenditures of the candidates themselves, and twenty states go so far as to limit the contributions that can be made by organizations or individuals *on behalf of* a candidate. Some states have passed specific prohibitions as well: 33 states outlaw campaign contributions by corporations; 10 states outlaw contributions from people or businesses holding state franchises, liquor licenses, and the like; and 5 states outlaw contributions from labor unions.

The problem with both federal and state regulations is that by and large they are quite ineffective. Basically, the financial limits set by these statutes, which were adopted decades ago, do not realistically reflect the greatly increased costs of today's campaigns. As a result, federal and state stipulations are evaded through several tactics. First, candidates or organizations may indicate only part of their actual expenditures or receipts when they file public statements. Second, the limits on spending by any one organization are circumvented by establishing a number of committees to help a specific candidate. None of the committees exceeds the legal limit on expenditures, but together they offer the candidate far more money for his campaign than the law technically allows. For example, federal law stipulates that a candidate for the House of Representatives may spend no more than $5,000 on his campaign, and a candidate for the Senate may spend no more than $25,000. Yet in 1960, one candidate for the House reported total expenditures of $62,228, spent mainly through auxiliary committees; similarly, a Senate candidate that year had a total of $103,734 spent on his behalf.

Third, federal and state prohibitions against contributions by corporations are evaded when corporation executives make sizable donations to various candidates and committees as individuals. While labor-union leaders are less apt to make sizable personal contributions, they can use union money for the "political education" of their own members. The AFL-CIO's Committee on Political Education, for example, cannot use union money to campaign among the general public, but it can use these funds to campaign among its union members on behalf of particular candidates.

These inadequacies of the present regulations have led to efforts to encourage individual donations to political parties and thus to minimize large-scale donations by wealthy individuals and groups. In 1967 the House and Senate considered administration-sponsored legislation embodying widespread election reforms, which would remove ceilings on total campaign expenditures and instead limit the contribution of each donor to $5,000— given to one candidate or spread among several—in each election campaign;

provide direct federal funds for presidential campaigns; and give individual contributors a tax credit for small donations. In the Senate a tax-incentive provision was proposed to allow a 50 percent credit on political contributions up to $50 in any one year, applicable to any candidate for local, state, or national office or any political committee formed to support such a candidate. Also proposed was a provision for federal subsidy of presidential campaigns to give assistance, based on congressional estimates of campaign cost limits, to candidates who did not accept private contributions for a prescribed period of time before and after the election. Republicans were united in opposition to the tax-incentive provisions because their party has not suffered from the serious campaign deficits that have plagued Democrats in recent years. Southern Democrats opposed federal funding for presidential candidates because they feared increased administration control over local affairs. Other opponents questioned the provisions for review and control over party expenditures, the possibility of unfair discouragement of third-party efforts, and potential presidential independence of state and local party organizations. At this writing, the bill is still pending in Congress.

The real problem is to reduce the parties' reliance on a small number of very large contributions. The consensus among political scientists is that it is unrealistic to expect federal and state legislation to do more than effectively publicize the receipts and expenditures of campaigns.

SUMMARY

In formal terms, our two major parties appear to be hierarchies of closely linked units, with power ascending upward from the precinct organizations through the county organizations and the state organizations to the national party committees.

In fact, however, power in our party system lies predominantly at the state and county levels, and both county and state organizations have substantial autonomy from the state and national organizations, respectively. Each layer of the party organization performs the crucial party functions for the offices at its own level—controlling the nomination of candidates, raising and distributing funds, conducting election campaigns, and distributing patronage and other rewards. Moreover, it is the state party chieftains, rather than the national-committee chairman, who control the national convention, and, similarly, it is the local party heads who usually wield power within the state arena.

The decentralization of our party system is a logical outgrowth of our federal system, our separation of government powers, and the emphasis of our political culture on the unique needs of each community and state in a diverse nation. Nonetheless, state and local organizations willingly form temporary confederations every four years to elect a President, partly because the national and state elective offices carry significant tangible benefits and partly because the fate of candidates at the top of the ticket affects the fortunes of state and local candidates as well.

Throughout our history, our national parties have met three criteria of competitiveness: they have divided the popular vote closely in most elections; the opposition party has posed frequent and serious electoral threats to the party in power; and the opposition has won at least occasional victories in any given period.

At the state level, party politics varies greatly from state to state, due to the absence of tight national control over state and local party organizations and to the autonomy of state governments. States can be classified as *one-party* or *two-party* systems according to the degree of party competition in the state. About half the states have two-party systems; about one-third have modified one-party systems; about one-sixth have truly one-party systems.

The degree of party competition within a state is influenced by the state's historical experience and its socioeconomic character. Two-party states tend to be the most urban, with the highest median income and the highest percentage of laborers and immigrants or their descendants. Modified one-party Republican states are the most rural and agricultural, with the smallest percentage of Negroes. The states of the Deep South owe their one-party Democratic systems to the historic impact of the Civil War and Reconstruction.

One-party states tend to be organized around one or two dominant interests, goals, ideologies, or traditions that unite a majority of the state's population. All one-party states have factions, and these groups tend to perform the regular party functions; in such states it is not the statewide elections but the party primaries or nominating conventions where the crucial choices are made. One-party states can be classified as *two-faction* or *multifaction* systems. Multifactional politics produces charismatic candidates and promises of patronage, rather than a clear liberal-conservative choice between candidates or coherent policy issues; shifting coalitions of politicians and interest groups; and increased conflict between the legislative and executive branches of the state government.

Two-faction systems, on the other hand, often resemble two-party competitive states in offering more clear-cut policy issues and liberal-conservative choices of candidates. However, two-faction systems still have substantially lower voter turnouts than two-party systems and generally lack a stable precinct organization.

In two-party systems, state parties function similarly to those at the national level in competing for control of state offices. Such systems are generally based on a significant statewide cleavage of interests along economic, religious, or ethnic lines. Two-party politics tends to be more programatic than one-party politics, with higher levels of voter interest and turnout. Within two-party systems political scientists have found "issue-oriented" parties and "job-oriented" parties. Issue-oriented politics is characterized by greater interest-group activity, a division of voters along socioeconomic and political lines and diminished party patronage. Job-oriented politics is characterized by the leadership of professional politicians who control significant patronage and by heterogeneous voter support for each party.

Though party power is greatest at the state level, party organization is most cohesive at the local level, partly because one-party domination is the rule in most localities. Local party organizations perpetuate themselves by serving two key functions. First, they provide tangible and intangible services to constituents, and they offer rewards of patronage—though diminished today—for party workers. Second, the local parties capitalize on the support they gain through their services in order to deliver the vote for the organization's candidate in the primary. The ward and precinct organizations do their most important work at this stage, where a small number of predictable votes is apt to bring victory for the organization because voter turnout is low. Some primaries determine the party's candidate for *public* office, while others choose officials for *party* posts. When these two types of primaries are related, factional conflicts often come to a head. Though insurgents occasionally triumph in the primaries, the regular party organization usually comes out the winner.

The American public has traditionally distrusted the professional party politician and the "closed" aspects of party politics, but we have been unwilling to link parties more closely to the government by setting up official rules for nominating and electing candidates. Instead, the public has helped to institute a series of reforms, which party leaders have sometimes turned to their own organizational advantage.

The public has tried to reform the nominating process by establishing the direct-primary system, used by most states today. The primary has democratized the nominating process in several ways: it has enlarged the electorate participating in the choice of party nominees; it has forced candidates to appeal to a broader audience; and it has helped amateur reform groups at times to defeat the party organization at the polls.

However, the primary system has accentuated the problems of decentralization by putting greater power over nominations at the local level and by undermining the functions of the party organization. Even the *preprimary convention*, adopted by party organizations in a few states to counteract these effects, has not been successful for parties with significant factionalism.

The public has also helped to establish controls over aspects of campaigns and elections, and here, too, party organizations have often been able to turn these regulations to their own advantage.

State voter registration laws vary from very lenient to very strict, reflecting the different balance in each state between party strength and public pressure. Party organizations prefer strict registration laws because they keep voter turnout low and maximize the influence of regular party supporters.

The form of the ballot and the timing of elections also affect party organization. About half the states use the "Indiana ballot," which encourages voting a straight party ticket and thus strengthens the dominant party in the state. The "Massachusetts ballot" helps the state's weaker party by encouraging voters to choose each candidate on his own merits. When state and local elections are held at the same time as national elections, the coattail effect of national candidates has maximum impact, voter turnout is increased, and local issues and loyalties are subordinated.

The public has traditionally been suspicious of the large sums of money required to finance campaigns, but our desire to keep parties separate from government has prevented our instituting official subsidies for running campaigns. Both major parties depend on large contributions from a few donors, rather than on many small contributions. Federal and state regulations of campaign financing have been ineffective and often unrealistic, and the problem today remains: how to reduce the reliance of both parties on a few major contributors?

THE
DYNAMICS
OF
VOTER
CHOICE

7

*Elections have been called the "great collective
events" of democratic society. Masses of
citizens go to the polls, pass judgments on their
political leaders, and determine who will hold
power until the next election. When the citizen
votes in this fashion, he must relate himself—
his interests, his loyalties, and his perceptions
of the candidates, the issues, the parties, and
the times—to the ballot choices confronting
him. What have social scientists discovered
about the basic characteristics of the American
electorate in this voting process? What factors
influence the individual's decision about
whether to participate? What factors influence
the partisan choices of those who do vote?
Finally, how do these findings square with our
ideal of a rational and responsible electorate?*

THE FLOW OF AMERICAN ELECTIONS

Though our largest and most visible electoral contest occurs only once every four years, when the President is selected, the American political system quietly generates a steady flow of elections year after year. Unlike the voters in many other democracies, who are presented with elections once every three or four years, the American voter is asked to go to the polls once or even twice a year.

The frequency of elections in this country stems partly from the separate jurisdictions and political offices that our federal arrangement gives the state and local governments; partly from the staggered terms of office established for executive and legislative branches by federal and state constitutions; and partly from the desire of state and local political leaders to hold their elections at different times from the national election, in order to minimize the effect of national issues in state and local elections.

Thus, in November 1964, the American voter chose a President and Vice-President, a United States congressman, and, in thirty-five states, a United States senator (since one-third of the Senate comes up for election every two years). In about half the states, the voter was also asked to elect a variety of state and local officials (governors and other elected executive officials, state legislators, mayors, city councilmen, sheriffs, etc.) and, in some states, to decide questions being put to local referendum ("Should the legislature authorize a state lottery with revenues for public education?").

The preferences of voters in presidential elections carry major political implications. In 1964, for example, 70.6 million Americans—62 percent of the adult population—chose between two candidates for President: the Democrat, President Lyndon B. Johnson, and the Republican, Senator Barry Goldwater of Arizona. The key issues of the campaign were, first, whether to maintain or escalate our war effort in Vietnam; second, whether to continue federal social-welfare programs or cut them back; and, third, whether to continue or reduce federal intervention to prevent infringement of civil rights by state and local authorities. Goldwater championed a strongly conservative tradition, while Johnson defended a middle-of-the-road and liberal tradition.

The 1964 election produced a landslide in which Johnson received an unprecedented popular-vote majority of 61.3 percent and carried 44 of the 50 states. This landslide exerted a dramatic "coattail" effect on the results of the 1964 congressional, state, and local elections, because many voters make their choice for President first and then vote for the congressional and local candidates on his ticket. Thus the Democrats also won 17 out of 25 governors' races, captured control of 35 state legislatures, and gained a huge majority in both houses of Congress. The public mandate implicit in Johnson's electoral triumph enabled him to win enactment in the Eighty-

An Apocryphal Story: The Coattail Effect

[Hymie] Shorenstein was a Brooklyn district leader forty or fifty years ago [who] ran his district with the traditional iron hand. One year he nominated a young man, who was making his first run for office, for the assembly. [The young man discovered after nomination that the party's campaign literature and posters concentrated on Al Smith, the Democratic candidate for President; the young assembly candidate was neither mentioned in print nor called upon to make speeches at the rallies. In desperation he went to see Shorenstein.]

"... I've been running for six weeks," pleaded the candidate, "and nobody knows it. No speeches, no rallies, no literature, no nothing. What should I do?"

"Go home," said Shorenstein.

"But—"

"Go home," repeated Shorenstein.

As the young man, dismissed, rose and started out the door, Shorenstein relented....

"Young man," he said. "You ever been to the East River?"

"Yes," came the answer.

"You see the ferryboats come in?" asked Shorenstein.

"Yes."

"You see them pull into the slip?"

"Yes."

"You see the water suck in behind?" the litany continued.

"Yes."

"And when the water sucks in behind the ferryboat, all kinds of dirty garbage comes smack into the slip with the ferryboat?"

"Yes."

"So go home and relax. Al Smith is the ferryboat. This year you're the garbage."

From Edward N. Costikyan, former district leader in New York County, *Behind Closed Doors*, 1966.

ninth Congress (1965–66) of more liberal socioeconomic legislation than had been passed at any comparable period since the crisis era of the first New Deal Congress (1933–34).

In the odd-year state elections of November 1965 and 1967, no federal offices were on the ballot, but voters were asked to choose governors, state legislators, mayors, and other local officials and to decide various referenda issues. Odd-year elections also have significant political implications—in particular, they offer clues to each party as to the trends in the electorate's preferences that may shape upcoming presidential elections and party contests at state and local levels.

For example, the 1965 election victory of liberal Republican John V. Lindsay as mayor of New York City, normally a heavy Democratic strong-

"I'm sure it has a lot of significance, if I only knew what."

Odd-year state elections are studied carefully by party leaders, but their portents are not always clear.

© 1967 Herblock in the Washington *Post*

hold, suggested that attractive candidates and liberal programs—especially in future presidential elections—could produce Republican successes even in urban areas where minority-group voters were concentrated.

In 1967, bitter mayoralty fights took place in Gary, Indiana, and Cleveland, Ohio—both involving Negro candidates running on the Democratic ticket in what were normally heavily Democratic cities. Both Negroes—Richard Hatcher in Indiana and Carl Stokes in Cleveland—defeated their opponents by winning overwhelming pluralities among Negro voters, who turned out more heavily than the whites, and by carrying 10 to 20 percent of the white vote. But the fact that a majority of the white, traditionally Democratic voters crossed over to the Republican side rather than see a Negro chosen as mayor suggested that the race issue would exert a major influence on traditional party voting lines during the next several years.

In the off-year national elections held in November, 1966—halfway between the presidential elections of 1964 and 1968—voters were asked to choose an entire United States House of Representatives, a third of the United States Senate, and various state and local officials, as well as to decide referenda questions. The results of the 1966 elections were significant in several ways. First, the Republican party was able to revive the two-party system that had been eclipsed by the extraordinary Johnson landslide of 1964. The Republicans gained 3 new Senate seats, 47 new seats in the House, and 8 new governorships—a victory that went beyond the gains normally expected for the minority party in the off-year elections, when the President is not on the ticket. Moreover, Republican prospects for the 1968 presidential election were significantly enhanced by the statewide or national victories of a number of strong possible Republican candidates for President or Vice-President: governors such as George Romney of Michigan, Nelson Rockefeller of New York, and Ronald Reagan of California; and United States senators such as Charles Percy of Illinois and Mark Hatfield of Oregon.

Finally, the 1966 elections suggested that the Ninetieth Congress would not be so docile as its predecessor in approving new Johnson legislation and that the conservative Republican–Southern-Democratic coalition (which had often prevented passage of socioeconomic legislation) would be revived in the 1967–68 session.

In addition to these November elections, contests to choose local school-board members and special district committees or to pass on bond issues are held at other times during the year. Thus, the American citizen is continually being called upon to vote in significant electoral contests that raise issues directly affecting his personal and group interests. Elected officials, party leaders, and interest groups carefully watch the outcomes of these elections, and, indeed, important modifications in executive programs and legislative actions often occur in response to the "voter mood" expressed in electoral results.

How do Americans respond to these calls to vote, and what factors influence their preference for one set of candidates and policies over another?

THE AMERICAN ELECTORATE AS A WHOLE

During the past three decades, political scientists, sociologists, and social psychologists have made significant advances in studying voting behavior scientifically. A variety of research techniques has been developed, from analysis of voting statistics in key election districts in order to measure changes in group or regional voting patterns over time, to preelection and postelection in-depth interviews of representative samples of the national voting population.[1] With such techniques, social scientists have identified a

[1] For the classic works, see Paul F. Lazarsfeld, Bernard E. Berelson, and Hazel Gaudet, *The People's Choice* (New York: Columbia University Press, 1948); V. O. Key, Jr., *Southern Politics in State and Nation* (New York: Vintage, 1949); Bernard E. Berelson, Paul F. Lazarsfeld, and William N. McPhee, *Voting* (Chicago: University of Chicago Press, 1954); Angus Campbell, Gerald Gurin, and Warren E. Miller, *The Voter Decides* (Evanston, Ill.: Row, Peterson, 1954); and Angus Campbell, Philip Converse, Warren Miller, and Donald Stokes, *The American Voter* (New York: Wiley, 1960), and *Elections and the Political Order* (New York: Wiley, 1966).

set of characteristics of American voting behavior that represents the foundation for understanding the electoral process in our political system:

1. *The participation in voting in the United States is relatively low.* "Despite the great public interest aroused by a presidential contest," the authors of *The American Voter* observe, "our national elections bring less than two-thirds of the adult population to the polls." [2] (It has averaged little more than 60 percent for presidential elections in recent decades and just over 40 percent for congressional elections.) Figure 7-1 shows these percentages from 1950 to 1966. In local elections for school boards, bond issues, local referenda and the like, held apart from national and statewide elections, turnouts range from 20 to 30 percent, rising to 50 percent levels only when the most heated political, racial, or religious issues are generated by an election.[3]

Voting turnout is substantially higher in other democratic nations. In recent national elections, the turnout has been 77 percent in Great Britain, 83 percent in Israel, 88 percent in West Germany, and 93 percent in Italy.

Our lower turnout can be explained partly by legal and personal factors. Careful estimates are that 3 to 5 percent of our adult population is prevented from voting because they have moved out of their state or community during the year and thus cannot satisfy residence requirements for voting in the national election.[4] Most states require that prospective voters register months in advance of a general election; such early registration discourages potential voters who lack the incentive to register when political activity and issues are far less intense than at election time. In European countries, voters have permanent national voter-identification cards; to vote, they merely show up on election day. Much of the differential between American and European voting turnout is explained by this deliberately cumbersome system set by American state laws. Some nonvoting is explained by the heritage and continuing residue of deliberate discrimination against potential Negro voters in the South. Federal-court decisions and voting acts, registration drives by civil-rights groups, and a general rise in the socio-economic level of the Negro community have increased Negro registration and voting sharply in the South in the past decade (Southern Negro registration rose from 25 percent of the eligible Negroes in 1956 to 46 percent in 1966), but the leading study of Southern Negro voting concludes that a combination of cultural and political factors still inhibits Negro voting participation.[5] However, since Southern Negroes represent only about 13 percent of the American adult population (a figure being reduced annually

[2] Campbell, *et al.*, *The American Voter*, p. 89.
[3] Alvin Boskoff and Harmon Zeigler, *Voting Patterns in a Local Election* (Philadelphia: Lippincott, 1964), pp. 17-21.
[4] Campbell, *et al.*, *The American Voter*, p. 90n.
[5] Donald R. Matthews and James W. Prothro, *Negroes and the New Southern Politics* (New York: Harcourt, Brace & World, 1966).

Figure 7–1   Voting Turnout in Presidential and Congressional Elections, 1950–66

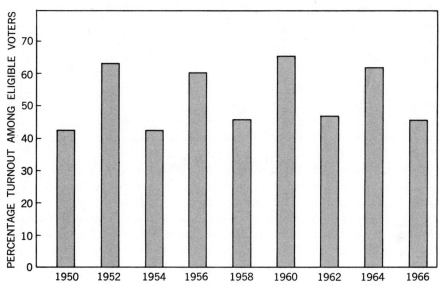

SOURCE: *Statistical Abstract of the United States*, 88th ed., Table 532 (1967), p. 377.

by Negro migration out of the South), discrimination against Negro voters in the South accounts for only a few percentage points in the overall national-turnout figures.

Finally, personal factors—illness on voting day, bad weather, business trips away from the home community and the like—obviously affect turnout. But these factors are also present for citizens in those democratic nations—some highly industrialized—with much higher voting turnouts.

Some political scientists have argued that our relatively low turnout rates reflect the population's general satisfaction with the way the American system is operating; that is, a large segment of our citizenry does not vote because they do not believe that this political act has vital consequences for their lives. In fact, Seymour Lipset has observed that *high* turnout is sometimes "a symptom of the decline of consensus." For example, voting turnout was extremely high in Germany and Austria just before these democracies broke down and the countries turned to fascism. Furthermore, argues Lipset, a "sudden increase in the size of the voting electorate" may signify a breakdown in effective government and in the regular party system; under such conditions the new voters injected suddenly into the voting process will have "social attitudes [that] are unhealthy from the point of view of the requirements of the democratic system." [6] Those who believe that our low turnout reflects our general consensus about politics would contend that our present levels of voting participation, coupled with the other means of participation available in our political system (such as membership in political interest groups), provide a stable and appropriate base for representative democracy.

On the other hand, some political scientists have noted that political participation through both voting and group memberships is heavily concentrated among the more well-to-do and the better-educated groups in American society; they question whether the low-turnout groups—the poor, the least educated, and the low-status minority groups in the population— are properly represented in our system.

We will return to this issue later, but the key finding to note here is that about 40 percent of our eligible voters in presidential elections and about 60 percent in off-year elections do *not* participate.

2. *The American electorate has a low emotional involvement in national elections.* Elections in many democratic nations generate high emotional involvement for much of the electorate. These people believe that each election could make important differences in their lives by affecting their property, freedom, or social status within the society.

In contrast, many Americans see elections as events that will *not* make a major difference in their lives. The high popular consensus on values and procedures that we described in Chapter 1 as a basic characteristic of the American political culture, coupled with the relatively similar policy positions taken by our two major parties (in contrast to the divergent and even conflicting positions among Western European parties, for example), leads many Americans to believe that their interests will be served even if they do not vote and even if the opposition party should win the election. Political scientists refer to this as the "low salience" of national politics for the American electorate. Later, in our detailed discussion of voting behavior, we will discuss which sectors of the electorate do tend to feel that their vital interests are involved in national elections and which sectors tend to regard elections and government policy either as unimportant or as unlikely to change their situation.

3. *Many voters lack familiarity with the leading issues, government policy toward them, and party positions on them.* Careful studies of voter-information levels have shown that a large proportion of the electorate is unfamiliar with both the facts and the political significance of leading issues in election campaigns.

One set of opinion polls found that only 55 percent of adult Americans knew how many United States senators there were from his state; only 47 percent knew the length of a United States representative's term; only 40 percent knew how many justices served on the Supreme Court; and only

[6] Seymour M. Lipset, *Political Man: The Social Bases of Politics* (New York: Doubleday, 1960), pp. 227–29.

"Nixon? He's wonderful, too. They're *all* wonderful—wonderful, warm people, and great, great Americans."

Most Americans have a low level of ideological and issue orientation in national elections.

Drawing by Stevenson
© 1967 The New Yorker Magazine, Inc.

23 percent could state correctly one provision of the Bill of Rights. Polls also show that leading Cabinet, congressional, and party leaders are less well known to adult Americans than are sports, comic-strip, and show-business celebrities. When the 1960 presidential campaign was under way, a third of the public could not name the Republican vice-presidential nominee and 6 percent could not name *any* of the four candidates for President or Vice-President.[7]

In one of the most detailed studies of voter-information levels, the Michigan Survey Research Center study of 1956 asked a cross-section of the electorate a set of questions about the most publicized, leading issues of public policy in the 1956 presidential campaign. All the questions were phrased simply, to let the respondents register their attitudes on each policy issue and state whether they knew what the federal government was doing with regard to it. Those interviewed were told that it was quite proper to indicate that they did not have an opinion on that question, if such were the case. Table 7–1 shows the survey's findings.

On the average, between half and two-thirds of the electorate held opinions *and* said they knew what government was doing on that issue.

To probe further the degree of familiarity about issues, the survey went on to ask those who satisfied these two conditions whether they knew the differences between the political parties on these issues and therefore could identify the party closest to their own views on that question. Though there was considerable variation from issue to issue, with party differences on domestic issues receiving greater recognition than those on foreign-policy issues, the survey found that on the average, only 40 to 60 percent of the *informed* segment of the electorate could identify party positions. Thus, only one-third of the national electorate held an opinion, knew what the

---

[7] These findings are reported in Fred I. Greenstein, *The American Party System and the American People* (Englewood Cliffs, N.J.: Prentice-Hall, 1963), pp. 12–14.

Table 7-1   Levels of Voter Knowledge in the 1956 Presidential Election

Issue	No opin- ion	Hold opinion but do not know what government is doing	Hold opinion and know what gov- ernment is doing	Total
Foreign policy				
Give aid to neutral countries	28%	19%	53%	100%
Send soldiers abroad	20	13	67	100
Economic aid to foreign countries	17	16	67	100
Act tough toward Russia, China	20	11	69	100
Avoid foreign involvement	14	15	71	100
Friendliness toward other nations	12	10	78	100
Domestic policy				
Firing of suspected communists	16	39	45	100
Leave electricity, housing to private industry	30	19	51	100
Segregation of schools	12	34	54	100
Influence of big business in government	28	18	54	100
Influence of unions in government	25	20	55	100
Insure medical care	12	29	59	100
Cutting taxes	19	18	63	100
Government guarantee of jobs	10	23	67	100
Racial equality in jobs and housing	14	19	67	100
Government aid to education	10	23	67	100

SOURCE: Angus Campbell, Philip Converse, Warren Miller, and Donald Stokes, *The American Voter* (New York: Wiley, 1960), p. 174.

government was doing on the issue, and recognized the relevant differences in party position. The general explanation of these findings is that many Americans have such a high commitment to their private concerns—family, job, religion, recreation, sports—that they ignore or "screen out" the barrage of reporting on public issues in the mass media and avoid acquiring information on them in books, from organizations, or in conversation.

However, these findings on factual knowledge and issue familiarity are subject to one important qualification. When a segment of the population or a particular organized group is directly affected by a political issue, its members become much more aware of this issue than of others, and they turn out in greater numbers to protect their position. A Negro voter may have neither factual nor structural knowledge of government issues, but he knew in 1964 who was "for" and "against" expanding Negro equality, just as senior citizens in 1964 knew who was "for" and "against" medical care for the aged.

4. *Ideological positions are weak among American voters.* Ideology is usually defined by social scientists as a structured and abstract perception of political problems, interests, forces, and events; it adopts a theory of social cause and effect and features a belief in the need for long-range plans or policies to protect or advance the cause believed in. How many American voters see the political world and the voting act in these terms?

In the most thorough study of the ideological factor in the electorate, the Michigan Survey Research Center found that only 2½ percent of their cross-section sample of the electorate and only 3½ percent of their sample of actual voters in the 1956 presidential election held political views that could be considered ideologically oriented.[8] These were people who "talked in terms of the liberal-conservative continuum, or one of the narrower domains of abstract content involved in current ideological controversy: trends in the relationship between federal power and local autonomy, the fate of individual incentive under government 'dole,' and the like." An example of an interview with a woman living in a Chicago suburb will indicate how generous the survey analysts were in bestowing the label of "ideological" on interviewer responses.

(I'd like to ask you what you think are the good and bad points about the two parties. Is there anything in particular that you like about the Democratic Party?) No. *(Is there anything at all you like about the Democratic Party?)* No, nothing at all.

(Is there anything in particular that you don't like about the Democratic Party?) From being raised in a notoriously Republican section—a small town downstate—there were things I didn't like. There was family influence that way. *(What in particular was there you didn't like about the Democratic Party?)* Well, the Democratic Party tends to favor socialized medicine—and I'm being influenced in that because I came from a doctor's family.

(Is there anything in particular that you like about the Republican Party?) Well, I think they're more middle-of-the-road—more conservative. *(How do you mean, "conservative"?)* They are not so subject to radical change. *(Is there anything else in particular that you like about the Republican Party?)* Oh, I like their foreign policy—and the segregation business, that's

[8] Campbell *et al.*, *The American Voter*, p. 249.

a middle-of-the-road policy. You can't push it too fast. You can instigate things, but you have to let them take their course slowly. (*Is there anything else?*) I don't like Mr. Hodge. (*Is there anything else?*) The labor unions telling workers how to vote—they know which side their bread is buttered on so they have to vote the way they are told to!

(*Is there anything in particular that you don't like about the Republican Party?*) Mr. Hodge! (*Is there anything else?*) I can't think of anything.[9]

The Michigan survey went on to develop a second category: near-ideology.[10] This included persons who used terms like "liberal" and "conservative" as general labels for the parties; who mentioned some ideological issues, such as "federal control of utilities" or protection of "individual rights"; or who referred to the Democrats as favoring "liberal legislation for the people" or a better "standard of living" for "the working class of people." The survey found that 9 percent of the electorate sample and 12 percent of the voter sample demonstrated these qualities of near-ideology.

Adding the respondents in the categories of ideology and near-ideology together, the Michigan study found that only 12 percent of the electorate sample and 15 percent of the voter sample had an ideological perception of the political world.[11] Table 7–2 summarizes these levels of conceptualization among voters in 1956. If the Michigan study is sound, 85 percent or more of American voters lack a substantial ideological orientation in their voting behavior.

5. *Party identification is the most important factor affecting a voter's behavior over time.* Most high-school civics texts and a good deal of American patriotic oratory describe the American citizen as someone who votes for "the man" or "the issues" rather than for "party labels." Yet a host of election studies shows that the psychological identification of voters with one of the major parties constitutes the single most durable, significant, and predictable factor in shaping the political perceptions and voting decisions of the great majority of American voters. The Michigan center interviewed samples of the electorate over a twelve-year period in order to discover what percentage of the voters regarded themselves as affiliated with either party and what the actual distribution of party identification was among voters. Table 7–3 on p. 240 shows the results.

Note in this table that the various levels of party identification remained roughly the same over twelve years even though some of the interviews were conducted just before the presidential election, some just before the off-year congressional elections, and some in periods between such elections. The general finding of the table as to the high level of partisan affiliation in the population becomes even clearer if we consolidate the figures for one year.

[9] *Ibid.*, p. 228.
[10] *Ibid.*, p. 230.
[11] *Ibid.*, p. 249.

Table 7–2   Levels of Conceptualization Among Voters in 1956

Classification	Percentage of total sample	Percentage of voters
Ideology		
Ideology	2½	3½
Near-ideology	9	12
Group Benefits		
Perception of conflict	14	16
Single-group interest	17	18
Shallow group benefit responses	11	11
Nature of the times	24	22
No issue content		
Party orientation	4	3½
Candidate orientation	9	7
No content	5	3
Unclassified	4½	4
	100	100

SOURCE: Angus Campbell, Philip Converse, Warren Miller, and Donald Stokes, *The American Voter* (New York: Wiley, 1960), p. 249.

In 1964, for example, 74 percent of the respondents regarded themselves as Democrats and Republicans, and another 12 percent considered themselves "independent" Democrats or Republicans. Only 10 percent regarded themselves as complete "Independents."

The partisan loyalties expressed in these voter self-descriptions are quite stable for the great majority of the electorate. Most voters (two-thirds in the Michigan sample) go through life from their first vote to their last identifying with the same party; a majority (56 percent in the Michigan sample) have never crossed party lines in a presidential election.

The importance of party identification lies in its heavy influence on a person's decision on whether to vote, on his perception of policy issues, and on his final choice of candidates. "Identification with a party," the Michigan studies concluded, "raises a perceptual screen through which the individual tends to see what is favorable to his partisan orientation." [12] The stronger a voter's party identification, the more completely he filters out aspects of issues or candidates that do not jibe with his party's position. A direct correlation has also been found between the voter's identification with a party and his expressed and measurable psychological involvement in political affairs.

[12] *Ibid.*, p. 133.

Table 7-3 The Distribution of Party Identification in the United States, 1952–64

	Oct. 1952	Sept. 1953	Oct. 1954	April 1956	Oct. 1956	Nov. 1957	Oct. 1958	Oct. 1960	Oct. 1961	May 1962	Aug. 1962	May 1964
Strong Democrat	22%	22%	22%	19%	21%	21%	23%	21%	26%	25%	23%	24%
Weak Democrat	25	23	25	24	23	26	24	25	21	24	24	22
Independent Democrat	10	8	9	6	7	7	7	8	9	7	7	7
Independent	5	4	7	3	9	8	8	8	10	9	11	10
Independent Republican	7	6	6	6	8	6	4	7	5	4	5	5
Weak Republican	14	15	14	18	14	16	16	13	13	15	16	17
Strong Republican	13	15	13	14	15	10	13	14	11	11	11	11
Apolitical (do not know)	4	7	4	10	3	6	5	4	5	5	3	4
Total	100%	100%	100%	100%	100%	100%	100%	100%	100%	100%	100%	100%
Number of Cases	1,614	1,023	1,139	1,731	1,772	1,488	1,269	3,021	1,474	1,299	1,317	1,465

source: Angus Campbell, Philip Converse, Warren Miller, and Donald Stokes, *Elections and the Political Order* (New York: Wiley, 1966), p. 13.

Conversely, the Michigan studies had this to say about the "independent voter":

> Far from being more attentive, interested, and informed, Independents tend as a group to be somewhat less involved in politics. They have somewhat poorer knowledge of the issues, their image of the candidates is fainter, their interest in the campaign is less, their concern over the outcome is relatively slight, and their choice between competing candidates, although it is indeed made later in the campaign, seems much less to spring from discoverable evaluations of the elements of national politics.[13]

6. *Despite the importance of party identification, the voting decisions of many Americans—and indeed their party identifications as well—are heavily affected by psychological and group-membership factors.* Civic texts and popular myth have also stressed that voters ought to be individuals whose basic criterion for bestowing their vote is "the public interest"—not "narrow" personal or group interests. Chapter 5 has shown, however, that Americans tend to view the public interest as an extension of their group interests, and it suggested that, except in national emergencies, it would be virtually impossible to define a concept of "public interest" that all Americans would agree upon. Election studies show that in fact few voters have a concept of general public interest in mind when they pull the lever in the voting booth. The Michigan survey found that 45 percent of its voting sample acknowledged making their decisions on election issues in terms of securing benefits to certain basic groups to which they belonged, and 22 percent made their decisions in terms of the "goodness" or "badness" of the times, as measured by its effect on them and their families.[14]

Thus, surveys of the American electorate as a whole reveal: low participation in elections in comparison with other democratic systems; low levels of familiarity with leading issues, government policies, and party positions; low levels of ideological orientation among voters; low emotional involvement in national elections; the central influence of party identification in structuring the vote; and a heavy role for psychological and group factors in influencing voter choices. Laymen and professionals may argue about the causes and meaning of such characteristics, but any informed analysis of American voting behavior must begin with these givens.

INFLUENCES ON THE INDIVIDUAL'S VOTING DECISION

So far, we have been looking at the characteristics of the American electorate as a whole. But what makes the individual American decide whether

---

[13] *Ibid.*, p. 143.
[14] *Ibid.*, p. 249. The remaining 33 percent divided into 15.5 percent who had ideological or near-ideological conceptions and 17.5 percent with no issue content.

or not to vote? And what factors shape the direction of his choice when he does cast a ballot?

To begin, we must recognize that voting is only one form of a citizen's political involvement. It falls along a spectrum of activity that ranges from highly passive, such as receiving political stimuli by not turning off a political discussion program when it happens to appear on the television screen after a favorite Western, to highly active, such as running for public office or heading a political party organization. Robert Lane has noted that the act of voting has certain prerequisites.[15] The citizen must: (1) relate himself to society (be aware of the fact of the election, its date, etc.), (2) affirm the value of voting (accept the fact that elections matter and are not sham procedures), (3) implement a political emotion (take action rather than remaining passive in his attitude), (4) make a concrete decision between the contenders, and (5) arrange for the voting act (plan to cast a vote, meet legal requirements, and expend the necessary time and energy).

Thus, a complex set of psychological and social forces shape the voting decision. Though social scientists have worked intensively to identify these factors and apply them to groups within the electorate, there is still much in voting analysis that must be treated tentatively and cautiously. In this section we will discuss the available voting-behavior studies under a scheme encompassing five types of factors: categoric, sociological, psychological, political-legal and issues and candidates. *Categoric* factors define basic population categories into which an individual fits. In this perspective, a person might, for example, be described as male, thirty-five, white, Irish-Catholic, a college graduate, a salesman, a suburban dweller, and so on. Most members of each category tend to share certain predilections and attitudes, depending on the issues and circumstances involved. *Sociological* influences are those arising from a person's direct face-to-face relationships with others in his daily life, from family members and work associates to local community figures whom he knows and who know him. *Psychological* factors are introduced with a person's political socialization in childhood, and they form his conception of his role in the political system. Such factors include a person's view of society and his sense of his power, duty, and self-interest in the election process. *Political-legal* factors—registration laws, community pressures, or the degree of interparty competition—are those that can either facilitate or impede voting turnout and can also affect the voter's partisan choice by favoring one party over the other in a given election area. Finally, *issues and candidates*—that is, a voter's judgment on public-policy questions and the personalities of the contending candidates—also play a role in the voting decision.

Figure 7–2 shows the components of these five types of factors and indi-

---

[15] Robert E. Lane, *Political Life* (New York: Free Press, 1965), p. 47.

Figure 7–2   Basic Factors Shaping the Voting Decision

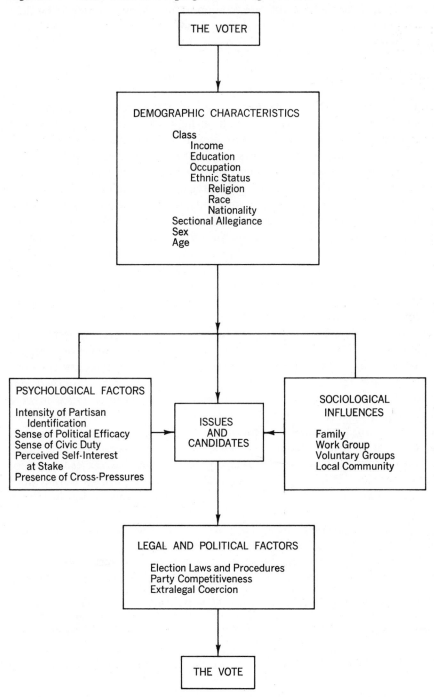

cates graphically how they influence (a) whether an individual will vote, and (b) which party or candidate to support in a given election if he does vote.[16] Let us begin by examining more closely the factors influencing voting turnout.

Voting and Nonvoting

Table 7–4 shows which categoric, sociological, psychological, and political-legal factors are associated with a high turnout among American voters and which are associated with lower turnout. As we see, a profile of the high-turnout voter consists of the following characteristics: categorically, he is generally at upper-class levels of society in income, education, occupational status, and ethnic prestige. In sociological terms, such a voter is closely integrated into community life: he is a long-time resident, a member of community groups, and the like. Psychologically, he has strong party identification, faith in the effectiveness of his vote, political self-confidence, and a lack of cross-pressures—that is, temporary conflicts—among his categoric identifications. Finally, in the political-legal sphere, he resides in a state whose laws, customs, and interparty competition stimulate electoral competition. The reverse characteristics produce the profile of the low-turnout voter.

A few of the factors shown in the table are so powerful as to affect turnout even when they are *not* supported by other factors. For example, the turnout of women is less than that of men in every category: income, education, age, religion, and so on. Similarly, income matters more than education: of those voters who had only a grade-school education *but* who were in the top quarter of the population by income, 83 percent turned out to vote in the 1944 presidential election—a figure only 4 percent lower than for those of the same income bracket with college educations.[17]

The presence of one-party or two-party systems has the same sort of across-the-board effect in state and local elections, especially during non-presidential years. That is, the greater the two-party competition in a state, the greater the voting turnout, regardless of other factors. Thus, the one-party Southern states are among the lowest of the fifty states in voting turnout for both primaries and general elections.[18]

Despite these exceptions, however, it is important to recognize that it is usually a complex *combination* of factors, rather than any one alone, that

---

[16] This figure does not attempt to portray the flow of communication to the voter or the complex sequence of interactions among the factors. For such attempts to diagram political behavior, see, for example, Lester W. Milbrath, *Political Participation* (Chicago: Rand McNally, 1965), p. 28.

[17] Lane, *op. cit.*, p. 50.

[18] Lester W. Milbrath, "Political Participation in the States," in Herbert Jacob and Kenneth Vines, *Politics in the American States* (Boston: Little, Brown, 1965).

determines whether or not a person will vote.[19] Businessmen and white-collar workers vote more than wage earners, for example, but this disparity applies mainly to voters in the age range of twenty-one to forty. The gap decreases as voters get older, until for fifty-year-olds there is little difference in voting turnout between businessmen and wage earners. Or, to take another example: urban areas in general produce higher turnout than rural areas. Yet the nation's highest and fourth-highest states in terms of voting turnout are Idaho and North Dakota—both highly rural, sparsely populated states. The explanation is that their lenient election laws greatly facilitate voting. Or, for a final example: high socioeconomic status tends to give rise to greater feelings of political effectiveness and civic duty than does low socioeconomic status, but other factors may produce these same feelings even for a person of low socioeconomic status (for instance, a politically active trade unionist or a postal worker).

What general observations can we make about voting turnout? First, the voting turnout in national and state elections has been rising gradually since 1920 (though it is still lower than that of the 1890's, which resulted from the fierce party battles of that era). Voting for President, for example, has climbed gradually from 44.2 percent of the voting-age population in 1920 to the 62 to 63 percent range in the 1960's. Though this trend may be due mainly to the generally rising levels of education and communication in the nation, it is significant that the increase in turnout is occurring largely among formerly low-turnout groups; this indicates that certain minority, lower-income, or less-educated groups are entering the electorate. Some other groups, especially those that already have high turnout, such as Jews and union members, have leveled off in their turnout percentages. And some groups, such as white-collar workers, may in fact be declining in turnout.

Second, groups with low turnout generally receive less attention to their claims for government assistance than those with high turnout. In a community in which Negroes and white families on relief do not vote in high percentages but white middle and upper classes do, local political leaders will be far more responsive to the needs and moods of the middle- and upper-class elements. A dramatic increase in Negro voting in a Southern community usually brings a sudden concern by the white elected officials for paving the roads in the Negro section and cleaning up dilapidated schools, and Southern officials have been known to learn how to pronounce "Negro" in place of "nigger" in the space of a few months. However, one cannot make a direct correlation between a group's voting level and government responsiveness to its claims. Even with low percentages, there still may be a voting majority of a group in a city or enough votes to hold the

[19] See Greenstein, *op. cit.*, pp. 19–20; Lane, *op. cit.*, pp. 45–51; Lipset, *op. cit.*, pp. 184–229; Milbrath, "Political Participation in the States," pp. 34–55.

Table 7–4   Factors Affecting Voting Turnout in American Elections

Factors	High turnout	Lower turnout

Categoric	High education
	High income
	Occupation:
	  Businessman
	  White-collar employee
	  Government employee
	  Commercial-crop
	    farmer
	White
	Second and third genera-
	  tion American
	Catholic or Jew
	Males
	Metropolitan-area
	  resident
	Northeastern or Mid-
	  western region
	Older voters
		Low education
		Low income
		Occupation:
		  Unskilled worker
		  Servant
		  Service worker
		  Subsistence farmer
		
		Negro
		First generation
		  immigrant
		Protestant
		Females
		Rural-area resident
		
		Southern or Far Western
		  region
		Young voter

Sociological	High exposure to political
	  information and stimuli
	Long-time resident in the
	  community
	Member of voluntary
	  organizations
	Married person
	High political interest in
	  work group
	Crisis political situation
		Low exposure to political
		  information and stimuli
		Newcomer to the
		  community
		Nonmember of volun-
		  tary organizations
		Single person
		Low political interest
		  in work group
		Normal political
		  situation

Psychological	Raised in family with
	  strong party identifica-
	  tion
	Holds strong party
	  identification
	Strong sense of political
	  efficacy
	Strong sense of civic
	  duty
	Believes personal interests
	  at stake in election
	No cross-pressures
		Raised in family with
		  weak or no party
		  identification
		Holds weak or no party
		  identification
		Weak sense of political
		  efficacy
		Little sense of civic duty
		
		Believes personal interests
		  not directly at stake
		Cross-pressures

Table 7–4 (Continued)

Factors	High turnout	Lower turnout
Political and legal	Resides in state with facilitative registration and election laws	Resides in state with restrictive and cumbersome election laws
	National election	State or local election only
	Close party competition	One-party state
	No community sanctions or violence against individual's voting	Community sanctions and/or violence against individual's voting

SOURCE: The categoric portion of the table is adapted, in part, from Seymour M. Lipset, *Political Man: The Social Bases of Politics* (New York: Doubleday, 1960), p. 189.

balance of power in a state election. And there are other forms of group action that capture government attention and produce program responses. As one militant Negro leader said in 1967, after the bloody street fighting in Detroit and Newark that summer, "When we want to reach whitey now, we get him on the Detroit-Newark 'hot line.' "

The Partisan Choice

As we noted earlier in the chapter, about two-thirds of the American voters identify with one party all their political life, and more than half have never switched their party allegiance even temporarily. Which categoric factors help to develop the continuing party loyalties of voters? And what is the impact of sociological and psychological factors on these categoric characteristics? Finally, in what ways do specific issues and candidates in particular elections modify the voter's traditional party allegiance?

Categoric factors

Class The American heritage of relatively high social mobility and strong social egalitarianism have combined to make our "class" factors less well-defined than the European brand. Nonetheless, class does exist in the United States, and its effect on voting can be measured for an individual or group by trained social observers. The components of class in America are education, income, occupation, and ethnic status (race, religion, and nationality). These factors are interrelated in their effect on partisan choice just as they were in their influence on voting turnout. In broad terms, the

"Come along, we're going to the Trans-Lux to hiss Roosevelt."

This 1936 classic by Peter Arno reflects the sharp class divisions between the parties in the Roosevelt era.

Drawing by Peter Arno
© 1936, 1964 The New Yorker Magazine, Inc.

greater a person's educational level, the higher his income, the better-paid and more prestigious his occupation, and the more socially approved his social status, the more likely it is that he will vote Republican; the reverse characteristics tend to produce Democrats. Moreover, this pattern has deep historical roots. As Seymour Lipset has written, "The Democrats from the beginning of their history have drawn more support from the lower strata of society; while the Federalist, Whig, and Republican parties have held the loyalties of the more privileged groups." [20]

The mutual reinforcement of class components is quite evident. A Negro youngster living in the South on a small rural farm is not likely to have the money to get the educational opportunity that could allow him to enter the executive world of the business corporation; even if he did break in on the basis of talent, his race would hinder his full advance upward. By contrast, a white Protestant child born to a wealthy corporate executive will be sent to the right preparatory schools and the right college, will enter the executive ranks of the corporation, and will enjoy a smooth transition upward if his skills justify a leadership role.

Several important points must be made about class factors in American voting, however. There are enough deviations from this general pattern to warn against any solidly deterministic theory. A wealthy corporation president, categorically speaking, should be Republican. But there are such individuals who vote Democratic because they grew up in the Democratic

[20] Lipset, *op. cit.*, p. 230.

"Roger and I have stayed in the Republican party because of the children."

This cartoon illustrates the class aspect of party identification in the United States even today.

John Ruge in the *Saturday Review*

solid South and developed a strong party identification, which was strengthened by careful cultivation of such individuals' continued interest by Democratic party officials. Or a wealthy individual may vote Democratic—and may even be a Democratic party leader in the nation—because he comes from an old, established family whose fortune was made generations ago, because he received a liberal education, because his ideological perspectives made him seek to be a patrician leader of the "lower class" party; examples of this tradition in the United States are New Deal Democrats such as Averill Harriman, heir to a railroad fortune, and Franklin D. Roosevelt, member of an old, wealthy New York family.

Class also has a subjective element—that is, whether an individual thinks of himself as "upper," "middle," or "lower" class and what effect this perception has on his political orientation. This element is in fact distinctive from—and sometimes at variance with—the objective components of class. For example, white-collar workers in a corporation may in objective socioeconomic terms (income, education, etc.) be in precisely the same class as factory workers. But the contacts of white-collar workers with management people at work lead many clerical workers to think of themselves as middle class instead of lower class and to lean toward managerial rather than labor-union viewpoints. Thus, white-collar workers vote Republican in greater percentages than do manual workers.

In general, urban residents were found to be more class conscious than rural residents, though this may again be a matter of lower-income, occupational, and ethnic levels being concentrated in the cities. Class consciousness and its effect on party choices go up in times of severe economic distress, such as the Great Depression. Thus, there was a greater division of the two parties along class lines in the late 1930's than had been the case in the 1896–1932 era, when groups such as poor Negroes had been voting for Republicans as the party of emancipation and many factory workers in Eastern cities had supported the Republicans because of the strong rural-Protestant cast of the Democrats at the time.

Still another component of class is ethnic-group status, defined here to include nationality, religion, and race. Certain ethnic groups today identify with the Democrats as the lower-class party even though *other* aspects of their class standing—income, education, and so on—would lead them to vote Republican. This is because these groups at one time had low socioeconomic status in this country, and the social identification of these ethnic voters and their offspring remains Democratic, partly because there are still ethnic class barriers in this country. It is also true that party identifications that were formed in the early years of a group's history are sometimes retained by individuals even after their economic or social status later rises.

In order to test whether the effect of ethnic-group membership on partisan choices could be distinguished from socioeconomic influences, the Michigan center in 1956 chose test samples of ethnic-minority members and matched them with a control sample of nonmembers from the same socioeconomic circumstances—that is, high-income Catholics were matched with high-income non-Catholics, low-income Negroes with low-income whites, and so on. They found that although members and nonmembers had the same socioeconomic situation, Catholics produced a 2.9 percent deviation toward the Democrats; Southern Negroes diverged 15.4 percent and Northern Negroes 11.6 percent; and Jews deviated 45.5 percent.[21] Thus, all these groups tended in varying degrees to vote more Democratic than those who were in the same socioeconomic situation but from ethnic minorities.

Under what circumstances is the ethnic-group interest perceived as salient in an election? We can distinguish a group's "recognition" interests (having its members chosen for public office) from its concrete "issue" interests. The presence on a ticket of members of the newly rising ethnic groups in American society has been shown again and again to garner votes from that group's members to support that ticket even for a party that may not be the one most consistent with the socioeconomic interests of that group. "Issue" considerations for groups can be illustrated by the concern of Jewish voters in 1948 that the national administration should have a favorable policy toward the newly created state of Israel.

The 1960 election is an important one to analyze for these ethnic-group factors.[22] Religious affiliation played a key role in 1960, when John F. Kennedy's Catholicism was considered sufficiently salient to increase Catholic Democratic votes from an estimated 63 percent "normal" Democratic party vote to 80 percent. At the same time, there were marked defections by Protestant voters, traditionally Democratic, who objected to the idea of a Catholic President. Among Southern Protestants, regular church at-

---

[21] Campbell, *et al.*, *The American Voter*, pp. 301–06.
[22] The data and analysis here come from Philip E. Converse, "Religion and Politics: The 1960 Election," in Campbell, *et al.*, *Elections and the Political Order*, pp. 96–124.

Ethnic Voting and the Balanced Ticket

Tammany Hall knew how to handle the many religious, ethnic, and cultural groups which make up the population of New York. Tammany always put "balanced" tickets into the field. If an Irish Catholic headed the ticket, a Jew was number-two man, and an Italian was not far behind. Sometimes, depending upon the stature of the individual candidates, this order was rearranged. (The Protestants? Unburdened by minority status and therefore relieved of the terrible pressure of trying to prove individual worth, they were busy making money in the banks, insurance companies, and brokerage houses.) On the basis of the "balanced" ticket, a young Jewish lawyer once became a magistrate because it was raining.

It was the night of the meeting in Tammany when designations for public office were announced. Three candidates for magistrate were to be named. They named the Irishman and the Italian, but, when they called out the name of the Jew who was slated for the job, there was no answer. It was a night unfit "for man or beast." The fellow made a mistake in thinking that the meeting would be called off. An alternate name was called out; still no answer. Finally Charley Murphy, the Tammany boss, a bit nettled, called out: "Is there a Jewish lawyer in the house?" A young fellow who had passed his bar examinations a few weeks before stood up.

He was named magistrate. Turned out to be a darned good judge, too.

From Harry Golden, *Only in America*, 1958.

tenders defected by 40 percent, those going "seldom" by 18 percent. Among non-Southern Protestants, "regular" church attenders defected by 37 percent, those who went "seldom" by 11 percent, and those who "never" went by 5 percent. These statistics do not mean that the voter's religion was the basic determinant of the 1960 vote. Party identification was *still* the most important single factor. But religious-group membership did raise the number of defectors from normal party positions considerably.

When we weigh the combined impact of the various components of class —income, occupation, education, and ethnic status—it. is fair to say that class has always been the primary categoric factor influencing the party identification of American voters.

Sectionalism   The region and type of community in which the voter lives can exert substantial impact on the voting decision. One aspect of geographic location of the voter is the creation of sectional loyalties—affiliation with the sectionally dominant party, which attracts even voters who would be expected by their class to identify with the other party. Usually, sectionalism has deep historical roots; the inhabitants of a section feel that their traditional "way of life" is being threatened by other areas of the nation. As a

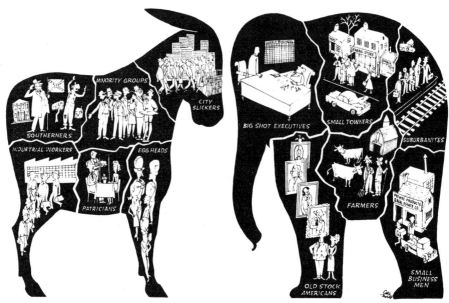

Drawing by Carl Rose
© 1962 by the New York Times Co.
Reprinted by permission.

Political X-Ray

This political "x-ray" shows which voting groups tend to vote Democratic and which Republican.

political force, sectionalism has played a major role in our electoral history, not just in the solidly Democratic South but with areas such as the Midwest and West. Key has noted that an important effect of sectionalism has been to unite different classes within our *national* party coalitions:

> Sectionalism . . . contributes to the multiclass composition of each of the major parties, a characteristic bewildering to those who regard only a class politics as "natural." A politics that arrays people of one section against those of another pulls into one party men of all social strata. A common interest bound the Southern banker, merchant, cotton farmers, and wage earner together.[23]

However, the force of sectionalism in American political life is now diminishing. This is partly a result of high population mobility between sections (Southern Negroes moving to the North, Northerners to the South, Southerners and Easterners to the West). It is also affected by the increasing nationalization of American values through the mass media, universal military service, job mobility, and similar factors. In the South, for example, Republican voting has steadily increased in the past two decades, at first

[23] V. O. Key, Jr., *Politics, Parties, and Pressure Groups*, 5th ed. (New York: Crowell, 1964), pp. 243–44.

How to Distinguish Democrats from Republicans

Although to the casual glance Republicans and Democrats may appear to be almost indistinguishable, here are some hints which should result in positive identification....

The people you see coming out of white wooden churches are Republicans.

Democrats buy most of the books that have been banned somewhere. Republicans form censorship committees and read them as a group....

Democrats give their worn-out clothes to those less fortunate. Republicans wear theirs....

Republicans employ exterminators. Democrats step on the bugs.

Republicans have governesses for their children. Democrats have grandmothers....

Large cities such as New York are filled with Republicans—up until 5 P.M. At this point there is a phenomenon much like an automatic washer starting the spin cycle. People begin pouring out of every exit of the city. These are Republicans going home....

Republicans study the financial pages of the newspaper. Democrats put them in the bottom of the bird cage....

On Saturday, Republicans head for the hunting lodge or the yacht club. Democrats wash the car and get a haircut.

Republicans raise dahlias, Dalmatians, and eyebrows. Democrats raise Airedales, kids, and taxes....

Democrats watch TV crime and Western shows that make them clench their fists and become red in the face. Republicans get the same effect from the presidential press conferences....

Republicans smoke cigars on weekdays....

Democrats make up plans and then do something else. Republicans follow the plans their grandfathers made.

From Will Stanton, "The View from the Fence or How to Tell a Democrat from a Republican," *Ladies Home Journal*, November 1962.

only for presidential candidates, but now also for congressmen, state legislators, mayors, and governors. Democratic gains in formerly one-party Republican states of New England, such as Maine, also illustrate this trend.

Sex   American culture, Lane has written, "emphasizes moral, dependent, and politically less competent images of women." [24] This leads not only to

[24] Lane, *op. cit.*, p. 215.

a lower voting turnout for women than men but also to a high conformity of married women to the party and candidate choices of their husbands. The only significant differentiating aspect of women in voting is that "when morality issues such as corruption or [liquor] prohibition have been salient in American elections, women have voted disproportionately for the more 'moral' candidate." [25]

Age   The young adult is likely to follow his parents' party identification in his earlier voting years, then to develop his own reasons for continuing or changing that loyalty as his class situation, residential setting, and other factors enter the equation.

Both the prevalence and intensity of party identification increase with a voter's age, as he builds increasing historical associations with one or the other party. This means that the older a national electorate, the more stable its voting patterns will be and the more voting will follow normal party divisions in the absence of cataclysmic events. The younger the electorate—and the American electorate is getting steadily younger as a result of our increased population under twenty-five—the more fluid and less party-influenced voting will be. Reducing the voting age below 21 years of age, as two states now do and as some writers have advocated to encourage civic participation among the young, would probably create even more fluidity than at present.

Sociological and psychological factors

Sociological and psychological factors are those that influence *how* a voter perceives the relationship between his categoric characteristics and the issues and candidates of particular elections. The key sociological factor involved in this process is group influence (family, work group, voluntary groups, and the community) on the individual.

The key psychological factors are the individual's sense of political efficacy (whether he thinks his vote will make a difference in government policies), his feeling of civic duty, his perception of whether his personal interests are at stake in the election, the intensity of his party identification, and whether he is subjected to cross-pressures in a particular election. On the whole, feelings of political efficacy and civic duty are strongest among better-income, better-educated segments of the population, as is the belief that personal interests are affected by elections. However, within middle- and upper-income groups, those individuals who score high in these feelings tend to vote in greater proportions than those with low feelings of efficacy and duty. In terms of voting choice, the key psychological factor is the voter's decision as to which of his many categoric characteristics takes predominance in the context of a given election. Because the voting act

[25] Lipset, *op. cit.*, p. 260*n*.

requires the individual to relate himself to the political system, it is his psychological *perceptions* of his categoric attributes that most political scientists consider the crucial element in voting choice.

Let us examine the impact of sociological and psychological factors in three types of situation. First, a voter's categoric attributes may be in permanent harmony. For example, most corporation executives have a high level of income and education, high occupational prestige, and high ethnic-group status. They vote Republican. For a person with such a happy conjunction of attributes, his sociological relationships merely reinforce his categoric predilections, and his psychological outlook is likely to make him a highly committed and often active party supporter.

Second, an individual may have permanent conflicts among his categoric characteristics, which he resolves through a psychological decision to consider one characteristic continuously dominant. For example, the rich corporation executive in Alabama may put his sectional background above his class status and vote for the Democrats instead of the Republicans.

Third, the issues or candidates in a particular election sometimes create temporary cross-pressures on a voter when two or more of his categoric identifications conflict. For example, his socioeconomic status might lead him to prefer one party's position or candidate, while his ethnic identification might sway him in the other direction. The person who is able to resolve this conflict usually does so by voting according to the categoric characteristic he perceives to be most directly affected by a particular election. For example, we saw that many Republican, upper-income Catholics defected to the Democrats in the 1960 presidential election because their paramount interest was in advancing the opportunities for a Catholic to become President of the United States.

A case study of the voting decision   To show the interplay of factors that shape the individual's voting decision, let us trace the components of a vote cast in 1964 by a real individual we will call David Farber.[26] Born in New York City in 1939, David's early childhood was spent in a Bronx apartment. His family was Jewish, his father an American-born garment worker and union member. David's mother and father voted consistently Democratic, regarding themselves as strong Democrats because of the New Deal's labor policy and Franklin Roosevelt's leadership of the anti-Nazi coalition in the Second World War. David knew his parents' party identification, but there was little political discussion in the family.

David attended public schools and graduated from a state university in 1959 with an engineering degree. He worked two years for a large electronics corporation at Cape Kennedy. After that he took a job with a medium-sized aerospace corporation located just outside of Los Angeles,

[26] From personal interviews by Alan F. Westin, 1964–67.

California. He registered as a Democrat in 1962 and has remained a registered Democrat to the present. If he had voted in 1960, he says he would have chosen John F. Kennedy over Richard Nixon.

From these characteristics, David Farber's presidential vote in 1964 seemed fairly predictable. A registered Democrat, from a strongly Democratic family, his father a union member, of Jewish religion, living in a metropolitan area, his vote should have been for Lyndon B. Johnson. Yet David Farber voted for Barry Goldwater in 1964, shocking his parents and friends considerably in the process.

At the issue level, David could give quite rational explanations for his Goldwater vote. When asked in 1964 what he regarded as the most important domestic issue, he described this as "centralization of government—we're going socialist too fast." He also cited "bad administration of welfare programs," "moving too fast on civil rights—you can't legislate equality," and "loss of American prestige in the world." When asked how he made up his mind in voting, David said he "decides on the basis of listening directly to the candidates; I don't trust the commentators and columnists."

How did David develop this Republican issue-orientation and ballot? The answers lie at the sociological and psychological levels. David works in a twelve-to-fifteen-man engineering unit; all his work associates are Republicans. David is the only Jew in the group, is known as such, but is well regarded as "one of the boys." Though he says that little or no "politics" is talked at work or at lunch, he recalled under questioning that there is a good bit of talk about high taxes, welfare "chiseling," Negro riots, and so forth. David hopes to move into the management ranks of the firm he works for, as a project administrator, and he has already handled several assignments as a work-team coordinator.

When asked what he thought of Goldwater's "extremism" and the "radical right" issue in 1964, David replied that he dismissed this as simply "propaganda." Since he was only in his early and mid teens when the loyalty-security furor and "McCarthyism" was at its height, David has no personal recollection of this issue of the 1950's. Two friends of the Farbers in their local community area are Birch Society members; while David doesn't feel at all attracted to their ideas, he finds them "nice people" to be with.

When asked whether he had ever experienced economic or social discrimination because of his Jewish name or identity, David said "definitely not." He believes that if a Jew experienced such discrimination in the United States today it would be unfair but it might well be because he had displayed some "undesirable traits."

In personal and family life, David belongs to no civic groups or social organizations. He does not belong to a Jewish temple or any fraternal groups. He lives in a predominantly Republican, middle-class, virtually all-white suburb in the Los Angeles County complex. He has no Negro friends or personal acquaintances. He reads no political magazines or intellectual journals, and his annual subscriptions are to *Time, Life,* and *Playboy*. His wife is a Democrat, with mildly liberal views, but she is not strongly political. David remarks, laughingly, that "we cancel each other's vote out regularly." They rarely discuss politics and lead a close family life, with frequent camping trips to the nearby mountains.

David Farber still retains a Democratic voting registration, primarily as a family inheritance. But in 1966, he voted for Ronald Reagan, the conservative Republican candidate for governor. In 1967, he said he distrusted not only President Johnson but also Vice-President Humphrey and Senator Robert Kennedy and believed he would support any Republican over Johnson in 1968.

To sum up, David is deeply influenced toward conservative ideas and Republican voting by his peers at work, his career ambitions in management, the aerospace-military industry he works for, and his desire to be accepted in a Gentile-dominated working environment. Because he has no significant exposure to Jewish religious activity or culture and no experience with discrimination, he has a very low ethnic identification. Because of this, and an insulation from liberal friends, he experiences no cross-pressures to the peer-group and community influences on him. In all likelihood, David will change his voting registration to Republican within the next decade and move where he "belongs" as a registered voter.

Issues and candidates in elections

So far we have examined issues and candidates primarily as they are made salient by an individual's categoric, sociological, and psychological characteristics. However, the way in which issues and candidates polarize the groups in the electorate along party lines merits additional discussion here.

Political scientists speak of a "normal" vote in national elections as one that reflects the dominant political cleavages in the country during that period. One party tends to be dominant in national elections for a relatively long time—often for several decades. During this period, as Chapter 5 discussed, the two parties remain competitive, but the opposition party wins only occasional victories. For example, as Figure 5–1 (page 175) showed, the Republicans won the Presidency in 7 out of 9 elections from 1896 to 1932 and controlled the House of Representatives in 13 out of 17 elections. Then, under the pressure of gradual but major changes in the composition of the American population or of some cataclysmic event, such as the Civil War or a major depression, a basic voting shift occurs that transforms the opposition party into the dominant one for a considerable period. For example, since the Great Depression brought the Democrats to power in 1932, this party has won the Presidency in 7 out of 9 elections and has controlled the House 16 out of 18 times (see Figure 5–2, page 175).

The fact that one party tends to maintain a national majority for several decades has been used by political scientists as a basis for categorizing presidential elections. One scheme identifies four basic types:[27] (1) a *maintaining* election, which registers the normal majority of the dominant party, as with Calvin Coolidge's Republican victory in 1924; (2) a *deviating* election, when some special event or personable candidate displaces the normally dominant party temporarily, as with Dwight Eisenhower's Republican victories in 1952 and 1956; (3) a *reinstating* election, when the normally dominant party is returned to office after a deviating election, as in the 1920 victory of Republican Warren Harding or the 1960 victory of Democrat John F. Kennedy; and (4) a *realigning* election, when a marked and enduring shift in party identification takes place in a segment of the electorate to transform the national minority party into the dominant one, as with the election of Democrat Franklin D. Roosevelt in 1932.

Though these classifications have been developed for national elections, they can also be applied helpfully to many local and state elections. For example, the victory of Republican-Liberal John Lindsay as mayor of New York in 1965 seems to represent only a deviating election. That is, a number of Jewish, Negro, Italian, and Irish voters temporarily deserted the Democrats to vote for Lindsay personally, but they did not appear to be changing their party identification at the city level for good. On the other hand, if Lindsay could reconstruct the New York City Republican party to attract influential leaders from normally Democratic ethnic groups, especially the Negro community, if he could win reelection as mayor several times and compile a successful record in office that would lead 1965 deviant voters to identify permanently with Republican programs, and if the Democrats in New York City remained disorganized and splintered, then the "deviating" election of 1965 would in retrospect be considered a "realigning" election— that is, the beginning of a permanent shift in voting alignment within the city.

What factors make voters deviate temporarily or decide to return to their normal vote in the next election? Obviously, one factor is the personality of the candidates in an election. When a voter sees a candidate as embodying highly admirable qualities of leadership and character—as Eisenhower was perceived in the elections of 1952 and 1956—independent voters or those with weak party affiliations tend to vote for "the man" rather than the "issues." That is, they view issues *per se* as less important than their confidence that their favorite candidate would make a good President.

On the other hand, when a voter has a strong party identification and issue orientation, these tend to outweigh his perceptions of the candidate's personality. In 1964, for example, many Democratic voters said they were not strongly impressed with Lyndon Johnson's personality, but they voted

[27] Campbell, *et al.*, *The American Voter*, Ch. 19.

their issue and party preferences despite this fact. The Michigan Survey Research Center concluded from its studies that "the further one moves from pure policy to pure personality," the further "Johnson's advantage [over Goldwater] declines." [28]

A second factor that helps to explain the deviation and return of voters from their normal patterns is the role of issues in national campaigns. One theory, by V. O. Key,[29] stresses that the electorate is far less stable between elections than the total voting figures from election to election would indicate. Key found that 11 to 22 percent of the voters in elections between 1936 and 1960 switched party affiliations from the last election, about 15 to 20 percent were new voters, and the remainder of the electorate, 58 to 74 percent, were "standpatters" who voted for the same party as they had at the previous elections. The basic characteristic of the switchers was their preference for the policy positions being expressed by the party to which they were switching their allegiance. In particular they believed that this party would best handle whatever they considered the most important issue of the campaign (such as war and peace, race relations, or inflation).

Key found that these switchers had about the same distribution of party identification, factual knowledge, and political interest as were found among the standpatters in each election. Switchers are *not* predominantly voters with low levels of interest and knowledge and weak party identifications; thus they are quite different from the "independent" voters described earlier in the Michigan studies.

Key concluded that the switchers and new voters frequently hold the balance of power in a presidential election. The administration must pursue policies that will hold as many of its standpatters as possible, minimize defections, and attract as large a percentage of new voters as possible. The opposition seeks to raise issues that will lead to massive switching, while holding its own standpatters. Key interpreted this pattern to mean that presidential elections do render an "issue-oriented" judgment on the policies of the preceding administration, and that this is a rational aspect of voting by "a responsible electorate."

How do "issues" become operative in elections? Before an issue can exert influence on the voter's choice, he must recognize it as a policy question, have at least a minimal intensity of feeling toward it, and perceive that one party represents his position on that issue better than the other does.[30]

Berelson, *et al.*, have offered a "life history" theory of how issues gradually come to influence elections.[31] They suggest that a political issue is

---

[28] Philip Converse, Aaze Clausen, and Warren Miller, "Electoral Myth and Reality," *American Political Science Review*, Vol. LIX (1965), p. 330.

[29] V. O. Key, Jr., *The Responsible Electorate: Rationality in Presidential Voting, 1936–1960* (Cambridge, Mass.: Harvard University Press, 1966), pp. 30–53.

[30] Campbell, *et al.*, *The American Voter*, p. 170.

[31] Berelson, Lazarsfeld, and McPhee, *op. cit.*, pp. 207–12.

generally raised first by a small segment of the population—usually by a "radical" group that may represent one wing of a political party—in response to some condition or event in the country. At first, neither major party will champion the issue. However, if the condition or event that precipitated the issue attracts growing concern among other sectors of the population, the cause then wins acceptance within one party as a "minor" issue to be raised along with many others in order to attract some new voters to that party or to prevent defections among its own party identifiers. Then, the issue may become a major policy argument of that party and will, at that stage, produce total opposition from the other major party. This is the period of maximum partisan disagreement over the issue. The issue may then begin to attract such broad support from the voters that it becomes accepted by the leadership of both parties; now it draws attack only from a minority "radical" wing of the opposition party. Finally, the dominant consensus ceases to be challenged even by this minority. Many issues in American national politics have gone through such a life cycle. For example, the federal social-security program of worker-government contributions for old-age payments was originally proposed by left-of-center reformers in the 1920's and early 1930's. It was taken up by Franklin Roosevelt's Democratic Administration in the 1930's, and was bitterly opposed by the Republicans in Congress and used as a national campaign issue. Nevertheless, social security was enacted because of public support for it. By the 1950's only a few right-wing Republicans were still calling for repeal of social security and the Eisenhower Republican Administration in the late 1950's even extended the program's coverage. By the 1960's, the basic social-security program was no longer a significant partisan issue.

In this analysis, the primary determinants of which issues are central in elections are *not* the parties but the "events and needs of society" and the positions of important groups in the population. On a given issue one party usually takes an enthusiastic stand in favor of change, while the other party rejects the need for this innovation. The key issues in national elections are those that have reached the peak of their life history—that is, their moment of maximum partisan disagreement. It is around these disagreements that "parties polarize and elections are in part decided." [32]

In conclusion, it is important to note that the evidence summarized in this chapter suggests that a person's voting choice is a complex response to a blend of candidates, issues, group interests, party loyalties, and the mood of the times—and we still know less about this intricate process than we wish. Although careful preelection surveys can sometimes predict the votes of many individuals within the context of a particular election, the behavior of the electorate stems from a mixture of motives and perceptions that warn sharply against simplistic theories of American voting patterns.

[32] *Ibid.*, p. 212.

SUMMARY

As background for understanding the behavior of the American electorate, we began this chapter by discussing the frequency and significance of American elections. Our federal system, our emphasis on checks and balances, and the desire of state and local officials to remain independent all encourage a variety of elections at all levels—presidential elections, odd-year state and local elections, and off-year national elections. The "voter mood" expressed in these elections affects the course of presidential and legislative policies and offers party leaders significant clues as to voting trends that will affect future elections.

Through a variety of research techniques, social scientists have discovered six characteristics of the American electorate as a whole: (1) Voting turnout in the United States is low, ranging from 60 percent in presidential contests to as low as 20 percent in local or state odd-year elections. (2) American voters lack a high emotional involvement in elections, partly because many voters feel that elections do not make a major difference in their lives. (3) Many voters often lack familiarity with the issues, their significance for public policy, or their relevance to party positions in election campaigns. (4) American voters lack substantial ideological orientation in their voting behavior. (5) Party identification is the most important factor affecting voting behavior. The stronger a voter's party identification, the more effectively he screens out opposing issues and candidates. Two-thirds of the electorate identify with one party all their political life; half the voters have never switched allegiance in a presidential election. And (6) sociological and psychological factors, such as group membership and self-interest, have an important impact on voting decisions.

Voting-behavior studies have suggested that five types of factors shape the individual's decision on whether to vote and on his partisan choice: (1) *Categoric* characteristics that define the basic population categories into which an individual fits: class (income, occupation, education, and ethnic status), residence, sex, and age; (2) *sociological* influences—those arising from face-to-face relationships with family, work group, and local community; (3) *psychological* factors that form the voter's conception of his role in the political system: his view of society, his sense of civic duty, and his sense of self-interest in the election's results; (4) *political-legal* factors that facilitate or impede voting turnout: registration laws, degree of interparty competition, community pressures; and (5) the particular *issues and candidates* of each election.

High voter turnout is generally associated with upper-class standing in income, education, occupation, and ethnic status; close integration into community life; strong party identification; strong feelings of political efficacy; the absence of cross-pressures among a voter's group identifications;

and legal requirements that facilitate voting. In general, a complex combination of factors determines whether a person will turn out to vote, but certain trends are powerful across the board: women vote less often than men; people of high incomes vote more often than those with low incomes; and turnout is greater in states with strong two-party competition than in one-party states.

In general, voting turnout has been rising since 1920, particularly among certain minority, less-educated, or lower-income groups. Nonetheless, government still gives less attention to the needs of groups with low turnout than to those of groups with high turnout.

Among the categoric characteristics that influence the voter's partisan choice, the primary factor is *class*. Voters with high income, social prestige, high occupational and ethnic prestige, and good educations are likely to vote Republican; those with the reverse characteristics tend to vote Democratic. Thus, the voter who is most likely to have a high turnout record is most likely to be Republican. Among class factors, ethnic-group identification is particularly salient in elections where the group feels that its "recognition" interests or "issues" interests are at stake.

A voter's perception of the relationship between his categoric characteristics and the issues and candidates of a particular election are influenced by two types of factors: the sociological influences of family, work group, and community; and psychological factors—primarily the voter's judgment as to which of the categoric characteristics should take precedence in an election when he makes his partisan choice.

When a voter's categoric characteristics are in permanent harmony, his sociological influences reinforce his partisan choice, and in psychological terms he is likely to be an active party supporter. When a voter's categoric traits are in permanent conflict, he makes a psychological decision to consider one of them paramount, and he chooses his party allegiance accordingly. When temporary cross-pressures arise in a given election, the individual who votes makes his choice according to the characteristic most directly affected by the election.

The final factors influencing the voter's partisan choice are the issues and candidates of each election. The results of national elections throughout our history indicate that one party tends to be dominant for a relatively long period of time, although close interparty competition continues to exist. A "normal" or "maintaining" election is thus one that reflects the dominant political attitudes of the period and gives the dominant party its normal majority. Gradually, however, under the pressure of major events or social trends, a basic shift in the preferences of some voters transforms the opposition party into the dominant one, in a "realigning" election. "Deviating" elections occur when "switchers" shift their party allegiance temporarily because of a special event or candidate; "reinstating" elections reflect the return of the normally dominant party to office. It is the party switchers and the new voters who hold the balance between the "standpatters" of both parties, and significant switching in voting occurs on the basis of the administration's performance in office on key issues.

For an issue to become operative in an election, the voter must be able to recognize the issue, consider it important to him, and believe that one party better reflects his own views than the other does. Major issues on the political stage generally follow a "life cycle," which begins when a fringe group of the population takes up a cause in response to a particular condition or event. If the cause begins to win support among other sectors of the population, one party is likely to champion it first as a minor issue that will attract party switchers and then as a major policy issue. If the other party resists innovation in this direction, the issue reaches its peak of maximum partisan disagreement. Gradually, both parties form a consensus on the issue, and it ceases to be a partisan question.

American elections reflect the American political culture by expressing the elements of conflict and consensus within the society, and the electorate mandate exerts a powerful influence on the course of elected government.

SELECTING
THE
PRESIDENT

8

The great prize in the American political system is the Presidency. This chapter discusses the two stages in the contest for presidential office: the politics of nomination and the politics of the election campaign. The chapter analyzes the two major forces in determining the election outcome: the party leaders and the masses of voters. How influential are an aspirant's showings in the primaries? What crucial functions do the party brokers perform? How do the voters' predispositions influence campaign strategies? The last section evaluates our institutional mechanisms for nominating and electing the President. What inequities exist in the present system? What political factors make reforms difficult?

Every four years the great drama of American politics reoccurs: the frenzied contest for power and the serious choice of the people; the bizarre and glorious spectacle of American democracy at its most important task —the selection of a leader who can drastically affect the lives of more millions of people than any other man in history. This process—indigenous, gradually evolved, and a complex reflection of American politics—is seldom understood abroad, and its profound meanings may escape the consciousness of the American himself. Drawn together in this "main event" of the American political system are all the participants in the American political process described in the preceding chapters on interest groups, parties, and voters.

One of the most important tests of a political system is its means of selecting a leader. Monarchies seek stability by gaining public acceptance of the legitimacy of hereditary succession, but such systems are prey to assassinations and revolutions to institute new monarchical lines. Moreover, while monarchs sometimes rule with strength and benevolence, they may as often be weak or arbitrary. Dictatorships face instability during the period of transition from one leader to another, and the system is sometimes strained by aspirants trying by violence or conspiracy to step in as leader prior to the death of the incumbent. In parliamentary systems the people vote on candidates for a representative assembly, from which the leader will emerge. In an essentially two-party system, as in England, their vote may in effect register their choice between two leaders offered by the parties. In multiparty systems, the people have little way of registering a choice of leadership, for the leader emerges in a bargaining process among the parties after the election. Moreover, in any parliamentary system, the leaders of the parties, from which a premier will be chosen, will be selected from among each party's experienced parliamentary élite by an internal party process in which the rank and file of the party have no direct participation.

In the United States, by contrast, the President is chosen by popular verdict. In 1960, for example, 12 million people voted in presidential primaries, and an uncounted number of others participated in the gamut of conventions; nearly 69 million voted in the election, and an estimated 3½ to 4 million participated in campaign activities.[1] When the vote was counted, the nearly 50 percent of the voters who lost quietly accepted the result and acclaimed the winner. This participation and acceptance of the result, repeated with no resort to force for a century, is a great exhibition of

[1] Theodore H. White, *The Making of the President, 1960* (New York: Atheneum, 1961), pp. 26–27. Much of the detail on the campaigns of 1960 and 1964 is drawn from this and White's companion volume, *The Making of the President, 1964* (New York: Atheneum, 1965).

popular government and rule of law. The result is achieved, perhaps, because not too much is expected of it: campaign issues are usually not deeply divisive, the differences between the parties are deliberately blurred by their attempts to form the largest possible coalition of voters, and the losers will have another chance four years later.

There was a time when the results of this system were criticized by many commentators. In 1887 Lord Bryce wrote a chapter on "Why Great Men Do Not Become President" and found that the Presidents after Jackson compared unfavorably with British prime ministers. But in 1962 seventy-five historians who were polled recorded that "great" or "near-great" Presidents had occupied the White House during thirty-five of sixty years in the twentieth century. Probably no one today would argue that a more satisfactory result had been achieved in any other democratic country. The change in the caliber of our Presidents since Bryce's day is probably due in large part to the greater responsibilities and challenges of the office in the twentieth century. Bryce contended that the competence required for the Presidency was similar to that required of a railroad executive. But today the American people demand a man who will, in their view, be able to carry out responsibilities far exceeding those of any other position in private or public life. Bryce argued that politics did not attract great men, but he wrote at the apex of industrial power in a prepolitical era; today the responsibilities and opportunities of the Presidency challenge the most talented and ambitious men to climb the ladder to nomination and from there to the Presidency.

THE LADDER TO NOMINATION

The nomination stage narrows the electorate's choice of a President to two men. What paths may a presidential aspirant take to reach this half-way station, and which aspirants are most likely to succeed in doing so? The events of 1960 and 1964 in the Democratic and Republican parties exemplify normal practice and show the range of possibilities for aspirants seeking nomination.

The Democrats in 1960

For 1964 the Democratic convention would be stage-managed for the nomination of the party's incumbent President—a reminder that the man in office can expect the nomination if he desires it and is eligible under the Twenty-second Amendment. But 1960 for the Democrats was a year that exhibited the varied routes to nomination. Five men were ready to climb the ladder to it. One—the twice-defeated Adlai Stevenson, former governor of Illinois but now a national figure and prominent Democratic spokesman—would offer his friends no leadership in their campaign for his renomination but would hope for a draft at the convention. Four others—John Kennedy, Hubert Humphrey, Lyndon Johnson, and Stuart Symington—would mount campaigns for the nomination. All four came from arenas of politics that had not been promising proving grounds for presidential nominations in the past. First, all were United States senators, and only one senator—Harding in 1920—had been nominated since 1884. Second, they had won distinction on the national political stage, and not since 1884 had such an aspirant—except for Truman, who moved up through the Vice-Presidency—gained a presidential nomination on the basis of such service. Eisenhower's experience was nonpolitical; Hoover's was administrative and generally regarded as nonpolitical; Hughes' was briefly judicial but primarily gubernatorial; Taft's was national but largely judicial and administrative rather than political. Neither Bryan nor Harding had achieved any national distinction in their positions in Congress, and McKinley had supplemented his congressional career with two terms as governor of Ohio. Bryce's comment in 1887 that experience in national policies would only create enemies and thus eliminate an aspirant seemed substantiated.

State politics had been the typical preliminary course run by aspirants for seventy-five years. The three Democratic Presidents during that time had achieved distinction as governors of New York (Cleveland and Franklin Roosevelt) and New Jersey (Wilson), and Democratic nominations had gone to other governors as well—Smith from New York, Cox from Ohio, and Stevenson from Illinois. After Bryan, only in 1924 did the Democrats fail to choose a governor when the nomination was open. The Republicans likewise had nominated governors from Ohio (Harrison and McKinley), New York (Hughes and Dewey), and Kansas (Landon), and their two Vice-Presidents who became Presidents had been governors—Teddy Roosevelt in New York and Coolidge in Massachusetts.

Did 1960 herald a new period? International events and the expansion of national domestic programs had made the national government the focus of attention, and national leaders—whether in the Vice-Presidency, the Cabinet, or Congress—were provided with opportunities superior to those of governors to win attention from a national constituency. Moreover, the gap between state experience and the qualifications for President created by the dominance of defense and international problems had become obvious. Some commentators were saying that neither party would ever again offer a candidate to the people who had no experience on the national stage.

All four of the active contestants had disabilities besides the traditional one of prominence in national politics. Kennedy was youthful, inexperienced (he piloted his first bill through the Senate in 1959), and a Catholic; Humphrey had antagonized the South, which had traditionally wielded power in Democratic conventions; Johnson was regarded as a Southerner who lacked appeal for Northern urban electorates and labor leaders; and Symington lacked glamour and had overconcentrated his attention on national defense.

Kennedy's success in overcoming his disabilities, thus destroying certain traditional political taboos, was to be a major breakthrough. In particular, his ability to overcome the religious taboo would suggest that other handicaps—of race, sex, section, and the like—might well be overcome by future aspirants. By broadening the pool of politically eligible candidates from which our leaders can be chosen, Kennedy's success was significantly to enhance our democratic process.

Each of the four senators publicly committed himself in the last half of 1959 to an effort to obtain the nomination. Each took the first step by establishing an organization with national headquarters. The Kennedy organization was the most thorough and systematic and the best financed— factors that contributed greatly to his success. In the first full-scale briefing of his aides, Kennedy made what was in effect

> a tour of America, region by region, state by state, starting with New England, moving through the Atlantic states and the Midwest, through the farm states and the mountain states, down the Pacific Coast, through the Southwest and then the South. "What I remember," says Lawrence F. O'Brien, director of organization and keeper of the political ledgers, "was his remarkable knowledge of every state, not just the party leaders, not just the Senators in Washington, but he knew all the factions and the key people in all the factions." [2]

Before the meeting had adjourned, the Kennedy strategy had been planned, and portions of the nation had been assigned to trusted lieutenants who would be responsible for winning the support of Democratic professionals in each area.

In our decentralized parties (described in Chapters 5 and 6) nominations are won by garnering the votes of the party leaders from states, cities, and counties who become delegates to the national conventions. In fifteen states and the District of Columbia, the delegates are chosen in a primary, but the significance of the primary in providing choices for the voters and in committing the delegates varies considerably among the states. In some primaries the candidate for delegate need not indicate his preference for a presidential candidate; and sometimes there is no contest for delegates because the primary merely approves the choices of the party organization. But in a number of states the primary provides an opportunity for popular expression on the presidential candidates. In California, Ohio, Wisconsin, and Minnesota, would-be delegates must commit themselves to a candidate, gain his consent, and run under his name. In New Hampshire and Florida dele-

[2] White, *The Making of the President, 1960,* pp. 54-55.

gates may run under a presidential candidate's name even without his consent. And in three states—Oregon, Maryland, and Indiana—which do not elect delegates by primary, a presidential-preference poll for voters binds the delegates on their first convention vote. In Oregon, state law requires that the Secretary of State put on the preference ballot the names of all persons he regards as candidates for presidential nomination, and in 1968 Wisconsin and Nebraska will also require that the names of all candidates go on the primary ballot.

In other states the delegates are chosen in a variety of ways, normally by a hierarchy of conventions beginning at the precinct level and running upward to a state convention. Although substantial numbers of party activists may participate in local conventions, the choice of delegates will be influenced, and frequently dominated completely, by the office-oriented party regulars. The system of indirect election of delegates strengthens the hands of the party leaders as selections of delegates are made at successively higher levels.

This was the setting in which the four men and the friends of the uncommitted Stevenson had to find support for the nomination. Two of the four—Kennedy and Humphrey—decided to enter the primaries. Both men sensed the need for demonstrating to the party regulars that they could win popular support in a campaign. Kennedy also needed to show that his religion would be no bar to a successful campaign against the Republicans. New Hampshire holds its primary early. For Kennedy it was favorable territory; he entered there and won easily. Humphrey similarly won the delegation from the District of Columbia. Humphrey regarded Wisconsin as favorable territory and entered there; Kennedy, knowing he must win support in hostile territory, decided to challenge Humphrey. Kennedy won a majority in the state, but his victory did not answer the question of whether he could attract non-Catholic votes: he carried the six Catholic districts of Wisconsin but lost the four Protestant ones. When asked what the Wisconsin result meant, Kennedy replied, "It means that we have to do it all over again. We have to go through and win every one of them— West Virginia and Maryland and Indiana and Oregon, all the way to the convention." Humphrey had decided to enter Protestant West Virginia, and Kennedy challenged him there. Humphrey had to travel by bus and had insufficient funds for the battle; Kennedy's friends from the East swarmed into the state, organized nine thousand local activists, bought newspaper space and television time, and spread his appeal—that a Catholic should not be denied the right to the Presidency—to every hamlet and crossroad. Kennedy triumphed with a massive majority.

This test before the populace led to Humphrey's withdrawal from the race and to confirmation of Kennedy as the man other candidates would have to beat. Kennedy continued to enter primary after primary to demonstrate further to the party brokers who would lead the convention that he could be a winning candidate. But, unlike Estes Kefauver, who had sought to climb the ladder by the primary route in 1952, Kennedy's organization men were also working directly to persuade the party leaders.

Johnson and Symington had sensed that they could not win by the primary route. Johnson moved in two ways: he remained in Washington to call attention to his superior political talents by carrying a legislative program through the Senate; meanwhile, his supporters aligned delegates in the South and West in order to form a base to build on after the first convention ballot. Symington cultivated the state and city party brokers who had been the bulwarks of Truman's strength, hoping that they would give him a base of support in case of a convention deadlock. Stevenson's supporters built an organization and worked to hold together some of his delegate support from other years. But neither Johnson's more than four hundred delegates nor a giant emotional display for Stevenson at the convention could overcome the solid achievements of Kennedy in winning primaries and persuading city, county, and state party brokers. He had the votes needed for nomination on the first ballot.

The Republicans in 1960 and 1964

Only two men had serious aspirations for the Republican nomination in 1960—Richard Nixon, congressman from a California district and then Vice-President under Eisenhower; and Nelson Rockefeller, aide to Presidents Roosevelt and Truman with responsibilities in international affairs, and to Eisenhower in executive positions, and governor of New York after the election of 1958. Both could be presented to the nation as candidates experienced in national affairs. Nixon had for years maintained close contact and friendship with the party professionals across the nation and could count on this base of support, largely conservative in its orientation, for the nomination. Rockefeller, from the liberal wing of the party, would have to assault this position, presumably through the primaries. In late 1959 he built an organization to take soundings throughout the country to see if he would have organization, voter, and financial support; his polls showed that he would not. Lacking support from the party regulars—who must ultimately bestow the nomination and who in this case distrusted a liberal from the Eastern establishment—Rockefeller withdrew at the end of the year. Then, after a series of international events convinced him that the nation was in peril, he reentered the campaign in the summer of 1960, calling in effect for a new deal by the Republican party, with a larger defense program, support for civil rights, medical care for the aged, and other social legislation. His late bid for the Presidency was almost without hope of success, but before his second withdrawal he had, by threat of a floor fight over the Republican platform, won Nixon's collaboration in obtaining more positive positions on civil rights and national defense than had been recommended by Charles Percy's platform committee.

Senator Barry Goldwater—leader of the right wing of the splintered Republican party—bitterly condemned the "Compact of Fifth Avenue" between Nixon and Rockefeller, which he considered the "Munich of the Republican party." He has insisted that the Republicans would have won in 1960 on their original moderate civil-rights platform. Goldwater left the convention as the idol of the Republican Right, and the stage was set for 1964. Rightist groups echoed his praises, Goldwater clubs emerged, and F. Clifton White, who had from 1950 to 1960 held a tight rein over the Young Republican organizations, began in 1961 to build from his numerous contacts a Goldwater-for-President movement. Goldwater could wait until 1963 to set up his own organization and incorporate White's movement into it, and not until January 1964 did he formally announce his candidacy. By then he was, as Kennedy had been in the Democratic contest in 1960, the front runner for the nomination.

Goldwater's major opponent was Rockefeller, reelected governor of New York in 1962 by a large majority and boasting a gubernatorial record of liberal policies and sound finance. Rockefeller had laid his plans early, had systematically constructed a home organization, and was definitely committed to the race by 1963. For him this was a battle of principle—against a man who would, as Rockefeller interpreted Goldwater's statements, make social-security voluntary, place the decision on whether to use nuclear weapons with military men in the field, and allow discrimination against Negroes to continue. But Rockefeller now had a disability greater than his liberalism and greater than Kennedy's Catholicism—his divorce and subsequent remarriage in 1963 to a divorcee.

There was also a third force trying to make itself felt in the race for the nomination. This was the Republican establishment, which was centered in New York but reached into the other Eastern cities; this group was composed of bankers, business leaders, and lawyers and had given support to Willkie, Dewey, and Eisenhower. Accustomed to moving with a world of change, they were frightened by Goldwater, but they believed that Rockefeller could not win and that a Rockefeller-Goldwater confrontation spelled disaster for the party. This group looked at a field of possibilities—Nixon, for whom they had no affection; Henry Cabot Lodge, Nixon's running mate in 1960, who was at the time ambassador to Vietnam; Governor Romney of Michigan; and Governor Scranton of Pennsylvania. In vain they tried to obtain Eisenhower's support for a suitable candidate; at times it seemed to be given, only to disappear a few days later. First Lodge and later Scranton offered some promise of a candidacy, but neither was able to move far.

As with the Democrats in 1960, the battle between the front runner and the opposition was fought in the primaries and with the power brokers. This battle in the primaries has been called a "duel to the death," but it was in fact indecisive. Rockefeller and Goldwater contested in the New Hampshire primary, and were both beaten by a write-in campaign for Lodge, led

Conrad in the Denver *Post*

"Someone's been eating my porridge," said the Daddy Bear.

This cartoon emphasizes Goldwater's early lead in the 1964 race for the Republican nomination, which he gained by carefully cultivating state and local party workers throughout the country.

by a small group of political amateurs. The three battled in Oregon, and the victory went to Rockefeller. Then came California, and though the Lodge forces now supported Rockefeller, Goldwater won with a 51.6 percent majority.

Like Kennedy, however, Goldwater was careful not to rely solely on his edge in the primaries. Working independently and systematically, the Goldwater forces—often new men in politics, with zeal and devotion to both the movement and the man—were working from the precincts up to bring state after state into line.

Rockefeller's candidacy was dead, and thirteen Republican governors, attending the annual governors' conference, frantically sought a candidate to oppose Goldwater. The result was an announcement by Scranton, who fought courageously for the remaining two months, as had Rockefeller in 1960. But it was a futile effort, for Goldwater already had the delegates. Even the efforts of the men of the establishment to put through some changes in the platform were shouted down from the convention floor.

The Convention Stage

National conventions have frequently been characterized disdainfully as a kind of circus, where the old comically join the young in parades, carrying banners, chanting slogans, and "whooping it up" for their candidate, and where crowds in the galleries put on emotional displays for platform planks or candidates. Other critics see conventions as shams, fronting for the

California

This cartoon emphasizes Goldwater's efforts in the state primaries. His victory over Rockefeller in the California primary virtually assured him of the nomination.

From *Straight Herblock*,
Simon & Schuster, 1964

"smoke-filled rooms" where bargains are struck among power-seeking politicians.

These characterizations are extravagant judgments that overlook the form and essence of a convention. Its form is not patently different from other large assemblies. Outwardly, a convention consists of from thirteen hundred to fifteen hundred official delegates from fifty states, the District of Columbia, Puerto Rico, and the Virgin Islands (the Democrats also include the Panama Canal Zone). This number is increased somewhat by the state practices of dividing their votes among "half-delegates" and sending alternate delegates (chosen primarily to honor more party leaders and offer them a part in the convention). The assorted delegates are surrounded by thousands of spectators—families of delegates, party enthusiasts from over the country, representatives from the communications industries, local party activists, and curious onlookers. The business of the convention, *except for* the choice of the candidate, is slowly worked out in committees. A credentials committee will check the credentials of each delegation and decide on contests between rival delegations from a state—as happened at the Democratic convention of 1964, for example, when rival delegations showed up for both Alabama and Mississippi. Sometimes the decision of the credentials committee on which delegation is to be seated will be appealed to the convention floor and will become an early test of power between competing factions.

A platform committee, with one or two delegates from each state or other area, will work for days prior to the convention's opening, holding

"How much did this enthusiastic reception cost us?"

Interlandi in the Los Angeles *Times*

hearings and hammering out the platform wording. All the divisions in the party are reflected here, and the committee's decisions mirror the forces that are dominant or the ingenuity of party leaders in devising language that compromises differences. These decisions too may be appealed to the floor by delegates strongly committed to principle.

When the convention opens, it proceeds with a conventional routine: the selection of the temporary chairman who delivers the keynote address, the report of the credentials committee, the selection of the permanent chairman, the report of the platform committee, and, finally, the nominating speeches and the vote on the candidates for President, subsequently repeated for the vice-presidential candidates.

The essence of the convention process is harder to grasp. Underlying all else is consciousness of the seriousness of the main business, the choice of a candidate. The stakes are high: victory in November, the liberal or conservative stance of the party, and the future fortunes of men who commit themselves on winning or losing sides. All know that this is something more profound than a circus or a conference of manipulators in a smoke-filled room. The contests that are mirrored in the convention reflect deep differences over men (Kennedy and Johnson in 1960), over principle (Rockefeller pushing Nixon to an agreement in 1960, and Rockefeller, Scranton, and associates battling the Goldwater platform positions on the floor of the Republican convention of 1964), and over interests (innumerable interests seeking commitments in the drafts of the platform committee and representation through a favorable presidential or vice-presidential candidate). The bitterest American political battles are those within the parties in the pre-convention and convention struggles.

Sometimes the choices of candidates have been determined or nearly determined before the convention meets. Nixon's and Goldwater's party victories needed only to be confirmed in the conventions of 1960 and 1964, and Kennedy's momentum had merely to be maintained in 1960. Only when the verdict at the grassroots—in the primaries and among the far-flung party brokers—is indecisive is there need for the issue to be determined by bargains at the convention.

Sometimes the convention could achieve agreement only on a dark horse—as in the choice of Harding by the Republicans in 1920 and that of Davis by the Democrats in 1924. But dark horses are less likely today. The Democrats took a step in this direction in 1936 by abolishing the convention rule requiring a two-thirds vote for nomination. (In the Democratic convention of 1924, a contest between the two leading contenders went through 103 roll calls because neither of them could ever poll the necessary two-thirds majority!) In both parties today the visibility of the nomination process—through primary campaigns and television reporting of conventions—and the knowledge that the people expect a man of national prominence reduce the chance that the party brokers will offer a dark horse to the electorate.

The convention reflects both the disunity and the unity of the party. It will leave some party leaders with wounded feelings and may even deepen conflicts within the party. The Goldwater group left the convention of 1960 with unusually bitter resentments, and the Eastern and Midwestern governors who were defeated in 1964 were unreconciled to the decision of their party. The divisions of 1960 foretold the struggles of 1964, and those of 1964 presaged deep conflict among the liberal, conservative, and moderate wings of the Republican party in 1968. But conventions also provide opportunities for salving wounds and reconciling differences. In 1960, for example, Rockefeller and Nixon compromised their differences, and Kennedy bridged the gap in his party by offering Johnson the Vice-Presidency. Moreover, the convention symbolizes the unity of the party and is a vehicle for arousing enthusiasm and reaffirming allegiance. The keynote address acclaims the party's virtues and the opposition's degradation; the usual motion to end the balloting with nomination by acclamation affirms the closing of the ranks; and the candidate's acceptance speech introduces him dramatically to the nation. The convention is a thrilling experience for the millions of party members who view it on TV and a call for them to join in a united march to victory.

The choice of the Vice-President

Vice-presidential candidates are usually hand-picked by the presidential nominees. Occasionally, however, there is a floor fight over the choice, and

Stevenson in 1956 left the choice entirely to the convention. In the past, in an effort to garner votes from a wide spectrum of voters, an important criterion for choosing vice-presidential candidates has been their ability to appeal to segments of the electorate other than those whose interests are reflected by the presidential candidate. In line with this ticket-balancing custom, Kennedy chose Johnson, and Nixon chose Lodge. Goldwater ignored this conventional political wisdom by choosing William Miller, whose appeal was to the same sector of the Republican party represented by Goldwater himself.

Two recent events may discourage ticket-balancing and encourage consideration of whether the vice-presidential candidate is potentially of presidential caliber: the Twenty-second Amendment, ratified in 1951, provides that no President can serve more than two terms; this encourages a presidential candidate, particularly an incumbent President, to choose a running mate he would choose to endorse—or even groom—as his successor. In addition, the assassination in 1963 underscored the national interest in choosing a vice-presidential candidate with competence for the Presidency. This new concern was reflected in Johnson's choice of Hubert Humphrey—the man he considered best qualified to succeed him—as his running mate in 1964. And future presidential candidates may be further influenced in this direction by increased voter concern.

An alternative: a national primary?

There are critics who belive that the convention system is insufficiently democratic to accord with the ideals of our nation. The only substitute that has been suggested—and the proposal has not received serious consideration in influential circles—is a national presidential primary. According to this plan, there would be a national primary day on which every registered Republican and Democrat would have the opportunity to vote for the candidate of his choice—an opportunity now available only to residents of New Hampshire, Oregon, and a few other states. Proponents of the plan argue that it would take power away from the politicians and bestow it on the people.

A national primary would present certain technical problems, however. First, which names would be listed on each party's ballot? Presumably each candidate would have to apply for listing or give his consent if others proposed his name. Such a procedure would eliminate "reluctant" candidates whose chances would initially appear to be slender but who might gain strength after others had dropped by the wayside. Would the ballot include every person who wanted to be listed, or would some means have to be devised to limit the slate to a number from which the voter could make an intelligent choice? Oregon, for example, allows its Secretary of State to draw up the slate, but it is difficult to imagine any national official being given such awesome power for a primary that determined the nomination.

And what would happen if—as would often be the case—no candidate received a majority? It would then be necessary to resort to a convention or to a complex and poorly understood system of preferential voting (in which each voter would express several preferences in numerical order and the votes would then be tallied by one of several known methods). Still another possibility in such an event would be a run-off primary between the two candidates receiving the most votes—with the possibility that neither of these candidates is the one a majority of voters would have preferred.

A national primary would have major substantive consequences. First, a national primary would increase the advantage of the candidate with personal financial resources and perhaps prevent the entry of men who can now raise money for a primary campaign in a few states. Even as is, a campaign for nomination can be very expensive—in 1964 approximately $5.5 million was spent in Goldwater's preconvention campaign, at least $3 million in Rockefeller's campaign, and over $800,000 in Scranton's.[3] Moreover, the physical strain of a national primary, and perhaps a run-off primary as well, followed by a national election campaign would be unbearable for some men who could otherwise be strong party candidates in an election.

Second, a national primary would weaken party unity and the moderating forces within the parties. It would tend to disintegrate parties, creating factional groups clustered around individuals rather than organizations and thus destroying the pivotal role of the party brokers as mediators. For example, a national primary could accentuate the regional differences that already weaken our national-party coalitions of state organizations. A Democratic national primary in which a Southerner competed with a Northeastern liberal and a Midwestern farm-labor candidate might well deepen the rifts that are now compromised within the convention system. Moreover, flamboyant party figures in the tradition of Huey Long or Joseph McCarthy might find it easier to disrupt the party, and perhaps win the nomination, through a primary than through a convention. The strength of the parties now rests in the state and local organizations; and it is unlikely that state and local leaders will be induced to give up the convention system, which gives them substantial influence over nominations, for a primary that dilutes their power.

Despite criticisms of it, the present system has very significant assets. Its great advantage, it has been said, is that

> It provides an opportunity and a means for the contending candidates, factions, and interests within a party to agree upon the terms upon which they will work together in a presidential campaign.
>
> . . .
>
> It needs to be remembered that the presidential electors are chosen within the states and that the extraordinary achievement of the convention—an

[3] Herbert E. Alexander, *Financing the 1964 Election* (Princeton, N.J.: Citizens' Research Foundation, 1966), pp. 17-30.

extra-constitutional, semiprivate gathering—rests in its capacity to assure that the branches of the party in each of the forty-eight states (fifty plus the District of Columbia) will support electors pledged to vote for its nominee.[4]

These advantages are best illustrated by examples of failure to achieve them. When in 1948 Truman's position on the racial issue went beyond what the Southern wing of the Democratic party found acceptable, the state party organizations of Alabama, Louisiana, Mississippi, and South Carolina put up a candidate of their own and cast the electoral votes of their states for him. When the differences between the Eastern wing of the Republican party and the Goldwater forces were not compromised by the party brokers in 1964, Rockefeller and Romney disassociated themselves from the Goldwater campaign, other party leaders sat out the campaign, and many Republicans stayed home on election day. When, on the other hand, the party brokers succeed in their convention tasks, the unity of the party is preserved, and the stability of the two-party system is maintained.

There is, moreover, a large measure of democracy in our present system. For democracy need not be plebiscitarian; it can equally well be representative. The existing system provides for the brokerage of differences within a broad arena of popular participation. Several factors—the primary contests, the open battle of contestants before the public over a period of months, the spotlight of TV and news commentators on the conventions, and the ever-present realization of the party leaders that a candidate must ultimately gain the approval of the voters in order to win—make the American nominating process more popular than the choice of a party candidate in any other country and a reasonable adaptation of the democratic ideal.

THE CAMPAIGN FOR ELECTION

The presidential aspirant who has gained his party's nomination has completed only half his task. After a brief rest, he must face the grueling time schedule and myriad political demands and tensions of the election campaign itself. The candidate devotes several weeks to consulting with party leaders, assembling a staff, and planning and organizing the campaign. About September 1 he will begin his speechmaking, and his campaign will gain momentum from then on. He will try to reach the peak of his campaign on the eve of election day—thus avoiding the error made by Thomas Dewey, defeated Republican candidate in 1948, who reached a climactic moment in his campaign several days before the balloting.

[4] V. O. Key, Jr., *Politics, Parties, and Pressure Groups,* 3rd ed. (New York: Crowell, 1952), pp. 475–76.

The Candidate's Audiences

Each candidate directs his campaign to many audiences. The national news media provide an opportunity to reach a national audience and to emphasize the aspects of the American consensus (peace, prosperity, etc.) that transcend class, section, or group interest.

More specialized appeals are also made to various groups. Messages are delivered to farmers, laborers, conservationists, and others; particular attention is given to the Negro vote and the "white backlash"; and campaign committees are set up to appeal to women, minority groups, and even—in recent years—to artists and intellectuals. But every appeal to one group is made with consideration of its effects on others: laborers cannot be promised enough to antagonize business, or farmers enough to arouse fears among city consumers. With national press and television coverage making what is said in one place news in every other, a candidate must constantly be aware of the divergencies, conflicts, and balances among the groups. Thus, the election campaign is a forum for amelioration, rather than aggravation, of group conflict.

Nevertheless, the significance of differentiated appeals as means of garnering votes is confirmed repeatedly in presidential elections. When Martin Luther King was arrested in October 1960 for refusing to leave a seat in a restaurant in Atlanta and was sentenced to four months of hard labor in the state penitentiary, presidential-candidate Kennedy promptly telephoned his sympathies to Mrs. King. The news leaked, of course; King was released, and his father, a Baptist minister, said, "Because this man was willing to wipe the tears from my daughter [in-law]'s eyes, I've got a suitcase of votes, and I'm going to take them to Mr. Kennedy and dump them in his lap." [5] A million pamphlets describing the incident were distributed among Negroes throughout the country, and their vote may well have been decisive in states like Illinois, where an estimated 250,000 Negro votes helped give Kennedy a 9,000-vote margin over his opponent.

Kennedy also had to make a specific appeal to a majority group—the Protestants. He met the issue of religion head-on—as he had in the West Virginia primary—before a meeting of Protestant clergymen in Houston:

> I believe in an America where the separation of Church and State is absolute —where no Catholic prelate would tell the President (should he be a Catholic) how to act, and no Protestant minister would tell his parishioners for whom to vote—where no church or church school is granted any public funds or political preference—and where no man is denied public office merely because his religion differs from the President who might appoint him or the people who might elect him.

Each candidate gives special attention to those combinations of interests and attitudes that are dominant in states regarded as strategic to his plan.

[5] See White, *The Making of the President, 1960*, pp. 322-23.

The 1964 Campaign: Johnson's Broad Appeal

The great theme of Barry Goldwater had developed gradually, so that it was not until October that one found the Prophet phrasing the question: "What's happening to this country of ours?"

But the great line of Lyndon Johnson happened, just like that, on a September morning as the street crowds boiled up around him in an engulfing demonstration at Providence, Rhode Island, halting his car and paralyzing his procession. Whereupon the President of the United States, transported, clambered atop his car, seized the bull horn and shouted: "... I just want to tell you this— we're in favor of a lot of things and we're against mighty few."

For Johnson was Peace and Prosperity; he was the friend of the farmer and the worker, of the businessman and the teacher, of the black and the white; he was Mr. Responsible, Mr. Get-Things-Done, Mr. Justice-for-All, Mr. President.

From Theodore H. White, *The Making of the President, 1964*, 1965.

Kennedy's electoral strategy, for example, was based on carrying nine states with large electoral blocs (New York, Pennsylvania, California, Michigan, Texas, Illinois, Ohio, New Jersey, and Massachusetts), totaling 237 electoral votes; he could win the election if Johnson could hold a substantial portion of the South or if they picked up additional states in New England or other sections of the country. Kennedy thus concentrated his appeal on the groups that had formed the core of the successful Roosevelt coalition: Northeastern liberals; minority groups such as the Jews, Catholics, Negroes, and the Irish; intellectuals; labor groups; and the Old South. Goldwater's strategy in 1964, in contrast, aimed at the South, the border states, the traditional Republican states in the West and Midwest, and big states like Ohio, Illinois, and California—with little or no hope for New York, Pennsylvania, and Texas. Goldwater therefore concentrated his appeal on the groups that could form the basis for a conservative coalition: farmers, some suburbanites, persons antagonistic to the welfare state, and those with "white backlash" attitudes.

While the candidate—like an uncertain suitor courting several maidens —seeks both to gain support and to avoid alienating various groups, he understands that basically votes come from individuals, and it cannot be assumed that all individuals in any group will vote the same way. As Chapter 7 has discussed, the voter is an independent unit, influenced not only by his group memberships but by his occupational interest, religion, race, and party affiliation, his family's party orientation, and many other factors. Coal miners showed they had minds of their own when the majority of them voted for Roosevelt in 1940 against the recommendation of their revered

"Never mind the fine print, son—how would you like to win that girl?"

Because of his positions on many issues, Goldwater's political appeal was narrower than Johnson's and focused heavily on the South.

From *Straight Herblock*, Simon & Schuster, 1964

leader, John L. Lewis; Negroes have spurned the advice of Adam Clayton Powell or Jackie Robinson, both of whom asked them at one time to vote Republican; and farmers have been impervious to the partisan preferences expressed by the heads of the major agricultural organizations.

There is another sense in which the candidate seeks support from different audiences. First, there are the party activists, whose enthusiasm must be kindled for the many tasks of the campaign. The great leaders of the party, party professionals in thousands of locations, leaders of favorable groups, and a multitude of party members must be motivated to ardent loyalty and zealous activity. Then there is the two-pronged appeal to the voters who are predisposed to vote for their party's candidate and to those who will make their decisions on the basis of the candidate's personality and his stand on the issues. Both parties must take account of party identification and candidate orientation. The Democrats, however, will give greater stress to the former, because the majority of the voters regard themselves as being Democrats; while the Republicans will emphasize the duty of the voter to select the superior candidate, because they can win elections only if they garner traditionally Democratic votes.

Campaign Techniques

Great changes have occurred in campaign techniques in recent years. McKinley conducted a "front-porch" campaign, arranging for delegations

The 1960 Television Debates: The Loser

Looking back now on all four of them, there can be no question but that Kennedy had gained more from the debates than I. While many observers gave me the edge in the last three, he definitely had the advantage in the first—and especially with the television audience. And as I have pointed out, 20 million people saw the first debate who did not bother to tune in the others....

I believe that I spent too much time in the last campaign on substance and too little time on appearance: I paid too much attention to what I was going to say and too little to how I would look. Again, what must be recognized is that television has increasingly become the medium through which the great majority of the voters get their news and develop their impressions of the candidates.... One bad camera angle on television can have far more effect on the election outcome than a major mistake in writing a speech which is then picked up and criticized by columnists and editorial writers. I do not mean to suggest that what a candidate says is not important; in a presidential election, in particular, it should be all-important. What I do mean to say is that where votes are concerned, a paraphrase of what Mr. Khrushchev claims is an "ancient Russian proverb" could not be more controlling: "one TV picture is worth ten thousand words."...

Looking to the future, the incumbent—or whoever represents an incumbent Administration—will generally be at a disadvantage in debate because his opponent can attack while he must defend. But joint TV appearances of candidates at the presidential level are here to stay, mainly because people want them and the candidates have a responsibility to inform the public on their views before the widest possible audience.

From former Vice-President Richard M. Nixon, *Six Crises*, 1962.

of party leaders to make the pilgrimage to his home; and the Republicans tried to keep Harding at home ("If he goes on a tour, somebody's sure to ask him questions, and Warren's just the sort of damn fool that'll try to answer," said one of the Republican professionals). Today the candidate goes to the people. Nixon in 1960 flew 65,000 miles, appeared in 188 cities at least once, made over 150 major speeches, and was estimated to have been seen by over 10 million people in the flesh.[6] Johnson, an observer noted,

> would reach down and clutch hands, first with his right hand, then with his left, then grab waving hands together in bunches and squeeze them. By evening his right hand was swollen and bleeding and Band-Aid covered an angry bruise at the base of his thumb. But he wanted the people close; he wanted to press the flesh.[7]

A major change has resulted from television, first used extensively in the campaign of 1952. The revolution in communications "probably profoundly

---

[6] White, *The Making of the President, 1960*, p. 317.
[7] White, *The Making of the President, 1964*, p. 385.

altered the nature of political power, by making it possible for national leaders to reach and influence mass opinion directly without heavy reliance on an intermediate network of party workers." [8] It has thus served to democratize further the presidential election, as well as the nominating process.

This does not mean that the parties do not intensively organize the party workers from national headquarters downward to local units, but it does signify greater reliance on direct candidate contact with the voter. In 1960 Kennedy and Nixon even engaged in a four-session debate televised before 60 to 75 million people. By election day the average voter has seen the candidate repeatedly—on the platform, shaking hands with people, talking with the press—and has made his own judgment of the man.

Modern campaigns are expertly planned in particulars and massive in their total impact. Idea men assist in the choice of themes and issues, the creation of symbols and phrases, and the weaving of these into speeches; public-relations experts plan for effective use of all the mass media and of

[8] Key, *op. cit.*, p. 499.

The 1960 Television Debates: The Winner

The four debates, and the first in particular, played a decisive role in the election results. Nixon knew it. Kennedy knew it. Their advisers and party leaders knew it. Their crowds reflected it. Their polls showed it. The on-the-spot surveys, the post-election surveys and the surveys of surveys all showed it.... [The debates] were a primary molder in the public mind of campaign issues and candidate images. They were a primary reason for the increasing interest in the campaign and the record turnout at the polls. And they were a primary factor in Kennedy's ultimate electoral victory....

He won [the debates] in part because he recognized the unprecedented impact certain to be made by the most historic debates since Lincoln and Douglas, and viewed by more than a thousand times as many people. He directed that his schedule be arranged so as to allow him the maximum time for briefing, preparation and rest before each encounter.... His only desire was to be properly prepared and informed. To this end, prior to the first debate, we reduced to cards and reviewed for hours the facts and figures on every domestic issue, every Kennedy charge and every Nixon countercharge. We threw at the Senator all the tough and touchy questions we could devise. One session was held on the sunlit roof of his Chicago hotel, another in his sitting room, the last in his bedroom after he had confidently napped for nearly three hours in the midst of a bed full of file cards. He had, in a sense, been preparing for this moment for years, in hundreds of rapid-fire question-and-answer sessions with newsmen, college audiences, TV panels and others.

From Theodore C. Sorensen, former special counsel to President Kennedy, *Kennedy*, 1965.

publicity techniques to create a favorable image for the candidate; professional poll takers employed by the parties use scientific techniques to test the attitudes of voters, particularly in strategic areas and on crucial campaign themes or issues; prominent leaders of groups are enlisted for statements, and auxiliary organizations are created to reach the rank and file of groups; the itineraries of presidential and vice-presidential candidates are carefully planned for maximum impact where the electoral results will be greatest; each appearance of the candidates is staged to show mass support; campaigns to register the party voters may be undertaken, and the party faithful will be stimulated to get out the vote on election day. There is much that is scientific in this process—for example, poll-taking as a guide for pinpointing efforts. But inescapably there is a massive appeal reaching, as we have indicated, to all audiences—to Alaska as well as New York, to multitudes of groups, and to the mind of the individual.

Such massive campaigns are expensive—increasingly so since the introduction and expanded use of television. National law prohibits any committee from spending more than $3 million in a campaign, but the parties escape this limitation by creating additional organizations. Money is spent by labor and miscellaneous organizations and by state committees, but the national party committees themselves spent approximately $20 million in 1960 and $25 million in 1964. Of the latter sum $11 million was spent for radio and television time. The parties spend comparable sums, with the Republicans normally spending more since 1932. The Democrats spent more in 1960, but the Republican expenditures were almost double those of the Democrats in 1964.[9] The effect of the heavy expenses is to create a fund-raising problem for each party, and normally both parties end a campaign in debt. As Chapter 6 discussed, President Johnson tried to meet this problem in 1967 by recommending to Congress that it enact legislation providing for government financing of presidential campaigns.

Campaign Effects

Although some studies have been made, we do not have information adequate for judging the effect of campaigning in changing votes. Probably this varies from one campaign to another, depending on such factors as the extent to which the candidate is known or the issues are clarified at the beginning of the campaign. Sometimes, as in 1936 and 1964, the results of the election have been determined before the campaign begins. On the other hand, in more closely contested races, campaigning has been reported as influential on the thinking of voters—as, for instance, Eisenhower's promise to go to Korea to seek an end to the war and the impression of competence given by Kennedy in the first televised debate with Nixon. Every candi-

---

[9] For these and other figures, see Alexander, *op. cit.*, and Report of the President's Commission on Campaign Costs, *Financing Presidential Campaigns* (April 1962).

date assumes that there are undecided or loosely committed voters who can be affected by some kind of appeal. He assumes also that enthusiasm must be created among those who are organized to get out the vote on election day.

Another kind of discussion centers on the contribution of the campaign to the education of the voter and the quality of the American dialogue on political matters. There is much ballyhoo, some overzealousness (as when some Republicans called Democrats "the party of treason" in 1952), some harsh language (as when Nixon called Kennedy a "barefaced liar"), and considerable inflation of claims—both by the in-party defending its record in office and by the out-party attacking it. But Americans expect their President to be a man of dignity and good judgment and one capable of avoiding serious mistakes; these expectations lead to cautiousness and restraint. Moreover, Americans over the past century have tended to become less strident and vituperative in their politics and to place a high premium on smooth social relations, though the new epoch of riots and demonstrations may aggravate tensions and deepen antagonisms in the politics of the nation.

The presidential campaign is a period when the entire nation is engaged in political dialogue. On the street, at coffee, in taxis, at home, across the bridge table—everywhere Americans meet—the dialogue is maintained. In the course of the dialogue Americans are educated—with a mixture of superficiality and profundity, but always with serious purpose—on the wide range of domestic and foreign issues felt by them to be meaningful and on the abilities of aspirants to their highest office. Moreover, the campaign is the nation's greatest instrument of political socialization—it educates children as well as adults in the mechanics and spirit of the political system. There is safety for the political system in this socialization and free discourse, and safety also in the people's habit of returning their attention to nonpolitical interests after the election. The revival every four years of this discourse and the complete dependence of the nation's would-be governors on the independent expression of the voter are also the apex of the democratic experience of the nation.

THE ELECTORAL SYSTEM

The people do not, of course, elect their President directly. They cast their votes for electors, who are by decisions of the state legislatures elected in every state on a general state ticket. The winning slates of electors gather in their respective state capitals in December to cast their official ballots for President and Vice-President.

Each state has as many electors as its combined number of United States senators and representatives. To win, a candidate must have a majority of the total electoral votes; otherwise, the election of the President is thrown into the House of Representatives, where each state casts one vote and the choice is made from the three highest candidates.

This system has been criticized on many grounds. The central criticism is that the man who leads in the popular vote may be defeated in the electoral vote. This happened to Tilden in 1876 and to Cleveland in 1888; also, in 1824 Jackson led in the popular vote but failed to get an electoral majority, and the House of Representatives selected Adams. Several factors can contribute to this result. One is the overallocation of electoral votes to small states. Alaskans in 1964 got 3 electoral votes with 67,259 popular votes being cast, while New York got 43 electoral votes with 7,156,715 votes cast, which meant 1 electoral vote for each 22,420 popular votes in Alaska but for each 166,437 votes in New York. A second factor is the uneven degree of voting within the states: Mississippi, Kansas, and West Virginia each have 7 electoral votes, but in 1964 more than twice as many people voted in Kansas and West Virginia as in Mississippi.

Yet the main cause of distortion in the electoral-vote system is that a state's vote is cast as a unit. For example, in 1960 over 3 million people voted for each of the candidates in California, but all the state's electoral vote went to the candidate who polled 50.1 percent of the popular vote. In effect, the system counts millions of people as voting for a candidate they did not choose.

Certain by-products of the system of unit voting have also been criti-

"Don't expect me to get this real accurate, Bub."

As this criticism suggests, the Electoral College distorts the popular vote for President.

From *The Herblock Book,* Beacon Press, 1952

cized. First, in "safe" states that traditionally vote for one party there is no incentive for a heavy voter turnout, and the development of two-party politics is impeded. Second, the unit rule gives disproportionate power at the nominating conventions to the big "swing" states—those states fairly evenly divided between Democrats and Republicans—because they can deliver large blocs of electoral votes in the election. Thus, the leaders of these states will have the advantage in the competition for nomination, the bargaining power of minorities and splinter groups from these states is increased in the nominating process, and the presidential candidates are encouraged to direct their appeal to the strong minorities in these states.

A second criticism of the Electoral College is that it allows an elector to make a free decision rather than reflecting the popular vote of his state. Although in accord with the intention of the Framers, free choice by the electors is inconsistent with popular choice of the President. Parties are careful to choose dependable persons as electors, and a few states require that an elector vote for his party's choice. On the other hand, some of the Southern legislatures have specifically authorized unpledged electors. In 1960 six of Alabama's electors, eight of Mississippi's, and one of Oklahoma's cast their votes for Senator Harry Byrd of Virginia, even though they had given no indication during the campaign that Byrd would be their choice.

Using unpledged electors is one technique for throwing an election into the House of Representatives. A more direct method would be to enter a third candidate. In addition to criticism of the Electoral College, there has been criticism of the constitutional rule for voting for President in the House. Each state would vote as a unit, which would give the same weight to Alaska as to New York and would deny a vote to any state whose delegation was evenly divided. In a vote in the House, a bloc of states could have a "swing" position, and this has been seen as a possibility for the Southern states—whose representatives, though not hopeful of electing a third-party candidate, could hope to strike a bargain with one of the major-party candidates.

Proposed Reforms

Constitutional amendments with respect to the Electoral College have been proposed in almost every Congress—151 such proposals were made between 1947 and 1963. Most of the recent ones have fallen into three categories.

The simplest proposal is that the Electoral College be abolished and that popular votes determine the result of the election. Such a plan would remove all the distortions in the counting of the popular ballot and also the threat that behavior of electors could thwart the expression of popular will. It is the only plan that assures that the candidate receiving the most votes wins the election. While on the surface the plan appears meritorious, there is strong opposition to it. The small states would lose the advantage of overrepresentation, as would the states with low voter turnouts. Second, a system of direct popular election would increase the pressure for uniform national requirements on voting; setting up such requirements would give the national government new powers of regulation over an area now left (with limitations) to the states and would raise controversial issues of states' and civil rights. Third, a system of direct election would remove the deterrence to the rise of third parties provided by the present winner-take-all rule.

An alternative proposal is proportional voting, frequently called the Lodge-Gossett plan after its main coauthors (formerly senator from Massachusetts and congressman from Texas, respectively). The plan would abolish the Electoral College and apportion a state's electoral vote in proportion to the popular vote—a candidate getting 52.46 percent of the popular vote in a state would get that percentage of the state's electoral vote. The political appeal of the proposal, in contrast to the popular-election plan, lies in its maintenance of the present allocation of electoral votes to the states and its avoidance of pressure to establish uniform voting requirements.

But because of the inequities built into the allocation of electoral votes among the states, even if each state's electoral votes were split to reflect its division of the popular vote, the national tallies of electoral and popular votes would still not jibe exactly. Thus, a minority candidate could still win an election. In fact, had the system been in use in 1880 and 1896 the Democrats would have won even though the Republican candidates had more votes. Devotees of the two-party system fear that third-party candidacies would be encouraged by the plan, even though its advocates have accepted an amendment to it requiring 40 percent of the electoral vote to win an election. Finally, political liberals object to the plan because it would weaken the power of the urban majorities in large "swing" states, which could no longer deliver large electoral blocs, and would strengthen the power of one-party states, which could still swing a large margin of electoral votes to a candidate.

A third plan is the district plan. The most prominent of these plans retains electors and provides that the two electors given equally to each state be elected statewide and the other electors be chosen from congressional districts. This plan too would not remove all possibilities for a "minority" President. Also, it would increase pressures for gerrymandering of congressional districts. The district plan would encourage the election of a President with an outlook similar to that of the House of Representatives. Not surprisingly, those political forces now favored by the composition of the House favor such a plan, and vice versa. Until now the plan would have favored Democrats over Republicans in general, and rural conservatives over urban liberals. Reapportionment on the one-man–one-vote principle may, however, change the composition of the House and modify the alignments on the district plan.

In recent congressional hearings considerable predominance of opinion for reform was expressed, but without agreement on method. There is a hazard for political stability in the possibility that the winners of a majority in an election would have to take a minority President. Yet a favorable political coalition in favor of reform has not been fashioned. In opposing a proposed reform, Senator John Kennedy spoke of the balance of power in a "solar system." He meant that the overrepresentation of rural areas and small states in Congress justified overweighting the influence of urban, liberal minorities in the Presidency. But these balances in the "solar system" may be affected in the future by the one-man–one-vote decisions, national pressure for voter registration in the South, and urbanization of the nation. Decisions on reform of the Electoral College may be affected by these changes; they could also be affected by the results of an election that produced a "minority" President.

The method of voting in the House of Representatives for the President is a separate issue and has not had the same attention as the other issues.

SUMMARY

The American system of choosing its national political leader is unique in the extent of direct popular participation. Moreover, the stability of our system is safeguarded in large measure by its consonance with democratic ideals, the opportunities it provides for mediation among leaders of each party, and the consequent readiness of losing candidates and voters to accept the electoral verdict peacefully.

Several aspects of the process for gaining presidential nomination and election contribute in our day to these results. First, the pool from which presidential candidates have been nominated has widened in recent years: though presidential candidates had traditionally come out of state politics, today's aspirants for nomination are likely to have experience in national politics, and this trend may even become a prerequisite in the future. In addition, Kennedy's success in winning the Democratic nomination proved that youthfulness and a minority background were not insurmountable handicaps.

Second, to gain the nomination, most aspirants must mobilize their organizations on several fronts simultaneously. They must make a good showing in the primaries, both to win delegates to the nominating convention and to convince the party brokers that they can win popular support in an election campaign despite their political handicaps. At the same time, candidates must work directly with the party brokers to win their personal support and the votes of the delegations they control.

Third, the party convention preserves party stability and democratic participation. It not only conducts the serious business of choosing candidates for the Presidency and Vice-Presidency but symbolizes the unity of the party and helps to arouse enthusiasm and loyalty among the party faithful. While the convention sometimes deepens conflicts within the party, more often it is a vehicle for reconciling intraparty differences—such as through compromises on the party platform—so that contending factions can work out the terms by which they will work as a united party during the campaign. The convention's relative success in mediating differences within the party, coupled with the broad popular participation in primaries and in choosing convention delegates, provides a substantial measure of representative democracy for our system.

Vice-presidential candidates are usually chosen by the presidential nominee, and the custom of "ticket-balancing"—choosing a Vice-President who appeals to a different segment of the voting population than the President does—has been a predominant criterion. The passage of the Twenty-second Amendment and the assassination of President Kennedy may discourage this custom in the future.

The alternative to the present system for nominating party candidates— a national presidential primary—has both procedural and substantive drawbacks. Among these, it would favor candidates with vast financial resources and might even prevent the entry of a candidate without substantial funds. And, second, a national primary would be a divisive force rather than a conciliatory one. It would weaken party unity and might well encourage personal factions, regionalism, and extremism.

In the campaign itself, the two candidates direct their appeal to several audiences simultaneously. First, they try to emphasize those aspects of the American consensus shared by all classes, groups, and sections. Second, they make more specific appeals to various interest groups, being careful not to promise too much to any one group or to antagonize competing groups in the process. Each candidate gives special attention to the dominant groups in the states that are crucial to his electoral strategy.

A candidate must also make differentiated appeals to party activists, who must be rallied for work in mobilizing votes; to voters who will support him out of traditional allegiance to their party; and, finally, to voters who will make their choice according to their evaluation of each candidate and the campaign issues.

Campaign techniques have been revolutionized by the use of television, which has helped to democratize both the nominating process and the election campaign; by the extensive and expert organization of modern campaigns; and by scientific procedures such as poll-taking. An inevitable outgrowth of these changes is a vast increase in campaign costs.

Our indirect electoral system for choosing the winning presidential candidate has been heavily criticized for two main reasons: first, the man who wins the popular vote may still be defeated if he loses the electoral vote; and, second, if no candidate receives a majority of the electoral votes, the

President is chosen by balloting in the House of Representatives—a procedure that gives each state only one vote, despite huge differences in the populations of our fifty states.

Several reforms of the system have been proposed: first, that the Electoral College be abolished and the President chosen directly by popular vote; or, second, that each state's electoral vote be divided in proportion to the way its popular vote splits for the presidential candidates; or, third, that two electors from each state be elected statewide, while the other state electors be chosen from congressional districts.

The problem with all these proposals is that each one would take influence away from some bloc of voters that is favored by the present system, and, not surprisingly, the blocs that would be adversely affected have prevented agreement on reform.

In fact, despite its inequities, the present system performs a crucial function: its overemphasis on the influence of urban, liberal minority groups in the large, industrial "swing" states helps to counteract the disproportionate influence of rural areas and small states in Congress. And the stability of our system is greatly enhanced by the checks and balances which ensure that each major group in our society is influential in at least one arena of our political "solar system."

III

THE PRESIDENT, CONGRESS, AND THE EXECUTIVE BRANCH

Part III introduces us to the institutional arenas of the American political system, and it is here that we see how our system's distinctive cultural and socioeconomic characteristics and our political process set boundaries on formal government action and shape the politics of its institutions. Chapters 9 and 10 explore the role of our President and the instruments at his disposal in the executive branch. Chapters 11 and 12 explore the distinctive internal procedures and power structure of Congress, as well as its relationship to the President, in a system with elaborate "checks and balances," with political parties that lack centralized discipline, and with multiple policy-making arenas and many political routes for reaching each one. The distinctive role of the bureaucracy in this system is discussed in Chapter 13.

THE PRESIDENT Mainspring of the System

9

In the conventional classification of governments, that of the United States is a presidential system. This designation emphasizes a crucial point: the most distinctive creation of the American system is the Presidency. The basic characteristics of this important office will be examined in this chapter. What are its component elements? How are they related to one another? What are the power resources of the Presidency? What are the limits upon these resources? How does the modern Presidency differ from the eighteenth- and nineteenth-century Presidency? What has caused these changes?

THE TWENTIETH CENTURY: THE ERA OF THE PRESIDENT

Within the broad limits of the Constitution, the expectations growing out of contemporary domestic and international conditions fix the functions of the President. What are these functions? They are discussed below under six headings; however, one must remember three things about any such list. First, the categories are largely conventional. Second, the President's roles are continually being elaborated on and modified by practice, statute, and necessity. Third, and most important, any list of functions is an analytical exercise, dividing reality into segments in order to describe it. But the President—one man—performs all six functions simultaneously. Thus, what he does in one role materially affects his success in the others. Woodrow Wilson's failure in the 1918 congressional elections to win the Democratic majority that he had asked for weakened his influence later at the Paris Peace Conference and his chances of winning Senate approval of the treaty he helped to write. This inseparability of functions is inescapable. Congress, executive officials, his party, the voters, and the governments of other nations condition their responses to the President upon how he is doing with each of the other groups. Foreign ministries watch American elections as barometers of presidential influence; Congress and administrators respond to presidential successes and failures in the world of diplomacy and with the electorate; and voters react to a President's ability to get what he asks from Congress and from other governments.

The President as Chief of State

As Chief of State the President is the ceremonial head, not only of the government, but of the nation. He embodies, in William Howard Taft's phrase, the "dignity and majesty" of the American people, for other nations and for Americans themselves. When he goes abroad, he ranks with kings above prime ministers, who are heads of government but not heads of state. When he is at home he receives distinguished visitors as the country's host, and his dinners for the diplomatic corps or for visiting rulers are state dinners, not mere public banquets. In performing a wide variety of rituals, significant and trivial, he is acting as *the* representative of the American people. This is the common denominator of such varied presidential actions as laying a wreath on the Tomb of the Unknown Soldier, greeting the president of India at the airport and riding with him to the White House, throwing out the first baseball of the season, congratulating the annual Peach Queen, or lighting the nation's Christmas tree. The authority for this function is almost wholly conventional and extraconstitutional. A nation requires symbols of its unity, its power, and its virtues, so we make the President, the First Lady, and their children our royal family *pro tempore*. We pick a President in a rough, partisan battle, but once he is elected we proclaim him President of all the people. Though he does not *exercise* all the power of the American nation, he *represents* it all. It has been proposed that the functions of the President as Chief of State be reduced or dropped because they waste the energies of an already overburdened man. Presidents, of course, do delegate the performance of many ceremonial duties to their Vice-Presidents and to members of the Cabinet. But they are wise to retain a good many of these responsibilities, for whatever contributes to the President's standing as the representative of the whole American people contributes also to the effectiveness with which he can perform his other roles. Thus, if he appears in the eyes of a majority of the country to be speaking on a matter of import not as the head of a particular administration but as the leader of the whole people, it matters little that his opponents see his actions as motivated by partisan considerations. They must respect the Presidency even if they dislike the man, and they must take care that attacks on the man are not seen as disparagement of the office. A classic example is John F. Kennedy's inaugural address. When he said, "Ask not what your country can do for you—ask what you can do for your country," he was appealing for support of his Administration's program but on terms that could not effectively be attacked on partisan grounds.

Thus the role of Chief of State, with all its trivialities, is important to the Presidency. Cherished symbols are a source of power, defined or not— particularly if the symbol is a living one.

The President as Chief Executive

The function of Chief Executive rests more clearly on the Constitution, but the language of the relevant provisions is ambiguous in two senses. First, it appears to grant the President more power than he actually has. The opening sentence of Article II reads: "The executive power shall be vested in a President of the United States of America." This appears to be a sweeping assignment. But other provisions of the Constitution and various statutes give a considerable share of "executive power" to Congress, particularly the Senate. On the other hand, the Constitution enumerates certain specific powers and duties of the President as Chief Executive that on the surface seem quite limited and even inconsequential:

> he may require· the opinion, in writing, of the principal officer in each of the executive departments, upon any subject relating to the duties of their respective offices . . . he shall nominate, and by and with the advice and consent of the Senate, shall appoint ambassadors, other public ministers and consuls, judges of the Supreme Court, and all other officers of the United

States, whose appointments are not herein otherwise provided for, and which shall be established by law . . . he shall take care that the laws be faithfully executed . . . .

But through both practice and statute, these simple directives have been the basis for almost the whole structure of what most citizens would understand by the phrase "the executive power." Thus there is considerable support in law and practice for the ordinary citizen's assumption that the President is responsible for anything that happens, or fails to happen, in the executive branch. The President cannot escape this responsibility, yet the gap between the popular assumption and operating reality—to be explored further in later pages—may at times be quite wide. This gap must be filled by a President's *political* skills if it is to be filled at all. It is ironic that the function of the Presidency that on first glance appears to be the most *administrative* requires for its successful performance the greatest *political* dexterity.

Constitutionally the heart of the Chief Executive's function is his duty to "take care that the laws be faithfully executed." Note that the President is not directed to execute the laws himself; rather he is instructed to see that others perform the execution faithfully. One would therefore describe these "others" as the President's subordinates. But we shall see that in reality this may not be accurate.

The execution of a law almost invariably involves some discretion. Even the most familiar of administrative activities, those of traffic policemen, involve some determination of whether the momentary double-parking of an automobile warrants the issuance of a ticket. If the traffic ordinances of a city cannot provide for all the contingencies surrounding their enforcement, the far more complex and technical legislation of the federal government is no less likely to involve discretion in its execution. Thus, with increasing frequency in recent decades, Congress has enacted statutes stating the conditions under which certain types of action shall be taken and authorizing the President or some subordinate executive to issue the regulations necessary to give effect to the statutes. These executive directives are referred to as "delegated legislation."

In order to "take care that the laws be faithfully executed," the President must supervise the broad discretionary choices of his ostensible subordinates, either in exercising authority granted to them by the Congress or in enforcing the laws through authority assigned to them by the President. The practice of "delegated legislation" has thus increased the President's responsibilities as Chief Executive more than it has increased his *authority* to discharge these responsibilities.

A President's formal control over his subordinates lies primarily in his powers of appointment and removal. To be able to pick one's subordinates and to replace them if they are not satisfactory would seem to be an elementary necessity for presidential control of the executive branch. Yet almost 90 percent of the more than 2 million civilian officials in the executive branch today are recruited by the Civil Service Commission or related personnel agencies and appointed under the merit system. Of the remaining 200,000 or so positions, about three-quarters are appointed by the heads of agencies or by the President himself. The remaining fourth can be appointed only with "the advice and consent of the Senate." Perhaps a thousand of these last positions involve significant policy-making authority. In 1965, the year following President Johnson's election (Eighty-ninth Congress, First Session), the nominations he submitted to the Senate fell into the following classifications:

	Number	*Percentage*
Commissioned officers in the armed forces	49,211	88
Postmasters	1,456	3
Other civilian positions, including judges	5,098	9
Total	55,765	100

The President's power of appointment is limited in three ways. First, the requirement of senatorial confirmation gives the Senate collectively—and certain powerful senators individually—bargaining power affecting some of the most important postions in the executive branch. In the case of Cabinet posts—the President's "official family"—the Senate normally confirms the President's nominations without difficulty, if only because in choosing men for these key positions Presidents avoid nominations expected to produce senatorial opposition. Offering an acceptable nominee may be the price he pays for passage of an important bill or for harmonious relations between Senators and the department concerned. In 1933 Franklin D. Roosevelt could have had almost anyone he wanted as Secretary of State, but when he appointed Senator Cordell Hull, a favorite among his colleagues on Capitol Hill, he assured smooth relations between the department and Congress. The President need not *con*sult with Senators on such choices, but he will avoid offering them *in*sult. Second, with respect to positions in a senator's own state that are subject to confirmation, the practice of *senatorial courtesy* frequently takes the appointing power out of executive hands. Under this custom the Senate will refuse to confirm a nominee to a federal position in a senator's state if the senator declares the nominee "personally obnoxious" to him. The complaining senator must normally be of the President's party, and the party must be in the majority in the upper chamber. The third type of limitation is an informal one. Even when the Senate's formal consent is not necessary, an appointment in a senator's state or sometimes one that is within the jurisdiction of an important Senate committee should not be made by the President or a department head until it has been cleared with the affected senator. Failure to observe this practice, especially if the senator is of the President's party, may limit the nominee's usefulness in dealing with Congress, affect the fortunes of the administration's legislative proposals, and handicap the agency's appropriation requests.

The removal power of the President is subject to a few formal limitations, but the informal constraints upon it are considerable. Formal restrictions apply only to the so-called independent agencies or multimember commissions whose functions the Congress and the Supreme Court interpret as being quasi-legislative or quasi-judicial. A familiar example of these is the Interstate Commerce Commission. For all such positions Congress may specify the grounds for removal and the procedures that must be followed to effect it. But even if Congress is silent, when the Court regards the agency's functions as being quasi-judicial it will not permit removal except for such causes as inefficiency, neglect of duty, or malfeasance in office.[1] Presidents may, of course, informally persuade unwanted officials to resign or, in some instances, even demand an undated letter of resignation as a condition of appointment.

No formal restrictions inhibit the President's power to remove an official he appoints whose functions the Court regards as purely executive. This doctrine was not explicitly accepted by the Supreme Court until 1926, but it is now firmly established.[2] Nonetheless, removal of executive officials is subject to restriction in practice. In essence, the President may remove any purely executive official *if he can afford the political costs.* That is, an official enters his office with the support of friends; if he performs his assignments successfully, he acquires additional support among members of Congress, among his associates in the executive branch, and among interests concerned with the operations of his agency. If the President wishes to remove him for reasons of policy—and those are normally the ones that produce difficulty—the chances are that these supporters of the official can create difficulties for the President. They may, for example, retaliate by opposing or reducing their support for other aspects of his program.

For this reason Franklin D. Roosevelt kept Jesse Jones as Secretary of Commerce and head of the Reconstruction Finance Corporation for several years despite their policy differences and despite actions on Jones's part that seemed disloyal. Jones had so strong a following on Capitol Hill and in the business community that only Roosevelt's certainty that Jones had secretly worked against him in the 1944 campaign finally persuaded the President to remove him. The harsh battle over Senate confirmation of Henry Wallace as Jones's successor was an index of the price Roosevelt paid. This element of political cost is the principal reason for speaking of the officials of the executive branch as only "nominal subordinates" of the President.

[1] *Humphrey's Executor* v. *United States,* 295 U.S. 602 (1935); *Wiener* v. *United States,* 357 U.S. 349 (1958).
[2] *Myers* v. *United States,* 272 U.S. 52 (1926). The court's opinion in this case, written by Chief Justice William Howard Taft, includes a historical account of the controversies over the removal power dating from 1789.

The President's control over officials in the executive branch also depends on his capacity to persuade them. "Persuasion" here is a broad term including not only explicit rational argument but, more significantly, the creation of a set of attitudes, an atmosphere in and outside the government in which officials will feel that it is right or at least prudent to accede to the President's preferences. In a dramatic form, this is what Franklin Roosevelt achieved in the executive branch during the critical days of the early New Deal. Men who did not know him were loyal to him and his wishes. Some who opposed his views went along because they had no real choice. This element of persuasion, though conspicuous in the President's relations within the executive branch, permeates all the Chief Executive's functions. As Professor Richard Neustadt briskly states, "Presidential *power* is the power to persuade." [3] The effectiveness of persuasion in one area, moreover, significantly affects its strength in another. Persuasion links with a special intimacy the President's role as Chief Executive and his third major function, that of Chief Legislator.

The President as Chief Legislator

Constitutionally the presidential role of Chief Legislator rests on three provisions. First, the Constitution requires that "he shall from time to time give to the Congress information of the state of the Union, and recommend to their consideration such measures as he shall judge necessary and expedient." This "message power" extends not only to the annual message on the State of the Union, which Presidents traditionally deliver at the opening of each session of Congress, but also to a large number of special messages—often a score or more in the course of a session. In 1966, for example, Johnson's special messages dealt with such diverse topics as civil rights, crime and law enforcement, transportation, consumer interests, food for peace, and electoral-campaign reform. Most of these special messages are sent to Congress rather than delivered by the President in person, and they are typically quite specific. In recent years, moreover, they have usually been accompanied by complete drafts of the legislation requested. Although formally introduced in Congress by members of the House and Senate, these are usually known as "administration bills." Together they constitute the most important part of the legislative agenda.

Second, the Constitution grants the President a veto power over legislation. He normally exercises this veto by returning any bill he declines to sign to the house in which it originated—within ten days of receiving it. The returned bill must be accompanied by a message stating his objections. If two-thirds of a quorum in each house votes to repass the bill, it becomes law despite the President's objections. The Chief Executive may use his veto in

---

[3] Richard E. Neustadt, *Presidential Power: The Politics of Leadership* (New York: Wiley, 1960), p. 10.

The President as Legislative Leader

The President cannot afford—for the sake of the office as well as the Nation—to be another Warren G. Harding, described by one backer as a man who "would, when elected, sign whatever bill the Senate sent him—and not send bills for the Senate to pass." Rather he must know when to lead the Congress, when to consult it and when he should act alone.

Having served fourteen years in the legislative branch, I would not look with favor upon its domination by the Executive. Under our government of "power as the rival of power," to use Hamilton's phrase, Congress must not surrender its responsibilities. But neither should it dominate. However large its share in the formulation of domestic programs, it is the President alone who must make the major decisions of our foreign policy.

That is what the Constitution wisely commands. And even domestically, the President must initiate policies and devise laws to meet the needs of the Nation. And he must be prepared to use all the resources of his office to insure the enactment of that legislation—even when conflict is the result. By the end of his term Theodore Roosevelt was not popular in the Congress—particularly when he criticized an amendment to the Treasury appropriation which forbade the use of Secret Service men to investigate Congressmen! And the feeling was mutual, Roosevelt saying: "I do not much admire the Senate, because it is such a helpless body when efficient work is to be done." And Woodrow Wilson was even more bitter after his frustrating quarrels—asked if he might run for the Senate in 1920, he replied: "Outside of the United States, the Senate does not amount to a damn. And inside the United States, the Senate is mostly despised. They haven't had a thought down there in fifty years."

But, however bitter their farewells ... Roosevelt and Wilson did get things done—not only through their Executive powers but through the Congress as well.

From Senator John F. Kennedy of Massachusetts, *Congressional Record*, January 1960.

a second way if Congress adjourns within ten days of his receipt of a bill: the President merely retains the bill unsigned—hence the term "pocket veto"—and Congress has no opportunity to override. When Congress remains in session the President has a third option: to allow a bill to become law without his signature by not signing it within the ten-day grace period. This weak protest is seldom used by contemporary Presidents.

Two factors in addition to the provision for congressional overriding restrict the scope of the veto power. In the first place, the President, unlike some state governors, must accept or reject a bill *in toto*. That is, he does not have the power of the *item veto*, permitting rejection of undesirable provisions in otherwise acceptable legislation. For example, in the early years of the foreign-aid program, when it was largely focused on Europe, a rider compelled President Truman either to accept a provision for aid to Franco Spain or to reject the whole legislation. Secondly, various legislative actions of consequence are not subject to the President's veto. Thus, it was decided early in the history of the Union that congressional resolutions proposing amendments to the Constitution need not be submitted to the President.[4] Another type of resolution, the *concurrent resolution*—which must be approved by both houses "concurring" on the substance—is also not submitted. Until fairly recently concurrent resolutions were used primarily to express congressional intent or preference and thus, though requiring the concurrence of both houses, lacked the status of law. In recent years, however, Congress has included in a number of statutes provisions for repeal or for overriding executive enforcement action by concurrent resolution—a kind of legislative veto. The constitutionality of these provisions has never been ruled upon by the Supreme Court.

Despite these limitations, the veto power is a formidable instrument. A presidential veto can outweigh the votes of 289 representatives and 66 senators. More important, since it is rarely certain that a two-thirds majority of both houses will be forthcoming to repass the bill, the threat of a veto by the President or his spokesmen frequently produces amendments or other modifications in a bill to make it acceptable. In 1967, for example, it was well known in Congress that the President would veto any bill that granted broad wire-tapping authority to enforcement officials. In consequence, efforts were made to develop a compromise measure that would meet most of the restrictions the President privately insisted upon. Thus the veto is not merely a negative instrument but has some positive utility for a President as well.

Third, the Constitution grants the President the power "on extraordinary occasions" to call Congress into special session. Today, when the legislature normally meets for eight or nine months of the year, this power is of slight consequence. Among the most famous special sessions was that beginning in March 1933, the so-called Hundred Days, when Congress rapidly enacted the early framework of Franklin Roosevelt's New Deal. The Constitution further provides that the President, when the houses of Congress are in disagreement over a time of adjournment, "may adjourn them to such time as he shall think proper." This power has never been exercised.

It would be inaccurate to assume that the function of Chief Legislator gives the President a high degree of control over Congress. The Constitution does make him a part of the legislative process, however, and popular expectations have obliged him to take an increasingly active part in the enactment of important statutes. In the past quarter-century Congress too has come to expect that the White House will be the chief source of its agenda, provider of grist for its committee mills and of topics for its debates. In

[4] *Hollingsworth* v. *Virginia*, 3 Dallas 378 (1798).

almost no other way could it respond in orderly fashion to the demands on the government. But the President needs a great deal more than his constitutional powers to get what he considers essential from the legislature. This is where the politics of the Presidency appears once again.

For the label "Chief Executive" to have any substantial meaning, a great deal of persuasion is required. A President can place some reliance on the ties of party, but these are often insufficient. He must engage in a variety of activities—directly or through his staff—that will induce congressional majorities, like executive subordinates, to feel it right or prudent to accept his minimum demands. This he may do by appealing for popular support in a nationally important speech, by eliciting editorial endorsement of his views, and even by trading improvements in the congressman's district for support on an administration bill. Here he faces the threat of a vicious circle. If he fails conspicuously with Congress, he will still be Chief of State but not an influential one; and he will still formally be Chief Executive, but he may not be able to count on the loyalty and zeal of his executive subordinates. If his support in the country declines, so will his fortunes in Congress, and so on. In seeking to avoid this ominous prospect, the President must effectively perform his fourth major function, that of Party Leader.

The President as Party Leader

Unlike the functions previously discussed, the role of Party Leader is wholly extraconstitutional. It does, however, reflect a constitutional arrangement— the fact that the Presidency (along with the Vice-Presidency) is the only elective office in the country requiring the support of a coalition of leaders in more than one state. Therefore, the "national party" of an incumbent President, while not his personal instrument, is indistinguishable from him; his fortunes with the electorate are essentially the party's fortunes. One of his and its chief concerns must be to keep this coalition intact and strong enough either to assure his reelection or to gain the nomination and election of a preferred successor. To do this, his personal popularity in the country is of course crucial. In addition, his use of patronage on state and local levels and his choice of policies to sponsor influence not only members of Congress who are part of his coalition but also the cohesion of supporting groups within the states. He is not completely free to choose whom he will deal with on patronage, of course, but his preference for one factional leader over another may have wide repercussions within a state as well as effects on "his" party. Thus, President Kennedy's decision in 1961 to bypass New York State Chairman Michael H. Prendergast and National Committeeman Carmine De Sapio contributed to the decline of this faction. Conversely, Kennedy's decision gave prestige and strength to the rival faction led by Mayor Robert F. Wagner of New York City and former governor Herbert Lehman.

The President as Party Leader

When the founding fathers outlined the Presidency in Article II of the Constitution, they left a great many details out and vague. I think they relied on the experience of the nation to fill in the outlines. The office of chief executive has grown with the progress of this great republic. It has responded to the many demands that our complex society has made upon the Government. It has given our nation a means of meeting our greatest emergencies. Today, it is one of the most important factors in our leadership of the free world....

There is a power in the course of events which plays its own part.... Justice Holmes' epigram proved true. He said a page of history is worth a volume of logic. And as the pages of history were written they unfolded powers in the Presidency not explicitly found in Article II of the Constitution.

In the first place, the President became the leader of a political party. The party under his leadership had to be dominant enough to put him in office. This political party leadership was the last thing the Constitution contemplated. The President's election was not intended to be mixed up in the hurly-burly of partisan politics. ... The people were to choose wise and respected men who would meet in calm seclusion and choose a President and the runner-up would be Vice President.

All of this went by the board—though most of the original language remains in the Constitution. Out of the struggle and tumult of the political arena a new and different President emerged—the man who led a political party to victory and retained in his hands the power of party leadership. That is, he retained it like the sword Excalibur, if he could wrest it from the scabbard and wield it.

From former President Harry S Truman, speech at Truman birthday dinner, May 1954.

In a sense, then, the President must be Party Leader just because he *is* President. He needs the party, and the party needs him—which is the chief reason, of course, why a defeated presidential candidate is no more than "titular" leader of his party. Even if he retains considerable popular following, he has little to give to the elements of the coalition that nominated him.

We should point out that the party that elects the President and the party of the same name in Congress are not identical. (This discrepancy will be examined in more detail in Chapter 11.) As a result, the sanctions and rewards at the disposal of an incumbent President are rarely sufficient to control fully the electoral fortunes of candidates for the House and Senate. In particular, the President's influence tends to be weak at the crucial nominating stage, where the candidates for Congress are chosen by "his" party. Nevertheless, candidates for the House and Senate do share certain common stakes with the President. First, in presidential elections the preponderance of voters tend to favor Republican candidates as a whole or Democratic candidates as a whole. This tendency can be a controlling factor in the election or defeat of a representative or senator, particularly in closely competitive areas. Only twice in more than a century and a quarter since the emergence of national political parties has the majority in the House not been of the same party as the President when both were chosen in the same election. In 1848 Zachary Taylor, a Whig, was elected President, though the Whigs failed to gain a majority in the House; in 1956 Dwight D. Eisenhower was reelected, but the Democrats retained a majority of seats in both houses of Congress.

Second, representatives and senators not only have personal ties and intangible loyalties to a common party—which are of real consequence—but have a substantial incentive to have the party appear united behind the President's wishes and policies. For they are affected by the fact that, as the most prominent member of his party, a President discredited or repudiated is a handicap to the whole ticket. Even legislators from one-party states, among whom these incentives are likely to be least compelling, are affected by these common stakes. For years many Southern senators have understood that the President and the Democratic leaders in Congress had to bring up civil-rights legislation. Though they knew they would have to oppose such bills and go through the forms of blocking consideration of them, they accepted the White House agenda as inescapable. As Party Leader, the President must attempt to exploit these *convergent* tendencies as fully as possible.

In a great many cases, however, common party stakes are not sufficient to assure a majority of votes in Congress for the President's plans. A Democratic President, for example, will need some Republican votes in Congress for certain of his measures. In particular, he will need them in the Senate for the two-thirds majority required by the Constitution for the acceptance of treaties. The President must therefore maintain cordial relations with at least a fraction of the "opposition" in Congress, even if his party is in the majority. Though he is a Party Leader, his partisanship must be limited. His role as Chief of State further checks his partisan behavior. The function of Party Leader, therefore, is essential, but it must be performed within severe limits.

The President as Chief Diplomat

The fifth major function of the President, that of Chief Diplomat, derives from two provisions in the Constitution: first, that "he shall have power, by and with the advice and consent of the Senate, to make treaties, provided two thirds of the senators present concur"; and, second, that "he shall receive ambassadors and other public ministers." These formal stipulations are of considerable consequence. The "right of reception," as it is sometimes called, makes the President legally the sole means of communication between

Gillam in *Judge*

"Blame the thing—I can't make it work!"

the government of the United States and all foreign powers. In addition, it confers the right, not seriously questioned since the early years of the Constitution, to grant or to withhold recognition of a government by receiving or refusing to receive its diplomatic representative. Ambassadors of foreign governments are accredited to the President; though they maintain informal contacts throughout the government, in principle they are instruments of communication and negotiation between him and the foreign heads of state. Similarly, American ambassadors abroad are not general representatives of this government but the President's emissaries.

To the extent that relations with other governments are restricted to communications between heads of state, the President's formal position is exclusive. These communications are important and extensive, but they do not cover the full range of foreign affairs. The making of a treaty, for example, automatically involves the Senate. The Senate does not have to give its consent to negotiation in its various stages; but Presidents, especially in recent decades, have found it prudent to work closely with senators, especially the members of the Committee on Foreign Relations. Securing a two-thirds majority in the Senate is not easy at best, and failure to consult with key senators in the process of negotiations may lead the Senate to reject the treaty outright or to attach amendments or reservations that will require extensive renegotiation before the President can ratify the treaty. When the treaty reflects a delicate balance of concessions among several governments, attempts at renegotiation to meet the Senate's reservations may

"One at a time, dammit, one at at time!"

The 1893 cartoon on the left and the contemporary cartoon on the right both illustrate frustrations of the Presidency. The earlier one shows President Cleveland trying to secure cooperation within his own Administration, while the present-day one shows the problems created by multiple foreign-policy crises.

Conrad in the Denver *Post*

be hopeless. Thus Woodrow Wilson's decision not to include any senator in the delegation to the peace conference at Paris in 1919 is usually regarded as a blunder that led directly to Senate reservations to the treaty that were unacceptable to Wilson, with the result that the treaty was never ratified by the United States.

Treaties are not the only form of contract between the United States and other governments, however. The Constitution clearly envisaged certain international alliances that were not to be subject to the kind of Senate action required for the ratification of treaties. Article I, Section 10, provides that "no state shall enter into any treaty, alliance, or confederation," and a separate clause of the same section declares that "no state shall, without the consent of the Congress . . . enter into any agreement or compact . . . with a foreign power. . . ." The implication is therefore that the United States may enter into a "compact" or "agreement" as well as a "treaty."

These *executive agreements*, as they have come to be called, have a long history, and in recent years a large proportion of the arrangements with other governments have taken this form. In importance and effect they are often as binding and permanent as treaties. Thus the so-called Hull-Lothian agreement of September 1940 amounted to a virtual alliance between the United States and Britain. It exchanged fifty overage American destroyers for ninety-nine-year leases to a series of naval bases on British territory in the western Atlantic. The executive agreement has sometimes been used to bypass the Senate, but it has become an increasingly common device even when it has required some later action by Congress, such as appropriation of money, to be effective. A simple majority of the Senate and House in support of an appropriation request may be more readily forthcoming than a two-thirds majority of the Senate in support of a treaty.

Presidents, moreover, enter into a large number of executive agreements on the basis of prior statutory authorization by Congress. The most familiar, perhaps, are those negotiated under the authority of the Reciprocal Trade Agreements Acts, the latest of which, enacted in 1963, produced the "Kennedy Round" of tariff agreements. Under these the President is authorized to agree to adjust tariff rates within limits set by law. The various foreign-aid statutes enacted since the late 1940's have carried similar provisions.

The important thing to note is that, whether treaties or authorized executive agreements are involved, both the Senate and the House share significantly in the making of foreign policy. The President as Chief Diplomat can do a great many things under his own powers, including carrying out diplomatic maneuvers that make war inescapable and signing agreements that Congress cannot refuse to implement without causing the country to appear ridiculous. But in a great many other matters a presidential policy is meaningless without the support of Congress—particularly in policies such as foreign-aid programs, where the chief instrument is money.

Thus the President's powers as Chief Diplomat, like his other powers, depend heavily on his power to persuade. In the realm of foreign policy, moreover, the complexity of his responsibilities is increased by the need to reckon not only with the intricacies of the American system but also with the political circumstances of the countries with which he is negotiating. A President repudiated or under fire at home is not likely to be highly influential abroad; conversely, one whose initiatives on the foreign scene are consistently ineffectual will have trouble persuading Congress. Wilson's cumulated frustrations from 1918 through 1920 are a classic example, one that very likely worries President Johnson as difficulties in Vietnam result in resistance to both domestic- and foreign-policy programs in Congress.

This need to lead—to be persuasive—both at home and abroad reflects the principal change in the President's function as Chief Diplomat since the Second World War. Before the end of that war it would have been conceivable for a President to say, as Warren G. Harding did in his inaugural address in 1921: "We seek no part in directing the destinies of the world." No President or serious aspirant for the White House since could have made such a statement unless he added, "But we have no choice."

The President as Commander in Chief

In discharging his diplomatic responsibilities, the President receives considerable assistance from the powers associated with his sixth major function. The Constitution describes him as "commander in chief of the army and

The President as Commander-in-Chief

Whenever normal agencies prove inadequate to the task and it becomes necessary for the Executive Branch of the Federal Government to use its powers and authority to uphold Federal Courts, the President's responsibility is inescapable.

In accordance with that responsibility, I have today issued an Executive Order directing the use of troops under Federal authority to aid in the execution of Federal law at Little Rock, Arkansas. This became necessary when my Proclamation of yesterday was not observed, and the obstruction of justice still continues....

The very basis of our individual rights and freedoms rests upon the certainty that the President and the Executive Branch of Government will support and insure the carrying out of the decisions of the Federal Courts, even, when necessary, with all the means at the President's command....

Now, let me make it very clear that Federal troops are not being used to relieve local and state authorities of their primary duty to preserve the peace and order of the community. Nor are the troops there for the purpose of taking over the responsibility of the School Board and the other responsible local officials in running Central High School. The running of our school system and the maintenance of peace and order in each of our States are strictly local affairs and the Federal Government does not interfere except in a very few special cases and when requested by one of the several States. In the present case the troops are there, pursuant to law, solely for the purpose of preventing interference with the orders of the Court.

From President Dwight D. Eisenhower, radio and television address, September 1957.

navy of the United States, and of the militia of the several states, when called into the actual service of the United States." Except for extreme circumstances, however, military power is primarily a base for diplomacy, and the President's activities as Commander in Chief and Chief Diplomat are essentially indistinguishable. Thus the movement of troops, ships, and aircraft into an area of international tension—the reinforcement of our garrisons in West Germany and Berlin, or the relocation of the Mediterranean Fleet— may be as essential to diplomatic strategy as negotiation. Also, the President can in effect ignore the constitutional power of Congress to declare war through his power to assign American forces according to the exigencies of the international situation even in times of nominal peace. The "war" in Vietnam, for example, has never formally been declared, although congressional appropriations have in effect ratified actions in that area by a succession of Presidents.

The close connection between the President's diplomatic and military functions give a new significance to his role as Commander in Chief. The Founders' fundamental objective was to ensure that military decisions would be subject to control by a civilian accountable to the electorate. This need is no less valid today, but the new American responsibilities in the world have added a further justification for the President's military role: national-security policy represents such a complex mixture of diplomatic and military planning and action that it must be coordinated and ultimately controlled by one man. The President could not direct the foreign policy of the country without having at least formal control over each of its parts.

The President's role as Commander in Chief includes more than strictly military or diplomatic actions. In purely domestic matters he may use the military to enforce federal statutes and court orders, as President Kennedy did in 1962 when he sent troops into the University of Mississippi; he may employ the army to ensure the performance of necessary government functions, such as the movement of the mails; or, at the request of state authorities, he may direct the military to suppress riots and other disturbances. Some of these powers are authorized by acts of Congress. When the President proclaims a national emergency or Congress declares war, moreover, a large number of other powers of domestic application, many of them relating to the military, may be invoked by the President on the basis of previous legislation or as a logical extension of his military powers. Thus, after declaring a national emergency before our entry into the Second World War, Franklin Roosevelt invoked his discretionary powers as Commander in Chief to create a series of executive agencies that had no authority from Congress (except that implied in subsequent appropriations for their continuance). After Pearl Harbor, Roosevelt as Commander in Chief issued the order that led to the evacuation from the West Coast states of more than 100,000 Japanese nationals and American citizens of Japanese parentage.

The President's function as Commander in Chief is thus a broad one, but the restraints upon it are also considerable. First, the President's problems in his relations with military subordinates—who often have ties with national or regional interest groups and Congress—are similar to those he faces with his civilian executives. He has much the same need to persuade; he has the power of reassignment and removal, but he can use the power only if he can afford the political costs. When President Truman in 1951 relieved General MacArthur of his command in the Far East because of the general's public criticism of the Administration's policies in the Korean War, he precipitated a storm of controversy and a full-dress Senate investigation.

A second restraint on the President as Commander in Chief is that he must share some military functions with Congress. The Constitution gives Congress not only power of the purse but the power "To declare war . . . To raise and support armies . . . To provide and maintain a navy . . . To make rules for the government and regulation of the land and naval forces."

As we have seen, the meaning of these provisions in practice is not necessarily what it appears to be. But they make it inevitable that United States "military policy . . . exists in two worlds," the world of international politics and the world of domestic politics.[5] The latter is necessarily involved, since government decisions concerning military procurement, the recruitment, training, and pay of military personnel, and the location of military installations touch sensitive nerves within the body politic.

"Weak" Presidents and "Strong"

The pivotal character of the modern Presidency means that the traditional distinction between "weak" and "strong" Presidents has less validity than it had in the past. To be sure, some Presidents may be aggressive in their relations with Congress, while others are far more retiring. And some Presidents may exploit to the full the sources of influence in their several roles, while others may underutilize them. But no President today can choose to be a James Buchanan or a Franklin Pierce—two Presidents usually characterized as weak in their relations with Congress and in the use of their initiatives. The modern President cannot escape the expectations that the system has created around his office. Truman and Eisenhower both entered the Presidency persuaded that the White House should not attempt to lead Congress, but both were obliged to try in some measure to do so.

On the other hand, a strong President, no matter how eager he may be to realize the potential influence of the office, is not in a position to command the system. He is expected to keep it moving in a direction and at a rate acceptable to the country and its allies, but he cannot compel Congress, the executive officials, or the party—to say nothing of the electorate or other governments—to respond as he wishes. He is free to try to persuade—to lead—and the country is likely to suffer if he does not attempt to do so. This is the essential meaning of the Presidency as the mainspring of the system: even if members of Congress, his nominal subordinates in the executive, the voters, and the governments of foreign countries do not respond to his leadership as he would wish, they nonetheless rely upon it.

THE SHIFT TO THE EXECUTIVE

Although based on constitutional provisions, the Presidency today is a far cry from its conception by the Founding Fathers. When they decided that the Constitution should deal first with Congress, second with the Presidency,

[5] Samuel P. Huntington, *The Common Defense: Strategic Programs in National Politics* (New York: Columbia University Press, 1961), p. 1.

The Case for a Strong Executive

While President I have *been* President, emphatically; I have used every ounce of power there was in the office and I have not cared a rap for the criticisms of those who spoke of my "usurpation of power"; for I knew that the talk was all nonsense and that there was no usurpation. I believe that the efficiency of this Government depends upon its possessing a strong central executive, and wherever I could establish a precedent for strength in the executive, as I did for instance as regards external affairs in the case of sending the fleet around the world, taking Panama, settling affairs of Santo Domingo and Cuba; or as I did in internal affairs in settling the anthracite coal strike, in keeping order in Nevada this year when the Federation of Miners threatened anarchy, or as I have done in bringing the big corporations to book—why, in all these cases I have felt not merely that my action was right in itself, but that in showing the strength of, or in giving strength to, the executive, I was establishing a precedent of value. I believe in a strong executive; I believe in power; but I believe that responsibility should go with power, and that it is not well that the strong executive should be a perpetual executive. Above all and beyond all I believe as I have said before that the salvation of this country depends upon Washington and Lincoln representing the type of leader to which we are true. I hope that in my acts I have been a good President, a President who has deserved well of the Republic; but most of all, I believe that whatever value my service may have comes even more from what I *am* than from what I *do*.

From President Theodore Roosevelt, letter to George Otto Trevelyan, June 1908.

and third with the judiciary, they were accurately reflecting the priorities and philosophy of their time. For the Philadelphia Convention of 1787 took place in the midst of the era of the legislature. In Great Britain, Parliament was fast becoming the dominant government institution. Other factors also encouraged the Framers to favor the legislature. First, the colonial assemblies had been highly effective instruments against the Crown and its representatives before and during the Revolution. Second, the Framers were guided by the patterns of the postrevolutionary state constitutions, which had tended to establish weak, multimember executives, because public sentiment was so strong against placing authority in the hands of any one person. Third, the Framers were probably influenced by the order of discussion in such familiar commentaries as John Locke's *Second Treatise on Civil Government* (1690).

Many of the delegates to the Philadelphia Convention wanted to create "a vigorous executive," but, knowing the dominant sentiment of the country, they had more trouble agreeing on this section of the Constitution than on any other. Both the temper of the times and political prudence dictated that the legislature should come first. Otherwise the proposed Constitution was unlikely to be accepted.

Today, the wording of the Constitution technically continues to give primacy to the legislature. But, if the Constitution were to be rewritten to reflect the practices actually followed today, the Presidency would come first. The new phrasing would allocate to Congress the power to criticize, to approve, to disapprove, and to modify proposals laid before it and the power to propose new lines of action in some areas of public policy. But it would designate the President as the leader in the most important matters of public policy, foreign affairs, and national security.

How did the Presidency change so tremendously? It was not changed suddenly; in fact it was not even changed by a series of overt, purposeful actions by Presidents, Congress, or the electorate. Three factors altered the Presidency: (1) a rapidly changing society, which has created problems too complex to be treated primarily through legislative actions; (2) crises at home and abroad; and (3) the political talents of Presidents sensitive to these changes and crises.

The Case for a Restrained Executive

The true view of the Executive functions is, as I conceive it, that the President can exercise no power which cannot be fairly and reasonably traced to some specific grant of power or justly implied and included within such express grant as proper and necessary to its exercise. Such specific grant must be either in the Federal Constitution or in an act of Congress passed in pursuance thereof. There is no undefined residuum of power which he can exercise because it seems to him to be in the public interest.... The grants of Executive power are necessarily in general terms in order not to embarrass the Executive within the field of action plainly marked for him, but his jurisdiction must be justified and vindicated by affirmative constitutional or statutory provision, or it does not exist....

Ascribing an undefined residuum of power to the President is an unsafe doctrine [that] might lead under emergencies to results of an arbitrary character, doing irremediable injustice to private right. The mainspring of such a view is that the Executive is charged with responsibility for the welfare of all the people in a general way, that he is to play the part of a Universal Providence and set all things right, and that anything that in his judgment will help the people he ought to do, unless he is expressly forbidden to do it. The wide field of action that this would give to the Executive one can hardly limit.

From former President William H. Taft, *Our Chief Magistrate and His Powers,* 1916.

Presidential Growth in the Nineteenth Century

The potential for growth in the Presidency became evident as early as 1803. President Jefferson was presented, as a result of the military and financial embarrassments of Napoleon, with an opportunity to purchase the vast domain of French Louisiana for the United States. As a constitutional theorist and "strict constructionist," Jefferson was certain that the President lacked constitutional authority to acquire territory. But he agreed to the transaction, though he sought the approval of Congress after the fact. His action was justified by Congress on the "new" ground that it was implicit in the President's power to make treaties. This justification by Congress points to an even more fundamental Jeffersonian innovation: his ability to translate into presidential power his popular following in the nation and the skills of his lieutenants in Congress. Since his day no President has succeeded in making the office effective without duplicating Jefferson's role as Party Leader.

In our second example, the successive crises of the Civil War, Abraham Lincoln took a series of executive actions, without prior congressional authorization, that constitutional lawyers have debated for a century. He spent federal funds, increased the size of the Army and Navy, established a military-draft system, and suspended the writ of habeas corpus, to mention only a few. Several of his actions were ratified after the fact by Congress— but not all of them. The Supreme Court, discredited by its proslavery decisions and loath to limit a President in wartime, did not declare any of the President's policies invalid until after the war.

At least some of Lincoln's acts violated the Constitution. In *political* terms, however, the secession of the Southern states and the later crises of the war itself required vigorous leadership and speedy action. Emergency may not have compelled the President to act unconstitutionally, but it did compel him to act. Although the Constitution nowhere explicitly provided for the contingencies of secession and civil war, it surely implied that in such circumstances the government would act and that leadership would come from the Chief Executive.

The effect of such extraconstitutional expectations can be illustrated by the 1902 strike of the United Mine Workers in Pennsylvania, during Theodore Roosevelt's first Administration. The strike dragged on for five months. By late summer the coal shortage had become severe, and the price of coal was rising rapidly. In early October, schools in New York City were closed for lack of coal. Republican leaders, including the President, were worried about the effects of these conditions on the impending congressional elections. Had the governor of Pennsylvania requested federal assistance to maintain order in the coal fields, the President could legally have sent in troops, but the strike remained relatively peaceful. No other constitutional or statutory basis for presidential intervention existed, and the Supreme

Court's view of the federal government's control over commerce was then too narrow to permit a presidential request for legislation.

The President nevertheless felt that he was expected to find a solution to the crisis. As he wrote to Senator Mark Hanna, "We have no earthly responsibility for it, but the public at large will visit upon our heads responsibility for the shortage in coal." [6] Working directly and through various intermediaries, Roosevelt finally induced the union and the coal operators to resume operations and to agree to accept the terms recommended by a commission he appointed. The requirements and needs of a changing society have, in effect, added such responsibility to the presidential office.

The Sources of Change in the Presidency

Although the evolution of the Presidency has been continuous, the rate of this change has varied. Despite the dramatic examples of Jefferson and Lincoln, the development of the Presidency was gradual throughout the nineteenth century. With the advent of the twentieth century, however, the significance of the Presidency began to expand at a tremendous rate as the inevitable result of changing economic and social conditions, both domestic and international.

What were these conditions? Since they affect all branches of government, why should they have changed the relative importance of the President in the constitutional scheme? Can we point to factors that have been peculiarly "presidential"?

The answer is that the elements of the modern Presidency are the result of socioeconomic change and increasing interdependence in the society, not of mere growth in the volume of federal government activities. When a society undergoes continual and rapid change and when shifts in one part of its structure produce strains and frictions in another, its government must supply the means for speedy action. It must provide effective ways to make adjustments, and it must set, or at least propose, priorities among alternative lines of action.

Neither legislatures, nor courts, nor bureaucracies are the most likely sources of such action. It is possible for Congress, especially through its leaders, to initiate some important governmental policies. For example, the civil-rights legislation enacted during the second Eisenhower Administration owed more to Lyndon Johnson's efforts as Senate majority leader than to presidential efforts. But legislative bodies rarely speak with one voice; no legislator, not even a distinguished senator, has the national standing of a President. As for the courts, they are inherently *reacting* institutions rather than initiating ones; they cannot speak until a dispute is brought before them. And bureaucracies, though they are often more inventive than their

[6] Quoted in Henry F. Pringle, *Theodore Roosevelt* (New York: Harcourt, Brace & World, 1956), p. 189.

GROWING EXECUTIVE POWERS

ORIGINAL CONCEPT OF U.S. PRESIDENCY

Don Hesse in the St. Louis *Globe-Democrat*

Overgrown

Many conservatives complain that the growth of the Presidency has distorted the Framers' concept of limited executive power.

critics recognize, lack the *political* authority essential for solving crises. The responses demanded by rapid change must come from a source capable of quick, decisive, and authoritative action. In the American scheme the Presidency is most likely to be that source. "What separates the major from the minor Presidents," a distinguished journalist has remarked, ". . . is ability to perceive and seize initiative. For the laws of Congress cannot define, nor can custom anticipate, the unknown—and this is where the great Presidents must live . . . ." [7]

Domestic factors enlarging the Presidency

The domestic factor most responsible for enlarging the Presidency is the network of interdependencies among producers, distributors, transporters, managers, workers, and consumers created by a highly industrialized economy. The elements of this network normally exist in tolerable harmony, but the system is not fully self-correcting. It involves a division of labor among participants who have yielded self-sufficiency in return for the higher productivity that goes with specialization. But a consequence of this division is that disturbance or failure at any point in the network affects the others in varying degrees. If private parties directly involved in the disturbance do not take corrective action, some of the parties—and the public—will expect the government to act, and the responsibility for initiating such action usually falls on the President.

[7] Theodore H. White, *The Making of the President, 1960* (New York: Atheneum, 1961), p. 369.

"Promise it won't rise any higher?"

Liberals, however, tend to argue that new domestic and international pressures require increased discretionary power for the President.

© 1964 by Bill Mauldin
From *What's Got Your Back Up?*
Harper & Row, 1961

Take the pricing policies of large corporations. In many industries a few large corporations are generally able to control the prices at which their products will sell, since the companies' predominance overcomes the price-setting effect of market demand. The price decisions of these corporations, especially for commodities that are the raw materials of many other industries, can have an important effect upon price levels throughout the economy.

As the effects of a price increase are felt in the cost of living or in declining exports, demands and proposals for corrective action begin to appear. These may come from the business community, from labor organizations, from academicians, and from a host of other sources; committees of Congress may hold hearings on "administered pricing" or on "labor monopoly," and various bills may be introduced into the House and Senate; specialists in various executive agencies are likely to study the problem, to assess proposed solutions, or to devise additional alternatives.

Any of these efforts may result in actions not directly connected with the President. The chances are, however, that if the problem persists he will be pressed to select and champion one or more proposals on which the executive branch and especially Congress can focus their attention. As the expectation grows that this is a matter for "the government," the President's feeling of responsibility for resolving the conflict increases. In particular, if his party depends heavily on certain groups in the electorate who show signs of defection because of the continued conflict, the President will be called upon as Party Leader to formulate some corrective action.

In a free society, not all the required corrective actions are taken by the federal government or by any government. Some are managed by individuals for themselves, some by corporations or other private groups, and some by state and local governments. But those needs that are beyond private means or beyond the public means of states and cities inevitably must be met by Washington.

As some of these functions of government and of the President become accepted, they may be partly formalized in continuing legislation. In the Employment Act of 1946 Congress accepted—hesitantly and somewhat reluctantly—a lesson of the depression of the 1930's: that the federal government cannot escape concern with the state of the economy. The act directed the President, with the assistance of a Council of Economic Advisers, to report at least annually on the condition of the economy and to propose measures to achieve the objectives of the act. The chief significance of the act is that it *institutionalized* and formally acknowledged the proposition that the government must assume a minimum degree of managerial responsibility for levels of employment and rates of economic growth. The act did formally what Theodore Roosevelt did personally and informally in the coal strike of 1902. It identified the Presidency, moreover, as the appropriate source of initiative for proposed programs.

As presidential responsibility and initiative are accepted in such critical domestic matters and as the office becomes increasingly pivotal in the political system, more and more groups turn to the President. Specialists who want to do something about the deterioration of our major cities, scientists who want to guide and protect the conduct and the application of scientific research in the United States, and citizens who see other problems that seem to call for coordinated action—all feel that the President's involvement and support would greatly enhance the chances of achieving solutions. The factors encouraging the focus on the Presidency thus tend to be cumulative.

International factors enlarging the Presidency

The domestic developments enlarging the Presidency have been heavily supplemented by the emergence of the United States as a superpower in a world changed almost beyond recognition from the one dominated only a few decades ago by a handful of European nations. Change and interdependence on the domestic scene have placed increased responsibilities on the Presidency; the same factors in international politics have had an even stronger impact. For if the United States is to be effective in its foreign relations it must, as nearly as possible, speak with one voice.

Looking at the United States in the 1830's, De Tocqueville attributed our relatively feeble executive power to the insignificance of our foreign relations. Observing that in "a nation without neighbors" the Chief Executive gains little standing from his responsibility for the conduct of foreign relations, the perceptive Frenchman understood that, conversely,

> If the existence of the Union were perpetually threatened, if its chief interests were in daily connection with those of other powerful nations, the executive government would assume an increased importance in proportion to the measures expected of it and to those which it would execute.[8]

The effects of the new international politics upon the Presidency are now so apparent, perhaps, that one is in danger of forgetting that they had their beginnings scarcely more than five short decades ago. As late as 1884 Woodrow Wilson, writing his classic study of the American system, *Congressional Government*, saw "Congress predominant over its so-called coordinate branches." The Presidency, he felt, was not a position of "recognized leadership in our politics"; it was "too silent and inactive, too little like a premiership and too much like a superintendency." In 1900, however, following the changes brought by the war with Spain, he prepared a new preface in which he pointed to the "greatly increased power and opportunity for constructive statesmanship given the President."

But Wilson knew that the effects of this enhanced presidential position would not be confined to the office itself. He anticipated that it might have a "very far-reaching effect upon our whole method of government," achieving an "integration" that he still found wanting in the operation of the system.[9] His anticipations were accurate; because the United States would never again be as removed from the rest of the world as it had been through most of the nineteenth century, the more prominent position of the Presidency would also affect the other branches of the government and perhaps provide a means of integrating the whole system.

The effects on the Presidency that Wilson anticipated have been persistent. They have been enormously stimulated, however, by American involvement in the two world wars. The kind of total national effort that these conflicts required concentrated authority and leadership in the Chief Executive. And the years since 1945 have seen relatively little shrinkage in the office.

The reasons that the Presidency grows as the importance of foreign relations increases are complex, and this growth cannot be explained merely by constitutional prescription or by the efficiency of the nation's speaking with a single voice. These are valid factors, to be sure, but there are no obvious explanations for their validity. Since the Logan Act of 1799, it has been a crime for anyone to encroach upon the President's exclusive right to negotiate with foreign powers. The spirit of this prohibition is fairly

[8] Alexis de Tocqueville, *Democracy in America*, Phillips Bradley, ed. (New York: Knopf, 1945), Vol. I, pp. 126 and 131.
[9] Woodrow Wilson, *Congressional Government* (New York: Meridian, 1956; 1st edition, Boston, 1885), pp. 22, 23, 52, and 141.

frequently compromised, both by members of Congress and by private citizens. Yet its purpose is seldom actually violated. Why?

In the international sphere both the prospects of change and the implications of interdependence are quite different from what they are on the domestic scene. Domestic political relations rest on an assumption of ultimate agreement among contestants, on acceptance of some final legitimate authority, and on an expectation of nonviolent processes of settlement. They tend, in other words, toward stability. In international political relations these stabilizing factors are either missing altogether or only moderately operative. The commitments of nominal friends—even such close allies as Britain and the United States—cannot be complete or wholly reliable. Allies are always in part rivals and even potential opponents, the prospects of violent action are always present, and complete agreement must be hoped for rather than assumed.

A nation whose neighbors cover the globe is thus exposed to constant change. Since any move tends to have far-reaching effects in such unstable relations, such a nation must be able to act quickly and decisively. Moreover, the nation must maintain a minimum degree of secrecy about its plans. This means that only a few people can participate in deciding matters of greatest import—those immediately associated with the office where quick and decisive action can best be taken. During the Cuban missile crisis of 1962, for example, the Kennedy Administration had to formulate its plans within a small group of presidential aides. Only afterwards were congressional leaders given secret briefings, and the press and public learned about the policies only after the decisions had been made and many of the key actions had already been taken.

It follows clearly that information about the international system and information about the prospects of change tend to converge at the same point—the Presidency. The nature of the international system thus affords no acceptable alternative to presidential responsibility and leadership.

Five broad aspects of diplomacy in the years since the Second World War have greatly augmented these tendencies in the American Presidency:

First, through circumstances beyond its control, the nation has found itself at the head of one system of alliances in a bipolar world. As the trustee of that system it must be sensitive to changes within any member nation, or between two members, because they may affect the structure of the system itself. For example, danger to Denmark need not immediately concern Italy, and, similarly, a dispute over Cyprus between Greece and Turkey need not directly affect Norway; yet both situations might constitute threats to the stability of NATO, for which the United States—particularly the President—is chiefly responsible.

Second, since the Second World War there has been a huge increase in the importance of multilateral diplomacy. Multilateral negotiation, inherently more complex than bilateral, is further complicated when much of it must occur, as in the United Nations, in the light of full publicity. Policy must thus reckon with the responses of all nations and individuals who are witnesses to the public proceedings.

Third, this period has produced significant changes in the number and character of the actors on the diplomatic scene. In little more than a decade membership in the United Nations has risen from 50 to 121. At the same time power within the United Nations has gradually shifted from the Security Council, where the great powers can dominate, to the General Assembly, where all the new nations formally stand on an equal footing with the most powerful of the older powers. In addition, many of these new nations, especially in Africa, are experiencing rapid internal change, which threatens both their own stability and the stability of their commitments in the international system. These factors all increase the complexities of American diplomacy.

Fourth, the rivalry of Russia and the United States for the allegiance of the uncommitted countries as well as the needs and demands of the "developing" nations have introduced essentially new instruments into diplomacy, chiefly economic aid in its various forms. These have been the major means of American-Soviet rivalry in the Middle East, in the Congo, and in Indonesia, for example.

Fifth, the making of foreign policy has been enormously complicated by rapid changes in military technology. Military power, of course, has always been the handmaiden of diplomacy, but until fairly recently the technology underlying such power was comparatively simple and changed relatively slowly. In an age of nuclear missiles and space vehicles, however, weapons systems may be obsolete within a few months of their production. Hence the frontiers of our military power and diplomatic influence are delineated on the drawing boards of engineers and through the simulations of computers. This means, moreover, that new considerations and new actors—scientists and military technologists—must be involved in foreign policy. A decision for or against a program of nuclear testing, for example, involves simultaneously estimating its effects on our structure of alliances, on the attitudes of the uncommitted nations, on the prospects of international arms control, and on our position in the rapid and unending race for technological superiority. These estimates can ultimately be made only by the occupant of the White House.

The interdependence of foreign and domestic factors

International and domestic factors are closely interdependent. To take a welcome and not entirely fanciful example: suppose that the two sides in the Cold War reached an agreement on the reduction and control of armaments that would reduce our expenditures for defense by several billion dollars. This step would involve more than a mere budgetary adjustment; it would jeopardize employment and earnings in wide sectors of American industry where resources are concentrated on defense production; it would threaten the financial prospects of universities now receiving millions of dollars in defense-related research funds; it would, in other words, involve the kinds of dislocation created by demobilization after a war. Coordinated presidential initiatives would be as necessary and as widely expected here as they were during the Depression.

This is an extreme example, but the interdependence of international and domestic factors already exists on a smaller scale. For instance, take the connection between the emergence of the new nations of Africa as important elements in international politics and presidential initiatives in American race relations. Or between concern for the foreign policies of the African nations and the price or wage decisions of American-owned corporations on which some underdeveloped economies are heavily dependent. These connections require that priorities be proposed, that coordinated action be taken, and that initiatives be promptly forthcoming —the same requirements, in short, that have contributed to the emergence of the Presidency in the purely domestic or purely international spheres.

SUMMARY

This chapter has explored the sources and the implications of the proposition that the modern Presidency has become the mainspring of the governmental system. The duties of the modern Presidency can be conveniently divided into six categories. First, the President's role as Chief of State makes him the one ceremonial representative of the entire American nation. Though his duties as Chief of State are largely symbolic, they contribute to his power by placing his position above the partisan battle.

The President's role as Chief Executive rests more directly on constitutional provisions, particularly his responsibility to "take care that the laws be faithfully executed." The congressional practice of issuing "delegated legislation"—broad directives that allow the executive branch to decide how to implement them—gives the executive branch considerable discretion in administering statutes. Nonetheless, it is the President's *political* skills that help him to approach filling the gap between public expectations of the President and his actual power.

The President as Chief Executive is limited by the formal and informal restrictions on his power to appoint and remove officials in the executive branch. His power of appointment is limited first by the fact that almost 90 percent of executive-branch officials are chosen through the merit system, and, second, by the need for Senate confirmation of many important policy-making positions and by the custom of senatorial courtesy.

The President's removal power is formally restricted only in regard to members of "quasi-legislative" or "quasi-judicial" agencies or commissions, but in fact he must often pay substantial *political* costs to remove even a purely executive official. Such an official is likely to have friends in Congress, throughout the executive branch, and among interest groups who could hamper the President's program in retaliation.

The President's role as Chief Legislator rests largely on two constitutional provisions. First, his duty to deliver an annual State of the Union message to Congress has led to the presidential practice of drafting detailed "administration bills," which make up the heart of the legislative agenda. Second, the President's right to veto legislation, though limited in several ways, still gives him substantial power to prevent unwanted legislation and to influence the content of statutes.

The President's role as Party Leader, though extraconstitutional, is nonetheless significant. His job is to keep the "national party" that elected him strong enough to reelect him or to elect a preferred successor from his party. Even senators and representatives from the President's party have an incentive to preserve the appearance of unified support for the President's programs. These common stakes stem partly from an intangible sense of party loyalty and partly from the fact that the fate of a presidential candidate in an election often affects the fates of the party's candidates for the House and Senate as well.

The President's role as Chief Diplomat stems from his constitutional right to "receive ambassadors and other public ministers" and from his power to make treaties with the advice and consent of the Senate. The President's "right of reception" makes him the sole means of formal communication with foreign governments and allows him to grant or withhold recognition of them as well.

The formal stipulation that two-thirds of the Senate approve treaties reflects the significant role of both the Senate and House in the making of foreign policy. The Senate is in practice involved in the negotiations of most formal treaties; and even executive agreements, though made by the President alone, often depend on the Senate and House for appropriations to put them into effect.

The President's role as Commander in Chief of the United States Army and Navy closely complements his role as Chief Diplomat, because military strategy is often a base for diplomatic negotiations. The new significance and complexity of our military establishment today have accentuated the importance of having one civilian—the President—with ultimate control over diplomatic and military strategy. The President may also use his powers as Commander in Chief in the domestic sphere to enforce federal statutes and court orders. His power, however, is limited by the power of Congress over the purse and to declare war.

It is important to remember that all six of the President's roles are interdependent: the degree of his effectiveness in one role largely determines his success in the others. Because his powers are subject to constitutional and political restraints, the politics of the Presidency is one of persuasion—the art of rational argument and the skillful creation of an atmosphere in which those participants on whom the President depends for success are induced to accept his initiatives.

Though the Founding Fathers had envisioned a government in which Congress would be dominant, the Presidency today has become the key element in the system. The primary domestic factor responsible for this change has been the rise of our highly industrialized economy, with its complex interrelationships among management, labor, and consumers. Since any disturbance in this intricate network has far-reaching effects, both the public at large and the affected interest groups have come to expect the President to take leadership in solving economic crises.

The Presidency has also been expanded by our vastly increased importance as a superpower in today's world. Several aspects of the contemporary international system encourage power in our government to flow to the President: our position as head of a system of alliances encompassing half the world; the increased importance of multilateral diplomacy; the independence of the Afro-Asian former colonies; the new importance of economic aid in American-Russian competition for the allegiance of the uncommitted nations; and, finally, rapid changes in military technology.

In both domestic and international affairs, the Presidency has been the branch best equipped for speedy action, for effective negotiation of adjustments to change, and for the identification of priorities among alternative lines of action.

The pivotal character of the modern Presidency in the American system has led some responsible observers to fear that, in Edward S. Corwin's words, "the Presidency is a potential matrix of dictatorship." [10] Others, however, fear that too large a gap between the expectations focused on the President and the power he can exercise may lead to a weakening or failure of the system. Both these concerns have some substance. However, a narrowing of the gap between expectations and effective influence might well reduce the likelihood of getting a dictator in the White House. How wide the gap is in fact depends in considerable measure upon the quality of the President's instruments for persuasion. These instruments thus deserve a close analysis, which the next chapter will undertake.

[10] Edward S. Corwin, *The President: Office and Powers*, 3rd ed. (New York: New York University Press, 1948), p. 353.

THE
INSTRUMENTS
OF
PRESIDENTIAL
LEADERSHIP

10

In order to close the gap between what is expected of him and what he can accomplish, the President requires more than skills of persuasion. He must be able to use a variety of leadership instruments. This chapter analyzes the range of presidential instruments—from institutional agencies such as the White House Office to informal practices such as the press conference. Our purpose is to evaluate how useful each instrument is in helping the President to discharge the demands that are imposed on him. To do so, we have asked two questions: What are the range and importance of each instrument's functions? How closely do its stakes and goals coincide with those of the President?

For the President to function as a "mainspring," he needs more than the opportunity for leadership and initiative. " 'Powers' are no guarantee of power." [1] Why should this be so?

First, for reasons of preference or personality, the President may not take the lead. In such circumstances the system partially compensates by providing other sources of initiative, chiefly Congress. These alternative points of leadership, however, lack the special resources of the Presidency and rarely can do for the system as a whole what the modern Presidency can under favorable circumstances.

Second, and more characteristically, the President's ability to persuade may not be sufficient to close the gap between what the system requires and what he can accomplish. To perform his six functions, the President must successfully persuade a motley assortment of individuals and groups whose consent or support is necessary for the accomplishment of his objectives. These people—including his nominal executive subordinates, a majority in the House and the Senate, the press, the electorate, and the governments of foreign nations—may not be susceptible to his attempts at persuasion. Their own objectives may be hopelessly at odds with his, or they may anticipate greater gain from rejecting presidential suggestions than from acceding to them. Reluctance or rebellion in one quarter, moreover, may spread rapidly to others, and the gap between public expectation of the President's role and his actual performance may be widened.

How wide the gap becomes depends not only upon the inclinations and skills of the President but also upon the availability of appropriate instruments for his leadership. The President's day contains too few hours for him to keep in touch unaided with all those whom he needs or who depend upon him—in and out of the country—and to perform all the acts of persuasion upon which his efforts depend.

There are an almost unlimited number of devices that may serve as presidential instruments, and they are by no means confined to government agencies. In appropriate circumstances a widely read newspaper columnist, an important friend in the business community, or one in the labor movement may be crucial to the President. But they are likely to be of less continuous importance than the official apparatus of the government. In this chapter, therefore, primary attention will be given to the official instruments of the President.

Broadly speaking, the usefulness to the President of any instrument of initiative depends on two factors: (1) the range and importance of its functions and (2) the degree to which its political stakes and goals approximate those of the President. Agencies that can serve as vehicles of presidential initiative may rely, in varying degrees, on sources other

[1] Richard E. Neustadt, *Presidential Power: The Politics of Leadership* (New York: Wiley, 1960), p. 10.

than the President for their prestige, influence, and political survival. To the extent that these other sources of support are at odds with presidential purposes, the agencies they affect will be too. If conditions are favorable, however, the President may use such instruments as channels for carrying out his decisions or as sources of advice to him or as both.

THE EXECUTIVE OFFICE OF THE PRESIDENT

The Executive Office of the President is the official designation for a collection of organizations and individuals, each formally charged with assisting the President in performing duties that are distinctively presidential. Created by President Roosevelt's executive order in 1939, the Executive Office now includes as its principal units the White House Office, the Bureau of the Budget, the Council of Economic Advisers, and the National Security Council. The agencies of the Executive Office employ upwards of 2,500 people, a large proportion of whom are professional specialists— lawyers, economists, statisticians, political scientists, journalists, and many others.

The White House Office

The heart of the White House Office—and of the entire Executive Office— is the President's personal staff, which numbers approximately twenty. This personal staff is a comparatively recent phenomenon; its growth is one index of the increased importance of the modern Presidency. At the turn of the century the President's immediate assistants were a secretary, a few clerks, and a messenger, all of whom were paid from the President's personal funds rather than by the government. The modern character of the White House Office dates from 1939, when it was greatly expanded as part of the creation of the Executive Office of the President.

A few members of the personal staff have sharply defined responsibilities, notably the Press Secretary and the Appointments Secretary. Recent Presidents also have designated one special assistant and one or more administrative assistants for liaison with members of Congress—discussing, negotiating, and soliciting support for the President's policies. Most of the President's assistants, however, work on *ad hoc* assignments; they may have a particular specialty, but they are also generally equipped to deal with a wide range of government problems, performing the anticipating, inquiring, investigating, and follow-up activities that constitute the heart of staff work.

The usefulness of the President's personal staff as a presidential instrument is potentially very great. The range of its concerns is as broad as its members and the President are prepared to make it. Their proximity to him and their identification with his fortunes, especially if they have long been among his intimates, are likely to minimize divergence from his purposes.

However, what the members of the President's personal staff can do for him they do as his auxiliary eyes and ears, not as instruments with power of their own. Their influence depends upon recognition of their competence as individuals and in particular upon the confidence the President appears to place in them.

The chief hazard of the personal staff from the President's standpoint is that its members may cease being his *auxiliary* eyes and ears and begin to do most of his seeing and hearing—and thus his choosing—for him. If the President delegates extensively and demands recommendations that reflect agreed staff positions, as was Eisenhower's practice throughout his Presidency, he is likely to lose touch with informative details and revealing conflicts. When that occurs, he is in danger of becoming a prisoner of his staff system rather than its master. As Neustadt aptly observes, "A President is so uniquely situated and his power so bound up with the uniqueness of his place, that he can count on no one else to be perceptive for him." [2]

The Bureau of the Budget

The oldest and most significant unit in the Executive Office is the Bureau of the Budget, created by the Budget and Accounting Act of 1921. Before the Bureau of the Budget was organized, no one in the executive branch, not even the President, reviewed the financial requests of departments and independent agencies; they were merely collected by the Treasury Department and forwarded to Congress for action. For almost two decades after its establishment the bureau was little more than a housekeeping device to promote economy and efficiency in the executive branch. The intimacy that was expected to exist between the President and the bureau, however, is suggested by the act's provision for presidential appointment of the Budget director without the advice and consent of the Senate. A more significant role for the bureau was symbolized in its transfer from the Treasury Department to the Executive Office of the President when that agency was created in 1939.

The contemporary Bureau of the Budget has four chief functions. First, it prepares and administers the budget. This includes assisting the President in setting general budgetary policies as well as in reviewing and approving, reducing, or (rarely) increasing the estimates submitted by the departments and agencies (subject to their appeal to the President). The

[2] *Ibid.*, p. 179.

bureau also apportions appropriations by controlling the rate at which appropriated funds may be spent.

Second, the bureau does legislative reference work, which includes reviewing agencies' requests for legislation in order to determine whether such proposals conform to the President's program and reviewing legislation passed by Congress and submitted to the President for his signature. The bureau, after clearance with other interested executive agencies, recommends that the President either sign or veto a measure and, if the latter, prepares a draft of a proposed veto message.

Third, the bureau studies the organization and management practices of executive agencies; it then sponsors improvements in these matters and prepares major reorganization plans, which the President is authorized to put into effect if they are not disapproved by a congressional concurrent resolution.[3]

Fourth, the bureau tries to improve financial-management practices, in cooperation with the Treasury and the General Accounting Office, and it reviews and coordinates the statistical services of the government.

If the President chooses to develop its potentialities, the Bureau of the Budget can be enormously useful as an instrument of initiative. A budget is a program. Its construction permits the bureau and the President to make a wide range of significant choices, both about the general level of expenditures in relation to the needs of the economy and about the relative emphasis that should be given to competing demands for public funds— civil versus military, one arm of the military or one proposed weapons system versus another, increased educational subsidies versus more funds for national parks, and so on. The execution of a budget after appropriations have been voted, moreover, can involve important opportunities for the control or alteration of the program by regulating the rate of expenditure. And preparing the budget and executing it give the bureau an acquaintance with the problems and shortcomings of all other executive agencies that is unparalleled in scope and detail anywhere else in the government.

An agency with these functions can be a major instrument for making nominal presidential subordinates in the executive branch into subordinates willing or obliged to execute the President's wishes. To execute its functions properly, the bureau must be sensitive to public demands, to the temper of Congress, and to the designs and desires of key senators and representatives in their relations with executive officials and with interest groups. For this reason a Bureau of the Budget functioning *in close alliance with the President* can be an unparalleled source of intragovernmental intelligence, program advice, and support for the President. Insofar as it operates in this fashion, moreover, the Bureau of the Budget comes to be relied upon both by the executive agencies and by Congress. Congressional

---

[3] On the "legislative veto," see Ch. 9, p. 302.

leaders as a matter of course may inquire of the bureau—among others—how important proposed legislation is to "the President's program" because they need to know presidential intentions in setting their own agendas and in fixing their own priorities.

The bureau's political risks and goals are compatible, but not identical, with those of the President. Its origin and its standard activities assure it some influence apart from presidential support. As a part of the bureaucracy it has its own stakes, its own risks and goals, in its relations with other agencies and with Congress. But programs and commitments that an agency develops in close association with the President can create joint stakes of greater magnitude. Thus, the Bureau of the Budget can be invaluable to the President who wants to take effective initiative.

The Council of Economic Advisers

The smallest and one of the youngest institutional staff units in the Executive Office is the Council of Economic Advisers. Created by the Employment Act of 1946, the council is composed of three members, professional economists of high standing, appointed by the President with the consent of the Senate. The President designates one of the three as chairman.

The functions of the council are to analyze trends in the economy, to appraise the adequacy of existing government programs in meeting the economic needs it identifies, and to recommend to the President policies necessary to achieve the goals of the 1946 act. In addition, the council prepares for the President the Economic Report, which the statute requires him to submit to Congress at the beginning of each session. The preparation of this report, like the writing of the annual budget message, gives the President the opportunity to assess broadly the existing policies and to specify the major guidelines for future government programs affecting the economy. As Neustadt says, the preparation of the report compels the President "to come to grips with those things he would want to make his own if he were free to interfere and pick and choose at will." [4]

The council, however, has limitations as a presidential instrument. First, its influence depends primarily upon its reputation for disinterested, professional competence. This influence is diminished if the council appears to be tailoring its advice to fit the administration's preconceptions. On the other hand, unless its members act before Congress and the country as spokesmen both for the President's economic program and for their own analyses, they may see his policies undermined and find their analyses ignored or misinterpreted.

This problem caused considerable difficulty in the early years of the

---

[4] Neustadt, *op. cit.*, p. 156.

council. The first chairman, Edwin G. Nourse, took the position that the advisers should not testify before Congress. Until his resignation in 1949 the council's relations with Congress and even with the White House deteriorated. In subsequent years council members have normally testified when asked by Congress. They have also taken the position that they should resign if they felt obliged to dissent from the President's decisions, although no such resignations have occurred.[5]

Second, economic considerations are not the only factors relevant to presidential policy choices. Thus the President cannot assume that the stakes of the council—in the long run professionally determined—are identical to his even when they are consistent with his. In this respect the council resembles the President's scientific advisers rather than the generalists on the White House staff: the members of the council give professional advice on technical questions, but "they are not across-the-board, general purpose counsellors and political intimates of the President." [6]

The National Security Council

Significantly different from the other institutional staff units in the Executive Office but equally important, the National Security Council (NSC) is composed of the President as chairman, the Vice-President, the Secretary of State, the Secretary of Defense, and the Director of the Office of Emergency Planning (a minor unit in the Executive Office). These members are provided for by statute, but in addition the President may invite other officials to attend its meetings.

The NSC thus bears a close resemblance to a Cabinet committee. The National Security Act of 1947 created the NSC to advise the President on the coordination of foreign, military, and domestic policies. It has a forty-person secretariat, and the special assistant to the President for national-security affairs directs the work of this group in support of the council.

The proceedings of the NSC are classified top secret for security reasons, which may account in part for the many disagreements about the council's value to the President. Critics argue that since most of its members must represent the special viewpoints of their agencies, agreements arrived at by the NSC are likely to be ambiguous compromises. Supporters, on the other hand, assert that the organization provides an essential arena for responsible discussion of the most critical military-diplomatic issues. Both views are partly correct.

Though the NSC's concerns are great, they are by no means equal to those of the President. And, like the Cabinet, its utility as an instrument

---

[5] Corinne Silverman, *The President's Economic Advisers* (University, Ala.: University of Alabama Press, 1959).

[6] U.S. Senate, Committee on Government Operations, Subcommittee on National Policy Machinery, *Organizing for National Security* (1961), Vol. III, p. 81.

The Role of the National Security Council

The National Security Council has never been and should never become the only instrument of counsel and decision available to the President in dealing with the problems of our national security. I believe this fact cannot be overemphasized.... I have the impression that many of the great episodes of the Truman and Eisenhower administrations were not dealt with, in their most vital aspects, through the machinery of the NSC. It was not in an NSC meeting that we got into the Korean war, or made the Korean truce. The NSC was not, characteristically, the place of decision on specific major budgetary issues, which so often affect both policy and strategy. It was not the usual forum of diplomatic decision; it was not, for example, a major center of work on Berlin at any time before 1961. The National Security Council is one instrument among many; it must never be made an end in itself.

But for certain issues of great moment, the NSC is indeed valuable. President Kennedy has used it for discussion of basic national policy toward a number of countries. He has used it both for advice on particular pressing decisions and for recommendations on long-term policy. As new attitudes develop within the administration, and as new issues arise in the world, the NSC is likely to continue as a major channel through which broad issues of national security policy come forward for Presidential decision.

From McGeorge Bundy, special assistant to the President for national security affairs, letter to Senator Henry M. Jackson of Washington, July 1961.

of presidential initiative is limited by the natural tendency of most of its members to represent the views and interests of their agencies. Nevertheless, if the President, either through council discussions or through his personal staff, can learn what these special concerns are and what controversies tend to be obscured in the agreements that are reached, he gains some advantage. He needs a consensus among his key military and diplomatic subordinates, but he also needs to know what issues are being avoided or minimized in achieving it.

Other Units

Of less importance as presidential instruments are four other units of the Executive Office. The Office of Emergency Planning advises the President on the planning and coordination of policy concerning a wide variety of emergencies, both natural disasters and the consequences of military actions. It was established as a successor to the Office of Civil and Defense Mobilization in 1961, when the operating responsibilities for civil defense were transferred from OCDM to the Department of Defense.

The Office of Science and Technology was created in 1962 to advise and assist the President in the effective use of science and scientists both in national-security matters and in domestic areas of concern to the government. Then in 1963 the Office of the Special Representative for Trade Negotiations was established to assist the President in connection with the trade-agreements program, and the following year the Office of Economic Opportunity was created by statute to carry out such aspects of the poverty program as the President assigns to it.

THE VICE–PRESIDENT AS EXECUTIVE

At a session of the Senate in the First Congress someone proposed that the Vice-President should be addressed as "His Superfluous Excellency." The characterization is overly harsh, but it points to the anomaly of a position that is close to power yet has little of its own. Many Vice-Presidents have been men of great ability, but none has quite escaped the handicap of being without a substantial independent source of power.

In his capacity as President of the Senate, the Vice-President, by long-established practice, is an outsider. Unlike the Speaker of the House, he derives little or no influence from his position as such. A former senator in the Vice-President's chair, especially one who is highly respected by his colleagues, such as Alben Barkley (Vice-President from 1949 to 1953), may derive some influence from his personal associations. But a man as gifted as Lyndon Johnson, who as majority leader was without doubt the most powerful man in the Senate, did not retain more than a shadow of his former influence when he was that body's presiding officer. Counselor and adviser a Vice-President may be, but not a Senate colleague or leader.

The Vice-President has few assured resources for effective influence. Even the political support he may have had at the nominating convention tends to dissipate like that of a defeated candidate for the Presidency— and for much the same reasons. He is not in a position to help anyone else except by borrowing influence from someone who has it. Perhaps the most likely source of influence is the President himself. The President's ability and willingness to grant such support are substantially limited; though, as we shall see shortly, this may be changing. Another possible source is the Twenty-second Amendment, which limits a President to two terms and may thus make the Vice-Presidency a promising place from which to run for President.

In the past, vice-presidential nominees have characteristically been chosen to secure a crucial bloc of convention votes for the presidential aspirant, to appease the party supporters of a defeated rival for the presidential

The Vice-Presidency: Filling the Post

The Vice-President-picking process invariably begins with a search for someone who will strengthen the ticket and invariably ends with a search for someone who won't weaken it. Those ruled out on my list were too liberal, too conservative, too inarticulate, too offensive to some groups in the party, too much like Kennedy in strengths and weaknesses or too young ("We don't want the ticket referred to as 'the whiz kids,' " I wrote). I placed at the top of my list, as did many others, the name of one man who had none of these disqualifications and many qualifications: Lyndon B. Johnson....

Despite the regional nature of his support for the Presidency, Johnson was more of a national figure than a Southerner. The youngest Majority Leader in history, a Senator's Senator who had accomplished more in the Congress during the previous eight years than Eisenhower, he certainly was no stranger to agriculture and the West. He had strong voter appeal in areas where Kennedy had little or none. He was a Protestant with a capital P. His work on behalf of foreign aid, social legislation and particularly civil rights had modified liberal opposition. His assistance with a Kennedy Congress would be indispensable.

Above all, Kennedy respected him and knew he could work with him. Lyndon Johnson was, in his opinion, the next best qualified man to be President. He admired from firsthand observation Johnson's tireless ability to campaign, cajole and persuade. He admired his leadership of the party during its dark days and his sure-footed finesse in the Senate. Referring to Johnson's powerful position when introducing him to a Boston audience in 1959, he had observed, "Some people say our speaker might be President in 1960, but frankly, I don't see why he should take a demotion."

From Theodore C. Sorensen, former special counsel to President Kennedy, *Kennedy*, 1965.

nomination, or to balance the national ticket geographically and factionally. Senator Kennedy, a liberal Catholic from Boston, chose as his running mate Lyndon Johnson, a defeated rival who was a Southerner, a Protestant, and a moderate in domestic politics. Johnson himself followed the tradition of the balanced ticket in 1964 by choosing as his running mate Hubert Humphrey, an outspoken liberal from Minnesota with ties to the intellectual community and some farm support. But both Kennedy's and Johnson's choices also suggested their desire to choose men of presidential stature, able to be effective successors in case of their own death or disability.

Such considerations are likely to be reinforced by the adoption of the Twenty-fifth Amendment in 1967. Designed primarily to meet the contingency of presidential disability, it provides that the Vice-President shall become Acting President (1) if the President informs Congress in writing that he is unable to perform his duties or (2) if the Vice-President and a majority of the Cabinet or other body authorized by law inform Congress in writing that the President is incapacitated (until the President similarly notifies Congress that no inability exists). If a dispute develops under the second provision, Congress is given twenty-one days in which to resolve it. (The amendment also directs the President to fill a vacancy in the Vice-Presidency by nominating a replacement subject to the approval of a majority of both houses of Congress.)

One cannot argue, however, that traditional practices have resulted in placing second-rate men in the post of heir apparent. Of the thirty-two men who have run for Vice-President on the tickets of the two major parties between 1900 and 1964, all but a handful have been men of competence, and some of them—such as Theodore Roosevelt (1900), Hiram W. Johnson (1912), Franklin D. Roosevelt (1920), and Earl Warren (1948) —have been unusually gifted.

In recent years Presidents have often taken advantage of the political advice of their Vice-Presidents, especially ones well acquainted with Congress, and have made some use of them within the executive branch. Most recent Presidents have invited Vice-Presidents to attend Cabinet meetings. The Vice-President may also be appointed to some posts of secondary but not negligible importance. For example, Vice-President Humphrey has served as chairman of the President's Equal Employment

---

The Vice-Presidency: The Scope of the Job

The Vice-President today really has his responsibilities at the option or, should I say, at the will of the President. You're the kind of a Vice-President that the President wishes you to be. That is, if you have the ability, if you have the desire. The President can make you a very busy Vice-President; he can make you an active Vice-President. He can make you one that is close in on the administration, or he can leave you without many duties except those we've listed under statutory responsibilities and the constitutional responsibility of presiding over the Senate.

... In recent years Presidents have seen fit to ask their Vice-Presidents to do more. Why? Because there's more to do in government today. It is utterly impossible for a President alone to undertake all of the many duties of his office without some assistance and help, and a Vice-President in many ways becomes like a special assistant to the President, [but] not an assistant President. I want to make that clear: there are no assistant Presidents; we have but one President, and we must adhere to that constitutional position of one President. But a Vice-President can be a helper to a President. He can be sort of a special assistant to a President, an adviser to a President.

From Vice-President Hubert H. Humphrey, interviewed on "At Issue: The Vice-Presidency," produced by National Educational Television, April 1965.

This cartoon illustrates the fact that the Vice-President travels as a spokesman for the President rather than as an independent political figure.

Drawing by Ivey; Ben Roth Agency

Council, a group that coordinates the efforts of various agencies in civil rights and nondiscrimination. Similarly, Vice-President Lyndon Johnson was made chairman of the President's Committee on Equal Employment Opportunity in 1961—a position that may have helped Johnson to establish politically useful connections with the Negro community. Presidents in recent years have increasingly used their Vice-Presidents also for ceremonial and quasi-diplomatic activities, illustrated by Humphrey's tour of European capitals in 1967 to explain the Administration's Vietnam policy. The Vice-President is by statute a member of the National Security Council, and it has recently become customary for him to preside in the President's absence.

Nonetheless, it is doubtful whether these activities of the Vice-President constitute a trend toward a substantial increase in the importance of the office. In all of them he acts essentially for the President rather than on his own. It is unlikely, moreover, that a President will regard his Vice-President as his alter ego, since differences between them in perspectives and goals are almost inevitable. A President who delegated substantial authority to his Vice-President would be making the grant to a man not subject to his removal power and would, at the same time, be building up the political prospects of a possible successor. But most Presidents, facing the Twenty-second Amendment's ban on more than two terms, are likely to conserve their own presumably declining influence by trying to keep all the aspirants guessing as long as possible. Nevertheless, the forces that

"And if I try harder, because I'm only number two—what number does that make *you?*"

This contrasting cartoon suggests that, despite his lack of independence, being "number-two man" gives the Vice-President an advantage over his competitors.

Jim Berry from Newspaper Enterprise Assoc.

make the Presidency the mainspring of the system make it desirable that a man of ability be ready quickly to take the place of a dead or disabled President. Future Presidents are therefore likely to maintain the practice of keeping their Vice-Presidents as fully apprised of current problems and policies as possible without jeopardizing the superiority of their own position.

THE CABINET AND ITS MEMBERS

The President's Cabinet has been an accepted part of the American government since the 1790's, though it is not mentioned in the Constitution and was not referred to in any statute until 1907. It is not a body whose members feel a strong collective responsibility and a mutual obligation and is at best of limited usefulness to the President as a source of advice; yet Presidents have, with varying degrees of regularity, retained the Cabinet meeting as part of their busy operations. The Cabinet is thus less than one's preconceptions might suggest and more than its disillusioned critics would grant. Its persistence is a reflection of certain needs of the Presidency itself, while its limitations derive from the considerations affecting the appointment of its members and from their status as departmental executives.

The Process of Appointment

A President does not have complete discretion in selecting his Cabinet officers. First, he is limited by party considerations. Not all the selections must be drawn from the President's party, but in fact almost all of them are. In the course of the nomination and election campaigns obligations have been incurred that have to be recognized, if only for the sake of harmony in the President's coalition. The President may feel obligated to a man even if the qualities that made him valuable in the campaign are not pertinent to his usefulness as a member of the Cabinet. For example, the Connecticut Democratic organization played so invaluable a part in mounting Senator Kennedy's drive for the nomination in 1960 that it would have been unwise for President-elect Kennedy not to have found a place in the Administration for Governor Abraham Ribicoff if he desired one.

Second, the Cabinet must reflect some recognition of geographical balance and of the party organizations in the larger states. North, South, East, and West must all be represented. Moreover, when a Department's activities are peculiarly concentrated in one section of the country, as those of Interior are in the West, its Secretary is expected to be either a resident of the area or publicly identified with it.

Third, several of the departments, notably Agriculture, Commerce, the Treasury, and Labor, are peculiarly identified with distinct segments of society. The relevant organized interest groups make every effort to secure an appointment acceptable to them. Normally they cannot force the President's choice, but the man designated is not likely to be clearly objectionable to them. This is understandable, since, for example, a Secretary of the Treasury who was regarded with hostility by the financial and banking community would find it nearly impossible to perform his statutory duties. This was presumably President Kennedy's reason for naming Douglas Dillon as Secretary of the Treasury. Though he was a Republican who had been ambassador to France and Undersecretary of State in the Eisenhower Administration, Dillon was highly respected in financial circles. Without this confidence a Secretary of the Treasury would also find rough going in his relations with Congress—where every Cabinet officer must earn his spurs. In fact, relations between key committees in the House and Senate and related interest groups are frequently so close that hostility toward a Cabinet officer from either group will almost certainly be reflected in a lack of friendliness from the other.

Fourth, real obstacles are presented by the unwillingness or inability of some of the most desirable men to serve. Few Cabinets are composed entirely of a President's first choices; he may be obliged to move fairly far down a preference list before he secures an acceptance. There are several reasons why men decline Cabinet posts: health considerations, problems of personal financial sacrifice, and, in the case of ambitious politicians, the fact that a Cabinet post tends to close a public career rather than further it—which may, for example, seriously restrict a President's ability to recruit able men from the Senate or the House.

Finally, a President must give general consideration to the public impression of his Cabinet. It may need socioeconomic balance or youthful vigor or solid respectability. An appearance of being above merely partisan considerations may be important. Thus, when Franklin Roosevelt in 1940 appointed two prominent Republicans, Henry L. Stimson and Frank Knox, as Secretary of War and Secretary of the Navy respectively, he in effect announced a government of national unity (which subsequently reduced partisan criticism of his wartime Administration).

Within these limits a President has some freedom of choice. But he may still be moving in the dark, even if the range of his personal acquaintance is broad. Franklin Roosevelt had met Harold Ickes for the first time only a few hours before he appointed him (a second choice) as Secretary of the Interior. And John F. Kennedy reportedly had seen Dean Rusk on only two occasions before inviting him to become Secretary of State, though he had been acquainted with Rusk's writings and with his reputation.

Given these features of their appointment, it is scarcely astonishing that Cabinet members do not constitute a group of colleagues with a sense of mutual obligation. They come together as comparative strangers, chosen for varying and even contradictory reasons. They owe no obligation to each other, and even their ties to the President may not be controlling if they regard their appointments as rewards for services rendered or if they look upon themselves as representatives of a particular clientele.

Departmental Executives as Councilors

The problem of the Cabinet member as a departmental executive is essentially that, as Richard Neustadt expresses it, he has five masters: the President, Congress (especially its relevant committees), his departmental clients, his staff, and himself.[7]

If a man cannot serve two masters without at least the appearance of disloyalty to one, his embarrassments with five would seem inescapable. Understanding the reasons for this situation not only will be a help in comprehending the limitations of the Cabinet but will also contribute to an understanding of some basic features of the government as a whole. A department Secretary (or the administrator of any other agency) cannot be entirely his own master, since each of the other four masters controls power resources he is sure to need at one time or another. Serving their expectations and demands is the price he must pay for drawing on their resources. First, he needs the President: without presidential endorsement

[7] Neustadt, *op. cit.*, p. 39.

The President and His Cabinet Officers

The task of seeing that the major policies are all of a piece and that, taken together, they are congruent with the strategic concept determined upon requires continuous superintendence which only the powers of the Presidential office can supply.

I do not mean just an office. I mean also a man and his full attention. The appreciations necessary to the strategic conception which is the basic element of our policy cannot be achieved by intermittent attention. They cannot emerge from briefings designed to reduce all complexities to a nutshell. They cannot be arrived at through policy papers designed to cover up dilemmas and smooth over the points of crux. The job cannot merely be distributed among subordinates.

If this central requirement of Presidential leadership and executive energy is not fulfilled, it is difficult to the point of impossibility to redress the lack at other points. A thousand committees may deliberate, 10,000 position papers may issue, and the bureaucratic mills may whir to unprecedented levels of output in memorandums, estimates, and joint reports—but little will come of it all if the exercise of the central authority vested in the President is faltering, intermittent, or ambiguous.

From Paul H. Nitze, president of the Foreign Service Educational Foundation, statement before the Subcommittee on National Policy Machinery of the Senate Committee on Government Operations, June 1960.

and initiative a Secretary's major proposals will be handicapped, and presidential support when he comes under attack from inside or outside the government may provide his margin of survival. But the President's resources are limited. If defending a member of his Cabinet would jeopardize a major part of his legislative program, for example, the President might be obliged to withhold that defense. He cannot fight all of a Secretary's battles, and one who is in constant trouble becomes a burden to him. So the departmental executive is obliged to court his other masters. If he fails to do so, Congress, especially through its relevant committees, may reduce his authority as well as his appropriations and enfeeble his efforts to initiate policy. His staff within the department may then withhold their support when they see him losing his influence with Congress; without them he will eventually be helpless. And client groups outside the government can give him trouble in Congress, elsewhere in the executive branch, and in the press.

The Cabinet as Council

Since Cabinet officers are often rivals in the inevitable jurisdictional conflicts that emerge in any government, they are not disposed to bring before the entire Cabinet major matters concerning their departments. They naturally prefer to get the President's attention alone. This circumstance, as Richard Fenno aptly puts it, "converts the meeting into a joint enterprise, in which 'joint' denotes a common determination to suppress vital issues and 'enterprise' consists in the great variety of devices for doing so." [8] Thus, when the Cabinet members in effect set the agenda for meetings, they almost inevitably produce an agenda of trivialities. Some contribution toward a more orderly procedure was made by Truman's device—extended by Eisenhower and retained in part by his successors—of circulating an agenda in advance and of making a record of decisions. But these changes do not go to the heart of the problem of the Cabinet as a council.

Fundamentally, the Cabinet as a council is only as useful as the President chooses to make it. For instance, if the President sets the agenda for a Cabinet meeting, he can presumably get a useful range of reactions on questions he wants discussed. (There are not many occasions when such

[8] Richard F. Fenno, Jr., *The President's Cabinet* (Cambridge, Mass.: Harvard University Press, 1959), p. 134.

The Cabinet Officer and His Subordinates

The military substitute for thought at the top is staff. Staff is of great importance. It performs the indispensable function of collecting the food for thought, appraising and preparing it. It is the means of carrying out decisions made. But, when it also performs the function of final thought, judgment, and decision, then there is no top—only the appearance of one. This can happen in a number of ways, but the most insidious, because it seems so highly efficient, is the "agreed" staff paper sent up for "action," a euphemism for "approval."

"One can always," I have said elsewhere, "get an agreed paper by increasing the vagueness and generality of its statements...." But a chief who wants to perform his function of knowing the issues, the factors involved and their magnitudes, and of deciding, needs, where there is any doubt at all, not agreed papers, but disagreed papers....

One fact ... is clear to anyone with experience in government: The springs of policy bubble up; they do not trickle down. When this upsurgence of information, ideas, and suggestions is vigorous, appreciated, and encouraged, strong, imaginative, and effective policies are most apt to result....

The chief must from time to time familiarize himself with the whole record; he must consider opposing views, put forward as ably as possible. He must examine the proponents vigorously and convince them that he knows the record, is intolerant of superficiality or of favor-seeking, and not only welcomes but demands criticism.

From former Secretary of State Dean Acheson, "Thoughts About Thought in High Places," *New York Times Magazine*, October 1959.

a meeting suits his needs, however. More frequently a strong President knows what he wants and is inclined to use the Cabinet to help him sell his views rather than to formulate them.) In addition, the President may be able to conduct the discussions so as to indicate fairly clearly the directions in which he wants the administration to move and to give the discussion a unity of purpose that Fenno calls "administrative coherence." [9] These two functions largely account for the persistence of the Cabinet council despite its other limitations, and the Cabinet as a council can be only what the President chooses to make it.

THE INDEPENDENT AGENCIES

Many important administrative activities of concern to the President are handled outside the twelve executive departments by *independent agencies,* which include from thirty to forty major units. Some are headed by single administrators, but some of the most important are headed by multimember commissions or boards. In order to evaluate their utility as instruments of presidential leadership, we must divide these agencies into two groups according to what they are independent *of.*

The larger group contains agencies that are merely independent of the executive departments. Although on a lower rank, these agencies stand in the same relation to the President as do the Cabinet departments; we shall refer to them as *executive agencies.* The heads of some of them, in fact, are a good deal more intimately associated with the President than are some department Secretaries.

The eight agencies in the second group, on the other hand, are in significant respects formally independent of the Chief Executive himself. These units, called *regulatory agencies,* are all headed by commissions or boards. They include what are sometimes known as "the big six": the Interstate Commerce Commission, the Federal Trade Commission, the Federal Power Commission, the Federal Communications Commission, the Securities and Exchange Commission, and the National Labor Relations Board. The other two are the Civil Aeronautics Board and the Board of Governors of the Federal Reserve System. The activities of all but the last include what the Supreme Court has designated as "quasi-judicial" functions.[10]

No agency in either group is independent of Congress. Creatures of legislation and dependent on annual appropriations, they are neither formally nor informally beyond the reach of Congress or its committees.

[9] *Ibid.,* pp. 91 ff.
[10] *Humphrey's Executor* v. *United States,* 295 U.S. 602 (1935).

The important questions to ask concerning these two sets of agencies are: (1) Why are they independent? (2) What does "independent" mean in fact? (3) What difference does their independence make to the President's leadership and to the functioning of the government generally?

The Independent Executive Agencies

One can identify at least half a dozen reasons for the independence of executive agencies.

Flexibility—freedom of initiative—is the first reason for independent status, especially for those agencies that are government corporations. The best-known example is the Tennessee Valley Authority, established in 1933 to develop the resources of a multistate region. Placing this function in one of the existing departments might have compelled its conformity to the department's management procedures, thus inhibiting imaginative operation.

A second reason for independence, which we may call departmental incompatibility, is illustrated by the Atomic Energy Commission. The commission was made independent, because, when the Atomic Energy Act was under consideration in 1945 and 1946, the prospect of control by the Defense Department—the only logical alternative to independence—was strongly and effectively opposed by groups of organized scientists and their allies in and out of the government.

Clientele relations, the third reason, largely account for the independent status of the Veterans Administration. Larger in number of employees than any Department except Defense and Post Office, the VA since its creation in 1930 has been the governmental arm of the American Legion and other veterans' groups, for whose members—and nonmember veterans—it provides a wide range of services. Any attempt to put the VA under the jurisdiction of one of the Cabinet-level departments would thus be politically difficult, because its clientele groups would fight strongly against losing privileged access to "their own" executive agency.

The fourth reason for independence—the need for independence of political parties—is exemplified by the Civil Service Commission. It is unique in that it could not constitutionally be made independent of the President, since to do so would encroach on his constitutional powers of appointment. Therefore, the Pendleton Act of 1883 explicitly subjected members of the commission to his removal power. But it also specified that no more than two of the commission's three members might be of the same party. The intent of this legislation was to make the commission independent of the political parties and of the electoral organizations associated with senators or representatives or the President.

A fifth reason is illustrated by the United States Information Agency (USIA), which is responsible for American propaganda abroad. An independent agency only since 1953, it was previously part of the Department of State. The Department of State, however, is primarily concerned with the formulation of foreign policy and with the conduct of diplomatic relations, and therefore its traditions are inhospitable to large operating programs such as that of the USIA. Since the latter's functions did not lend themselves to location in one of the other departments, independence became the only feasible alternative.

Finally, a housekeeping agency such as the General Services Administration is independent principally because it is a service agency for the whole executive branch and thus cannot easily be located in any of the regular departments. Created in 1949, it procures and manages most government buildings, rental space, and various supplies and services. It also is responsible for the management and preservation of government records.

As instruments of presidential initiative these agencies do not differ fundamentally from the executive departments. The President's relations with their administrators present the same characteristics and the same problems as do his relations with his Cabinet executives—and for essentially the same reasons.

The Independent Regulatory Agencies

Most of the controversy concerning independent agencies has been concerned with the *regulatory agencies*, chiefly because of the importance of their activities in the government and in the economy. This is best explained by the circumstances of their creation and the conditions of their operation.

Independence is a relatively recent issue in connection with these commissions. The first of them, the Interstate Commerce Commission, was established in 1887 and modeled after comparable bodies in the states, which were normally not subordinated to the state governors. By the time the second regulatory commission was established—the Federal Trade Commission, in 1914—the ICC had become sufficiently respected to provide a pattern for imitation.

Two major factors account for the respect accorded the independence of the ICC, and they are almost precisely duplicated in the history of most of the other commissions. The commission device itself is often a compromise measure, which the affected industry agrees to on the well-grounded expectation that once the agitation dies down the commission, cut off from the main stream of political life—independent of the President and of any systematic supervision by the whole Congress—will be compelled to come to terms with the regulated interests. The industry may then criticize specific actions of the commission but will strongly oppose any attempts of outsiders to place the agency in one of the "political" departments. Its "independence" will be defended in terms of high principle. In this way a commission tends to become a protector of the interests it was established to regulate, guarding against glaring excesses but generally doing little that is clearly unacceptable to the industry.

The second factor accounting for the independence of the regulatory commissions is their judicialized procedures, which also follow the pattern set by the ICC. All but one of them, the Federal Reserve Board, tend to consider cases brought by complaining parties rather than to initiate proceedings themselves; they handle cases in a formal adversary proceeding resembling a lawsuit; and they tend to make rules case by case, like a common-law court. The basic pattern was deliberately adopted by the ICC in its earliest days as a defense against the tendencies of the courts and the bar to restrict its jurisdiction and powers. It succeeded so well that it became the model for the comparable agencies established between 1914 and 1938.

Those who insist that the regulatory agencies must be independent of the Chief Executive rest their case on the quasi-judicial function of these commissions. However the term "quasi-judicial" may be understood—and it has never had precise definition by the Supreme Court—it is not a logical justification of independence. If it refers to the fact that those agencies have power to determine the rights of citizens, the same may be said of most governmental agencies that enjoy no such independence. If the term refers to the courtlike procedures of the commissions, it is clear that these rest on convention rather than on necessity. More important, these same kinds of function have for decades been carried on within the executive departments without difficulty.

The basic problem presented by the regulatory agencies is that their policies directly affect the government's ability to discharge its economic responsibilities, but their independence hampers the President in his use of them as instruments of his general policy. "Separation from general economic policy is more difficult in an age when government underwrites a minimum standard of living and a commitment to high employment, and when it is deeply involved in the economy for reasons of national security and foreign policy." [11]

This point is nowhere better illustrated than by the Board of Governors of the Federal Reserve System, which differs in important respects from the other commissions. The Federal Reserve Board (FRB) is composed of seven men appointed by the President with the advice and consent of the Senate for staggered terms of fourteen years, with a chairman designated by the President from among its members. It is essentially the governing board of a central banking system whose powers are granted by statute. The financial support of the FRB, however, comes not from congressional appropriations but from payments made by banks that are members of the Federal Reserve System (including all of the national banks and about one-

[11] Merle Fainsod, Lincoln Gordon, and Joseph C. Palamountain, Jr., *Government and the American Economy*, 3rd ed. (New York: Norton, 1959), p. 59.

third of the state banks in the country). It is thus independent of the congressional power of the purse and of presidential control, except for the President's appointment and removal powers, whose potency, as we have seen, is limited.

The powers of the FRB over the money and credit supply can profoundly affect the state of the economy. The relations between the FRB, on the one hand, and the President, the Secretary of the Treasury, the Council of Economic Advisers, and related agencies, on the other, are thus a delicate matter. Disagreement could have major implications for the economy, but whether in such a contingency a President would claim a power of removal is highly conjectural—and whether he would be upheld by the Supreme Court is even more so.

The independent commissions may be beyond the reach of the President's removal power, but he has other partially effective means of influence. The most readily available means in the long run is the power of appointment, but the long run may be very long indeed, because commission members serve overlapping terms of considerable duration. Thus a President limited to eight years in the White House may not be able to appoint a commission majority sympathetic to his views before he himself is forced to retire. Presidential appointments of commissioners, moreover, are subject to at least as severe limitations—particularly those imposed by client groups—as presidential appointments of Cabinet members. Since 1950 the President has been empowered to designate the chairman from among the commissioners for all commissions except the ICC. Since the chairman is normally the commission's chief executive, this power may be an important means of affecting policy—particularly if the President also makes a point of offering policy suggestions and soliciting advice.

The President has a few additional formal powers affecting all the commissions. In particular he may request a commission study of any subject in its jurisdiction. The request in most cases is not binding, but it is unlikely to be ignored by any commission. Conformity both to these requests and to a President's views on general policy becomes far more likely if a popular President with a strong congressional following makes these views public, since no commission could long withstand open opposition from both the White House and a sizable segment of Congress.

The independent commissions are thus not completely independent of the President, but the notions of independence and bipartisanship reinforce the commissions' tendency to ignore a President's stake in their policies and actions. Despite this fact, he will be held responsible for the economic consequences of their policies. He may also suffer politically from revelations that overdependence of a commission on its clientele has resulted in misconduct. It is significant that both the Truman and the Eisenhower Administrations were seriously embarrassed by scandals in the independent commissions.

A President therefore encounters difficult problems in employing the regulatory commissions as instruments of his initiative. But they are so important to him and to his program that an energetic President is almost obliged to try to induce them to accept his leadership, even though he may not be able to gain all that is expected of him by his larger constituency.

UNOFFICIAL AND SEMIOFFICIAL INSTRUMENTS OF LEADERSHIP

The unofficial and semiofficial instruments of presidential leadership are too varied to catalogue completely, but a few examples will illustrate their range.

The "Kitchen Cabinet"

In their search for disinterested advice and for assistants whose attachment to the Chief Executive's stake in office is as complete as can be, most Presidents since Andrew Jackson, especially forceful ones, have created *kitchen cabinets* composed of persons who had no official place in the White House entourage. This term was first used contemptuously of the four men whom Jackson, ignoring his Cabinet, relied upon both for advice and for confidential assistance. All four had worked assiduously for his election in 1828. Lincoln had a similar group around him as did Theodore Roosevelt. Franklin D. Roosevelt's original "brain trust," none of whom had Cabinet rank, was a comparable group, and his use of men like Robert Sherwood and Judge Samuel Rosenman in the drafting of his speeches involved the same kind of relation. More specialized roles, involving not only advice but actions as presidential agents, were played by Colonel E. M. House in Wilson's Administration and by Harry Hopkins in the war years of Franklin Roosevelt's Presidency. Kennedy made use of a series of informal advisers, mostly, but not exclusively, from university circles. The Johnson Administration has not been as close to the academics, but it has used comparable alternatives. For example, Clark Clifford, a Washington lawyer and close friend of the President, has been used for advice, legislative liaison, and special missions. He chaired a special panel to review CIA activities and represented the President in diplomatic efforts to secure support for Johnson's Vietnam policy.

The growth of the White House staff and the Executive Office has so established the "institutionalized Presidency" in the past three decades that some observers predict the disappearance of this kind of adviser. This seems unlikely, however, since Presidents will continue to need advice and assistance that is unaffected by continuing connections within the government.

Even the White House staff, whose personal loyalties can be counted upon with considerable confidence, may in time become enmeshed in continuing relations among themselves and elsewhere within the government that unwittingly influence their counsel. The "institutionalized Presidency," therefore, is unlikely to do away entirely with the kitchen cabinet.

Ad Hoc Commissions

Presidents from the time of Washington have appointed *ad hoc* commissions, usually without statutory authorization, to investigate some factual situation and often to recommend appropriate action. As recently as Theodore Roosevelt's day, however, this practice produced protests in Congress. It was argued that without legal authorization such bodies were unconstitutional. In 1909 Congress attempted by statute to prevent Theodore Roosevelt from using the device. The President signed the measure but announced his intention of ignoring it. Since that time the presidential commission has become accepted.

Presidents may appoint these *ad hoc* commissions merely as fact-finding instruments, as devices for avoiding premature commitments on a troublesome problem, or as a harmless means of pacifying an insistent reform group. But the most interesting cases are those in which the *ad hoc* commission actually becomes an instrument of initiative. Ideally such a commission is composed of prominent citizens and technical experts of unimpeachable disinterestedness who are asked to study and make recommendations on a problem that is somewhat controversial but one on which detached men of intelligence are likely to agree on a certain solution—the one the President favors. Their report then has important news value. The President in turn can borrow the prestige of the commission's members to lend support to the policy he expected them to favor.

A classic example is President Roosevelt's Committee to Investigate the Rubber Situation, appointed in 1942. The problem grew out of the critical shortage created by the Japanese seizure of the rubber-producing areas in the Far East at a time when facilities for making synthetic rubber in the United States were almost nonexistent. The committee reported that the immediate answer was to conserve rubber by rationing gasoline, a highly controversial measure. The committee's report contained no surprises, but it helped materially in compelling the contending interests to accept a workable program of conservation, including gasoline rationing. More recently, President Johnson has appointed commissions on the question of government support for the construction of a supersonic jet transport, on the problem of revising the Selective Service law, and on the causes of Negro riots in the cities.

The Press Conference and the Presidential Pulpit

The President's regular meetings with the White House correspondents are an illustration of an informal practice, developed in response to new conditions, that has become so completely a presidential institution that he could not abolish it if he wished to. The press conference was begun by Theodore Roosevelt, who, when he described the White House as "a bully pulpit," revealed his own conception of the President as teacher to the nation. But not until Franklin Roosevelt's Presidency did the conferences reach something like their contemporary form and importance. In fact, they may have reached the peak of their value to the President in those years. They were neither televised nor broadcast, and F.D.R. often talked off the record about events and problems with a candor possible only because his remarks were not for direct quotation. He was the master of the situation, whereas subsequent Presidents have been constantly in danger of becoming its victims. They have been compelled, especially with the advent of television, to make public shows of these meetings. An offhand, ill-considered response to an unexpected question can have serious political and diplomatic repercussions, and the way in which the President handles himself before the press affects his standing with all the spectators in and out of Washington whom he needs to persuade.

The other chief danger of the institutionalized press conference is that if it is held with too great regularity it loses much of its public audience, for its effect depends in part on novelty and infrequency. For this reason President Kennedy wisely limited the occasions on which his press conferences were carried "live." Similarly, President Johnson had a series of unannounced "spot" conferences for press people regularly attached to the White House before he had one of the full-dress sessions in the State Department auditorium. A President constantly "going to the people" is in danger of losing their attention.

The Congressional Party Leaders

Presidents are obliged to maintain contact with Congress, and they have devised a wide variety of means for doing so. Maintaining this contact is the chief function of one or more members of the White House staff; the President's calendar of appointments regularly includes conferences with senators and representatives; and at critical stages in his legislative program the White House switchboard may be busy with his calls to wavering members of Congress. But in the last thirty years, as the Presidency has come to occupy a larger and larger place in the system, weekly conferences at the White House with the principal "elective" leaders of his congressional party concerning the President's legislative program have become a Washington institution.

These congressional leaders are not merely the President's agents on Capitol Hill. They have their own stakes—in their constituencies and in Congress. But, for reasons that will be more closely examined in Chapter 12, they have *some* stake in the President's position and in their somewhat privileged relations with him. On the President's side these relations are of enormous value. The congressional party leaders are channels of persuasion and negotiation and sources of valuable intelligence. To the degree that the President can carry them with him, they are instruments of his influence on Capitol Hill that are very nearly indispensable. Most Presidents also find it useful to cultivate key committee chairmen and the leaders of the opposition party. But it is the elective leaders of the President's party whose concerns most nearly approximate the President's, and they are in a position to facilitate the whole gamut of his legislative program.

AN OVERVIEW OF THE INSTRUMENTS OF LEADERSHIP

Few instruments of presidential initiative are ready made and consistently reliable. But, in order to prevent an intolerable gap between what is expected from the President and what he is able to produce from the system, he must employ his ingenuity in exploiting the partially reliable devices available to him.

The gap, in some degree, will always be present. No set of formal procedures will close it, since neither the political stakes nor the functional range of the instruments the President can use are equivalent to his own. Nonetheless, such instruments can be indispensable means of bringing presidential—and governmental—performance into some conformity with contemporary requirements. Clearly, the relative independence of the major regulatory commissions at best increases the awkwardness of the President's situation and at worst may frustrate his designs. But the problem of achieving effective leadership would not be wholly eliminated even if these functions were made a part of the executive. The President would still need to persuade these new "subordinates" that their stakes were convergent with his.

Persistence of the gap in some degree, moreover, stimulates political inventiveness and the search for formulas of adjustment and is thus an assurance of vitality—to say nothing of the freedom to dissent. In governing, as in individual experience, creativeness emerges from the tensions between aspiration and possibility, provided they are not so great as to produce only frustration.

Attempts to keep the President from narrowing the gap are in part efforts to insulate private interests from more inclusive public claims. They are also reflections of divergent views concerning the Presidency. In a far deeper sense they represent a continuing dispute over the range of responsibilities that shall be conceded to government as an institution. These conflicts are inevitable in a society responding to changes as rapid and extensive as those the United States has experienced in the twentieth century. In fact, such conflicts are at the heart of the political contest. The President's search for and experiments with the instruments of initiative, therefore, are in a sense the central features of our society's search for means of dealing with the complexities of the contemporary world.

SUMMARY

The presidential instruments of leadership help close the gap between what is expected from a President and what he is able to achieve. The usefulness of each instrument depends on (1) the range and importance of its functions and (2) the similarity of its political stakes and goals to those of the President.

Several units are included in the Executive Office of the President. The President's personal staff is potentially an extremely useful instrument, because its concerns can be as broad as the President wishes to make them and because it is closely identified with the President's own risks and goals.

The Bureau of the Budget can also be an enormously useful presidential instrument. First, construction and administration of the budget allow the bureau and the President to make important decisions about the level and rate of expenditures and about the relative financial emphasis to be placed on competing programs. Second, the bureau is an excellent source of intragovernmental intelligence, advice on programs, and support for the President.

The Council of Economic Advisers helps the President specify broad guidelines for government programs affecting the economy. The Council is limited as a presidential instrument, however, partly because its influence depends on its professional disinterestedness and partly because the President must ultimately use political as well as economic criteria in making policy choices.

The usefulness of the National Security Council as a presidential instrument is limited by the tendency of its members to represent the views and interests of their separate agencies; however, the NSC discussions help the President to find out what kinds of issues are being avoided or minimized in achieving a consensus within the group.

The Vice-President is handicapped as a presidential instrument even though he derives his influence almost entirely from the President himself. There are inevitably differences in perspectives and goals that keep the

President from delegating substantial power to the Vice-President or making him an heir apparent.

The Cabinet is limited as a presidential instrument mainly by the politics of appointing its members and by their roles as departmental executives. In appointing a Cabinet member, the President must meet several requirements: he must reward party supporters, provide geographic balance, find candidates acceptable to the "clientele" groups of the department, and consider the overall image of the Cabinet.

Cabinet members thus have no obligations to one another, and even their obligations to the President may not be controlling. For each Cabinet executive is also responsible to Congress, which controls appropriations and influences the department's programs, to his departmental clients, who have influence in Congress and elsewhere in the executive branch, and to his staff, whose support he needs to execute policies.

In terms of their usefulness as presidential instruments, the independent agencies can be classified as either executive agencies or independent regulatory agencies. The executive agencies are closely associated with the President and are thus more accessible instruments than the independent regulatory agencies. The President's relations with administrators of the executive agencies have the same characteristics and problems as his relations with Cabinet executives.

The independent regulatory agencies, on the other hand, are substantially independent of the President, partly because of their "quasi-judicial" functions and partly because of their close relations with the "clientele" groups they regulate and with Congress. The President has only partially effective techniques for influencing the policies of an independent agency, which often bear directly on his programs.

The unofficial instruments of presidential leadership include: (1) the "kitchen cabinet," an advisory staff that is completely dedicated to the President's stake in office; (2) *ad hoc* commissions, through which the President can sometimes gain support for his policies by borrowing prestige from an impartial, technically competent outside group; (3) the press conference, which helps the President to maintain his role as a popular leader; and (4) the congressional leaders of the President's party who have some stake in the status of the President's programs in Congress and in their privileged relations with him.

None of these instruments alone, nor all of them together, can fully and permanently solve the President's problem of making his authority equal to his responsibility. If used with skill, however, they can be valuable, and to meet his obligations a President must try to adapt them to his purposes.

PRESIDENTS, CONGRESSES, AND CONGRESSMEN

11

This chapter is based on a fundamental fact: the political stakes and risks of congressmen differ significantly from those of the President. The chapter will begin by exploring the constitutional and political sources of these differences. It will then examine how the system of "checks and balances" transforms these differing political stakes into areas of potential conflict between the President and Congress. The final section examines how well Congress and its members fulfill the criteria of "responsiveness" and "representation": What factors affect the recruitment of congressmen? What is the proper role of the legislator? Which biases in the composition of Congress affect its representativeness?

The first Administration bill to reach the floor of the House of Representatives after President Kennedy was inaugurated in 1961 was a controversial measure to provide short-term relief to farmers producing grain for animal feed. The President faced the humiliating prospect that his initial legislative request would be defeated in the House. The key to success or failure lay not with representatives from farm states but with a handful of New York City Democrats, indifferent to the bill as such but angry about the Administration's handling of patronage appointments. Threatening until almost the last minute to oppose the feed bill, they did ultimately vote for it, but the narrow 209–202 margin by which the bill passed indicated clearly how close the President had come to embarrassment.

This episode illustrates a fundamental fact of the American system: the House and Senate share with the President many of the basic functions of governing, notably the enactment of legislation; but their stakes and their risks, even within the same party, may be sharply in conflict with his. This, in practice, is what "checks and balances" mean.

One of the characteristic tests of a President's performance is how well he gets along with Congress. Since the President's legislative program sets the principal agenda for the legislature, how much of it Congress enacts becomes as much a popular measure of performance as the baseball player's batting average. The implicit assumption is that somehow a President ought to find ways of getting from Congress what he thinks the country needs. But he may not possess the means for such achievement.

The differing stakes of the President and Congress sometimes make it difficult for the President to lead even his own party in Congress.

Sanders in the Greensboro *Daily News*

354

The member of Congress has his own tests of performance to meet, and he may not be able to do so by consistently supporting even a President of his own party. He may have his own conceptions of appropriate public policy based on long experience on a legislative committee; he may have his own distinctive ties to various interest groups; above all, he has his own political career to make or maintain, and that depends heavily on the "batting average" he has in his constituency. For, as the veteran New York representative Emanuel Celler suggested in the title of his autobiography, "You never leave Brooklyn." [1]

THE SOURCES OF CONGRESSIONAL-PRESIDENTIAL CONFLICT

The fundamental sources of the recurrent conflict between the President and Congress can be classified generally as either constitutional or political.

Constitutional Sources

Perhaps the greatest ambiguity in the Constitution is the question of which takes precedence, the Chief Executive or Congress. When the two are in conflict, which shall prevail? A "vigorous executive" was designed by the

[1] Emanuel Celler, *You Never Leave Brooklyn* (New York: Day, 1953).

"First—you have to get their attention."

State of the Union messages are one instrument for bridging the gap between the President and Congress.

Conrad in the Denver *Post*

Founders, but the legislature was granted a series of nonlegislative functions (to be discussed shortly in more detail), which limits that vigor.

By a narrow vote the Constitutional Convention decided to separate the legislative and executive branches by prohibiting any person's simultaneously holding an office in the executive branch and being a member of either house of Congress. That decision virtually precluded the government's developing ministerial responsibility in the legislature, as the British were then beginning to do. This decision also made it less likely that the two branches could be fused by the development of strong, centralized control of both the White House and Congress. The possibility was made even more unlikely by the arrangement of unequal terms—six years for senators, four for the President, and two for representatives—and by the provision that only one-third of the Senate should be replaced at each biennial election. Legislative elections every two years assured the possibility that at the midpoint of each presidential term the President and a majority in the House or in both chambers might be of opposing political parties. This has occurred no less than fifteen times—at roughly one-third of the midterm elections—in the course of our history. Such party division increases the probability of conflicts between President and Congress. To complicate matters, since only one-third of the Senate is replaced at each election, popular support registered for a President in his own and in the House election may not immediately be reflected in the composition of the Senate.

Political Sources

The political sources of the separatism between the President and Congress—that is, their differing stakes and risks—derive from a single fact: the forces—the organizations and the attitudes—responsible for the election and especially the nomination of members of Congress differ significantly from those forces that put a President in the White House. In an election the presence of the party label may make the results look harmonious, but in nominations—especially those made through the characteristic device of the direct primary—a variety of factors, often wholly unrelated to national or presidential considerations, may account for the outcome. Moreover, the effective electorate—those actually voting in midterm elections—is characteristically not a representative cross-section of the presidential electorate. Many more voters in presidential elections are normally uninvolved in politics, loosely identified with a party, and likely to be swayed by the candidate's personal characteristics. In midterm congressional elections more voters have the reverse characteristics and, in addition, are concerned with purely local issues. This means that the political risks of a President and a member of Congress, even from the same party, are far from identical.

This basic political source of separatism is reinforced by the internal power structure in Congress, to be discussed in more detail in Chapter 12.

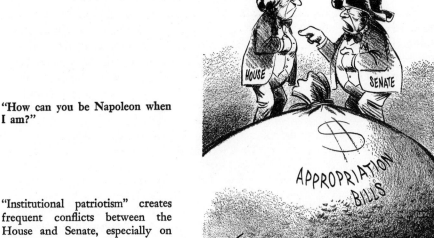

"How can you be Napoleon when I am?"

"Institutional patriotism" creates frequent conflicts between the House and Senate, especially on money issues.

Don Hesse in the St. Louis *Globe-Democrat*

Also working for separatism is a factor that can best be described as *institutional patriotism,*[2] which affects not only the relations between the President and Congress but also those between the Senate and the House and between committees in the two chambers. Institutional patriotism represents the normal tendency of influential persons in an organization to identify with it, to accept its distinctive codes and outlooks, and to mistrust the behavior of adjacent, and in a sense rival, organizations. The phenomenon can be seen in the clashes between legislative committees in the Senate and in the House as well as in the thinly disguised resentment that members of the House feel on occasion toward the Senate, and vice versa.

For example, for fifteen weeks—from April 10 to July 20, 1962—no appropriation measures were enacted by Congress. Money bills were passed by the House and were amended in the Senate as usual. But they could not be enacted until the differences between the versions passed by the House and the Senate were ironed out in conference committees composed of members of the Appropriations Committees of both houses. The conference committees did not meet, because Clarence Cannon of Missouri, chairman of the House Appropriations Committee, had demanded that the meeting places and the chairmen for the conference committees should alternate between the House and Senate. Since by ancient tradition such committees have always met on the Senate side of the Capitol and have been chaired

[2] Donald R. Matthews, *U.S. Senators and Their World* (Chapel Hill: University of North Carolina Press, 1960), pp. 101–02.

The President and Congress: The President as Pivotal

During my years in the Senate I have come to understand that the presidency is the ultimate source of action. The Senate is not. It may have been in 1840, but it isn't today. Take the labor bill, for instance. In 1958 I had worked for two years on a labor reform bill. President Eisenhower made one fifteen-minute speech which had a decisive effect on the House. Two years versus one fifteen-minute speech. I worked a year on a proposal to send an economic mission to India. The State Department opposed it, and it was defeated in the conference. I worked for a year on a bill to change the Battle Act to allow a greater economic trading with countries behind the Iron Curtain, such as Poland. The President withdrew his support on the day of the vote. We were defeated by one vote. All of the things that you become interested in doing the President can do and the Senate cannot, particularly in the area of foreign policy. There is, in fact, much less than meets the eye in the Senate, frequently. It's the President who controls and can effect results, play on the vital issues of national security, defense and foreign policy. We play, constitutionally, a secondary role in the United States Senate.

From Senator John F. Kennedy of Massachusetts, "Why Go Into Politics," in James M. Cannon, ed., *Politics U.S.A.,* 1960.

by senators, Carl Hayden of Arizona, chairman of the Senate Appropriations Committee, refused to agree to this proposal. He was supported in the Senate in a bipartisan defense of Senate prerogatives. "The Senate refuses to become Cannon fodder," declared Everett Dirksen, the Republican leader. In the end Cannon and his committee dropped their demands.

As the New York *Times* commented, "The prestige at stake was institutional." [3] If this sort of thing can occur between the Senate and the House, it is clear that it can happen even more easily between Congress and the President (plus others in the executive branch), whose stakes and circumstances are so markedly different.

The institutional patriotism that divides President and Congress also reflects a genuine legislative uneasiness at the twentieth-century shift of government initiative toward the President. Increased initiative from the White House does not, of course, narrow the range of things that Congress *can* do; but it does restrict what Congress is *likely* to do. In consequence congressional speeches for several decades have deplored the loss of legislative independence, have criticized presidential encroachment, and have demanded a restoration of Congress' "proper" role. Much of this is mere rhetoric; still more is a disguise for interest groups who hope to improve

[3] New York *Times*, July 21, 1962.

their ability to get what they want by championing the legislature's "constitutional prerogatives." But much reflects a genuine concern.

Nonetheless, the initiative in legislative matters has not entirely shifted from Congress. Thus one must include among the political sources of separatism the substantial degree to which Congress remains an alternative channel of initiative within the government. This alternative channel frequently competes with the presidential one, such as when an interest group that is unable to accomplish its purposes through the executive attempts to achieve them through Congress and its committees. For example, in 1962 the President and the Secretary of Defense decided that the B-70 bomber would not be put into production because it would be obsolete before it could become fully operational. The Chairman of the House Armed Services Committee, Carl Vinson of Georgia, was able to force formal reconsideration of this decision and to gain an agreement that a limited number of planes would be produced for reconnaissance. Vinson clearly spoke for that section of the Air Force committed to the B-70 as a strategic weapon, and it is likely that he was representing the manufacturers of the B-70 as well.

Congress as an alternative channel of initiative may play a clearly con-

The President and Congress: Congress as Pivotal

[INTERVIEWER]: How do you use the Presidency, in Theodore Roosevelt's phrase, "the bully pulpit," to move [Congressmen] who are really kind of barons and sovereigns in their own right, up there on the Hill? Have you any way to move them toward a course of action which you think is imperative?

KENNEDY: Well, the Constitution and the development of the Congress all give advantage to delay. It's very easy to defeat a bill in Congress and much more difficult to pass one.... [It is a difficult] struggle for a President who has a program to move it through the Congress, particularly when the seniority system may place particular individuals in key positions who may be wholly unsympathetic to your program, maybe even though they're members of your own party in political opposition to the President. This is a struggle which every President who's tried to get a program through [Congress] has had to deal with....

They are two separate offices and two separate powers, the Congress and the Presidency. There's bound to be conflict. But they must cooperate to the degree that's possible. But that's why no President's program is ever put in [completely]. The only time a President's program is put in quickly and easily is when the program is insignificant. But if it's significant and affects important interests and is controversial ... then there's a fight and ... the President is never wholly successful.

From President John F. Kennedy, interviewed on "A Conversation with President Kennedy," produced by ABC, CBS, and NBC, December 1962.

structive role. In the late 1950's critics in Congress persistently questioned the adequacy of the Administration's capacity for fighting a limited conventional war and eventually produced modifications in the policy.[4] Senators, even when not members of the Foreign Relations Committee, have on more than one occasion suggested useful new departures in foreign policy. And congressional committees, such as the Subcommittee on National Policy Machinery of the Senate Committee on Government Operations in 1960 and 1961, have contributed significantly to the clarification of policy issues within the government.[5]

No member of Congress, however, and none of its committees speaks from a position comparable to the President's. No leader in Congress can commit both chambers to an agenda, to say nothing of committing them to a legislative program. Initiatives coming from Capitol Hill, therefore, lack the range and the resources of those from the White House. They may be sufficient to impose modifications in presidential proposals, but if they are constructive proposals of any breadth their success is likely to depend on their being taken up by the President and incorporated in his program.

THE NONLEGISLATIVE AND SEMILEGISLATIVE FUNCTIONS OF CONGRESS

The tendency toward conflict that is fostered by the differing political risks and stakes of the President and members of Congress is reinforced by the existence of a considerable number of nonlegislative or semilegislative congressional activities. Many of them are part of the constitutional "checks and balances," which encourage separatism between President and Congress.

Amending the Constitution

By constitutional arrangement and judicial interpretation, Congress is the national agency that deals with amending the Constitution. The two methods of proposing amendments—by a two-thirds vote in each house (the only method actually employed thus far) or by calling a convention at the request of two-thirds of the state legislatures—put Congress at the center of things. The President may urge that an amendment be proposed, he may express his dissatisfaction with one already proposed, or he may even actively attempt to defeat an amendment under consideration by Congress; but resolutions proposing amendments are not submitted for his

---

[4] Samuel P. Huntington, *The Common Defense: Strategic Programs in National Politics* (New York: Columbia University Press, 1961), pp. 145–46.

[5] U.S. Senate, Committee on Government Operations, Subcommittee on National Policy Machinery, *Organizing for National Security* (1961), 3 vols.

signature. Congress also chooses whether the ratification shall be by three-fourths of the state legislatures or by conventions in three-fourths of the states.

Electing the President and Vice-President

The Senate and House both have electoral functions. One with symbolic importance is the requirement that responsibility for counting the electoral votes for the two offices lies with the President of the Senate, "in the presence of the Senate and House of Representatives." Somewhat more substantial are the powers of the House to elect the President and of the Senate to choose the Vice-President if no candidate receives a majority of the electoral votes. The choice of a President has not been thrown into the House since 1824, but the special position that this provision gives the legislature, especially the House, is one of the subtle factors contributing to its collective self-regard.

Impeaching and Judging

The judicial functions of the two chambers have a similar effect. The House has the sole power of impeachment and the Senate the sole power to try impeachment charges. Only twelve impeachments, nine of them involving judges, have come to trial. President Andrew Johnson was impeached but acquitted in 1868. One can readily agree with Thomas Jefferson's judgment that impeachment is "the scarecrow of the Constitution," so infrequently is it used, but the mere existence of the power has relevance to separatism.

More important, the houses of Congress have the right, affirmed by the Supreme Court, to imprison for contempt a person who refuses to obey its legitimate demands—for example, to appear before it or one of its committees, to answer questions, or to supply evidence. Since the Court held in 1821 that such imprisonment could not extend beyond the adjournment of the house by which it was ordered,[6] Congress has by statute made this kind of contempt a criminal offense, enforceable in the regular courts.

Finally, the Constitution gives each house exclusive power, not only to judge the elections by which its prospective members have been chosen and to decide whether it will seat them, but to punish a member for a breach of its rules, including improper conduct; and it may censure or even expel one of its number. Challenges to election results—usually by the losing candidate—are fairly common, but refusal to seat an elected candidate and censure or expulsion of sitting members are rare. The House took such an unusual action in February 1967, when it refused to seat Adam Clayton Powell of New York. Powell was disqualified not for any election irreg-

---

[6] *Anderson* v. *Dunn*, 6 Wheaton 204 (1821).

ularities but for personal misconduct—the misuse of public funds for private purposes and criminal contempt of court in connection with a libel case against him in his home district. A dramatic case of this kind in the Senate was its censure of the late Senator Joseph R. McCarthy of Wisconsin for abuse of Senate committees. And in 1967 the Senate voted to censure Thomas A. Dodd, Democrat of Connecticut, for his personal use of campaign funds and for behavior unbecoming the office of senator.

Approving Treaties

Although making treaties is a less significant aspect of foreign policy than it was several decades ago, it is not a minor matter. In 1966, for example, the Senate received twenty-one presidential requests for its consent to the ratification of treaties. Moreover, when one contemplates the significance that the Nuclear Test Ban Treaty of 1963 may have in the foreign relations of the United States, it is clear that treaties are still of considerable importance.

For present purposes, however, the importance of the Senate's executive functions in treaty-making is their potential for conflict with the President. The Senate, especially its Committee on Foreign Relations, has an almost proprietary interest in all phases of foreign policy. For years an assignment to the Committee on Foreign Relations has been one of the two or three most sought-after positions in the Senate, and its members are likely to be treated with special deference by the Secretary of State and others in the executive branch concerned with foreign policy. This state of affairs sometimes results in a mutuality of concerns between the two groups. But at least as frequently it has had the opposite result. For the Foreign Relations Committee, like most executive agencies, has two masters: first and foremost, the Senate as a whole and, second, the President and his Secretary of State. If the committee is to be effective in the Senate, therefore, it must at least on occasion stand up to the executive, such as when it cuts the requested foreign-aid program. To retain unimpaired its standing in the Senate, it must also extract concessions from the executive. Thus the intimate involvement of the Senate in treaty-making may induce conflict by entangling general foreign-policy questions with the institutional patriotism of the Senate and with the senators' political risks, which differ from those of the President.

Approving Presidential Appointments

The Senate's role in the essentially executive function of appointments, discussed briefly in Chapter 9,[7] also contributes to the separatism of the President and Congress, reflecting their different stakes. The expectation of the

[7] Ch. 9, pp. 298–99.

"Did you ever have one of those days when you didn't know whether to advise or consent?"

Drawing by Richter in the *Saturday Review*

Founders was that the Senate would act as a council to scrutinize presidential selections in order to discourage favoritism and to keep out the unfit. In practice, this function has sometimes given the Senate a strong influence over the President; less often it has had the reverse effect.

In the first place, Presidents may on occasion use appointments as the *quid pro quo* in bargaining for support of legislation, but senators may make a change in administration policy the price of support of a nomination. Second, an appointment or two each year may stir up considerable controversy. Such controversy may stem from party or factional rivalry. For committee hearings—in which outsiders and representatives as well as senators may testify—and floor debates on nominations offer opportunities for opponents to attack administration policies by challenging nominees. The source of the hostility might also be an interest group. A group that is part of an agency's clientele and fears that its influence with the President's nominee may be inadequate may persuade a friendly editor or member of Congress to oppose the nomination. Such a situation is especially likely if the President's intent in making the nomination is to alter some of the established policies of the affected agency.

Controversy over a nominee may also represent defense of the Senate's institutional patriotism. An example of this was the Senate's reaction to President Eisenhower's nomination of Lewis L. Strauss as Secretary of Commerce in 1958. As the Republican chairman of the AEC from 1953 to 1958, Strauss had antagonized Democratic Senator Clinton Anderson of New

Mexico, who had become chairman of the Joint Committee on Atomic Energy in 1955. Anderson charged that Strauss had not been candid in his relations with the joint committee. The hearings on Strauss's nomination dealt almost entirely with his past record and his alleged personal deficiencies rather than with his ability to meet the problems of the Department of Commerce. The Senate voted by a narrow margin against confirmation of Strauss. This vote partly represented a policy protest by the Democratic majority on the recurrent issue of public ownership of power systems. But more conspicuously it supported the charges of Anderson and other senators that Strauss had failed to show a proper respect for the Senate.

The institution of *senatorial courtesy* is a third feature of the Senate's role in presidential nominations, one not generally anticipated in 1787. The precedent for the practice was established in 1789, when the Senate rejected Washington's nominee for naval officer for the Port of Savannah "apparently for no other reason than that the man was not acceptable to the faction in Georgia which her Senators chanced to represent." [8] Since then Presidents have rarely failed to clear with senators of their own party nominations for positions in their states.

The practice of senatorial courtesy has persisted for two reasons. First, a senator's concern over appointments in his state reflects the difference between his political stakes and the President's: he needs to be alert to the danger that the President, intentionally or not, may build up within the senator's state an opposition to the senator's party or factional organization. Second, the practice itself testifies to and reinforces the Senate's institutional solidarity. Otherwise uncongenial senators will grant this curious form of veto to one another in order to avail themselves of its protection on another occasion.

Finally, the Senate can affect nominations indirectly without exercising its formal veto. Some men decline a presidential offer at the outset out of reluctance to run the gantlet of the Senate's advice and consent. Not infrequently, moreover, a President withdraws a nomination after it has been made, usually at the formal request of the nominee, when it becomes evident that Senate resistance will be formidable. Even if confirmation is won, controversy warns the official that if he is to lead a reasonably successful political life he should give considerable respect to the views and desires of key senators.

Supervising the Executive Branch

The lesson in legislative-executive protocol learned by an appointee in a confirmation struggle is in most cases amply reinforced in his subsequent relations with key members of the House and the Senate, especially mem-

[8] George H. Haynes, *The Senate of the United States* (Boston: Houghton Mifflin, 1938), Vol. II, pp. 736–37.

The Dangers of Legislative Encroachment

The President is responsible for the administration of his office. And that means for the administration of the entire executive branch. It is not the business of Congress to run the agencies of government for the President.

Unless this principle is observed, it is impossible to have orderly government. The legislative power will ooze into the executive offices. It will influence and corrupt the decisions of the executive branch. It will affect promotions and transfers. It will warp and twist policies.

Not only does the President cease to be master in his own house, but the whole house of government becomes one which has no master. The power of decision then rests only in the legislative branch, and the legislative branch by its very nature is not equipped to perform these executive functions.

To this kind of encroachment it is the duty of the President to say firmly and flatly "No, you can't do it." The investigative power of Congress is not limitless. It extends only so far as to permit the Congress to acquire the information that it honestly needs to exercise its legislative functions. Exercised beyond those limits, it becomes a manifestation of unconstitutional power. It raises the threat of legislative dictatorship and that's the worst dictatorship in the world.

From former President Harry S Truman, speech at Truman birthday dinner, May 1954.

bers of the subject-matter committees and the appropriations subcommittees. Checking on the actions of the executive branch and criticizing its policies are a normal part of the legislature's functions in all constitutional governments. But the distinctive features of the American system result from the different risks of the elected executive and the elected legislators.

The formal source of the problem lies in one of the great ambiguities of the Constitution. Article II clearly contemplated the creation of executive departments by acts of Congress. What Congress may create, it may abolish or alter; what Congress may alter or destroy, it may restrict and instruct. So essentially runs the argument. But what then becomes of the executive power that is "vested in a President" and of his duty to "take care that the laws be faithfully executed"? No executive subordinate can be entirely sure whether he is ultimately responsible to the President or to Congress.

The legislature can legitimately inquire into the use of the power and funds it grants. The usual view, in fact, is that the President and Congress "share" responsibility for administrative supervision. But when the stakes of power between the President and Congress diverge, conflict is likely. Control then tends to be exercised by the legislature, its committees, or their chairmen.

Legislative domination of executive agencies normally increases with the length of time these agencies work with particular members of Congress. Take the case of Representative Carl Vinson of Georgia. Elected to Congress in 1914, he served continuously for fifty years. From 1931 to 1965, moreover, he was chairman or ranking minority member of the House Naval Affairs Committee and of its successor after 1947, the Armed Services Committee. Small wonder if Vinson considered Presidents, Secretaries of Defense, and their immediate subordinates as recent arrivals and temporary occupants of executive positions, amateurs who had not been around long enough to know what they were doing. Vinson's case is exceptional only in degree.

The fundamental factor encouraging legislative supervision of administrative agencies to become close and detailed, and to threaten or displace presidential influence, is the nature and location of each legislator's political risks. Administrative officials are in a position to help or hurt individuals or interest groups important in the constituency of a member of Congress by awarding a contract, moving or eliminating a field office, or enforcing more vigorously the regulations under which an industry operates. Since the political career of a member of Congress rests primarily on individuals and groups in his constituency, he is almost compelled to try to influence such executive decisions in a way that will protect his position. His failure to affect these decisions may cause him serious trouble, for in the next election—especially in the primary—an opponent may successfully accuse him of neglecting or selling out the interests of his constituency.

Congressional supervision of administration, largely because of its electoral implications, is not confined to the language of authorizing legislation or of appropriation acts. This supervision is frequently the main theme of exchanges with executive officials in committee hearings; it is contained in the language of committee reports; it forms a large part of the less-public stream of communications, by letter and by telephone, between members of Congress and executive agencies; and it supplies much of the content of speeches on the floor of both houses. Any administrator who ignores these expressions, especially when they come from an influential representative or senator, must be prepared with an effective defense.

Conducting Investigations

The purposes of congressional investigations are numerous. Their classic functions are legislative—that is, Congress must be able to find its own facts on a given problem if it is to legislate on it. Furthermore, as we have just seen, Congress must be able to find out whether the laws are being enforced as they were intended and whether appropriations are being used properly. Finally, given the constitutional power of each house of Congress to discipline its own members, investigations into the merits of charges against a member are a natural part of legislative prerogatives. These purposes are the chief reason for the courts' reluctance to impose restrictions on congressional investigations, since it would be difficult to limit excesses without handicapping the achievement of legitimate purposes.

Attacking the administration

Most investigations, however, are directed more toward persuading the electorate than toward informing the legislature. This feature is most noticeable when a partisan or interest-group objective is served by an attack on the administration through an investigation. It is particularly likely to occur when the majority in one or both houses is not of the President's party, though an opposition majority in Congress is not essential. If an investigation's sponsors can make charges so serious that refusal to investigate them would imply acknowledgment of guilt, a minority may be able to cause an administration acute embarrassment. This was the kind of circumstance that opened "the McCarthy period," when in 1950 the junior senator from Wisconsin publicly charged the Secretary of State with having ignored evidence that 205 communists were employed in the State Department. It was also part of the reason for Republican desires to prolong the 1964 investigation of the affairs of Robert G. Baker, secretary to the Senate Democrats before revelations of questionable business activities forced his resignation. For Baker had been a protégé of Lyndon Johnson. Or if some dramatic event demands a public explanation, or even a scapegoat, the President's party in Congress may be obliged to support an investigation. This was essentially the setting for the first congressional investigation of the executive—the inquiry into the disastrous failure of the expedition led by General St. Clair against the Indians in the Western Reserve during Washington's first Administration.

Investigations aimed at embarrassing the administration have been the setting for a classic type of conflict experienced by most Chief Executives: a Cabinet officer is called upon to testify or to supply documents to a committee, and the demand is rejected by the President, who claims "executive privilege," arguing that communications between him and his advisers are privileged or that disclosure would not in his judgment be in the public interest. Washington set the precedent in 1796 when he declined to supply the House with papers relating to Jay's Treaty. Most Presidents since then have had occasion to invoke "executive privilege" against the demands of congressional investigations. Congress has frequently challenged the claim but has found no way to enforce its protests.

Supporting the administration

Congressional investigations may also support the President's program. The early New Deal legislation regulating stock exchanges and public-utility holding companies gained invaluable support from the series of investigations conducted under Senate auspices from 1933 through 1935. Furthermore, even investigations into sensitive areas may avoid strictly partisan results and embarrassment to the administration if congressional leaders handle them with care. The potentially explosive Senate inquiry into President Truman's dismissal of General MacArthur in 1951 is a good example. The care with which Senate leaders conducted these hearings avoided what might have been a free-for-all, damaging to the national security as well as to the President.

Publicizing the chairman

Not infrequently a legislative investigation may have as its chief result, if not its primary objective, promotion of the personal political fortunes of one of its members, usually the chairman. Any senator or representative may introduce a resolution establishing an investigating committee, and, by custom, if the resolution is adopted its sponsor is made chairman. If its hearings make the headlines—and the television screens—the chairman of the committee may suddenly become a major national figure. Thus the investigations of interstate crime under the chairmanship of Senator Estes Kefauver lifted him out of comparative obscurity and made him a popular aspirant for the Presidency in 1952 and 1956. Representative Richard Nixon's prominent part in the Alger Hiss case in 1948 as a member of the House Un-American Activities Committee contributed to his rapid rise in national politics.

Investigations and the rights of citizens

The congressional investigations especially likely to provoke controversy and criticism are those aimed at influencing public opinion, particularly when they are also associated with "scapegoating" and achieving notoriety for the chairman. In such investigations the committee may sacrifice the privacy of a witness and brand him as "guilty" of improper or illegal behavior without his having the benefit of protections available to him in a court of law. Although such a committee pronounces no formal sentence of fine or imprisonment, permanent damage to the witness' reputation and even loss of his livelihood may occur—which has led critics to charge that investigating committees performing in this fashion are usurping a function that properly belongs to the courts.

Although in recent years most committees criticized for this sort of action were investigating alleged subversive activities and associations, an investigation of any topic may be subject to such abuses. For example, even the Senate investigations in the 1930's of stock-exchange and investment-

"Fair is fair."

ANIMALS WILL KINDLY FOLLOW THEIR OWN RULES OF PROCEDURE

The Senate has consistently declined to set strict rules of conduct for its investigating committees.

From *Herblock's Here and Now,*
Simon & Schuster, 1955

banking practices were as abusive of privacy and the elements of fair play as any recent exposures.

The tendency toward excesses is not peculiar to special or select committees set up for the purpose. The committees most widely criticized in recent years for invasion of private rights have been standing committees or subcommittees: the House Committee on Un-American Activities, the Subcommittee on Internal Security of the Senate Judiciary Committee, and the Permanent Investigating Subcommittee of the Senate Committee on Government Operations.

Every citizen has an obligation to supply any government agency with information that it may legitimately request, and the presumption is in favor of Congress when a point is in dispute. There are, however, circumstances in which a witness may legitimately refuse to answer a committee's questions. First, he may decline to answer by invoking the Fifth Amendment's privilege against self-incrimination. Resort to this privilege means only that answering *might tend* to incriminate, but in the eyes of most citizens, unfortunately, it is often tantamount to an admission of guilt. Second, a witness may refuse to answer if the question is irrelevant to the authorized subject of the investigation.[9] The difficulty with both rights, however, is that a recalcitrant witness must be prepared to face an indict-

---

[9] *United States* v. *Rumely,* 345 U.S. 41 (1953); *Watkins* v. *United States,* 354 U.S. 178 (1957).

ment for contempt of Congress and to justify his refusal to the satisfaction of the courts.[10] Beyond these two privileges, the witness essentially has no rights except those granted him by the committee.

Two important questions are suggested by this persistent conflict between the investigating function of Congress and private rights. First, why cannot the witness be guaranteed the safeguards he would have in court, such as the right to legal counsel and the right to cross-question others? One must keep in mind that the purpose of a court trial is to determine whether it has been proved that a particular set of acts was committed and whether it has been established beyond reasonable doubt that the accused person committed them. Judicial safeguards were developed on the assumption that it is better for a guilty man to go free than for an innocent man to be punished. A legislative investigation to establish the need for a change in the statutes, however, need only indicate that without such change certain undesirable results *tend* to occur. To require the committees to observe courtlike procedures would delay and complicate the useful function of establishing the need for legislation. Hence the reluctance of the courts to require additional restraints on investigative committees.

Second, why cannot Congress itself impose effective restraints on these committees or establish an alternative method of investigating that will be free of their deficiencies? One frequently hears the suggestion that it is up to Congress to use its powers of investigating more responsibly, as if that required merely an act of will. Unfortunately matters are not that simple. In the first place, authority in Congress (discussed further in Chapter 12) permits such restraints only in the most extreme cases. For example, in the early 1940's a House investigation of the Federal Communications Commission was severely criticized both because of its tactics and because its chairman, Representative Eugene Cox of Georgia, clearly had initiated the inquiry in order to "punish" the FCC for referring to the Attorney General evidence of illegal activity by Cox. As criticism mounted, Speaker Sam Rayburn persuaded Cox to withdraw as chairman. Even the Speaker of the House could only *urge* the withdrawal of Cox, himself a highly influential representative. Second, and more fundamental, both the weakness in the congressional structure of authority and the casual acceptance in Congress of the vagaries of investigations reflect once again the fact that the political risks of a congressman ultimately lie in his local constituency. Most senators and representatives look to the day when they can strengthen their political fortunes by heading an investigation of national importance. Even if they have no such ambition, they know that their threat to institute an investigation can be a means of protection against their opponents in and out of the government. They are therefore unlikely to

[10] *United States* v. *Barenblatt*, 360 U.S. 109 (1959).

oppose another member's investigation for fear of limiting their own ability to use this device for political self-protection.

The conflict between investigations and private rights and the conflict between the President and Congress thus have a common source—the congressman's localized political risks.

CONGRESSIONAL CAREERS AND CONGRESSIONAL ROLES

The characteristic operations of Congress, especially its recurrent conflicts with the White House, are thus a composite of constitutional arrangements, reinforced and supplemented by the decentralized, localized political risks faced by representatives and senators. These characteristics make the personal qualities of members important in the operation of Congress, since they allow more freedom of action to the individual member than does a more disciplined legislature such as the British Parliament.

Any institution is affected by the characteristics of the people who are drawn into it. A college in which most of the students are only interested in having fun for a few years before going to work, in finding a marriage partner, and in making "good contacts" will differ sharply from one where the students' primary objectives are to equip themselves to understand the world they live in, to appreciate the fragile quality of the things that make a civilized man, and to prepare for a career that will be of some value to society. To discover what a senator or representative does and what kind of place Congress is we can usefully ask two questions. First, what variations exist in the qualities that are useful or necessary for getting elected? Second, what variations are there in the "uses" to which a congressional position is put—in what the members expect to get out of it?

Recruitment Qualifications

All senators and representatives must meet certain formal qualifications. Members of the House must be at least twenty-five years of age, senators at least thirty; representatives must have been citizens for at least seven years, senators for at least nine years; both must be residents of the state from which they are chosen, and, by tradition, most representatives live in their districts. The typical member of Congress, in addition, has been resident in his state and locality for a major part of his life. He has, furthermore, been actively involved in the organizational life of the community—its business, civic, religious, and fraternal organizations—and usually its political institutions. Characteristically he is ambitious, and his personal life is relatively free of what his locality would regard as scandalous moral behavior, although some variation may exist in the latter respect. Beyond these rather standard qualities we encounter considerable variation, due primarily to the social structure of the community or locality and to the peculiarities of its party system.

The influence of social structure

Social structure is an important factor in recruitment. First, it will govern the occupational alternatives open to a man of ability and aspiration. In a poor, rural, nonindustrialized area these will be limited, and a political career—especially one that leads to Washington—is likely to be prized and respected. Thus the Southern states have sent to Congress a disproportionately large number of men with unusual political and parliamentary skills. On the other hand, a prosperous, urban, industrial area will provide a wide variety of occupational channels for able and ambitious men; if the people of the area regard these channels as more desirable, the most talented men will not be attracted to a political career. Some of the most prosperous areas in the North, especially suburbs like Westchester County, New York, often have been represented in the House by men whose talents by any criterion were considerably below those of many of their constituents and of their colleagues in the House. On the other hand, in an urban area containing sizable numbers of comparatively recent immigrants, politics may be more open to talented members of those groups than business or the other professions.

If the social structure of an area is relatively homogeneous in occupation, income, and religion, race, or nationality, its representatives will require somewhat different skills from those of men elected from areas with greater diversity. The politically significant cleavages *within* such homogeneous areas are likely to be few. Usually they are, in fact, one-party areas. Therefore, as long as a man adequately reflects the dominant characteristics of the area, the qualities important to his political advancement are peculiarly personal—his manner, "personality," family connections, and so on. Homogeneity in social structure, moreover, is sometimes less important than the homogeneity of the population that actually votes. In those states of the South where Negroes and a considerable portion of lower-income whites have not been part of the actual electorate, the characteristics needed by the member of Congress are essentially personal. In more heterogeneous districts, on the other hand, how the aspirant is identified on either side of the cleavages and resulting issues in the constituency may be the controlling factor. He will therefore require more skill in recognizing and accommodating the claims of rival interests in his constituency than will a member of Congress from a more homogeneous district.

In this respect there are fewer differences among senators than among representatives, since almost all statewide constituencies show a considerable degree of internal diversity. Take, for example, the division between urban and rural populations, a cleavage related to a wide range of political issues in the country, from farm price supports and urban renewal to foreign aid and minimum wages. Only four states in 1960 did not include at least one Standard Metropolitan Statistical Area (that is, at least one city of 50,000 inhabitants or more). Although some of the remaining forty-six states had sizable populations outside the metropolitan areas, in most of them a senator needed at least a minimum number of city votes to assure his election. By contrast, in 1966 nearly half the House districts were outside metropolitan areas.

The significance of this pattern is that, first, the Senate has been more oriented toward urban interests than has the more rural House. Second, the heterogeneous constituencies of the Senate have been much more responsive to changes in the society and the world than the more homogeneous constituencies—especially the rural ones—of the House. For these reasons the Senate over the past thirty years has generally given far more support than the House to legislation attempting to deal with the problems of our industrial society—public housing, urban renewal, social security, minimum-wage standards. For essentially the same reason, the House has been a good deal less ready than the Senate to accept the new position of the United States on the international scene and the politics that have grown from that position—participation in the United Nations and related agencies, support of "neutralist" nations, economic assistance to underdeveloped countries, cultural-exchange programs, and the like. Finally, since Senate constituencies more closely resemble the President's heterogeneous one, that body has normally been more responsive to his programs and policies.

The influence of party systems

The state and local party system also helps to determine what qualities are needed for entrance into Congress. The character of the effective electorate—those who actually vote—has already been mentioned. In addition, variations in party structure, in party competition, and in party nominating processes can influence the kinds of skill congressmen need have. A well-organized party at the state or local level can actively recruit, groom, and support candidates for public office, including Congress. The qualities the party seeks are not uniform, of course, but they are likely to include the ability to work effectively as part of the organization. The candidate of such a party must make considerable personal effort to get himself elected, but he usually can rely on the organization and the pull of the party label to get out the vote in the general election. In a nomination contest—even one involving a direct primary—he can rely for assistance on a continuing organization.

Where no such organization exists—as in most one-party areas, South and North—an aspirant for Congress is likely to need personal qualities and skills that will substitute for those a party organization might provide. His chief obstacles, almost by definition, will be in the primary, where the party label is of no assistance. Unable to rely on a continuing organization, he is obliged either to build his own or to cultivate a slapdash, hell-for-leather mass appeal. Thus it is the degree of strength of the state party institutions that largely determines whether the "skills" of the demagogue are an asset or a handicap in seeking public office. The Huey Longs, the Gene Talmadges, and their ilk are not an accident on the political scene: where party organization is weak or nonexistent, one can expect all sorts of extraneous factors—a flamboyant personality or popularity as a banjo-playing radio entertainer or a fire-and-brimstone preacher—to be converted into a political career. Ronald Reagan, George Murphy, and Pierre Salinger were more likely to be products of California politics, with its weak parties, than of the more disciplined system of a state like Pennsylvania.

The party connections of senators are usually different from those of most representatives because of the personal power of a senator on the national scene. The facts that there are only two senators from each state, that they influence executive appointments, and that they hold office for six years automatically make each senator a factor to be reckoned with in his state's politics. In consequence, senatorial nominations—even in states with weak party organizations—normally go to men who have achieved political prominence as governors, as other statewide officials, or as representatives in Congress. Only a small proportion of senators lack considerable prior political experience. And a well-organized state party is likely to regard a Senate nomination as one of the prize places on its ticket.

The degree of party competition in the constituency affects the attitudes, if not the personality characteristics, of members of Congress. In those constituencies where the margin of victory is slight—one-third to one-half the House seats and a slightly smaller proportion in the Senate—a congressional incumbent approaches a reelection campaign acutely aware that his political survival might well turn on how his party label currently appears to the movable electorate. If he and the President are of the same party, the strength of the party label—especially in a year when a President also seeks reelection—will depend in part on these voters' responses to the President and to what he has done. In such circumstances the recruitment process is likely over the long run to turn up men whose views resemble those of the President. The problems that are most conspicuous in closely contested constituencies, therefore, are likely to be those that are the more acute national issues of domestic policy.

The Uses of Congressional Office

The role that a man will play in Washington is also affected by what he wants from his position. These objectives will in turn go a long way toward making the House or Senate what it is on the national scene. Here again we find a general difference between House and Senate. Senators, by and large, have "arrived" while the representatives are more likely to be still "on the move." A senator may want to become a federal judge, or his state's governor, or a Cabinet member—and, of course, if he comes from a large state he may have presidential ambitions; but for the most part the Senate is the capstone of a career. Those contented with a Senate career may play a variety of roles reflecting personal and interest-group commitments.

A senator with presidential aspirations is likely to be what some senators call a "show horse." That is, he will attempt to use the Senate to gain the national reputation essential to being nominated. He may try to exploit the chairmanship of a dramatic investigating committee, he may talk to the galleries on all manner of subjects, and he is likely to spend a good deal of his time traveling about the country rather than in the Senate. The "show horse" is likely not to be highly influential within the Senate. In any case, he presents a sharp contrast to the Senate careerist, the "work horse."

Some representatives also enter the House at the peak of a career. Representatives elected by party organizations in large cities may even be sent to the House as a place of semiretirement from the rigors of local politics. But a good many representatives are "on the move." One indicator of this movement is the House turnover rate: in each Congress from 15 to 25 percent of the representatives are serving for the first time. A representative may move on to the Senate, to another national office, or to state or city office. In recent years about one-quarter of the senators have come to the upper chamber directly from the House. (Movement the other way has occurred only rarely since John Quincy Adams went from the Senate to the House in 1831.) The representative's style of behavior will depend primarily upon where he must appeal in order to gain the objective he is ultimately aiming for. In an extreme case his future may lie in hands almost indifferent to his House performance. Thus in New York City for some years the most coveted party prizes have been the principal state and city judgeships, since they pay well, involve long tenure, and afford ample patronage to the party in the form of clerkships, bailiwicks, and similar positions. For many representatives from New York City, mostly Democrats, the House becomes a waiting place until they get a chance at one of these court posts. They are part-time legislators with little interest in the House. Whatever the aspiration of the ambitious representative, however, the odds are that the influences controlling his prospects are predominantly in the state or locality.

Almost all representatives, even if they seek only reelection, are hungry for opportunities to make a name. Few of their constituents know them, and, unlike senators and governors, they cannot hit the headlines almost at will. This eagerness to become known makes representatives somewhat more ready to accept the preferences of the party leaders in the House; it also may tie the representative fairly intimately to an incumbent senator; and it may provide some leverage to the President, especially one in the same party. But the net effect of the need to become better known is for the representative to be drawn toward persons and activities in his locality that will enhance his reputation; his role in the House may thus become of limited national value.

THE QUESTION OF REPRESENTATION

Given this variety in the skills, backgrounds, and goals of the men who are recruited into Congress, one may well ask where the function of representation fits in. At minimum the idea of representation implies that the government, and especially the legislature, will be so structured that no significant interest in the society fails to get at least a hearing.

Responsiveness and Responsibility

Beyond this minimum, the notion of representation becomes complicated by the associated idea of self-government. We all realize that 195 million people or even 112 million voters cannot govern themselves. They cannot directly set public policy and enact laws. Most voters are satisfied with being able to choose periodically which of two or more sets of aspirants for public office seems likely to make the most acceptable kinds of decisions. Collectively, then, they designate elected officials to represent them.

But, although the people of a nation cannot govern themselves in the literal sense, a significant proportion of them still have firm views on public questions, especially those questions bearing directly on their sources of livelihood and personal welfare. Since they designate "representatives" to make public choices for them, does this mean that on those questions where the voters hold fairly firm views the representatives must follow the preference of their constituents? Almost by definition, one's opinions on matters directly affecting his own welfare are basically selfish and therefore probably cannot take into account conflicting preferences and long-term consequences. Must the representative reflect these "broader" factors in his choices and thus appear to "sell out" at least some of his constituents? If so, in what sense can he be called a representative? (On the American national scene, of course, this question is especially complicated. When representatives, senators, and Presidents disagree, who is in fact truly representative?)

A classic statement of this problem was written two years before our Declaration of Independence by Edmund Burke, British statesman, philosopher, and, at the time, member of Parliament for Bristol. Burke conceded that a representative was obliged to keep in close touch with his constituents and to concern himself with their needs. But he argued that, as a member of a national legislature—"a deliberative assembly of one nation, with one interest, that of the whole"—he could not simply act as the voters' agent but had to exercise his judgment. If necessary he had to sacrifice his constituents' demands to what he viewed as the national interest. If his constituents did not approve his actions, they in turn could vote him out at the next election. (They did.)

In actual fact members of Congress must be both agents and "governors." Given the localized political risks in connection with renomination and reelection, a United States legislator today would be courting disaster if he took as outspoken a position as Burke's, but he is often applauded if he speaks in *general* terms of his high Burkeian duties.

To a remarkable degree members of Congress are not only agents but errand boys for their constituents. Their offices are distribution centers for government publications, welcoming committees for groups of irate citizens or voyaging sightseers in Washington, and even informal employment agencies for federal job seekers. They are expected to help get voters' sons out of (or into) the Navy, the Army, the Marines, or the Air Force. They must "open doors" in the executive establishment for constituents seeking a government contract, loan, or favorable administrative ruling. They are obliged to look after the interests of local industries before legislative committees and administrative agencies, to contribute money and time to district causes, and to offer ceremonial congratulations to winning football teams, high-school graduating classes, and successful garden clubs. Many representatives require their staffs to scrutinize the personal news in all local papers and then send congratulatory notes.

Most senators and representatives also spend a good deal of their own time and that of their limited staff on constituent mail. Prompt and careful responses to communications from constituents are usually considered essential to maintaining one's place with the voters. This is a relatively easy task for some, such as a number of representatives from the South whose constituents rarely write. For others the volume of mail amounts to thousands of letters each day when there is controversy on an issue. The problem of how to answer abusive mail is tricky. One representative is reported to deal with it by sending the following form: "Dear Sir:

The Congressman as Agent

The primary and overriding duty and responsibility of each Member of the House and the Senate is to get reelected.... It would be ridiculous for anyone to think otherwise or for a Member to do otherwise, for if a Member was not interested in reelection, there would be no point in his starting in the first place to seek the public office....

When questions of national interest conflict with the desires of one's constituents, the national interests suffer. For instance, I represent a district that is interested in the bread-and-butter issues of life—housing, jobs, and education. My constituents don't care whether I vote for, or against, or not vote at all on tidelands oil, surplus wheat, industrial monopolies, or the oil-depreciation allowance. In these areas, I exercise my personal judgment. However, Representatives from those areas that have the problems of tidelands oil, surplus wheat, industrial monopolies and oil-depreciation allowances feel obliged to vote either according to what their constituents want or what the money boys who bankroll their campaigns demand.

To sum it up, the politician holding a seat in the United States Congress has a two-pronged responsibility that is obvious: commitment to the interest of his constituency and to the national welfare. How he performs in the first instance defines his life expectancy as a Member of Congress; how he performs in the second is his legislative voting record.

From Representative Adam Clayton Powell, Jr., of Manhattan, "The Duties and Responsibilities of a Congressman to the United States," *Esquire*, September 1963.

Today I received a letter from some crackpot who signed your name to it. I thought you ought to know about this before it went any further." [11]

Members of Congress also gain an impression of constituent opinion by reading local newspapers and noting positions adopted by local groups. Advice (rarely instructions) from close supporters in the local organization, party or personal, is sought and weighed. As frequently as possible visits to the home area are used to gain fresh impressions. Some senators and representatives even try to poll their constituents by mail ballot.

In every constituency there are some legislative matters on which constituency opinion is so clear and so solid that the member of Congress has no option. A representative or senator from the Deep South or the urban centers of the North, for instance, needs no communications on a racial issue.

But most legislative questions are not of this order, and the legislator often has no choice but to be a Burke. Frequently it is on questions of the greatest consequence—including many matters of foreign policy, such as the supplying of nuclear weapons to a multinational organization—that

[11] Neil MacNeil, *Forge of Democracy: The House of Representatives* (New York: McKay, 1963), p. 141.

constituency guidance is slight. On other issues, such as aid to church-sponsored schools, opinions and demands are so divided, even among supporters, that however the legislator votes—or even if he fails to vote—he risks trouble. His choices here may produce constituent reactions that threaten his political survival, but he can only guess at them at best. On many of these issues—as well as on some where constituency preferences seem fairly clear—he makes the choices that in his judgment are best for the nation. (In all probability, if voting in Congress on foreign aid at any time since 1950 had scrupulously mirrored mass sentiment in the country, funds for that program would have been slight or nonexistent.) And, on issues on which constituent opinion is not rigid, a congressman, especially one with high prestige, may in the course of time actually *lead* public opinion.

Thus the legislator as representative is responsive to a wide range of views but chiefly to interests that can affect his political future. These interests are characteristically those held by organized groups, but a forward-looking representative may anticipate the responses of various interests—and even the emergence of new groups. Urban renewal may look like a good thing, for instance, until property owners or tenants threatened by dispossession organize to defeat its supporters.

The personal judgments of the legislator take on added importance

The Congressman as Legislator

We have much leeway in voting, but we can't go against the district too often, I think. On *really* important issues I always vote my conviction regardless of the pressures which are put upon me. On less important votes politics may be followed on an expedient basis. I think members have to decide where they are going to make their stand and at what point the issue isn't too important. Sometimes it is easier to follow what your district wants you to do.

People vote for you for an infinite variety of reasons. No one action you take will make or break you, but too many wrong actions are likely to prove costly. What I am saying is that you can be independent to a point, but if you continually vote against what you are expected to vote for, you will have a lot of trouble staying here.

I think you can vote pretty nearly the way you want to vote on issues. The people don't expect you to agree with them on every issue, and they respect you for arriving at your independent judgment. You must demonstrate that you are conscientious, however, and that you are able to arrive at a reasonable and intelligent judgment.... The important thing is that you state your position clearly and defend it before them.

Congressmen quoted anonymously in Charles L. Clapp, *The Congressman*, 1963.

because of the second feature of the system—responsibility to the electorate. For when elections permit remarkably full comment and discussion, representatives seeking reelection are held responsible at the ballot box for their political judgments—both their actual choices and what the voters *think* those choices have been. At times legislators may be the political victims of consequences completely beyond their control, as voters react against the condition of the economy and the state of the world. This exposure to the whims of the electorate, however, is an inescapable cost of a system that seeks stability by channeling grievances toward the ballot box.

Responsiveness and the Composition of Congress

A prerequisite for stability in a representative system is that a demand felt by any appreciable number of citizens must not go unheard or be compelled to seek subversive means of expression because it is denied spokesmen in the government.

This does not mean that Congress must be an exact cross-section of the electorate. In fact its members are disproportionately drawn from certain sectors of the population. The average age of the members of Congress—about fifty for representatives and sixty for senators—is ten to twenty years older than the average age of the voting population. The overwhelming majority of Congress are men—in 1967 Congress included only one woman senator and eleven women representatives. Moreover, the members of Congress have had much more formal education than the average citizen: less than 10 percent of the population of voting age has had four or more years of college training, but well over 80 percent of the representatives and senators have attended college, and approximately one-half have earned advanced degrees.

These differences from the population at large are of little consequence for the representative requirement suggested above. The politically relevant attitudes and demands of women are not different from those of men, and, except for a few local situations, there is no such thing as a distinctive "women's vote." It is unlikely that even the higher average age of members of Congress, as compared with the electorate, affects the representativeness of the legislature, since American political cleavages normally do not occur along age or generational lines. Differences of education in themselves present no problem. In any group and in almost any social situation people tend to look to the most skilled for leadership and advice. Political skills—for example, in speaking and organization—are likely to be associated with educational accomplishment.

Other respects in which the composition of Congress differs from the general population may be of more consequence. Differences of viewpoint according to social class—however that troublesome concept is defined—

are by no means uncommon in the United States. Members of Congress, as one would expect from the figures on their educational attainments, are drawn overwhelmingly from the middle and upper strata of society (as measured by their occupations in private life). A considerable majority also come from families of comparable status. Thus the law, business, banking, and the other recognized professions account for the private occupations of most members. A small number, a little more than 10 percent, call themselves farmers, and wage-earners are few and far between, as are leaders of organized labor.

Undoubtedly this occupational or class bias tends to favor the political attitudes of the higher social strata. The tendency is constrained to some extent, however, by the fact that the overwhelming majority of these men have spent a substantial proportion of their lives in politics and in public office—and expect to spend more. They cannot afford, therefore, to ignore the demands of any significant group of voters in their constituencies. Nonetheless, some irreducible minimum of class bias may remain: farm laborers, sharecroppers, and various groups among the urban poor who do not or cannot vote are no threat to the elected legislator and have no means of being politically effective between elections.

Normally the underrepresentation of Catholics and Jews in Congress, especially in the Senate, is of minor consequence. Most issues in American politics, especially at the national level, have not split the population along religious lines. Similarly, few consequences of any importance derive from the disproportionately large number of representatives and senators who are of "Yankee" stock or are descended from the old immigrant groups from northwestern Europe.

The unrepresentative character of Congress in respect to race, however, is not only conspicuous but also a source of difficulty in a time when cleavage on racial lines is growing. Negroes constitute more than 10 percent of the population, but from Reconstruction until 1966, when Edward W. Brooke was elected from Massachusetts, the Senate included no Negroes. Recently Negroes have accounted for about 1 percent of the House membership—6 congressmen out of 435 in 1967–69. Fundamentally the underrepresentation of Negroes stems from two factors: first, the still quite extensive disfranchisement of Negroes in the South; and, second, the fact that many white voters are unwilling to cast their ballots for a Negro running for a major office against a reasonably acceptable white. Thus Negroes are elected to the House only from a few large cities containing congressional districts whose voters are overwhelmingly Negro. On the other hand, many white members of Congress, especially in the North, have sizable numbers of Negro voters in their constituencies, so Negro claims have not gone unrepresented in Congress, especially in the past decade, though Negro voters have not been represented proportionately.

The preference of Negro groups in recent years for gaining their objectives through the courts and the importance of the Negro vote in presidential elections indicate that the judicial and executive branches of the government have been considerably more responsive to the Negro than the legislative branch. From the standpoint of the system's stability, the importance in presidential elections of the Negro vote in such large states as New York, Illinois, and Michigan may well be great enough to compensate for the bias against Negroes in the composition of Congress. This consideration should be borne in mind when one hears outcries against the "power of minorities" under the present method of electing Presidents. If this counterbalance were removed, the Negro might well be consigned to a kind of political ghetto, with the explosive implications like those evident in the last years of most African colonies.

The gerrymander and the urban-rural cleavage

The important point about the biases in the composition of Congress is that none of them—with the possible exception of the Negro problem—is frozen into the system. If they should threaten the stability of the political system, they can be altered relatively easily. As changes occur in the prestige structure and the value system of society, patterns of congressional membership will change; if new kinds of cleavage occur in the nation's politics, membership patterns will undoubtedly be modified almost imperceptibly and without official action.

This cannot be said of the biases in the distribution of Senate and House seats in relation to area and population. In the Senate, of course, the bias stems from the constitutional guarantee of equal representation of all states regardless of population—often described as the one unamendable provision of the Constitution. This meant in 1965 that at one extreme the two senators from Alaska represented 253,000 people, the two from Nevada 440,000 and the two from Vermont 397,000, while at the other extreme New York's two senators represented over 18,000,000, California's approximately the same number, and Pennsylvania's over 11,000,000.

Political cleavages between small and large states as such are not characteristic of American politics; past divisions have normally been regional or sectional. Increasingly, however, the sharpest divisions are between sizable urban populations and those in small towns and rural areas. Because the Senate gives disproportionate weight to the less populous states, it gives an advantage to the interests that are strongest in the rural and smaller urban areas. But, as explained earlier in the chapter, this bias is growing smaller as most states develop sizable urban concentrations of population whose demands senators cannot ignore.

The situation in the House, however, is somewhat different, for political rather than constitutional reasons. To be sure, the Constitution provides

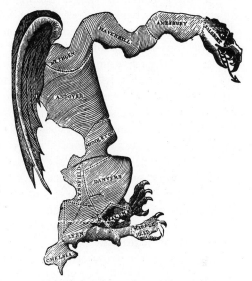

The Gerrymander

This famous political cartoon of 1812 introduced the word "gerrymander" into the American political vocabulary: it illustrates the contorted legislative boundaries drawn by Republicans to produce sizable majorities in the Massachusetts legislature.

New York Public Library Picture Collection

that each state shall have at least one representative. This meant in 1967 that the smallest of New York's forty-one districts contained more people than the whole state of Alaska. But aside from this special provision, the seats in the House are apportioned among the states in proportion to population.

The Constitution requires that after each decennial census Congress shall apportion seats by statute among the states according to population. Up through the census of 1910, when the House reached its present size of 435, the conflicts over this decision were eased by increasing the number of seats. In 1920, following a tentative decision to create no additional seats, Congress deadlocked and no reapportionment was carried out. In 1929, therefore, a statute fixed the number of seats at 435 and established a system of automatic reapportionment if Congress fails to act. Under this system, after each census the President notifies Congress of the number of representatives each state would be entitled to under each of two complex methods of calculation. If Congress fails to act within sixty days, the reapportionment occurs automatically according to the method used after the previous census.

In 1842 Congress required that members of the House be elected by districts whose boundaries would be fixed by the state legislatures, and representation by district has remained the norm, though it is no longer required by law. It is the drawing of the district boundaries that has produced the chief bias in House representation. The major means of discrimination is the gerrymander.

The gerrymander is named after Elbridge Gerry, governor of Massachusetts in 1814, who was responsible for creating a district in that state whose distorted shape was said to resemble a salamander. "Gerrymander" refers to the drawing of legislative district lines so as to grant undue advantage to the party in control of the legislature that does the districting. One way to do this is to gather as many as possible of the opposition party's voters into one district, so that in all the other districts they constitute a hopeless minority. This was the device used by the Republicans in California after the 1950 census to create the Twenty-sixth District, heavily Democratic (by more than 60 percent even in the Republican landslide of 1956), which left six of the remaining eleven districts in Los Angeles County safely Republican.

The second way is to carve out of an area that strongly favors the opposition party one or more districts that can safely be counted on by the party controlling the legislature. For example, after the 1950 census the Republican legislature of New York was able to create a new district by carving out a narrow strip across heavily Democratic Kings County (Brooklyn); the new district voted Republican in four of the five subsequent elections.

A consequence frequently associated with the gerrymander is that some districts in the same state have contained huge populations, while others were relatively small. Thus in 1960 the largest district in Texas, the Fifth (Dallas), contained over 950,000 people, more than four times as many as the smallest district in the state. Not surprisingly, the huge Dallas district, created by a legislature dominated by Democrats, was one of the two Republican districts in the state during the mid-1960's. From time to time in the past the congressional statutes apportioning representatives among the states required state legislatures to create districts as nearly equal in population as possible and composed of compact and contiguous territory, but since 1911 none of these provisions has been specified in the law.

Since the state legislatures, together with state governors, are responsible for drawing congressional-district boundaries, they are the ultimate source of malapportionment in the House of Representatives. Until recently most of these legislatures have themselves been unbalanced in favor of rural and small-town areas, a bias that has come from two sources: state constitutions and legislative practice. The constitutions have provided for representation in one chamber on the basis of area rather than population, and often they have guaranteed some minimum representation per county in the other chamber, regardless of population. Legislative practice in many states has compounded the constitutional imbalance by the "silent gerrymander"—the failure of a legislature to redistrict despite a state constitutional mandate. Thus the state legislative districts in Tennessee had not been changed between 1901 and 1962. Since population in all states has been shifting to urban areas during the last sixty years, the two sources of bias have resulted in overrepresentation of thinly populated sections. A study published in 1961 estimated that over the country as a whole counties with less than 25,000 population in 1960 had almost twice the representation to which they were entitled on a strictly proportional basis, while counties with 500,000 or more in population had only three-quarters of their just representation.[12]

The House of Representatives that resulted from these imbalances has thus almost inevitably favored rural and small-town areas. That is, it has been disproportionately composed of men from districts in which the most critical domestic issues of the day—urban renewal, race relations, social security, and the like—have little or no importance. Moreover, as we noted earlier, such areas of thin and declining population are likely to be those least informed and least sensitive to the contemporary requirements of international affairs. The representational bias of the House has thus been a potential threat to the adaptability of the political system.

In a series of decisions beginning in 1962 the Supreme Court has acted to correct this situation. In that year it effectively outlawed the "silent gerrymander" by directing the state of Tennessee to redraw its state legislative districts, as its constitution required.[13] Two years later the Court ruled that representation in both houses of state legislatures must be based on population, regardless of provisions to the contrary in state constitutions,[14] and efforts to amend the Constitution of the United States so as to overrule this decision have not succeeded so far. In 1967 the Court declared that it would not permit marked deviation from the principle of "one man, one vote," when it rejected a Florida apportionment plan in which some districts were overrepresented by more than 18 percent and others were underrepresented by more than 15 percent.[15] Finally, the Court since 1964 has broken with precedent by deciding whether the congressional districts created by the states meet the requirements of the Constitution. It rejected the districting in Georgia, which discriminated against the urban areas, stating that "as nearly as practicable" district boundaries must be so drawn that district populations are approximately equal.[16]

These actions by the Court have given the underrepresented sectors of the population a means for correcting the bias of the House of Representatives against the areas of population growth and concentration, so ultimately the House will be more capable of dealing with the issues characteristic of such areas.

---

[12] Paul T. David and Ralph Eisenberg, *Devaluation of the Urban and Suburban Vote* (Charlottesville, Va.: University of Virginia Press, 1961), p. 9.
[13] *Baker* v. *Carr*, 369 U.S. 186 (1962).
[14] *Reynolds* v. *Sims*, 377 U.S. 533 (1964).
[15] *Swann* v. *Adams*, 87 S. Ct. 509 (1967).
[16] *Wesberry* v. *Sanders*, 376 U.S. 1 (1964).

SUMMARY

Persistent tensions between the President and Congress are a conspicuous feature of the American system. The sources of these strains are partly constitutional and partly political. Politically, these strains reflect the local risks to which a senator or representative is exposed; and they also mirror the general tendency for the political stakes of the President and those of the member of Congress to be different. These differences in stakes have in some ways been accentuated by the biases in our system of representation. Such factors produce senators and representatives with a variety of skills and goals, and this significantly affects the kinds of role that members of Congress will choose to play and the responsiveness of the system as a whole.

The resulting differences in political outlook are converted into potential conflicts between the President and Congress by the constitutional system of checks and balances. The Constitution grants the President many legislative functions, and, conversely, it assigns to the House and Senate many nonlegislative and semilegislative powers.

The American scheme thus makes of Congress an alternative channel of initiative within the government. The resulting difficulties are great both for most members of Congress and for the President. The senator or representative is almost obliged to exploit such opportunities as are available to him, while the President, given the expectations focused on him in the country and in Congress itself, must try in turn to persuade Congress to accept his initiatives.

How these attempts turn out, of course, depends in considerable measure on the skills of the political actors. The outcome will also reflect, however, characteristics of the legislative process itself and of the power structure within Congress. These matters will be examined in the next chapter.

CONGRESS
The Power Structure and the Legislative Process

12

Chapter 12 examines the power structure of Congress, the ways in which it favors or hampers various interests, and its impact on legislative procedure. The most profound influence on the structure of Congress is the decentralization of our party system and the localized risks of each legislator. This chapter examines this influence by asking several questions: What role does party actually play in the legislative process? What institutions compensate for the lack of centralized parties? What powers do elected and seniority leaders command? What are the effects of the congressional power structure on the procedures for enacting legislation? Finally, what are the prospects for change in congressional structure and procedures?

The machinery of the House and Senate is not a neutral registering device. Like any other human institution, it has a power structure that favors some kinds of people, interests, or enterprises and hampers or excludes others.

The representative or senator who enters Congress must come to terms with this internal structure. How effectively he is able to satisfy the demands coming from his constituency and to meet his political risks will depend—as in the case of the President or any other official—on his ability to get this structure to work on his behalf. As an individual, and especially as a new member of Congress, his resources are limited. Because he cannot dominate the structure, he finds that he must yield to the demands of those who do if he is to influence it in any degree. This is the chief source of leverage against him that is available to those leaders who occupy key points in the legislative system, including the President indirectly.

Viewed as a whole, Congress is a remarkable, even an admirable, institution. It reflects the diverse goals and risks of its members and the variety of demands on its attention from the White House, the executive agencies, and interest groups. Through a process of conflict, search, negotiation, and compromise it arrives at the legitimate rules that guide the country's complex affairs.

THE STRUCTURE OF POWER

The most characteristic comment on the political parties in the House and Senate is that they are undisciplined, as a casual reading of the press reports of any congressional session will reveal. On most votes in either house the majority and the losing side both include some members of each party. Although there are votes on which a *majority* of Republicans opposes a majority of Democrats, those on which *all* the members of one party oppose all members of the other normally occur only when the principal officers of each chamber are being chosen at the beginning of each Congress. Party discipline, of course, can be measured only on "yea-and-nay," or roll-call, votes, on which each member casts his vote as his name is called. ("Yea-and-nay" votes are constitutionally required only on motions to override a presidential veto, but they may be demanded on other matters by one-fifth of those present.) On all other votes it is impossible to tell who favored which position.

The Partisan Frame

Given the local nature of political risk in Congress, discussed in Chapter 11, the degree of bipartisan voting should not be astonishing. But it can easily be exaggerated. *The fact is that most members of Congress vote with the majority of their fellow partisans most of the time.* Both the records and the statements of senators and representatives show that they do not like to vote against a majority of their fellow partisans and particularly their party leaders. Many legislators will go to considerable lengths—and even run heavy risks—to avoid doing so. (One way of avoiding such recorded opposition is to accept a *pair*, under which a member agrees not to vote if a member on the other side is obliged to be absent.)

The basic reasons for this partisan predisposition are three. First, most members have a sense of party loyalty and identification that is reinforced by long experience in electoral contests and by a vague sense of party tradition. When Republican orators speak of "the party of Lincoln" or Democrats of "the party of Jefferson, Wilson, and Franklin D. Roosevelt," they refer to a very real—although imprecise—sentiment. Second, the members of Congress have some stake in the popular standing of the party label, as we have already seen. Even those from safe districts have something to gain from their party's being "in control" of the government. Third, all manner of opportunities, favors, and advantages are at the disposal of the party's leaders, and these may be withheld from a member who too frequently votes "wrong."

Despite the evidence of a lack of party discipline, therefore, the partisan frame is real. It both reflects and reinforces the structure of power in Congress.

"Elective" Leaders and "Seniority" Leaders

It is valuable to distinguish two types of leader within the Congress. First are the *elective leaders,* who are chosen by the members of the party caucus or conference in their respective houses or are designated by such a leader. Second are the *seniority leaders,* the chairmen and ranking minority members of the standing committees. A seniority leader reaches his position by virtue of having continuously been a member of a committee for longer than any other senator or representative of the same party.

One can identify certain broad differences between the two types. First, the elective leader is likely to stand toward the center on the spectrum of his party's attitudes. His influence depends heavily on persuasion and on the respect his colleagues feel for him as a person. An extremist normally cannot establish these relations of confidence. If one does reach this sort of position, as occasionally happens, he is likely to be an ineffective leader. The seniority leader, on the other hand, reaches his position by a route beyond control of the chamber. Hence the accidents of elections, deaths, and resignations can bring to seniority positions men who occupy an extreme position—usually conservative—in their parties.

Second, the elective leader is a generalist, concerned with the total legislative product of his chamber and of the party, with overall strategy—including the President's—and with the political problems of most of his fellow partisans in the chamber. The seniority leader, on the other hand, is a specialist. He has reached his position by staying on a committee for years, and his influence in the house depends considerably on his presumed expertness in the area of his committee's work. He is closely associated with the "clients" of his committee, among the interest groups and in the executive branch, and his congressional world is likely to be confined to his committee, its jurisdiction, traditions, and prerogatives.

Third, both types are likely to be skilled parliamentary tacticians, but the seniority leader can more easily be something of a tyrant within his bailiwick. His stock in trade conspicuously includes the power to prevent things he opposes or to hold them up until his terms are met. The elective leader, on the other hand, is more concerned with getting things done and must therefore rely more heavily on positive inducements. His opportunities for dictation are relatively few.

The House of Representatives

In the House the principal elective leader on the majority side is the Speaker. Although his is a constitutional position and he is thus formally elected by the whole House, he is chosen in fact by the majority caucus. Once nominated, he is automatically elected, since voting is along strict party lines. A House member's failure to vote for his party's nominee invites loss of the benefits that come from seniority within the party. The Speaker is a man of considerable seniority in the House, though not necessarily the most senior. Both parties in recent years have followed the practice of promoting their floor leader (discussed in the next section) to Speaker when that post becomes vacant, a natural development. The occupants of these two positions on the majority side must work in close harmony to be effective. Thus for more than two decades the House Democratic leadership was the team of Sam Rayburn and John W. McCormack. Rayburn was the senior and more influential; but they were a team.

Although the Speakership is, like most of the leadership posts in both houses, more than the sum of its formal powers, let us begin by examining what these powers are.

The Speaker of the House, like his counterpart in the British House of Commons, presides over House sessions and is expected to interpret and enforce the rules with fairness to all sides. Most modern Speakers would agree with Joseph W. Martin that, "In order to retain his effectiveness, a Speaker has to be fair." [1] But the American Speaker is a political official and is expected, within these rules, to aid the fortunes of his party. Next in line

[1] Joseph W. Martin and Robert J. Donovan, *My First Fifty Years in Politics* (New York: McGraw-Hill, 1960), p. 181.

of succession to the White House following the Vice-President, the Speaker is a figure of genuine importance in Washington.

During the nineteenth century the formal powers of the Speaker gradually became formidable indeed. He appointed all standing committees and their chairmen, although in doing so he was expected to respect the claims of seniority. He was chairman of the powerful Committee on Rules. Finally, he had an almost unlimited power to recognize members on the floor of the House, even though he was expected to use this power to grant a fair hearing to all sides and to reflect the views of a genuine majority. During the period from 1903 to 1910, when the Progressive movement created cleavages, especially among the dominant Republicans, Speaker Joseph G. Cannon increasingly used these powers against the Progressives without regard for the powers' implied limitations. Understandably, in 1910 a group of Progressive Republicans, led by George W. Norris of Nebraska, allied with the minority Democrats to remove the Speaker from the Rules Committee, to make appointment of committees and their chairmen elective, and to restrict sharply the power of recognition.

The centralization of power in the Speakership up to 1910, however, reflected the inescapable fact that a body as large as the House cannot function like the legendary town meeting with a fluid leadership under a neutral moderator. In consequence, the Speakership has informally regained most of its former influence. As a member of the House the Speaker can vote on any issue and can participate in debate—privileges used sparingly by most Speakers to emphasize the party stakes in a particular legislative question. The Speaker still has significant powers of recognition; his decisions on the rules of debate, though fairly closely limited by precedent, are rarely overridden; he refers bills to the standing committees—a matter of consequence when the precedents are unclear; he appoints all select and special committees and the House members (called *managers*) of the Senate-House conference committees that iron out differences in the bills passed by the two chambers; and he appoints the chairman of the Committee of the Whole. The House uses the device of constituting itself a Committee of the Whole during what is usually the most critical phase of debate. In committee the rules of debate are more informal, no roll-call votes are taken, and 100 members rather than 218 are sufficient for a quorum. Since the chairman of the Committee of the Whole must frequently make decisions crucial for the fortunes of legislation, his appointment—usually for no longer than debate on a single bill—is of some consequence.

The floor leader

The floor leader, a party post filled by caucus election, has few formal powers. He is normally the chief strategist and tactician on the floor for his party. On the majority side the chief function of the floor leader is to set the schedule for debate, along with the Speaker, the Rules Committee, and to a lesser extent the minority leader. But his influence on the House time-table, crucial in any legislative body, is still considerable. He normally holds no committee position, but on the majority side he tends to be the Speaker's alter ego, and on the minority he is his party's prospective candidate for Speaker.

The whips

"Whip" is a name also taken from the British system, where the position is the chief instrument for imposing party discipline. In the House, however, the whip has no such function but acts as assistant floor leader. He and his assistants send out weekly notices of the legislative program, try to see that members are on hand for key votes, and arrange pairs. Most important, they run *whip checks*—polls of the party members—to estimate for the principal leaders the voting intentions of their "followers" on pending bills. But the most that a whip, a floor leader, or even the Speaker is likely to do to pressure a party colleague is to say, "We really need your help on this one. I hope you can see your way clear."

The party committees

Each party in the House has a number of committees that collectively are a part of the elective leadership. The most important of these are the two Committees on Committees. Established after the "Revolution of 1910" to nominate members of the standing committees, they in effect make the choices, since their slates are never rejected by the caucus or the House. By virtually unalterable convention the minority's Committee on Committees nominates for the minority positions on the standing committees—which are by equally strong tradition always bipartisan—although technically the majority's committee could choose the minority members as well. The unwritten rule of seniority, which is rarely violated, provides that a member cannot be removed from a committee except at his own request or if his party's proportion in the House is reduced in an election, in which case its proportion on committees is cut and the most junior member is dropped. Turnover after elections creates vacancies, to which both new and reelected members aspire. In choosing whom to assign to such openings, the Committees on Committees exercise significant powers. The members of the Republican Committee on Committees are elected by the delegations from the many states with Republican members. The Democrats since 1910 have made the Democratic members of the House Committee on Ways and Means their Committee on Committees, a custom that puts a premium on Democratic membership on this already powerful standing committee.

Getting the right committee assignment has enormous significance for a representative's career in the House. Assigning coveted committee posts to "deserving" members and getting satisfactory committees—especially those handling the most important business of the House—are also matters of great consequence to the leadership. In both parties, therefore, the principal elective leaders play an important—though unofficial—role in making the committee slates. In neither party can they have a completely free hand in appointments, but their "suggestions" are rarely ignored, and they have an effective veto on nominations from other sources. As Joe Martin said, "In the four years that I served as Speaker, no Republican went on an important committee without my approval." [2]

The Democratic and Republican Congressional Campaign Committees date back almost a century. In each party they are composed of one representative from each state having a party member in the House, and they are usually chaired by a comparatively senior member from a safe district. They supply services and limited financial assistance to candidates of the party in elections, but not in primaries.

Each party also now has a Policy Committee. These committees—earlier called Steering Committees—have in fact done no steering and almost no policy-making. For the minority party in Congress or for the party out of the White House, the Policy Committee, like the caucus, may be a reasonably effective means of developing party positions. The chances are, however, that it will function as the instrument of the principal elective leader or it will become a dead letter. The latter is more likely on the majority side, since the Speaker and the floor leader, in collaboration with the President and the Rules Committee, make party policy and will not welcome an alternative and less easily controlled instrument. The lesson to be learned from the history of steering committees, policy committees, and caucuses is that the sources of party disunity are not removed by creating forums for discussion and voting.

The Rules Committee

In a category by itself is the House Rules Committee. It is a standing committee of the House and thus technically is not part of the "elective" leadership. Its functions, however, are so critical to the operations of the majority's elective leaders and are so different from those of the other standing committees that it requires separate discussion.

The most important duty of the House Rules Committee is to propose to the House what are known as *special orders*, or *rules*, which in effect set both the *time* and the *terms* of debate on a bill. The importance of the special order is suggested by the fact that most major legislation is considered under

[2] *Ibid.*, p. 181.

"Play ball!"

This liberal cartoon views the Rules Committee as an undemocratic institution blocking Congress from voting on key legislation.

© 1964 by Bill Mauldin
From *What's Got Your Back Up?*, Harper & Row

this procedure. The alternative, generally speaking, is for a bill, once it is reported by a standing committee, to wait its turn on one of the four House calendars, or lists of pending bills. The only exceptions to these procedures are the bills reported by certain committees in addition to Rules—notably Appropriations and Ways and Means, which can be considered almost at once. But the power of the Rules Committee to set the terms of debate is of importance even for these committees. For the rule reported by the committee not only may make a particular bill the order of business but also may set a limit on the time for debate, specify what amendments may be considered, what votes may be taken, and what motions shall be in order. Any standing committee will prefer to the vicissitudes of ordinary procedure a special order that restricts or prohibits unwelcome amendments on the floor. (Rules allowing considerable time and opportunity for amendment are usually called *open* rules; those severely limiting members on these counts, *closed* or *gag* rules.)

The chief sources of controversy over the committee are its negative powers: it may refuse to grant a rule, thus usually preventing a bill's consideration; it may agree to grant a rule only if the sponsoring committee changes certain provisions of the bill; or it may report a rule that favors certain amendments unwelcome to the sponsors.

Throwing Out the Brake Pedal

This conservative cartoon portrays the House Rules Committee as a valuable check on hasty legislative action.

Knox in the Nashville *Banner*

If the majority of the Rules Committee and the principal elective leaders of the majority party work in harmony—if the Speaker controls the committee—the resulting control of the House agenda and the other standing committees is impressive. Normally such cooperation would be assumed, since the majority party always has twice the representation on Rules that the minority has. The Democratic elective leaders, however, through the workings of the seniority rule and related factors, have been plagued by a frequent refusal of the nominal majority on the committee to support them. Thus from the late 1930's until 1961, when the Democrats nominally controlled Rules with a membership of eight to four, two conservative Southerners on the committee, voting with the four Republicans, were able to bottle up or force severe changes in measures desired by Democratic Presidents and congressional leaders.

In 1961 the Democratic elective leaders waged a battle to reform the Rules Committee by enlarging its membership from twelve to fifteen—adding two Democrats and a Republican. The leadership could then count on a majority of eight to seven. Members of President Kennedy's staff worked hard for this bill, and the President's prestige and program were both at stake. After a vigorous fight, the House adopted this proposal for a two-year period by a vote of 217 to 212 (with the vast majority of Democrats and a trickle of liberal Republicans in favor, and the vast majority of

Republicans and all the Southern Democrats opposed). In 1963, again with the President's active support, the House made the committee's enlargement permanent. This time the vote was 235 to 196, with a small majority of the Southern Democrats supporting the Administration.

The continued strength of the Rules Committee reflects a number of factors. First, neither party's elective leaders wish to eliminate or seriously weaken it. Functioning cooperatively, it is too valuable an instrument of control. Second, most rank-and-file members and even other committee chairmen have little inclination or incentive to buck Rules on a particular issue. This accounts for the infrequent resort to the *discharge petition*, a device requiring the signatures of a majority of the House (218 members) in order to take a bill from a committee and bring it before the House. The elective leadership understandably dislikes this sort of repudiation of central control of the agenda, and the committee chairmen fear this kind of challenge to their prerogatives. Thus a member who sponsors or even signs a discharge petition is inviting leadership disapproval or even later retaliation. Finally, the Rules Committee can perform a very useful function as a whipping boy—that is, it can refuse to report a bill for which there may be intense interest-group or even popular demand but which has provoked vigorous opposition. By refusing to grant a rule the committee thus saves the House members from the pain of publicly choosing between proponents and critics of the measure. For example, during the 1961 Rules Committee struggle "Judge" Howard W. Smith of Virginia, chairman, threatened to embarrass members of the House by reporting out two highly controversial bills. The protective function of the Rules Committee also helps the Speaker, which is one reason no Speaker is likely to assume membership on Rules. If he can get what he really wants from the committee, he is delighted to escape some of the pressure that he would feel if the decisions were clearly labeled as his.

The Senate

The President pro tempore

Like the House, the Senate elects a presiding officer, a position provided for in the Constitution. Though he follows the Speaker in line of succession to the Presidency, the President *pro tempore* is not the equivalent of the Speaker of the House. Since he presides in the absence of the Vice-President, whose position is of no consequence in the Senate's power structure, he has no significant function to perform, although he may have *personal* influence in the chamber. Most important, he has no control over the Senate's time-table. Such powers are lodged elsewhere or are controlled by the Senate rules, which are made to protect the chamber majority against a presiding officer of whom it disapproves or who may not even be of its party.

The floor leader

In both Senate parties the key elective leader is the floor leader (majority leader or minority leader). The majority leader is potentially the more influential, especially if the President is also of the same party, but the minority leader is often of only slightly less consequence. In both parties the floor leader is elected by the caucus or the conference.

The Senate floor leader cannot be described by a statement of formal powers. By convention the principal function of the majority leader is to set the Senate's schedule in consultation with others, including the minority leader. The necessity for such consultation reflects two major facts. First, a senator is one of a relatively small and select group, and his name is likely to be known both by constituents and by the Washington community. Only the more prominent and senior representatives are likely to enjoy such personal repute. Senators regard themselves as ambassadors of sovereign states, jealously guarding their equality of status. Second and equally important, the Senate, being less than one-fourth the size of the House, operates much more informally and with far less dependence on its rules. The setting of the schedule and a great many other matters of less import are handled by *unanimous consent*. This means that any senator can block the majority leader's proposed schedule by objecting to his request for unanimous consent. Hence the minority leader—as well as other key senators—must be privy to the majority leader's intentions. Since the rules and customs of the Senate practically prohibit any limitation on the *length* of a debate—except by unanimous consent—the Senate majority leader's scheduling function, unlike that of his counterpart in the House, is largely confined to fixing the *order* of consideration.

Nonetheless, the majority leader is still the principal influence on the schedule, which is a crucial source of control in any legislative body. A majority leader interested in maximizing his power, therefore, will guard this prerogative carefully and exploit it to facilitate his objectives. Like the House majority leader, he cannot indefinitely refuse to schedule a bill in which any significant minority of the Senate is interested, but the time he chooses to call it up may affect its chances. For this reason he is almost certain to be kept informed of the legislative projects, although not necessarily the strategies, of his colleagues, especially in his own party. The majority leader's control of the schedule is only infrequently challenged, especially from within his own party, because the floor leader can retaliate against a challenger by withholding favors and assistance in connection with his legislative projects.

Largely because of the informality of the Senate's procedure, the floor leader, especially on the majority side, takes a more continuous and overt part in the management of affairs on the floor than does his opposite number in the House. Lacking both the close control that may be provided by the

The Majority Leader: "The Servant of the Senate"

The more I go into the problem, the less power I find that the Leader has. I've studied the rule books really hard ... and I find that, as far as the power of the Leader is concerned, it is no greater than that of any individual Senator.

The Leaders on both sides—that is, both parties—get by on the basis of courtesy, self-restraint and accommodation. If we did not operate in that manner, it is quite possible that at some time the Congress could become an anarchic body ... because it is the Senate as a whole which controls what should be done, not the Leadership. The Leader is the servant of the Senate....

My job, as I see it, is to represent the Senate to the White House, and to represent to the Senate the views of the White House. And to do that I have called eight or ten informal caucuses this year of the Democratic members to report to them, insofar as I could, on the conversations which were carried on at the White House Leadership meetings....

[The power to schedule legislation] doesn't give me any leverage, because I don't seek any leverage from it. What I try to do, as soon as legislation is passed out of a committee and has its O.K., is to bring it up on the floor as soon as possible, regardless of whether it is legislation proposed by a Republican or a Democrat, regardless of whether I think it's good or bad, in my personal opinion. I think it's the policy committee's duty to exercise this function, and it's my responsibility to follow that committee's wishes.

From Senate Majority Leader Mike Mansfield of Montana, copyrighted interview in *U.S. News & World Report*, September 1962.

House Rules Committee and the collaboration of a powerful Speaker, the Senate floor leader is obliged to be on the floor most of the time. The majority leader's ability to exercise parliamentary initiative is assured in part by the convention that whenever he rises from his seat the presiding officer will recognize him.

Like their counterparts in the House, the elective leaders in the Senate have a variety of informal means of influence, which *in toto* can be impressive if they are skillfully exploited. In the first place, the floor leader has a substantial influence on committee assignments, which are quite as important to senators as to representatives. The floor leader can use this influence both to affect the composition of key committees and to create obligations to himself. Thus Lyndon Johnson, who elevated the position of majority leader to a peak of importance during his tenure, adopted the practice of assigning most freshman senators to at least one major committee. By abandoning the practice of making them serve an apprenticeship on minor committees, Johnson undoubtedly made these men grateful to him. Similarly, a floor leader can grant or withhold a wide variety of other favors, ranging from advice on a legislative problem or help in the home constituency to the allocation of space in the Senate office buildings. Such favors can be converted into valuable support on the floor.

The floor leader of the President's party has an inescapable stake in the President's program. He is not a pliant presidential tool, but he must represent the President if he is to be leader of the Senate party. This point was dramatically underscored by Senator Knowland in February 1954. Having decided to vote against President Eisenhower's position on an important issue of foreign policy, just before the final roll call he yielded his seat to Senator Saltonstall, the Republican whip, and explained to the Senate: "I have left the desk of the majority leader because I wish to make it very clear that what I say is not said as majority leader, but . . . in my capacity as an individual Senator." [3] The floor leader has his own political problems, both in his constituency and in the legislature, which may compel him to

[3] *Congressional Record*, Eighty-third Congress, Second Session (February 26, 1954), p. 2371.

The Majority Leader: "The Leader of the Senate"

I think that the Majority Leader is more than the leader of the majority. He is actually the leader of the Senate. As chairman of the Policy Committee, perhaps his most important function is programming the bills that come out of committee and ultimately become law....

The Majority Leader, through his power of recognition and through the persuasion that he must exert, quickly determines whether he can lead the Senate. And no leader of any party can necessarily lead the Senate, because the Senate doesn't vote on party lines, as you would expect in an ordinary parliamentary body....

[Basically, the Leader's job is] persuasion with colleagues on both sides of the aisle.... About all the leader can do is recommend....

A good leader should not only know more about the workings of the committee and how the members arrived at the content of the bill as finally recommended, but he must also know the problems of each individual State and the temperament of each individual Senator....

You have to understand what actuated the House when it sends over the bills that it must originate, such as appropriations and tax bills. You must understand the reasoning behind their reductions or their increases....

And then you have to take those factors and get them into the entire machinery of the Senate—100 members—and see how you think they would be accepted....

What we have tried to do is determine what the leadership thinks is possible and desirable, and present it to the group and hope that they will agree.

From Senate Majority Leader Lyndon B. Johnson of Texas, copyrighted interview in *U.S. News & World Report*, June 1960.

reject or modify the President's requests. When he does champion a presidential proposal, he must rally Senate support largely by persuasion and negotiation. But in a subtle fashion his standing as floor leader, and thus his ability to solve his problems, depends on the progress of the President's program. The stakes of the contemporary majority leader thus make him a rival of the seniority leaders, and his problems resemble those of the President.

This new character of the floor leader's role, even if he is not of the same party as the President, has given him new national prominence. He gets more attention in the press than most senators and all representatives except the Speaker. National publicity in turn has contributed to the stature of the position. Finally, floor leaders, like other elective leaders of the President's party, can augment leverage with their colleagues through association with the President, as we shall see later.

The whips

The position of the whips in the Senate basically corresponds to their position in the House. The whip in both Senate parties is normally the second-ranking elective leader. Like the House whip, he checks voting intentions, gets members on the floor for key votes, and arranges pairs. The Senate whip also is normally the assistant floor leader, taking the leader's chair whenever the latter leaves the floor. Given the involvement of the floor leader in Senate floor activities, this function adds to the whip's importance and normally makes him the floor leader's closest associate. In consequence the whip is frequently regarded as the most likely successor to the floor leader.

The party committees

The two Senate Committees on Committees perform the same functions as their House counterparts, and they vary in size from eight to fifteen or more members, depending on the size of the legislative party and the kinds of factions within it. As in the House, the principal elective leaders have a good deal of influence over the selections that are made.

The Senate parties also have their party Campaign Committees, whose functions are essentially the same as those in the House. They vary in size from five to eight members, who normally serve for two years and are usually chosen from among senators in whose states no senatorial vacancy is scheduled to occur for at least two years.

The party Policy Committees in the Senate are a good deal more important than those in the House. A major reason for this is that the Senate majority has no scheduling body like the House Rules Committee. The Majority Policy Committee is by no means the equivalent of the Rules Committee in the lower chamber, but, as a body of influential senators, it is consulted by the floor leader in making his scheduling decisions. Second, in a chamber whose procedures depend so heavily on informal understandings, the Policy Committee can be a valuable source of intelligence and advice to the majority and minority leadership. In addition, through the floor leader, the committee is likely to be more quickly and completely informed than the rest of the Senate concerning the President's legislative intentions—especially if he is of the same party. Thus senators eagerly seek assignments to these committees.

The Policy Committees do not make policy in the substantive sense, and a glance at the membership of recent committees indicates why. A committee containing such contrasting types as John Tower and Jacob Javits or John Pastore and Richard Russell would scarcely be expected to agree on many controversial matters. But on the majority side they can discuss, influence, and even agree on matters of schedule. Southerners on the Democratic committee may go along with a majority leader's decision to *call up* a civil-rights bill, even though they will *oppose* the measure on the floor. Members of the Majority Policy Committee rarely support attempts on the floor to upset the majority leader's decisions on the order in which bills shall be considered. The Majority Policy Committee thus performs a policy function that is procedural rather than substantive.

The Standing Committees

The seniority leaders and the seniority rule

The chairmen and ranking minority members of the standing committees of Congress are collectively referred to as *seniority leaders*. There are sixteen committees in the Senate and twenty in the House, not counting a few "select" committees and a number of joint committees of the two houses. The chairmen and ranking minority members reach their positions through the operation of the unwritten but almost inflexible *seniority rule*. Once a man is on a committee, if he is consistently reelected and if he lives long enough, he will eventually find himself at the top of the list and the committee's chairman when his party is in the majority.

The seniority rule is one of the most criticized features of Congress, and the arguments against it are impressive. The first objection is that the rule merely rewards the capacity of a man to survive physically and politically—regardless of his competence.

The second argument is that the seniority rule makes it likely that the views and policies of committee chairmen will be out of step with sentiment in the country, particularly as reflected in presidential elections. For in order to be reelected enough times to become a committee chairman, a senator or representative must come from a constituency that consistently and overwhelmingly favors one party. Such "safe" constituencies are in many cases

CONGRESSIONAL COMMITTEE POSTS

SENIORITY SYSTEM

"It's a hell of a way to run a railroad."

Many liberals have criticized the seniority system, but Congress has been unable to arrive at a satisfactory substitute for accomplishing its work smoothly.

From *The Herblock Book,* Beacon Press, 1952

relatively untouched by the leading contemporary issues, either because their populations have no experience with such problems or because their effective electorates are agreed on maintaining the status quo. Conversely, legislators from closely competitive constituencies, in which the major questions of the day are likely to be conspicuous features of congressional campaigns, are discriminated against in the congressional power structure.

The seniority system, according to this argument, further biases congressional action because safe constituencies are not evenly distributed throughout the country. Among the Republicans, they are concentrated primarily in the Midwest and among the Democrats primarily in the South, and the dominant political attitudes in these areas are more conservative on many issues than the country as a whole. Thus, in 1962, of the twenty standing committees in the House, ten of the chairmen came from the South, and eleven of the ranking minority members came from the Midwest; the proportions in the Senate were comparable. Critics argue that these restrictive tendencies are encouraged because once a man has been appointed to a committee his succession to the chairmanship leaves him under obligation only to those influences in his constituency responsible for his successive elections. And, since their powers are considerable, committee chairmen can resist change and can impose on the country policies that fall short of contemporary needs.

The seniority rule, however, does not lack defenders, especially in Congress, and their arguments have some substance. First, it is suggested that the obstructive tendencies of chairmen are exaggerated. Long experience in Washington can give them as broad a view of public policy as anyone in the government, and even if they lack such a view they cannot indefinitely prevail in the committee, and still less in the chamber, against a determined majority that includes the elective leaders ready to use presidential leverage. One reason for this is that the committee chairmen, even though their direct ties are primarily to their constituencies, have some stake in a party record; if the party in the next election is reduced to a minority, they will lose their chairmanships even if they retain their congressional seats.

Second, defenders of the seniority rule point to the virtue of an automatic rule for settling potentially explosive problems with a minimum of difficulty. This, of course, is why the seniority criterion is used for handling such matters in many social groups. In institutions such as Congress or its parties, where centralized authority is limited, the absence of some automatic arrangement would invite prolonged and bitter controversy in the opening weeks or months of a Congress, which might make cooperative enactment of a legislative program almost impossible. The defenders argue that no alternative system has been proposed that would work as smoothly as the seniority rule and would have no equally objectionable consequences. Open election in a party caucus would invite chaos, and its results could easily be as inequitable as the present ones. Election by the committee members would be likely to increase the committees' independence of the elective leaders. The defenders of the seniority system react with equal skepticism to the suggestion that the majority party's Committee on Committees should choose chairmen strictly on the basis of "merit." Whose criteria of "merit" are to be controlling? And how is "merit" to be distinguished from mere preferences among alternative policies?

Fundamentally the persistence of the seniority rule reflects the familiar pattern of localized political risks of congressmen. Until congressional careers—especially nominations—come to depend on some central party leadership, no authority within Congress or within the government is likely to have the power to replace the seniority rule. It is well to remember that when Speakers had the authority to appoint House committees and their chairmen, they normally respected the claims of seniority or met with trouble. A successful challenge to the seniority rule, after all, would be a threat to the authority of all seniority leaders, and in resisting this challenge they would be supported by a large fraction of Congress. The partial exceptions serve to confirm the rule. In 1957 Senator John F. Kennedy was appointed to the Committee on Foreign Relations over Senator Estes Kefauver, who had a seniority advantage of four years. This would have been unlikely if Kefauver had not for years been in the bad graces of influential senators, especially the important Southern Democrats.

The committee, particularly if it is an important one, becomes for most members the means to a career *within* Congress. Thus not only the seniority

"I guess you can't stop progress, but I promised my constituents I'd do my best!"

The risks of congressmen are predominantly local: their primary goal is to be reelected by their constituents.

Jim Berry from Newspaper Enterprise Assoc.

leaders but also most of those within striking distance of such a position would feel their prospects threatened by a direct challenge to the rule. Interests become vested and loyalty to the standing committees develops, especially if they are the means to achieving personal goals.

The basis of committee power

The method of selecting seniority leaders is particularly important, because the standing committees are of major consequence in the operation of Congress. The power of the committees depends upon four closely related factors:

Expertise First, the committees are in an important sense composed of experts—notably the experienced members of the more significant committees. The committee system basically reflects the need for specialized counsel in any sizable legislative body dealing with a variety of complicated subjects—although such counsel need not come exclusively from members of Congress. In the early years of the Republic, Congress relied almost entirely on advice directly from the executive, especially the Treasury. There were few committees continuing from one session to the next. Reliance on the executive branch diminished, however, as the vigor of the Presidency declined under Madison and Monroe. By the beginning of John Quincy Adams' Administration (1825) the essential features of the standing-committee system were well established.

Committee expertise is developed, not only from continuous experience with bills on a given subject, but also by the processes of selection for committee membership. Members of Congress frequently try to get appointed to committees whose subject matter is of interest to them or important to their constituencies. Thus the members of the committees dealing with agriculture normally come from farm areas, and each is likely to be the spokesman for a major crop—wheat, corn, cotton, cattle, tobacco, dairy products, and so on. The Committees on Interior and Insular Affairs, especially in the Senate, are heavily weighted with men from the public-lands states. For their part, the elective leaders and sometimes the committee chairmen—though they rarely have a free hand—try to designate men whose judgment and willingness to work they have confidence in and try especially to prevent the appointment of men who appear unreliable. A man is unlikely to get on the Senate Finance Committee or the House Committee on Ways and Means, both of which deal primarily with taxation, if the leaders are doubtful of his judgment and "soundness," especially in financial matters. Thus "self-selection" and the leaders' choices encourage expertness.

Committees are expert in more than one way, however. At their best, the committees combine their expertise about the substance of legislation with the skill of the elected politician in judging the possible political effects of a proposal upon their constituencies and upon the country. Few "outside" specialists, except the President and some of his associates, can offer this combination, and this kind of expert is highly valued by his colleagues in Congress.

Monopoly of the legislative routine   Second, the committees collectively almost completely monopolize the basic, routine steps in the legislative process. That is, with rare exceptions all legislation proposed to either house is considered in standing committee before the chamber itself takes any action concerning it. Such domination of routine matters fosters expertness in the use of the institution's machinery. More important, it affords control of the gateways to action. The committees may not be able to prevent action, but they can usually influence its speed and character. The standing committees thus have much in common with the subordinate units of the executive bureaucracy, discussed in Chapter 10.

Clientele relations   Third, the committees have relatively stable and close relations with their "clients" in the executive branch and with interest groups affected by their decisions. These relations can constitute a firm triple alliance, with each partner depending on the others for support. The executive agencies are scrupulously attentive to the wishes of the committees that supervise them, and, conversely, within Congress these agencies are likely to be regarded as the "property" of the committees with jurisdiction over them. Interest groups for their part are enormously concerned about appointments to the committees in which they are interested, and they sponsor and oppose candidacies before the elective leaders and the members of the

Committees on Committees in order to assure the "right" sort of committee. They succeed often enough to make it inaccurate to think of group-committee relations as primarily a phenomenon of pressure. Many of these groups do not need to use pressure; they tend to work with the committees as partners. Such clientele relations are an effective defense against outside efforts to restrict a committee's prerogatives or to alter its decisions.

Authority   Finally, these three factors result in the tendency for each house to respect the authority of its committees. Particularly if the committee offers a unanimous recommendation, the natural disposition of members is to say, in effect, "The committee members are the ones who looked into this question. They ought to know." This occurs most frequently, of course, on routine bills, but even on matters of considerable controversy a bill that passes the House or Senate usually retains the essential form given it by the committee.

Committee rankings

Not all committees in the House and Senate are equally important or powerful. In each chamber, in fact, a fairly definite and stable prestige ranking exists. The high-prestige committees are of course the ones to which appointment is most desired, and once a member achieves a place on a top committee he rarely changes. Hence the average seniority of the members of the more important committees is significantly higher than the average for those committees lower in the prestige ranking. In the Senate, year in and year out, three committees stand at the top of the list: Foreign Relations, Appropriations, and Finance. In 1967 the average years of service on these committees ranged from thirteen to over seventeen. At the other extreme, the averages for the Committees on the District of Columbia, on the Post Office and Civil Service, and on Public Works were between five and eight years, although even these committees may be of great importance to particular senators.

In the House, three committees also are regularly at the top of the prestige ranking: Rules, Appropriations, and Ways and Means. In 1967 the members of these committees on the average had served continuously in the House for between eleven and thirteen years. Lowest averages were found on the Committees on Interior and Insular Affairs, on Post Office and Civil Service, and on Education and Labor, whose members averaged between four and six years of continuous service.

The chairman's power

Within the committee system the powers of the individual chairmen are formidable, although they vary somewhat from person to person and from committee to committee. The chairman usually calls committee meetings, largely sets the agenda, and rules on matters of order with an authority as firm as the Speaker's. The committee staff is primarily under his direction, except for the small fraction of it allocated in effect to the ranking minority member. The chairman usually appoints all subcommittees—a matter of considerable consequence, since a subcommittee and especially its chairmanship in a major standing committee, such as House Appropriations, may be more important than many of the lesser standing committees of the chamber. Standing committees tend to accept the determinations of their subcommittees in the same way that the House or Senate tends to accept committee decisions.

The chairman speaks for the committee in negotiations with the majority elective leaders (and the ranking minority member with the leaders on his side). He normally represents the committee on the floor, and when debate is limited—as it usually is in the House—he and the ranking member in opposition allocate the time among the committee members wishing to speak. Once a bill is passed, he and the ranking minority member are usually appointed to the conference committees that iron out differences between House and Senate versions of a bill. These formal powers of the chairman (and his minority colleague) are reinforced by such informal factors as the experience and parliamentary know-how of a senior legislator.

Even when a chairman cannot induce his colleagues to take a positive action that he favors, he can ordinarily prevent committee action that he opposes. Revolts against chairmen are rare, but they do occur. For example, in September of 1966, in an action that foreshadowed the controversy over the seating of Representative Adam Clayton Powell at the beginning of the Ninetieth Congress, the members of the House Committee on Education and Labor rebelled against Powell's autocratic domination of it. They changed the committee's rules so as to eliminate the chairman's traditional power to appoint staff, to approve expenditures, and to set the timetable for hearings and reports on bills.

Congressional Staff

The legislative branch employs approximately 25,000 people, ranging from pages on the Senate floor to highly responsible professionals. Two sets of staff significantly influence congressional decisions—the personal staffs of the representatives and senators and the staffs of the standing committees.

Each member of Congress is granted an allowance for hiring a personal staff, whose number varies with the size of his constituency. This staff handles mail, assists with visitors and telephone calls, writes speeches, handles constituents' problems with the executive agencies, helps with committee work, supplies material during floor debates, and advises on political problems in the constituency. The key people in this group are the one or two top aides to each member, usually called *administrative assistants*. Many of these, especially on the Senate side, are well-educated and able men with long experience on Capitol Hill or in the executive branch. Some, in fact, are relied upon heavily by their employers and carry considerable influence with them.

Since the beginning of the twentieth century all standing committees of Congress have had regular clerical or professional staffs, and some committees have enjoyed such assistance since the 1850's. The professional staffs of the committees do not legally have permanent tenure, but continuity has become the practice, and they are an influential part of the congressional structure. Partly because of such continuity, many of the committees have attracted and retained highly competent people. These men have contacts throughout the government and among relevant interest groups. They carry on or commission research, plan hearings, draft bills, amendments, and reports, assist in floor action and on conference committees, and conduct inquiries within the executive agencies under their committees' jurisdictions. In addition, any committee or member of Congress can call upon the research facilities of the Legislative Reference Service in the Library of Congress and the bill-drafting skills of the lawyers in the offices of the House and Senate Legislative Counsel.

The problem of congressional staff is essentially a question of how much. Without competent staff neither individual members nor committees could function effectively. But with too much, especially too many experts, the danger would arise that the decisions of Congress were in fact made by staff rather than by elected representatives.

Tension and Leverage Within the Power Structure

The most conspicuous feature of the congressional power structure is the absence of a clear and stable hierarchy. There is little that resembles a chain of command in either house, especially in the Senate, and, of course, neither house is consistently superior to the other. As one might expect in a legislature that reflects localized risks of a decentralized party system, power is dispersed in several directions.

The chief centers of power in each house are the principal elective leaders and the individual seniority leaders, especially the committee chairmen. In fact, particularly among the President's fellow partisans, elective and seniority leaders tend to become competing, even contesting, centers of power. Symptoms of the conflict are easily seen. For example, on several occasions attempts have been made in the Senate, especially among the Republicans, to reconstitute the Policy Committee so that it might include all the party's seniority leaders *ex officio*. Thus far these efforts have been successfully resisted by the elective leaders.

With the administration increasingly fixing the major features of the congressional agenda, the principal elective leaders of the presidential party almost inescapably develop stakes in the Chief Executive's program. The seniority leaders, on the other hand, are involved in only a segment of the President's program at most; moreover, they would stand to lose in the long run by consistently accepting presidential proposals, for they would encourage the expectation of subordination to the elected leaders and would gradually lose the capacity to bargain on behalf of their "clients."

This tendency toward bipolarity should not be exaggerated, however. As old colleagues and friends, elective and seniority leaders may easily have more in common as legislative politicians than they share with a President. This is especially true during periods when they are officially in opposition to the White House. But even elective leaders belonging to the same party as the President cannot be simply his spokesmen. They must represent their chambers with the President as well as represent him in the halls of Congress.

When the elective leaders and the appropriate seniority leaders are in agreement, the rank-and-file representative or even senator may have little option but to go along. When a seniority leader and the elective leaders are opposed, however, the member's choices may be painful, for he usually needs aid from both centers of power to help his constituency. Both sets of leaders, moreover, have means of influence upon him. With respect to members of his committee a chairman can grant or withhold favors, from favorable handling of a pet bill to assignment to a desired subcommittee. Especially in the House, where the majority of the members serve on only one committee, a chairman can make an enormous difference in a colleague's career. Chairmen of major committees with a broad jurisdiction, such as Appropriations or Rules, have power well beyond the committees' membership. Failure to appropriate for a project important in one's constituency or refusal to grant a rule for a desired piece of legislation may be severe sanctions. Elective leaders, on the other hand, influence committee assignments, can put in a good word at the White House, and control the chamber's agenda. They can help to get a favored bill out of committee, they can run interference with the Rules Committee in the House, they can support or reject a request for suspension of the rules or unanimous consent, and they can grant or withhold a variety of means to enhance one's standing in his constituency.

No reliable generalization can be drawn about which set of leaders tends to predominate. The precedence between elective and seniority leaders and the quality of the competition between them depend heavily on the skills and dispositions of the individuals involved. The powers of the elective leaders, even of the Speaker to a considerable degree, are a composite of persuasion, obligation, bargaining, and authority. An able and aggressive man can do much with these powers, but a maladroit or unassertive man can fail to exploit them without seriously risking loss of his post. Since the strength of elective and seniority leaders is so often nearly equal, the elective leader tends to rely on persuasion and behind-the-scenes bargaining in his relations with a committee and its chairman. And with a committee chairman of high prestige and seniority, particularly in the Senate, a more junior floor leader will have to be more a petitioner than a bargainer. On the other hand, the seniority leaders do not consult together or act collectively on matters of substantive policy, so they tend to be isolated in a contest with a floor leader unless the prerogatives of committees or their chairmen are attacked. Moreover, the principal elective leaders in the party of the President, through their regular weekly sessions at the White House and through their generally easy access to the President, gain a broad strategic advantage from their firsthand knowledge of his plans and preferences. Similarly, the White House legislative staff may provide an effective complement to the elective leaders' efforts through the favors it can offer. But a committee chairman who rarely feels a need for presidential assistance, such as Senator Russell of Georgia, Chairman of the Armed Services Committee, will not be easily dissuaded from a decision to hold up an administration bill, and his powers may well be sufficient to prevail in the committee and on the floor.

THE STRUCTURE IN ACTION: LEGISLATIVE PROCEDURE

Types of Legislative Action

In each house the formal actions taken through the power structure involve four different classes of proposal. Within each class the number of each proposal indicates the order in which it was introduced in the chamber. A *bill* is a general statutory proposal and is designated H. R. 1, H. R. 2 or S. 1, S. 2, depending on the house in which it is introduced. A *joint resolution*, designated H. J. Res. 1 or S. J. Res. 1, is normally a proposal on a limited matter, but in substance it is often difficult to distinguish from a bill. It requires approval by the Senate, the House, and, except when it proposes an amendment to the Constitution, the President. If passed, a joint resolution becomes a law, as does an enacted bill. A *concurrent resolution*, labeled H. Con. Res. 1 or S. Con. Res. 1, requires only the concurrence of the other chamber. In principle it deals with matters within the authority entirely of Congress rather than of the government as a whole. It is commonly used to express a congressional preference or to correct errors in bills passed by both houses and not yet signed by the President. Its most significant use, however, as pointed out in Chapter 9,[4]

---

[4] See p. 302.

is to permit Congress to disapprove presidential reorganization plans and to terminate certain powers granted to the President by statute. When used in this way it constitutes a kind of legislative veto. Finally, a simple *resolution*, designated H. Res. 1 or S. Res. 1, deals with matters entirely within the competence of one house: its rules and orders, the establishment of a committee, authorization to print reports, and the like.

Origins of Legislative Proposals

A legislative proposal can be introduced into Congress only by a senator or representative. The nature of its actual sponsorship, however, will make a great deal of difference in its chances for adoption. For in a given session several thousand bills and resolutions are introduced, but only a small fraction emerge from the committees, and a still smaller fraction are acted upon by the houses. A bill that is literally the project of an individual legislator, especially if it is controversial, is not likely to survive unless its sponsor is influential and has the strong support of legislators in both houses, of relevant interest groups, and of the affected executive agencies. Getting such support may take years of agitation, negotiation, drafting, and redrafting in the light of new evidence and the attitudes of influential people. If the actual sponsor is a standing committee or its chairman, the bill's chances are obviously better. One reason committee assignments are of such importance to a member of Congress is that a committee is more likely to support a proposal if the sponsor belongs to the committee. On the other hand, a sponsor who is able to get his proposal included among administration measures greatly increases its chances, since the President's program constitutes the heart of the agenda for Congress and its committees. Without such support, in fact, a legislative project may never get out of the discussion stage. For example, a number of major items in the New Deal—the TVA, social security, and others—had been proposed and debated in Congress for years without success before President Roosevelt made them a part of his program.

The sponsor of a bill (except tax legislation, which must originate in the House) must also choose carefully the chamber in which the bill is to be introduced; a favorable vote in the first chamber may assure quick passage by the second, whereas bitter debate or hostile committee treatment may damage its chances irreparably.

The Committee Stage

Review and report of a bill by a standing committee follow essentially the same procedures in both Senate and House. Most bills, of course, expire at the time they are referred to a committee—they are pigeonholed. On many of those that survive, including most that involve any controversy, public hearings are held, and the "staging" of these may be critical. For hearings serve quite as often to mobilize and test support for a measure— or to demonstrate opposition to it—as to inform the committee and Congress. Interest groups do their most conspicuous work at the hearings, although this is not usually the point at which their influence with the committee is most important.

If a bill goes any further than hearings, it is usually taken up in a committee's *executive session*, with outsiders, except professional staff, excluded. There it is discussed provision by provision, altered, amended, and voted upon. If no version can be worked out that a majority of the committee will support, at least for purposes of getting the bill out of committee, its progress is ended. In the executive session a bill's supporters will make every effort to get a unanimous report, or one supported by the largest possible majority, in order to improve the bill's chances once it reaches the floor. Any legislator attempting to defeat a bill unanimously supported by a standing committee will have to appear to his colleagues to be more of an expert on the substance of the measure than those on the committee.

The committee's intense and often conclusive work at this stage is one justification for the common assertion that the committees are "little legislatures." But a committee does not work in isolation. The elective leaders of both parties may try to persuade the committee—through its chairman or individual members or even through its staff. Interest-group representatives, executive officials, and members of the White House staff may be similarly active, in collaboration or in opposition to one another. The elective leaders are almost compelled to be active in this way, if only to get a bill of some sort to the floor.

Getting to the Floor

A bill favorably reported out of committee to either chamber goes on the calendar. In the Senate, the rules provide that during the first two hours of a legislative day the bills on the calendar are called in the order in which they were reported. Only the most uncontroversial measures are handled in this way, however, for a bill is usually passed over at this stage if any senator objects to its consideration. In most cases the majority leader, after the consultations discussed earlier, moves the consideration of a bill. This is a powerful prerogative. For example, a controversial bill originating in the Senate that is not called up until late in a session is virtually doomed. Under the rules any senator can call up any bill on the calendar, and this device sometimes succeeds over the majority leader's objections, but a senator who attempts it invites retaliation from the leader.

In the House, matters are more complicated. When the Rules Committee operates in close cooperation with the Speaker and the majority leader, their collective control of the order in which bills are considered, the timing of debate, of the moves that are in order on the floor, and even of the content of a bill reported to the House, is almost complete. When the elective leaders do not control the Rules Committee, however, it may be induced to act only after elaborate negotiation, if at all.

There are other routes to the floor of the House, but they are more hazardous. For example, since 1909 the House rules have contained a provision for Calendar Wednesday. This procedure provides that every Wednesday is to be devoted to the standing committees, to be called in alphabetical order, whose chairmen may call up any bills reported by their committees. Such bills then become the business before the House. In recent years the House, on motion of the majority leader, has usually dispensed with Calendar Wednesday by unanimous consent, thus attesting to the effectiveness of the elective leaders' control of the agenda.

Consideration on the Floor

To the layman the debates that occur once a bill becomes the pending business before the House or Senate may appear to be the most important phase of the legislative process. It is true that they provide a climax to the proceedings, but the words spoken on the floor rarely determine any votes. Too much has occurred previously, too much has been said in hearings, in Capitol Hill offices, and in the press, for persuasion in debate to be critical. This does not mean that all minds are made up as debate begins. Often as the debate proceeds a great deal of behind-the-scenes maneuvering by the leaders, the White House staff, and interest groups is concentrated on members known or suspected to be uncertain.

Nor does this mean that debate is a mere ritual. For the great discussions in Congress, though they occur infrequently, are in some measure national debates. Members of the attentive public are in an important sense participants. The discussions these debates precipitate are an essential part of the consensus-building required for effective representative government. They provide for the discerning administrator a foretaste of the conflicts he will inherit at the enforcement stage. For the sponsors of the bill, floor debates, like committee reports, help to build the record that the courts will examine in determining "legislative intent." For political leaders of all kinds, the debates help to build personal and party "records" and to define issues. In a representative system such communication is not a mere formality. Finally, drawn-out debate can build up the suspense surrounding a pending decision and can contribute subtly to the effectiveness of off-stage maneuvering.

Senate debate

The forms and conventions of debate differ sharply in the two chambers. In the Senate the custom of unlimited debate is distinctive. Despite this custom, the majority leader is usually able to arrange a fixed time for voting on a bill or an amendment. Here his negotiations with the minority leader become critical. When he rises to ask unanimous consent to such a limitation, any senator may still defeat the move by objecting. As we have seen, however, the instruments of pressure in the floor leader's hands are substantial, and a tentative objection is frequently withdrawn after some persuasion—on or off the floor. Such informality and personal negotiation would be impossible in a body much larger than the Senate. Its virtual absence today in the House is almost wholly a consequence of that body's much larger size.

Unlimited debate in the Senate, in the absence of unanimous consent, provides the means for the *filibuster*, the attempt by one or a few senators to prolong debate in order to bring about the defeat of a measure or prevent it from coming to a vote. The most characteristic use of the tactic is to hold up all other Senate business for so long—especially toward the end of a session when a great many essential measures are awaiting action—that the leaders will be forced to drop the bill. Some of the most spectacular physical performances in American history have been one-man filibusters. One of the classic solo filibusterers was Senator Huey ("The Kingfish") Long of Louisiana, who in June 1935 spoke for fifteen and one-half hours. Long's 1935 record was broken by Senator Wayne Morse, who on April 24-25, 1953, spoke continuously for twenty-two hours and twenty-six minutes against an offshore-oil bill. More common and generally more effective are the filibusters planned and staged by a group of senators.

A filibuster can be defeated in various ways, none of them easy. Since the filibusterers must keep the right to the floor, any of a number of parliamentary missteps can occur that an alert opposition can exploit. Second, the filibusterers can be worn down physically if their opponents insist on keeping the Senate in continuous session, night and day, but this tactic is almost as hard on the other side. Finally, the Senate rules provide for *cloture*, a vote to limit the debate, but the requirements for its use are so stringent that the maneuver is almost useless. A petition supporting a cloture motion must first be signed by one-sixth of the Senate members. Two calendar days must elapse before it may be called up, and then two-thirds of the members present must vote to bring debate to a close. But each senator may still speak for an hour on the bill after cloture has been voted. Finally, cloture may not be applied to a debate on changing the Senate's rules, so the chances of making it easier to invoke are not great. Since cloture was first adopted in 1917, there have been thirty-eight attempts to apply it, only seven of which have succeeded, the most recent in 1965.

A dramatic example of successful cloture took place on June 10, 1964, when the Senate broke a seventy-five-day Southern filibuster against the 1964 Civil Rights Bill by a vote of 71 to 29. This represented the first time cloture had ever been successfully invoked to end a Southern filibuster against proposed civil-rights legislation. The bipartisan majority consisted of 44 Democrats and 27 Republicans, led by Floor Leaders Mike Mansfield and Everett Dirksen. Only 23 Democrats (including 21 Southerners) and 6 Republicans (all from Western states) opposed cloture.

In recent years filibusters have been employed principally by Southerners opposing legislation on racial matters, but over the years they have been resorted to by senators of all camps, on all manner of questions and for a wide variety of motives. The roster of great filibusterers includes such diverse figures as Norris of Nebraska, La Follette of Wisconsin, and Thurmond of South Carolina, as well as Morse of Oregon and Huey Long of Louisiana. This suggests a major reason why getting a two-thirds vote for a cloture motion is rare. Senators of all persuasions are reluctant to establish a precedent that would weaken an instrument they might wish to use for their own purposes later on. Nonetheless, criticism of the filibuster from within and outside the Senate has been increasingly severe. Proposals to amend the Senate rules so as to allow a majority a reasonable opportunity to restrict debate have been agitated for in almost every session for the past three decades.

House debate

Only limited dilatory tactics are possible in the House. For more than a hundred years it has been possible to close debate by a simple majority vote (on a motion for "the previous question"). More characteristically, however, the special orders adopted on the motion of the Rules Committee place a limit in advance on the length of debate. When a bill is taken up on the floor, the House usually first converts itself into the Committee of the Whole, where, as noted earlier, the procedural requirements are simpler and proceedings are more informal than in the House proper. Here all proposed amendments are debated, under a rule limiting speeches to five minutes each, and acted upon (without roll-call votes). An amendment rejected in the Committee of the Whole is lost. But when the Committee "rises" at the conclusion of the debate and "reports" to the House, a roll call may be demanded (usually by any member) on any amendment adopted in the Committee of the Whole. Thus the House as such can reject what the House as committee has tentatively accepted. Further debate, however, is normally not permitted under the rule, and usually only two more record votes are taken. One generally occurs on a motion to recommit the bill to the standing committee—with or without instructions to the committee. (If adopted, a recommittal motion in effect kills a bill for the session.) One may also occur on final passage of the bill.

Uses of the Vote

Determining the "meaning" of the votes in the House or Senate provides almost as much of an occupation for pundits and publicists as does the interpretation of an election—and the pitfalls are equally great. Most citizens, of course, are unaware of how their senators or representatives vote, even on roll-call votes. But the politically active—interest groups, party sponsors, and, in particular, the aspiring primary- or general-election opponents of the legislators—know.

Roll calls, therefore, are regarded with great respect by most members of Congress. In announcing the weekly program a majority leader is expected to indicate whether and when he anticipates such record votes. This practice not only warns members to be present but gives them time to decide whether they will be present. For the issues on which a member of Congress does not vote may be more revealing of the conflicting demands upon him than the questions on which he is recorded. For example, an elective leader of the President's party, caught between presidential preferences and constituency demands, may find it convenient to be off the floor when the question is decided.

Sponsors or opponents of a measure, including the leaders, may use the demand for a "yea-and-nay" vote as a tactical maneuver. Members caught by conflicting demands may be willing to vote one way if they are not individually recorded, even though they would feel obliged to vote the opposite way on a roll call. Roll-call votes may also be used as delaying devices, especially in the House, where a record vote takes up to forty-five minutes to complete. Finally, a record vote may be used when there is no question about the outcome but the sponsors desire a public indication of an overwhelming majority. Thus on a foreign-policy question, for example, a nearly unanimous record vote shows the solidarity of Congress on the matter.

How informative the roll-call vote is to the outsider normally depends on the stage at which the vote is taken. A vote on final passage is usually less revealing than one taken earlier in the proceedings, since a member subject to conflicting demands may, for example, vote against an amendment and then, finding it certain that the measure is going to pass however he decides, vote the other way on the final roll call. Or he may support a bill on final passage only after its provisions have been drastically restricted by an amendment for which he voted.

The Conference Committees

The Constitution makes no provision for handling disagreements between the two chambers on legislation, yet it is rare that a measure of any consequence passes both houses in the same form. The joint conference committees, appointed separately for each bill, are provided for in the rules of each house. (The house in which a bill originated, of course, may simply vote to accept the amendments added in the other, thus making a committee of conference unnecessary.) No fixed number of *managers* on behalf of the House and Senate is stipulated in the rules, because the members from each house act as a unit, a majority on each side determining what compromises will be accepted. In consequence, though the Speaker of the House and the floor leaders in the Senate are required by tradition to include among the managers the seniority leaders of the standing committees that have handled the bill, they may influence the outcome by appointing a large number of managers. Each house normally assigns from three to nine members.

The proceedings of conference committees are not public, but they are often closely followed by those concerned, including the White House. Thus the leaders or sponsors may deliberately accept an unwelcome amendment at the debate stage in one house in the expectation that the managers can be persuaded to drop it in conference. Under the rules, conference committees are not supposed to deal with provisions of a bill that are not in dispute between the two houses; in practice, however, they may alter agreed-upon provisions, insert new material, or sometimes write a wholly new bill.

The reports of conference committees are submitted to the two chambers, where they must be accepted or rejected without amendment. Rejection sends the bill back to conference, with or without instructions from the objecting house. But the pressure to get some sort of bill passed is so heavy at this stage that the reports are normally accepted. Following such acceptance the enrolled bill is sent to the White House.

The President's Choice

The formal options open to the President at this stage—signature, the two kinds of veto, and allowing it to become law without his signature—have already been discussed.[5] Four additional matters should be mentioned here. First, when a highly controversial bill has passed Congress—or when a bill requested by the President appears to fall short of his requirements—pressures on him to sign or veto can be enormous. Congressmen, executive officials, party leaders in the states, and interest groups are all likely to try to persuade him directly or indirectly. He is obliged to weigh the consequences, for the country and for his administration, as best he can. If he reluctantly decides to sign a bill—or to allow it to become law without his signature—he may issue a statement of his objections and call for appropriate modifications at a later legislative session or through other means.

Second, the President may use the veto message as a campaign document. Since the days of Jackson's battle over the Bank of the United States, Presidents often have directed their veto messages as much to the voters

---

[5] Ch. 9, pp. 300–01.

as to Congress. Whether a veto is sustained or not, the message transmitting it—and the debate that usually follows in Congress—is often an important part of the President's effort to maintain his initiative.

Third, the President may occasionally sign a measure but issue a statement giving his own interpretation of an ambiguous provision. Presidential interpretation of such a passage may not prevent Congress from enacting a more objectionable provision at a later date, when the balance of forces in Congress has changed, but it lends the weight of the President's prestige to the view he prefers and puts administrators, as well as legislators, on notice of his intentions.

Finally, if the President signs a bill that he wishes to have treated as a major element in the administration's record, he may turn the signing ceremony into a victory celebration. Various guests will be invited to the ceremony, chiefly members of Congress who have played a major part in the enactment. As the news cameras click, the President, surrounded by these dignitaries, will sign the bill, using as many pens as possible, so that each of his more important guests may have one as a souvenir of the great occasion. As noted in Chapter 9, such ceremonies are not inconsequential. They are among the flattering gestures that strengthen loyalty to the President, and they illustrate the subtle ways in which the symbolism of the President as the central actor—even in legislation—is reinforced.

SUMMARY: ASSESSMENT AND CHANGE

In this chapter we have tried to show that the individual member of Congress, even if he merely wants to reflect the demands of his constituency, must reckon with the power relations in the legislative process. These relations are so intricate and the points of leverage so numerous that it is often far easier to prevent action in Congress than to take it.

In recent decades, proposals have increasingly been made to reduce this complexity and to make positive legislative action easier. These proposals all suggest greater centralization of power and responsibility. Some would attempt to set up "programatic" parties, complete with frequent conventions, platforms to which members of Congress would be committed by unspecified instruments of discipline, and the like. Others would provide means for strengthening the President's legislative role.

In the absence of some devastating crisis, however, wholesale revisions in the structure of power underlying the legislative process are unlikely. It is more likely that these relations will undergo a gradual, unplanned modification, leading to far more centralization than prevails today. This trend is exemplified by the marked presidential involvement in legislation that has developed in recent decades. It is also indicated by the emergence of the elective leaders, especially in the President's party, as rivals to seniority leaders and as legislators whose roles and sources of power are molded by their stakes in the President's agenda.

One should not forget, however, that the difficulty of change in the legislative process is much more than a matter of custom or the inability of unenlightened men to see what would be most efficient. The careers, goals, and powers of important men are at stake. Important interests in the country, moreover, some of them organized and some not, gain considerable advantage from the status quo. These are not positions that are apt to yield to direct assault, though they might be reduced through small increments of change.

Meanwhile it is equally clear that Congress, for all its peculiarities, is neither moribund nor ineffective. The basic functions of a representative legislature under a constitutional system are (1) to give its assent to changes in the legal rules of the society, (2) to give a fair hearing in the process to differing interests, so that the resulting rules may approximate a consensus as nearly as possible, and (3) to inform itself both of the need for new rules and of the effectiveness with which existing ones are being administered. By these standards Congress—with its conflicts, its bewildering mixture of individual goals and loyalties, local demands, and national instruments—is probably the most effective legislative body in the world today.

BUREAUCRACY
The
Continuing
Executive

13

Chapter 13 discusses the political role of the bureaucracy in carrying out the decisions made by the elective branches of government. The chapter first describes a model of bureaucracy and then examines the ways in which the federal bureaucracy follows and differs from this model. First, the major activities of the bureaucracy are described to show how they inevitably become policy-making itself. Then several factors that shape bureaucratic decision-making are examined: What are the effects of bureau autonomy on hierarchy in the executive branch? How does Congress influence policy-making in the bureaucracy? And how do the patterns of civil-service recruitment affect the perspectives and goals of the bureaucracy?

The glamor of great election contests, the recurring conflicts between the President and Congress, and the occasionally dramatic decisions of the Supreme Court tend to obscure a basic fact: only rarely do the President, Congress, and the Supreme Court actually carry out the things they decide upon. For the identification and analysis of problems, as well as for the suggestion of alternative means of dealing with them, they must rely on the bureaucracy, the employees who carry on the day-to-day activities and much of the forward planning of the government. Collectively these employees constitute the *continuing executive*.

For a number of reasons bureaucrats warrant separate treatment in a discussion of the national government. First, their activities have significant consequences, whether they are seeing that the mail gets through, tracking down a nationwide ring of automobile thieves, keeping unwholesome food out of trade channels, conducting research on cancer, advising on a land-reform program in Iran, or reviewing your income-tax return. Second, their problems in the governmental process are often different from those of the President and Congress. And, third, they exercise broad powers. In consequence, the fact that they are constitutionally under the Chief Executive may say very little about the influences to which they are in fact responsive.

THE NATURE OF BUREAUCRACY

In ordinary parlance the term "bureaucracy" is one of abuse. Analytically, however, *bureaucracy* is a neutral term, referring to the particular institutional form that legal authority tends to take in large organizations. Legal authority in turn is a right to command that is derived from general rules formulated through known and standardized processes. Distinguishable from, for example, authority based on tradition (as with the chief of a primitive tribe) or on the holder's personal qualities (as with the leader of a street-corner gang), legal authority is characteristic of large, complex organizations. Thus, bureaucracy tends to be a conspicuous feature of modern industrialized societies—not only in government but in many corporations, universities, churches, foundations, and even professional baseball teams.

Bureaucracy, especially in government, has three basic characteristics. First, it involves a specialization of duties, subdivided and assigned to particular jurisdictions or offices, which are usually arranged in a hierarchy. A modern army, with its many activities arranged in units, each part of a larger one and all headed by a commander in chief, is an obvious example. Second, the behavior of the people occupying these various offices is guided by known, general rules, but this guidance ordinarily does not extend to every detail of conduct in the office. The rules deal with the relations both among parts of the organization and of the organization to those outside it, and they can be changed only by legal authority. Third, the power that is legitimately exercised is an attribute of the *office* with its legally defined duties, not of the person who holds it. Thus, when I am told to make a change in my income-tax return, my obedience is not to a certain dark-haired man named Samuel Jones, who lives in a California-style ranch house in the suburbs and grows those handsome begonias; it is to the Deputy Assistant District Director of Internal Revenue, enforcing the directives of the Regional Commissioner, the Commissioner of the Internal Revenue Service, and the Secretary of the Treasury.

This discussion of bureaucracy in the abstract suggests why administrative action in a large organization like the executive branch tends to take bureaucratic form. Without a standard arrangement of offices or jurisdictions and without the guidance of general rules, subdivision of duties would be unpredictable, not only to the outsider but also to their co-workers. An examination of how and why administration in the federal government follows or differs from this model will contribute to an understanding of the continuing executive and of the government as a whole.

THE SIZE AND COMPOSITION OF THE BUREAUCRACY

The United States Government is by any standard much the largest employer in the country. The total number of civilian employees in the executive branch varies slightly from month to month and year to year, but for more than a decade it has been approximately 2½ million. (If we were to include the uniformed personnel of the military services, since technically they are part of the bureaucracy, this would bring the total to somewhat more than 5 million.) Thus the executive branch of the federal government has more civilian employees than the combined total (approximately 2 million) for the steel industry and the automobile industry.

These figures point to an enormous and continuing problem of organization. And they indicate the critical importance of means for communicating to the central points in the system the most significant problems of current administration. Further, they suggest that in a great many matters initiative must be taken in positions organizationally far removed from the White House and from Capitol Hill. Finally, these figures indicate the importance of devices to help assure that those bureaucrats who make significant choices

A "Board" in Place of the Cornerstone

This conservative cartoon depicts bureaucracy as a poor substitute for free enterprise.

Knox in the Nashville *Banner*

are responsible not only to their superiors but to the values and standards of society.

These problems, although common to the whole bureaucracy, are concentrated in particular portions of it. Nearly half the *civilians* in the executive branch (42 percent) are employed in the Department of Defense; another quarter are in the Post Office Department; and 7 percent work for the Veterans Administration. These agencies, the three largest in the government, thus account for three-quarters of all the civil servants in the executive branch. The other ten departments and several dozen independent agencies share the rest. The vast majority of civil servants are scattered over the country. Only about 10 percent of the total are located in the Washington metropolitan area. Of the other 90 percent a good many have probably never been in the capital except as tourists.

It would be misleading to speak of a "typical" bureaucrat. In the first place, by no means all civil servants are white-collar workers with clerical desk jobs. About 30 percent are blue-collar employees, the majority of them working in arsenals, shipyards, and other such establishments operated by the armed services. Included in the remainder, moreover, is an enormous variety of the most skilled personnel in the society: about 10,000 mathematicians and statisticians, nearly 50,000 professional medical people, and several thousand chemists and physicists, psychologists, veterinarians, librarians, lawyers, economists, and engineers.

THE FORMS OF ADMINISTRATIVE ACTION

It is possible to classify the activities of administrative units into four broad types, though any unit may engage in several activities involving a wide variety of occupations. For example, the enforcement activities of the Food and Drug Administration require the services of chemists, biologists, physicians, lawyers, and accountants, among others.

Law Enforcement

Perhaps the most familiar stereotype of government administration is the policeman since the most elementary function of government is the maintenance of peace and order. The detection, apprehension, and prosecution of those who have violated the law is also the most ancient form of administrative or bureaucratic action. Of course, under our federal system most crimes against persons or property are the concerns of the states and the localities, but a considerable number of federal statutes carry criminal penalties. A conspiracy in restraint of trade involves criminal penalties under the antitrust laws; deliberate failure to report taxable income is similarly punishable, as are the importation of narcotic drugs into the country without a permit and attempts to defraud the government.

The prosecution of alleged violations of federal law is chiefly the responsibility of the Department of Justice and its United States attorneys. This department, and especially the Federal Bureau of Investigation, also does much detection and apprehension work, particularly in connection with some of the more serious crimes such as kidnaping. But most other agencies in the executive branch that have enforcement responsibilities do their own detection and frequently participate in the prosecution phase.

The most important point to note is that enforcement—like other forms of administrative action—inevitably involves choice. Partly because the staff and financial resources of any agency are limited, the administrators must choose which lines of enforcement to emphasize, which of many likely types of violation to investigate, which apparent violations are clear enough to be referred to the Department of Justice, which should be settled without formal prosecution, and so on. For example, the Internal Revenue Service must make a series of decisions on 60 million or so individual and corporate income-tax returns filed each year. Which ones are to be examined closely? How many of a violator's previous returns should be reopened? Do the violations appear to have been deliberate, requiring criminal prosecution, or were they errors made in good faith, calling for only a financial settlement?

Such choices necessarily set policy. Hence they inevitably lead to the questions of how the choices are made and under what limitations. They raise, in other words, the central problems of organization, communication, and responsibility.

Administrative Legislation

Determining policy is a relatively obvious feature of administrative legislation. It derives chiefly from the increasingly common congressional practice of enacting legislation that sets only broad policies, leaving to the executive branch the formulation of detailed rules and regulations for making such policies effective. The courts early declared that such delegation of legislative power did not violate the constitutional separation of powers, provided that the statutes contained appropriate standards to guide administrative discretion.[1] Such quasi-legislative power, though always a feature of administration to some degree, has increased enormously as government has become involved in the highly complex, technical, and rapidly changing problems of contemporary society.

This administrative power may take the form of *rules* or *regulations* applicable to a whole class of persons or situations, which is administrative legislation in the strict sense.[2] Or it may take the form of *orders* or *directives* applying to particular persons, organizations, or situations. Thus, standards of composition or purity may be set for drugs that may be sold in interstate commerce; safety devices may be prescribed for commercial aircraft; aid may be granted to Iron Curtain countries if it is "in the interests of national security"; and so on. The congressional standards guiding these administrative determinations may be fairly precise, but they are apt to be quite general.

When the guiding standards are vague and the decisions to be made in issuing rules and orders are of major consequence to important interests in society, administrative legislation may be highly controversial. For in a good many cases Congress in effect passes on to the administrator unresolved and politically explosive conflicts thinly disguised by ambiguous verbal "standards." For example, the responsibility of the Department of Health, Education, and Welfare to determine when a school district had effectively desegregated inevitably transferred to the department all the controversy associated with this explosive issue. Sometimes this shifting of the contest to the administrative arena is inescapable, given the technicality of the problems involved; but it often may be the result of a compromise necessary to pass the legislation.

---

[1] *Grimand* v. *United States*, 220 U.S. 506 (1911). See also *Field* v. *Clark*, 143 U.S. 649 (1892), and *Hampton and Co.* v. *United States*, 276 U.S. 394 (1928). But compare *Schechter* v. *United States*, 295 U.S. 495 (1935). For further details on administrative legislation see Ch. 19.

[2] Since 1935 all such actions of general application have been published in the *Federal Register*, issued daily in Washington.

". . . sure, we've complied; here's our Negro!"

This sympathetic comment on the dilemma of Commissioner of Education Howe illustrates the problems of executive officials in policing compliance with their agency's directives.

Baldy in the Atlanta *Constitution*

Administrative Adjudication

Quasi-judicial administrative action [3] takes two forms: the first involves decisions on charges of law violation. An example would be a charge by the Department of Agriculture that a licensee handling poultry in a regulated market had violated trading regulations. The second form of administrative action involves decisions in disputes between individuals or organizations both subject to an agency's jurisdiction. Examples would be disputes between unions and employers involving charges of unfair labor practices or disputes between rival claimants to a television station.

The procedures of administrative adjudication, along with those of administrative legislation, have been highly controversial for more than two decades. Efforts have been made to make these actions conform to the procedures of the courts, to "judicialize" them, particularly in cases where the same agency issues the rules and adjudicates disputes arising under them. The important point is that administrative adjudication frequently requires the making of choices of great consequence not only to the immediate parties but to society in general.

Direct Operations

No single term adequately covers the enormous range of enterprises and services performed by and for the federal government. Such direct opera-

[3] See also Ch. 10, p. 345; further details appear in Ch. 19, pp. 621–26.

tions, however, constitute a very large part of government administrative activity.

The Post Office service is the most obvious example, but the list also includes the operation of the national parks, the generation and sale of electric power by the Tennessee Valley Authority, the protection of bank deposits through the Federal Deposit Insurance Corporation, the supply of hospital and medical services for veterans and their dependents, the management of a pension system covering some 60 million people under social security, and the operation of the most extensive medical-research facilities in the country. With all these the list is still far from complete.

The making of policy through the exercise of choice is an inescapable part of all these operations. Some activities, especially old and established ones, are fairly far removed from controversy, and the choices are therefore of limited consequence. Other choices, however, may affect the livelihood of individuals, corporations, and whole states. And these economic dependencies may make it difficult or impossible to make decisions that may otherwise be called for. Military requirements, for example, may indicate the wisdom of eliminating further production of an aircraft or missile. But, if the economy of a whole area, such as Southern California, is heavily dependent upon such production, military needs may not be the controlling factor in the decision.

THE FACTORS AFFECTING BUREAUCRATIC PERFORMANCE

Since the making of policy inevitably stems from the exercise of choice in the bureaucracy, let us examine the pattern of these choices and the influences to which they respond.

Organizational Forms

The organization of the bureaucracy—the units into which a department is divided, the duties assigned them, and the way in which they are related to one another—is a fundamental determinant of its performance, of what kinds of choice are made and how. "Organization" has been usefully defined as "the structure of authoritative and habitual personal interrelations in an administrative system." [4] In Chapter 12 we saw some of the consequences of organization in Congress. It is clear that one form of "authoritative and habitual" relations encourages certain kinds of choice and certain criteria of selection, while another form fosters altogether different emphases and choices.

[4] Dwight Waldo, *The Study of Public Administration* (New York: Random House, 1955), p. 6.

Take the familiar example of organization in student government. On most college campuses representatives on the governing body are chosen in one of three ways: by classes, by schools, or by social units (fraternities and sororities). The goals, the perspectives, and the habitual relations in each type of unit are somewhat different. Hence the selection of one or another of these units of organization as the basis for electing representatives tends to give priority to a distinctive set of interests.

In talking about administrative organization it is customary to distinguish four alternative emphases in structuring units and their relationships to other units: (1) *function*, or *purpose*, such as transporting and delivering the mail; (2) *process*, such as accounting or biological research; (3) *clientele*, such as veterans or exporters; and (4) *place*, or *geographic area*, such as the Missouri River Basin. If the major divisions in an organization emphasize one criterion, their subdivisions will follow one or more of the others. Thus the *function* of handling the mail may be subdivided into the *processes* of finance, real estate management, transportation, and so on.

The major units of the federal bureaucracy are the departments and the independent agencies. They have various bases of organization, usually function or clientele. (Geographic area is comparatively rare as a primary basis of structure, since most departments and agencies are at least nominally nationwide organizations.) However, since the twelve Cabinet-level departments owe their establishment and development to essentially political factors, none of them falls neatly into any one of the four categories of organization.

The oldest (1789) is the Department of State (first known as the Department of Foreign Affairs), whose major responsibility is the function of foreign policy. The Department of the Treasury (1789) is also chiefly functional; it is primarily concerned with managing the government's finances but includes such activities as the Secret Service. The Department of Defense (1947) is basically a functional unit. Two of its three principal constituent units date from the early years of the Republic: the Department of the Navy (1798) and the Department of the Army (1789, originally called the Department of War).

The Department of Justice dates from 1870, although its head, the Attorney General, has sat in the Cabinet as the President's principal legal adviser since 1792. From the beginning it has been the law office of the executive branch. It is in that respect a process unit, but it also operates the federal prisons and the Immigration and Naturalization Service and includes the Federal Bureau of Investigation.

The Post Office Department, primarily functional, was created in 1872, although the office of the Postmaster General dates from 1789 and its incumbent became a member of the Cabinet in Jackson's time.

The Department of the Interior (1849) has long been a kind of catchall for a variety of rather unrelated activities, but its growth from the General Land Office and the Office of Indian Affairs has continued to associate it primarily with problems, especially natural-resource problems, west of the Mississippi. Although broadly a functional unit, it comes closer than any other department to specialization by geographic area.

Since its creation in 1862 the Department of Agriculture has been primarily a clientele department, though it was not of Cabinet rank until 1889. Much the same can be said of the Department of Commerce (1913), although it is scarcely the sole spokesman for the business community in the executive branch, and it contains a number of activities only slightly connected with the affairs of its clients. The Department of Labor (1913) occupies a somewhat comparable position. This department has a relatively small staff and has been weak at times, reflecting the struggle of the labor unions to gain acceptance and legitimacy.

The Department of Health, Education, and Welfare (1953), even more than Interior, is basically a collection of functions, a kind of holding company for several rather unrelated activities. Its principal units are the Public Health Service, the Office of Education, the Social Security Administration, and the Food and Drug Administration.

The Department of Housing and Urban Development (1965) is also composed basically of a cluster of preexisting agencies: the Housing and Home Finance Agency, the Urban Renewal Administration, the Public Housing Administration, among others. Its creation, however, reflected recognition of the new importance of urban and metropolitan areas in today's society.

Finally, the Department of Transportation (1966) includes in a single agency most of the federal government's wide-ranging activities supporting or regulating means of transportation, such as the Federal Aviation Agency, the Bureau of Public Roads, and the safety functions of the Civil Aeronautics Board and of the Interstate Commerce Commission.

No two departments or independent agencies are organized identically, even in formal terms. Characteristically, however, they include three types of unit: (1) the Secretary (or his equivalent in the independent agencies) and one or more undersecretaries and assistant secretaries, who share nominal responsibility for supervising sectors of the department's activities; (2) a number of auxiliary or housekeeping activities for the whole department, such as personnel, budgeting, accounting, and the like; and (3) the major operating units, usually called bureaus. There are about 350 of these in the executive branch, ranging in size from fewer than 100 employees to more than 5,000.

The autonomy of the bureau

The bureau is the fundamental unit of the federal bureaucracy. It tends to be relatively indestructible and somewhat isolated from the remainder of the department.

Several factors account for these characteristics of the bureau. First, historically, many bureaus grew out of the recognition of a particular need followed by the initial recruitment of a small staff of specialists to deal with it; from the beginning they had few ties with the department in which they were located. For example, soon after we began to export livestock to Europe in the 1870's our shippers encountered European import restrictions aimed at excluding certain diseases common among cattle in this country. State efforts to eradicate the diseases failed, and in 1884, after considerable agitation in and outside the government to protect this export market, Congress established by law a Bureau of Animal Industry, to be located in the Department of Agriculture, and gave it authority—which was gradually expanded—to suppress livestock diseases. It continued as a bureau from 1884 to 1953, when its functions were reassigned by the Secretary of Agriculture, acting under reorganizing authority granted by Congress.

Second, distinctive patterns of recruitment and promotion contribute to a strong *esprit de corps* in each bureau. The Bureau of Animal Industry became a major center for research in animal diseases, as well as a regulatory unit, and as such it was a magnet for able and well-trained veterinary scientists all over the country. A current example of bureau *esprit* is provided by the Forest Service, which recruits most of its professional staff from the few leading schools of forestry in the country. Its upper echelons are composed of graduates of these schools who have spent their lives in forest management. Not unnaturally, they regard their location in the Department of Agriculture as nothing more than a matter of housekeeping convenience and thus have no special ties to the department as a whole.

Third, the chiefs of these bureaus often occupy their positions for a long time. Although only about one-third are appointed under civil-service procedures, a good many are in fact career men in their bureaus. Compared with Secretaries and sub-Cabinet departmental officials appointed by the President, who average only two or three years in office, bureau chiefs average five years or more in their positions and fifteen or more in the federal service. Standing committees of Congress, including appropriations subcommittees, usually give polite attention to a Secretary and his immediate associates, but they regard the long-term bureau chief as the one who really knows the answers—an attitude doubtless shared by the chiefs themselves.

Fourth, when both senior committee members and bureau officials continue in their positions for years, long acquaintance tends to develop into "authoritative and habitual interrelations"—a kind of informal organization not normally shown on the charts. This pattern encourages the bureau to act independently of its parent department.

Fifth, each bureau tends to acquire one or more clientele groups, which establish customary relations with it. Some bureaus may have a very wide variety of client groups. Those of the Forest Service, for example, would include the leading schools of forestry, the professional organizations of foresters, sectors of the lumber industry, sportsmen and livestock raisers'

"They act as if they've been doped."

Critics of government regulatory commissions during the Eisenhower era alleged that they were overly solicitous of the interests they were to regulate.

From *Herblock's Special for Today,*
Simon & Schuster, 1958

groups whose members use the facilities of the national forests, and officials and organizations in communities economically dependent on the forests. Similarly intimate relations develop between congressional committees and many of these outside interest groups, which are "clients" of the senators and representatives as well. This triangular relationship may be completely harmonious, or it may, especially in the case of regulatory functions, contain potential hostility. But, as Chapter 10 pointed out in discussing the independent regulatory agencies, the relationship normally tends toward stability.[5] Especially in the face of a threat to bureau autonomy or to established practice it may become an impressively strong "triple alliance." [6] Typical is the ability of the Interstate Commerce Commission and its client groups— particularly the railroads and the truckers—to influence Congress to deny the President authority to designate the commission's chairman.

Finally, these factors both account for and reinforce the tendency of Congress to "freeze" bureaus into the executive structure and to insulate them from other influences. Given the characteristic history noted above, it is not surprising that many bureaus are provided for by statute, which normally means that they cannot be abolished, nor can their powers be altered or transferred without subsequent statutory authority. Laws establishing bureaus also frequently grant various powers quite explicitly to the

[5] Pp. 344–45.
[6] The phrase in this context is from Marver H. Bernstein, *The Job of the Federal Executive* (Washington: Brookings Institution, 1958), p. 86.

bureaus and their chiefs. The more precisely these laws specify what a bureau chief shall do and how he shall do it, of course, the more meaningless is a department head's power to "supervise" the bureau. An alternative arrangement would be for Congress to direct the President to set up an activity where and in the form he deemed appropriate. In wartime, in fact, the President has been given such power. Another alternative would be for Congress to grant authority for an activity to a department and allow its Secretary to delegate and organize this authority as he saw fit. Historically this has not been customary, but in recent years Congress has granted such powers to the Secretaries of a number of departments. However, Congress still creates some bureaus by statute, and sometimes grants a Secretary the power to reallocate activities but significantly exempts certain bureaus from this authority.

For example, the Office of the Comptroller of the Currency, created by statute in 1863, is a bureau in the Department of the Treasury. It controls the establishment and consolidation of all national banks, regulates their creation of branches, and supervises their overall operations, chiefly through its bank examiners. Like a regulatory commission, which it resembles, the Office of the Comptroller of the Currency has developed over a century a stable set of relations with its clients, the national banks and their trade associations. In 1950, when a presidential reorganization plan proposed to give the Secretary of the Treasury general power to reallocate the department's activities, opposition pressures from both clients and bureau led Congress to exempt the Office of the Comptroller from this authority.

Presidents, secretaries, and bureau chiefs

The partial autonomy of the bureaus largely explains the inability of Cabinet members to function as disinterested presidential counselors. As Chapter 10 indicated, a Secretary is dependent not only upon the President but upon Congress (especially through its standing committees), upon his department's personnel, and upon his department's client groups.[7] These ties of staff, congressional committees, and clients, however, belong to the bureau rather than the department because of the continuities and the concentrated experience to be encountered in the bureaus. A Cabinet officer freshly arrived on the scene and relatively inexperienced in the ways either of Washington or of his department inevitably relies on the career people, especially the bureau chiefs. If he wishes to make an impact in his position, he must draw on the substantive ideas of his staff, secure their guidance in formulating his strategies, and persuade them to make his ideas and plans their own. If he has no such ambitions, he leaves the bureaus to their chiefs. But either way he depends on the bureaus.

A Cabinet officer must be able to go it alone, without appreciable presidential help, in a contest with elements in Congress and with various interest

[7] P. 339.

groups. But a Secretary is likely to discover soon that the loyalties of his staff are in pawn to the various triple alliances of the bureaus in his department. Thus, in order to get the cooperation he needs to put his program into effect, the Secretary must join one or more of these alliances himself. For example, for years one of the strongest such alliances in the Department of Agriculture was that involving the state colleges of agriculture, the American Farm Bureau Federation, and the department's Federal Extension Service. The last is a bureau that administers a grant-in-aid educational program for farmers in cooperation with the state agricultural colleges and the state and county units of the Farm Bureau. For years, the Extension Service was virtually the only channel of direct contact between the department and the nation's farmers. Under the New Deal, Secretary of Agriculture Henry A. Wallace tried to create new direct channels to farmers in order to execute the new agricultural programs. But despite the crisis of the Depression (and later the Second World War), no Secretary was able to conduct these and related programs without using the Extension Service to the extent demanded by its sponsors, who included members of Congress.

A bureau chief in charge of a new or controversial undertaking may need the Secretary, much as the latter may need the President. This is most likely to occur in connection with the jurisdictional rivalries that almost inevitably occur within—and particularly between—departments. A classic case is the recurrent hostility between the Bureau of Reclamation in the Department of the Interior and the Corps of Engineers in the Department of the Army, both of which engage in dam construction and related projects for developing water resources.[8] The corps is the center of perhaps the strongest alliances on the Washington scene. The Bureau of Reclamation, on the other hand, is less strongly fortified, so it almost inevitably depends on the Secretary of the Interior and through him on the President.

Nonetheless, the chief of an established bureau, even if he encounters jurisdictional conflicts, can "go it alone" by drawing on the kind of informal relations that make the bureau the key unit of the bureaucracy. For this reason bureau chiefs have less need of the Secretary than the Secretary has of the bureau chiefs or the President. For example, as head of the Department of Justice the Attorney General is more likely to draw on the prestige enjoyed in Congress by the Federal Bureau of Investigation and its chief, J. Edgar Hoover, than vice versa. Similarly, the Secretary of Agriculture has more need of the alliance with interest groups and congressional committees established by the bureau chief of the Forest Service than the chief has of either the Secretary's or the President's political resources.

The politics of reorganization

Some critics of the bureaucracy imply that there is a perfect solution to the problem of its organization if only the powers-that-be in Washington had

[8] See Ch. 20, p. 667.

the wit to discover it and the courage to adopt it. Such a solution, however, is an illusion.

In an enterprise as complex and extensive as the federal government, it is imperative that the strains and demands on the political system be handled as smoothly and as promptly as possible. To do so in a system that relies on presidential initiative, two broad criteria of good organization must be met. First, the various activities in the bureaucracy should be arranged so that the most important problems will be easily identified and the insights for dealing with them will be promptly generated. Second, the units in the bureaucracy should be so located in the executive hierarchy that the issues most needing decision by the President will reach him easily and quickly. Otherwise, important questions may be delayed or buried elsewhere in the structure, or when problems finally reach the President the essential choices will have been obscured by prior compromises.

Both criteria imply that good organization should reflect changing needs and issues at any given time. In a world of constant change an organization appropriate today may be inadequate a year from now. Thus, organization tends to be a continuous process of adapting as effectively as possible to current and anticipated needs.

Reorganization to foster appropriate perspectives in agency relations is illustrated by the 1940 transfer of the Food and Drug Administration from the Department of Agriculture to the Federal Security Agency (predecessor of the Department of Health, Education, and Welfare). When the Food and Drug Administration was located in the Department of Agriculture and controlled by congressional committees that were closely identified with food producers and processors, it tended to overemphasize such commercial matters as the adulteration of insecticides and fertilizers. Locating it in the Federal Security Agency and subjecting it to a different set of congressional committees shifted its emphasis to the practices of food growers and processors that were potentially harmful to humans.

In the past three decades Congress has implicitly acknowledged the validity of these premises by granting to successive Chief Executives contingent powers of reorganization. Beginning in 1932 Congress passed a series of statutes authorizing the President to submit reorganization plans to Congress that would go into effect in sixty days if Congress did not exercise its "legislative veto." Some statutes have specifically exempted from reorganization as many as seventeen agencies, both independent commissions and bureaus within departments. But current legislation formally exempts only certain courts and the General Accounting Office and provides that no department may be abolished, that no temporary agency may have its life extended, and that no term of office may be increased.

The *unwritten* exemptions to a President's reorganization powers, however, are extensive. As long as Congress retains a legislative veto over such

The Politics of Reorganization

A rumor to the effect that the Children's Bureau may be a casualty of the contemplated reorganization of the huge Department of Health, Education, and Welfare has shocked and disturbed child-welfare authorities across the nation.

The proposed plan, it is said, calls for the transfer of children's health services, presently in the bureau, to a separate department of health which would include all of HEW's varied health programs. Child-welfare services would be taken from the bureau and placed in a reorganized welfare department.... This would leave the Children's Bureau a shadow of its present self....

The possibility of such changes has caused great consternation among leading pediatricians and other believers that the present Children's Bureau should be built up and expanded—not fragmented or weakened.... Dr. Robert Cook, professor of pediatrics at Johns Hopkins Medical School in Baltimore, reached by telephone, admitted he had heard the rumor about the bureau "and it doesn't sound good." ... To downgrade the bureau now would, in his opinion, "be like taking a winning team and breaking it up." ... Dr. Robert Parrot, director of the Children's Hospital in Washington, D.C., was of the same opinion.... "If [the proposed reorganization] in any sense means the dissolution of the bureau and losing the focus on children in the shuffle, I would not be for it."

Secretary of Health, Education, and Welfare John W. Gardner is already being made aware of this rising sentiment. "Vigorously protest proposed transfer of U.S. Children's Bureau health programs to U.S. Public Health Service," read a telegram from George J. Hecht, chairman, American Parents Committee and publisher of *Parents' Magazine.*

From Josephine Ripley, "Children's Bureau Shift Fought," *The Christian Science Monitor*, April 1967.

---

proposals—and that is likely to be a very long time—the alliance systems of a great many bureaus and agencies will be sufficient to jeopardize or defeat any reorganization plan threatening those systems. For example, even though it is not covered by statutory exemptions, the Federal Bureau of Investigation could prevent its being transferred to the Treasury Department and being made a division of the Secret Service; the Forest Service could still obstruct a transfer to Interior; the Marines could thwart any attempt to combine them with the Army; and any of the "big six" independent regulatory commissions could resist transfer to one of the executive departments.

Thus, the politics of reorganization makes the powers of the Chief Executive insufficient by themselves to permit full satisfaction of the two criteria of organization. To satisfy these criteria the President must rely also on the persuasion, bargaining, and maneuvering essential to executive leadership.

The Patterns of Civil-Service Recruitment

The processes and patterns of recruitment significantly affect the values, perspectives, and goals that mold an institution. This should be evident from our discussion of congressional careers in Chapter 11.[9] In contrast with the relatively informal recruitment of members of Congress, however, entrance into the civil service is quite formal and institutionalized.

One informal factor of consequence does affect the recruitment of civil servants. Government employment carries less prestige than do occupations in the private sector of society, especially in the more industrialized sections of the country. This is far from the case in all societies, and it may be in the process of change in the United States. But the civil service, even in the federal government, does not get its full share of the ablest and most ambitious young people in the country, although it does include a large number of dedicated men and women of topflight ability. The proportion of the latter is undoubtedly lower than it might be because of the lower prestige of public employment. Salary differentials, especially in the top positions, give private occupations another advantage over the civil service, but they probably are a less fundamental factor.

Before the 1880's the federal bureaucracy was recruited almost exclusively on a partisan basis, called the *spoils system*. With every change of President, incumbent civil servants, often in fairly large numbers, were displaced by those of the President's party, those associated with his faction, and those associated with local party organizations or with members of Congress important in the President's entourage.

Until fairly recently many features of government operation were tolerably compatible with that mode of recruitment. First, the government was a small show by modern standards. Even in 1933 total employment in the executive branch was less than 600,000, almost half of whom were in the Post Office. Second, technical specialization had not proceeded very far, in keeping with the relatively uncomplicated, almost peripheral role of government in the society.

Third, the functions of the bureaucracy as a source of initiative, of policy proposals growing out of technical preoccupation with various features of a sensitively interdependent society, were relatively slight.

The spoils system did not mean, however, that competence was completely neglected in appointments. Moreover, many technical employees were retained in successive administrations and even gradually moved up to positions of considerable responsibility as the value of their experience and accumulated knowledge was recognized. But spoils and partisan attachments were by far the dominant recruitment factors.

The turn of the tide came in 1883 with the passage of the Pendleton Act,

[9] Pp. 371–76.

In Memoriam—Our Civil Service
as It Was

This anti-Jackson cartoon illustrates the rise of the patronage
system in national government
during the 1830's.

Thomas Nast in *Harper's Weekly*

creating the Civil Service Commission and providing for recruitment by
open competitive examination. This legislation climaxed twenty years of
agitation by reformers. They were aided by the assassination in 1881 of
President James A. Garfield by a demented aspirant for a government post
who held the President responsible for his failure to secure an appointment.
But the inefficiencies of an unrestrained patronage system in a period of
increasing government responsibility and complexity would eventually have
made the change inevitable.

In 1883 the competitive service covered only about 10 percent of the
employees in the executive branch. But steady expansion by executive order
and statute over the years has brought between 80 and 90 percent of federal
employees under the competitive provisions of the Civil Service Act. More
than 90 percent of federal employees are chosen by merit systems if one
includes those independent of the Civil Service Commission, such as the
Foreign Service of the State Department, the FBI, the TVA, the Atomic
Energy Commission, and the commissioned medical officers of the Public
Health Service.

In the executive branch of the federal government, therefore, recruitment by patronage has disappeared except for a relatively small number of posts, including approximately 1,100 Cabinet, sub-Cabinet, and similar top-level positions.

The problems of neutrality

A prime goal of the reformers who promoted the merit system was neutrality. They argued that if appointees to the government service could be selected on a basis of competence alone, through the device of open competitive examination, the civil service would put its skills at the disposal of whichever political party had received the voters' mandate and would loyally carry out the policies arrived at by the political officers of the government. Furthermore, recruitment through the competitive system would remove the partisan incentive to create unnecessary government jobs. More important, appointees would no longer feel obligated to their political sponsors in Congress and in the local party organizations.

These worthy objectives have been partially attained since 1883 by extending the coverage of the competitive system and by instituting additional devices aimed at insulating the bureaucracy from partisan politics. Conspicuously, the Hatch Act of 1939 in effect prohibited all executive employees, whether under civil service or not, from engaging in any partisan activity other than voting and discussions in the privacy of one's home. A second Hatch Act extended these limitations to state and local employees paid from federal funds.

Agency and professional politics   Partisan activity is not the only form of politics. The units of the executive branch, as we have already seen, have inevitable ties with committees of Congress and with interest groups; they are inescapably involved in the contests of influence between the President and his opponents in Congress. Paradoxically, greater technical competence and the virtual elimination of partisanship have increased the importance of professional and bureau ties.

Thus the pursuit of neutrality through the competitive system has created new problems. Neutrality toward political parties does not necessarily mean neutrality toward professional goals and agency politics. Agency goals, moreover, may not be as broad and flexible as the governmental situation requires.

With the unit-by-unit growth of the bureaus, recruitment into the federal service has tended to emphasize specialization—foresters into the Forest Service, chemists into the Food and Drug Administration, and so on. To counter these tendencies, efforts have been made in the past four decades to recruit able young generalists with liberal-arts educations directly from the colleges and universities as the nucleus of the government-wide career

The Tension Between Specialization and the Broad View

Two contradictory forces are at work which severely complicate the problem of leadership [in the federal bureaucracy]. On the one hand, increasing specialization in all professions makes technical expertise an essential prerequisite for anyone who seeks a position of influence within his or her profession. On the other hand, in this age of large-scale organization and increasing specialization, we face a more urgent need than ever before for people who are capable of practical action in complicated areas requiring deep knowledge of several related disciplines. A person who has climbed the ladder within his profession may be incapable later in life of thinking in broad terms about what Secretary Gardner called "the largest questions facing our society." And, the person who dabbles in a number of disciplines may find that despite his good intentions he lacks the depth, experience and expertise required to relate various complex fields....

In the final analysis, however, leadership is essentially an attitude of mind.... Today, more than any other type of leader, we need the man who can relate diverse and complicated fields, the man who has specialized but also remains a sophisticated generalist. This is where attitude of mind comes in. The men and women who can achieve expertise but retain flexibility, who can define alternatives and still put their hand to the task of implementation—these will be the leaders of the future.

From Joseph W. Barr, undersecretary of the Treasury, address at De Pauw University, March 1966.

service. Though these efforts have been partly successful, the careers open to generalists are more likely to be bureau careers, or at most department ones, rather than government-wide ones. Some individuals with initiative do move from agency to agency, especially in Washington. But, for those who do not change agencies, advancement tends to depend on identification with the norms and objectives of the bureau or agency. Such identification once again reinforces the politics of the triple alliance of bureau, client group, and congressional committee.

These tendencies toward separatism and "agency self-government" are most conspicuous in the highly independent specialized corps in the executive branch. The Foreign Service and the Federal Bureau of Investigation have their own systems of recruitment, promotion, and retirement. The commissioned corps of the Public Health Service (a bureau), in addition to conducting its own recruiting system, has succeeded in arranging the statutes so that the President must appoint the Surgeon General (chief of the bureau) from among the personnel of the commissioned corps. The problems of such separatism are similar to the problems of civilian control of the military, which are also specialized corps. Without effective civilian controls, the policies generated by the military corps tend to reflect its own perspectives rather than the values and needs of the political system as a whole.

Neutrality and active recruitment   The concept of neutrality may also be at odds with the goal of high competence. The problem is that a competitive examination to separate the competent from the incompetent produces top quality civil servants *only* if adequate numbers of very able people are eager to enter public employment. Unfortunately, this has seldom been the case, and the merit system is particularly inadequate in a virtually full-employment economy, where industry and professional firms actively attempt to recruit the ablest young men and women in the country. In this context, government recruitment must be equally active.

The efforts aimed at recruiting able young generalists for careers in the federal government have attempted to meet this problem in part. The latest version of these, functioning since 1955, is the Federal Service Entrance Examination, open to young people who have completed or are about to complete four years of college or the equivalent.

Congress and recruitment policies

Some of these shortcomings of the recruitment system are, of course, fostered and reinforced by persistent attitudes in Congress. Although they have gradually accepted the merit system, members of Congress have nonetheless been fearful that it might become a presidential instrument. This fear is illustrated by the restrictions they placed on political activity by government employees in the 1939 Hatch Act. The act was intended to prevent the employees of New Deal emergency agencies not under civil service from working in electoral campaigns against members of Congress who opposed President Roosevelt. Similarly, members of Congress usually expect civil servants to keep clear of a President's shadow. (The tendency of bureaucrats to do so depends in part on a President's skill and standing.) Somewhat inconsistently, many members of Congress—partly because of the delegated powers that bureaucrats exercise—also look with suspicion and condescension on civil servants, who have "never carried a precinct." Some congressmen feel further that the bureaucracy can be improved only at the expense of congressional power.

These attitudes also explain the tendency of Congress to treat government employment as a form of charity, illustrated by the institution of veterans' preference, which grants extra points on examination scores to veterans trying for civil-service jobs and gives veterans preference over nonveterans when dismissals occur through personnel cuts in the bureaucracy.

Recruitment and the loyalty program

A critical and revealing problem affecting recruitment into the civil service is the federal loyalty-and-security program. Although it had its counterpart in the Second World War, it is primarily a product of the Cold War. It began in 1947 when President Truman issued an executive order requiring that all present and prospective government employees submit to a loyalty check. Successive versions of this order under Truman and Eisenhower increased the severity of the criteria for clearance, which reached a peak in 1953, when an Eisenhower order required that employment of any person must be "clearly consistent with the interests of national security."

No one would deny that positions involving access to highly confidential information should be reserved for persons whose loyalty and reliability are above question. Spying and subversion are not illusions. They occur not only through the deliberately disloyal but also through the emotionally unstable and those whose habits may make them vulnerable, for example, to blackmail. But all government positions need not be subject to the same precautions.

Hence, a loyalty-security program presents three problems: (1) defining which positions are sensitive and which are not; (2) defining which associations and actions are disloyal; and (3) determining the procedure and the character of the evidence to be relied upon in loyalty-security actions.

The first problem, deciding which positions are sensitive, seems simple, but in an atmosphere of semihysteria—such as prevailed in the late 1940's and in the "McCarthy years" of the early 1950's—it may not be. In the setting of the Alger Hiss case, of the widespread belief that the Soviet Union had secured the secrets of the atom bomb through espionage, and of the readiness by radical right-wing elements in the country and in Congress to see communists on every hand, it was far from simple.

The second problem, standards, is at best troublesome. A man who in his mature years is a member of the Communist party may present a security risk, but what of the man who for a brief time in his college years was active in "radical" causes? Or what about the man who has publicly taken unpopular positions, such as criticizing American actions in Vietnam? And how would one deal with the person whose sister or brother-in-law is a member of an organization that openly supports the foreign policy of Communist China?

The third problem, procedure and evidence, is obviously complex. To require a formal hearing for all loyalty-security cases would be cumbersome. Yet labeling a person as a "security risk" imposes serious economic and social penalties on him, not the least of which is that he may subsequently be unable to secure employment even outside the government. To permit a defendant to confront his accusers and to test the evidence against him might very well compromise the system of informants used, for example, by the FBI. But restriction of this opportunity raises the nasty question of whether the constitutional rights of American citizens are not seriously jeopardized. Do we not violate the concept of due process when a person is in effect publicly branded as a "security risk" through an investigative procedure in which he has no voice?

These problems have implications for the bureaucracy as a whole. When "sensitive positions" are loosely defined and when safeguards concerning standards and evidence are weak, an atmosphere of mutual suspicion is fostered in the service itself. In such an atmosphere the initiative and imagination needed from the bureaucracy is discouraged. Suppose a foreign-service officer's 1943 report from China, arguing that support of the government of Chiang Kai-shek is a waste, were rediscovered in 1954. If investigators use the report, not as an example of a realistic or even a mistaken or incomplete judgment, but as proof of subversive intent, what is the result? Any prudent man will avoid speaking candidly except on the most mundane matters.

The effects on recruitment are equally serious. An atmosphere of suspicion and conformity is not one eagerly sought by inventive and able men. And a clearance program that turns on dubious or unvalidated evidence may deny to the government the services of an able and imaginative man who has acquired enemies in the course of his career.

No one can be certain how many genuinely disloyal or risky persons

From *Herblock's Here and Now,*
Simon & Schuster, 1955

"That's the kind we want—you can see just what he's not thinking."

Critics of the loyalty-security program in government have stressed that its procedures encourage bureaucratic mediocrity.

have been dismissed or denied employment under this program. It is clear, however, that the number is small, that the overwhelming majority of civil servants are loyal and responsible, and that the few cases of disloyalty have usually been discovered by ordinary police work rather than by loyalty-security checks.

Tenure and turnover

A concomitant of recruitment by merit in the civil service is security of tenure. If arbitrary removal of civil servants were possible, so the argument goes, political-party preference could creep in through the back door though barred at the front. Hence, under the civil-service rules and statutes, after an employee has served for a probationary period of one year—during which he can be dropped without ceremony—he acquires civil-service status. Except in loyalty-security cases, he cannot be dismissed by his superiors without a complicated scheme of hearings and appeals. This system adequately takes care of eliminating obvious incompetents, but it may be too cumbersome to deal with the merely mediocre. This is suggested by the fact that the annual rate of dismissal for cause is only about one-half of one percent.

Despite protections against arbitrary dismissal, however, security in a government job may be less complete than in many private bureaucracies. The chief reason for this is that a government employee's tenure exists only as long as the job does, and the existence of the job depends on congressional authorizations and appropriations. The committees that at least nominally deal with legislation on recruitment, levels of pay, and conditions of work for the civil service proper and for the postal workers are the Senate and House Committees on the Post Office and Civil Service. These committees normally give a sympathetic ear to the representatives of employee organizations, to veterans' groups, and to the Civil Service Commission, in roughly that order. But it is the Committees on Appropriations and the program committees—all of which rank above the Civil Service Committee in prestige and power—that actually set the programs of the operating agencies and grant their funds. The Appropriations Committees in particular characteristically favor the reduction of programs and the restriction of personnel. They may also impose explicit limits on personnel levels, restrict or eliminate certain kinds of jobs, and even at times encroach on the jurisdiction of the Civil Service Committees by setting general rules for all executive employees.

The elimination of positions by Congress is called a *reduction in force*—in Washington jargon, "to rif" or "to be riffed." Reductions in force are governed by a complex set of rules, essentially involving competition within the affected agency among individuals with the same skills occupying positions in the same pay class and grade.

When a reduction in force occurs, a displaced employee may accept demotion to a lower position in the same agency. A slight reduction at the top of an agency, therefore, may affect jobs all along the line. In general, persons with civil-service status displace those without, employees with veterans' preference are favored over those without it, and persons with greater seniority outrank those with fewer years of service. Persons released through a reduction in force are given reemployment preference over new recruits, so a large proportion may remain in the service by shifting to another bureau or agency.

Thus the common notion that no civil servant is discharged or leaves for any reason other than death or retirement is wide of the mark. Turnover in the bureaucracy occurs at an annual rate of 20 to 25 percent, representing between 400,000 and 500,000 persons per year. About half this total represents voluntary withdrawals other than retirements.

In sum, recruitment and related practices reinforce bureau and professional ties and foster alliances with congressional committees. The "neutral" civil service has helped to make the bureaucracy a partially independent force in the governmental system, counted upon as a source of initiative by both President and Congress, dependent to some degree on both, and able at times to play one off against the other.

Judicialized Restraints

The policy choices made by bureaucrats are normally subject to review in the courts, but in fact relatively few bureaucratic actions are challenged, since the heart of administrative decision-making involves negotiation and informal settlement.

Over the years the courts' treatment of administrative decisions—especially those by quasi-judicial agencies—has varied. Until the mid-1930's the courts tended to regard administrative determinations with suspicion; they sometimes ignored the findings of fact made by administrators and even retried cases *de novo*—that is, they heard them as if no other tribunal had previously done so. Gradually, however, the Supreme Court and the lower federal bench began to confine review to determining whether decisions had involved a fair hearing after proper advance notice to all parties and whether they were supported by "substantial evidence" consistent with statutory standards.

Congress from time to time has also imposed judicialized restraints on the bureaucracy through legislation applicable to particular agencies or to the entire service. The most important example of the latter sort is the Administrative Procedure Act of 1946.

This legislation resulted from agitation by the American Bar Association, beginning in 1933, against (1) the growth of administrative discretion; (2) the "mixture" of quasi-legislative and quasi-judicial functions in the same hands, particularly when the same unit served as both "prosecutor" and "judge" in administrative determinations; and (3) what they regarded as the inadequacy of court review. In 1940 Congress, whose numerous lawyer members usually give the organized bar an attentive ear, passed in response a severely restrictive statute known as the Walter-Logan Bill. This bill, which President Roosevelt vetoed with a message of sharp rebuke, would have imposed a rigidly uniform procedure on all administrative rule-making and would have exposed almost all administrative determinations to a long series of judicial appeals *before* they could take effect.

The Administrative Procedure Act of 1946 was a much-modified version of the Walter-Logan Bill. It had four major provisions: (1) it required notice and hearing before the issuance of rules of general application; (2) it required that orders to particular persons or organizations be issued only after decision through courtlike procedures specified in the Act; (3) it required the appointment, under the Civil Service Commission, of independent "hearing examiners" to conduct all preliminary proceedings in isolation from the rest of an agency; and (4) it granted the courts broad powers of judicial review.

Most observers hold that the Administrative Procedure Act did little more than codify the judicialized practices previously followed in most administrative agencies. More important, the courts, and especially the Supreme Court, have continued to maintain the generally respectful view of administrative decision-making that they assumed after 1937. Nonetheless, judicialized restraints are a real influence upon the actions of the continuing executive.

SUMMARY: BUREAUCRACY AND THE PROBLEM OF CHOICE

The characteristics of the federal bureaucracy differ in important respects from those specified in the model of bureaucracy at the beginning of this chapter. Specialization of duties and jurisdictions has proceeded far, but the element of hierarchy typically extends little beyond the bureau level. Authority is an attribute of the bureaucratic office, and its exercise is constrained by public, general rules. But these rules only partly prescribe the relations among different parts of the bureaucracy and the bureaucracy's relations with the President, Congress, and interest groups.

Both the President and Congress have legal or politically effective controls over the bureaucracy. Certain bureaus operate as subordinates of the President or of the department Secretary. Other bureaus look to Congress and its committees for guidance. Still other agencies have considerable independence of both the President and Congress. The tendencies toward bureau autonomy, toward a collection of bureaucracies rather than a single bureaucratic structure, are thus strong.

The bureaucracy, especially in these quasi-autonomous units of the continuing executive, is inevitably involved in the making of policy, since all forms of bureaucratic action—law enforcement, administrative legislation, administrative adjudication, and direct operations—involve choices among alternative policies. This pattern is particularly clear in administrative legislation, because in recent years Congress—because of the technicality or controversial nature of the problems involved—has tended to pass legislation stipulating only broad policies. Specific implementation is left to the bureaucracy.

What factors guide and limit the policy choices of the bureaucracy? First, the organizational emphasis of an administrative unit is a fundamental determinant of performance. The major units of the federal bureaucracy— the departments and the independent agencies—are usually organized on the basis of function or clientele.

A bureaucracy in a system relying on presidential initiative should be organized so that, first, important problems can be easily identified and dealt with and, second, the issues needing a President's decision will reach him promptly. In recognition of this need, Congress has granted Chief Executives contingent powers of reorganization; but there are significant unwritten exemptions to these powers, because the alliance systems of many bureaus and agencies are powerful enough to thwart any reorganization that threatens them.

A second factor influencing policy choices is the system of recruitment in a bureaucracy. Since the 1880's the merit system has gradually become the primary means for recruiting civil servants, thus virtually eliminating political partisanship within the bureaucracy.

The combined effect of organizational forms, recruitment methods, and the notion of civil-service neutrality has been to ensure that the principal criteria for policy choices are professional. But organizational criteria, derived from identification with the bureau and its goals, are also influential. Given the somewhat unpredictable relations among the President, Congress, and interest groups, career bureaucrats inevitably search for contacts and support among all three that will minimize threats to a bureau program. Agencies whose actions are readily subject to court review may seek protection through the judiciary.

The pattern of relations among a bureau and its executive-branch superiors, Congress, and its interest clientele depends basically upon the size of the stakes that each feels in the bureau's functions. An agency performing a routine set of activities may be virtually an appendage of Congress or a captive of its clientele or both. But when a bureau program is a matter of consequence to the objectives of the President, he is compelled to try to make the agency a genuinely presidential instrument. A President with effective influence in Congress will encounter less difficulty in persuading the bureaucrats; their preoccupations with stability and organizational survival will incline them toward him.

The continuing executive remains a distinctive sector of the governmental system. Its powers are formally dependent upon authorization from elsewhere in the structure, but the diffusion of initiative within that structure, the rivalry and conflict among its parts, and the authority that derives from technical skill give the bureaucracy a degree of power and autonomy not evident from the formal structure.

IV

LIBERTY,

JUSTICE,

AND

LAW

The diffusion of policy-making arenas and the many routes for reaching them in the American political system are clearly underlined when we study our court system. Both state and federal courts are squarely in the middle of the political process— and both offer interested parties a variety of avenues for seeking victory in the political sphere. Chapter 14 discusses the structure and procedures of the state and federal court systems; Chapter 15 explores the political implications of the Supreme Court's controversial power of judicial review; and Chapter 16 analyzes the types of lawyers and judges our system tends to produce. Finally, Chapters 17 and 18 examine some of the court system's significant output—the substantive policies that have emerged in civil liberties and civil rights.

THE FRAMEWORK OF THE AMERICAN LEGAL SYSTEM

14

After constitutions have been adopted and amended, after leaders have been elected and installed in office, after legislation has set the basic lines of advantage and disadvantage for contending interest groups, and after administrators have applied these rules in the executive process, the American political system provides one more arena in which citizens and groups can press their claims or challenge the validity of government action: the legal arena. This chapter examines the basic framework of our legal system by asking three basic questions: What are the major functions of law? What are the distinctive ground rules of the American judicial system? And what institutional forms does this system take?

When the average college student thinks of law, his greatest difficulty is in clarifying his confused impressions about congressional civil-rights statutes, Nevada divorces, Supreme Court rulings on literary censorship, and Perry Mason trial tactics. As it happens, defining and classifying law is a troublesome problem for legal scholars and jurists as well. Which forms of official action rise to the "dignity of law" and how different layers in the legal system should be classified have proved such complicated questions that the law has been aptly called a "seamless web" of rules, relationships, rights, and duties.

The complexity of analyzing the law has led to several types of classification. Law may be analyzed according to the political jurisdiction that promulgates it (that is, federal law, state law, or local law); or according to the subject matter governed by the law (for example, criminal law, civil law, international law, or constitutional law); or according to the type of source it issues from (for instance, constitutional law, statutory law, administrative law, or common law).

As these classifications suggest, what we call law is made at virtually every level of government and by almost every type of official. It can range from the solemn declaration of American society's insistence upon freedom of religion to special city ordinances granting marching privileges to St. Patrick's Day paraders. Thus, the most useful way to consider law in the American political system is to examine what *functions* it performs. That is, in what ways does the law regulate the daily lives of every American citizen?

THE FUNCTIONS OF LAW: OF FORD CARS, TARPOTS, AND SCHOOL PRAYERS

Law as Regulator of Property and the Marketplace

In Capital City, Louisiana, in 1954, a year of hot competition among auto dealers, the Capital City Ford Agency placed advertisements in the local newspaper announcing: "Buy a Ford now and when the 1955 Fords come out, we'll trade even for your '54 Ford."

Mr. Johnson, a local resident who read this ad, bought a 1954 Ford from the agency, drove it happily until the 1955 models appeared, and then presented his '54 for an "even trade." To Johnson's dismay, the manager of the agency refused to swap. He told Johnson that despite what might have been said in newspaper ads or during conversations with salesmen, the contract Johnson had signed at the time of purchase had said nothing about trades in 1955. Johnson should have read the contract, since a written contract stipulates the obligations of seller and buyer. Johnson responded to this lecture on contract law by suing the agency for breach of agreement in the Louisiana courts.

This is a typical problem for the law as regulator of private bargains and the marketplace—a role vital in all countries, whether their economic arrangements are capitalist, socialist, or communist. In this case, the basic rule that contract law establishes is that the written agreement between two freely contracting, adult parties is the best proof of their intentions and defines the rights of the parties toward one another. The stability of business relations would be threatened by allowing buyers to use oral promises or general publicity by the seller as a basis for altering the terms of a formal agreement read and signed by the parties. In addition, American contract law does not regard newspaper ads as legally binding offers to sell merchandise; the ads are really only invitations to come in and offer to buy. Advertisers can then conclude the agreement by accepting the offer, or they can refuse to do so for many valid reasons, such as exhaustion of stock, a mistake in price in the advertisement, and the like.

On the other hand, what about Johnson's specific situation? The Capital City Ford Agency had not published a vague ad offering to sell Fords "at low, *low* prices" or to give "the best deal in town." Rather, the ad had made a very specific offer: to allow all purchasers of the 1954 model to make an even trade for a 1955 car. Johnson was able to show that he had read the ad, had gone to the agency directly as a result of it, and had purchased the car with the understanding that the even-trade arrangement was in force.

The Louisiana courts decided for Johnson.[1] The judge's opinion noted that it would be an unfair enrichment of the car agency to let it lure buyers into making purchases by advertising promises that were deliberately left out of the agency's contracts.

Contract law is only one facet of the law's role as regulator of property and the marketplace. Other "private-law" aspects of this role include the rules governing the creation of estates in land, the use of property in trust, the laws of inheritance, and many other facets of commercial life. In addition, there is a "public-law" side to this role of law that includes business antitrust laws; labor-management laws; laws regulating government contracts; the complex network of price, wage, and rationing controls in emergency periods; and the controls over rates, routes, subsidies, and licenses for the large part of industry supervised by federal and state regulatory commissions. The public-law sector limits the private bargains and marketplace ethics of individuals, corporations, or labor unions in

[1] *Johnson* v. *Capital City Ford Co.*, 85 So. 2d. 75 (La. App. 1955).

order to protect the public's basic interest in industrial peace, fair competition, stable prices, shared resources in economic crisis, and open entry to industries under government licensing. The law here protects all the "Johnsons" and operates by public initiative rather than private lawsuit.

The following case illustrates this public sector of marketplace law. During the 1950's, the Colgate-Palmolive Company conducted a nationwide television campaign for Rapid Shave shaving cream. The filmed commercial claimed that Rapid Shave had powerful "moisturizing" properties and, to prove this, it showed the cream being applied to what the announcer said was sandpaper. A razor swiftly shaved the paper clean of the "sand" particles, and the announcer told viewers that beards "as tough as sandpaper" would be shaved equally well if this shaving cream were used. Actually, sandpaper was not used in the commercial. Instead a plexiglas mock-up was used that looked like sandpaper, and its sand-substitute was easily removed by the razor.

In 1962 the Federal Trade Commission directed Colgate-Palmolive to stop showing its sandpaper commercials. The FTC acts under congressional laws giving it power to prevent "unfair or deceptive" advertising, especially for food, drug, and cosmetic products. The FTC claimed that Rapid Shave could not possibly shave real sandpaper in the manner and time shown by the commercials, nor could it shave a beard "as tough as sandpaper" as claimed.

"It turns up in some of the jumbo, giant, more-colossal-than-ever cartons."

Control of misleading packaging and labeling is part of the public sector of marketplace law.

From *Straight Herblock*, Simon & Schuster, 1964

Colgate-Palmolive, however, argued that technical problems in television caused sandpaper not to look like sandpaper when it was photographed, thus requiring some type of simulation. Furthermore, the use of "simulated materials"—such as dry ice in chocolate syrup to depict steaming coffee—was a common practice in television. Finally, they argued that simulation was lawful as long as nothing false was said about the product's properties.

The FTC was not persuaded. It ruled that advertisers must find ways to portray the qualities of their products that were true demonstrations. Such true demonstrations were not beyond the technical capacities of television photography, and use of falsehoods to sell a product was not justified by the product's genuine merits.

Law as Regulator of Family and Social Relationships

In 1947 a wealthy American woman was married in New York to Mr. W-D, a former Russian nobleman who had become an American citizen. During their courtship, Mr. W-D had stated that he was a prominent figure in European and American society circles, that he had always earned his own living and had never taken money from a woman, and that his purpose in marrying Mrs. W-D was to contribute to her happiness and to perform faithfully all his husbandly duties.

In 1949 Mrs. W-D sued in the New York courts to have the marriage annulled on the ground of fraud. According to Mrs. W-D, her husband's self-portrait had been wholly deceptive. He had been married previously and had been paid a large sum of money by his former wife as an "inducement" to give her an uncontested divorce; he was considered a fortune hunter and was not acceptable in European and American society; he had married Mrs. W-D primarily to get money to keep himself and his relatives in luxurious style without working, and he had done no work since the marriage; he had tried to get Mrs. W-D to give him money for a nonexistent business prospect and had attempted to collect commissions from the contractor who remodeled Mrs. W-D's house; and he had failed in his husbandly duties because he was, in Mrs. W-D's words, "a hypochondriac given to fits of uncontrollable temper and to periods of sexual impotency." Mrs. W-D asked the court to dissolve the marriage as one that had never been validly contracted.

The trial court, after hearing the testimony of both parties, ruled that Mrs. W-D's allegations were true and granted her an annulment. Mr. W-D carried the case to the Court of Appeals of New York, the highest tribunal in that state, where the decision was reversed.[2]

The Court ruled that annulment for fraud under New York law must be based on misrepresentations on matters "vital to the marriage relation-

[2] *Woronzoff-Daschkow* v. *Woronzoff-Daschkow*, 303 N.Y. 506 (1952).

ship," such as a wife's not telling her husband-to-be that she was already pregnant by another man. Another example would be the refusal of one party to fulfill a premarriage promise to follow a civil marriage with a religious ceremony deeply desired by the other party. But premarital falsehoods about character, fortune, health, or "marrying for money" are insufficient to void the marriage. The Court argued that Mr. W-D never promised to "support" Mrs. W-D, and this would have been unnecessary, given her wealth. He *had* earned his living before marriage, whatever might be said of how he had done it. While he lied when he said that he had never taken money from women, "premarital falsehoods much graver than that are insufficient for the judicial voiding of a marriage." As for his husbandly duties, there was no evidence that he refused to perform them, and the parties to a marriage must take one another "in sickness and in health." Thus, the Court ruled that Mr. W-D had performed the "fundamental duties of the marriage relationship" and an annulment for fraud could not be granted.

While regulation of the family was once governed exclusively by church law and church tribunals, most family matters are now regulated by the statutory and court-made law of the state. In addition to questions of valid marriage, annulment, divorce, and support after separation, domestic-relations law deals with the legal and economic relations between husband and wife and with relations between parent and child. The latter range from questions of legitimacy, adoption, and custody upon separation to issues of parental responsibility for the contracts, torts, and crimes of the child. Family law, sociologists suggest, reflects a society's changing morals and values; and debates among judges, legislators, religious leaders, and the public over the rules for marriage, divorce, or adoption are usually heated. Should the state forbid marriages between freely consenting members of different races? Should divorces be permitted for such grounds as mental cruelty or incompatibility or only for such grave offenses as adultery? Should the law require that a child given out for adoption be placed only with a family of the same religion as that of the child's parents —or as that of the mother if the parents were of different faiths?

Law as Assessor of Private Risks and Liabilities

While putting a new roof on an apartment house in Holyoke, Massachusetts, in 1941, the employees of a roofing company set up a tar kettle in the backyard of the property. The kettle was made of heavy metal and stood about three feet high. A smaller pot containing the tar was in the center of the kettle; around this pot, inside the kettle, was the fire that melted the tar and kept it hot.

On the day in question, the roofers finished using the hot tar shortly before noon. They put out the fire and covered the top of the kettle with a flat piece of sheet metal, held down by a slab of wood. At about three-thirty that afternoon, the six-year-old son of one of the tenants was playing on the flat roof of a low garage close to the spot where the tar kettle had been placed. One of the boy's playmates offered him a penny if he would jump on top of the tar kettle from the garage roof. The boy jumped, hit the cover on its side, and fell into the kettle. Though the fire was out, the tar left in the inner pot burned the boy severely, and he died soon afterward. At the time of the accident, the workmen were all occupied on the roof of the apartment house.

The boy's father sued the roofing company for damages, alleging that the child's death had been caused by the negligence of the company in not protecting the kettle more securely or having it guarded. Children were known to play in the yard, and anyone who set up such a potentially dangerous instrument as a kettle of hot tar should have exercised more care than was taken here. As the child's parent, the father asked the court to award damages for the suffering and death caused by the roofing company's creation of such a hazard.

The Supreme Judicial Court of Massachusetts ultimately ruled in favor of the roofer.[3] His men had protected the kettle adequately against children playing on the ground, the Court said, and could not reasonably be expected "to anticipate or to guard against the bare possibility of injury to some child jumping through the cover into the pot from an adjoining roof."

This case shows the role of law in dealing with injuries done to persons and property in society. The law redresses injuries in two ways: through criminal prosecutions, where the government punishes those responsible for causing harm to another in a way forbidden by law, and through *tort* actions, where the injured party brings a private suit for damages (or other special relief) when the injury was either unintentional or intentional but not criminal. Tort law protects not only property and the physical person but intangible rights such as those of privacy and reputation.

As the above decision demonstrates, proof of negligence is at the heart of tort law. In this case, the Massachusetts courts were aware that if unreasonable requirements were imposed on roofers—or on automobile drivers, store owners, airlines, home owners, or newspapers—society would risk being frozen into a costly oversecurity. Tragic as injuries can be, the care required by law must take into account the need for social progress, reasonable precaution, unreasonable conduct by the injured party, the function of damages, and similar considerations.

However, negligence is not always required for an injured party to recover damages, for society can decide that a person who carries on dangerous activities, such as keeping wild animals or storing volatile

---

[3] *Marengo v. Roy*, 318 Mass. 719 (1945).

explosives, must compensate anyone injured through these hazardous instrumentalities. Society can also leave injured parties to be compensated by means other than lawsuit, such as through private insurance or workmen's-compensation programs.

Law as Assessor of Offenses Against Society

The Direct Sales Corporation of Buffalo, New York, a firm that sold drugs by mail at wholesale prices, was indicted in 1941 for conspiracy to violate the Federal Narcotics Act. The indictment charged that, over an extended period of time, the wholesaler had sold morphine to a South Carolina doctor named Tate in quantities so much greater than a doctor could prescribe in normal practice that the wholesaler must have known Tate was distributing the morphine illegally. During 1939, the wholesaler sold Dr. Tate, a practitioner in a small rural community, between 5,000 and 6,000 tablets a month; the average doctor's normal *yearly* supply was between 200 and 400 tablets. The government's evidence showed that Tate, among other shady medical customers of the wholesaler, was selling the morphine at high prices to addicts. (Tate was tried and convicted separately.)

In this case, the basic issue was whether the defendant (the wholesaler) had sufficient criminal intention and knowledge of the offense being committed by Tate to make him guilty of conspiracy with the doctor. At the trial and on appeal, the wholesaler's defense was that the sales were perfectly legal. Dr. Tate had ordered the drugs on the official blanks prescribed by federal law; no maximum amount to be sold to any one doctor was set by law. Since the wholesaler's sales were themselves legal, it was argued, there could be no conspiracy conviction just because Dr. Tate had used the morphine tablets illegally. The wholesaler's lawyers placed heavy reliance on a 1940 case in which the United States Supreme Court had reversed the conviction of a supplier who had sold yeast, sugar, and large cans to men known by the supplier to engage in the illegal manufacture of alcohol. Such knowledge, the Court had said, was not enough to make the supplier part of a conspiracy, even though the supplies sold *were* used to manufacture whisky illegally.

In the drug case, however, the jury found the wholesaler guilty, and the Supreme Court affirmed the conviction in 1943.[4] The justices argued that in the 1940 alcohol supplier's case the goods sold were harmless in themselves and could have been used for purposes other than illegal distilling. But morphine is an inherently dangerous commodity whose distribution to doctors is regulated by law. This put the wholesaler on stricter notice that purchases in suspiciously large quantities would be for

[4] *Direct Sales Corporation v. United States*, 319 U.S. 703 (1943).

illegal purposes. The wholesaler undoubtedly knew that the customers for morphine distributed illegally were drug addicts, and the wholesaler's knowledge of Dr. Tate's excessive purchases constituted enough criminal intention to sustain the conspiracy conviction.

Criminal law, as Professor Herbert Wechsler of Columbia Law School has observed, "is the law on which men place their ultimate reliance for protection against all the deepest injuries that human conduct can inflict on individuals and institutions." Professor Wechsler continues:

> By the same token, penal law governs the strongest force that we permit official agencies to bring to bear on individuals. . . . If penal law is weak or ineffective, basic human interests are in jeopardy. If it is harsh or arbitrary in its impact, it works a gross injustice on those caught within its toils. . . . Nowhere in the entire legal field is more at stake for the community or for the individual.[5]

The major aspects of criminal law are three. (1) The definition of crimes: Is it murder for a doctor to shorten the life of an incurably ill patient at the patient's request? Is it arson to burn down one's own house? (2) The processes of investigation and trial by which guilt or innocence is established: Is telephone-tapping a legitimate police method? What is the proper test for insanity? (3) The punishment that is imposed after conviction: What kind of punishment? How much? For what purposes?

Law as Restrainer of Government and Distributor of Power in the State

In 1951 the Board of Regents of New York, which supervises education throughout the state, composed a special prayer that was recommended to local school officials for recitation during the school day: "Almighty God, we acknowledge our dependence upon Thee, and we beg Thy blessings upon us, our parents, our teachers and our country."

In 1958 in the community of New Hyde Park, a suburb of New York City, the local board of education directed that each class say the prayer aloud at the beginning of school. Children could be excused from saying the prayer upon the written request of their parents and could either stand silently or leave the room during the recitation. School personnel were forbidden to comment on such nonparticipation.

A group of five parents—one Unitarian, two Jews, one Ethical Culturist, and one agnostic—brought suit in the New York courts, challenging the Regents' Prayer as a violation of the United States Constitution. The First Amendment, they noted, forbids the federal government to make any law "respecting an establishment of religion or prohibiting the free exercise thereof"; this prohibition applies to the states through the Fourteenth

---

[5] Herbert Wechsler, "The Challenge of a Model Penal Code," *Harvard Law Review,* Vol. LXV (1952), pp. 1097–98.

Amendment. The protesting parents said that the use of government authority and public funds to institute an official prayer in the schools established a religion as forbidden by the Constitution. (Previous Supreme Court rulings had stated that it was an "establishment of religion" for the state to use its funds or official powers to teach religion in the public schools or compel observance of patriotic ceremonies when these violated the religious principles of the school children.) Furthermore, the introduction of an official prayer could only have divisive effects among children of different faiths and would embarrass those, both believers and nonbelievers, who could not subscribe to the prayer. The New York courts, from the local court to the New York Court of Appeals, upheld the prayer as a valid nondenominational exercise of patriotic and religious character. The parents appealed the case to the Supreme Court of the United States.

The Court had to decide whether the language of the "establishment" clause, the discussions surrounding its adoption, its interpretation by previous Supreme Courts, government practice as to religious observances, and the specific facts of the New York prayer recitation made it a valid public ceremony or an invalid establishment of religion. The majority of the Court held that the practice was unconstitutional.[6] The ceremony was clearly "a religious activity," wrote Justice Hugo Black for the majority; and "it is not part of the business of government to compose official prayers for any group of the American people to recite as part of a religious program carried on by government." In addition, there is an "indirect coercive pressure upon religious minorities to conform" in such a situation.

As often happens, particularly in sensitive constitutional-law cases, the Supreme Court was not unanimous. Justice Potter Stewart wrote a dissent that cited the long history of religious observances carried on in Congress, presided over by American Presidents, marking the daily opening of the Supreme Court, and capped by the addition in 1954 of the phrase "under God" to the nation's pledge of allegiance to the flag. It is misapplying a "great constitutional principle," he argued, to hold that New York establishes an "official religion" when it lets "those who want to say a prayer say it."

At the heart of the case was the conflict between the legislative, or "popular" majority's desire to use public institutions for the observance of dominant ideas and opinions and the desire of minority groups to keep compulsory or discriminatory practices out of the public sector.

The New York school-prayer case is a classic illustration of constitutional law in action. The federal Constitution and the fifty state constitutions grant specific powers to government and also place specific limits on government's authority to act. What the government can and cannot do, and which branch of the government can do what, is thus the heart of

6 *Engel* v. *Vitale*, 370 U.S. 421 (1962).

"Nice kitty can't come in?"

The school-prayer case aroused sharp liberal-conservative disagreement. Here, a liberal comment.

From *Straight Herblock,*
Simon & Schuster, 1964

constitutional law. In the American system, the interpretation of the Constitution's meaning on these issues lies mainly with the courts. In cases properly brought before the courts, judges review the actions of Presidents, Congresses, Interstate Commerce commissioners, governors, city councilmen, and police officers to ensure that all these officials act lawfully—that is, only in pursuance of constitutional power.

THE GROUND RULES OF THE AMERICAN COURTS

The Objectives of Legal Procedure

When the American judicial system deals with civil lawsuits and criminal prosecutions, its procedures are directed toward two different (though complementary) objectives. First, the judicial tribunal seeks to "find" what the facts are. To do so it must do more than decide whose version of an automobile accident, a political riot, or a sit-in demonstration to accept as accurate; it must also decide which facts are legally "relevant" to each case. For example, if Daphne Smith sues Philip Jones for $350 damages, alleging that Jones carelessly hit her motor scooter with his Caramba-35 sports car, there are a host of facts about Jones that could be introduced into evidence. Jones (1) is 46, (2) wears bifocals, (3) sells insurance, (4) is a Mason and a Presbyterian, (5) had a toothache on the day of the accident, (6) hates motor scooters, (7) was thinking about a French movie he had recently seen while he was driving on the day of the accident,

"You stay out of our public schools!"

Here, a conservative comment.

Knox in the Nashville *Banner*

(8) is slightly neurotic and takes tranquilizers, (9) votes Republican, (10) was driving a sports car that needed a motor tune-up, (11) was driving 35 miles per hour in a 20-mile zone, and (12) has reflexes that are a little slower than they used to be when he plays tennis with his son. Some of these facts, such as 4 and 9, would be excluded by the courts as evidence because they are irrelevant; some, such as 10 and 11, are crucial to the decision of the case; and some, such as 2, 5, 6, 7, and 12, may or may not be relevant, depending on what their significance turns out to be at the trial. Fact-finding is thus a complicated and sophisticated problem even in relatively simple cases.

The second function of the judicial tribunal is to determine what the law is. This is not simply a matter of looking up the legal precedents and constitutional and statutory provisions that apply directly to the dispute at hand and applying them to the facts. Often courts find that there are no laws or precedents that cover precisely a new situation that comes before them or that precedents are in basic conflict on a given point. In addition, one of the parties may claim that the statute or official action involved in the case violates the constitution of the state or federal government; this requires the court to rule on the meaning and scope of the constitutional clause that has allegedly been violated and to determine whether the challenged act falls within its scope. Sometimes the court may feel that the legal rule followed by prior courts should be changed, either because the existing rule was originally arrived at through errors of judgment or history or because new socioeconomic conditions seem to require a different rule.

In the American court system, facts are generally supposed to be determined by a jury composed of twelve people drawn from the local community and reflecting its knowledge and opinions. Questions of law, as to both legal rights and courtroom procedure, are the province of the judge. This division of functions lengthens trials, stresses emotional and dramatic appeals, forces the explanation of technical or legal matters in general terms, requires one continuous hearing in open court, and gives community sentiments a significant influence over the legal rules (since a jury can simply find individual or group defendants with whom it sympathizes to be "innocent" even though they clearly committed the acts with which they were charged). Jury trials can sometimes be waived by defendants in criminal cases or by consent of both parties in civil cases. To ensure speed and avoid certain kinds of prejudice, the modern trend is to have many cases tried by the judge alone, who then rules on both the factual and legal issues. Out of the 6,000–7,000 civil cases tried annually in the federal district courts in the middle 1960's, for example, more than half were heard by the judge alone.

The "Case and Controversy" Rule

In the United States, fact-finding and law-determining by courts are reserved for what are known as "genuine cases and controversies." That is, before a dispute can be brought into court, it must be *a real contest between opposing parties over a genuine controversy that is appropriate for judicial resolution and ready for legal decision.*

"A real contest between opposing parties"

In American courtroom trials, the opposing parties themselves determine which witnesses to call, which documents to offer in evidence, what questions to ask opposing witnesses, and what legal claims and supporting arguments to assert. The judge presides as an essentially neutral umpire. He does not make an independent investigation of the facts (as is done in many European countries). Except for an occasional question, he does not conduct examinations of the witnesses, nor does he introduce evidence or control what goes into the lawyers' briefs. This system, the "adversary theory of justice," rests on the assumption that the true facts and the real issues will emerge from the gladiatorial encounter of opposing parties and their trained lawyers in the open courtroom.

In this system, the judge and jury depend on the dedication of each side to produce the best factual presentation and strongest legal arguments for each side. However, there are times when both the plaintiff and the defendant are really on the same side and are seeking to set up a case in which a decision helping their interests will be made without the opposing interests being actively represented. For example, if a state government passes a special tax on manufacturing companies, a stockholder of such a company could sue the company's treasurer to secure a court order restraining payment of the tax on the ground that it is unconstitutional. In such a case the stockholder would be the plaintiff and the treasurer would be the nominal defendant. The treasurer would thus have to "defend" the constitutionality of the tax, something he might do with less than his last measure of devotion and zeal. The *real* parties in such an issue are the company and the state, and our theory about adversary proceedings is that the state must be made a party to the suit if true adverse interest is to aid the judge and jury.

"A controversy appropriate for judicial resolution"

Most of the disputes that arise among individuals, groups, and government agencies can be brought into the courts for adjudication if one of the parties desires a judicial ruling. It is clearly in the best interests of a democratic society to minimize tests of force and revolutions against government by providing ready access to the courts for the airing of grievances and the legal determination of rights. As a result of this liberal policy, the American courts are jammed with all types of lawsuit, involving matters of money and property (a suit to force someone to stop driving his car across the plaintiff's lawn); reputation (a suit to recover money damages from a local newspaper because one of its columnists called the plaintiff a "local Hitler"); constitutional rights (a suit to have a town ordinance forbidding drinking on the beach declared an unconstitutional violation of the residents' liberty); and the distribution of power between government units in a federal system (a suit to decide whether the federal or the state government has the right to determine the racial admission policies of Mrs. Murphy's boarding house).

However, there are some disputes that courts will not decide—that are not considered justiciable questions. Sometimes this is because the issues are really private and not government affairs. You cannot sue your neighbor to make him stop frowning as you go by his yard or to compel him to let his children play with yours. However, many questions that were once considered private and nonjusticiable—such as the hiring policies of employers or the admission policies of theater owners—have been accepted for review by the courts as a result of legislation or changing court doctrines that grant new legal rights or impose new legal obligations.

The other main type of nonjusticiable case is that involving "political questions." In a 1962 decision,[7] the Supreme Court identified two kinds of "political questions." The first involves issues on which the Constitution or laws give final say to a "coordinate political department"—the President

---

[7] *Baker* v. *Carr*, 369 U.S. 186 (1962).

or Congress in the federal system. The leading example is the field of foreign relations, where the courts' lack of secret information, its lack of expertise in diplomatic affairs, and the grave consequences of interfering in delicate international negotiations or agreements all make it wise for the courts to reject lawsuits to halt foreign aid, to force the recognition of Communist China, or to prevent the signing of a test-ban treaty. Has a state properly ratified a proposed constitutional amendment? Do a state's government institutions constitute a "republican form of government" as stipulated by the federal Constitution? These are both questions on which Congress— by accepting the ratification or seating the congressional delegation from the state—has final say.

The second category of political questions, the Supreme Court said, encompasses those in which there is "a lack of judicially discoverable and manageable standards" for solving the problem. The best example in this category used to be the drawing of boundaries by state legislatures for districts to elect state legislators or United States congressmen. In a famous 1946 case,[8] the Supreme Court held that this was a "political thicket" that the federal courts should not enter, since there was no standard for determining the exact degree of equality required by the Constitution for a fairly apportioned system and because the federal courts could not force districting on a fairer basis if the state legislature simply ignored the court's ruling. In the *Baker* v. *Carr* decision, however, the Court overturned this ruling and held that denial of the citizens' rights to equality in voting could be dealt with by the federal courts. Between 1962 and 1964, apportionment systems in more than twelve states were declared unconstitutional, and five states themselves moved to reapportion their legislative districts to provide greater fairness in representation.

"A controversy ripe for adjudication"

The final basic requirement for bringing a lawsuit in the American judicial system is that the case be "ripe" for courtroom adjudication. This means that all steps have been taken, short of going to law, to assert one's rights and that the regular procedures for hearing and appeal before government administrative bodies have been used to give government a chance to know and resolve the problem itself. For instance, a Negro teacher who wishes to sue the State of Mississippi for denying her the right to vote must first apply to the state voting registrar to be registered and be refused for an improper reason. Until she is officially refused (or until the registrar deliberately evades her and refuses to pass on her application), she has not "exhausted her administrative remedies" and is not ready to bring a lawsuit in either the state or the federal courts.

[8] *Colegrove* v. *Green,* 328 U.S. 549 (1946).

In discussing these three requirements for bringing a lawsuit in the American courts, it is important to distinguish the lack of a "genuine case and controversy" from the exercise of "judicial self-restraint." If there is no case and controversy, the court dismisses the complaint. When a court exercises "judicial self-restraint," however, it acknowledges that the rights of opposing parties in an appropriate and ripe controversy are at stake, and it hands down a decision on the merits of the dispute. But the court decides that the action taken in this matter by elected officials of government is not so unreasonable and arbitrary as to be unconstitutional.

Trial and Appellate Stages

Assuming that a genuine case or controversy exists, a dispute can move through two phases of the American judicial process—the *trial* and the *appeal*. There is diversity among the states, but the following is the basic pattern.

A trial can be either a civil lawsuit or a criminal prosecution. Let us take the civil lawsuit between John T. Anderson and the Running Waters Bubbler Company, arising because Anderson feels that the company sold him a defective water bubbler for his office. The case begins when Anderson—called the *plaintiff*—files a *complaint* in the proper state court describing the purchase of the bubbler, its defects, and the refusal of the company to repair it, replace it, or refund his money. Anderson asks the court to award him $175, the original cost of the bubbler. The company will file an *answer* giving its version of the facts or a *motion to dismiss*, which says that even if all the facts stated by Anderson are true he has no legal claim to recovery.

If the case is not dismissed, the lawyers for Anderson and the company will each make an *opening statement*. One judge will usually be presiding at the trial, and there may also be a jury of twelve persons, who were drawn from a larger panel of potential jurors called by law to "do jury duty." (If there is no jury, as we have noted, the judge rules on both the facts and the law in the case.) After the opening statements Anderson presents his case by introducing documentary evidence (the contract of sale for the bubbler, the inspection report of the repairman, and the like) and calling witnesses. The company lawyer has the right to cross-examine these witnesses to bring out conflicts in their stories, show their biases or mistakes in observation, and so on. After Anderson has presented his case, the company can again move to have the case dismissed, this time on the ground that the evidence does not satisfy the burden of proof on the plaintiff to demonstrate his case sufficiently to justify a jury verdict in his favor. If the judge agrees, he will dismiss the case.

But if the dismissal motion is denied, the bubbler company then calls its witnesses and presents its evidence, subject to cross-examination by Anderson's lawyer. After this presentation, either party can move for a *directed*

A Critique of Our Jury System

If a surgeon were to call in twelve men untrained in surgery, give them an hour's talk on the instruments used in appendectomies, and then let them remove a patient's appendix, we would be appalled. Yet similar operations on men's legal rights are performed every day by juries, amateurs entrusted with the use of legal rules which lawyers and judges understand only after long special training.

No sensible business outfit would decide on the competence and honesty of a prospective executive by seeking the judgment of twelve men and women, taken from a group selected almost at random—and from which all those had been weeded out who might have special qualifications for deciding the question. Yet juries chosen in this way are given the job of ascertaining facts on which depend a man's property, his reputation, his very life.

That man may be you, for no one is immune from lawsuits. Your landlord may sue you on your lease.... The driver whose car you bumped one Sunday afternoon may bring an action against you for a broken leg.... If any such case is tried before a jury, the decision will depend on that jury's verdict. The way jury trials are conducted is, then, a pretty serious business for every one of us....

Although trial by jury can be improved, in my opinion it will remain the weakest spot in our judicial system—reform it as we may.

From Appellate Judge Jerome Frank, "Something's Wrong with Our Jury System," *Collier's*, December 1950.

verdict, on the ground that with both sides of the case presented, the jury could not reasonably find for the other side. This directed verdict can then be appealed to a higher court.

If this motion is not granted, each side makes a *closing argument* to the jury, summing up the evidence and making its legal arguments. Then the judge delivers a *charge to the jury*, explaining the legal rules (in this instance about contracts, warranties of good performance, standards of good performance, and the like) and the issues of fact raised by the testimony. Following the charge, the jury retires to the jury room, deliberates on the case, and brings in its verdict. It can find for either the plaintiff or the defendant in general terms, or in certain kinds of case it can specify the amount of money that should be awarded ("$50,000 to the plumber whose arm was injured in the elevator crash"). In civil cases in some states the jury's verdict must be unanimous, or ten out of twelve; in other states only a simple majority is required. The losing party can then move for a new trial, on the ground that some error of procedure or of law was made during the trial, or for a *judgment notwithstanding the verdict*, on the ground that the jury's verdict was against the evidence and the judge should enter an opposite verdict. If these motions fail, the judge fixes the judgment, and the losing party may then move to have the verdict appealed to a higher court, on the ground that substantial legal errors were made at the trial.

There are a few important differences in the criminal prosecution. Let us take the case of *Illinois* v. *Leonard Lightfingers*, involving shoplifting in violation of a state statute against petty larceny. The prosecution is usually initiated by the presentation of the alleged facts by the district attorney to a grand jury (which returns an *indictment*) or, in some states, to a judge (who issues an *information*). Either brings the defendant to trial. Once the case has begun, the stages are substantially the same as in a civil case. However, the burden is on the government to prove the defendant's guilt "beyond a reasonable doubt"—not simply to support a verdict that he "probably" did it. The jury's verdict must always be unanimous. If Lightfingers is found guilty, the sentence is usually set by the judge (though in some states the jury does this) within the terms set by the petty-larceny statute (which might read "two to five years in the state prison and/or $5,000 fine"). The defendant may appeal his conviction, but the government cannot appeal an acquittal, since federal and state constitutions prohibit putting a person twice into jeopardy for the same offense.

In both the state and federal judicial systems, the trial courts are often packed with the drama and power of real life. Spectators often fill the court-room, witnesses will pour out impassioned stories in their "own words," lawyers often conduct probing cross-examinations, stirring appeals are made to the jury or the judge to avenge society or strike blows for liberty or protect the security of investments, and weeks may be consumed in this turbulent trial process.

The *appellate* courts present a very different picture. If the appellate court grants a request for review, each side files a written brief describing the facts of the case, the main points of the trial in the lower court, the legal issues being asserted on appeal, and the controlling legal precedents and policy considerations as each side sees them. The oral argument, which takes place before three or more judges in the appellate courts, rarely lasts more than from one to two hours for a case, even in major constitutional cases. There are no witnesses and no jury, and fresh documentary evidence is usually not produced. The lawyers for the opposing parties present their legal positions in an atmosphere of intellectual analysis. The judges typically interrupt the lawyer often to ask probing questions about the precedents for his position and the public-policy consequences of its adoption by the court.

After the oral argument, the judges retire to hold private conferences about the cases presented to them and to debate the issues. Their decision is reached by majority vote, and the majority usually issues a written opinion "for the court" (written by one judge in the majority) stating their judgment and justifying their views. A judge who does not agree with the majority can record his opposing vote and write a *dissenting opinion;* judges who agree with the decision of the majority but not with its exact line of

"It's nothing personal, Prescott. It's just that a higher court gets a kick out of overruling a lower court."

Drawing by Harris in the *Saturday Review*

reasoning can write a *concurring opinion.* After the first appellate court in the state or federal judicial system has decided an appeal, the losing party can try to carry the appeal to a higher appellate court. If the issues are of major importance and fall within the categories set by state and federal law, the case can go to the highest court in that jurisdiction—state cases to the state supreme court and federal cases to the United States Supreme Court. If a federal constitutional issue is involved, the decision of the state supreme court may be reviewable by the United States Supreme Court.

THE ORGANIZATION OF AMERICAN COURTS

The State Courts

There are dozens of different types of courts in the judicial systems of the fifty states, and each state has developed its own way of initiating trials and hearing lawsuits, providing routes of appeal, and establishing a final court of review. Most states have six types of court, with varying names, forms, and combinations.

Sometimes appointed but usually elected for short terms (from two to four years), the *justices of the peace,* or magistrates, decide minor civil cases (usually when the sum involved does not exceed a specified limit, such as $150 or $250) as well as minor criminal offenses (known as misdemeanors, such as speeding violations). "J.P.'s" usually do *not* have law degrees; their judicial functions, which usually also include performing marriages and issuing fishing permits, are only part of their overall work.

Sometimes called city courts, police courts, or small-claims courts, the *municipal courts* are usually the first judicial courts in the state system. They generally hear civil cases where the sums involved are less than a specified limit (normally $500 to $1,000), and minor criminal offenses, such as violations of city ordinances against littering the streets, disturbing the peace, or failing to provide proper fire exits in a theater.

County courts, or superior courts, are where major civil cases and serious criminal offenses receive their initial hearing. Here trial by jury usually makes its appearance, and here the great bulk of cases is found. It has been estimated that 95 to 98 percent of the cases decided in the county courts are not appealed further. In most states judges are elected to the county or superior courts, with terms averaging from five to ten years.

The modern trend in judicial organization has been to create *courts of special jurisdiction* to deal with such problems as domestic relations, juve-

---

The Importance of the State Courts

The work of the Supreme Court, especially significant, as, of course, it is, must not divert attention from the vital importance of the work of the state courts in the administration of justice. Actually the composite work of the courts of the 50 States probably has greater significance in measuring how well America attains the ideal of equal justice for all. We emphasize this when we remind ourselves that the Supreme Court is intruded between the state courts and litigants in a very narrow class of litigation. That, of course, is the class of cases in which the state courts deal with federal questions. This intrusion is required because the Supreme Court has been assigned the unique responsibility for umpiring our federal system. That role has always been and remains the Court's most important function....

It is important, however, to stress how infinitesimally small is the class of cases as to which the state courts have to share judicial power with the Supreme Court because they raise federal questions. I suppose the state courts of all levels must decide annually literally millions of controversies which involve vital issues of life, liberty, and property of human beings of this Nation. Even the yearly total of decisions handed down by the highest courts of the 50 States must run into the tens of thousands. Yet only a dribble of this vast number raises any federal question.

From Justice William J. Brennan, Jr., speech to the Pennsylvania Bar Association, February 1960.

niles, orphans, and probate (wills and estates), though county courts still handle these matters in some states. The new courts will often have more informal procedures than the county courts; the judges will usually have special training or experience in the problems treated; and special services will be offered by the court (such as counseling and psychiatric interviews).

Sometimes called the appellate division or the district court of appeals, the *intermediate courts of appeals* review appeals from cases decided by the municipal, county, and special courts and sometimes from cases decided by state regulatory agencies. The courts of appeals are geographically distributed through the state, in districts or regions, and judges at this level (whether elected or appointed) usually serve for relatively long terms, averaging from seven to twelve years.

The *state supreme court*, sometimes known as the court of appeals, is the court of last resort in the state judicial system. Cases are accepted for review in this court at the discretion of the judges; only a few classes of case have a *right* to be reviewed in the state high court. Decisions of the high court are final as to the meaning of the state constitution, state statutes, state trial practice, and the like; the United States Supreme Court—as we shall see—will not review these matters unless substantial federal constitutional rights have been denied by the state law or its interpretation.

The Federal Courts

Beside the state courts stand the courts of the United States. Article III of the federal Constitution spells out nine categories of case that may be brought to the federal courts for decision. Two of these categories depend on the nature of the case: eligible for review are cases "arising under this Constitution, the laws of the United States, and treaties made . . . under their authority" or cases involving "admiralty and maritime jurisdiction." The remaining seven categories involve the types of parties who may bring suit. Included are (1) cases "affecting ambassadors . . . ministers and consuls"; (2) cases "between two or more States"; (3) cases "between a State and citizens of another State" (limited by the Eleventh Amendment in 1798 to cases in which a state is the plaintiff); (4) cases "between citizens of different States"; (5) cases "between citizens of the same State claiming lands under grants of different States"; (6) cases "between a State, or the citizens thereof, and foreign States, citizens or subjects"; or (7) cases "to which the United States shall be a party."

At the trial level in the federal system are the federal-district courts, of which there are eighty-six distributed throughout the fifty states, with at least one in each state.[9] From one to eighteen judges are assigned to each district court, according to the amount of legal work arising there. In gen-

[9] There are five additional district courts, one each in the District of Columbia, Puerto Rico, the Canal Zone, Guam, and the Virgin Islands.

eral, a single federal-district judge hears motions and presides at trials, but if a party challenges the constitutionality of a federal statute three district judges will hear the case.

District-court business divides into civil and criminal cases. *Civil cases* (about 79,000 cases in 1966) derive from private disputes between citizens of different states involving $100,000 or more and suits in which the federal government is a party. The major types of case dealt with in the federal courts involve matters of contract (insurance claims, suits under defense contracts); torts (for injuries sustained on ships, airplanes, collisons with mail trucks); real property (leases or sales of federal land); and statutory actions (arising under federal statutes regulating antitrust, patents, taxes, civil rights).

Criminal cases (about 29,300 cases in 1966) involve prosecution of individuals or organizations for violations of federal laws. The violations most frequently prosecuted are embezzlement and fraud against the United States, liquor-law violations, interstate auto theft, and larceny. Other major violations include subversive activities, illegal use of narcotics, and forgery.

The Importance of the District-Court Judge

The District Court for the District of Massachusetts seems to me to offer at least as wide a field for judicial service as the Court of Appeals for the First Circuit. The District Court gives more scope to a judge's initiative and discretion. His width of choice in sentencing defendants is the classic example. But there are many other instances. In civil litigation a District Judge has a chance to help the lawyers frame the issues and develop the facts so that there may be a meaningful and complete record. He may innovate procedures promoting fairness, simplification, economy, and expedition. By instructions to juries and, in appropriate cases, by comments on the evidence he may help the jurors better to understand their high civic function. He is a teacher of parties, witnesses, petitioners for naturalization, and even casual visitors to his court. His conduct of a trial may fashion and sustain the moral principles of the community. More even than the rules of constitutional, statutory, and common law he applies, his character and personal distinction, open to daily inspection in his courtroom, constitute the guarantees of due process.

Admittedly, the Court of Appeals stands higher than the District Courts in the judicial hierarchy, and Congress by attaching a larger compensation to the office of Circuit Judge has expressed its view of the relative importance of the two courts. Yet not all informed persons would concur in that evaluation. My revered former chief, Judge Augustus N. Hand, always spoke of his service in the District Court as being more interesting as well as more revealing of his qualities, and more enjoyable, than his service in the Court of Appeals.

From U.S. District Judge Charles E. Wyzanski, Jr., letter to Senator Leverett Saltonstall of Massachusetts, January 1959.

After a civil or criminal case has been determined by a federal-district court, the losing party can appeal the decision to the United States Court of Appeals. The United States is divided into eleven judicial circuits, each with its own courts of appeals composed of from three to nine judges and a chief judge. Here cases are usually heard by three judges, though in particularly important cases all the judges in a court of appeals will sit *en banc*. Cases come to the courts of appeals not only from the district courts but also from regulatory agencies, such as the National Labor Relations Board or the Federal Securities and Exchange Commission. By congressional statute regulatory-agency cases go directly to the courts of appeals, because the agencies are presumed to have determined the facts already, and the role of the courts of appeals is to see that no errors of law or procedure have occurred.

In 1966 the courts of appeals disposed of more than 6,500 cases, the majority of which came from the district courts and the regulatory agencies. Only a few started directly under special statutes. In 1966, 1,400 of the total were appeals in criminal cases, an increase of 20 percent over the preceding year.

The Supreme Court

At the top of the federal judicial system is the United States Supreme Court, the final judicial authority on federal law and on disputes over the meaning of the United States Constitution. "The judicial power of the United States," says Article III of the Constitution, "shall be vested in one Supreme Court, and in such inferior courts as the Congress may from time to time . . . establish." The number of justices on the Supreme Court has been a matter for regulation by Congress. Between 1787 and 1869 the Court's size varied from five to ten. Congressional motives for changing its size were often frankly political. Since 1869, however, we have had a nine-man court. In 1937, after the Court had struck down a series of major New Deal statutes, President Franklin Roosevelt sponsored legislation to provide "youth and energy" on the Court by giving the President authority to appoint a new justice whenever an incumbent justice reached the age of seventy and did not retire. This plan would have authorized a possible maximum of eighteen justices. F.D.R.'s opponents attacked the plan as "Court-packing," and its resounding defeat in 1937 suggests that a nine-man Court has become an established political tradition.

The Supreme Court has two kinds of jurisdiction. In cases involving foreign diplomats or involving a state as a party, the Supreme Court has *original jurisdiction*. This means that the justices get the case directly and hear it as a court of "first instance," finding out what the facts are as well as determining the law. Only a trickle of cases today go directly to the justices under original jurisdiction. These cases, however, are often legally important and politically explosive. In recent years the Court has decided

Figure 14–1   The Federal Judicial System

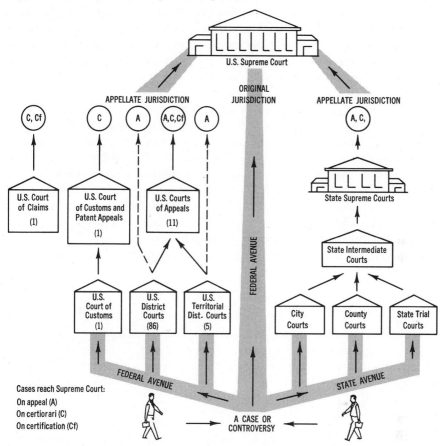

suits between states over land boundaries, water rights, and taxing authority, involving hundreds of millions of dollars—such as the conflict between Arizona and California over water rights to the Colorado River.[10] Important litigation between the federal government and states in the last three decades has included such matters as the fight between the federal and state governments for title to the rich oil deposits under the tideland waters off California, Texas, Louisiana, and Florida. In 1966 the Court sustained the major provisions of the Voting Rights Act of 1965 under its original jurisdiction.[11] This was the only case of this type to be dealt with by the Court during the 1965–66 term.

In all other cases, the Supreme Court has *appellate jurisdiction*—that is, it reviews decisions that have already been made by trial courts and by lower appellate tribunals. As Figure 14–1 indicates, there are two main ave-

[10] *Arizona* v. *California,* 373 U.S. 546 (1963).
[11] *South Carolina* v. *Katzenbach,* 383 U.S. 301 (1966).

nues of appellate jurisdiction, one for cases from the federal-district courts and courts of appeals and the other for cases from the state courts. Since the Supreme Court is the final tribunal in the federal judicial system, its review of lower federal-court cases is logical and necessary, and it has given rise to little dispute in our constitutional history. Supreme Court review of state-court decisions, on the other hand, has been highly controversial, as Chapter 16 will discuss.

The Supreme Court's appellate jurisdiction was left by Article III to be set up "with such exceptions, and under such regulations as the Congress shall make." Under this congressional power, successive judiciary acts since 1789 have defined the rules by which cases are brought to the Supreme Court; in particular these acts have tried to confine Supreme Court review to those appeals that are truly important for developing a consistent and effective constitutional law for the nation. Yet this congressional power is also the lance with which Congress can threaten the Court when the justices hand down rulings that congressmen bitterly oppose.

The only punitive exercise of this kind occurred in 1869. The Habeas

---

The Appellate Role of the Supreme Court

The Supreme Court is not, and never has been, primarily concerned with the correction of errors in lower court decisions. In almost all cases within the Court's appellate jurisdiction, the petitioner has already received one appellate review of his case. The debates in the Constitutional Convention make clear that the purpose of the establishment of one supreme national tribunal was, in the words of John Rutledge of South Carolina, "to secure the national rights & uniformity of Judgmts." The function of the Supreme Court is, therefore, to resolve conflicts of opinion on federal questions that have arisen among lower courts, to pass upon questions of wide import under the Constitution, laws, and treaties of the United States, and to exercise supervisory power over lower federal courts. If we took every case in which an interesting legal question is raised, or our *prima facie* impression is that the decision below is erroneous, we could not fulfill the Constitutional and statutory responsibilities placed upon the Court. To remain effective, the Supreme Court must continue to decide only those cases which present questions whose resolution will have immediate importance far beyond the particular facts and parties involved. Those of you whose petitions for certiorari are granted by the Supreme Court will know, therefore, that you are, in a sense, prosecuting or defending class actions; that you represent not only your clients, but tremendously important principles, upon which are based the plans, hopes, and aspirations of a great many people throughout the country.

From Fred M. Vinson, "Work of the Federal Courts," *Supreme Court Reporter,* 1949.

Corpus Act of 1867 authorized the Supreme Court to hear direct appeals from military actions in Southern states during Reconstruction if the plaintiff filed a writ of habeas corpus. William McCardle, a Southerner being held by federal army officers in Mississippi contended that his imprisonment was improper because the Reconstruction Acts were unconstitutional.[12] Afraid that the Court might declare the Reconstruction program unconstitutional, Congress repealed the Court's jurisdiction under the 1867 act. The case was then dismissed by the Supreme Court, stating that the removal of its jurisdiction was a valid exercise of Congress' authority under Article III.

The Court has never said that Congress could shut off appellate review completely or eliminate appeals from a given class of cases, but the assumption that Congress might be able to do so has prompted several efforts in the past decade to eliminate appellate jurisdiction in specific areas in which the Court has taken an unpopular stand. These efforts are hampered by the prospect of the chaos that would be created by allowing the Supreme Court only original jurisdiction, leaving fifty state supreme courts and eleven federal circuits all to apply different rules of law. The force of political tradition will also help to protect the Court's appellate jurisdiction on such matters unless it acts in total disregard of political realities.

The Supreme Court's appellate jurisdiction is made up of obligatory and discretionary cases. *Obligatory* cases come either on appeal from state or federal courts (where it is claimed that federal constitutional rights were violated) or by a little-used procedure called *certification*, in which a federal court of appeals certifies a new and difficult question directly to the Supreme Court for decision. In practice, however, the Court can dismiss cases that come to it on appeal if it finds that they do not present a "substantial federal question"; so the "obligatory" jurisdiction of the Court is really discretionary. *Discretionary* cases are presented by *petitions for certiorari*, which ask the justices to examine a state or federal court's record in a case for errors. The Court can simply refuse to grant certiorari if it thinks the claim has no merit or if it does not want to consider a case at the time.

During the 1965–66 term, 2,683 cases were filed in the Supreme Court. Of these, 2,185 were denied review, and 342 were decided on their merits. The Court handed down 107 decisions, with full opinions, of which 41 were constitutional issues and 66 nonconstitutional issues. As Chief Justice Fred Vinson once explained, the Supreme Court does *not* sit to provide one last opportunity for litigants to retry their cases; the function of the Court is to interpret the Constitution of the United States, to assure uniformity of judgments in the federal and state courts on these principles, and to oversee the federal legal system.

The Court's discretionary jurisdiction allows it to concentrate on the important issues that demand time and care. Cases decided with full opinions

---

[12] Ex parte *McCardle*, 7 Wall. 506 (1869).

Keppler in *Puck*   Our Overworked Supreme Court

An 1885 cartoon shows that the Supreme Court's calendar was crowded even then.

by the Court provide the primary legal and educative impact of the justices on the political process. In its 1965–66 term, for example, the Court explained why payment of a poll tax as a prerequisite to voting violated the equal-protection clause of the Fourteenth Amendment; [13] why statements obtained from a suspect during "custodial interrogation" are inadmissible unless the accused person has been informed of his rights to be silent during all stages of the investigation and to be represented by counsel; [14] why the 1950 Subversive Activities Control Board provision requiring registration by each member of communist-action organizations violated the member's privilege against self-incrimination; [15] why the "two-for-the-price-of-one" advertisement of a paint company was deceptive under Section V of the Federal Trade Commission Act; [16] why the conviction of Negro civil-rights demonstrators for breach of peace at a Louisiana library violated their rights to free expression; [17] and why a publisher violated the federal obscenity statute by mailing an "obscene" advertisement of his magazine, even though the Court did not find the magazine itself to be obscene.[18]

[13] *Harper* v. *Virginia State Board of Elections,* 383 U.S. 663 (1966).
[14] *Miranda* v. *Arizona,* 384 U.S. 436 (1966).
[15] *Albertson* v. *Subversive Activities Control Board,* 382 U.S. 70 (1965).
[16] *Federal Trade Commission* v. *Mary Carter Paint Company,* 382 U.S. 46 (1965).
[17] *Brown* v. *Louisiana,* 383 U.S. 131 (1966).
[18] *Ginzburg* v. *United States,* 383 U.S. 463 (1966).

THE RELATION OF LAW TO POLITICS

The institution of judicial review has made the American legal system an inescapable part of the nation's political process. This statement may appear to contradict the common American assumption that "politics" should halt at the courtroom door in both "private law" (contracts and torts) and "public law" (governmental action), but in fact both statements are valid. That the rulings of the courts should be free from the dictation of political party leaders or from political favoritism is not only the ideal of our system but very largely our practice. There are, however, legitimate ways in which the courts interact with the political order.

First, the courts are part of the continuous process of forming public policy. New York passes a law on school prayer; school administrators for the state and local district apply the law; then some parents challenge it in court. In this case the court strikes down the law. The legislature and school districts react; a new religious exercise may be drafted and instituted; an attempt may be made to secure a constitutional amendment to allow religious exercises in public schools; or a campaign may be launched in Congress to limit the appellate jurisdiction of the Supreme Court on school religious-practice cases. These new measures will in turn be presented to the courts for review, and the courts' response to them will produce new legislation, new administrative practices, and new political alignments and intergroup struggles. The role of the courts as a participant rather than the ultimate arbiter of the political struggle becomes even clearer when the courts are only interpreting statutes or executive regulation; then, the legislatures and executives can alter or overturn the courts' rulings simply by amending their own actions.

Second, the courts can enlarge or narrow the arena of political decision. In matters such as civil rights, labor-union control, or antitrust laws, the courts often decide which level of government—federal, state, or local—has primary jurisdiction in determining the rights and duties of groups and individuals. If Little Rock is supreme, Negroes will attend formerly all-white schools; if the State of Arkansas is supreme, the schools will remain segregated; if the United States has primary authority, the schools will be desegregated. By defining the arena of struggle, the court directly affects who wins, since the size of the arena determines the relative power of business groups, civil-rights groups, or labor groups in relation to the governing authorities.

Another way in which the courts affect the political process is by altering the timing of political struggle. The courts can freeze political disputes for several years while they are being considered in the courts, or they can prevent elected officials from taking action while new statutes or constitutional amendments are secured to supply the authority denied by courts. This may be a good thing, requiring a reform movement or a repressive movement to go back to the electorate for a mandate or to redraft its key measures in more careful terms. It may also be harmful, causing serious problems to go unsettled for a dangerously long time or hampering reform movements in achieving social progress while the public is attentive and enthusiastic about reform.

SUMMARY

Law can be classified in many ways, but the most useful way to examine its role in the political system is through a functional analysis of how law gives order and predictability to American affairs. Some major functions of law are the regulation of property and the marketplace, the regulation of family and social relationships, the assessment of private risks and liabilities, the determination of offenses against society, and the restraint of government power.

The ground rules of the American courts are directed toward two basic objectives for civil lawsuits and criminal prosecutions alike: determining the facts of the case and ascertaining what the law is. In order to be heard in court, a case must represent a real contest between opposing parties over a genuine controversy that is appropriate for judicial resolution and ripe for legal decision at the time. Under this "case and controversy" doctrine, American courts have refused to decide cases manufactured by two friendly parties (because this runs counter to our adversary theory of justice); personal disputes that are not subject to legal determination; and "political" issues.

Cases that meet the case-and-controversy requirements are examined by the courts first in a trial stage and then, if the losing party wishes to pursue the matter and has legal grounds for doing so, in an appellate proceeding. After the appellate court has given its ruling, the loser can try to take his case to the next higher appellate court. Generally speaking, the highest court for state cases is the state supreme court; the highest for federal cases is the United States Supreme Court. But when major federal constitutional issues are involved, a decision by the state supreme court may be reviewed by the U.S. Supreme Court.

As this procedure suggests, there are myriad state courts within the fifty states. But six types are most common: on the lowest rung, the justices of the peace; then the municipal courts, the county or superior courts, the courts of special jurisdiction, the intermediate courts of appeals; and, finally, the state supreme court. The primary route of judicial action is from the county court to the state supreme court.

Standing beside the state courts are the federal courts, which offer a separate judicial avenue open to nine categories of cases specified in the national Constitution, such as cases between two or more states, cases to which the United States government is a party, or cases between citizens of different states. At the bottom of the federal ladder are the eighty-six district courts scattered through the fifty states, which handle both civil and criminal cases. The vast bulk of federal cases receive final settlement at this level. But some cases are appealed to one of the eleven federal courts of appeals.

At the top of both the federal and state systems stands the United States Supreme Court, which has original jurisdiction over certain types of case as well as general power of review over decisions by the federal courts of appeals and over decisions of state supreme courts on cases that raise questions of federal constitutional law. The Supreme Court's primary work is in reviewing the cases that come up from the lower courts, rather than in deciding cases of original jurisdiction. Though the Supreme Court justices try to accept only cases raising the most important constitutional questions, the Court still passes on an extraordinary range of issues each year.

Thus, the American courts play an important—and legitimate—political role in a society with a written constitution and a federal structure. The instrument of judicial review allows the courts to influence the political system in several ways, and the next chapter will examine further the implications of this court power. What is important to note here is that, although Americans want their courts to be free of "politics" in the sense of party dictates or political favoritism, our culture has always supported the larger political role of the courts in our system.

JUDICIAL REVIEW AND THE POLITICAL PROCESS

15

*Chapter 14 has described the ground rules of
our judicial system as a significant arena of
American politics. This chapter will examine
the primary instrument through which the
courts influence our political system: judicial
review. What major theories of law guide
judicial decision-making? How did the courts
develop their powers of judicial review? The last
section analyzes the role of the Supreme Court
—the fountainhead of judicial review in America.
Which aspects of its role have remained
constant and which have changed since the
"constitutional revolution of 1937"? What
major trends in American political life have
triggered these changes?*

BASIC THEORIES OF LAW

One of the most important keys to understanding the American system of judicial review is the classic debate over the nature of law. In democratic systems, law embodies two values that are in constant tension. On the one hand, law is the process that gives stability to personal and property relations in a society, providing continuity with the past and permitting citizens to predict the probable legal consequences of their actions. Law is thus an instrument of the status quo. On the other hand, law must provide for social change, not only through the general statutes passed by elected organs of government but through the specific rulings of courts and administrative agencies. Law must therefore be an instrument of transition, adjusting older rules to the changing power relations and shifting ideals of society.

Still another tension is built into legal systems. The ideal of judging is that all those who come before the courts to assert their rights or defend their interests are entitled to equal treatment under the existing rules. The law must not distinguish between rich and poor, white and black, Gentile and Jew, liberal and conservative, pacifist and militarist, Northerner and Southerner. But to adhere to equality, especially in the public-law sector, judges and other lawmakers must have some concept of justice that defines the relations of individuals, groups, society, and the state. By what standards is justice measured, and what happens when statute law or constitutional law conflicts with the judge's deep conviction that the law as enacted is unjust?

While the lawmaker's allegiance to party, economic interest groups, religion, race, and class will affect his view of these conflicts, he will also be guided by some basic approach to the legal system—a unifying idea about its nature, purposes, and possibilities. Men have debated theories of law for thousands of years. Over six hundred years ago, the clash of theories was recorded in a fourteenth-century law case. After the trial had been completed in the royal court of Common Bench, one of the presiding judges asked, "Plaintiff, will you say anything else . . . ?" Thorpe, the plaintiff's lawyer, replied, "I think you will do as others have done in the same [type of] case, or else we do not know what the law is." One justice replied, "It is the will of the Justices." "No," interjected the Chief Justice, "law is that which is right." [1] Today, the main contending theories of law can be grouped under three headings: the *natural-law* concept, the *positive-law* concept, and the *sociological* or *developmental* concept.

---

[1] *Langbridge's Case*, 19 Edw. III 375. Quoted in Harold Berman, *The Nature and Functions of Law* (Brooklyn: Foundation Press, 1958), pp. 21–22.

481

The Natural-Law Tradition

The natural-law tradition is as ancient as the Greek philosophers and as modern as the Nuremberg trials of the Nazi leaders for "crimes against mankind." It assumes that there are fundamental and absolute concepts of law and justice that men can know and apply to their political and social affairs. The validity of a legal system, and of every decision taken under it, rests on the harmony of its rules and regulations with the principles of natural law. One main school of natural law is religious and rests on man's presumed ability to discover fundamental, rational principles of right and wrong by which to test man-made laws. In this way, man participates in God's divine reason. Another school, sometimes called "rationalistic natural law," sees natural law as flowing from a rational universe and from man's self-developed moral codes. But both schools of natural law would agree that a constitutional clause that forbade anyone to practice anything but the national religion, or a systematic national program to destroy a racial or ethnic group, or the replacement of independent courts with a party-tribunal system would violate all natural-law standards. The essential point is that a higher morality limits all powers of government.

The Positive Theory of Law

Positivism, the second major theory of law, maintains that law is what the supreme political authority in the state commands and can enforce. While positivism sometimes cites a moral justification for its position—that it brings order out of the violent relations of men and protects property— the basic view of the positivist is that law must be separated from standards of morality set by authorities other than the sovereign. This criterion makes for certainty about what is binding law and provides stability by rejecting any outside test of validity. The role of judges according to positivist theory is to apply the laws of the sovereign, not to substitute their own notions about what is wise.

The positivist theory can be used by almost any political system. In a theocratic state, positive law would be the command of the church authorities; in a monarchy, the will of a king; in a totalitarian system, the command of the leader; in a democracy, the acts of the elected government. Positive law can thus be reactionary, reformist, or even revolutionary. Its essential point is that human political institutions are the sole source and measure of law.

The Sociological Theory of Law

A third basic theory defines law as a gradual, organic growth of rules developed by men in specific societies in order to adjust conflicting interests peacefully. Law is viewed as growing out of family relations in primitive societies, then out of tribal customs, and so forth. It develops stage by stage in response to changes in technology and the organization of society. The moral aspirations of the society as well as the particular policies of the sovereign are embodied in law.

Sociological theory also stresses the realistic analysis of how lawgivers and law-interpreters adjust conflicting interests in society. When legislation is proposed to create a federal loyalty program, sociological theory sees both legislators and judges weighing the need of the state to protect itself from internal subversion against the equal need of the democratic state for freedom of expression and social criticism. Thus sociological theories probe the economic, ideological, psychological, or class factors that influence judges and try to bring these into clear focus, so that society can decide whether these factors are the desired criteria to be applied by the judges.

The essence of sociological theory, therefore, is that law is a product of particular societies and an instrument for reconciling conflicting interests.

Theories of Law and the American Legal Tradition

Each of the three theories in fact represents an idealized concept of law rather than what law actually was or is. In democratic societies, the three ideas tend to be blended inseparably in popular attitudes toward law. Positive law is seen as the normal foundation of statutory and administrative law; sociological analysis is used to describe and criticize the decisions of the lawmakers and law-interpreters, and natural law is invoked as an ideal—especially in the courts—by those who believe their rights have been fundamentally violated. Positive law stresses stability, order, and the legitimacy of authority unless overruled by political processes. Natural law stresses morality, reason, and restraint on the uses of power. Sociological theory stresses realism, criticism of law, and the need to accommodate both positive and natural law by adjusting conflicting interests in light of the best historical and political experience of society.

American law from colonial times to the nuclear age has been shaped by all three juristic theories. Natural-law ideas in the writings of John Locke, Thomas Jefferson, and Tom Paine, among others, were a major ingredient in America's revolutionary ideology. Statements that rulers could not abridge the "rights of mankind" and the "laws of Nature and Nature's God" permeated the major documents of our colonial era. Once the nation was established the United States Supreme Court began to interpret many of the broad clauses of the Constitution protecting individual rights—"due process of law," "equal protection of the law," "deprivation of liberty," and "obligation of contracts"—as shorthand terms for a body of natural-law principles that could be used by judges to restrain offending government officials.

At the same time, the idea that even the Constitution and the Supreme Court cannot justify violations of "higher law" has been another significant legacy of the natural-law heritage. No free man need obey "a covenant with Hell," the antislavery leaders said of the Constitution after the Dred Scott decision in 1857 seemed to give permanence to slavery. Today, freedom riders and sit-in demonstrators against segregation often maintain that "unjust" laws need not be obeyed, and these demonstrators are prepared to violate segregation rules even if the Supreme Court should not uphold the right of Negroes to conduct such demonstrations.

The positivist tradition in the United States can be seen in the nineteenth-century movement to limit the common-law rules inherited from British law and applied by "aristocratic" judges. State legislatures adopted codes spelling out rules for major legal issues of property and procedure. These codes represented an attempt not only to rationalize the American legal system but also to protect the political and legal reforms of the Jacksonian movement from the hostile interpretations of conservative judges. The positivist tradition in American law is also reflected in the assumption by many Americans that law can legislate morality in matters ranging from the drinking of liquor and respect for religion to the elimination of "dangerous" ideas about politics, economics, or society.

Finally, the sociological contribution to American law can be seen in the writings of Oliver Wendell Holmes, Jr., Roscoe Pound, Jerome Frank, and a steady stream of influential legal thinkers who changed the entire tone and outlook of American law between 1900 and the present. Their powerful analyses of how judges really decide cases, how flexible the Constitution must be in the face of new national crises, and the basic role of legislation in adjusting conflicting group interests have become the common language of law taught in the law schools and understood broadly by the population.

The three legal theories are also at work in the day-to-day operations of lawmaking at the legislative level in the United States. When a city council considers a fair-housing law, advocates of legal guarantees of racial equality in housing will clash with defenders of the individual's right to dispose of his house or to rent his apartment as he chooses, and the legislative debate will typically ring with appeals to "higher rights" or "fixed constitutional limits" or "balancing the interests." But it is in courts that this debate presents itself most often.

The great majority of American judges are obviously molded by their times in their choice of juristic theories. In the eighteenth century, when Nature and Nature's God were invoked to justify the creation of a new governmental system, all factions within the Supreme Court talked in terms of judges who applied the great principles of natural law that had been written into the Constitution. Today, when judges are evaluated in a climate of legal realism, they must also consider whether subjectivity and

judicial manipulation are influencing their opinions on constitutional decisions. Indeed, judges attack one another directly and forcibly for "judicial
legislation." Thus, while a few judges may transcend their eras, the juristic
theories of most judges reflect the dominant attitudes of society toward
the role of law.

We must remember of course that most judges—at least some of the
time—are primarily influenced by factors other than juristic theory: their
own socioeconomic background, their ideological stance, their relation to
the factions of the Court, their own political ambitions, their attitude
toward minority groups, and their policy judgments on specific legislative
programs. Only a few rare spirits are able to govern themselves consistently
by a general juristic theory. Nevertheless, the concepts of self-control and
impartiality remain the ideal of our legal system and the standard of
measurement for great judges.

JUDICIAL REVIEW: THE AMERICAN JUDGE
AS PHILOSOPHER–KING

Theories of law and of judicial decision-making become matters of great
political impact when the courts exercise their special power of *judicial
review*. Judicial review is the power of a court to inquire whether a law,
executive order, or other official action conflicts with the written constitution and, if the court concludes that it does, to declare it unconstitutional
and void. Two quite different situations must be distinguished: (1) the
power of courts to pass on the acts of coordinate branches of the same
government, such as federal courts judging acts of Congress or actions of
the Secretary of Defense, or the Illinois courts passing on the validity of
Illinois statutes or of executive orders of the governor; (2) the power of
the federal courts to determine whether acts of a state branch of
government conflict with the federal Constitution. In the first instance,
judges are given special authority over the acts of elected branches in the
same government. In the second, judges apply the law of all the people of
all the states—the federal Constitution—to acts of a lesser sovereignty, the
member state. A famous comment of Justice Oliver Wendell Holmes, Jr.,
in 1913 explained the significance of this difference: "I do not think the
United States would come to an end if we lost our power to declare an
Act of Congress void. I do think the Union would be imperiled if we
could not make that declaration as to the laws of the several states."

Supreme Court review of state-court decisions has been a stormy issue
since the days of Thomas Jefferson. States'-rights advocates contended in a
series of famous cases during the first decades of the Republic that in

Judicial Review: A Narrow Interpretation

The Supreme Court too often has tended to adopt the role of policy-maker without proper judicial restraint. We feel this is particularly the case in both of the great fields we have discussed—namely, the extent and extension of the federal power, and the supervision of state action by the Supreme Court by virtue of the Fourteenth Amendment. In the light of the immense power of the Supreme Court and its practical non-reviewability in most instances no more important obligation rests upon it, in our view, than that of careful moderation in the exercise of its policy-making role.

We are not alone in our view that the Court, in many cases arising under the Fourteenth Amendment, has assumed what seems to us primarily legislative powers.... We do not believe that either the framers of the original Constitution or the possibly somewhat less gifted draftsmen of the Fourteenth Amendment ever contemplated that the Supreme Court would, or should, have the almost unlimited policy-making powers which it now exercises. It is strange, indeed, to reflect that under a constitution which provides for a system of checks and balances and of distribution of power between national and state governments one branch of one government—the Supreme Court—should attain the immense, and in many respects, dominant, power which it now wields.

From *The Conference of Chief Justices: Report of the Committee on Federal-State Relationships as Affected by Judicial Decisions*, August 1958.

a federal union with sovereign states, each state must have the final word on matters that lie within its territorial borders. But the Supreme Court held that where a "substantial federal question" is determined by a state court, the need to protect the citizen's federal constitutional rights and to provide uniform interpretation of the Constitution throughout the Union required the United States Supreme Court to pass upon these questions. The Court was supported by the language of the Constitution in Article VI, which provides that the Constitution and federal statutes and treaties "shall be the supreme law of the land" and that "judges in every state shall be bound thereby, anything in the Constitution or laws of any State to the contrary notwithstanding."

While federal judicial review of state-court decisions is grounded in the explicit language of Article VI, nothing in the Constitution specifies that the Supreme Court has the power to declare acts of Congress or the President unconstitutional. However, the Constitution uses language that supports judicial review as a "logical consequence" of our constitutional system. This suggestive language is found in the statement of Article VI that federal laws made "in pursuance" of the Constitution are the "supreme law of the land" and in the power given the Court by Article III to determine "all cases . . . arising under this Constitution. . . ."

In the famous case of *Marbury* v. *Madison* (1803),[2] when the Supreme Court first exercised the power of judicial review of national acts, Chief Justice John Marshall's opinion for the Court relied on three key arguments: (1) a written constitution is superior to all acts of government made under it; (2) our government is a system bound by law; and (3) the sworn duty of federal judges is to follow the Constitution, enforce only constitutional laws, and determine which law prevails when there is a conflict.

Actually, Marshall's argument is not without its weak points. When there is a genuine disagreement between the elected branches of the federal government and the Court about the constitutionality of a measure, why is the judge's oath more sacred than that of legislators and executives? Why shouldn't each branch be the final judge as to the constitutionality of measures under its own jurisdiction? Why should the expertness of judges in reading legal documents make them expert in construing a constitution, which represents both a framework of government and a division of power in a system? Most of Marshall's critics were willing to concede that legislative and executive acts affecting the *judicial* branch (as in *Marbury* v. *Madison*) could be resisted by the Court if found to be unconstitutional; but, as Senator Benjamin Wade of Ohio was to say in

[2] 1 Cranch 137 (1803).

Judicial Review: A Broad Interpretation

It is emphatically the province and duty of the judicial department to say what the law is. Those who apply the rule to particular cases must of necessity expound and interpret that rule. If two laws conflict with each other, the courts must decide on the operation of each. So if a law be in opposition to the constitution; if both the law and the constitution apply to a particular case, so that the court must either decide that case conformably to the law, disregarding the constitution, or conformably to the constitution, disregarding the law, the court must determine which of these conflicting rules governs the case. This is of the very essence of judicial duty. If, then, the courts are to regard the constitution, and the constitution is superior to any ordinary act of the legislature, the constitution, and not such ordinary act, must govern the case to which they both apply....

The judicial power of the United States is extended to all cases arising under the constitution. Could it be the intention of those who gave this power to say that in using it the constitution should not be looked into? That a case arising under the constitution should be decided without examining the instrument under which it arises? This is too extravagant to be maintained.

In some cases, then, the constitution must be looked into by the judges. And if they can open it at all, what part of it are they forbidden to read or to obey?

From Chief Justice John Marshall, *Marbury* v. *Madison*, 1803.

1858: "I deny the doctrine that Judges have any right to decide the law of the land for every department of this Government."

From Marshall's day to the present, the question of whether the Framers really intended the Court to have this power has been warmly debated. The two most persuasive statements on the founding of judicial review—in the works of Professors Charles Beard and Edward S. Corwin—agree that judicial review is justified, but for different reasons. Beard searched through the records of the Constitutional Convention and some contemporaneous sources and concluded that twenty-five of the fifty-five men at the convention, including the leaders at that meeting, "favored or at least accepted some form of judicial control." The idea was in close harmony with the dominant purpose of the Framers, which was to set up a governmental system that would protect property interests and provide checks upon either monarchy or democracy. Corwin, however, has argued that nothing in the Constitution represents the judgment of a majority of the convention on what to do about judicial review of national legislation. Rather, Corwin felt, judicial review developed from the strong popular desire to check the abuses of legislative power by the state legislatures after 1787 and from the logical unfolding of the kind of government that the Constitution had called into being.

Today, of course, hardly any commentators seriously contend that the Court should give up a "usurped power." But critics of the Court's "seizure" of authority are particularly concerned about *how* the Court is using this far-reaching power at any given moment. As for the Supreme Court, it refers to this power with majestic assurance today. In 1958, when the Court struck down its eighty-second congressional provision, Chief Justice Earl Warren discussed the Court's authority in this tone:

> We are mindful of the gravity of the issue inevitably raised whenever the constitutionality of an Act of the National Legislature is challenged. . . . [But] the Judiciary has the duty of implementing the constitutional safeguards that protect individual rights. . . . The provisions of the Constitution are . . . vital, living principles that authorize and limit governmental powers in our nation. They are the rules of government. When the constitutionality of an Act of Congress is challenged in this Court, we must apply these rules.[3]

The impact of judicial review on our political process can be most clearly seen by examining the constant and the changing elements in the role of the Supreme Court since 1790. The impact of Supreme Court rulings on politics is reflected in the continuing controversy over the Court's proper role, and the impact of political change on the Court is reflected in turn in those aspects of its role that have undergone basic change since 1937.

[3] *Trop* v. *Dulles*, 356 U.S. 86 (1958).

THE SUPREME COURT: FOUNTAINHEAD
OF JUDICIAL REVIEW

The United States Supreme Court presents students of American government with a challenging paradox. On the one hand, some liberal critics of the Supreme Court have long described it as our most archaic and aristocratic political institution. Nine men—who were never elected to their office, whose terms are for life, and who can be removed only for "high crimes and misdemeanors"—are authorized to declare unconstitutional the acts of popularly elected Presidents, Congresses, governors, state legislatures, and mayors. That a powerful nation with a vigorous two-party system and a majoritarian ideology should continue to allow nine elderly lawyers to exercise such a veto power on the most sensitive issues of our society has often been portrayed as an incredible denial of American democratic principles.

Critics of the Supreme Court during the ninteenth and early twentieth centuries received the "classic rejoinder," usually from conservatives. They were reminded that the American republic was created by a written constitution that deliberately limited the power of the national and state governments. The Constitution also guaranteed Americans certain fundamental rights of liberty, property, and equality that no elected officials or majority vote could take away. To enforce these limitations, the Framers set up an independent judiciary to articulate the ideals of limited government and constitutional rights and to strike down government measures that violated the Constitution. This was to keep the majority within constitutional boundaries and protect minority rights.

The difficulty with the "classic rejoinder" today is that it simply no longer describes the spirit or the influence of the Supreme Court. The justices now give little comfort to conservative and well-propertied groups in the nation. Their rulings on matters such as antitrust laws, industrial regulation, civil liberties, or civil rights have often been *more* liberal in recent years than the positions of the elective branches of state and national governments.

The debate over the Supreme Court and judicial review is therefore no longer one between democratic critics and conservative defenders. It is a distinctly new and more subtle controversy, one brought into its sharpest focus by the basic question: What is new since 1937, and what has remained constant in the role of the Supreme Court in American government? The year 1937 is pivotal, since this was when President Franklin Roosevelt led New Deal liberals in a full-scale attack on "the nine old men," culminating in the famous but unsuccessful "court-reform" proposals. It was also the year in which the Supreme Court majority, without the addition of any new Roosevelt appointees, upheld the New

Deal economic program, thus changing its basic constitutional philosophy on the reach of federal and state legislative power over economic affairs and marking the beginning of a new era in the Court's doctrines on property rights and civil rights. Let us look at those elements that have remained constant and those that have changed since 1937.

Constant Elements in the Court's Role

1. *Procedures and traditions.* The Court still decides cases with the same procedures and traditions as it did in the pre-nuclear age. The justices still form a small committee and still function as a closed, corporate entity, steeped in the learning of the law and operating through the ancient traditions of the Anglo-Saxon legal system. Even though the justices now have law clerks and secretaries to assist them, most of the work of the Court is as personal and as painfully slow as it has ever been. While the law clerks write memoranda summarizing the cases that come by the thousands to the Court, each justice personally considers whether to vote for or against accepting each case for consideration. Oral argument before the United States Supreme Court remains the Socratic exchange so familiar in the courts of England and the United States throughout the formative years of this judicial system. While the briefs of counsel have grown longer, they still consist of about the same kind of appellate argument that Supreme Courts received in 1830 or 1890. The justices still write their

---

Preparing a Supreme Court Opinion

When one starts to write an opinion for the Supreme Court of the United States he learns the full meaning of the statement of Rufus Choate that "one cannot drop the Greek alphabet to the ground and pick up the Iliad." It takes the most painstaking research and care. Mr. Justice Cardozo was not far wrong when he said, "A Judge must be a historian and prophet all in one." In the average case an opinion requires three weeks' work in preparation. When the author concludes that he has an unanswerable document, it is printed in the print shop in the Supreme Court building and circulated to each of the Justices. Then the fur begins to fly. Returns come in, some favorable and many otherwise. In controversial cases, and all have some touches of controversy, the process often takes months. The cases are often discussed by the majority both before and after circulation. The final form of the opinion is agreed upon at the Friday conferences. Of course, any Justice may dissent or write his own views on a case. These are likewise circulated long before the opinion of the majority is announced.

From Tom C. Clark, "The Supreme Court Conference," *Federal Rules Decisions,* 1956.

own opinions (aided by law clerks, who do research and some drafting).

Secrecy still surrounds the Court's deliberations, and neither the press nor Congress can probe into the internal processes of the Court's decision-making, as is done with executive, administrative, or congressional procedures. Finally, the justices' life tenure creates a sense of independence from party pressures and a mood of dedication to principle that—while they do not guarantee either intellect or wisdom—do make the Court the most "long-range minded" of our national institutions in its approach to policy issues. This may give way to intense partisanship or ideological militancy in some justices, and even in some Court majorities (as in 1857 over slavery or in the 1930's on New Deal reforms), but the dominant tradition has been independence from party or intraparty factional positions.

2. *The types of Court justices.* No person who is not a lawyer has yet to sit on the Supreme Court, though there is no constitutional or statutory bar to appointing a political scientist or a constitutional historian. If one studies carefully the pre-Court professions of the justices, the same basic types of the 1860's or 1920's are those that populate the Court today. There have been the former members of the President's administration, drawn from Cabinet and executive officials. There have been the powerful party figures, men who must be rewarded for service to the President's party. There have been the powerful members or immediately retired members of Congress, of whom some are appointed to the Court for party reasons and some in order to eliminate their obstruction of the President's program in Congress. There are also prominent members of the bar and judges of the federal and state courts appointed to the Court, again usually for broad party and sectional reasons. Occasionally, there have been law professors.

The present Supreme Court reflects these patterns. Earl Warren was a Republican governor of California and the Republican vice-presidential nominee in 1948; President Eisenhower rewarded him for his service by appointing him Chief Justice in 1953. Hugo Black, a Democratic senator from Alabama between 1928 and 1938, was appointed by President Franklin D. Roosevelt at least partly because of Black's yeomanly service in the Senate on behalf of New Deal measures, including support of the President's Court-reform proposal of 1937. Roosevelt also appointed William O. Douglas, who, though a law professor at Columbia and Yale in his early career, was a member and then chairman of the Securities and Exchange Commission during the New Deal. Of the remaining three Eisenhower appointees still on the bench, John M. Harlan was a Wall Street lawyer and protégé of Republican party leader Thomas Dewey; Eisenhower had earlier appointed Harlan to the federal court of appeals. William J. Brennan, Jr., was a judge of the Supreme Court of New Jersey, and, as an Irish-Catholic Democrat, he represented a bid by Eisenhower for the votes of Catholics and "Eisenhower Democrats" in the upcoming 1956 election.

An Attack on Judicial Dissent

Dissent has a popular appeal, for it is an underdog judge pleading for an underdog litigant. Of course, one party or the other must always be underdog in a lawsuit, the purpose of which really is to determine which one it shall be. But the tradition of great dissents built around such names as Holmes, Brandeis, Cardozo, and Stone is not due to the frequency or multiplicity of their dissents, but to their quality and the importance of the few cases in which they carried their disagreement beyond the conference table. Also, quite contrary to the popular notion, relatively few of all the dissents recorded in the Supreme Court have later become law, although some of these are of great importance.

There has been much undiscriminating eulogy of dissenting opinions. It is said they clarify the issues. Often they do the exact opposite. The technique of the dissenter often is to exaggerate the holding of the Court beyond the meaning of the majority and then to blast away at the excess. So the poor lawyer with a similar case does not know whether the majority opinion meant what it seemed to say or what the minority said it meant. Then, too, dissenters frequently force the majority to take positions more extreme than was originally intended....

The *right of dissent* is a valuable one. Wisely used on well-chosen occasions, it has been of great service to the profession and to the law. But there is nothing good, for either the Court or the dissenter, in dissenting per se. Each dissenting opinion is a confession of failure to convince the writer's colleagues, and the true test of a judge is his influence in leading, not in opposing, his court.

From Justice Robert H. Jackson, *The Supreme Court in the American System of Government*, 1955.

Potter Stewart was a federal court of appeals judge and former practicing lawyer. Kennedy appointee Justice Byron White was formerly Deputy Attorney General, and Abe Fortas was a Washington lawyer who had served President Johnson as a close political adviser. Thurgood Marshall, who was the first Negro on the Court, had served as Solicitor General in the Johnson Administration.

3. *Internal divisions over constitutional questions.* When the Supreme Court in the 1960's divides 5–4 or 6–3 on major constitutional issues, and when the justices exchange frank and passionate majority and minority opinions, this reflects a tradition started in 1810, when Justice William Johnson, a Jeffersonian appointee, began to dissent systematically and forcefully from the Supreme Court majority led by Chief Justice John Marshall. Ever since then, splits within the Court on leading issues and on basic philosophy have been a regular feature of our constitutional system.

Some commentators have deplored these divisions, have criticized the formation of "cohesive blocs" within the Court, and have called for a show of constitutional harmony within the Court to reassure the public that constitutional law is above personal or ideological differences. But in fact divisions among the Court's Justices are really a sign that the fiercely held views in the country at large on various sides of great questions are represented within the Court. At best this dialectic of debate can be translated into constitutional terms that will lend themselves to resolution or compromise. To contend for a unanimous bench is to confuse constitutional adjudication with mathematics or good-fellowship.

4. *Confrontation with highly volatile sociopolitical issues.* In fact, the constitutional decisions of the Supreme Court represent a history of almost all the great political, socioeconomic, and intergroup conflicts in American domestic affairs. No sooner has a major issue arisen when the individuals or interest groups that lost the fight in the political arena have rushed into court to seek vindication of "their rights" under the Constitution. If rebuffed by the courts, they have usually kept trying.

This "court-seeking psychology" of Americans can be explained in many ways. Some see it as a reflection of an "ideological split personality"

A Defense of Judicial Dissent

Disagreement among judges is as true to the character of democracy as freedom of speech itself. The dissenting opinion is as genuinely American as Otis' denunciation of the general warrants, as Thomas Paine's, Thomas Jefferson's, or James Madison's briefs for civil liberties.

Democracy, like religion, is full of sects and schisms. Every political campaign demonstrates it. Every session of a legislature proves it. No man or group of men has a monopoly on truth, wisdom, or virtue. An idea, once advanced for public acceptance, divides like an amoeba. The ifs and buts and howevers each claim a party; and what was once a whole is soon carved into many separate pieces, some of which are larger than even the original....

The law will always teem with uncertainty ... under the democratic scheme of things. The truth is that the law is the highest form of compromise between competing interests; it is a substitute for force and violence—the only path to peace man has yet devised. It is the product of attempted reconciliation between the many diverse groups in a society. The reconciliation is not entirely a legislative function. The judiciary is also inescapably involved. When judges do not agree, it is a sign that they are dealing with problems on which society itself is divided. It is the democratic way to express dissident views. Judges are to be honored rather than criticized for following that tradition, for proclaiming their articles of faith so that all may read.

From Justice William O. Douglas, "The Dissenting Opinion," address to the American Bar Association, September 1948.

between liberalism and conservatism in the American people, others as a filling of the policy vacuum created by our weak party system, others as a heritage of legalism and moralism from the Puritan tradition, and still others as the special instrument used by conservatives to ward off liberal legislative policies for more than a century and now used by liberals with equal delight to thwart the will of conservative majorities in the state and federal legislatures.

Whatever the reasons, the Supreme Court has always been where the action is. Between 1790 and 1860, the Court issued key rulings on the volatile issues of states' rights over commercial regulation and taxation, legislative regulation of property rights and contracts, and the status of slavery in the Union. Between 1865 and 1920, the Court dealt with Reconstruction and the rights of the newly freed Negro, the regulation of corporations in the formative period of American capitalism, the relations of labor and management, state and federal taxing powers, and civil liberties during wartime. Between 1920 and 1937, the justices ruled on the central questions of industrial depression and recovery, social welfare, labor relations, agricultural policy, and the boundaries of state and federal power over economic affairs. From 1937 to the present, the Court has issued important rulings on Cold War loyalty-security measures, segregation and racial discrimination, church-state relations, labor-management affairs, state procedure in criminal investigations and trials, and many other issues.

The Court as a whole has pursued three basic concerns in its constitutional jurisprudence: (1) balancing the parts of the federal Union, (2) fostering a "sound" economic order, and (3) protecting individual rights to property and liberty. In each era, the Court has given its own reading of what the Constitution said and intended on each of these matters, adjusting precedents to changing socioeconomic and technological conditions. The Court has had to interpret and reinterpret certain constitutional clauses that have been the battleground of debate decade after decade.

Before the Civil War, the two main provisions were the *commerce clause* (giving Congress the power "to regulate commerce with foreign nations, and among the several States, and with the Indian tribes") and the *contract clause* (forbidding the states to pass any law "impairing the obligation of contracts"). The commerce clause required the justices to rule not only on which regulations of interstate sales of goods, transportation, and business firms Congress could make but also on which state regulations of multistate or intrastate commerce interfered with freedom of interstate movement. Through the contract clause the Court became the judge of legislative land grants and their revocation, debtor and creditor laws, and state regulation of chartered corporations.

Following the Civil War, the commerce and contract clauses were joined on the Court's most active constitutional agenda by two powerful clauses put into the Fourteenth Amendment in 1868. These forbade states to deny any person "life, liberty, or property, without *due process of law*" or to "deny to any person . . . the *equal protection* of the laws." The due-process clause became the Court's primary standard for judging the "reasonableness" of state legislation governing labor conditions, welfare, taxation, and administrative regulation of industry. Similarly, the Court used the equal-protection clause to strike down state actions that were said to discriminate unfairly against a particular business activity. Negro civil rights, fairness in criminal procedure, and freedom of expression were only rarely considered under the due-process and equal-protection clauses before 1920, and the Court usually found that restrictive actions of states were constitutional.

In the post-1937 period, the contract clause has become almost a dead letter in constitutional litigation, but the commerce, due-process, and equal-protection clauses are still among the Court's basic tools. The interpretations have changed—today the due-process clause is used primarily to test state measures dealing with religion or free speech and to require states to adhere to high standards of fairness in criminal procedure; the equal-protection clause now safeguards Negroes and other minority groups far more than it does corporations; and the commerce clause is used primarily to strike down state taxing and business-regulation measures that seek to Balkanize the national economy. But the essential point is that the shifting policy issues of American society have been tested again and again according to a handful of major constitutional clauses. These were drawn by the Framers in broad enough language for each successive Court majority to be able to use them as guidelines for adjusting constitutional standards to changing social conditions.

Of course, the fact that great issues are always *brought* to the Court does not mean that Court must try to *settle* every explosive question. Some of the Court's severe "self-inflicted wounds," remarked Charles Evans Hughes in 1928, were caused when the justices failed to realize when to avoid, delay, or moderate judicial intervention in political conflicts. Hughes cited the Court's decisions supporting slavery in 1857, denying the legality of federal paper currency in 1870, and striking down the federal income tax in 1895 as the three most serious examples of Court venturesomeness leading to a collapse of public confidence in the Court. Yet the dominant tradition of the Court has been to accept and decide most explosive issues. Thus the Supreme Court of the 1960's is squarely in the Court's historical mainstream when it makes headlines with constitutional rulings on communist-control measures, race relations, legislative districting, movie censorship, and antitrust cases.

5. *Sharp public controversy and "Court-curbing" campaigns.* Because it has always dealt with the crucial issues of the day, and because its rulings have injured or thwarted powerful political, economic, and social movements, the Supreme Court has consistently been the target of passionate

attacks and efforts to limit its powers. Between 1800 and the 1820's, Jeffersonians bitterly assailed the Court and argued that it lacked the power to decide whether acts of Congress were constitutional, whether federal law was supreme over state law, or whether the President had exceeded his constitutional powers. Between 1830 and 1850 the Jacksonians protested Supreme Court interference with state regulation of commerce. Court decisions on slavery cases were also protested, both by the North (whenever the Supreme Court upheld the rights of slaveholders) and by the South (when the Supreme Court did not act strongly enough in enforcing slavery through the federal court system).

Between 1850 and 1875, a peak of controversy over the Court was reached, with attacks on the Court's 1857 Dred Scott decision upholding slavery [4] and with the 1866–68 fight between the Radical Republicans in Congress and the Supreme Court justices over the constitutionality of Reconstruction measures. (We have already discussed congressional action against the Court over the McCardle case in Chapter 14.) The years from 1880 to 1900 featured the protests of farmers, Populists, and early labor-movement leaders against what they called the "corporate bias" of the federal judiciary; in 1896 the Supreme Court became a major issue in the presidential campaign.

From 1920 to 1925 the Progressives launched a full-scale attack on the Supreme Court's economic doctrines, challenging the "anti-labor," "anti-liberal" bias of the justices. In the presidential elections of 1912 and 1924, third parties (the Bull Moose movement in 1912 and the La Follette Progressive movement in 1924) promised, if they were elected, to provide checks on an overbearing Supreme Court. Various proposals were advocated in Congress during this era for overturning decisions of the Supreme Court. Between 1925 and 1937 came the clash between the New Deal and the "nine old men," when a majority of the Supreme Court erected a wall of constitutional doctrines against which most of the key New Deal measures rammed in vain before 1937.

Finally, the period from 1937 to the present has been marked by repeated crises about the Supreme Court's civil-liberties and civil-rights decisions. The most important of these protest movements, the so-called "Court-curbing attack of 1957–58," came from Southern congressmen, internal-security stalwarts, and some business groups, who unsuccessfully challenged the Court's decisions on loyalty-security measures, congressional investigations, desegregation, labor relations, and antitrust. In the late 1960's forces led by conservative Senator Everett Dirksen attempted to overturn the Court's one-man–one-vote ruling on legislative reapportionment, but this movement also failed.

Thus, to say that the Supreme Court of the 1960's has been a "con-

---

[4] *Dred Scott* v. *Sanford*, 19 How. 393 (1857).

troversial agency" is to say that the justices are running true to historical form.

6. *The power and the great vulnerability of the Court.* In the 1960's, with newspaper headlines and hour-long network-television programs devoted to the Court's major rulings, with Presidents, Congresses, governors, and state legislatures being forced to accept Court decisions on their powers, the Court seems to be an immensely powerful institution. And so it seemed when the Jeffersonians, Jacksonians, Populists, and New Dealers protested the Court's immense effect on the economic and political issues of their day. Yet, ironically, the Supreme Court is a highly vulnerable institution.

Constitutional amendments can overturn unpopular rulings. Congressional statutes can reverse the Court's decisions when these rest on interpretation of federal statutes. Congressional control over the Court's appellate jurisdiction can be used to cut off the Court's review of specific areas of controversy or to threaten the Court. Presidents can seek to change the voting balances within the Court in their appointments of new justices. State and federal officials can mount embarrassingly effective resistance to the Court's orders, ranging from subtle inaction to open defiance, since the justices must ultimately depend on elected officials to enforce their orders. The bar and bench can raise influential protests against the Court's legal arguments and professional competence. And every Supreme Court is acutely sensitive to continuous, widespread mistrust of its decisions by the general public.

For these reasons the Supreme Court, when confronted by the determined will of dominant opinion in the nation, has always modified its disputed doctrines to conform to these forces. Such modifications in Court policy occurred when the Court faced Radical Republicans in 1866–68, when it faced New Dealers in 1936–37, and when it faced the "Court-curbers" of 1957–58. As Thomas Reed Powell once said, the Court knows how to execute the "switch in time that saves nine." Here, too, the justices of the 1960's are in the same ambiguous and challenging position as their predecessors. If they use the Court's symbols and authority wisely and with political skill, they can be a tremendous force in our national life; if they go too far, they risk swift and effective reprisals.

We have now seen that many elements that uninformed critics have called "revolutionary" innovations of the post-1937 or post-1957 Court have really been present since its founding. However, the Court since 1937 *has* been a new institution in several basic respects, and it is to these that we turn now.

New Elements in the Court's Role

1. *The beneficiaries of the Court's decisions.* Throughout the history of the Court until 1937, those who profited most from the Supreme Court's

SUPREME
COURT

NEW TERM

"Umph! You still hanging around?"

Before 1937, as this New Deal cartoon shows, conservatives saw the Supreme Court as an important check on the reformist programs of the elected branches.

Duffy in the Baltimore *Sun*

rulings were New England businessmen, Western land speculators, Southern planters, slaveholders, new industries that followed the Civil War (the railroads, manufacturing companies, and so on), banking interests, public-utility holding companies—in short, the propertied elements in American economic life.

The Supreme Court's definitions of property rights, limited government, and states' rights produced an ideal set of ground rules for those running a capitalist system. They provided the fiscal stability, credit guarantees, protection of contracts, employer control over work conditions, and reliance upon private initiative and welfare that stood as a barrier to many farm, labor, and middle-class reform movements from 1800 to 1937.

Spokesmen for the business community understood that the Supreme Court was "their" institution in the nation's government structure and defended it staunchly. During the 1840's, for example, Daniel Webster, the dean of corporate counsel in the pre-Civil War era, commented that the nation's "chartered interests" knew that their "only security is to be found in this tribunal," with its checks upon the "unlimited despotism" of state governments and the "leveling ultraisms of anti-rentism or agrarianism." At the peak of American capitalist expansion, the Supreme Court in one term (1895) struck down the federal income tax, dismissed prosecutions against the sugar trust, and upheld the contempt conviction of American Railway Union President Eugene Debs. The president of the Fourth National Bank of New York responded by telling an applauding audience of commercial leaders: "I give you, gentlemen, the Supreme Court of the

Liberals, on the other hand, viewed the pre-1937 Court as a barrier to vital economic-recovery programs.

Seibel in the Richmond *Times-Dispatch*

United States—guardian of the dollar, defender of private property, enemy of spoilation, sheet anchor of the Republic!"

In 1911, when the Supreme Court cut sharply into the sweep of the Sherman Antitrust Law, one of the Standard Oil executives capped the outpouring of corporate praise for the Court's decision by saying, "I am for the Supreme Court every time. For more than a hundred years it has been at work and it has never made a mistake." In 1936 the president of the Crucible Steel Corporation indicated business' appreciation of the judiciary: "The judiciary has again proved itself to be the bulwark of defense against the subtle and skillful manipulation of democratic processes to achieve unsanctioned theories."

Today, however, American business is saying very different things about the Supreme Court. In 1960, for example, the vice-presidents and general counsel of fifty of the nation's largest and most powerful corporations were asked what they thought about the United States Supreme Court.[5] Two-thirds of the counsel were deeply hostile to the Court. A leading industrial-manufacturing corporation's general counsel explained:

> I think the informed businessman is pretty well discouraged with the Warren Court. In matters affecting business, the Court has pretty well swept aside what was left of constitutional safeguards in the field of taxes and government regulation. The bloc of four with which the Chief Justice is usually found

[5] This mail questionnaire was conducted by Alan F. Westin in 1960; replies in author's possession.

is quite beyond the pale of reason in the eyes of most of the men with whom I discuss these matters.[6]

Most corporate spokesmen speak of the Court today in the sad, sometimes sharp, tones of a man who sees his former mistress bestowing her favors on strangers. For its part, the post-1937 Supreme Court majority often treats the rigid property-rights doctrines of the nineteenth- and early twentieth-century justices as rather embarrassing reminders of an indiscreet liaison in its youth. This rift in the classic love affair between business and the Supreme Court is one of the most significant aspects of the present Supreme Court's relation to the government and to public opinion.

The main complaint of business today is that the Supreme Court does not limit the power of the federal government to tax broadly, to regulate industry closely, and to supervise labor relations in detail. In recent Supreme Court cases involving labor-management relations, labor and management each win about half the cases each term. Even this, however, is not satisfactory to business, since the cases it loses are usually those in which it had hoped to see the Court establish doctrines that would turn back, or at least prevent, the further expansion of federal jurisdiction over industry.

On the other hand, a new set of beneficiaries has replaced business. Today, this group includes Negroes, persons claiming that their civil liberties have been infringed upon by elected majorities (communists, syndicate leaders, balky college professors, people who are loyalty-security risks, and so on), and spokesmen advocating that their right of religious freedom has been improperly limited (Jews, Seventh-Day Adventists, Unitarians, humanists, and atheists).

Not unexpectedly, the major shift in the beneficiaries of judicial review has brought a dramatic change in the roster of court defenders and attackers in the public arena. As we noted at the beginning of this section, from the early Republic until the 1930's it was the liberals who criticized the Court as undemocratic and the conservatives who defended it as a badly needed brake on popular democracy. Today, however, the liberals defend the Court as a wise check on mass passions and a protector of human rights against "populist sentiment." The groups supporting the Court at legislative hearings and in the popular media are the Americans for Democratic Action, the National Association for the Advancement of Colored People, the AFL-CIO, the American Jewish Congress, the American Civil Liberties Union, and similar groups in what is usually called the liberal-labor ("Lib-Lab") coalition. It should be noted, however, that these groups are not defending their economic interests but rather are protecting their broad ideological interests or their social status. Labor-union testimony on behalf of the Court, for example, has dealt not with its labor rulings but with its civil-rights and civil-liberties decisions.

6 *Ibid.*

Conversely, it is now the key elements of the *conservative* camp—groups such as the American Legion, many leaders of the American Bar Association, state and local law-enforcement officials, Southern political leaders, conservative Republicans, and many businessmen—who cry that the Court is tampering with the wise conclusions of the people's representatives.

One explanation for the reversal of attitudes may well be that whether a group approves or disapproves of a political institution usually depends on whether that institution appears to be serving the particular interests of the group at that moment. Perhaps, then, the liberals have only recently become defenders of the Court because they had to wait from 1790 until the 1940's to find a set of justices whose decisions would serve their interests and to whom they could give their allegiance.

Groups who do not feel that the Court is protecting their interests often conduct vigorous campaigns either in Congress or in the public arena for action that would in effect reverse the Court's decisions. The business community, for example, has had a good deal of success in "the congressional court of appeal," which is why businessmen have not sought punitive measures against the Court, such as changing the basis of judicial review, limiting the Court's jurisdiction, or changing the basis of judicial appointment.

Today, the Supreme Court decisions that affect business mainly concern federal regulatory actions, federal tax laws, and federal regulation of labor relations. Decisions in these areas turn largely on interpretation of federal statutes—the National Labor Relations Act, the Social Security Act, wage and price statutes, the basic enabling statutes of the major regulatory commissions, and so on. Business soon discovered a safety valve: when the Supreme Court handed down a decision it did not like, it could ask Congress to rewrite or repeal the statute. Between 1944 and 1960 about sixty Supreme Court rulings were either directly nullified or severely limited by congressional action resulting from pressure by the business community.

On the other hand, few decisions of the Court on civil-liberties or civil-rights issues have been affected by such reversal campaigns. In recent years, decisions on issues such as federal loyalty-security programs, passports, school prayer, legislative reapportionment, school desegregation, and public accommodations have been the targets of such efforts, but the liberal allies of the Court have been able to defend it successfully from these attacks.

2. *The Court's areas of intervention.* Prior to 1937, the bulk of the Court's politically sensitive constitutional rulings were in the field of property controls—taxation, regulation of commerce, labor relations, antitrust, farm programs, and so forth. There were comparatively few cases involving criminal procedure (selection of juries, evidence rules, searches and seizures, etc.), and state criminal cases were generally left as the state supreme courts had decided them. In the 1960's, by contrast, the Court decides few constitutional cases affecting property rights; instead, almost half of the cases it

Jensen in the Chicago *Daily News*

Three Is Growing into a Crowd

Today, conservatives attack the Supreme Court for intruding on legislative and executive authority.

has decided with full opinions in its last two or three terms have been liberty, equality, and fair-procedure cases.

There is a variety of reasons for this change. First, the justices themselves washed the property cases out of their stream of constitutional decisions with the basic judicial doctrine adhered to since 1937: federal power to regulate the economy is essential to managing an industrial economy and is authorized by the Founding Fathers in their broad charter. This power should not be constricted by judge-made interpretations of what would be good for the nation. Thus, all the staples of pre-1937 jurisprudence—direct and indirect controls on commerce, the power to regulate shipment of goods in interstate commerce but not production for commerce, federal power over manufacture but not agriculture—have been reduced to this simple inquiry: Did Congress use its broad power reasonably? And the Court has not found an unreasonable use of federal legislative power in property cases since 1937.

Another reason for the shift in agenda is that the Court majority has enunciated constitutional doctrines that have opened up broad avenues of access to the Supreme Court for minority groups. Beginning with the Gitlow case in 1925, the Court ruled that the freedoms guaranteed in the First Amendment (freedom of speech, press, assembly, and religion, and the bar against religious establishment) were part of the due process of law that the states could not infringe under the Fourteenth Amendment. This meant that the Court would now agree to review cases of state action alleged to violate

"Can you see me now?"

Liberals, on the other hand, now defend the Court as a protector of individual rights.

From *Herblock's Special for Today,*
Simon & Schuster, 1958

First Amendment guarantees, something it had generally not done before. The Gitlow concept has been steadily widened, and the Court now polices a tremendous part of state-government action under the Fourteenth Amendment. In addition, in 1938 the Court virtually invited minority groups to litigate by its famous comment in the Carolene Products [7] case that judicial intervention against legislative will was justified when the political process was unavailable for relief—such as when Negroes and other racial minorities, political radicals, or labor-union organizers were oppressed by hostile local majorities.

The new religious, racial, and liberal groups that sprang up after the First World War have accepted with alacrity the Court's invitation to litigate. Many of these groups have perfected the techniques of the "test case" and are quite skilled in bringing to the Supreme Court cases that would probably never have been the subject of a Supreme Court ruling had it not been for their initiative. Before 1937 businessmen, corporations, business associations such as the American Anti-Boycott League or the National Association of Manufacturers, and some labor unions and groups like the Consumers League largely shaped the test cases. Now it is such groups as the NAACP, the ACLU, Protestants and Other Americans United for Separation of Church and State, and the Anti-Defamation League that appear as the parties or as "friends of the Court" in the leading cases each term.

[7] *United States* v. *Carolene Products Co.,* 304 U.S. 144 (1938).

Another major factor affecting the agenda of the Court is that in economic affairs the country is largely on a social-welfare–capitalist plateau. There have been no radical departures from American economic-organization and welfare laws since 1938. Labor, management, and government do a perpetual gavotte in collective bargaining, but without creating situations that produce constitutional tests. The major domestic conflicts affecting our society have been matters of *status*, not property: the problems of communism, loyalty, and internal security that reached their peak in McCarthyism involved the definition of political deviation and the limits of liberty; the revolution in race relations since the Second World War and in religious interrelations forces the Court to probe our concepts of equality.

3. *The Court's atmosphere and doctrinal ethos.* This is a delicate but vitally important point. Before the 1930's, the Supreme Court talked about constitutional law in highly traditionalist terms. As Justice Owen Roberts put it, the function of the United States Supreme Court was to lay a challenged statute or executive order beside the Constitution to see whether the former squared with the latter. According to this mechanistic notion of jurisprudence, the justices merely fed a statute into the judicial slot machine and pulled the lever: if it came up three lemons or three cherries, it was constitutional; if it came out two lemons and a cherry, it was not constitutional.

Since the late 1930's, however, a majority of the Supreme Court has been discussing the role of the Court, the meaning of the Constitution, and the principles of American constitutional order in terms of sociological realism (discussed earlier), which sees the role of the Supreme Court as part of the larger governmental process, not as a separate "platonic council." Several generations of legal debate have culminated in a Supreme Court that accepts a modern, liberal style of judicial review—including discussion of economics, references to political history, use of sociological treatises, and the absence of appeals to precedent as wholly controlling. The techniques by which the Court works today clash with the fundamentalist's notion of what the judiciary should do in our system. For the Court now says in essence, "Look, we have no magic clothes on; we are not emperors, simply lawyers trying to apply the rules of the Constitution in a reflective and responsive manner consistent with the intention of the Framers and with the needs of modern public policy. We are not gods; neither are we men with as many pressures upon us as those who legislate. Our function is to uphold the great balances of American government—as Justice Robert Jackson put it, the balances between federal and state authority, liberty and order, human rights and property rights." One cannot read a contemporary Court decision without realizing how important is this difference of today's tone and style in the justices' explanation of their case to the public. Ironically, it is this realistic and pragmatic judicial style that gives those who challenge the Court one of their primary weapons—for this style undercuts the assumption that justices are Platonic philosophers.

SUMMARY

Judge-administered law in a democratic state is expected on the one hand to encourage stability and predictability and on the other to accommodate shifts in the values and power balances of the society. The need to balance these competing goals makes the attitudes of the American judge in reaching decisions a central element in our judicial system. The Anglo-American legal tradition offers its judges three theories about their proper role in passing on the acts of elected branches of government:

According to the *natural-law* tradition, a higher morality limits all powers of government, and judges should strike down legislation that violates these norms (as the judges perceive them). According to the *positivist* tradition, however, judges are obliged to uphold those acts declared by the supreme political authority in the state through established legislative procedures; judges should not substitute their own notions of proper policy for those of the sovereign authority. According to the *sociological* theory of law, judges should decide cases according to whether statutes are consistent with the basic values and the historical and contemporary traditions of society. The American judicial tradition has incorporated aspects of all three theories, but disagreement over which approach should be dominant still marks intra-Court debates.

In the United States the issue is posed most sharply when judges exercise the power of judicial review. This power allows federal or state courts to determine the constitutionality of acts by the elected branches of government at their own level, and it also allows federal courts to pass on the constitutionality of state-government actions. The power of federal courts to review state actions is clearly indicated in the United States Constitution, but the power of the Supreme Court to review acts of Congress and the President is less clear.

Nonetheless, this power has gradually accrued to the Court on the basis of implied provisions in the Constitution, early Court decisions under John Marshall, and our favorable political values. Today, though the wisdom of specific decisions is often disputed, there are no significant attacks on the Court's power of judicial review per se.

The significant influence of the Supreme Court on our political system has made its role a highly controversial one throughout its history. In the final section of the chapter, we examined which aspects of the Court's role in the political system had remained constant since 1790 and which had changed significantly. We chose 1937 as the dividing line between "old" roles and "new" roles because this date marked a basic shift in the primary issues confronted by the Court and in its relation to the sociopolitical forces in our national life.

Six features were shown to be basic constants. The Court's authority to exercise the power of judicial review has continued to put before the justices the major sociopolitical issues of the day: our consensus politics and public attitudes toward the Constitution have continued to create expectations that the justices would decide such issues when they reached the Court. Both the operating procedures and the types of men chosen to be justices have remained basically the same before and after 1937. The Court's rulings have continued to generate sharp controversy in the press and public opinion, since groups whose interests were not advanced by judicial decisions have challenged the doctrines, personnel, or powers of the Court. Finally, we saw that the Court, while it continues to have major impact on the nation's political system, is still a vulnerable institution that must depend on the elective branches to carry out its rulings and is subject to formal and informal reprisals if it moves too far away for too long a time from dominant opinion in the nation.

On the other hand, three major changes have taken place in the political role of the Supreme Court since 1937. The Court's main emphasis in constitutional decisions has shifted from issues of property to issues of liberty, equality, and due process. In this shift, the main beneficiaries of the Court's constitutional rulings are no longer propertied and business groups and their conservative allies but minority racial, religious, and ideological groups and their liberal allies. These minority groups and liberals have become the Court's principal defenders against "Court-curbing" efforts by some conservative groups. Finally, the dominant philosophy within the Court on its role in the American political system has changed since 1937 from one based on legal traditionalism and "law-finding" to one of legal realism, seeking democratic justifications for the Court's continuing influence in the political system.

LAWYERS
AND
JUDGES
IN THE
POLITICAL
SYSTEM

16

In addition to having its own sphere of jurisdiction, special institutions, and operating rules, the American legal system has two distinctive sets of actors who play the principal roles in this arena. The first actor is the lawyer. What special roles do lawyers play, and what accounts for their disproportionate influence on our politics? The second actor is the judge, whose role is clearly distinct from that of legislator, executive, or administrator. What types of men do our judicial selection and control processes bring to the federal bench? What different roles do federal judges play, and what factors within and outside the courts explain continuing differences of opinion as to the "proper function" of judges?

AMERICAN LAWYERS:
THE BRIDGE BETWEEN GOVERNMENT AND SOCIETY

Lawyers play a unique role in the American political system and one far out of proportion to their numbers or wealth. Lawyers can be thought of as a bridge between the general citizenry and the huge, impersonal government. The complexity of business and legal affairs makes the expert advice of a lawyer so useful that the legal profession is constantly performing the role of middleman in the governmental process.

Though lawyers make up less than 4 percent of the work force in the United States today, they have a total monopoly on judicial offices (above the justice-of-the-peace level), and they occupy more than 50 percent of the legislative and executive posts in our national, state, and city governments. They have maintained this predominance ever since colonial days; thirty-one of the fifty-five Framers of the Constitution were trained in law. In the years since national independence, about 66 percent of United States senators, 55 percent of congressmen, and 60 percent of state governors have been lawyers. (By contrast, a little over 10 percent of the members of the Supreme Soviet and about 50 percent of the members of the British House of Commons are lawyers.)

This disproportionate influence of lawyers in public life can be traced to several factors. First, it is easy for lawyers to run for public office or to serve in government for a time and then reenter professional life, usually with enhanced career prospects. This contrasts with the professional problems that ventures in public service create for owners of businesses, doctors, dentists, skilled workers, and others. Political campaigning itself serves as free advertising for young lawyers, even when they are not elected, and many members of the bar start running for local office almost as soon as they hang up their shingles. Second, a large number of posts within the legislatures, executive offices, and regulatory agencies have traditionally gone to men with legal backgrounds, since questions of constitutional law, statutory construction, and common law are central to decisions in these areas. This is closely connected to the third factor—our law-oriented and court-seeking approach to public-policy questions. Fourth, lawyers are led into politics because two main sources of the rewards they seek are controlled by political parties: appointments to judgeships and the distribution of high-paying legal work for lawyers in private practice (such as being named executors of trusts and estates when no one has been chosen by the deceased, guardians of minors, or referees in bankruptcy cases). To secure such appointments, it has been common for lawyers to start working early in their careers at the local party headquarters and to make party activity a regular part of their schedules. Finally, after studying the legal system intensively in law school and after struggling with the law's application in practice, many lawyers

508

come to hunger for a primary role in the lawmaking process. The desire to shape the law directly in legislatures, executive offices, or from the bench is virtually an occupational urge of lawyers.

On the whole, has this gravitation of lawyers toward public life been beneficial or harmful to our political system? Critics portray the legal profession as inherently conservative or even reactionary, arguing that training in the evolution of law and the importance of precedent make most lawyers suspicious of social reform and legislative experimentation. When they are in executive positions, lawyers usually adopt narrow, procedurally focused approaches, and too often they prove unresponsive to the swift movement of domestic events or the subtleties of international relations. These critics point to such "legalistic blunders" as Secretary of State Bryan's preoccupation on the eve of the First World War with signing arbitration treaties to make war "impossible" or Secretary of State Dulles' insistence in the 1950's on forcing Arab-Asian nations to join paper defense pacts. In addition, say opponents, the impact of lawyers on the drafting of statutes in the legislature has produced overcomplicated, legalistic, and unwieldy statutes.

Supporters of the legal profession, on the other hand, begin by asking what other professional or occupational group has a better record in terms of integrity, creativeness, and dedication. Lawyers also meet several important criteria for public officials: respect for constitutional procedures, skill in drafting laws to express the meaning of their sponsors, concern for the peaceful adjustment of conflicting economic and social values, and high regard for fair play and due process. Such supporters would offer the careers of such men as Henry Stimson or Dean Acheson as evidence that lawyer-diplomats can be superb negotiators and foreign-policy leaders. Most important, supporters would note that the archconservatism and isolationism that marked so much of the bar in the 1870–1930 period are no longer present. Today, many lawyers approach public service with a philosophy of sociological jurisprudence, a commitment to social welfare and internationalism, and a dedication to the cause of civil liberties and civil rights greater than that of most business and professional groups.

A Portrait of the American Legal Profession

In 1967 the leading directory of lawyers in the United States, Martindale-Hubbell, listed about 300,000 members of the legal profession. While found in both small towns and major cities, lawyers have tended to concentrate in major urban centers of commerce and government. A survey of the professional status of lawyers during 1966 indicated that 71 percent were in private practice, of which about two-thirds worked alone and one-third worked in law firms; 14 percent worked for the government, of which about 5 percent were judges or court officers; 10 percent were employees in private industry; and about 1 percent were teachers in educational institutions.

Within this division of the legal profession, some political scientists have speculated that there is a shadowy but important class stratification.

> The upper class, of course, is made up of the partners of the large firms, counsel for big corporations, and government lawyers at the Attorney General, Solicitor General, and Assistant Attorney General rank. The upper middle class might be viewed as composed of professors at Ivy League and other prestige law schools, government counsel just below the Assistant Attorney General rank, and partners in established and prosperous but not necessarily large urban firms. Country lawyers and professors at lesser-known law schools make up the lower middle class together with the highly mobile associates in the bigger offices. In the lowest class in the profession are those attorneys who specialize in criminal law, divorce cases, and personal injury suits . . . men like Clarence Darrow, Melvin Belli, and Jerry Geisler. There is . . . a distinct tendency within the legal profession to look down on these lawyers, and . . . [their failure to become] Supreme Court justices indicates that the bar has made its notions of social status felt.[1]

The basic pattern of specialization indicated by the 1967 trends is relatively new, dating largely from the 1930's. Between the founding of the Republic and the close of the Civil War, however, the great bulk of lawyers were in individual and general private practice. Land titles and local commercial transactions were the main staples of law business, along with the bundle of personal and family affairs that inevitably required legal forms or proceedings. A firm with six lawyers was considered a giant in the 1850's. In this era, the famous trial advocates—men such as Luther Martin, Daniel Webster, and Rufus Choate—argued all types of cases and for whichever client hired their services first. Lawyers were usually active in political-party affairs, and it was largely from the party-centered but "independent" bar that judgeships were filled and executive appointments were made.

Between 1870 and 1930, profound changes took place in the bar, spurred by the expansion of manufacturing and commerce, the need for new legal forms to serve growing American capitalism, and the rise of critical labor-management relations. In this era, top legal talent gravitated to large urban firms devoted exclusively to servicing large corporate clients. Lawyers also joined the law departments of the corporations themselves, working up to the post of general counsel for railroads, banks, and steel companies. The leaders of this corporate bar—men such as Joseph Choate, Elihu Root, John W. Davis, and George Wharton Pepper—dominated the profession in this era of business hegemony in American life. Judges at both the state and national levels were drawn heavily from the new corporate bar, and when corporate lawyers went to court to challenge regulatory measures limiting their corporate clients, counsel found the bench sympathetic to their views on constitutional issues. Nothing approaching the size, talent, and resources

[1] Walter F. Murphy and C. Herman Pritchett, *Courts, Judges and Politics* (New York: Random House, 1961), pp. 122-23.

A Fine Point of Law

Lawyers have traditionally been the object of satire by cartoonists: here William Sharp caricatures two lawyers debating during a trial.

William Sharp

of the corporate bar was available to support government, labor, farmers, or minority groups during this period, and it was in these years that the legal profession became most closely identified with strongly conservative "big business."

The American Bar Association became the symbol of legal conservatism in America. Founded in 1878, by 1936 the ABA spoke in the name of the entire American legal profession, although its membership consisted of only 17 percent of the practicing bar. During these fifty years, ABA leaders were usually drawn from a coalition of Northern corporation lawyers and Southern lawyer-politicians. The Bar Association's political ideology is suggested by its opposition to a proposed federal amendment forbidding child labor, its support for injunctions against union picketing and strikes, its opposition to regulatory agencies, its campaigns to soften the antitrust laws, and its approval of wide-ranging "antiradical" and loyalty-oath laws.

However, organizations representing lawyers underwent important changes after 1937. Through its energetic recruitment policy and its decision to democratize its House of Delegates, the American Bar Association had grown to more than 124,000 members by 1967, about half the active profession. The ABA has become increasingly liberal in its policy positions during the 1950's and 1960's, admitting Negro lawyers to membership, opposing federal bills to curb the Supreme Court for its liberal civil-liberties decisions, endorsing civil rights for all minority groups, and promoting a strongly internationalist "World Peace Through Law" program. Many of the bar's progressive attitudes are expressed by large and influential bar associations at the city and state levels.

This trend in the ABA has been paralleled by the increasing numbers of lawyers who work for the government, providing a continuing pool of talented counsel to defend the government's interests in the courts and legislatures, and by the new importance of labor-union lawyers. Many labor unions now have full-time law departments, and the new respectability of the union lawyer today was symbolized by the appointment of Arthur Goldberg, formerly general counsel of the United Steelworkers of America and the AFL-CIO, to the Supreme Court in 1962.

Another development in the legal profession during recent years has been the growth of legal staffs within civil-liberty and minority-group organizations, who now bring test cases on behalf of liberty and equality claims as the corporate bar once did between 1870 and 1937 in behalf of property interests. Men such as Robert Carter and Jack Greenberg of the NAACP, Leo Pfeffer and Will Maslow of the American Jewish Congress, Hayden Covington of Jehovah's Witnesses, and Osmund Fraenkel of the American Civil Liberties Union typify these "civil liberty" and "civil rights" advocates. Finally, the liberalizing role of law schools and of law professors has grown significantly in the past three decades. The attitudes of the majority of law teachers reflect the spread of legal realism and of the public-policy responsibility of the law, and two generations of law students have already been shaped by the teaching and writing of legal realists in law schools across the country.

AMERICAN JUDGES: POLITICS AND THE ROBE

Public Expectations of the Judge

Americans view the process of judging as a special government function, and they view judges as a class apart from other actors in the political process. Whenever public confidence in the political process is shaken, it is traditional to call in judges to restore integrity and find the truth without favor. Thus judges (and legislators) were used to determine the victor in the disputed presidential election of 1876, to investigate and clean up baseball after the Black Sox scandal of 1919, to determine the cause of our devastating loss at Pearl Harbor in 1941, to prosecute on behalf of the nation in the Nuremberg war-crimes trials in 1946, and to chair the commission set up in 1963 to investigate the assassination of President Kennedy.

Judges, according to our civic myth, are supposed to be "above politics." This means that, first, they should be selected from the best men available, without regard to political affiliation or prior party service. Second, "political" influences—whether of personal ideology, party, or interest groups—should not affect their decisions in specific cases. And, third, they should be immune from political reprisals for unpopular rulings or controversial judicial philosophies. How does our actual system of selecting and controlling judges conform to these assumptions?

The Need for Judicial Self-Discipline

It is asked with sophomoric brightness, does a man cease to be himself when he becomes a Justice? Does he change his character by putting on a gown? No, he does not change his character. He brings his whole experience, his training, his outlook, his social, intellectual, and moral environment with him when he takes a seat on the supreme bench. But a judge worth his salt is in the grip of his function. The intellectual habits of self-discipline which govern his mind are as much a part of him as the influence of the interest he may have represented at the bar, often much more so....

To assume that a lawyer who becomes a judge takes on the bench merely his views on social or economic questions leaves out of account his rooted notions regarding the scope and limits of a judge's authority. The outlook of a lawyer fit to be a Justice regarding the role of a judge cuts across all his personal preferences for this or that social arrangement....

Need it be stated that true humility and its offspring, disinterestedness, are more indispensable for the work of the Supreme Court than for a judge's function on any other bench?

From Justice Felix Frankfurter, "Some Observations on the Nature of the Judicial Process of Supreme Court Litigation," *Proceedings of the American Philosophical Society,* 1954.

The Pattern of American Judicial Recruitment

In most Western European democracies judges are part of the career civil service. A candidate for judicial office, after graduating from law school, presents himself for a special examination designed to measure qualities that are thought to produce good judges, as distinct from good lawyers. Once appointed by the executive, the young man begins as a judicial officer and moves upward from the lower to the higher courts, through promotions based primarily on evaluations by the ministry of justice or a judicial council, neither of which relies heavily on political criteria. In keeping with the concept of a "nonpolitical" judiciary, European courts (with a few exceptions) do not have the power of judicial review over the constitutionality of legislation, which minimizes party conflict over judicial appointments.

In the United States we followed a different path. According to our common-law tradition, the role of judging was seen as a creative art performed by men who mixed technical knowledge of the law with a political sense of the community's mores and needs. Men drawn from community affairs were seen as best fitted for such a role. This tradition was supported by the bar, which not surprisingly favored experience in the practice of law as the prime requisite for judges, and by the American public, who distrusted the idea of a judiciary made up of career civil servants. Furthermore, after our unpleasant colonial experience with judges who were considered pliant tools of the British Crown, the Framers of the American Constitution decided to free the judiciary from close reliance on either the executive or the legislative.

THE SELECTION AND CONTROL OF FEDERAL JUDGES

The rules for the selection of federal judges have remained the same since the early days of the Republic. The Constitution provides that justices of the Supreme Court shall be appointed by the President with the advice and consent of the Senate. But, unlike the provisions for the President and members of Congress, the provisions for justices specify no requirements of age, citizenship, period of residence, or even legal training. Constitutionally, a twenty-five-year-old French lady pediatrician without legal education could serve on the Supreme Court of the United States if she were nominated by a President and confirmed by the Senate. The Constitution gives Congress the power to establish lower federal courts; beginning with the Judiciary Act of 1789, congressional statutes created the federal-district and circuit judgeships and provided that appointments for these offices (as well as for special federal tribunals, such as the court of claims) be made by the President with the advice and consent of the Senate. All federal judges are given life tenure once their appointment has been confirmed.

The process of federal judicial appointment follows a classic pattern.[2] When a federal vacancy occurs, the President consults with a variety of persons (determined by his own inclinations and his sense of political prudence). These will usually include members of his official family (especially the Attorney General), leaders of his party, influential senators, spokesmen for national and state bar associations, leaders of important interest groups, and, sometimes, individual members of the federal judiciary. Since the start of the Cold War, FBI security checks are also secured for leading prospects. An important point to note is that *party affiliation is the single most conspicuous factor in federal judicial appointments.* An average of about 90 percent of the federal judges chosen by Presidents from George Washington to Lyndon Johnson have come from the President's own party, as part of the system of rewards for political service. For example, under Republican President Warren Harding, 97.7 percent of the judges appointed were Republicans; while under Democratic President Woodrow Wilson, 98.6 percent were Democrats.[3] Supreme Court appointments have reflected the pattern of the

[2] For an excellent analysis of the selection process, see Harold W. Chase, "Federal Judges: The Appointing Process," *Minnesota Law Review,* Vol. LI (1966), pp. 185–221.
[3] See Ben R. Miller, "Federal Judicial Appointments," *American Bar Association Journal,* Vol. XLI (1955), p. 125.

A Judge Should Be a Party Man

In the ordinary and low sense which we attach to the words "partisan" and "politician," a judge of the Supreme Court should be neither. But in the higher sense, in the proper sense, he is not in my judgment fitted for the position unless he is a party man, a constructive statesman, constantly keeping in mind his adherence to the principles and policies under which this nation has been built up and in accordance with which it must go on; and keeping in mind also his relations with his fellow statesmen who in other branches of the government are striving in cooperation with him to advance the ends of government. Marshall rendered such invaluable service because he was a statesman of the national type, like Adams who appointed him, like Washington whose mantle fell upon him. Taney was a curse to our national life because he belonged to the wrong party and faithfully carried out the criminal and foolish views of the party which stood for such a construction of the Constitution as would have rendered it impossible to preserve the national life. The Supreme Court of the sixties was good exactly in so far as its members represented the spirit of Lincoln.

From letter by President Theodore Roosevelt, July 1902, in Henry Cabot Lodge, *Selections from the Correspondence of Theodore Roosevelt and Henry Cabot Lodge, 1894–1918,* 1925.

federal judiciary as a whole, with about 90 percent of the justices between 1789 and 1968 coming from the President's own party. The party out of power in the White House often calls on the President to distribute federal judgeships more "equitably," especially when a large number of additional judgeships are created by Congress to be filled all at once. But the prevailing philosophy has been: "More than enough good men for these judgeships can be found in our party." President Kennedy, for example, had sent eighty-two nominees for judgeships to the Senate by 1962; eighty-one were Democrats, and the other was a member of the Liberal Party of New York (which supported Kennedy and the state Democratic ticket in the 1960 elections).

The primary effect of this partisanship is that when the White House is occupied for long periods of time by one political party, the federal judiciary becomes solidly packed with its adherents. When Grover Cleveland, Woodrow Wilson, Franklin Roosevelt, and Dwight Eisenhower came to the Presidency, for example, each after more than a decade of White House control by the opposing party, they confronted a judiciary in which 80 to 90 percent of the judges were from the opposing party. It is true, of course, that the American party system is broad enough to produce very liberal Republicans and very conservative Democrats and that the real socio-economic views of justices like Harlan Stone (a liberal Republican) or James McReynolds (a conservative Democrat) were what mattered in their decisions. But *most* judges reflect fairly closely the median positions of their party. The tendency for the judiciary to remain in the hands of the opposition during the early years of an administration thus provides a check on a popular movement that gains control of the Presidency and Congress at the same time. Seen from another perspective, however, reform Presidents such as Jefferson, Jackson, Lincoln, Wilson, and Franklin Roosevelt, during the important first years of innovation, had their legislative programs harshly treated by federal judges with partisan and ideological hostility to the reform measures.

The Selection of District-Court Judges

As we saw in Chapter 14, the district courts represent the lowest level of the federal judicial system, and the authority of a district judge lies wholly within the boundaries of a single state—sometimes within a single county. Even though this judge will be the final voice of federal law in over 90 percent of the cases brought before him, American practice by the 1840's had established the principle that district-court appointments were primarily the choices of the party controlling the state, not of the President—reflecting the primacy of state party organizations in the American political system. The state party exercises its power over these judicial appointments through the rule of "senatorial courtesy," discussed in Chapters 9 and 11.

When one or both United States senators from a state with a district-court vacancy belong to the same party as the President, he must accept the nominee of the senator or senators. When both senators belong to the opposition party, the President has to find someone acceptable to those senators and to the state leaders of the President's party. In practice, then, the Constitution's mandate of nomination by the President and confirmation by the Senate has been reversed; the local senators nominate and the President acquiesces or conducts limited negotiation.

This practice has been defended on several grounds. Local senators are presumed to know better than a President or an Attorney General who are the best-qualified candidates for judicial office in their states. Furthermore, senatorial choices are more likely to reflect the spirit and attitudes of the local community. The crux of the matter, however, is the fact that federal judgeships pay quite well, are lifetime jobs, command enormous prestige, and are eagerly sought after by lawyers. Since these positions are one of the top rewards a local party can bestow on party contributors and workers, the local parties have fought tirelessly to retain control of them. Critics of senatorial initiative in district-court appointments maintain, on the other hand, that this process lowers the quality of federal judges by limiting presidential choices, fosters patronage and payoffs, and often installs local prejudice in the federal courthouse.

The problems of Presidents over senatorial control are illustrated nicely by two incidents. In 1929 President Herbert Hoover announced publicly that he would restore confidence in the federal judiciary (somewhat shaken by scandals in the Harding Administration) by refusing to appoint anyone as federal judge as a reward for party activity and that the recommendations of party organizations would be accepted only if nominees were "highly qualified." The showdown on Hoover's policy came in 1929. The senior Republican senator from Pennsylvania, Daniel Reed, backed by the state organization, "nominated" Albert Watson, a state-court judge from Scranton, for a district judgeship. Leaders of the state bar and even the senior judge of the federal-circuit court protested informally to the White House that Watson was inferior material. Hoover delayed appointing Watson for several months. At this point, Senator Reed told the President that if Watson's name was not sent to the Senate promptly, the Pennsylvania delegation in Congress would not support the President on key legislative matters.

Hoover reluctantly sent Watson's name up, and Attorney General Mitchell made a lukewarm endorsement of him as the "best available." The Judiciary Committee hearings disclosed that Watson's practice consisted primarily of uncontested divorce cases; that he had argued only six cases in court in twenty-six years at the bar; and that he was opposed by three-fourths of the active lawyers in the district. The governor who had appointed him to his state judgeship wired opposition to the federal appointment. Several progressive Republicans such as La Follette and Norris called on the Senate to reject the nomination and end local-party dictation of district judges. Watson was confirmed, 53–22.

Another revealing instance took place in 1959, when President Dwight Eisenhower sent thirteen lower-court nominations to the Senate. For most of the congressional session, the Senate Judiciary Committee took no action on them. It turned out that the Senate majority leader, Lyndon Johnson of Texas, had his own candidate for a district-court vacancy in that state, but Eisenhower had nominated someone else. Even though Johnson was a Democrat and not entitled to "automatic-nomination" power, his influence led the Judiciary Committee to keep Eisenhower's thirteen nominees waiting. Unable to break the deadlock, Eisenhower arranged to have his Texas nominee withdraw, and Senator Johnson's choice was named to the post. Within three days the thirteen judges had been approved by the Senate Judiciary Committee and confirmed by the Senate.

No studies have ever been made of the backgrounds of a significant sample of district judges. There have been distinguished men throughout the country and throughout our history who have served on the district bench, some for their whole careers and others on their way up to higher-court appointments. Twenty percent of the Supreme Court justices have come from the lower federal-district courts. Furthermore, there is no evidence that party influence in electing district judges has produced a system of judicial payoffs through favors in decisions. Nevertheless, it is true that district judges rather naturally tend to be lawyers of local fame rather than statesmen with national reputations. Also, local influences exert more pressure on district judges than on the upper-court judges. Yet it is important to note that in highly controversial cases involving racial discrimination in the South, most Southern district-court judges have applied federal antidiscrimination laws despite the hostility from local political leaders toward such rulings.

The Selection of Appellate-Court Judges

Since the jurisdiction of a court of appeals covers more than one state, the senators of one state cannot control presidential choices as they can with district judges. A demonstration of this came in 1955, when President Eisenhower named the Solicitor General of the United States, Simon Sobeloff of Maryland, to the court of appeals for the Fourth Circuit. This circuit covers Maryland, West Virginia, Virginia, North Carolina, and South Carolina. Since Sobeloff had called for implementation of the school-desegregation order and had defended the Supreme Court against charges of "judicial legislation," many Southern senators opposed his confirmation. They managed to delay Judiciary Committee consideration of the nomination for a year. When Eisenhower and a bipartisan Senate group were able to force the nomination out of committee and onto the Senate floor, the Senators from North Carolina, South Carolina, and Virginia announced that Sobeloff was "personally obnoxious" to them and should be rejected. Nevertheless, Sobeloff was confirmed.

There are several significant differences between appeals-court and district judges. First, district judges tend to come directly from law practice, with much prior experience in party service but not in public office. By contrast, one study has indicated that about 85 percent of appeals-court judges have had some prior experience in state or national office. Of these more than half had served as federal-district or state-court judges.[4]

Second, district judges tend to be more susceptible to ideological and political influence from local party leaders and the informal power structure of the community. Appeals judges, on the other hand, travel throughout their areas and develop social bonds with the élite of law schools, the federal executive, legal associations, and so on. They command greater prestige among lawyers because they are generally concerned with appeals on constitutional issues. These factors make appeals judges a more independent and distinguished group than district judges. An appeals judgeship becomes the "career" office of talented men in the closing decades of their lives. With their long tenure in office, the appeals-court judges leave a clear imprint not only on the quality of federal justice in their regions but often—as with men such as John J. Parker, Learned Hand, Jerome Frank, Calvert Magruder, and Charles Clark—on the development of federal law as a whole.

[4] Cortez A. M. Ewing, *American National Government* (New York: American Book, 1958), pp. 384–86.

The Selection of Supreme Court Justices: Nine Men at the Top

It is traditional for students of American government to say that the men appointed to the Supreme Court are, more than any other actors in the federal judicial system, the free choices of Presidents. This clearly was not the case, however, during the first century of the Court's existence. Between 1789 and 1894, eighty-four men were nominated to be justices (excluding several who were nominated but declined to accept). Of these, twenty were not confirmed by the Senate, either by direct vote against confirmation or by deliberate failure of the Senate to act (causing appointments to lapse or forcing nominees to withdraw). This rejection rate is higher than that for lower judicial posts, since most challenges or rejections are reserved for appointments that will have a major impact on the political scene. The first Senate rejection occurred in 1795 over President Washington's attempt to promote John Rutledge from associate justice to Chief Justice. Rutledge, while a firm Federalist, had delivered a speech opposing Jay's Treaty, and the Federalist majority in the Senate opposed his confirmation. This established the precedent that the Senate would base its decision on each judge on both professional and political criteria. Other rejections added further grounds: expression of Senate opposition to the President by denying him important appointments; refusal to confirm appointments just before a presidential election when it was likely that the opposition party, which already controlled the Senate, would gain the White House as well and thus have a chance to name the justice themselves; vendettas over patronage between the President and powerful senators from the nominee's home state; and, on rare occasions, a belief that the nominee lacked ability as a lawyer and statesman. Party issues and executive-legislative tensions were the dominant factors between 1789 and 1894, and Presidents seemed to be rather accustomed to having nominees to the Supreme Court turned down.

The situation since 1895, however, has been quite different: forty-six men have been nominated to be justices, and only one was rejected by the Senate. This was John J. Parker, a federal court-of-appeals judge named by President Herbert Hoover in 1930. Parker was principally opposed by Negroes, labor unions and Republican progressives—groups who feared he would be a social and economic conservative. Despite the harmony of this second period, however, the Senate has frequently held far-reaching committee hearings and general debates over the socioeconomic beliefs of nominees. Thus, protests against Louis D. Brandeis' liberalism in 1916, Charles Evans Hughes' conservatism in 1930, John M. Harlan's internationalism in 1955, and William J. Brennan, Jr.'s, attitudes on internal-security issues in 1957 produced Senate fights of varying intensity, although all the nominees were confirmed.

The rejection of only one nominee since 1895 has led some commentators to suggest that a lessening of partisan response in the Senate, coupled with somewhat greater presidential concern with selecting men of at least minimum professional reputation, has given Presidents in the twentieth century more freedom in Supreme Court nominations than in any other federal judicial selections. However, others suggest that Presidents have been "prepackaging" their nominations by avoiding candidates who would be objectionable to the Senate.

Characteristics of the justices

Several studies [5] made prior to 1962 examined the backgrounds of the ninety-four Supreme Court justices appointed since 1789. These surveys indicated the following facts about composition of the Court:

1. About 91 percent were from socially prominent, politically influential, and upper-middle-class families. About 60 percent of these families were quite active in politics and had a strong sense of civic participation.[6]

2. All the ninety-four justices included in these surveys were white. Eighty-three were Protestant, five were Catholic, and four were Jewish.[7] Eighty-eight percent were of Northern European descent, primarily English, Welsh, Scotch, and Irish.[8]

3. All the justices had been lawyers. Prior to their appointment to the Court, about half were primarily pursuing political careers (United States senators and representatives, governors, or officials in the federal executive branch); about one-fourth were primarily state or federal judges; and the remaining fourth were in private law practice or were academicians. Well over 50 percent had served in a judicial capacity, although only slightly more than 25 percent had had extensive judicial careers. All but one had actively participated in politics or in some public service in government.[9]

4. By party affiliation, almost half the justices have been Democrats, over one-third have been Republicans, and thirteen were Federalists.[10] As noted earlier, almost 90 percent came from the appointing President's own party.

5. Justices have been drawn rather evenly from the major regions of the country in each decade in our history. However, because of their concentration of legal talent and their political importance, the four largest states of the period—New York, Ohio, Massachusetts, and Pennsylvania—have supplied well over one-third of the justices. (These same states have also produced most of our Presidents.) [11]

---

[5] John R. Schmidhauser, *The Supreme Court: Its Politics, Personalities, and Procedures* (New York: Holt, Rinehart and Winston, 1960); Henry J. Abraham, *The Judicial Process* (New York: Oxford University Press, 1962).

[6] Schmidhauser, *op. cit.*, p. 32.

[7] Abraham, *op. cit.*, p. 69.

[8] Schmidhauser, *op. cit.*, p. 37.

[9] Abraham, *op. cit.*, p. 57.

[10] *Ibid.*, p. 73.

[11] *Ibid.*, p. 68.

Using these data, one scholar has drawn the following composite picture of the Supreme Court Justice.[12]

> White; generally Protestant . . . ; fifty to fifty-five years of age at the time of his appointment; Anglo-Saxon ethnic stock . . . ; high social status; reared in an urban environment; member of a civic-minded, politically active, economically comfortable family; legal training; some type of public office; generally well-educated.

While background does not always determine judicial philosophy, the above findings suggest that the Supreme Court has been dominated by the gentry in our early history and by the "professionalized upper-middle class" in recent times. Thus, if the Court is the "keeper of the American conscience, it is essentially the conscience of the American upper-middle class," conditioned by the "conservative impact of legal training and professional legal attitudes and associations" and propelled by "individual social responsibility and political activism."[13]

But, when the figures are broken down by period, it becomes clear that

[12] *Ibid.,* p. 58.
[13] Schmidhauser, *op. cit.,* p. 49.

"Should be a good fit . . . it took us 177 years to make."

Gene Basset. Scripps-Howard Newspapers

the "democratization" of the Supreme Court is under way. In terms of religion, five Jews and five Catholics have been appointed since 1895, almost one-fourth of the justices for that period. While conservative corporation lawyers filled the Court heavily between 1890 and 1930, the period since 1930 has brought to the Court active liberals who were senators, governors, attorneys general, labor and civil-rights lawyers, and law professors.

Of course, the Supreme Court is not required to be a representative body, and its members need not register the religious, racial, sectional, class, or nationality percentages of the nation in each era. Yet, if the Court is to enunciate the constitutional credo of the nation and if it is to be increasingly concerned with the questions of status in our rapidly changing society, it seems fitting that it include persons whose backgrounds are varied as the nation is varied. This was clearly in Lyndon Johnson's mind when he appointed Thurgood Marshall in 1967 to be the Court's first Negro justice. To insist that a given seat be reserved for a Catholic, or an Italian, or a Negro would weaken the dignity and independence of the Court and limit the President. But this factor is certainly considered by Presidents and their advisers, and the growing concern for minority representation on the Court has become part of the ethos of appointment policies.

Alternative roles for the justices: three prototypes

Of the ninety-nine men who have sat as Supreme Court justices between 1789 and 1967, at least half can fairly be described as men of modest intellectual powers, lacking deep cores of self-consciousness, and not terribly troubled by the dilemma of exercising judicial review in a society valuing majority rule. These justices were carried along by the dominant currents of opinion in their time, and for them the process of judging generally consisted of applying rather clear precedents to specific problems. It may surprise some readers to learn that the giants of the Supreme Court—Marshall, Story, Miller, Holmes, Brandeis, and so on—are exceeded in number by distinctly average judges such as Bushrod Washington, Thomas Todd, Nathan Clifford, Ward Hunt, William R. Day, Edward T. Sanford, or Harold Burton.

This leaves between thirty and forty justices who were truly influential in American constitutional history. Some were powerful inside the Court, gathering colleagues into cohesive majorities or into minority blocs. Some were powerful in terms of their appeals outside the Court, usually in dissent, calling for new doctrines and criticizing the prevailing constitutional philosophy of the majority.

Looking at these influential justices, one can see three main prototypes of basic judicial philosophy. First is the *True Believer*, who views the Constitution as setting forth certain rights that are entitled to absolute protection by the judiciary. He wants the Supreme Court to exercise its

The True Believer

I do not agree that laws directly abridging First Amendment freedoms can be justified by a congressional or judicial balancing process....

To apply the Court's balancing test under such circumstances is to read the First Amendment to say, "Congress shall pass no law abridging freedom of speech, press, assembly and petition, unless Congress and the Supreme Court reach the joint conclusion that on balance the interest of the government in stifling these freedoms is greater than the interest of the people in having them exercised." This is closely akin to the notion that neither the First Amendment nor any other provision of the Bill of Rights should be enforced unless the Court believes it is *reasonable* to do so. Not only does this violate the genius of our *written* Constitution, but it runs expressly counter to the injunction to Court and Congress made by Madison when he introduced the Bill of Rights. "If they [the first ten amendments] are incorporated into the Constitution, independent tribunals of justice will consider themselves in a peculiar manner the guardians of those rights; they will be an impenetrable bulwark against *every* assumption of power in the Legislative or Executive; they will be naturally led to resist *every* encroachment upon rights expressly stipulated for in the Constitution by the declaration of rights."

From Justice Hugo Black, dissenting in *Barenblatt* v. *United States*, 1959.

powers fully to defend such rights whenever the elective branches of state or national government or private parties infringe upon them. The True Believer has sometimes been a liberal in his socioeconomic outlook, such as the first Justice John M. Harlan (1877–1911) or Justice Hugo Black, who joined the Court in 1937. Other True Believers have been socio-economic conservatives, such as Justices James Wilson (1789–98), Stephen Field (1863–99), and George Sutherland (1922–38). But, whatever their place on the ideological spectrum, all these men have seen the Supreme Court as a place where truth is defended and error lashed, where the Constitution embodies the "American way," and where Presidents and Congresses and governors are commanded to cease tampering with the fundamentals of the Republic.

The second prototype among the influential justices has been the *Institutionalist*. Sometimes Institutionalists are men whose personal attitudes on social or economic questions would make them liberals, such as Justices Samuel Miller (1862–90), Louis D. Brandeis (1916–39), and Felix Frank-furter (1939–62); others would be classified as conservatives, such as Chief Justice Charles Evans Hughes (1930–41), Justice Oliver Wendell Holmes, Jr. (1902–32), and the second Justice John M. Harlan, who joined the Court in 1955. But the basic assumption of all Institutionalists is that the Constitution created various powers and guaranteed various rights that often

The Institutionalist

As a member of this Court I am not justified in writing my private notions of policy into the Constitution, no matter how deeply I may cherish them or how mischievous I may deem their disregard.... It can never be emphasized too much that one's own opinion about the wisdom or evil of a law should be excluded altogether when one is doing one's duty on the bench. The only opinion of our own even looking in that direction is whether legislators could in reason have enacted such a law....

The admonition that judicial self-restraint alone limits arbitrary exercise of our authority is relevant every time we are asked to nullify legislation. The Constitution does not give us greater veto power when dealing with one phase of "liberty" than with another.... Judicial self-restraint is equally necessary whenever an exercise of political or legislative power is challenged.... Our power does not vary according to the particular provision of the Bill of Rights which is invoked....

Before a duly enacted law can be judicially nullified, it must be forbidden by some explicit restriction upon political authority in the Constitution. Equally inadmissible is the claim to strike down legislation because to us as individuals it seems opposed to the "plan and purpose" of the Constitution. That is too tempting a basis for finding in one's personal views the purposes of the Founders.

From Justice Felix Frankfurter, dissenting in *West Virginia State Board of Education* v. *Barnette*, 1943.

come into conflict under the actual pressures of governing, and that the Court ought to defer to the elective branches of government unless clearly defined constitutional rights have been directly violated. Such judicial conduct breeds responsibility among elected officials, avoids public over-reliance on courts, and maximizes the authority of the judiciary when it does strike down popular acts as unconstitutional. Where the True Believer is likely to gird his loins happily for showdowns between the Court and Congress or the Court and the President over assertive judicial rulings, the Institutionalist typically regards this as a disaster, to be entered into only when unavoidable.

Between the True Believers and the Institutionalists is a smaller number of justices, the most individualistic (even quixotic) of all. These are the *Selective Interventionists*, who believe that the Court's basic role is to maintain the crucial equilibrium in American government between majority rule and minority rights, national and state authority, and public and private sectors, adhering to the spirit that the Framers intended but adapting to the challenges of drastically different conditions. The Selective Interventionist sees both True Believers and Institutionalists as overly rigid. The Interventionist decides in each momentous case whether to wield the judicial veto or defer to elected authority by weighing key imponderables:

Can the political process correct itself? Will the Court's mandate be obeyed? Is public opinion amenable to constitutional change in this area? Of the Selective Interventionists, Justices Joseph P. Bradley (1870–80), Benjamin N. Cardozo (1932–38), and Robert H. Jackson (1941–54) are leading examples.

Proposed Reforms of the Federal Judicial-Selection Process

Two main reforms have been proposed in recent years to "take the federal judiciary out of politics." The dominant groups behind these proposals have been the American Bar Association and conservative business and civic groups. The first reform would require that justices of the Supreme Court have prior experience as judges of the state or lower federal courts. The assumption here is that such prior service would reveal the nominee's judicial temperament and would prepare him for service on the nation's highest court.

But critics of this proposal point out that since state parties and individual senators heavily influence the selection of state and lower federal judges, the actual effect of this plan would be to limit the choice of Supreme Court justices to judges acceptable to the powers that be at the state level. The net impact would undoubtedly be to produce far more con-

The Selective Interventionist

The political function which the Supreme Court, more or less effectively, may be called upon to perform comes to this: In a society in which rapid changes tend to upset all equilibrium, the Court, without exceeding its own limited powers, must strive to maintain the great system of balances upon which our free government is based. Whether these balances and checks are essential to liberty elsewhere in the world is beside the point; they are indispensable to the society we know. Chief of these balances are: first, between the Executive and Congress; second, between the central government and the states; third, between state and state; fourth, between authority, be it state or national, and the liberty of the citizen, or between the rule of the majority and the rights of the individual.

I have said that in these matters the Court must respect the limitations on its own powers because judicial usurpation is to me no more justifiable and no more promising of permanent good to the country than any other kind. So I presuppose that a Court that will not depart from the judicial process will not go beyond resolving cases and controversies brought to it in conventional form, and will not consciously encroach upon the functions of its coordinate branches.

From Justice Robert H. Jackson, *The Supreme Court in the American System of Government*, 1955.

servative justices. In addition, no one has proved that prior experience on trial or appellate courts necessarily prepares a man for the special constitutional decision-making and balancing of values required for Supreme Court adjudication. Most of the great justices, for example—Marshall, Story, Curtis, Campbell, Miller, Bradley, Hughes, Brandeis, Frankfurter, Jackson—had no prior judicial experience. Moreover, the Court in its best periods has had members from diverse careers—some from Congress, some from the executive, some directly from legal practice, and some from state government—each offering a different perspective to the group.

The second proposal has been that Presidents clear all their nominees for the federal bench—from district courts to the Supreme Court—with the American Bar Association and the state bar association from the nominee's home state. Informal consultation with bar associations and bar leaders has been traditional, but in the 1950's, the American Bar Association pressed for formal submission of projected appointees to its Standing Committee on the Federal Judiciary. Under President Eisenhower the Attorney General's office began this as a general practice in preparing its appointment lists, but neither the Eisenhower nor Kennedy Administrations promised to abide automatically by the recommendations. While it uses the Bar Association rating as one guide to the competence of a nominee, the Department of Justice is aware that the Bar Association's ideological and policy stands influence its appraisal of nominees and that there are other considerations in selecting judges than professional standing *per se*. Probably the present system—friendly liaison between the Department of Justice and bar associations, but no veto power—is the wise accommodation.

Controls over the Federal Judiciary

How to exercise control over the performance of federal judges without impairing judicial independence has been a serious problem in the American legal system. First, it is important to note that control of federal judges once they have been appointed has been minimal. Judges of the district courts, courts of appeals, and Supreme Court have life tenure. There is no compulsory retirement age. The presiding judges or senior judges of courts have no disciplinary powers over junior colleagues, nor can a majority of the judges on a court take disciplinary action against a fellow member. Judges can be removed only by impeachment for "high crimes and misdemeanors," initiated by majority vote of the House of Representatives and requiring a two-thirds vote of the Senate (after full trial) to convict. Of course, a federal judge who breaks federal or state laws can be prosecuted by the appropriate courts, but only his resignation or impeachment would automatically remove him from the bench.

As a guarantee against punishing judges for unpopular decisions, this system has worked well and deserves continued support. Only one Supreme

Court justice has ever been impeached. Samuel Chase, a strong Federalist partisan, was accused by the Jeffersonians controlling Congress in 1805 of delivering political speeches from the bench and bullying defendants during sedition trials. Chase was narrowly acquitted. From then on, in Jefferson's words, impeachment was "not even a scarecrow" to frighten judges whose rulings offended Congress or the administration.[14] In recent years, some irate congressmen have tried to have the entire Supreme Court impeached for the 1954 desegregation rulings. Others have demanded impeachment of individual justices, such as Justice William O. Douglas for granting a stay of execution to the convicted atomic-espionage defendants Julius and Ethel Rosenberg. In the past decade, a vigorous campaign to impeach Earl Warren was conducted by the extreme right wing who opposed the Chief Justice's positions on civil liberties and civil rights. These threats have never been taken seriously by the justices, however, or by the majorities in Congress, and security from ideological reprisals through impeachment has encouraged the independence and sometimes the venturesomeness of the federal judiciary.[15]

Once we move away from ideological matters, however, there is some question as to whether the system for removing federal judges has worked well. As one recent commentator has noted: "A Federal Judge may suddenly become afflicted with a helpless insanity or blindness, deafness or senility; he may be convicted of murder, arson, or burglary; he may rend asunder the Canons of Judicial Ethics; or he may even be guilty of selling his Justice." [16] Yet only the awkward and complicated instrument of impeachment is available to remedy these situations if the judge refuses to resign. The problem of judges staying on the bench after their physical or mental powers have failed has been met partly by providing for liberal pensions upon voluntary retirement and partly through the informal pressures fellow judges usually bring to bear in such cases. These solutions are far from perfect, however, and willful but feeble-minded judges have plagued the federal bench on several occasions. Justice Stephen Field, for example, hung on at least two years longer than he was able to remain awake in the courtroom or follow issues sensibly in conference, but he was determined to stay on the Supreme Court longer than John Marshall; he did, to the enormous discomfort of his colleagues and the bar. This problem remains unsolved, but, many would say, it is not serious enough to warrant new measures.

A more serious problem has been control of judicial misconduct and

---

[14] The only other politically inspired impeachment in American history was the conviction in 1862 of a Tennessee district-court judge, West H. Humphrey, for supporting secession.

[15] Indirect controls on judicial behavior, such as campaigns to curtail a court's jurisdiction or to reverse its decisions by constitutional amendment, legislation, and the like have been discussed in Chapter 14.

[16] Joseph Borkin, *The Corrupt Judge* (New York: Potter, 1963), p. 192.

corruption. During our history, congressional committees have held fifty-five full-dress investigations (for possible impeachment) into alleged misconduct by federal judges. About a third of the investigations involved drunkenness and tyrannical behavior, but almost two-thirds involved corruption—misusing judicial powers over trusts, estates, and receiverships for personal gain or selling decisions in cases. Of the fifty-five investigations, nine resulted in impeachments,[17] eight produced official censure by the congressional committee but not impeachment, sixteen produced resignations from judges to avoid impeachment, and twenty-two resulted in judges being absolved of charges. A leading student of corruption in the federal judiciary has noted that the thirty-three judges whose cases indicated corruption by no means exhaust the list.[18] Other federal judges [19] were allowed by Congress to resign before official inquiries were begun because of the need to preserve public confidence in the courts. Nonetheless, thirty-three plus is clearly a tiny fraction of the federal judiciary in our history, and the standard of integrity and judicial propriety among federal judges has probably been far higher than at the local- and state-court levels.

But even a few tainted judges are too many, and those who feel that impeachment is inadequate as a remedy have suggested several new techniques. One is that the House of Representatives continue to investigate cases as it now does in considering impeachment but that charges be prosecuted by the Attorney General and judged by an *ad hoc* court composed of three court-of-appeals judges nominated by the Chief Justice of the United States. Such a proposal passed the House of Representatives in 1937 and again in 1941, but the resolutions never passed the Senate. Critics have argued that the potential threat to judicial independence and separation of powers was too great and that impeachment—or its threat—was sufficient.

Other proposals have been to give the Supreme Court authority to direct investigations through special referees, to require judges to file data on their financial dealings with any persons or companies involved in federal-court matters, or to adopt at the federal level the plan used by Britain and by Massachusetts, New Jersey, Texas, and other states, which permits removal of judges by the executive, upon the recommendation of both houses of the legislature.

[17] Of which four judges were acquitted, four were convicted, and one resigned before a vote.
[18] Borkin, *op. cit.*, p. 204.
[19] Statistics are not available.

THE SELECTION AND CONTROL OF STATE–COURT JUDGES

How do the features of national judicial selection and control compare with those of the states? Unlike the federal system, based on executive appointments approved by the legislature, the dominant state selection method is popular election. This system spread throughout the states as a product of the Jacksonian movement of the 1830's and 1840's, with its emphasis on democratization of government and electoral control by the public. The movement's key objectives were to recapture the judiciary from conservative classes, from the aristocracy of the bar, and from the influences of special-interest groups. The Jacksonians also stressed limited tenure for judges, in order to keep the judiciary responsive to dominant public opinion and to prevent hardening of the judicial arteries.

Today, two-thirds of the states use election for most or all of their judges, sometimes on so-called nonpartisan ballots (no party label given) but more frequently on regular party ballots. The elective term for all state judges averages six years, but in many states life tenure or long terms are provided for supreme-court judges or judges at the intermediate appellate levels.

Several hybrid systems are used by a few states to combine the best features of the appointive and elective plans for judges. In 1934 California adopted a plan in which the governor presents one candidate for appellate-court posts to a special commission composed of the chief justice of the state supreme court, the presiding justice of the district court of appeals for the area, and the state attorney general. If the commission approves the nominee, he is appointed for one year. At the end of that time, he runs for election on the statewide ballot for a twelve-year term. Only his name appears, without party label, and in this form: "Shall _____ be elected to the office of _____ for the term prescribed by law?" If he is defeated, the governor designates a new judge for one year until the next election.

A second variation is the Missouri plan. Adopted by constitutional amendment in 1940, this provides that three candidates for all appellate courts and some trial courts in the state are nominated by special nominating commissions. The chief justice of the state supreme court, three lawyers elected by the state bar, and three nonlawyers appointed by the governor make up the leading commission for appellate court nominations, with members, unsalaried, serving for six-year terms. The governor must appoint one of the three persons nominated by the commission for one year. At the end of that year the judge must be elected on a nonpartisan ballot, with a "Shall he be retained?" question as in California. Between 1940 and 1960, only one of forty-four appointments was rejected by the electorate, even though the state changed parties frequently at local and state levels.

In practice, the various appointive, elective, and hybrid systems for judicial selection and control used by the states are much the same. That is, it is the leaders of the political parties who are decisive in selecting the candidates who run for election or are appointed by governors. Furthermore, party competition is rare; usually, in two-party states, the parties get together, distribute judgeships according to the party ratios in the area, and then endorse one another's choices. It has been suggested that bar associations draw up a panel of names from which election or appointment would be made, but this would only transfer the political struggle to within the bar association, and—as with recommendations for federal judgeships—the associations' nominations would undoubtedly be influenced by the ideological and policy positions of the bar.

SUMMARY

Our focus in this chapter has been on those actors in the American political system charged with the special responsibility for translating the rule of law into practical reality for American government.

We have analyzed the two principal groups of actors in the American legal system—lawyers and judges. As a professional group, lawyers gravitate naturally to political activity and government service, partly because there is a premium on their legal training and partly because political activity enhances legal careers. Though the lawyer's political role has generally been a conservative one—because most lawyers represent propertied clients—the ultraconservative ideology that marked the American bar between the 1880's and 1930's is no longer dominant today, and important segments of the bar are devoted to government legal service, minority-group representation, and reform movements. However, lawyers today continue to serve the same role of middleman between government and society that they occupied in the early years of the nation.

In the American judicial system, judges are lawyers who have ascended to the bench. Though the general public sees the judicial function as "nonpolitical," the selection process for the federal judiciary assures that almost 90 percent of those selected are of the same party affiliation as the President nominating them. The judicial-selection process also produces lawyers who have been politically active before appointment, either in party activity, elected government service, or politically appointed posts in executive agencies. On the whole, the lawyers who make up the American bench are middle and upper-middle class in social origin and represent fairly closely the progress of religious, ethnic, nationality, and racial groups into other positions of political importance.

The role of judge allows considerable latitude in judicial philosophy. The major types, whom we have called the True Believers, the Institutionalists, and the Selective Interventionists, can be found today as throughout our national history.

An important area of controversy in an analysis of the American judiciary is the problem of establishing rules to control the judges as they perform their roles. Although most state-court judges are elected or appointed to serve for a limited term, federal judges serve on the bench for life and can only be removed through the complex mechanism of impeachment. Problems of judicial misconduct or loss of ability to perform effectively due to age or illness must be balanced against the need to protect judges from reprisals for unpopular decisions.

In 1830, De Tocqueville observed that the United States was unique in the way that the "customs and technicalities" of the legal profession were introduced "into the management of public affairs." [20] This remains the impact of lawyers and judges to this day.

[20] Alexis de Tocqueville, *Democracy in America*, Phillips Bradley, ed. (New York: Knopf, 1945), Vol. I, p. 290.

PROPERTY,
LIBERTY,
AND
DUE PROCESS

17

*No study of the American political system
would be complete without analyzing the way
constitutional rights are defined and enforced
in the United States. Although we recognize
the moral dimension of constitutional rights and
the special role of the judiciary in this area, our
emphasis is on the development of these rights
as part of the political process, because the
intergroup, institutional, and cultural forces at
work here are the same as in economic and social
issues. Who enjoys constitutional rights and
who does not? The answers are part of the
policy output of our political system. This
chapter deals with the rights of property,
liberty, and due process, while Chapter 18
discusses civil-rights, or equality, issues.*

The founders of the American nation drew their conception of liberty and property from John Locke, who believed that the basic purpose of creating government was to secure the individual's life, liberty, and property. Liberty and property were regarded by most of the Framers as inter-related rights. The man with property—wealth, land, or a prosperous business—could exercise his liberty to disagree with government or with dominant public opinion, since he did not risk his family's economic welfare by dissenting. Property was also believed to give men the leisure to develop themselves into better-informed citizens. A final element in this propertied-middle-class perspective was the belief that widespread ownership of property by the citizenry, especially ownership of land, would inhibit the rise of both an urban proletariat and a radical peasantry seeking central-ized government or the "leveling" of property.

Americans have remained convinced to this day of this basic interrelation of personal liberty and personal property. Then and now, however, debate begins with the inescapable question: How far may liberty or property be limited by government in the public interest, as defined by the elective branches of government? When the government goes too far, we expect the courts to intervene, but just what constitutes an infringement of "our rights" arouses passionate debates.

THE RIGHTS OF PROPERTY

To avoid misunderstanding, let us define what is meant by "property" and its "rights." When people talk about *property*, they refer to the temporary possession or the full ownership of valuable things. These may be *tangibles*, such as houses, horses, or Ford Mustangs, or *intangibles*, such as stock in General Motors, patents for new atom-smashers, or franchises to drill for oil. Owners must have freedom to sell, exchange, and pledge their property, and these transactions must be protected by law. Property owners also seek the right to pass property on to their heirs, to make gifts during their lifetimes, and to engage in business ventures. They must also have the right to invoke the law to make another party to a contract live up to their agreement. Finally, property must be held without fear of arbitrary government confiscation.

All these property rights were well established by British common law in the American colonies long before the Constitution was written. But common law also firmly established that property rights were *not* absolute. Property could not be used in ways that conflicted unduly with

533

the rights of neighbors, with the rights of the public, or with the paramount rights of government. For example, a man who whipped his horse could be fined for abusing his property; a man who burned rubber in his backyard could be punished for creating a nuisance in the neighborhood. Contracts calling for illegal acts or for taking advantage of minors were not enforceable in the courts. Contracts in restraint of trade were invalid, and making them could be punished by law. And an owner was required to give up his land (for compensation) when government needed it to build a highway, public building, or military installation.

Two main points must be kept in mind in examining the present framework of American property rights. First, many public measures that affect property and wealth are viewed by the courts today as essentially administrative or legislative matters with which judges will not interfere. As long as the rates are not found to be "confiscatory" (and rates as high as 90 percent are not so considered), levels of income taxation cannot be challenged successfully in the courts; this is a matter for debate in Congress and for decision in the executive branch. Similarly, the courts have ruled against opponents of foreign aid who have tried to withhold a portion of their federal income tax corresponding to the percentage of the annual federal budget that goes to foreign aid.

Second, the growing need for positive government in a modern, interdependent, industrial society has led the courts to allow expansion of many of the powers of government to deal with property rights in ways that nineteenth-century Supreme Court majorities forbade. The revenue needs of government have led to federal and state taxation of more and more types of property and economic activity, and taxation carries with it the power to encourage, discourage, or even destroy a given activity or type of ownership. Despite these vast expansions of power, however, there remain vital constitutional limits beyond which the taxing and police powers may not go. There are also important constitutional rules about how valid measures must be framed and administered if they are to be upheld.

We can identify three basic sets of property guarantees in the federal Constitution that are still significant. First are the clauses inserted specifically to protect property rights against government invasion. These include the *contract clause* ("no State shall . . . pass any . . . law impairing the obligation of contracts") and the *just-compensation clause* ("private property . . . [shall not] be taken for public use, without just compensation").

Second are the provisions inserted to protect the basic rights of both property and liberty from infringement by arbitrary procedural act of the government. These include the guarantees to each person of "due process of law," of his own "privileges and immunities," and of "equal protection of the laws."

Third are the clauses written primarily to protect individual liberty but in practice applied to give important protections to holders of property as well. These include the guarantees of free speech and free press and the protections against "unreasonable searches and seizures" and self-incrimination.

It is important to note the legal distinction between property rights for individuals and those for corporations. Some property rights—to make contracts, to engage in business, and to be free from arbitrary confiscation and regulation—have been held to apply to both individuals and corporations. Thus, giant firms such as Standard Oil of New Jersey or Bell Telephone are treated as individual "persons" under the contract, due-process, equal-protection, and just-compensation clauses. However, the courts will often apply a less sweeping standard of protection to corporations than to individuals, even when constitutional clauses apply to both. For example, the Supreme Court has ruled that corporations are entitled to some protection against "unreasonable searches and seizures" under the Fourth Amendment but that they can "claim no equality with individuals in the enjoyment of [this] right to privacy." [1] Still other rights—such as the privileges-and-immunities clause of the Fourteenth Amendment and the self-incrimination clause of the Fifth Amendment—have been construed as applying only to individuals, either because the courts have interpreted this as the intention of the Framers or because such is the essential nature of the right.

One area that illustrates the rise of property issues is that of just compensation. Normally, when local, state, or federal governments exercise the sovereign's right to eminent domain in order to acquire private property for public projects, they pass a statute authorizing a specific program and appropriate money to compensate persons whose property must be taken for public use. Government appraisers inspect the property to determine its fair market value so that the owner can be reimbursed. If the owner feels that the government estimate is too low, he can challenge the appraisal in the courts. Recent court decisions have upheld wide discretion in government to take private property by eminent domain for purposes of beautification and recreation in addition to government business in the narrow sense.

Another key area of property rights concerns due-process limits on the powers of local, state, or federal governments to regulate property. *Substantive* due process requires that government action interfering with liberty and property rights be based on rational ways of achieving valid public purposes. Thus, courts have upheld the right of governments to regulate property within their jurisdictions in such a way as to eliminate nuisances and bar undesirable business activity. This regulation falls under the police power of governments and their obligations to protect their citizens and to develop their cities properly. Governments also have the power to destroy without compensation property, such as diseased food,

[1] *United States* v. *Morton Salt Company*, 338 U.S. 632 (1950).

that is dangerous to public health, safety, or morals. Substantive due process thus safeguards the individual by ensuring that if the government interferes with liberty or property rights, it is doing so for worthwhile purposes that reflect community beliefs and it has chosen acceptable means for achieving its goals.

Procedural due process, on the other hand, safeguards the individual by ensuring that the *process* by which the government affects an individual's liberty or property rights follows certain procedural rules. Procedural due process requires that notice, fair housing, and impartial appeal be given to all persons whose liberty or property rights are affected by government action or programs. Take, for example, the homeowner who finds that his house has been assessed by the city at a far higher value than he thinks proper, or a major airline that wants to obtain permission from the Civil Aeronautics Board to fly the New York-to-Miami passenger run, or a drug manufacturer who seeks to challenge the Food and Drug Administration's seizure of one of his products as impure. The key question for each will be what kind of hearing he can have to present his case to government officials. Judicial definitions and state and federal legislative enactments have evolved a general code of procedural rights to govern the regulation of property in the administrative process. Persons whose rights have been or will be affected must be given an opportunity to appear before the officials responsible for making these decisions, to be represented by counsel, to introduce evidence in support of their cases, and, usually, to know and comment about the witnesses and evidence adverse to them. In general the judiciary no longer substitutes its judgment about matters such as utility rates or television franchises for those of the regulatory agencies, as it did before 1937, but individuals can still appeal most administrative decisions to the courts. Court rulings overturning administrative decisions that it finds unjustified or improper still provide a major protection of property.

The exercise of property rights has been increasingly limited by the growing commitment of American society to racial and religious equality. In recent years, American law has narrowed the power of property owners to use or dispose of their property in ways that directly discriminate on the basis of race, color, or religion. Courts have not only upheld the power of legislation to forbid discriminatory practices in public accommodations and housing but have also ruled that the states, even by popular referendum, cannot adopt new laws to give property owners "absolute discretion in the resale or rental of housing." In a major 1967 case, the Supreme Court overturned such a California referendum amendment as a violation of the equal-protection clause of the Fourteenth Amendment.[2] The amendment, known as Proposition Fourteen and supported by conservative real-estate

[2] *Reitman* v. *Mulkey*, 387 U.S. 369 (1967).

interests, repealed fair-housing laws previously enacted by the state legislature to prevent discrimination in the sale or rental of private housing accommodations. The Court held that a state is guilty of discriminatory action if it has the power to prevent such conduct but does not do so. Proposition Fourteen amounted to "a significant state involvement" in the promotion of racial discrimination, because it established "a purported constitutional right to discriminate in the private use of property on grounds which would be unavailable under the Fourteenth Amendment should state action be involved."

But, despite such limits, the general position of property holders in the American system remains quite secure, especially compared to that of property holders in most other countries of the world. The basic political and ideological commitment of the American people is to a mixed economy, featuring a primary private sector (regulated by the government) and a small but important publicly owned sector. Americans still accept the free-enterprise system, extoll the role of a propertied middle class in promoting political and economic stability, support the usefulness of much corporate bigness to provide efficiency and create new products, and insist that government provide due process in executive agencies and the courts before limiting property rights. It is on this basis that our present structure of property rights has been erected, has flourished, and continues to enjoy widespread public support.

LIBERTY RIGHTS IN AMERICA: THE DILEMMAS OF FREEDOM

Justice Robert H. Jackson once characterized the American approach to liberty issues by noting:

> Liberty is not the mere absence of restraint [and] it is not a spontaneous product of majority rule. . . . It is achieved only by a rule of law . . . in rationally and dispassionately devised rules which limit the majority's control over the individual and the minority.[3]

While the tensions between liberty and order are as old as government, securing "liberty under law" in an age of nuclear warfare, subversive activities, racial tensions, industrial empires, densely packed cities, interstate crime syndicates, and huge government is an awesome task even for a nation that has struggled with liberty issues for almost two centuries.

When we deal with liberty issues, our "official" national philosophy is expressed by the First Amendment to the Constitution:

---

[3] *The Supreme Court in the American System of Government* (Cambridge, Mass.: Harvard University Press, 1955), pp. 76-7.

Congress shall make no law respecting an establishment of religion, or prohibiting the free exercise thereof, or abridging the freedom of speech, or of the press; or the right of the people peaceably to assemble, and to petition the government for a redress of grievances.

There are other parts of the Constitution that contribute to our definition of liberty, of course, such as the narrow definition of treason, the prohibitions against bills of attainder (laws that impose punishment on a person or group without a trial) and against *ex post facto* laws (making acts criminal offenses retroactively). But it is primarily the "first freedoms" of the First Amendment—religion, speech, press, and assembly—that constitute the "sacred bundle" of free expression and conscience. They protect the rights of individuals to hold, advocate, and publish their ideas freely, whether religious, political, social, or literary, and to conduct public meetings and organize groups of individuals to urge the acceptance of these ideas by government or society. As a corollary, the First Amendment denies Congress the power to impose an official set of religious, political, or social doctrines to which citizens must subscribe. In addition to the rights of freedom of speech, press, religion, and assembly, two other liberty rights—freedom of association and the right of privacy—have come to be included in the bundle of liberties guaranteed by the First Amendment as necessary to expression and conscience, even though the terms "association" and "privacy" do not appear in the Constitution.

We should also note that the First Amendment's guarantee of free expression and conscience is a restraint not only on the entire federal government but on state governments. Since the 1920's, the federal courts have agreed to review state actions affecting First Amendment freedoms to see if these actions violate the Fourteenth Amendment's guarantee of state "due process of law." In addition, every state constitution contains provisions similar to those of the First Amendment, and these guarantees are applied in the state courts.

Freedom of Expression

In our analysis of liberty issues, we will deal first with freedom of expression —speech, press, and association. A central factor in the Court's decisions in free-expression cases has been its distinction between issues that do not involve loyalty-security matters and those that do. We will maintain this distinction in our discussion, and we begin with those issues of speech, press, and association that do *not* involve the loyalty-security context.

The limits of free speech

"Speech" ranges across a wide spectrum, from the conversations of a husband and wife in their living room to the political candidate's voice on a loud-speaker reaching thousands of persons packed into a city square. Society regulates all these speeches in some way, from forbidding the husband and wife to speak so loudly during an argument that they disturb the neighbors to punishing the political candidate if he incites his audience to march on opposition-party headquarters and "smash it up a little." How much freedom of speech one can enjoy depends on what one says, where, when, how, and even about whom.

In light of this reality, the Constitution's provision that no law shall be passed "abridging the freedom of speech" is starkly absolute. A few philosophers and judges, such as Professor Alexander Meiklejohn and Justice Hugo Black, have argued that the Founding Fathers really intended all speech to be immune from licensing, censorship, or penalty. The Supreme Court, however, has not accepted this view and has traditionally thrust some speech outside the warm shelter of the First Amendment, either by saying that some types of talking are not "speech" or that some laws regulating speech do not "abridge" it. Justice Frank Murphy, one of the Court's most fervent defenders of maximum free speech, expressed this limiting principle for the Court's majority:

> There are certain well-defined and narrowly limited classes of speech, the prevention and punishment of which have never been thought to raise any constitutional problem. These include the lewd and obscene, the profane, the libelous, and the insulting or "fighting" words—those which by their very utterance inflict injury or tend to an immediate breach of the peace.[4]

The Court's approach to deciding whether something is speech or "nonspeech" is illustrated by the way it has categorized cases in the area of incitement to riot.

On one hand, the Court reversed the conviction of Father Terminiello, an ex-priest whose record as an anti-Semite and racist led hundreds of citizens in Chicago to demonstrate outside a hall that he had hired for a speech.[5] The demonstrators shouted opposition to Terminiello's views, tore at his followers when they entered the building, threw rocks in the window, and tried to break into the hall en masse, but they were restrained by the police. Inside, Terminiello made a speech denouncing Jews as "slimy scum" and attacking the New Deal as a Jewish and communist plot. These remarks stirred some hostile listeners in the audience to shout, which led to their removal from the meeting hall. Terminiello was convicted for breach of the peace; at the trial, the city judge instructed the jury that speech which "stirs the public to anger, invites dispute, brings about a condition of unrest, or creates disturbance" warrants conviction. The Supreme Court reversed the conviction, holding that the judge's definition of illegitimate speech was far too broad to be constitutional.

[4] *Chaplinsky* v. *New Hampshire*, 315 U.S. 568 (1942).
[5] *Terminiello* v. *Chicago*, 337 U.S. 1 (1949).

In a contrasting case,[6] a Syracuse University student named Feiner made a speech on a street corner in which he called the mayor of Syracuse a "champagne-sipping bum," denounced the American Legion as a "Nazi Gestapo," and urged American Negroes to "rise up in arms and fight for their rights." A crowd gathered, blocking the sidewalk, and several persons in the audience protested to the police to get that "son of a bitch" off the soap box or they would. The police arrested Feiner when he refused to stop voluntarily, and he was convicted of disorderly conduct. In this case, the Supreme Court upheld the conviction. It accepted the judgment of the jury and the state courts that the speaker's remarks were creating public disorder and held that the state was empowered to avert that danger.

The Court's decisions in these two cases suggest several questions that might be asked in deciding future free-speech cases: Did the defendant hire a hall and speak only to people who chose to attend, or did he speak on a street corner to passers-by? Did the judge properly interpret the statute prohibiting disorderly conduct? And, finally, did the police make some effort to protect the speaker before hauling him down?

In most free-speech cases, however, the Supreme Court is concerned with drawing the line between regulations of speech that "abridge" it and regulations that do not. The general principle is that wholesale restrictions on speech will be viewed by the Court as dangerous and unacceptable. "Reasonable" procedures would be acceptable, however. For example, city licensing laws that require a speaker to submit his remarks in advance for censoring by the police would abridge freedom of speech because they make the police a general censoring agency. But a licensing statute that gave the parks commissioner the right to decide which of several parks facilities would be assigned for a particular rally would not abridge speech, unless discrimination—by the assignment, say, of hippies to far-away parks—were proved. Laws would abridge if they forbade all picketing in labor disputes but not if they only regulated the noise level and physical blocking of pickets to prevent the picketing from becoming coercive. Federal laws requiring lobbyists to register and disclose facts about their clients, funds, and activities do not abridge when applied to persons communicating directly with congressmen on matters of pending legislation; they would if the same rules were applied to representatives of civic organizations that publish their views on pending legislation and seek to influence the general public.

In deciding whether government measures abridge freedom of speech, a central criterion is the clear-and-present-danger test. In 1919 the Supreme Court upheld the conviction, under the 1917 Espionage Act, of a man mailing leaflets urging workers to refuse to join the military service during the First World War.[7] Justice Oliver Wendell Holmes, Jr., held that the

---

[6] *Feiner v. New York*, 340 U.S. 315 (1951).
[7] *Schenck v. United States*, 249 U.S. 47 (1919).

man's action did not fall under the category of constitutionally protected free speech, because, in distributing his leaflets, the man created a "clear and present danger" that military service would be obstructed. Such obstruction was a "substantive evil" that Congress had a right to prevent. Holmes said that questions of free speech were thus a matter of proximity and degree, noting, "The most stringent protection of free speech would not protect a man in falsely crying fire in a theatre and causing a panic." Since then, the concept of clear and present danger has been used to examine the effects of speech on society in a wide variety of situations as a rule for judicial measurement of statutes.

In cases not involving loyalty-security, the clear-and-present-danger test has been used on quite a few occasions to free defendants. For example, whether statements made outside the courtroom about the conduct of judges or judicial proceedings constitute "contempt of court" is governed by the clear-and-present-danger test. In a 1962 case,[8] a judge in a Georgia community impaneled the grand jury to look into what was called "Negro bloc voting" in the county, on the assumption that corruption and bribery might be present. The county sheriff, in public statements and an open letter to the grand jury, said that the investigation was really an effort to intimidate Negro voters. The sheriff was convicted of contempt on the ground that his statement implied that the judge lacked integrity and impeded the grand-jury investigation. The Supreme Court reversed the conviction, holding that there was no proof that these expressions had impeded the jury or would create a clear and present danger of doing so.

Freedom of the press

The "press" in America takes in everything from the mimeographed leaflet of a neighborhood "Save Our Schools" group to the New York *Times,* Doubleday Book Company, Columbia Broadcasting System, and Paramount Pictures. Each method of expression, the Supreme Court has said, is entitled to the guarantees of liberty of expression, but these guarantees vary in meaning according to the type of communication involved.

The Court faces two central problems in free-press cases: first, the banning, licensing, or censoring of publications before they appear and, second, the punishment of authors or publishers for bad content after publication.

Burning and banning in America   The basic rule as to prepublication restraints on the press was laid down by the Supreme Court in a famous 1931 case.[9] The State of Minnesota forbade, as a nuisance, the future publication of a weekly newspaper in Minneapolis that specialized in gaudy

[8] *Wood* v. *Georgia,* 370 U.S. 375 (1962).
[9] *Near* v. *Minnesota,* 283 U.S. 697 (1931).

attacks on what it called "grafters," "corrupt" officials, and "Jewish gangsters" in that city. The Court overturned the injunction, stating that the press was constitutionally immune from advance censorship, or "prior restraint," except in wartime or when the publication was obscene or incited readers to violence. *After* publication, however, newspapers were liable to prosecution or private damage suit for what they had published.[10]

In regard to books, a 5–4 majority of the Court in 1957 upheld a New York statute that permitted city officials to bring an injunction proceeding against persons selling "indecent" books or other materials.[11] Under the statute, a court trial was to be held within one day to decide whether the material was indecent; if the court upheld the complaint, the material would be destroyed. The Court's majority argued that such action was justified because the city officials were seizing already published material, not enjoining future issues of a publication because previous issues were considered objectionable. The minority saw this as akin to "book burning" and said that the law should put the seller on trial, not the book.

The basic rule as to handbills and leaflets is that these are a useful means of expression that may not be hindered by the government when they are for political, religious, or civic purposes. Thus, in a case involving a Jehovah's Witness who was selling religious literature door to door, the Court struck down a city ordinance forbidding the distribution of any publications unless authorized by the city manager.[12] To the city's argument that a "sanitary problem" was presented in cleaning up such literature, the Court held that pamphlets and leaflets "have been historic weapons in the defense of liberty, as the pamphlets of Thomas Paine and others in our own history abundantly attest," and their circulation may not be sacrificed to "sanitation." The distribution of *commercial* handbills, however, can be regulated. A supermarket that printed its Thursday specials on one side of a leaflet and a verse from Genesis on the other would not squeeze through the gate to immunity.

In ruling on motion pictures, the Court has barred state censorship based on grounds such as "sacrilege," "immorality," or "a threat to public order." Since 1952, the Supreme Court justices have gathered in the Court's conference room for private showings of films such as *The Miracle, M, The Moon is Blue, Native Son, La Ronde, Lady Chatterley's Lover,* and *The Lovers* and have struck down state refusals to license all these films. However, a 5–4 majority of the Court held in 1961 that the First Amendment did not forbid state laws requiring the submission of films for licensing before exhibition.[13] The Court did not say what standards of review could constitutionally be used in such a licensing system, only that licensing could be required.

[10] *New York Times* v. *Sullivan*, 376 U.S. 254 (1964).
[11] *Kingsley Books, Inc.* v. *Brown*, 354 U.S. 436 (1957).
[12] *Lovell* v. *Griffin*, 303 U.S. 444 (1938).
[13] *Times Film Corporation* v. *Chicago*, 365 U.S. 43 (1961).

"I enjoyed censoring the movie so much, one of these days I'd like to censor the book."

During the 1940's and 1950's police forces in some communities were given the authority to censor motion pictures.

From *Straight Herblock*, Simon & Schuster, 1964

Issues and dilemmas of obscenity   The second area of controversy in free-press cases involves restraint by punishment after publication. In this area, after ruling that obscenity is not constitutionally protected speech, the Court has struggled primarily to frame constitutional standards for defining "obscenity." In the leading cases of the late 1950's, the Court held that the standard for recognizing obscenity should be: "Whether to the average person, applying contemporary community standards, the dominant theme of the material taken as a whole appeals to prurient interests." (Webster's *Dictionary* defines "prurient" as "itching; longing; of persons having lascivious longings; of desire, curiosity, or propensity; lewd.")

When this test was used in two 1957 cases involving state prosecution of a bookseller for knowingly selling obscene literature and a federal prosecution for using the mails to distribute obscene literature,[14] the Court upheld both convictions *without* making an independent judgment on the obscenity of the materials, as it would have done, for example, in cases on movie censorship.

During the 1965 and 1966 terms, the Supreme Court attempted to deal again with the problem raised by state and federal efforts to control obscenity. In a case involving the conviction of a publisher for violation of the federal obscenity statute, the Court held that the questionable material was not obscene, but that the advertising used to promote it was "permeated with

---

[14] *Alberts* v. *California*, 354 U.S. 476 (1957); *Roth* v. *Unitea States*, 354 U.S. 476 (1957).

the leer of the sensualists," causing the publisher to be guilty of "the sordid business of pandering." [15]

In a companion case, the Court reversed a civil judgment of obscenity against the book *Fanny Hill*.[16] In doing so, Justice Brennan attempted to define further standards of obscenity, although his line of argument did not command a majority of the Court. He stated three criteria, indicating for the first time that all three must be satisfied before the material can be condemned as obscene: (1) the dominant theme of the material taken as a whole must appeal to a "prurient interest in sex"; (2) the material must be "patently offensive" in affronting contemporary community standards relating to the description or representation of sexual matters; and (3) the material must be utterly without redeeming social value.

Though the 1957 decisions established the constitutionality of obscenity legislation, the guidelines have proved difficult to apply. In 1967 the Court heard arguments in several cases that dealt with the issues of how much knowledge a vendor must have of the contents of a particular publication before he can be convicted of selling obscene matter and whether it is prior restraint for a judge in a rural county to enjoin national-magazine publishers from permitting certain issues to enter the county. Unfortunately, however, the Court reversed the convictions in all cases on the grounds that the "girlie" magazines in question were not obscene,[17] without explaining this decision.

Looking at the law of free press as a whole, it is clear that the public's attitude toward the scope of frank expression in matters of sex, morals, manners, and language has grown steadily more liberal since the Second World War. The Supreme Court has been both register and catalyst in this liberalizing process. Clearly, judicial action has opened avenues that would have remained closed because of local or state censorship, and the Court's rulings have enjoyed enough public support to prevent attempts to overturn them by constitutional amendment. The major effect of judicial rulings has been to place this debate where it really belongs—in the realm of individual judgment, family control, and civic-group influences—rather than to let it be a matter of general law, usually administered on a set of lowest-common-denominator standards by persons without appreciation of creative literary and aesthetic functions.

Freedom of association in a nation of "joiners"

Private, voluntary groups of all kinds play a central role in the nation's politics. As a result, freedom of association—though not mentioned in the

[15] *Ginzburg v. United States*, 383 U.S. 463 (1966).
[16] *A Book Named "John Cleland's Memoirs of a Woman of Pleasure" v. Attorney General*, 383 U.S. 413 (1966).
[17] *Redrup v. New York, Austin v. Kentucky,* and *Gent v. Arkansas*, 386 U.S. 767 (1967).

Constitution—has become a vital extension of the rights of free speech, press, and assembly. Yet American law has always recognized that group activity adds elements of size, power, and coordination that are not present when the same number of persons function separately. For better or worse, groups have a "multiplier" effect.

The main constitutional problems of free association (apart from the problems of loyalty-security) concern the authority of government to outlaw groups, to limit their activities, or to penalize membership in them. In a leading case on freedom of association, *NAACP v. Button*,[18] the Court in 1963 struck down a Virginia statute convicting the NAACP chapter there of violating several prohibitions on soliciting and managing law cases for group interests rather than for those of the specific client. The Court held this to violate the NAACP's right as a civic group to defend its interests and those of its members through the courts. In a series of earlier cases, the Court had also refused to permit Alabama to force the NAACP to produce the names and addresses of its members and agents within the state,[19] saying that "freedom to engage in association for the advocacy of belief and ideas is an inseparable aspect" of "liberty." In both NAACP cases, the Court said that anonymity was vital to effective association and that the right of members of the NAACP to privacy in association could not be invaded on the basis of the interests asserted by the states.

Another key aspect of associational freedom is the right to solicit members. In 1945 the Court struck down a Texas law requiring that all labor-union organizers coming into the state to solicit members apply to the Texas secretary of state for an organizer's card.[20] Thomas, a CIO organizer from Detroit, had deliberately addressed a meeting of refinery workers and invited them to join his union and had not applied for a card. The Court majority argued that freedom of speech and assembly rights are abridged even by such limited speech and assembly procedures.

It should be noted, though, that federal and state labor-relations statutes have been upheld, although they place many restrictions on what union representatives (and employers) may say and do in the course of organizing or collective bargaining.

Freedom of Expression and the Loyalty-Security Context

As we noted earlier, the outcome of cases involving free speech, free press, and free association is significantly affected if these cases involve loyalty-security matters. We use the term "loyalty-security" to highlight the fact that American public opinion and government policy have tended to merge the question of loyalty—which relates to the allegiance a citizen must give his country by word or deed—with that of security—which involves con-

[18] 371 U.S. 415 (1963).
[19] For example, *NAACP v. Alabama,* 357 U.S. 449 (1958); 360 U.S. 240 (1959).
[20] *Thomas v. Collins,* 323 U.S. 516 (1945).

crete dangers to the nation, such as espionage, sabotage, sedition, and planned penetration of government to manipulate policy-making. American society has generally insisted on strict loyalty tests and disloyalty penalties for persons who sharply challenge the dominant national consensus and has then called this a *security* matter.

Perhaps the best way to explore this field is to summarize some of the major loyalty-security measures that have been applied by government from 1940 to the present. (Some of these measures have proved unenforceable, and the use of some others has been judicially limited. The Court's positions in this area will be discussed later.)

1. In 1940 Congress passed the Smith Act, or the Alien Registration Act, the first national sedition law passed in peacetime since the short-lived act of 1798. This 1940 act forbids persons to advocate or teach the overthrow of any government in the United States by force or violence, or to publish matter so advocating, or to organize any group for that purpose, or to become a member of any group that so advocates. Conspiracy to accomplish these purposes is also a crime. Many states adopted "Little Smith Acts" in the 1940's.

2. Beginning in 1940, the federal government initiated various programs for testing the loyalty of federal employees. The basic outline of these programs has remained the same under Presidents Truman, Eisenhower, Kennedy, and Johnson. The Attorney General has drawn up a list of subversive organizations to guide loyalty-security officials. Applicants for employment and existing employees list their associations, and field investigations are made by the FBI and civil-service investigators into a person's life and associations. If "derogatory information" is turned up, a hearing occurs at which the employee hears the charges against him and can give testimony and present other witnesses. He cannot get the investigation reports, nor can he learn who has said what about him or cross-examine informants. Various higher appeal boards are available, with the Secretary of the department or head of the agency in which the employee works having final judgment on the issue of loyalty-security. Loyalty-security programs are also in force for persons who work in corporations doing government work that involves classified information. An estimated million employees are covered here. Many states have set up parallel loyalty programs for all their employees (including teachers), and loyalty oaths or tests are often employed in the state licensing of professional groups.

3. The McCarran Internal Security Act of 1950, passed in reaction to the outbreak of the Korean War, is a long and involved measure, the central part of which requires that any organization found to be "communist" by the Subversive Activities Control Board (after full hearings) must register with the Attorney General, disclose the names and addresses of its officers, account for its moneys and expenditures, and identify all its mail and broadcasts as coming from "X, a communist organization." Members of a reg-

istered organization are forbidden to hold nonelective federal posts, apply for or use a passport, or work in defense plants.

4. Both federal and state governments have enacted miscellaneous measures setting loyalty-security requirements for government benefits and penalizing communists in various ways. For example, passport regulations and federal grants to college students have had loyalty provisions attached, and some states withhold welfare payments or social-security benefits from communists. Almost a third of the states bar the Communist party from the ballot.

5. The 1920's saw the beginning of widely publicized and far-ranging investigations of "subversive groups" and "subversive persons" by congressional and state legislative investigating committees. These committees were typified on the national scene by the House Committee on Un-American Activities and the Senate Permanent Investigating Committee (under Senator Joseph McCarthy) and by state committees in the early 1950's.

6. After the Second World War, there was a sweeping trend toward the installation of loyalty-security standards by private groups as a criterion for determining officership, membership, or employment status. Many business corporations, labor unions, educational institutions, the press and television, religious groups, and civic associations came to consider loyalty as something to check into when hiring a new executive, choosing a baritone to sing the praises of the sponsor's shaving cream or razor blades, or deciding whether to expel a "left-wing" minister from the church.

It should be noted carefully that all the restrictions discussed above are directed at *expression*—that is, the advocacy—of *ideas* by speaking or writing or by joining organizations that are advocating those ideas. We are not dealing in this discussion with the state and federal measures that punish *acts* against the safety and security of the nation, such as treason, espionage, disclosure of atomic secrets, theft of government property, sabotage, perjury, acting for a foreign agent without registering, securing access to classified areas or secrets, inciting to violence, and so on. The Supreme Court, like virtually all Americans, has no trouble in recognizing the need to punish acts against the nation; it is the loyalty-security measures restricting speech, press, and association that create the controversy.

Communism and the American consensus

The basic question underlying the debates on loyalty-security measures in the past four decades has been: What is the Communist party, and how should it be treated? A related question has been: What about persons who are not members of the Communist party but who cooperate with or sympathize with it to some degree? Three main positions have developed among Americans on these issues.

The first position, "No Rights for Revolutionaries," sees the American

Communist party as a dedicated, conspiratorial movement directly controlled by the Soviet Union to serve the interests of Soviet foreign policy. The Communist party works underground at such tasks as espionage and secret penetration of government and key civic groups; it also openly maintains a political party and protest movement in order to bring in recruits for the underground apparatus. In addition, the Communist party creates and manages a series of "front groups" or "progressive" coalitions in which non-communists are attracted to work with communists for such broad "common objectives" as peace, civil rights, and labor. The result, it is said, is a core of disciplined agents ready to topple the American system at a signal from Moscow.

The advocates of this position therefore assert that we should use all possible legal measures to punish and exert pressure on the communists, through loyalty oaths, loyalty investigations, prosecutions of top leadership and local leaders, enactment of full-disclosure laws and registration requirements, penetration by FBI agents, congressional investigations, and the like. Another key reason for these measures is to keep weak-minded "dupes" and well-meaning "liberals" from being pulled into the communist camp. When asked whether pursuit of such loyalty-security measures is not imitating the communists themselves and curtailing freedom of expression and association, the supporters of this position reply that the communists cannot claim those rights in our country, since communists would be the first ones to abolish all civil liberties if they came to power.

The second position supports "Freedom for the Thought We Hate." Its central thesis is that the American Communist party has been a weak, wholly discredited movement in this country since the late 1940's. The United States is a rich, stable society, facing no internal crisis such as Russia faced in 1917 or Germany faced in the early 1930's. There is no evidence to indicate that drastic loyalty-security measures are needed to prevent a few thousand party members from toppling the United States.

Instead, advocates of the second position contend that we should maintain FBI surveillance and the laws punishing *acts* against national security, but we should let the activities of the communists that are above ground continue as proof that ours is a free society and that we can meet ideas on the field of reason. Keep the ideological pressure on, but do not institute loyalty-security oaths and forced-confession procedures that will create a climate of fear and a stifling of free thought among genuinely independent thinkers. It is these persons and not spies and hidden party members who are usually turned up by federal employee loyalty-security programs. Furthermore, creating a vast loyalty-security apparatus, it is said, inevitably strengthens the hands of right-wingers and reactionaries in America, because they use the loyalty-security measures to discredit liberals, democratic socialists, pacifists, and others as being "tools of the communists." This second position concludes that we institute loyalty-security measures at a far greater peril to ourselves than to the communists, since they are delighted to pose as martyrs and to point to the "class terror" and "persecution" in capitalistic societies.

The third position, "Limited Loyalty-Security Measures for Revolutionaries," lies between the views described above. According to it, the Communist party as a conspiratorial movement should be controlled, but its role as a social-protest movement should be protected. Exponents of this position fear "witch-hunting" and know the dangers of official thought control. But they do not believe that the machinery directed against *acts* of disloyalty is sufficient to protect government and civic processes from communist penetration. Communists must be barred from holding posts in government because they will use these posts to advance Soviet, not American, interests. And communists must also be kept from certain key sectors of private life, such as defense industries, where national security is directly at stake.

Therefore, they argue, *some* loyalty-security measures are necessary. But we must limit them to the area of genuine security need; draft precise legislation focused on communists and fascists; provide full due process in administering this loyalty-security machinery; and guard against overzealous cru-

Loyalty-Security: Limited Measures for Revolutionaries

There is no more fundamental axiom of American freedom than the familiar statement: In a free country we punish men for the crimes they commit but never for the opinions they have. And the reason this is so fundamental to freedom is not, as many suppose, that it protects the few unorthodox from suppression by the majority. To permit freedom of expression is primarily for the benefit of the majority, because it protects criticism, and criticism leads to progress.

We can and we will prevent espionage, sabotage, or other actions endangering our national security. But we would betray our finest traditions if we attempted ... to curb the simple expression of opinion. This we should never do, no matter how distasteful the opinion may be to the vast majority of our people....

And what kind of effect would these provisions have on the normal expression of political views? Obviously, if this law were on the statute books, the part of prudence would be to avoid saying anything that might be construed by someone as not deviating sufficiently from the current Communist-propaganda line. And since no one could be sure in advance what views were safe to express, the inevitable tendency would be to express no views on controversial subjects.

The result could only be to reduce the vigor and strength of our political life—an outcome that the Communists would happily welcome, but that freemen should abhor.

From President Harry S. Truman, veto message on the Internal Security Act of 1950, September 1950.

saders employing the machinery to punish dissent. Advocates of this third position would argue that measures such as the Smith Act, the Communist Control Act of 1954, state sedition laws, and denaturalization for "mental reservations" would be *illegitimate* loyalty-security measures because they do not really meet a security need and because their impact on free expression is too great. A limited federal loyalty-security program for employees in sensitive posts of government, on the other hand, would be proper. In this way, we respond effectively to the special character of the Communist party in a revolutionary age, but we protect both our reputation for freedom and our own precious rights.

Communism and the Supreme Court

Since the Russian Revolution of 1917, public opinion in this country—mirrored in Supreme Court decisions—has swung from one extreme to the other in its position on loyalty-security measures. From the First World War to 1927, a majority of the Supreme Court upheld the convictions of persons for antiwar and antidraft statements that allegedly violated the federal espionage and sedition acts or for left-wing speeches that conflicted with state antisedition laws in a dozen or more cases.[21] Many important statements about free speech and its importance to a free society were made in these cases, sometimes in the opinions of the majority and sometimes in concurring and dissenting opinions by justices such as Holmes and Brandeis, but all the defendants still went to jail. Convictions of various "radicals" were frequently reversed, however, and some antiradicalism laws were struck down.

Between 1927 and 1947, in a climate of general relaxation on loyalty-security issues, the Court began to interpret loyalty and security needs more narrowly. In 1927 the Court threw out the conviction of an organizer for the Industrial Workers of the World under a Kansas "criminal syndicalism" act, finding no valid evidence that the IWW advocated violent change of government.[22] During the 1930's the Court framed limits on state loyalty-security action and freed several admitted Communist-party members through the application of the clear-and-present-danger test.[23] During the Second World War the Court continued to free defendants in loyalty-security cases and to hold the government to tight constitutional limits in order to protect freedom of expression.[24]

Between 1947 and 1955, however, the Court stopped freeing defendants

---

[21] *Debs* v. *United States*, 249 U.S. 211 (1919); *Abrams* v. *United States*, 250 U.S. 616 (1919); *Gitlow* v. *New York*, 268 U.S. 652 (1925).

[22] *Fiske* v. *Kansas*, 274 U.S. 380 (1927).

[23] See *Stromberg* v. *California*, 283 U.S. 359 (1931); *DeJonge* v. *Oregon*, 299 U.S. 353 (1937); *Herndon* v. *Lowry*, 301 U.S. 242 (1937).

[24] See *Schneiderman* v. *United States*, 320 U.S. 118 (1943); *Taylor* v. *Mississippi*, 319 U.S. 583 (1943); *United States* v. *Lovett*, 328 U.S. 303 (1946); *Baumgartner* v. *United States*, 322 U.S. 665 (1944).

Loyalty-Security: The Clear-and-Present-Danger Test

Fear of serious injury cannot alone justify suppression of free speech and assembly. Men feared witches and burnt women. It is the function of speech to free men from the bondage of irrational fears. To justify suppression of free speech there must be reasonable ground to fear that serious evil will result if free speech is practiced. There must be reasonable ground to believe that the danger apprehended is imminent. There must be reasonable ground to believe that the evil to be prevented is a serious one.... The wide difference between advocacy and incitement, between preparation and attempt, between assembling and conspiracy, must be borne in mind. In order to support a finding of clear and present danger it must be shown either that immediate serious violence was to be expected or was advocated, or that the past conduct furnished reason to believe that such advocacy was then contemplated.

Those who won our independence by revolution were not cowards. They did not fear political change. They did not exalt order at the cost of liberty. To courageous, self-reliant men, with confidence in the power of free and fearless reasoning applied through the processes of popular government, no danger flowing from speech can be deemed clear and present, unless the incidence of the evil apprehended is so imminent that it may befall before there is opportunity for full discussion.

From Justice Louis Brandeis, concurring in *Whitney* v. *California*, 1927.

and all but abandoned the clear-and-present-danger test. This was the era of Alger Hiss's conviction for perjury in denying that he had given government secrets to a communist agent. During this period Harry Gold, David Greenglass, and Julius and Ethel Rosenberg were convicted for giving atomic secrets to the Soviet Union; and the Cold War boiled up into the bloody Korean "police action" of 1950–52. Strong public hostility was registered against communists and "pro-communists." In almost all these loyalty-security cases between 1947 and 1955, the defendants went to jail. While there were strong debates within the Court on the constitutionality of many of these measures, the Court did not declare a single federal loyalty-security act or prosecution to be unconstitutional, and only a few state actions were held invalid, usually on procedural rather than substantive grounds.

From 1955 to the present, however, we have had a period of relative relaxation, ushered in by the easing of Cold War tensions after the death of Joseph Stalin, the official censure of Senator Joseph McCarthy by his Senate colleagues, and the assumption of the administration of loyalty-security measures by the Republicans under Eisenhower (thus softening party conflict over this issue). During this time, the Supreme Court began to free defendants and to strike down some loyalty-security laws or practices. For

Still the Cornerstone

Crawford in the Newark *News*

During the 1950's liberals applauded the Supreme Court's rulings freeing defendants in loyalty-security cases on the ground that their constitutional rights had been violated.

example, the convictions of several Communist-party defendants under the Smith Act were thrown out because the judge at the trial did not instruct the jury that advocacy of the overthrow of the government as an "abstract idea" is lawful.[25] State sedition laws have been declared invalid as duplicating and conflicting with the federal Smith Act.[26] Federal employee-loyalty programs have been cut back sharply in coverage and held to increasingly strict requirements of procedural fairness.[27]

In 1967 the Court in a 5–4 decision declared unconstitutionally vague New York State's Feinberg Law, requiring school and college teachers to sign a statement saying they were not communists and providing that teachers could be removed for "the utterance of any treasonable or seditious word." [28] It struck down the law's provision that public employment could be denied to Communist-party members, on the ground that the law did not specify that such employees must agree with the party's illegal aim before they could be dismissed. The decision followed a series of loyalty-oath decisions in the past decade in which the Court struck down state programs on narrow grounds, while upholding the right of the states to bar subversives from their payrolls.[29] In the 1967 case, the Court firmly upheld New York's

[25] *Yates* v. *United States,* 354 U.S. 298 (1957).
[26] *Pennsylvania* v. *Nelson,* 350 U.S. 497 (1956).
[27] *Peters* v. *Hobby,* 349 U.S. 331 (1955); *Cole* v. *Young,* 351 U.S. 536 (1956); *Vitarelli* v. *Seaton,* 359 U.S. 535 (1959); *Greene* v. *McElroy,* 360 U.S. 474 (1959).
[28] *Keyishian* v. *Board of Regents,* 385 U.S. 589 (1967).
[29] *Speiser* v. *Randall,* 357 U.S. 513 (1958); *First Unitarian Church* v. *Los Angeles,* 357 U.S. 545 (1958); *Cramp* v. *Board,* 368 U.S. 278 (1961); *Schware* v. *New Mexico,* 353 U.S. 532 (1957). See also *NAACP* v. *Button,* 371 U.S. 415 (1963) for commentary on standards of vagueness in the area of free expression.

Strange Ditch Diggers

Conservatives, on the other hand, attacked these Court rulings because they resulted in the freeing of communists or alleged communists.

Sandeson in the Fort Wayne *News-Sentinel*

right to protect its educational system from subversion but noted that "even though the governmental purpose be legitimate and substantial, that purpose cannot be pursued by means that broadly stifle fundamental personal liberties when the end can be more narrowly achieved." [30]

During this period the Court reversed convictions for contempt when the House Committee on Un-American Activities asked a witness such wide-ranging questions about his connections with communist activities that the witness could not be sure just what the committee was investigating and thus could not know what he was risking if he refused to answer.[31]

At the same time, however, the period from 1955 to the present has been marked by some other Supreme Court decisions that have *upheld* loyalty-security laws and prosecutions. Prosecutions under the Smith Act for "knowing membership" in the Communist party were upheld [32] in 1961, but in 1965 the Court ruled that requiring individual members of the Communist party to register under the Subversive Activities Control Act of 1950 violated the member's privilege against self-incrimination, since he would then be liable under the Smith Act for punishment as a party member.[33] After the Supreme Court's 1965 ruling, the government offered an FBI agent, who had been posing as a party member, to register for the party. In 1967 the United

[30] See *Shelton* v. *Tucker*, 364 U.S. 479, at 488–89 (1960).
[31] *Watkins* v. *United States*, 354 U.S. 178 (1957).
[32] *Scales* v. *United States*, 367 U.S. 203 (1961); *Communist Party* v. *Subversive Activities Control Board*, 367 U.S. 1 (1961).
[33] *Albertson* v. *SACB*, 382 U.S. 70 (1965).

States Court of Appeals held that this was not good enough, affirming that the provisions of the 1950 law were "hopelessly at odds" with the Fifth Amendment.[34] These decisions have begun to chip away at the excesses of the 1946–54 loyalty-security programs by finding errors in their basic constitutionality. However, the observation of Professor John P. Frank is often a ruefully realistic one: "The dominant lesson of our history in the relation of the judiciary to repressions is that courts love liberty most when it is under pressure least."

The Right to Be Left Alone: Privacy and the Constitution

Like freedom of association, privacy is nowhere mentioned in the First Amendment. When most students of the Constitution think of privacy, they probably do so in terms of the Fourth Amendment to the Constitution, which provides that "persons, houses, papers, and effects" shall be secure from unreasonable searches and seizures.

We have already examined one aspect of civic privacy—freedom of association. In cases presenting other aspects of privacy, the Supreme Court has upheld ordinances that forbade "raucous" sound trucks from broadcasting throughout the city or through residential areas, and it has indicated that limitation of all sound trucks to certain hours would be also constitutional.[35] The Court has also upheld the right of home owners to post "No trespassing" or "No soliciting" signs to exclude door-to-door advocates of religion and politics, as well as the Fuller Brush man or the student working his way through college by selling magazine subscriptions.[36] In both these cases, active or aggressive speech was constitutionally limited because of society's interest in peace and privacy within the home.

In another group of cases involving privacy, the Court has not found enough social utility to limit speech in the interests of repose. In the District of Columbia in the 1950's buses (a public utility) began to broadcast soft music and occasional commercial announcements during their rides. When a law suit was brought by passengers complaining that this made them a "captive audience" on a public utility and invaded their privacy interests in reading, thinking, or sightseeing on the buses, a majority of the Court refused to recognize their claims.[37]

Viewed as a whole, what seems to be happening is that the idea of privacy, formerly treated as an outgrowth of one's *property* rights (home, car, office, business secrets, reputation, papers, and the like), has in recent years

---

[34] *Communist Party v. United States,* 35 L.W. 2509 (1967).
[35] *Kovacs v. Cooper,* 336 U.S. 77 (1949).
[36] *Breard v. Alexandria,* 341 U.S. 623 (1951).
[37] *Public Utilities Commission v. Pollak,* 343 U.S. 451 (1952).

increasingly been interpreted by the courts as a *liberty* right that may not be invaded without due process of law.[38]

Such a development fits the analysis of many political scientists that the equilibrium among privacy, publicity, and secrecy is one of the key relationships that must be maintained if a free, pluralistic society is to prosper. As Professor Edward Shils has put this, an important goal of a liberal society is to achieve *civility*, a state that exists when there is *privacy* to nourish individual creativity and group expression; *publicity* of information to inform government and the public of the facts necessary to form wise judgments on public affairs; and certain areas of *secrecy* for government operations, to preserve the integrity of internal policy-making. "Freedom," says Shils, "flourishes in the indifference of privacy." [39]

God and Caesar: Religion and the First Amendment

The First Amendment forbids laws "prohibiting the free exercise of religion" and laws "respecting an establishment of religion." The two provisions interact, since establishing one religion as the official faith of the nation or a state would deny religious liberty to citizens of other faiths or of no faith.

In the Supreme Court, the free-exercise clause has been the shield primarily of small sects and nonbelievers. Few recent cases have involved direct denials of religious expression to Protestants, Catholics, and Jews. Those faiths can generally depend on their status as major, "recognized" religions to secure their freedom of operation. However, when Jewish groups and some Protestant denominations have tried to invoke the principle of free exercise of religion to challenge *general* government regulations—as in the school-prayer case, released-time systems for religious education, or Sunday-closing laws—the Court has not accepted their position. As we will see, those issues have been fought on the battleground of the nonestablishment clause.

In defining "free exercise," the Court has held that religious beliefs and opinions are inviolate but religious practices may be regulated by federal and state police power. To safeguard religious belief, the Court has struck down laws requiring door-to-door religious solicitors to secure a police permit and laws taxing such activity; [40] it has invalidated requirements that children of Jehovah's Witnesses salute the flag in school despite their religious scruples against this ceremony; [41] and it has refused to permit the federal government to make it a requirement of naturalization than an alien swear he will defend the country by bearing arms when this violates his religious

[38] Alan F. Westin, *Privacy and Freedom* (New York: Atheneum, 1967).
[39] Edward Shils, *The Torment of Secrecy* (Glencoe, Ill.: Free Press, 1954), p. 22.
[40] *Murdock v. Pennsylvania*, 319 U.S. 105 (1943); *Follett v. McCormick*, 321 U.S. 573 (1944).
[41] *West Virginia State Board of Education v. Barnette*, 319 U.S. 624 (1943); see also *Holden v. Board of Education, Elizabeth*, 46 N.J. 281 (1966).

principles.[42] But laws outlawing practices such as polygamy, snake-handling, parades without a license, and sales of religious newspapers on the streets by children have all been upheld over the protests of Mormons, snake-worshippers, and Jehovah's Witnesses.[43]

Halfway between the guarantee of religious freedom and the ban on establishment lies the immunity of churches from government interference in their internal affairs. The Court has held that government may not by statute or judicial decision determine which of two disputing factions within a church is entitled to church property or to control over appointments and communicants. Those are matters for the church authorities to decide.[44]

In the field of nonestablishment, the Supreme Court in 1947 laid down a classic definition of this constitutional clause:

> Neither a state nor the Federal Government can set up a church. Neither can pass laws which aid one religion, aid all religions, or prefer one religion over another. Neither can force nor influence a person to go to or to remain away from church against his will or force him to profess a belief or disbelief in any religion. No person can be punished for entertaining or professing religious beliefs or disbeliefs, for church attendance or non-attendance. No tax in any amount, large or small, can be levied to support any religious activities or institutions, whatever they may be called, or whatever form they may adopt to teach or practice religion.[45]

It is over this clause that the four great faiths of America—Protestants, Catholics, Jews, and secularists—have confronted one another in passionate debate over the boundary lines between religion and the state and the preferment of one religious viewpoint over another. When faced with applying this rule to varied church-state contacts, the Court since 1947 has run a rather zigzag course. Current rulings hold that the nonestablishment principle forbids such policies as sectarian instruction on school property during school hours,[46] officially composed nondenominational prayers for school-children,[47] and statutory requirements for Bible-reading and recitation of the Lord's Prayer in public schools.[48] It does *not* forbid state subsidy of bus transportation of children to parochial schools (since this aids the child and not the church),[49] or programs that allow those children requesting it to leave school early for religious instruction.[50] Laws requiring that stores and businesses be closed on Sunday have been upheld in the courts as general-

---

[42] *Girouard* v. *United States,* 328 U.S. 61 (1946).

[43] *Reynolds* v. *United States,* 98 U.S. 145 (1879); *Prince* v. *Massachusetts,* 321 U.S. 158 (1944).

[44] *Watson* v. *Jones,* 13 Wall. 679 (1872); *Kedroff* v. *St. Nicholas Cathedral,* 344 U.S. 94 (1952).

[45] *Everson* v. *Board of Education,* 330 U.S. 1 (1947).

[46] *McCollum* v. *Board of Education,* 333 U.S. 203 (1948).

[47] *Engel* v. *Vitale,* 370 U.S. 421 (1962).

[48] *Abington School District* v. *Schempp; Murray* v. *Curlett,* 374 U.S. 203 (1963).

[49] *Everson* v. *Board of Education.*

[50] *Zorach* v. *Clauson,* 343 U.S. 306 (1952).

welfare regulations against the protest that these discriminate against the Jews and Seventh-Day Adventists, who celebrate the Sabbath on other days of the week and thus "pay a penalty" under the Sunday laws.[51]

Liberty Rights and the Law: Conclusion

"My freedom to swing my arm," Justice Holmes once said, "stops where the other man's nose begins." This epigram describes many of the themes in this section on liberty. Where all are lined up in a congenial circle swinging their arms more or less in rhythm, there is small risk of collision, and liberty under these conditions has been fairly well secured in America. And there has generally been no denial of liberty *as a principle* in setting certain careful rules about consistently careless or deliberately aggressive arm-swinging. Limits on free expression that would incite to riot, on libel or on profanity, and the like protect society's nose and its process of arm-swinging as well. These rules must be carefully focused on the excesses, however, and administered with a deep awareness of the overriding need to protect free expression.

But the real testing time for liberty rights comes when their exercise collides with other values cherished by society—such as privacy, morality, public order, or internal security. And there has been continuing tension in American society over how best to deal with those who swing their arms in unorthodox ways or with revolutionary zeal. This clash between our middle-class consensus and the radical dissenters is our special dilemma in liberty matters. Most Americans do *not* believe in a toleration that rests on faith in the ability of a free society to withstand strong expressions of dissent from within. Thus we have too often imposed standards of loyalty when all that was objectively needed was laws insuring security. On the other hand, the leading groups in the nation and the courts seem to understand better in the 1960's than they did in the 1950's that it is as dangerous to muzzle free expression as to neglect controls on subversive activities, and this suggests that important progress is being made.

DUE PROCESS IN A FREE SOCIETY

Justifications for Due Process

Most observers of American government realize that there is an inevitable tension between due-process rules and the freedom of government authorities to investigate, prosecute, and punish various antisocial activities, from gambling and petty theft to murder and espionage. Two perennial questions

[51] *Sunday Closing Law Cases*, 366 U.S. 420, 582, 599, 617 (1961).

"Smile."

Renault in *Frontier*. Ben Roth Agency

As this cartoon suggests, liberals have supported efforts by the courts and legislatures to curtail "police brutality."

are: How much does due process handcuff law enforcement and threaten public safety? Are these restrictions on law enforcement necessary?

Three justifications for due process make up the classic rationales. First, due process is an essential ingredient of truth-seeking. The requirements for habeas corpus,[52] speedy trial, cross-examination of one's accusers, the privilege against self-incrimination, jury trial, and similar rights are vital to the exposure of falsehood, bias, mistake, coerced confessions, and government persecution, all of which impede the true determination of facts and motives, of guilt or innocence.

Second, due process is a safeguard against a police state. By forbidding police questioning of prisoners for days without rest or food, juries that exclude Negroes, or dismissal of government employees for "disloyalty" without fair hearings, due process helps to maintain the balance of power between the government and the private sectors of society. The public's knowledge that government must follow the rules of due process or be brought to account is essential to the confident exercise of free speech, free press, and political opposition, to the prevention of racial and religious discrimination, and so on.

Third, due process preserves individual dignity. Requiring accused persons to give testimony against themselves, secreting cameras in public bathrooms to catch sexual deviates, or allowing penniless defendants to stand trial in major criminal cases without lawyers would display callous disregard for the dignity of individuals.

[52] The stipulation that the government must produce an arrested person in court and specify the charge on which he is being held.

"Quick! While I keep 'em down, run and bring each of them a lawyer—and don't forget ours!"

Conservatives, on the other hand, have feared that court rulings expanding the rights of suspects would hamper police performance.

Brooks in the Birmingham *News*

In many instances, these three justifications of due process support one another harmoniously. In other situations, however, the three rationales may conflict, and society must decide which is the paramount consideration. For example, if truth-seeking is the prime goal, then a person who knows most about an event—the defendant or the prime witness—should be required to testify about it, or the jury should be able to draw unfavorable inferences about his silence, and legislative committees should be able to cite for contempt a person obstructing an important inquiry.

But, if individual dignity and the limitation of government power are the primary considerations, then government should be required to make a positive case or gather facts for legislation with its own witnesses and evidence, rather than forcing persons to incriminate themselves with their own testimony. Similarly, evidence illegally obtained—for example, by hiding microphones in a bedroom, pumping the stomach of a suspect who swallowed morphine capsules when police apprehended him, hypnotizing a prisoner to tell what he really did, or searching a business office without first securing a warrant—should be excluded as court testimony. Here, when perfectly solid evidence of a real crime is barred from court in order to deter police misconduct and protect individual dignity, truth is sacrificed to serve other due-process values, and criminals may walk off scot free.

Weighing the requirements of due process against those of public order is not the monopoly of any single branch of government in the federal or the state systems, but the courts have traditionally been the most influential interpretive and "enforcement" agency in this field. There are several reasons for this: (1) due process very often involves the conduct of courts themselves and of courtlike procedures; (2) lawyers have been a powerful force in supporting due-process values before the public and in bringing these issues to the courts; and (3) the basic rules of due process often require judicial elaboration and application to changing conditions. (What is an "unreasonable" search and seizure, for example, or "excessive" bail, or an "impartial" jury, or "cruel" punishment?)

Since the federal government and the states have their separate constitutions, there are fifty-one due-process systems in America, each setting rules for its own government procedures and each receiving authoritative interpretation from its highest court. However, the Fourteenth Amendment to the Constitution, adopted in 1868 to ensure that all American citizens enjoy certain basic national rights, includes a provision forbidding any state to "deprive any person of life, liberty, or property without due process of law." Under this clause, the United States Supreme Court reviews cases in which state procedures are alleged to violate due process, and if the justices decide this is a matter requiring national uniformity, the Court will enforce "federal minimums" on every state, regardless of the state's own constitutional position on the issue. A majority of the Supreme Court has ruled that due process as required in the Fourteenth Amendment encompasses those *substantive* rights of the first eight amendments to the Constitution that have traditionally been considered basic to our system of "ordered liberty." The Court has also held that the states must meet federal minimums for some of the *procedural* rights in the Fourth through Eighth Amendments—security against unreasonable search and seizure; the right to counsel from time of arrest through trial and appeal; and the ban against trying a person twice for the same crime.

Thus, the Supreme Court's role is not identical in federal and state due-process cases. When *federal* action is involved, the Supreme Court rules on the basis of constitutional clauses setting specific procedures for federal officials. The justices also act as the final authority in the federal judicial system in "maintaining and establishing civilized standards of procedure and evidence" and in seeing that "justice is done." When the Supreme Court reviews *state* action, however, the primary role in setting "civilized standards" lies with the political and judicial authorities of the state. The United States Supreme Court intervenes to upset state procedures only when the state's action violates fundamental national ideas of fairness, just treatment, and ordered liberty.

Nonetheless, the Supreme Court has enormously broadened its due-process review of state action in the past three or four decades, setting federal minimums for more and more state law-enforcement and hearing procedures. This reflects many factors, such as growing national uniformity and loss of state immunity throughout American society, increased public concern over local injustices in police practices and trial methods, and the expanded role of the Supreme Court in the civil-liberties field.

The law of due process can be divided into two main areas: (1) issues relating to criminal control in the judicial arena, including law-enforcement practices that lead up to judicial trials, and (2) issues relating to legislative and administrative proceedings, especially semitrials (to be discussed later in this chapter). Since the problem of crime and the apparatus of criminal justice in America provides the background for most due-process conflicts, a brief look at this area follows.

The Criminal-Justice System in America

The criminal-justice *system* reflects the way society assigns the responsibilities for enforcing standards of conduct necessary to protect its members from those who would violate the basic rules of group existence. The functions of the system range from investigation, apprehension, and prosecution to judicial determination and detention. The thread that ties the system together is the criminal-justice *process*—the decision-making network through which justice is applied to those charged with a crime.

Since the days of Jesse James and frontier lawlessness, American society has been plagued with the problem of crime. Even in the early nineteenth century, city dwellers were concernd with crime in the streets. Each new immigrant group found crime a means of entrance into a society that placed restrictions on legitimate access to its rewards and benefits. The turn of the century witnessed growing urban unrest plus new problems of labor violence and the beginnings of organized crime. On the other hand, certain crimes of the mid-twentieth century are relatively new. For example, white-collar crime—income-tax evasion, corporate theft—is steadily increasing.

Constantly changing social and economic conditions directly affect crime. Urbanization, deprivation, and discrimination encourage criminal acts. Increasing affluence in the society at large increases the frustration of those persons unable to achieve it, contributing to a steadily rising crime rate, which, in this country in 1965, totaled nearly 2,800,000 personal and property crimes.[53]

The sophisticated organization of crime in contemporary America adds to the problem. According to the Federal Bureau of Investigation, the core of organized crime consists of twenty-four groups operating as criminal cartels in the large cities of the nation.[54] A survey of seventy-one cities in

[53] Report of the President's Commission on Law Enforcement and the Administration of Justice, *The Challenge of Crime in a Free Society* (1967), p. 18.
[54] *Ibid.*, p. 192.

Are Some More Equal than Others?

In theory, all Americans charged with a crime are, so far as the law is concerned, equal before the bar of justice in every American court. This is guaranteed by the "due process" and the "equal protection" clauses to the Constitution, and the inspiration comes from the Bible: "You shall do no injustice in judgment; you shall not be partial to the poor or defer to the great, but in righteousness shall you judge your neighbor." Justices of the Supreme Court and of many state courts take oaths to "do equal justice to the poor and to the rich."

Unfortunately, despite all these guarantees and safeguards, the poor often meet with less than the same justice....

When the police conduct a roundup of "suspects," they generally do so in poor neighborhoods, rarely in middle-class communities. As a result, more poor than rich are arrested for crimes they did not commit. We do not know how many of these people lose or fail to obtain jobs because of an "arrest record" resulting from guiltless involvement in such episodes. Nor do we know how many poor people are even aware of their rights in such situations: for example, their right to consult an attorney, to sue for false arrest, or to have their arrest records expunged (in jurisdictions which have procedures permitting this). Moreover, psychologists and sociologists tell us that young people who are close to choosing criminal identities may have this choice confirmed by their repeated treatment as criminal types.

From Justice Arthur J. Goldberg, "Equal Justice for the Poor, Too," *New York Times Magazine*, March 1964.

---

the United States in 1965–66 revealed that in 80 percent of those with populations of over 1 million, the police agencies indicated the presence of organized criminal syndicates. However, organized crime is not merely a big-city problem:

> In one Eastern town . . . the local racket figure combined with outside organized criminal groups to establish horse and numbers gambling grossing $1.3 million annually, an organized dice game drawing customers from four states and having an employee payroll of $350,000 annually, and a still capable of producing $4 million worth of alcohol each year. The town's population was less than 100,000.[55]

Although there is some debate about the extent of organized crime and about whether there is one national syndicate or a series of loosely structured alliances, there is no debate about the fact that organized crime has worked its way into areas such as loan-sharking, gambling, prostitution, narcotics, labor-racketeering, and even legitimate business. It participates in virtually every illegal activity that offers maximum profit at minimum risk of

[55] *Ibid.*, p. 191.

interference from the law, and it offers goods and services that Americans desire even though they are illegal.

There are more than 2,800 activities that federal law defines as criminal and a much higher number of state and local ones. Some crimes are spontaneous, while others are systematically planned; some are willingly undertaken by both buyer and seller; some are violently imposed upon their victims; all vary with sex, age, location, and situation.

The crimes the American public fears most are those that most affect their personal safety—at home, at work, or in the streets—especially crimes of violence. Yet these crimes constitute only 13 percent of crimes committed. Americans are generally more tolerant about crimes against property, which comprise the other 87 percent,[56] partly because they are less personally frightening. This ambivalence about certain types of crime—off-track betting, income-tax evasion, prostitution, and traffic violations—is caused in part by the pleasure of the average citizen in seeing someone "beat the system," even though they know it is wrong to do so. Every person has probably committed some "little crime" for which he experiences pleasure or gain and does not expect to be caught or punished. This ambivalence about crime affects public attitudes about police investigation and about punishment.

Every criminal-justice system consists of six components: police agencies, prosecutors (or district attorneys), courts, probation agencies, correctional institutions, and parole agencies. Each component deals with situations that call for decision-making. They respond by investigating, assembling and assessing facts, reaching conclusions, taking or recommending action, and observing the results of their actions to determine whether earlier decisions should be reassessed or modified.

The criminal-justice system in America is a product of our complex relationship of state and federal authority. Most crime in the United States falls under local jurisdiction; the federal government usually has jurisdiction only over crimes that involve sabotage, federal property, violations of federal statutes, or limited areas that, because of their interstate character, involve both federal and state jurisdiction. Thus, complete jurisdiction over the assassination of President Kennedy in 1963 lay in the hands of the Dallas police force; it was not until after this tragedy that it became a federal crime to assassinate a President.

On the state and local levels, the police function in American society is decentralized and overlapping, scattered in hundreds of city police departments, county sheriffs' offices, state highway patrols, county- and state-prosecutors' offices, special port or transit authorities, state attorneys general, and city jails and state penitentiaries. Thus, 420,000 police officers

---

[56] See Federal Bureau of Investigation, *Uniform Crime Reports* (1965), p. 51. It is important to note in all figures on crimes that these reflect only crimes that are **reported**.

in the United States operate out of 40,000 separate law-enforcement agencies.[57]

On the federal level, law enforcement is primarily the responsibility of the United States Department of Justice. Since its organization in 1870, the department has grown into a full-scale agency responsible for co-ordinating the peace-keeping, investigative, prosecutive, and corrective functions of federal law enforcement as well as the legal affairs of the federal government. Under the jurisdiction of the department are the Attorney General; the Solicitor General; eight divisions (including anti-trust, civil rights, and internal security); the Federal Bureau of Investigation and the Federal Bureau of Prisons; the Immigration and Naturalization Service; the Parole Board; and ninety-one offices of United States attorneys and United States marshals throughout this country and its territories.

A basic historical theme of American political thought has been our distrust of a system that would centralize the power of law-enforcement agencies. However, no society can be secure when crime threatens the daily life of its members. The importance of this issue is evidenced by the attention of both government and civic groups in the late 1960's to the need for upgrading law enforcement in America. A presidential commission on law enforcement and the administration of justice was set up in 1965, and it devoted two years to the study of the problems raised by crime and the need for effective law-enforcement procedures. The federal government focused on the need to aid state and local law-enforcement agencies through programs of federal grants-in-aid, and public attention was drawn to proposals for expanded training programs and technological innovations that would aid in more effective crime prevention, detection, and control.[58] How can we expand protection of public order while preserving (and extending) the guarantees of due process? The possibilities can best be seen by examining some of the key stages of the criminal-justice process.

Investigation

As law-enforcement agencies move through the stages of the criminal-justice system, the conflicts over due process take specific forms. A central issue of criminal procedure is the investigative function of law enforcement. As fans of "The FBI" and "New York Police Department" know so well, police investigation runs a wide gamut, from tedious week-long shadowing of subjects to spectrographic analysis of dried bloodstains by the police lab. Whenever such investigative activity is held to constitute a "search and seizure," federal and state constitutions require that police go before a judge in a secret proceeding in advance (if there is time to do so), satisfy

[57] The President's Commission on Law Enforcement and Administration of Justice, *The Challenge of Crime in a Free Society* (1967), p. 91.
[58] See, for specific recommendations, *The Challenge of Crime in a Free Society.*

the judge that a crime has been or is about to be committed, and specify why a search of a specifically designated place or the seizure of a particular object is necessary to the solution of the crime.

Much police investigative activity—for example, shadowing, looking through a window, photographing premises from outside, and planting informants within gangs or subversive organizations—has been held to fall outside the category of searches and seizures. All these activities can be carried on without getting a warrant.

Supreme Court rulings on wiretapping have distinguished between cases where police entered the premises to install listening or tapping equipment and those where they did not. The Court has held that the former constitutes illegal search and seizure unless done by judicial warrant.[59] But it has ruled that tapping telephones through connections further along the lines,[60] listening to conversations from outside a room with sensitive microphone devices, or planting microphones on police agents or informants to get evidence are all constitutional.[61] In practice, however, this ruling is partly cancelled out by a congressional statute that has been held to forbid the presentation of wiretap evidence in federal trials;[62] in addition, several states have adopted court-order controls for wiretapping, while two have banned such evidence completely from state courts.[63]

Even if an investigative activity is held to be a search and seizure, there are some situations in which police can act without first obtaining a judicial warrant. The main instances are when a person consents to a search by police, when criminal evidence comes into view of the police during the regular patrols (such as marijuana seen on the back seat of a parked car), or "when the search is incident to a valid arrest," such as in police pursuit of bandits who have just held up a drugstore. In a 1963 decision, the Supreme Court explained that such on-the-spot searches were proper to prevent escapes, the use of weapons, and the destruction of evidence.[64]

The reason this problem has given state and federal courts such trouble (and has produced such conflicting rulings)[65] is that state and local police are reluctant to get judicial warrants before engaging in searches; this is due in part to police stubbornness and in part to the need for speed and secrecy. Also, in some cases the police may not have enough facts to satisfy a judge that a crime has been committed and to specify what they

[59] *Silverman* v. *United States,* 365 U.S. 505 (1961).

[60] *Olmstead* v. *United States,* 277 U.S. 438 (1928).

[61] *On Lee* v. *United States,* 343 U.S. 747 (1952).

[62] *Nardone* v. *United States,* 302 U.S. 379 (1937).

[63] See Alan F. Westin, "Wiretapping: The Quiet Revolution," *Commentary,* Vol. XXIX (1960), p. 333.

[64] *Ker* v. *California,* 374 U.S. 23 (1963).

[65] See, for example, *United States* v. *Rabinowitz,* 339 U.S. 56 (1950); *Brinegar* v. *United States,* 338 U.S. 160 (1949); *Henry* v. *United States,* 361 U.S. 98 (1959).

are seeking to find. (Federal agents follow warrant procedures more often, reflecting the generally higher standards of professional and ethical conduct in federal law enforcement.)

Continuing police misconduct in this respect has presented courts with a troublesome dilemma. Decades of experience have shown that private law suits, administrative discipline, or criminal prosecutions of the police for illegal actions are hopeless remedies. Juries do not like to award damages to "criminals" against police officers, and district attorneys or attorneys general usually do not discipline or prosecute their own sub-ordinates when this "overzealous" activity produces solutions to crimes and, often, public applause for catching criminals. Thus, beginning in 1914 for federal proceedings [66] and in 1961 for states,[67] the United States Supreme Court has held that evidence obtained by illegal search and seizure violates due process and may not be used in criminal trials. The justices decided that if police officials know they will *lose* cases resting upon illegally obtained evidence they will be deterred from acting illegally. "Letting the criminal escape because the constable blundered" has been criticized as both dangerous and unnecessary, but the Supreme Court—and even many students of law enforcement—remain convinced that this is the only way to control police misconduct and that the rule presents no serious bar to effective investigations.

Detention

Once persons are arrested by police and "taken down to headquarters," two main issues of fair procedure arise, both growing out of the constitutional guarantee that persons need not give self-incriminating testimony. The first involves coercion of confessions by improper police methods. The use of drugs for narcoanalysis or the hypnotism of prisoners is for-bidden, and lie-detector tests can be administered only with the prisoner's consent (and are not admissible as evidence). Extraction of confessions by any kind of force or threat is outlawed, whether obtained through physical mistreatment or more subtle techniques, such as warning a prisoner that the police cannot protect him from the mob outside unless he confesses at once. Confessions obtained involuntarily are excluded from federal or state trials as a matter of due process. The Court usually orders a new trial when such a confession was a central part of the conviction.

The Court has found it very difficult to set boundary lines on just how much questioning of a detained prisoner and what kind, short of torture, amounts to coercion. How long the prisoner is questioned, whether he was of normal mentality, what conditions he was questioned under, whether he was subjected to physical or psychological discomfort, and what he

[66] *Weeks* v. *United States,* 232 U.S. 383 (1914).
[67] *Mapp* v. *Ohio,* 367 U.S. 643 (1961).

was told by his examiners are all relevant factors in determining coerciveness.

The second main issue arising during detention is that of a timely arraignment. After a person is arrested, federal and state statutes generally provide that he must be brought "without unreasonable delay" before a judicial official, who holds a hearing on the probable cause for detention, informs the prisoner of his rights, and decides whether to return the prisoner to jail or release him on bail until the trial. Ever since the 1940's, the Court has been concerned with due-process guarantees during detention, has openly refused to accept the judgment of the trial jury and the state courts about the "facts" of procedural safeguards, and has made an independent study of the trial record to determine voluntariness of confessions and due process.

In 1964 the Court began to use the due-process clause to develop a firm constitutional standard of voluntariness, holding that a detained person was entitled to a lawyer during the pretrial proceedings [68] and that the Fifth Amendment privilege against self-incrimination was applicable to state cases.[69] In 1966 the Court handed down a landmark decision, declaring that statements or confessions obtained from a suspect during interrogation in the station house or jail were inadmissible unless the prosecution had employed specific procedural safeguards: (1) the suspect must be informed of his right to remain silent; (2) he must be told that anything he says can be used against him; (3) he must be advised of his right to consult with an attorney and to have him present during the interrogation; (4) if he is indigent, a lawyer must be appointed for him; (5) if a suspect submits to the interrogation without counsel, the prosecution must be able to prove that these warnings were given and intelligently waived; (6) if the suspect indicates a desire to be silent at any stage during the interrogation, questioning must cease, *even if silence was waived at an earlier stage;* (7) if the suspect asks for a lawyer, questioning must cease until he has conferred with one.[70]

Critics of the Court's decisions in these cases, including many law-enforcement officials, argue that the hours of questioning before arraignment are vital to the investigative work: guilty persons are more likely to reveal inconsistencies, give leads, and make confessions before they return to their cells; conversely, the ability to question for a reasonable length of time before having to charge a suspect formally often leads police to conclude that the detained person is not guilty, and he is let go. However, most persons arrested for crime do not know of their constitutional rights to silence and counsel, and they are deeply intimidated by the fact of detention and the physical presence of police interrogators. The establish-

[68] *Escobedo* v. *Illinois,* 378 U.S. 478 (1964).
[69] *Malloy* v. *Hogan,* 378 U.S. 1 (1964).
[70] *Miranda* v. *Arizona,* 384 U.S. 436 (1966).

ment of these new standards by the Court thus contributes to the dignity of the individual and helps assure that truth-seeking and law enforcement will rely on the best process in the long run.

Trial and appeal

Due process provides a code of working rules for virtually every aspect of criminal trial and appeal, from the way in which a trial is initiated (by indictment of a grand jury or on a finding of "probable cause" by a magistrate) to the procedures for asking a state supreme court or the United States Supreme Court to reconsider its "final" ruling once again. In brief outline, defendants in the federal and state courts enjoy the following due-process rights: to have a definite charge lodged against them, to have a speedy and public trial, to have legal counsel for the defense, to be present at the trial, to compel witnesses to appear, to cross-examine hostile witnesses, to refuse to testify at all themselves, to be tried by an impartial jury and judge in a courtroom atmosphere free from intimidation or terror, to be presumed innocent until proven guilty beyond a reasonable doubt, and to appeal to higher courts to correct errors of fact-finding or law made at the trial. Let us examine one of these basic trial rights—the assistance of counsel—to observe the conflicting values involved and the judicial choices at work.

The right to counsel illustrates how American society has changed its notions of what constitutes fundamental fairness in criminal procedure. Before 1938 the Sixth Amendment's provision that the accused was entitled to "the assistance of counsel for his defense" had been held to require court appointment of a lawyer in federal trials for defendants without funds *only* in capital cases. In 1938 the Supreme Court held that counsel must be present (unless intelligently waived by the accused) "in all criminal proceedings" in the federal courts.[71] In 1963 the Supreme Court decided that counsel was constitutionally required for defendants in all state criminal cases as well.[72] As we have just noted, the Court expanded this ruling in 1964 and 1966 to provide that counsel be present at various stages of the judicial process from the time of arrest. Today, a combination of privately supported legal-aid societies, "public defender" organizations, and court-appointed lawyers provide counsel for indigent defendants.

Punishment

The Eighth Amendment states that "cruel and unusual punishments" may not be inflicted on criminals; this amendment has been held to outlaw

---

[71] *Johnson v. Zerbst,* 304 U.S. 458 (1938).

[72] *Gideon v. Wainwright,* 372 U.S. 335 (1963). Before 1963 defense counsel was required in state trials (under the Fourteenth Amendment) only in special cases, such as when legal issues were so complicated that a layman could not be expected to protect his interests intelligently or when the defendant was young or illiterate.

torture, the wearing of heavy chains on hands and feet during prison terms, and deliberately slow execution. Execution by new methods such as gas and electrocution has been upheld, and the death penalty itself is constitutional, though it has been abolished by legislation in several states. Recently, the Supreme Court used the cruel-and-unusual-punishment standard to strike down a federal statute taking away the citizenship of military personnel convicted by court-martial of wartime desertion.[73] Denationalization, said the Court, constitutes "the total destruction of the individual's status in organized society. It is a form of punishment more primitive than torture, for it destroys for the individual the political existence that was centuries in the development."

Due Process and Semitrials

The central purpose of the criminal trial is to determine the guilt or innocence of a defendant. As the titles of criminal cases indicate—*United States* v. *Leonard Lightfinger* or the *California* v. *Watery Cellars Construction Company*—these are adversary proceedings, with "government" arrayed on one side and private parties on the other. The pace of trial and appeal is deliberately slow, and when the moment comes for final decision, presumptions of innocence are deliberately placed on the defendant's side of the scale.

In *semitrials*—proceedings conducted by executive and legislative agencies —most of the key characteristics of criminal proceedings are absent or greatly modified. The purposes of a semitrial are executive or legislative: to protect government secrets and policy-making processes from foreign agents (in employee loyalty-security hearings held by executive agencies), or to remove undesirable aliens from the country (in deportation hearings), or to collect, evaluate, and publicize facts that may require legislative action (in legislative committee hearings). Even some judicial proceedings—for example, those of juvenile court—can have the characteristics of semitrials. In order to protect the public in these cases, government agencies often find themselves having to probe guilt or innocence—that is, to secure the facts, examine motives, choose between conflicting accounts of witnesses, and make findings of responsibility in a procedure resembling the judicial trial. And the results of semitrials are often quite severe for individuals or organizations—dismissing government employees with the stigma of "disloyalty" on their records, deporting persons who may have lived in the United States for many years and have businesses and families here, forcing witnesses (by subpoena) to testify at legislative investigations and expose their activities to widespread public view, or ending a franchise on which the holder may have spent great sums of money (and which may be worth millions of dollars).

[73] *Trop* v. *Dulles,* 356 U.S. 86 (1958).

Because semitrials do not formally determine criminal guilt or impose the kind of punishment that requires full due process, the Supreme Court has held that semitrials need only be "fair" hearings. What constitutes fairness will vary with each type of situation.

Disputes have involved such due-process problems as whether there must be a definite and supported charge, whether defendants should have the right to confront hostile witnesses and cross-examine them; what rules of permissible evidence will be followed; and whether there should be presumptions of innocence and burdens of proof. How these rules of fairness have been applied in semitrials can be seen by sampling two leading areas of controversy: deportation hearings and juvenile proceedings.

In the leading Supreme Court case on deportation, an 1893 decision,[74] the justices held that the federal government's right to expel foreigners living in the United States who had not become citizens through naturalization "is as absolute and unqualified as the right to prohibit . . . their entrance into the country." Deportation is "not punishment for crime," however; this means that neither Congress' rules governing deportation nor the proceedings held by officers of the Immigration Service are subject to the due-process limitations of criminal trials. This difference has had a significant effect on the procedures and outcomes of semitrials. For example, in criminal trials it is illegal to punish an activity retroactively if it was lawful at the time it was conducted; but in semitrials an alien who joined the Communist party in this country in 1922, when it was lawful, can now be deported under a 1950 statute retroactively making membership grounds for deportation.[75] Second, in criminal trials a person can be punished only for "knowing" membership in a subversive or illegal organization; but aliens can be deported even for "innocent" membership in the Communist party—even if they left the party when they found out that it advocated the overthrow of the government.[76] Third, aliens can be held without bail throughout the hearings on deportation.[77] Fourth, secret evidence from informers or government undercover agents is allowed at semitrials. Fifth, the agency's decision need not prove guilt "beyond a reasonable doubt" but need only be based on "substantial evidence" in the record.[78]

However, the seriousness of deportations has led the Court to say that a fair hearing is required. This has been interpreted to mean that "hearsay" evidence may not be used and vague charges will not be tolerated.[79] The Immigration Service must follow its own rules of procedure, and failure to do so will violate the rights of the alien. And any person

[74] *Fong Yue Ting* v. *United States*, 149 U.S. 698 (1893).
[75] *Harisiades* v. *Shaughnessy*, 342 U.S. 580 (1952).
[76] *Galvan* v. *Press*, 347 U.S. 522 (1954).
[77] *Carlson* v. *Landon*, 342 U.S. 524 (1952).
[78] *Ibid.*
[79] *Jordan* v. *DeGeorge*, 341 U.S. 223 (1951).

held for deportation who claims that he is really a citizen (through birth, marriage, naturalization, etc.) is entitled to a regular trial in the courts to determine whether he is a citizen.[80]

There are signs that the deportation issue may be reopened again in the late 1960's, especially since the Supreme Court has held the related act of denaturalization to be a cruel and unusual punishment that Congress could not impose without a judicial trial, even for wartime desertion by servicemen,[81] and since, in 1967, the Court declared unconstitutional the Federal Nationality Act of 1940, which deprived citizens of their nationality if they voted in a foreign election. The Court's landmark ruling made a person's citizenship an inviolate right, guaranteed by the Fourteenth Amendment, which Congress could not take away for any reason unless the individual gave his consent.[82]

In its 1965 term the Court seemed on the verge of setting new standards for those proceedings that are distinct from criminal law. In one case, the Court limited application of Rule 42a of the Federal Rules of Criminal Procedure, permitting summary conviction without a hearing, after notice, for contempts "committed in the actual presence of the court," to conduct threatening the judge or disrupting court proceedings; [83] and, in another, the Court held that federal judges could not impose sentences of more than six months for criminal contempt unless the defendant had been offered a jury trial.[84] In 1967, the Supreme Court handed down a landmark 5–4 decision dealing with the juvenile court—long considered "civil" court because of its attempts to provide guidance and rehabilitation for the child rather than to impose punishment. The Court ruled that juveniles must be afforded due-process guarantees, including the rights to counsel, to confrontation and cross-examination of witnesses, and to appellate review and transcript, as well as the privilege against self-incrimination.[85] Although the Court realized the implications for such a decision on reformation in the nation's three thousand juvenile courts, Justice Fortas' opinion pointed out that "the Bill of Rights is [not] for adults alone. . . . Under our Constitution, the condition of being a boy does not justify a kangaroo court."

Due Process: Meeting Ground for Liberals and Conservatives

In the conflict between "liberty-firsters" and "property-firsters" over the primacy of Lockean principles, due process—justice—may well be the meeting ground of the two warring camps. It is interesting to note that

[80] *Ng Fung Ho* v. *White*, 259 U.S. 276 (1922).
[81] *Kennedy* v. *Martinez*, 372 U.S. 144 (1963).
[82] *Afroyim* v. *Rusk*, No. 46, 1966 Term (1967).
[83] *Harris* v. *United States*, 382 U.S. 162 (1965).
[84] *Cheff* v. *Schnackenberg*, 384 U.S. 373 (1966).
[85] In re *Gault*, No. 116, October Term, 1966 (1967).

interest groups that usually agree on very little of substance often stand together in defending due process. When the Supreme Court has condemned illegal searches and seizures, the liberal weeklies and civil-liberties organizations have been joined by the *Wall Street Journal* in their hurrahs for the Court. When the Court ruled that due process was needed to some extent in federal loyalty-security hearings, conservatives from the American Bar Association stood beside leaders of Americans for Democratic Action and the American Civil Liberties Union in voicing approval. The basic reason is that the due-process rules enunciated in "communist cases" or "racketeer cases" become precedents for antitrust cases as well, and the procedures set for witnesses called before "anticommunist" investigating committees become guidelines for hearings on drug companies, missile manufacturers, labor unions, private foundations, civil-rights groups, and university professors. The basic trend over time has been for due process to receive a fairly high bipartisan and bi-ideological support in America, despite occasional public hostility against the rules when they interfere with the speedy apprehension and conviction of especially detested offenders.

SUMMARY

The rights of property, liberty, and due process are constant battlegrounds in the American political system. In the most obvious sense, this is because a natural tension exists between such competing values as individual pursuits and community interests, dissent and conformity. These rights are also highly controversial because civil-liberties issues are so often issues of economic and political power: he who has power usually has his constitutional rights well protected; he who challenges the predominant powers must *struggle* to secure those rights, appealing in particular to agencies such as the courts and to the public belief in civil liberties—a continuing though uneven force in our political culture.

In the area of property rights, we described the way American politics and law in the past three decades have limited many of those rules protecting an owner's freedom to use private property that prevailed before problems such as national depression, World War II, urban crises, and racial justice made it clear that increased social controls over property were vital to the successful management of a democratic society. Yet we also saw that the constitutional rights to contract, to receive just compensation for property taken by the government for public use, and to secure substantive and procedural due process and equal protection under the law have remained strong and meaningful in our system.

In the area of liberty, we concentrated on the First Amendment guarantees of free speech, press, assembly, association, religion, and privacy because these are the bedrock of free expression. We showed in each of these areas that neither the courts, nor elected agencies, nor dominant public opinion in the United States has supported *absolute* rights of expression. In each area, the courts have engaged in a process of weighing the social value to the democratic process offered by certain kinds of "offensive" speaking, writing, meeting, and so on against the harm allegedly done to the values of public order and community moral standards. The distinct trend in all of these areas in the past decade has been to extend the claims of free expression. This has been done primarily by Supreme Court rulings but with sufficient support from the legislatures and public opinion to keep these decisions from being overturned or ignored. Even in loyalty-security questions—the most sensitive of all issues to popular fears of nonconformity and dissent—the relaxation of Cold War tension during the past decade has seen many of the extreme measures of the late 1940's and early 1950's either struck down as unconstitutional or softened considerably through judicial and executive interpretation.

Finally, we have treated due process as the most widely respected area of civil liberties. Both liberals and conservatives in America share a recognition that fair procedure serves vital goals in our system: as the soundest way to find the truth, as a system that respects individual dignity, and as a process that sets essential limits on the police power of government. Yet there are sometimes conflicts among these values, and the problems of large-scale modernized crime, subversive activities, and government regulation of organizational affairs create additional problems of balance throughout the process of criminal-justice, from investigation and detention to trial, appeal, and punishment. Here, too, we have seen that the trend of the past decade has been to expand greatly the protection of persons accused of crimes, being tried in the courts, or facing semitrials. Many of these expansions of due-process rights, such as the right to counsel and restrictions on police interrogation, have represented responses to the claims of the poor and minority groups that they have not received the same due process as the well-to-do and the well-respected in our society. Whether the balance has swung too far toward protecting the accused is now a subject of intense public debate, but what is most significant is the way the new rights of due process have led to experiments in many law-enforcement agencies with practices that, perhaps for the first time in our history, are truly consistent with the words and intent of the Constitution.

CIVIL RIGHTS The Dilemmas of Equality

18

Throughout the nineteenth century, American egalitarianism was so radical that it was the despair of European conservatives and a polestar for subject nationalities everywhere. Yet even then the United States had allowed a double standard—providing one law for whites and another for blacks—to adulterate its tradition of equality. This discrepancy was to stain our law, politics, and culture down through the twentieth century. We will trace four major periods in the history of the double standard, and we will survey the key civil-rights issues of the 1960's. To what extent has the double standard been eliminated? What are the areas of continuing crisis? What are the recent shifts in the civil-rights movement?

EQUALITY AND THE GOVERNMENTAL PROCESS

Equality issues become matters of government action in two major ways. First, governments define in constitutional clauses, laws, administrative regulations, and court decisions those who are entitled to enjoy various rights and privileges within the nation or a state and on what terms. Federal provisions specify, for example, who can be a citizen of the United States and who can serve on federal juries. State provisions determine who can vote in Tennessee, be a judge in Wisconsin, practice pharmacy in Maine. All these government acts involve classification through law, the inclusion and exclusion of categories of people, and the setting of various qualifications for the exercise of rights. And many other public laws involve equality judgments. Every tax statute distinguishes among types of taxpayers in matters of rate, deductions, and exemptions. Every zoning law elevates one type of business activity or building style or civic use over competing interests. Eighteen-year-old males are called up for military service with the United States, but seventeen-year-olds are not; and the huskiest twenty-year-old girl will have to volunteer if she wants to be in the nation's armed forces. The same equality issue is raised in each instance: Is the classification fair and reasonable, or does it embody distinctions that are legally improper?

Second, government enters the equality struggle by setting minimum equality standards in the private sector. When powerful private groups engage in practices that directly affect the economic, social, or political well-being of the public, government often steps in to set rules of entry or even forbid discrimination. The hiring and promotion policies of corporations, the admission practices of labor unions, the selection standards of private colleges and universities, the practices of real-estate brokers and rental agents, and the guest regulations of public-service facilities such as railroads, restaurants, hotels, theaters, and buses are all private activities that have come under government regulation to ensure equality, because the policies of these private agencies affect public well-being. Local and state authorities traditionally intervene in these matters under their constitutional power to protect the health, safety, morals, and public order of their communities or under their power to set standards for corporations and associations chartered by the state. The federal government has drawn its primary authority in this area from the effect of private activities on interstate commerce, interstate travel, the national armed forces, federally financed or federally assisted programs, and the specific provisions of the Constitution specifying the rights of citizens.

THE RISE AND FALL
OF THE DOUBLE STANDARD, 1781–1963

Our national experience with the problem of equality can be divided into four primary periods: 1781–1863, the era of white egalitarianism and Negro slavery; 1863–83, the period of temporary racial harmony; 1883–1941, the era when the double standard for white and black was grafted onto the American system despite universal freedom; and 1941–63, the era when the double standard was finally rejected by American law, politics, and civic opinion.[1] Throughout this survey, we will contrast American equality practices in regard to religion, nationality, sex, and sometimes property with those that have dealt with race (which we use to include the term "color"). Only with such a survey of basic trends can the civil-rights issues of the late 1960's be adequately understood.

The Early Double Standard: Of Free Men and Slaves, 1781–1863

In 1781 the majority of Americans in this young republic were white, of English or Northwestern European backgrounds, and Protestant. Apart from Indians, there were 3¼ million Americans: 2 million free persons, 600,000 Negro slaves, 300,000 indentured servants, 250,000 debtors and vagrants being held to "involuntary labor," and 50,000 convicts shipped to the colonies by Great Britain.

The leaders of the American states defined their ideas of equality in several major documents of national constitutionalism: the Declaration of Independence, the Articles of Confederation, the federal Constitution, and the various state constitutions.

The Declaration of Independence represents the most famous and comprehensive statement of the American ideal of equality: "We hold these truths to be self-evident," the colonists stated in 1776, "that all men are created equal." The Declaration reflected two central aspects of the American tradition of equality: first, the equality of men in the eyes of their Creator and of the law and, second, the duty of government to protect the inalienable rights of its citizens.

These principles were expressed in many of the state constitutions and bills of rights instituted between 1776 and the adoption of the Articles of

---

[1] For excellent works on the equality theme in American history, see Gunnar Myrdal, *An American Dilemma* (New York: Harper & Row, 1944); C. Vann Woodward, *The Strange Career of Jim Crow* (New York: Oxford University Press, 1957); Robert J. Harris, *The Quest for Equality* (Baton Rouge: Louisiana State University Press, 1960); John Hope Franklin, *From Slavery to Freedom: A History of American Negroes*, 2nd ed. (New York: Knopf, 1956); Milton Konvitz, *A Century of Civil Rights* (New York: Columbia University Press, 1961).

Confederation in 1781. Virginia's Bill of Rights (1776) declared that "all men are by nature equally free and independent," and the Massachusetts Declaration of Rights of 1780 used almost identical language. These declarations were implemented by the Virginia and Massachusetts constitutions, and in the famous Quock Walker case of 1783,[2] the Supreme Judicial Court of Massachusetts held that slavery violated that Commonwealth's equality guarantee.

This was not the interpretation that Virginia, with one-third of the slaves in the Republic, put on her declaration of equality. While many leading Virginians deplored slavery, they expected slavery to die out gradually as an uneconomical and illiberal system.

When the national union was being constructed, the issue of slavery threatened to prevent agreement between South and North. The "solution" that saved the day was that the Founding Fathers simply remained silent in our national charters about the standard of equality of the Declaration of Independence and the state bills of rights. Thus, the word "equality" does not appear in any reference to persons in the Articles, the Constitution, or the Bill of Rights. Instead, a clear distinction was enunciated between free persons and those not free. The Articles of Confederation provided that the privileges and immunities of "free citizenship" in each state were available to the "free inhabitants of each of these States, paupers, vagabonds, and fugitives from Justice excepted." The Constitution made provisions for "all other persons" not "free" in its three-fifths compromise for taxation and representation, in its clause barring federal interference with "importation of persons" before 1808, and in its requirement that persons "held to service or labour" must be "delivered up" if they escaped to other states.

Admission to citizenship

The Constitution provided that those who were granted citizenship by a state automatically became "citizens of the United States"; this meant, in practice, that all "free whites" in the new republic became citizens. As for new immigrants, a congressional act in 1790 provided that any "free white person" who resided in the United States for five years could become a naturalized citizen by asking to have citizenship conferred on him in federal or state courts.

The single restriction on equality for white immigrants in this period was the Alien and Naturalization Acts of 1798. Passed by the Federalists out of hostility to the liberal French émigrés who fled to the United States during the 1790's and became leading Jeffersonian Republicans, the Naturalization Act increased from five to fourteen years the period required for

[2] See Henry S. Commager, *Documents of American History*, 5th ed. (New York: Appleton-Century-Crofts, 1949), p. 110.

residence before acquiring citizenship. This legislation was repealed in 1801 by the Jeffersonian-controlled Congress, and throughout the remainder of the pre-Civil War period no restrictions—political, religious, racial, national, or any others—were imposed on free immigration and naturalization.

It was the status of the free Negro that created the great controversy in citizenship. By the early 1800's, almost 100,000 Negroes had been freed by their owners, had purchased their freedom, or had simply escaped to Northern and Western communities. They paid taxes, were allowed to vote, and even held public offices in some Northern states. Whether they were citizens of the United States, however, was hotly argued by pro-Negro and anti-Negro forces. The crucial test came in 1857, in the famous Dred Scott case.[3] Scott, a slave, had been taken by his owner from the slave state of Missouri into territory that had been declared free land by the Missouri Compromise, a congressional act of 1820. Scott sued in federal-district court, claiming that by his presence in free territory he had become a free man. The Supreme Court held that Scott could not maintain his suit, since no Negro, free or slave, could become a citizen of the United States. Chief Justice Roger Taney based this conclusion on various clauses in the Constitution indicating that slavery was a lawful institution in those states approving it and that Negroes were not intended to be citizens. Thus "they had no rights which the white man was bound to respect."

Voting and equality

Out of 2 million free Americans in 1781, only 120,000 were voters. This was a result of qualifications set for voting by the states, under the prevailing theory that suffrage was not a right of citizenship but a privilege conferred on those persons who met certain high standards. Generally, these standards restricted suffrage to males over twenty-one years of age, residing in the voting district, and having a certain minimum of property—usually land or a considerable income from property—to guarantee a "stake in society." Colonial restrictions on voting by Catholics, Jews, Quakers, debtors, and others were either dropped by the state constitutions in the 1780's or became dead letters until formally repealed at later dates.

The first wave of suffrage reform came between 1780 and 1800, when six of the thirteen original states either abolished the economic qualification entirely or limited it to the payment of taxes. By the 1820's, nine newly admitted states had no economic qualifications, and three others set only taxpaying requirements. Following the wave of Jacksonian "popular democracy," all states had abandoned property-holding qualifications by 1852, and only seven states continued taxpaying requirements. By the late 1850's, the only "stake in society" required for voting by a white adult male resid-

---

[3] *Dred Scott* v. *Sanford*, 60 U.S. 393 (1857).

ing in the state was enough concern with the problems of government to go to the polls on election day.

Again, the line between white and black was drawn sharply. When there were relatively few free Negroes in Northern states, Negroes were allowed to vote, and many did so in New York, Pennsylvania, Maryland, and North Carolina from 1776 to the 1790's. Between 1800 and 1830, however, free Negroes were gradually denied the franchise by constitutional change in every state outside New England. In New York after 1823, for example, Negroes had to meet a special $250 property-ownership qualification and a three-year residence requirement that did not apply to whites. By the Civil War, America's 500,000 free Negroes were disfranchised in all but a few states.

Equal administration of justice

"Administration of justice" refers to the treatment received by minority-group members from the police and the courts, as well as the protection given to them by public authorities against mob violence. The years from 1825 to 1855 have been called the "time of the mob" in American history because of the widespread riots, whippings, tarrings and featherings, beatings, destruction of property, and expulsions from communities that crowds of the citizenry inflicted upon groups that incurred their ire. The chief victims of this mob action throughout the nation were (1) Irish and German Catholics, who were feared as economic competitors by many "old-stock" workingmen and hated by some for their divergent religious and social mores; (2) the Mormons, who were viewed as dangerous because of their religious doctrines, land-holding policies, and antislavery sentiments; (3) the Masonic Order, which was denounced as a secret society plotting to overthrow the Republic; (4) the Abolitionists, who were mistreated in the North as well as the South for their ideas about forcibly ending slavery; and (5) free Negroes living in Northern and Middle Atlantic states, who were victimized by Northern white bigots. Many local elected authorities and small militias of this period were unable or unwilling to control mob action against groups that stood for principles repugnant to community morality; in addition, major political movements in the 1840's (the Native-American party) and the 1850's (the Know-Nothings) openly advocated both legal and direct-action measures against "aliens, Masons, Papists, and foreigners."

This widespread street fighting and violence, in direct disregard of the legal rights of victimized groups to hold their own views, underscores an important aspect of the problem of equality—that formal rights are value-less if the government does not enforce legal guarantees against physical violence and threats by angry majorities.

Looking back over the period of 1781–1863, we see clearly the emergence of the two contradictory trends in our tradition of equality. On the one hand, the practice of equal treatment for religious and nationality groups was steadily widened, and economic and party distinctions were abolished in bestowing citizenship rights. But, on the other hand, we maintained a tradition of unequal treatment and second-class citizenship for Negroes, not only by upholding slavery in the South but also by mistreating free Negroes in most of the Northern states. The double standard had been born, and a nation entered a civil war with the crisis between slavery and freedom at the heart of the conflict.

Experiment in Racial Harmony, 1863–83

The first two decades after the Civil War saw a major expansion of the constitutional guarantees of equality in America. While the Emancipation Proclamation in 1863 declared slaves in the seceded states to be free, it was the Thirteenth Amendment in 1865, outlawing slavery anywhere in the United States, that guaranteed what the Supreme Court called "universal civil freedom" for every American. The Fourteenth Amendment, adopted in 1868, declared:

> All persons born or naturalized in the United States and subject to the jurisdiction thereof, are citizens of the United States and of the State wherein they reside. No state shall make or enforce any law which shall abridge the privileges and immunities of citizens of the United States; nor shall any State deprive any person of life, liberty, or property, without due process of law; nor deny to any person within its jurisdiction the equal protection of the laws.

In the Fifteenth Amendment, ratified in 1870, the Republicans completed their constitutional work by providing that the right to vote could not be abridged by either the federal government or state governments "on account of race, color, or previous condition of servitude."

All three Civil War amendments gave Congress the power to enforce their provisions by appropriate legislation. Congressional majorities in the late 1860's and 1870's did pass a series of civil-rights statutes spelling out the rights of the new Negro freedman and providing penalties for denial of these rights. Two of the most important of these congressional statutes punished private conspiracies that attempted to deny persons their constitutional rights (the "Anti-Klan" Act of 1871) and forbade owners of public-accommodation facilities to deny service to persons because of "race or color" (the Civil Rights Act of 1875).

Between 1865 and the early 1880's, the egalitarian spirit of the civil-rights movement was reflected in widespread Negro voting throughout the South, the presence of Negroes beside whites in theaters, hotels, restaurants, and public-transportation companies from Maine to Florida, the presence of

Negroes in federal and state offices, judicial enforcement of citizenship rights for Negroes in the courts, and active Negro civil-rights organizations and protest movements. In the rural South and in some of the more exclusive Northern establishments, Negroes were still denied their rights by local authorities or were refused entry to public-accommodation facilities. But the clear national trend in these years was toward exercise of civil rights and white acceptance of Negro patronage, and no Southern state maintained, in law or fact, a Jim Crow society. Behind these advances, operating both as moral prod and legal shield, were the federal civil-rights statutes and the ultimate threat of federal force.

The Double Standard Restored and Enshrined, 1883–1941

The era that followed, however, proved to be a disastrous milieu for the efforts of Negroes to achieve full citizenship. The period of the 1880's through the 1920's was one of expanding capitalism and a free-enterprise philosophy that led middle-class Americans to distrust government—especially federal government—intervention in "private affairs." It was also a period in which the Southern states were returned to full participation in national political life, with the removal of federal Reconstruction forces as part of the "compromise" that gave the Republican, Hayes, victory over the Democrat, Tilden, in the electoral photo-finish race for the Presidency in 1876. As the 1880's and 1890's wore on, race relations were deeply affected by burgeoning élitist ideas in American life, such as belief in Anglo-Saxon racial superiority, the Darwinian notion of the "survival of the fittest," the "white man's burden" to rule colonial peoples, anti-Semitism, and fears of mass immigration to the United States of "inferior" peoples from Eastern and Southern Europe and the Orient. These isolationist and antiforeign sentiments grew more pronounced after the Spanish-American War in 1898.

The impact on racial equality of these sentiments was registered in our basic constitutional policies in two distinct phases. Beginning in 1876 and culminating in the *Civil Rights Cases* of 1883,[4] the Supreme Court struck down as unconstitutional the key federal laws forbidding *private* denials of civil rights. The justices did this by sharply limiting the "privileges and immunities" that went with national citizenship, and by interpreting the ban on *state* denials of rights in the Fourteenth and Fifteenth Amendments to refer only to the actions of state-government officials. The Court ruled that discrimination by corporations and persons licensed by the states was not covered by the amendments and that inaction by the state in dealing with mob violence and intimidation of citizens did not require federal interference. Justice Joseph Bradley commented for the Court that the Negro

[4] 109 U.S. 3 (1883).

had to cease being "the special favorite of the law" and take on "the rank of a mere citizen." Justice John Marshall Harlan was the lone dissenter.

The *Civil Rights Cases* had two effects. First, the Court's ruling destroyed the delicate balance of federal guarantees, Negro protest movements, and private enlightenment that had produced peacefully integrated public facilities throughout the nation in the 1870's and early 1880's. Second, it affected national politics by denying Congress the power to protect the Negro's right to equal treatment and wiping the civil-rights issue from the Republican party's agenda of national legislative responsibility; at the same time, it affected Southern politics by making anti-Negro positions a promising way for politicians to woo "poor whites" in order to win elections.

Even after the *Civil Rights Cases*, however, the situation of Negroes was not impossible. For the ruling did not bring wholesale imposition of segregation in public facilities in either the North or South. During the late 1880's, Negroes shared places beside whites in many Southern restaurants, streetcars, public halls, and theaters. But Democratic and Populist leaders in the South increasingly found the Negro a prime target. Between 1887 and 1891 eight Southern states passed laws *requiring* railroads to maintain white and Negro passengers in separate cars and then waited to see how these laws would be received by the Supreme Court.

In 1896 the Supreme Court upheld railroad-segregation laws in the leading case of *Plessy* v. *Ferguson*.[5] Although these laws represented state action, the Court held, they were not discriminatory because whites were separated from Negroes just as much as Negroes were separated from whites. "If one race be inferior to another socially," Justice Brown concluded, "the Constitution of the United States cannot put them upon the same plane." As in the *Civil Rights Cases*, Justice John Marshall Harlan was the sole dissenter. Pointing out that the known purpose of the segregation laws was to force Negroes out of white facilities, Harlan stated that these laws violated the personal liberty of white as well as Negro citizens and used race as an unreasonable classification, denying equal protection of the laws.

Under these narrow constitutional interpretations, the chalk line of rigid racial segregation was methodically drawn by law, by custom, and, where necessary, by force throughout the Southern and border states and by more subtle (but still effective) social discrimination throughout most of the North.

Public accommodations. Racial segregation was required by law in the South for almost every form of contact between whites and Negroes except walking on the street. Negro accommodations were invariably inferior, and Negroes had to pay equal prices for unequal facilities, such as dirty "Jim Crow cars" on the railroads, the back "Jim Crow room" in restaurants, or the "Nigger gallery" at theaters. Although eighteen Northern states had

[5] 163 U.S. 537 (1896).

passed laws forbidding discrimination by public-accommodations owners, these laws rusted quickly with neglect during this era, and most leading Northern hotels, restaurants, and theaters refused with impunity to serve Negro customers. Segregation became so much the national mode that the Wilson Administration in 1912–14 instituted segregation in the lunchrooms, rest rooms, and shops maintained by the federal government itself for federal employees and visitors. Washington, D.C., thus became a completely Jim Crow capital.

Voting. The Southern Negro was methodically pushed away from the polls by a combination of restrictive laws and official discrimination. The legal devices included requirements that prospective voters pay a poll tax or own land, or demonstrate reading and writing skills to the satisfaction of local (white) registrars, or be able to explain the state constitution to the satisfaction of these registrars. A study showed "virtually no" Negroes voting in the all-important Democratic primary in the Southern states in the 1930's and only 100,000 voting Negroes in general elections.[6] In the North, however, Negroes did vote, and, as whole wards or congressional districts became populated primarily by Negroes, their interests received some protection in Northern communities.

Housing. The South created separate "Negro quarters" in this era through local ordinances forbidding mixed neighborhoods and through local zoning controls. As Negroes moved North, they found that economic and social pressures channeled them into urban Negro ghettos, such as New York City's Harlem and Chicago's South Side. Restrictive covenants signed by home owners forbidding the sale of property to Negroes hampered Negro access to the newer parts of Northern cities and the rising suburbs. The Federal Housing Administration actively encouraged "homogeneous" neighborhoods and restrictive covenants in these years, and it approved restrictive practices by banks and real-estate agents.

Education. The public schools of the Southern and border states were strictly separated into white and Negro systems. Had these been truly "separate but equal," there might have been the period of educational progress and self-improvement that Negro leaders such as Booker T. Washington called for. But the undisputed fact is that Southern states starved Negro education in this era, providing generally older, more dilapidated, and more overcrowded school plants for Negroes, hand-me-down books, lower-paid Negro teachers, and "agricultural and mechanical colleges" for Negro higher education. And, in Northern urban centers, residential segregation, coupled with the prevailing concept of the "neighborhood school," produced a high degree of school segregation.

The administration of justice. In the South Negroes were excluded from service on grand juries and trial juries by local sheriffs and judges, who made

[6] U.S. Department of Justice, *Protection of the Rights of Individuals* (1952).

up the jury lists. This ensured all-white juries not only on cases involving Negro defendants or Negro civil-rights claimants, but also on cases involving white officials or private vigilantes indicted for anti-Negro acts. Moreover, public officials and civic leaders tolerated Ku Klux Klan terroristic activities and mob lynching throughout the South; lynchings averaged 100 per year in this period. The great majority of the victims were Negroes, and there were few convictions of the lynchers. Newspaper stories and official surveys documented widespread police mistreatment of Negroes arrested on suspicion or accused of crimes or picked up merely to keep them "in their place." Most important psychologically was the etiquette of inferiority adopted by Southern public officials when dealing with Negro citizens. Negro men were called "boy" or by their first names, and Negro women "girl" and "auntie," depending on their age, not only on the street but in public proceedings. Any notion that Southern law in this era was impartial toward Negroes in result or process is wholly mistaken, despite individual acts of kindness or paternalism toward Negroes from white persons or government charities.

Employment. Racial discrimination permeated employment patterns. Negroes were the last hired by industry and the first fired when agricultural depression struck in the 1920's and industrial depression occurred in 1929–33. Negroes were forced to work for lower wages than whites in the same jobs. When employment opportunities returned after the Depression, most of the opportunities for Negroes came in the "dirty and dangerous" specialties, and a combination of employer and union bars kept Negroes from most of the upward-moving industrial jobs. Some improvement came in the late 1930's as Negroes moved into auto production, machine tools, and similar industries. But when it came to white-collar and technical positions most national corporations had a strict "no Negroes" policy, and Negroes were completely barred from sales or executive positions.

The national military services. During the First World War Negroes were segregated in the Army, Navy, and Coast Guard, and Negro units were usually assigned to menial jobs such as mess duty and camp clean-up. As late as the eve of the Second World War, a government study found that Negroes were wholly excluded from the Army Air Corps, Marine Corps, and the Tank, Signal, Engineer, and Artillery Corps of the Army.[7]

In sum, the United States' treatment of its Negro citizens between 1883 and 1941 was nothing less than shameful. To be sure, some Negro Americans achieved success in the arts, education, law, business, science, and sports despite total segregation in the South and racial ghettos in much of the North. And groups such as the Urban League and the National Association for the Advancement of Colored People were formed in these years to press for civil rights and to assist Negro self-development. Also, there were many

[7] U.S. Civil Rights Commission, *Freedom to the Free* (1963), p. 114.

white Americans and groups such as the Catholic Interracial Council, the American Jewish Committee, and the Congress of Industrial Organizations (CIO) who fought beside Negro spokesmen to oppose segregation. But the twin promises of the Declaration of Independence and the Fourteenth Amendment—that Americans would be regarded as equal before the law and that government would protect this equality—were not only ignored but openly flouted by American law, politics, culture, and social thought in these years.

Because the double standard followed lines of color, other nonwhite groups also found the 1883–1941 era difficult. American Indians were treated as "Negroes" and segregated in Southern and Southwestern states when they left the federal Indian reservations. Widespread discrimination existed against Chinese- and Japanese-Americans on the West Coast and against Mexican-Americans in the Southwest. For all nonwhite citizens, second-class status was the rule.

However, the progress of minority religious and nationality groups in the 1883–1941 era provided a vital contrast to this pattern. Unlike nonwhite citizens, Catholics and Jews among the old stock and the new immigrants from Southern and Eastern Europe faced no *legal* discrimination and only occasional hostility in the administration of law. As a result, with their basic self-respect preserved, and with access to white schools, economic opportunities, and strong organizations to advance their cause, white minority groups as a whole prospered along with white Protestant Americans. They quickly took up political and civic activity in the cities and learned to protect their interests when attacked.

It was *social* rather than legal discrimination that white minority groups encountered in this era—and in strong doses—as ideas of Anglo-Saxon racial supremacy, anti-Semitism, and anti-Catholicism spread throughout the majority culture. Many public-accommodations facilities in the late nineteenth century began to bar Catholics and Jews. "No Jews or Dogs Allowed" was a sign printed and sold in dime stores and posted in those establishments that preferred open declarations to a quiet but equally strict policy. "No Catholics Need Apply" appeared in the newspaper ads and bulletin notices of many employers. Refusal to hire Catholics and Jews for white-collar, sales, and executive posts in local and national businesses was commonplace. Many leading professional schools, such as those for medicine, engineering, and architecture, established quotas for Jewish and Catholic applicants. Restrictive covenants binding home owners not to sell to "Negroes, Jews, Roman Catholics, Indians, Mongolians, or other non-Caucasians" covered vast areas of the country. Most important, anti-Semitic and anti-Catholic sentiments were widely accepted "genteel" views in this era, held in the best circles of society and not just limited to the Klan, the German-American Bund, or Gerald L. K. Smith's Christian Nationalists.

For women, this was a time of major advance in civil rights. The

Supreme Court held in 1875 that nothing in the Fourteenth Amendment gave women the right to vote, and that this matter was up to each state. While a few states gave women the vote in the nineteenth century (especially the progressive Western states, where women were in shorter supply), it took the militant suffragette movement decades to win the ballot for women generally. Using street parades, publicity, lobbying, hunger strikes in jail, and even handcuffing themselves to legislators' desks and the doors of city halls, the suffragettes finally won adoption of the Nineteenth Amendment, ratified in 1920, forbidding the federal government or the states to deny the vote to anyone "on account of sex."

The Fall of the Double Standard: American Egalitarianism Redeemed, 1941–63

Just as the larger national and international climate between 1890 and 1940 was not auspicious for the Negro in America or for the social position of white minority groups, so that climate during 1941–63 was just the opposite— a milieu in which all national and international influences exerted constant pressure *against* the double standard and in support of those seeking full civil rights for every American. The Second World War, for example, discouraged the double standard in several ways: first, the pressing need for military manpower and for civilian factory workers militated against discrimination and segregation; second, the war put a high premium on national unity; and third, it became crucial to distinguish our attitudes and policies from the racism and anti-Semitism of the fascists we were fighting.

After the Second World War, colored peoples in Asia, the Middle East, and Africa won their independence; their achievements, their importance to our economic and political interests, and their unshakable hostility to anti-Negro practices within the United States influenced American officials concerned with foreign policy and much of the American public as well. Furthermore, American racial policies made us vulnerable to adverse propaganda in the post-1946 rivalry between the United States and the Soviet Union in Western Europe as well as in the new nations. On the domestic scene, migration of Negroes to Northern communities and the growing economic and political influence of white minority groups strengthened the political position of those opposed to segregation on both moral grounds and those of self-interest. And, as in the 1870's, the fight against discrimination once again began to interest white Protestant liberals, whose attention had been caught up by economic recovery in the 1930's and the war in the 1940's.

Chipping away at "separate but equal," 1941–53

Between 1941 and 1953, the United States Supreme Court, the federal executive branch, and the Northern states became newly critical of official segregation and social discrimination. In a series of important rulings, the Supreme Court outlawed racial discrimination in the Southern Democratic primaries on the ground that the primary was an integral part of the official election process;[8] struck down segregation of passengers in interstate travel as a "burden on interstate commerce";[9] held that it would be unconstitutional for federal or state courts to uphold covenants containing racial or religious restrictions because doing so would constitute "government action";[10] and ruled that hereafter federal courts would demand genuine equality in the separate schools provided for Negroes.[11]

Presidential action between 1941 and 1953 contrasted sharply with the passiveness of the White House in civil-rights matters during previous decades. Under pressure of a threatened march on Washington by Negroes in 1941, President Franklin D. Roosevelt issued an executive order forbidding discrimination in defense industries or government employment and created a federal Fair Employment Practices Committee to deal with the problem through public hearings, inquiries into complaints, and recommendations to the parties.[12] (The committee was abolished in 1946 through Southern and conservative-Republican teamwork in Congress. In 1946 President Harry Truman created the President's Committee on Civil Rights;[13] its report in 1947, *To Secure These Rights*, surveyed American civil-rights practices and called for wide-scale remedies to fulfill American ideals.

In 1948 President Truman issued an executive order ending "separate but equal" recruiting, training, and service in the United States Army.[14] Another executive order in 1948 declared that federal jobs were to be distributed without regard to "race, color, religion, or national origin," and established a Fair Employment Board to oversee the policy.[15] In 1951 a presidential order created the Committee on Government Contract Compliance, requiring businesses holding contracts with the federal government to follow fair-employment policies.[16]

When President Eisenhower took office in 1953, he continued to use executive authority in key areas of civil rights. In 1953 he created the President's Committee on Government Contracts,[17] with power to receive complaints about discrimination by government contractors; the agency placing the contract investigated these complaints, and the underlying sanction was cancellation of the contract.

[8] *Smith* v. *Allwright*, 321 U.S. 649 (1944).
[9] *Morgan* v. *Virginia*, 328 U.S. 373 (1946).
[10] *Shelley* v. *Kraemer*, 334 U.S. 1 (1948).
[11] *Sweatt* v. *Painter*, 339 U.S. 629 (1950).
[12] Exec. Order 8802, *Federal Register*, Vol. VI (1941), p. 3109.
[13] Exec. Order 9808, *Federal Register*, Vol. XI (1946), p. 14153.
[14] Exec. Order 9981, *Federal Register*, Vol. XIII (1948), p. 4313.
[15] Exec. Order 9980, *ibid.*, p. 4311.
[16] Exec. Order 10308, *Federal Register*, Vol. XVI (1951), p. 12303.
[17] Exec. Order 10479, *Federal Register*, Vol. XVIII (1953), p. 4899.

Outside the South state and municipal governments also became active in protecting civil rights. In 1945 New York and New Jersey passed fair-employment laws, giving authority to state commissions to issue cease-and-desist orders enforceable in state courts against employers who were found to have engaged in discrimination. By 1953 six other Northern states had passed similar laws. In the eighteen states with public-accommodation anti-discrimination laws, complaints of violations began to be pressed, heard, and attended to. Other state laws forbade discrimination by public educational institutions.

The great contrast to these developments occurred in Congress. From 1946 to 1953, Congress refused to enact antilynching or anti-poll-tax laws, to create a new federal FEPC, or to enact any of the other measures recommended by the President and civil-rights groups. By 1953 it seemed that federal progress would stop once the outer limits of executive authority were reached and that nothing could be done about the all-pervasive system of Jim Crow in the South.

The great breakthrough, 1954–63

On May 17, 1954, the Supreme Court, in *Brown* v. *Board of Education*,[18] held that segregation in state public education was inherently discriminatory and unconstitutional. In a companion case, the Court struck down school segregation by federal authorities in the District of Columbia.[19] These rulings at one stroke transferred the legal sanction and moral authority of the nation's basic law from the segregationist forces to the civil-rights advocates.

However, the justices faced the new problem of implementing their decree in the District of Columbia and the twenty-one states with segregated public schools. Recognizing the complexity of the task, the Court took a year to hear arguments from the interested parties (Negro plaintiffs, Southern attorneys general, the United States government, and various other groups) and, in 1955, provided its blueprint for change. School authorities would not be required to give full and instant compliance but could work out, under the supervision of the lower federal courts, transitional programs that led "with all deliberate speed" to desegregated school systems.[20]

For almost two years after the initial Brown ruling, it seemed as though school desegregation might come peacefully to the nation. By the end of the 1956 school year, 699 school districts, principally in the border states and in a few "outer" Southern states such as Texas and Tennessee, had

[18] 347 U.S. 483 (1954).
[19] *Bolling* v. *Sharpe*, 347 U.S. 497 (1954).
[20] *Brown* v. *Board of Education*, 349 U.S. 294 (1955).

admitted Negro pupils to formerly all-white schools. Even more important, 690 of these had been integrated without court injunctions.

By 1956, though, the South had recovered its balance. Southern public officials, private anti-integration groups such as the White Citizens Councils, and Southern white public opinion decided that the Supreme Court's mandate could be evaded. Southern intransigence took five main forms:

1. Public schools in many Southern communities were closed by law or local school-board decision to prevent desegregation.

2. Negro students and parents were intimidated and threatened by violence in many Southern states. Since local officials were unwilling to act to prevent this harassment, President Eisenhower was forced to send federal troops to Little Rock, Arkansas, in 1957, and President Kennedy had to send federal marshals and later combat troops to the University of Mississippi in 1962 to enforce school desegregation.

3. Laws were enacted in many Southern states to allow school boards to assign students to particular schools and to set up complex procedures for Negro parents seeking to transfer their children to schools outside their neighborhood. Such pupil-placement laws became the backbone of *tokenism*, a practice that allowed a very few Negroes to attend white schools but kept the vast bulk of the school system thoroughly segregated.

4. Vigorous anti-Supreme Court campaigns were mounted by Southern segregationists, and congressional legislation was introduced to curb the power of the Court on such matters as public education.

5. Many Southern states moved to harass or ban the NAACP in their states because of the crucial role played by that group in the court battles for civil rights. Legislative investigations, statutory provisions, and criminal prosecutions were used to drive the NAACP out of the South. The Supreme Court struck down such measures as improper applications of the states' powers to resist integration and to punish legitimate Negro organizational activity,[21] but the drain on civil-rights funds and time while these cases were being fought in court hurt the NAACP nonetheless.

The federal courts had spelled out what the rights of Negroes were, but what the civil-rights cause really needed was national legislation implemented by executive power. The period from 1957 to 1963 brought both. In 1957 the growing civil-rights movement, the increasing importance of Negro voters in key Northern states, and pressure from world public opinion finally provided enough impetus to compel Congress to pass a civil-rights act.[22] The 1957 law had four major provisions: (1) the federal government could sue for civil injunction in federal-district courts when any person was deprived of his right to vote; (2) federal-district courts were given jurisdiction over these proceedings without being required to wait

---

[21] See *NAACP* v. *Alabama*, 357 U.S. 449 (1958).
[22] 71 Stat. 634 (1957).

until state remedies had been exhausted; (3) the United States Civil Rights Commission was created, a bipartisan body authorized to investigate reports of civil-rights denials and to appraise federal-government policies to protect these rights; and (4) the Civil Rights Section of the Justice Department was expanded into a full division with an assistant attorney general at its head.

In 1960 Congress passed another civil-rights act,[23] which allowed federal voting referees to be appointed by federal-district courts where a "pattern or practice" of discrimination was found. These referees were given the power to order the admission of qualified voters to the voting rolls. Though the 1957 and 1960 acts represented only a start, they were the first congressional actions on civil rights in more than eighty years and broke the legislative logjam.

Between 1954 and 1963, significant steps were also taken through executive action. The Kennedy Administration created the Committee on Equal Employment Opportunity by merging the Committee on Government Employment Policy and the Committee on Government Contracts.[24] This new, more powerful committee could investigate federal agencies on its own initiative and issue orders of compliance. The same executive order required a nondiscrimination clause in all contracts with the United States government as well as the submission to the government of reports on compliance with fair-employment policies. Other executive action by President Kennedy included the creation of a commission to deal with discrimination in federally assisted or owned housing.[25]

Meanwhile, the Supreme Court continued its own efforts to extend the new equality standard by striking down racial discrimination in legislative voting districts,[26] by compelling desegregation of interstate public-accommodation facilities,[27] and by upholding the voting-protection provisions of the 1957 Civil Rights Act.[28]

State action outside the South also continued to increase protection of civil rights, providing for fair-housing, fair-employment, and public-accommodation legislation; in many states commissions were established to enforce these laws. Voluntary actions of private business, labor, religious, and civic groups gave major support to the civil-rights movement by eliminating discriminatory practices and lending moral and financial support on all fronts.

By 1963 American constitutional law had unequivocally outlawed racial segregation by government or in privately owned public facilities. Both national political parties were pledged to securing civil rights for all minority

[23] 74 Stat. 86 (1960).
[24] Exec. Order 10925, *Federal Register*, Vol. XXVI (1961), p. 1977.
[25] Exec. Order 11063, *Federal Register*, Vol. XXVII (1962), p. 11527.
[26] *Gomillion* v. *Lightfoot*, 364 U.S. 339 (1960).
[27] *Bailey* v. *Patterson*, 369 U.S. 31 (1962); *Turner* v. *Memphis*, 369 U.S. 350 (1962).
[28] *United States* v. *Raines*, 362 U.S. 17 (1960).

groups. The governing boards of American religious bodies fought racial discrimination, and public-opinion polls showed support both North and South for the Negro cause. Yet, despite these encouraging trends, it was clear that the deeper racial conflict in the United States was far from resolved.

A NEW ERA OF CONFLICT AND RESOLUTION, 1963–65

The 1963 Civil-Rights Upheaval

During the "long, hot summer" of 1963, Negro demonstrators were packed in the streets of America from Boston to Birmingham. Saying they had "lost faith in the white power structure of America," they demanded breakthroughs in five major areas.

The first area of protest, because of its symbolic importance, was continuing segregation in American education. Although nine years had passed since the Brown decision, integrated schools in the South reflected the triumph of tokenism. Only four-tenths of 1 percent of Negro children in the Deep South in 1963 were in integrated schools, and in three states not a single Negro child was enrolled in a white school.[29] In the North, *de facto* segregation existed in most schools, despite court actions in major Northern cities to compel redistricting to achieve more racially balanced schools. Affirmative action by cities—such as pupil transfer and "busing"—in order to even out racial imbalance could not offset the effect of increasingly dense Negro populations in the cores of Northern cities, white migration to the suburbs, the placing of white children in private and parochial schools, and the resistance of white parents to school-integration measures. As a result, *de facto* segregation actually *increased* in the 1961–63 period.

The employment situation was equally bleak. Automation hit Negroes hardest, and unemployment rates, especially among unskilled and youthful workers, rose rapidly. Many important labor unions continued to pursue official policies of discrimination in membership and apprenticeship programs. Tokenism in the corporate world was still standard operating procedure, despite efforts on the part of some leading corporations to adopt fair-employment policies.

The third area of major upheaval in 1963 was housing. Despite executive and state action on fair-housing laws, residential segregation increased steadily. The white population moved out of the inner city, urban renewal tended to become "Negro removal," and new, high-cost apartment buildings kept Negroes out of the more fashionable private projects within the

---

[29] Southern Education Reporting Service, *Statistical Summary of School Segregation-Desegregation in the Southern and Border States, 1963–64,* p. 63.

A Southern White on Negro Rights

What can be done to ease racial tension in the rural South and to improve the lot of southern Negroes?...

First of all, the incredible complexity of the Negro problem in the rural South must be recognized. Regardless of how many civil-rights campaigns are conducted, the problem is going to be around for generations to come, just as the vexing problem of Harlem will be around for generations to come.... Our race problem must be recognized for what it is: a dilemma to which there is no quick solution.

Secondly, the utter hopelessness of the Negro's economic future in the rural South must be recognized. Without extensive landholdings, skills, or opportunities for employment, he is caught in a poverty cycle from which he is powerless to escape. Although the proposal sounds drastic, a deliberate effort must be made to move as many Negroes as possible out of the rural South. If the Negro is going to be saved, he will be saved in the metropolitan areas of this country which offer jobs in factories and offices.

Finally, a program of cultural and economic rehabilitation must be inaugurated for those Negroes who remain in the rural South. Though it may seem brutal to the doctrinaire, this program must be carried out at first within a framework of segregation. The ministry of hundreds of Booker T. Washingtons is needed, and responsible Negro organizations should provide it.

From Clayton Sullivan, Mississippi clergyman, "Speaking Out," *Saturday Evening Post*, April 1965.

city core. Displaced and newly arrived Negro families had to move into areas of heavy Negro concentration in the cities. Would-be Negro suburban home owners were firmly barred by the practices of real-estate agents, lending agencies, and local home owners. The Levittowns and other working-class suburban communities remained for whites only. Increasing "ghettoization" of Negroes in the Northern cities or predominantly Negro suburbs brought with it all the other vestiges of segregated life.

Fourth, the refusal of public-accommodation facilities in Southern and border states to serve Negroes was a flagrant insult that added to Negro unrest. Although Congress clearly had the power to regulate these facilities under its authority over interstate travel, it took no action to alleviate the situation.

The fifth area of protest was the increasingly violent harassment of civil-rights workers and Negro spokesmen in the South during the early 1960's. Beatings, bombings, and shootings were commonplace. The lack of adequate protection from law-enforcement officers—indeed, the frequent harassment by these officers themselves—made the concepts of due process and justice a mockery. The list of civil-rights murders was long and increasing in frequency, and the persons responsible for such crimes, if caught, were not punished. This was the year Medgar Evars, state leader of the NAACP in Mississippi, was ambushed and killed outside his home. No one was ever convicted for the crime. Although such murders were given national and worldwide attention, the system of "Southern justice" usually brought acquittals for the guilty persons from the all-white juries that heard their cases. Reports issued by the Civil Rights Commission, documenting such abuses in great detail, stressed the need for state and federal action to provide the protection due every American citizen.

These substantial civil-rights grievances began to produce campaigns of "direct action" by Negroes and their white supporters. These campaigns were in large part the logical culmination of a variety of nonviolent protest techniques that had been developed during the late 1950's and early 1960's.

In 1955, for example, the local Negro community of Montgomery, Alabama, mounted a year-long boycott of segregated city buses, and a federal-court injunction finally forbade discriminatory seating. The legal and spiritual success of this boycott set a pattern for similar boycotts of dime stores, department stores, buses, and markets in other Southern communities.

A Southern Negro on Civil Rights

You may well ask, "Why direct action? Why sit-ins, marches, etc.? Isn't negotiation a better path?" You are exactly right in your call for negotiation. Indeed, this is the purpose of direct action. Nonviolent direct action seeks to create such a crisis and establish such creative tension that a community that has constantly refused to negotiate is forced to confront the issue....

I must confess that over the last few years I have been gravely disappointed with the white moderate. I have almost reached the regrettable conclusion that the Negroes' great stumbling block in the stride toward freedom is not the White Citizens' "Counciler" or the Ku Klux Klanner, but the white moderate who is more devoted to "order" than to justice; who prefers a negative peace which is the absence of tension to a positive peace which is the presence of justice; who constantly says, "I agree with you in the goal you seek, but I can't agree with your methods of direct action"; who paternalistically feels that he can set the time-table for another man's freedom; who lives by the myth of time and who constantly advises the Negro to wait until a "more convenient season."

Shallow understanding from people of good will is more frustrating than absolute misunderstanding from people of ill will. Lukewarm acceptance is much more bewildering than outright rejection.

From Martin Luther King, Jr., letter from Birmingham City Jail, April 1963.

A second technique was developed in 1960, when the first "sit-in" was conducted at the Woolworth lunch counter in Greensboro, North Carolina. "Sit-in," "sleep-in," "read-in," "pray-in," and "swim-in" soon became part of the language of the protest movement. The third tactic used by civil-rights groups was the "freedom ride," which tested and exposed segregation in interstate travel and in Southern terminal facilities—practices clearly illegal under Supreme Court rulings.

The immediate stimulus for the 1963 protest campaign, however, was the confrontation between Dr. Martin Luther King, Jr., and the police of Birmingham, Alabama. When King failed to get Birmingham city officials to pursue a "minimum program" of racial justice, he protested by leading several thousand Negro residents, including school children, in orderly street marches. The demonstrators were brutally swept off the streets by high-pressure fire hoses, herded off the march routes by snarling police dogs, and repeatedly shocked with electric cattle prods. Pictures of Negroes being subjected to this treatment were flashed around the world via newspapers and television. More than 2,500 demonstrators, including Dr. King, were arrested and jailed. Like an atomic chain reaction, Birmingham set off street demonstrations by masses of Negroes and white allies in North and South. Negro leaders united to serve notice on the white communities that militancy would increase and that "normal" business and civic affairs could no longer continue without sincere efforts being made to meet Negro demands for

"Those Alabama stories are sickening. Why can't they be like us and find some nice, refined way to keep the Negroes out?"

When their quest for equality reached the North in the 1960's, Negroes discovered that, in practice, Northern communities were often as restrictive as Southern ones.

From *Straight Herblock,* Simon & Schuster, 1964

fair treatment and legal rights. On August 28, 1963, to symbolize this new spirit of unity, 200,000 marchers assembled in Washington, D.C., to demand a strong, omnibus federal civil-rights law and remedial action by local and state governments throughout the North.

The Legislative Breakthrough of 1964

Not quite one year later, after long and embittered battles in both houses of Congress, including a protracted fight against Southern filibusterers in the Senate, a bipartisan coalition produced the Civil Rights Act of 1964,[30] the most comprehensive civil-rights law since the ill-fated experiments of the 1870's. The major provisions of this act (1) prohibit racial discrimination in all public accommodations affecting interstate commerce and all publicly operated facilities; (2) create a federal Fair Employment Practices Commission to enforce standards of fair employment in businesses and labor unions with more than a hundred employees (gradually reduced to twenty-five by 1968); (3) authorize the executive to halt federal funding of state or private programs where racial discrimination exists; (4) prevent voting registrars from adopting different standards for white and Negro applicants, require literacy tests to be in writing, and make a sixth-grade education a "rebuttable presumption" of literacy; (5) extend the life of the federal Civil Rights Commission; (6) establish a Community Relations Service to mediate racial disputes; and (7) authorize the Attorney General to bring enforcement suits against public-accommodations owners who discriminate and on behalf of the persons whose constitutional rights have been violated in school-segregation, or similar, cases.

The most visible results of the 1964 act occurred in public accommodations. Many owners of segregated facilities opened their doors to Negroes; others converted their facilities into "private clubs," refusing service to nonmembers, and still others resisted the law openly. In 1964, however, the Supreme Court unanimously upheld the constitutionality of the public-accommodations provision.[31] And, on the whole, voluntary compliance with this provision was remarkably good in the South as well as in the North, where de facto discrimination had existed. Compliance spread slowly but steadily during the late 1960's.

Other provisions of the 1964 act, however, were inadequate in many ways. For example, the provisions dealing with voting rights could not prevent Negroes from being so intimidated by their local communities that they did not register to vote, even though they were freer to do so by law. Nor did the new bill deal with the problems of housing or violence against Negroes and civil-rights workers. As if to underscore this situation, one month after the passage of the bill, three young civil-rights workers in

[30] 79 Stat. 437 (1964).
[31] Katzenbach v. McClung, 379 U.S. 294 (1964).

"Naturally the Southerners will object."

Southerners have viewed federal civil-rights legislation as a basic threat to their private-property rights.

Brooks in the Birmingham *News*

Mississippi were kidnaped and murdered; later that fall, a Washington, D.C., Negro educator, Lemuel Penn, returning from two weeks in Army summer camp, was shot and killed on a Georgia highway. Even the issues such as fair employment, which were dealt with in the act, ultimately depended on more far-reaching economic solutions rather than on civil-rights measures. Unless ways could be found to reduce the unemployment situation and increase the pool of jobs for all American workers, Negroes might win a "fair share" of "not enough to go around."

The 1965 Civil-Rights Campaign

In 1965 the problem of voting rights became more acute as state and local authorities in the South continued to interfere with efforts by Negroes to register and vote and harassed civil-rights workers attempting to mount a massive voter-registration campaign. Strict discriminatory requirements set by local authorities, impossible literacy tests, and lengthy, often unfavorable court action successfully prevented voting by Negroes. Dr. King, hoping to make the voting-rights drive one of national concern, headed a voting-rights protest campaign in Selma, Alabama. Peaceful marches, sit-ins at local courthouses, and demonstrations were marred by a series of violent attacks, mass arrests, and murders. State troopers, acting on orders from Governor George Wallace, used tear gas, night sticks, and whips to halt a march, severely injuring many marchers. Around the nation, sympathy marches, sit-ins, and demonstrations were held, pickets maintained a round-the-clock vigil at the White House, and a wide range of national leaders as well as private citizens demanded remedial action.

Responding to this heightened national attention and concern, President Johnson announced plans for a 1965 Voting Rights Act. After bitter congressional debate and the second successful cloture vote in two years by the Senate, Congress approved the voting legislation and the President signed into law the most comprehensive voting-rights legislation in ninety years. The Voting Rights Act of 1965 [32] (1) suspended literacy tests or other qualifying devices for voters where they were found to foster discrimination; (2) authorized the appointment of federal voting examiners who could order registration if federal courts determined they were needed, or if the Attorney General had received at least twenty valid complaints from residents of a voting district, or if the Director of the Census determined that less than 50 percent of the persons of voting age in any voting district were registered or had voted in the presidential elections of 1964; (3) made approval by federal court or the Attorney General essential before new state or local voting laws could take effect; (4) allowed states to contest the action of federal examiners, but only if they could prove in a federal court that there had been no voting discrimination during the past five years; and (5) declared that the payment of poll taxes abridged the right to vote and authorized the Attorney General to institute suits challenging poll taxes in the states.

CIVIL RIGHTS AND AMERICAN GOVERNMENT: THE CONTINUING AGENDA

The mid-sixties marked an important shift in the struggle for equality in the United States. More civil-rights legislation was on the books than at any other time since Reconstruction, and many Negroes had advanced their socioeconomic as well as their legal status. Yet progress in the area of civil rights was erratic, and the "racial crisis" had become a central issue of American politics in virtually every local community as well as on the national scene. A look at current gains and failures in the campaign for Negro equality sets the scene for our analysis of the current civil-rights dilemmas.

Gains in Civil Rights

Employment. In 1950, only 9 percent of the total Negro labor force were in white-collar occupations; in 1965 this had increased to 16 percent. Unemployment rates for Negroes declined from 11 percent in 1962 to 8.3

[32] 79 Stat. 437 (1965).

percent in 1965, while the corresponding figures for whites remained about the same.[33] Increasing numbers of technical jobs opened up for skilled workers, and highly trained Negroes could choose among desirable offers in business, government, and education.

Public accommodations. A survey of desegregation in public-accommodation facilities in the South as of 1967 showed that many restaurants, hotels and motels, hospitals, and theaters had opened their doors to Negroes.[34] (This trend, however, was limited mainly to the larger cities, where anonymity protected the Negro from intimidation, and to nationwide chain facilities such as Holiday Inn and Howard Johnson. In the small Southern towns, intimidation, discrimination, and segregation continued.) The public-accommodations section of the 1964 Civil Rights Act was reinforced by the passage of similar statutes in many states, and changing community mores led to greater acceptance of desegregated public facilities throughout the nation.

Voting. By the late summer of 1966, over 2,700,000 Negroes—about 53 percent of the Negro voting-age population—were registered to vote in eleven Southern states.[35] Although this was considerably lower than the percentage of white registration, it represented an increase of about 10 percent over the number of Negroes registered to vote in 1964, prior to the Voting Rights Act. In some Southern counties the Negro electorate gained the majority position and became a force to be reckoned with by potential candidates for office.

Political entry. Increased Negro political activity throughout the country led to increased selection of Negroes as party nominees and increasing victories of these candidates. After the elections of 1966 there were 123 Negro state representatives and 31 state senators in the legislatures of twenty-seven states. As recently as 1960, by contrast, there had been only 30 Negro state representatives and 6 state senators within state legislatures. In 1966 particularly notable examples of this trend were the election of Edward Brooke, the first Negro United States senator since Reconstruction, the election of Negroes to the Georgia legislature, and the victory of Negro candidates for sheriff in some Southern counties. In 1967 Negro mayors were elected in two major Northern cities—Cleveland, Ohio, and Gary, Indiana.

Federal programs and community organizations. One response to civil-rights demands was fresh government attention to the problems of the economically disadvantaged. The poverty program established local, community-based projects designed to improve the educational, employment,

---

[33] Bureau of Labor Statistics, U.S. Department of Labor, *Special Labor Force Report No. 69* (1966), pp. A-10, A-11.

[34] New York *Times*, May 29, 1967.

[35] Voter Education Project, Southern Regional Council, Inc., *Voter Registration in the South* (Atlanta, Ga., 1966).

and overall economic opportunities of deprived citizens throughout the nation. Despite criticism of both their ends and means, poverty program projects such as Head Start, VISTA, and the Job Corps were important and effective training laboratories for minority-group members, helping them to develop technical skills and to gain experience in the administration of the affairs of their own community with federal financial assistance.

Areas of Continued Crisis

Speaking at Howard University in 1965, President Johnson noted that "freedom is not enough. . . . You do not take a person who for years has been hobbled by chains and liberate him . . . and then say, you're free to compete with all the others, and still justly believe that you have been completely fair." Observing that Negroes are trapped in "inherited, gateless poverty," he continued:

> It is not enough just to open the gate of opportunity. All our citizens must have the ability to walk through those gates. . . . [But] the isolation of Negroes from white communities is increasing rather than decreasing. . . . Negro poverty is not white poverty . . . there are deep, corrosive obstinate differences which are not racial, but the consequence of ancient brutality, past injustice, and present prejudice.

Unemployment and economic progress. In the fifteen-year period between 1949 and 1964, the median annual income for nonwhite families in the United States increased from $1,650 to $3,800, while the median annual income for white families rose from $3,200 to more than $6,800. Although the middle-class Negro had benefited economically in the late 1960's, lower-class income levels and job opportunities had worsened. The uneducated, unskilled Negro faced increasing difficulties as technological advances removed many unskilled jobs from the market and increased educational requirements for jobs. In 1965, 50.7 percent of all Negroes who were employed were unskilled, as compared to only 17.6 percent of whites.[36] Nearly 20 percent of the unemployed Negroes lacked any previous work experience. In the South, even the trained, well-educated Negro faced severe problems finding a job appropriate to his background.

Housing. Eighty percent of the Negro population of the United States lives in the city, while sixty percent of the white population resides in the suburbs. In both city and suburb in every region in the country, racial separation in housing is still the accepted pattern. Discriminatory policies of housing builders, real-estate brokers, lending institutions, and local government officials often close ranks to exclude poor and nonwhite families from suburban developments and to keep them in specified areas of the community. Urban renewal and highway construction often displace large

[36] *Special Labor Force Report No. 69*, p. A-22.

The Only Man Who Can Untangle It

Conservatives have tended to argue that slow progress in civil rights is the only sure path to equality.

Marcus in the New York *Times*

numbers of low-income, nonwhite families who cannot afford to relocate anywhere but in the already overcrowded nonwhite sections of the city. Although federal housing policies and executive orders in recent years have been designed to promote equality in housing, they have often been denied meaningful sanctions or effective enforcement. Rent-supplement programs and Federal Housing Administration programs have often failed to support low-income housing for both city and suburb, or such housing has been constructed in predominantly Negro or white areas of the city, thus promoting almost totally nonintegrated occupancy. The failure of government to act decisively in the area of housing and the tight coalition of builders and brokers supporting discriminatory policies has meant that established residential patterns remain self-enforcing barriers to real equality.

Education. Although education is one of society's major routes of upward mobility, a 1966 survey by the United States Office of Education found that "when measured by that yardstick [segregation], American public education remains largely unequal in most regions of the country, including all those where Negroes form any significant portion of the population." [37] Thirteen years after the Brown decision, only 15.9 percent of Negro students in the South—and only 4.9 percent in five states of the deep South—attended integrated schools. [38]

The problem of school segregation in the South was matched by growing *de facto* segregation in other parts of the country. For the population shifts that were rapidly producing Negro cities and white

[37] James Coleman, *et al., Equality of Educational Opportunity*, U.S. Office of Education, No. 3 (1966).
[38] *Ibid.*

"What do you mean, 'not so fast'?"

But for Negroes who have spent generations unsuccessfully pursuing equality this argument has hardly been persuasive.

© 1963, The Chicago *Sun Times*. Reproduced by permission of Wil-Jo Assoc., Inc., and Bill Mauldin.

suburbs were simultaneously leading to almost totally separate schools for white and Negro students. In 1966, 65 percent of all Negro first-grade students in the United States attended a school that was 90 percent or more Negro, while 80 percent of white first-graders attended schools that were 90–100 percent white.[39] For example, in 1966 in Baltimore, 92.3 percent of the elementary-school Negroes were in schools composed mostly of Negroes, while 67 percent of the white students were in schools that were 90 percent or more white. In Pittsburgh the percentage of Negroes in mostly Negro schools increased from 51 percent in 1950 to 82.8 percent in 1965; in Cincinnati it rose from 70.7 percent in 1960 to 88 percent in 1965.[40] A 1967 Civil Rights Commission report concluded that the impact of school segregation goes far beyond the question of equal educational facilities to issues of achievement levels, job opportunities, and the Negro self-image—in short, to the question of equality on all levels.

Justice. "Justice for all" still received only limited support in many areas of the country in the late sixties. In 1965 the Civil Rights Commission prepared a report on law enforcement [41] that underscored the problems of violence, intimidation, and unfair legal processes existing in the South. It

[39] U.S. Civil Rights Commission, *Racial Isolation in the Public Schools*, Vol. 1 (1967), p. 2.
[40] *Ibid.*, pp. 4, 6.
[41] U.S. Civil Rights Commission, *Law Enforcement: A Report on Equal Protection in the South* (1965).

recommended broad federal legislation to protect persons attempting to exercise constitutional rights, but a decline in white support for the civil-rights movement during the middle and late sixties caused the defeat of such legislation. This lessening of national attention on Southern law-enforcement practices reduced pressure on local and state officials to conform to broad standards of due process. Despite court decisions requiring equality in jury selection, few Negroes were actually chosen for jury duty, thus removing a potential safeguard for due process in the judicial arena. Even volunteer attorneys working to defend the rights of Negroes and civil-rights workers were threatened by increased efforts in many Southern states to bar them from practice. In the North, Negroes also encountered problems in securing due process and impartial justice. The rioting that plagued many of the nation's cities during the middle and late 1960's was distinctive for the violence of Negro hostility toward the police; tense relations between the police and Negro slum communities marked most American cities.

For example, the arrest of a Negro for drunken driving in the Watts section of Los Angeles by a white motorcycle policeman sparked a riot in the summer of 1965 that lasted for more than a week. The toll of the upheaval was high: 34 dead, 1,032 wounded, $40 million worth of property damage, and 3,952 arrested. Similar riots ripped with explosive force through major and minor cities throughout the United States. In 1967, riots in Newark and Detroit were at least as serious. Studies of the causes of such outbreaks revealed consistent findings: in communities with consistently high unemployment, low income, high percentages of broken families, substandard housing, and increasing racial isolation, the bitterness and frustration of the residents was likely to erupt in violence.

Competing Theories for Achieving Racial Equality

Attempts to find adequate solutions to the problem of achieving true racial equality in America during the last decade have resulted in several contrasting theories. Even if "full equality" for the Negro becomes completely accepted by American society, what does "full equality" mean, and what measures can be adopted to bring this condition into being?

One approach, accepted by many Americans as both right and practical, is the policy of *equal opportunity*. According to this position, entrance into education, public and privately owned housing, public and private employment, labor-union membership, and other sectors of national socio-economic life should be based strictly on "merit," without regard for race, color, religion, or nationality. Our goal should be a *color-blind* society.

In areas such as voting or access to public accommodations, this approach works quite well because Negroes can be elevated to a plane of true equality through judicial and legislative action. However, in situations where past practices against Negroes have built up situations of "frozen discrimination," this color-blind approach could take generations to succeed, and Negroes would continue to be hampered by limited educational, housing, and employment opportunities. Two approaches have been advanced to combat the effects of "frozen discrimination"—both resting on the assumption that to achieve true racial equality and intergroup harmony a society must be both *color-conscious* and *color-blind*.

The first approach is *planned integration*. This involves the establishment of quotas based on racial percentages in the local community to achieve balanced racial policies. For example, in housing, an area where discrimination affects Negroes particularly sharply, advocates of this approach point out that housing developments now open on a nondiscriminatory basis are always in danger of becoming all Negro. Decent housing is so infrequently available to Negroes that good housing in low and middle price ranges quickly attracts many Negro customers. White families begin to feel uneasy when the proportion of Negroes rises above 40 percent and soon move out, leaving the development to become virtually all Negro. Since this pattern is such a fundamental fact of white behavior, planned-integration advocates stress that the only hope for equality in housing rests on adopting some sort of quota system. Critics of the plan reply that denial of an apartment or home to a Negro who is already hard pressed to find decent housing is unconstitutional when done by government and, when done by private parties, perpetuates an inferior, "don't tip the white man's supremacy" role for Negroes. These critics suggest that enforcement of complete antidiscrimination policies throughout the community—letting natural desires for "own group" and "mixed group" clusters in housing work themselves out—is the only way to proceed. Recently, integration-minded builders and private "fair-housing committees" have attempted to keep communities balanced interracially by helping Negroes find apartments and homes in formerly all-white communities and asking Negroes to refrain from filling up Negro sections in the suburbs or renovated sections of the cities. It remains to be seen whether this type of voluntary solution can overcome the powerful psychological drive for self-segregation.

The second approach involves so-called *compensation programs*, which call for government and private employers to overcome existing employment imbalances by making extra efforts to hire qualified Negroes. According to this program employers would give preference to Negro applicants over whites when the qualifications of both are equal and would decide on a certain number of Negro employees to be added each year to their work forces. This approach would be necessary only until Negroes truly have a chance to enter the system on an equal-opportunity basis. Its advocates are convinced that this is the only way to prepare Negroes for the major changes taking place in the American economy.

They urge accompanying measures such as job training and *re*training, government antipoverty campaigns, and the establishment of special schools for Negroes in the ghettos, with Negro parents sharing in the administration of the schools. Critics of this type of program, however, see it as perpetuating racial standards, deepening the conflict between Negro and white work competitors, and destroying initiative by creating Negro expectations of paternalistic treatment from whites. The solution here, these critics argue, is a combination of total nondiscrimination, major government and private programs of education, training, and employment of job seekers, and determined efforts by Negroes themselves to win recognition of their talents within the new milieu of equality, which encourages Negro self-respect and initiative.

Recent Shifts in the Civil-Rights Movement

A frontier problem of equality in the coming decade involves the techniques of protest used by Negroes and their white allies. Martin Luther King expressed the prevailing view of most civil-rights groups in 1963 when he noted realistically that only "pressure" had brought Negroes their present civil rights. "We know through painful experience," he said, "that freedom is never given voluntarily by the oppressor; it must be demanded by the oppressed." In keeping with this view, the techniques of "pressure" have gone through several phases between 1941 and the present. Between 1941 and 1953, Negro pressure was exerted primarily through legal test suits sponsored by the NAACP, through negotiation and bargaining with Northern white businessmen and public officials by the National Urban League, and through local lobbying for civil-rights legislation by Negro political and civic leaders in Northern communities. Between 1954 and 1964 these techniques were reinforced by the new methods we have discussed earlier—sit-ins, boycotts, large-scale street demonstrations. These tactics were completely nonviolent and any ensuing violence came from those attacking the demonstrators. Negro demonstrations generally took place in the South and, in almost every instance, used clearly legal means of protest under existing Supreme Court rulings. Only techniques such as the sit-in, which involved trespass on an owner's property and refusal to move when ordered to do so, were of questionable legality. However, the Supreme Court upheld such techniques in several cases during 1965 and 1966.[42]

After 1963, protests moved into the North as well, and more militant techniques of "direct action" began to be used, especially by the newer groups such as CORE and SNCC. These included such measures as halting

[42] *Cox* v. *Louisiana*, 379 U.S. 536 (1965); *Brown* v. *Louisiana*, 383 U.S. 131 (1966).

traffic by lying across the roadway, mass telephone campaigns, picket lines at schools and public offices to prevent employees of these institutions from entering until grievances were settled, lying down at construction sites to protest job discrimination or forming "human walls" across the driveways of restaurants and supermarkets where it was felt that too few Negroes were employed. These tactics were designed to break through community apathy to focus attention on continuing forms of racial prejudice. Militants argued that it was immoral for whites to remain "neutral" and go on with "business as usual" when discrimination existed; if constantly harassed by these protests, these people would be aroused to change existing policies. Finally, in 1966, the militants—CORE and SNCC—split openly with the established NAACP and the Urban League as well as with the middle-ground movement of Dr. Martin Luther King's Southern Christian Leadership Conference. These militant groups called for a program of "Black Power"—a rejection of the method of nonviolence and of the goal of integration. Black Power advocates urged Negroes to concentrate on building political, economic, and cultural strength in all-black movements in isolation from white society, so that they could bargain for equality with the "white power structure" on equal terms. The splits in the Negro civil-rights movement seem to presage a permanent development, with radical, moderate, and conservative wings destined to serve different constituencies within the Negro community.

These techniques raised the question of how far civil-rights militants should go—legally and morally—in support of their claims. Many felt that the earlier protests, directed against public officials and civic leaders who flatly refused to obey the nation's laws, were specific, nonviolent, limited in their effect to those engaging in discriminatory acts, and a necessary basis for court cases to challenge the legality of discriminatory policies. However, when more militant tactics were used, innocent people were also affected, and many believed that the boundary line had been crossed from proper to improper conduct. Frightened by riots that were becoming a fact of life as the 1970's approached, alarmed by Black Power and Negro expressions of hatred for whites, many white Americans withdrew support and sympathy from the civil-rights cause. In return, many Negroes began to believe that "Whitey" would never provide the employment, education, and housing opportunities to break the bonds of poverty for Negro masses in the ghettos.

By the late 1960's, the Negro civil-rights conflict had become the most explosive issue on the nation's domestic agenda. Most experts believed that the policy of passing antidiscrimination laws had ended, at least for the time being. Broad federal measures of this kind had already been enacted for voting, public accommodations, and employment; attempts during 1966–68 to extend these policies to housing, to protection of civil-

Civil Rights: The Negro Militants

One of the tragedies of the struggle against racism is that up to now there has been no national organization which could speak to the growing militancy of young black people in the urban ghetto. There has been only a civil rights.movement, whose tone of voice was adapted to an audience of liberal whites. It served as a sort of buffer zone between them and angry young blacks. None of its so-called leaders could go into a rioting community and be listened to....

Integration ... speaks to the problem of blackness in a despicable way. As a goal, it has been based on complete acceptance of the fact that *in order to have* a decent house or education, blacks must move into a white neighborhood or send their children to a white school. This reinforces, among both black and white, the idea that "white" is automatically better and "black" is by definition inferior....

From birth, black people are told a set of lies about themselves.... It takes time to become free of the lies and their shaming effect on black minds. It takes time to reject the most important lie: that black people inherently can't do the same things white people can do, unless white people help them.

The need for psychological equality is the reason why SNCC today believes that blacks must organize in the black community. Only black people can convey the revolutionary idea that black people are able to do things themselves. Only they can help create in the community an aroused and continuing black consciousness that will provide the basis for political strength.

From Stokely Carmichael, national chairman of SNCC, "What We Want," *The New York Review of Books*, September 1966.

rights activists, and to jury discrimination met a stone wall in Congress, where a mood of "we have enough civil-rights legislation" was plainly in command. Though some expansions of antidiscrimination laws—such as against racial discrimination in the sale or rental of housing—took place at the state and local level in this period, even this response was increasingly seen by experts as ineffective by itself in dealing with the basic needs of the Negro community.

The real issues of civil rights were economic, political, and psychological. Economically, the question was whether the United States could and would commit the massive funds necessary to provide permanent jobs, decent housing, and effective education for the Negro poor in the cities. Given the financial drain of the Vietnam war, such an effort would require increased taxes, new programs, and extensive federal-state-local-private collaboration far beyond the resources and programs of the mid-1960's.

Politically, the question was whether the Negro could be given the kind of participation in aid programs that would transform Negro involvement and commitment to Negro allegiance to change through orderly processes. Economic aid itself, no matter how large, would be inadequate for the civil-rights problem unless Negroes could achieve the personal dignity and self-respect, group organization, and political participation that would develop Negro *citizens* instead of welfare *subjects*.

Psychologically, the question was whether white and black Americans could move from the hostility and fear of the mid-1960's to a new sense of national cooperation. The wave of white hostility to Negro demands for economic and social opportunity that marked the "white backlash" after 1966 and the advocacy by radical Negroes of "guerilla war" in the cities to force social change were ominous warnings that the situation might get worse before it would get better. A hundred-years' debt of injustice, disadvantage, and neglect had finally come home to be paid. Whether white America would pay that debt as the price of peace in the nation or justice to black Americans was the pivotal question of our party politics, our economic planning, and even our foreign relations.

Civil Rights: The Negro Moderates

I would contend that "black power" not only lacks any real value for the civil-rights movement, but that its propagation is positively harmful. It diverts the movement from a meaningful debate over strategy and tactics, it isolates the Negro community, and it encourages the growth of anti-Negro forces....

The quasi-nationalist sentiments and "no-win" policy lying behind the slogan of "black power" do no service to the Negro. Some nationalist emotion is, of course, inevitable, and "black power" must be seen as part of the psychological rejection of white supremacy, part of the rebellion against the stereotypes which have been ascribed to Negroes for three hundred years. Nevertheless, pride, confidence, and a new identity cannot be won by glorifying blackness or attacking whites; they can only come from meaningful action, from good jobs, and from real victories such as were achieved on the streets of Montgomery, Birmingham, and Selma. When SNCC and CORE went into the South, they awakened the country, but now they emerge isolated and demoralized, shouting a slogan that may afford a momentary satisfaction but that is calculated to destroy them and their movement. Already their frustrated call is being answered with counter-demands for law and order and with opposition to police-review boards. Already they have diverted the entire civil-rights movement from the hard task of developing strategies to realign the major parties of this country, and embroiled it in a debate that can only lead more and more to politics by frustration.

From Bayard Rustin, executive director of the A. Philip Randolph Institute, " 'Black Power' and Coalition Politics," *Commentary*, September 1966.

SUMMARY

This chapter has traced the American tradition of equality from its earliest formulation in the Declaration of Independence to the civil-rights problems of the 1960's. The basic aim of the chapter's historical discussion has been to show how deeply racial discrimination has permeated our culture, law, and politics and to show why the current civil-rights issues represent a far more intransigent problem than those successfully solved by the United States in regard to white immigrants or religious minorities.

The period from 1781 to 1863 was characterized by an early double standard: whites made broad gains in access to citizenship and voting rights as well as religious and ethnic equality, while continuing to maintain and defend Negro slavery. The Civil War, however, brought a period of egalitarianism that included the Negro as well. The Thirteenth, Fourteenth, and Fifteenth Amendments outlawed slavery, made Negroes free citizens, and gave them the right to vote. Legal equality for Negroes was coupled with social harmony, and widespread integration of whites and Negroes existed in public accommodations and schools throughout the South.

Between 1883 and 1941, however, we returned to the double standard with renewed vigor: we continued to extend equality for whites while establishing a constitutionally sanctioned, politically enforced, violence-ridden system of segregation and discrimination—openly in the South and indirectly in the North—for the new Negro citizen. Two key Supreme Court rulings helped to bring this situation about: first, the *Civil Rights Cases* of 1883, in which the Court declared unconstitutional the federal laws forbidding private denials of civil rights, and second, *Plessy* v. *Ferguson*, in which the Court upheld even state denials of civil rights as being "nondiscriminatory." With these decisions, rigid racial segregation and discrimination began to be established in public accommodations, voting, housing, education, the administration of justice, employment, and the national military service.

Other nonwhite groups also received second-class status during this period. But white religious and national minorities, on the other hand, faced no *legal* discrimination. As a result, although they faced strong social prejudice, they were able to advance their cause through their access to white schools, their economic opportunities, and their political and civil-rights organizations.

It was the period from 1941 to 1963 that saw the fall of the double standard and the elevation of the American Negro to a plane of *legal* equality with whites. The Supreme Court passed several rulings outlawing various aspects of racial discrimination or segregation—culminating in the landmark decision in *Brown* v. *Board of Education* that segregation in public education was unconstitutional. In this period Presidents Roosevelt, Truman, Eisenhower, and Kennedy—in sharp contrast to preceding Presidents, though with varying degrees of initiative—used the executive order to forbid discrimination in areas under executive jurisdiction and to establish presidential commissions to protect civil rights. After being silent on civil rights for more than eighty years, Congress passed two bills, in 1957 and 1960, giving federal protection to would-be Negro voters in the South.

Yet the period from 1963 to 1965 was a highly turbulent one in which Negro demonstrators protested strongly against the segregation and discrimination that in fact persisted in education, employment, housing, and public accommodations, coupled with the harassment of civil-rights workers. In response, the most comprehensive civil-rights act since the 1870's was passed in 1964 outlawing discrimination in public accommodations, employment, and voting. The provisions of the act were buttressed by the Voting Rights Act of 1965.

How "equal" are Negroes and whites today? On one hand, Negroes have made significant gains of equality in employment, public accommodations, voting, and government-aid programs. On the other hand, Negro unemployment and the gap between white and Negro incomes has continued to increase, Negro housing has become worse, public education for Negroes is becoming more segregated outside the South while failing to achieve its overall educational goals, and early efforts to give Negroes a participatory role in local programs have had only limited success. Alienation between white and Negro communities has increased, and the steady waves of riots and rebellions in American cities have demonstrated that the problem of Negro equality cannot be "contained" even by tanks and federal troops.

The journey to full equality by a heterogeneous society with a long heritage of racial discrimination will not be easy, especially when the problems are complicated by radical technological and socioeconomic changes in American life. Militants will be needed to press for the content and not just the forms of equality; but the moderates will be needed to find workable solutions and to prevent the struggle from embittering the whole of American civic life. Whether white America finds the will and the techniques to build racial justice for all is the central domestic issue of our times.

JOB-MOBILE

MB ABOARD IF YOU WANT A JOB!

N ON
TIONS 1523 COLUMBIA AVE. James H.J. Tate, Mayor

V

GOVERNMENT
IN
ACTION

Parts I through IV have dealt mainly with the "inputs" of our political system—the influence on government decisions of our political culture, interest groups, voters, parties, and political officials. All this influence is ultimately focused on securing certain rights and benefits from the government. Part IV discussed some of our constitutional rights; Part V examines in detail the legislative policies and administrative methods that secure benefits for the American people. Chapters 20 through 23 discuss government policies regarding the economy, natural resources and technology, welfare benefits, and defense and foreign policy. Chapter 24 then examines the financing of these policies. Three questions are central to Part V: What roles has contemporary society thrust on our political system? What problems do these new roles create? And how do groups and officials influence government policy-making?

GOVERNMENT AND THE ECONOMY

19

How much government intervention in the economy is appropriate? This chapter examines the history of this basic American issue and then discusses how programs are established and administered. Have we ever had a truly laissez faire government? What roles do interest groups play in establishing government programs? What safeguards ensure that government agencies administer programs fairly, and how does politics affect this process? The chapter also discusses five major roles of government in the economy today. What general patterns of public policy have emerged? What kinds of benefits are sought for the American people through these patterns? And, finally, what is the role of private initiative in such an economy?

In *The Federalist,* James Madison emphasized economic factors in explaining why men in society split into contending groups:

> The most common and durable source of factions has been the various and unequal distribution of property. . . . A landed interest, a manufacturing interest, a mercantile interest, a moneyed interest, with many lesser interests, grow up of necessity in civilized nations, and divide them into different classes, actuated by different sentiments and views.

"The regulation of these various and interfering interests," he added, "forms the principal task of modern legislation." [1]

Madison's contemporaries advocated a more positive and selective role for government in the economy. Hamilton proposed that government promote finance and manufacturing, while Jefferson desired that government advance the interests of agriculture "and of commerce as its handmaid."

The Constitution itself was an economic document. It reconciled sectional interests, as in the compromises on commerce, and contained many decisions favorable to property rights. It granted Congress the powers of regulation that Madison foresaw would be needed—to "regulate commerce" and to "coin money" and "regulate the value thereof." Buttressed by Justice John Marshall's opinions, the Constitution was to free the commerce of the nation from state restraints and thus open one great national market for goods. In short, it provided the basis for a national economy, with national protections for capital and commerce and the power to regulate them.

Issues concerning regulation and promotion of economic interests have been dominant in American politics, partly because conflicts over religion, form of government, or foreign policy—which have split men into bitter factions in other countries—have been largely absent from the American political arena. Moreover, there has been a general consensus in favor of the capitalistic system, which has narrowed and moderated the contest among "the various and interfering interests" and permitted the development of policy in durable patterns.

HISTORICAL TRENDS IN THE ROLE OF GOVERNMENT

Since the founding of the nation, the consensus on capitalism—reflected in safeguards for property ownership and for private contracts—has been accompanied by an acceptance of certain traditional functions for govern-

[1] *The Federalist,* No. 10.

ment, such as the provision of a monetary system, a postal system, and other facilities of commerce. Even in the early years of the nation men were generally willing to accept an even larger role for government if it would advance their interests. Prior to the Civil War, sections and groups struggled for the national government's support of their interests on four major economic issues: (1) tariffs for protection of home production; (2) development of the West—which involved internal improvements, sale of land in small portions or at low cost, and grants of land to homesteaders; (3) easy credit terms versus sound banking; (4) free labor versus slave labor.

Recent historical research has shown that in this period men also sought state legislation to advance their economic welfare. Legislatures provided for internal improvements—roads, canals, and, for a period, railways—to advance agriculture, commerce, and industry. Numerous laws were passed also for the licensing of occupations, inspection of goods, protection of debtors, and other purposes, all of which involved detailed regulation of economic pursuits. Louis Hartz has concluded that in our early history people saw no threat to their personal liberty in government legislation to promote their economic interests.[2]

During the nineteenth century, however, two changes occurred. First, political power was democratized; that is, control of all branches of government, except the federal courts and some state courts, passed to the people directly. Second, economic power became concentrated in giant financial and industrial enterprises. Thus political power, widely dispersed, and economic power, highly concentrated, came into conflict. The diffused political power was reflected in successive demands for government regulation—from members of the Grange, from the Populist and Progressive movements. Faced with this situation, those whose economic interests were threatened by regulation embraced as a means of defense the ideology of laissez faire, which holds that government should not intervene in the economy.

It is important to note that the laissez faire theorists did not want the elimination of all government regulation. They knew that government, in protecting property rights, in effect "regulated" them—that is, it determined which property rights would be protected and to what extent and which contracts would be enforced. What they desired was a line of protection against regulations that they thought were unreasonable, and they found this bulwark in the courts, particularly the Supreme Court.

At first the Supreme Court upheld regulatory statutes, declaring in 1877 that "for protection against abuses of legislatures the people must resort to the polls, not to the courts."[3] Attorneys representing the losers

---

[2] Louis Hartz, *Economic Policy and Democratic Thought: Pennsylvania, 1776–1860* (Cambridge, Mass.: Harvard University Press, 1948).
[3] *Munn* v. *Illinois*, 94 U.S. 113, 134 (1877).

History Repeats Itself   Ehrhart in *Puck*

This 1889 cartoon compares the robber barons of the Middle Ages with the robber barons of the late nineteenth century.

in legislative battles were persistent, however, and in a short time they gained the support of the Supreme Court. For the next half-century (from about 1887 to 1937) the Court became the arbiter of conflicts over the proper function of government in the economy, and in the main its decisions upheld the position of the laissez faire theorists. The Court limited the power first of the state legislatures and then of Congress, which in the twentieth century began to pass regulatory legislation similar to that previously enacted by the states.

The Court was able to exercise this function through the due-process clauses of the Fifth and Fourteenth Amendments. It interpreted these clauses to mean that the legislatures could not pass laws that would deprive people of acquired property rights or certain economic liberties except for proper purposes and by proper means. The Court elaborated a set of guiding principles for determining in specific cases which purposes and means were constitutional. Thus, for instance, the right to engage in an occupation could be legally infringed by license requirements for learned professions or for supplying utility services. It could also be infringed to prohibit businesses, such as liquor or prostitution, that were regarded as inherently damaging to the community—but not to interfere with "ordinary" business such as conducting employment agencies or selling ice. According to judicial doctrine, liberty of contract, which affected wages, hours, and

---

The Case Against Government Intervention in the Economy

The American system ... is founded upon a particular conception of self-government in which decentralized local responsibility is the very base. Further than this, it is founded upon the conception that only through ordered liberty, freedom and equal opportunity to the individual will his initiative and enterprise spur on the march of progress. And in our insistence upon equality of opportunity has our system advanced beyond all the world....

There has been revived in this campaign ... a series of proposals which, if adopted, would be a long step toward the abandonment of our American system and a surrender to the destructive operation of governmental conduct of commercial business....

Every step of bureaucratizing of the business of our country poisons the very roots of liberalism—that is, political equality, free speech, free assembly, free press, and equality of opportunity....

Economic freedom cannot be sacrificed if political freedom is to be preserved. Even if Governmental conduct of business could give us more efficiency instead of less efficiency, the fundamental objection to it would remain unaltered and unabated. It would destroy political equality. It would increase rather than decrease abuse and corruption. It would stifle initiative and invention. It would undermine the development of leadership. It would cramp and cripple the mental and spiritual energies of our people. It would extinguish equality and opportunity. It would dry up the spirit of liberty and progress. For these reasons primarily it must be resisted.

From Herbert Hoover, presidential campaign speech in New York, October 1928.

---

prices, could be regulated by legislation only if the legislation were enacted for certain paramount public interests, such as protection of health.

Critics within the Court and outside it objected to the Court's writing of selective laissez faire into the Constitution under the rubric of due process and to its erection of a set of doctrines for determining which exceptions were legitimate. Informed observers could see that on the great economic confrontations of the day—labor versus capital, consumers versus utility monopolies—the Court's constitutional principles in effect gave victory to one side against the other. And, by upholding principles of selective laissez faire, the Court was in fact imposing its view of the proper relationship of the government and the economy. Dissenters within the Court argued that the Court should not rely on ideological principles to pass judgment on the relation of the government to the economy. Justice Holmes contended that "a Constitution is not intended to embody a particular economic theory." Thus, argued Holmes, issues of economic policy were outside the jurisdiction of the courts altogether. A more moderate attack came from men such as Justice Brandeis, who felt that the legitimacy of legislation should be determined empirically: Was the legislation in question a *reasonable* means of correcting an existing evil? Brandeis thought also that much deference should be given to the legislature's judgment on what was reasonable.

The Great Depression, however, shattered the Court's edifice of constitutional principles. Not only labor and consumers, who had suffered judicial defeats in the past, but investors, whose interests had been protected by the Court, looked to government for remedial legislation. A change of view was presaged by a 1934 Supreme Court decision, announced by Justice Roberts, upholding a minimum-price law for milk, although milk was not included in the traditional special category of public utilities.[4] Then, in 1937, the Court decided that the government could set minimum wages for women, thus reversing its old view,[5] and in 1941 it upheld a congressional act setting maximum hours and minimum wages for both male and female employees.[6]

[4] *Nebbia* v. *New York*, 291 U.S. 502, 536 (1934).
[5] *West Coast Hotel Co.* v. *Parrish*, 300 U.S. 379 (1937).
[6] *United States* v. *Darby*, 312 U.S. 100 (1941).

The Case for Government Intervention in the Economy

I feel that we are coming to a view through the drift of our legislation and our public thinking in the past quarter century that private economic power is, to enlarge an old phrase, a public trust as well. I hold that continued enjoyment of that power by any individual or group must depend upon the fulfillment of that trust....

Every man has a right to his own property; which means a right to be assured, to the fullest extent attainable, in the safety of his savings.... If, in accord with this principle, we must restrict the operations of the speculator, the manipulator, even the financier, I believe we must accept the restriction as needful, not to hamper individualism but to protect it....

The responsible heads of finance and industry, instead of acting each for himself, must work together to achieve the common end. They must, where necessary, sacrifice this or that private advantage; and in reciprocal self-denial must seek a general advantage. It is here that formal Government—political Government, if you choose—comes in. Whenever in the pursuit of this objective the lone wolf, the unethical competitor, the reckless promoter, the Ishmael or Insull whose hand is against every man's, declines to join in achieving an end recognized as being for the public welfare, and threatens to drag the industry back to a state of anarchy, the Government may properly be asked to apply restraint. Likewise, should the group ever use its collective power contrary to the public welfare, the Government must be swift to enter and protect the public interest.

From Franklin D. Roosevelt, address at the Commonwealth Club, San Francisco, September 1932.

The Court has now scrapped most of the limitations on regulatory power that it had established after 1880. There are still major limitations in favor of property, such as the Fifth Amendment prohibition against appropriating property without just compensation or the judicial rule that utility rates fixed by public agencies must be fair and reasonable. But the Court has substantially adopted the view of Justice Holmes that the Constitution does not embody any economic theory, thereby reverting to the view of 1877 that economic policy is to be determined through the political process rather than by the courts.

Today the issues of economic policy are viewed differently from the way they were seen in the judicial setting of 1887–1937. First, the Court, and indeed most commentators on public issues, used to posit only two interests—the public interest and a conflicting private interest. Today, however, it is recognized that there are many "various and interfering interests" and that regulatory legislation may in effect advance some private interests at the expense of others. The meaningful protections for the various interests are found, not in judicial doctrines, but in the legislative and administrative processes of government, where all interests can obtain a hearing and consideration of their demands for government action or inaction.

Second, we now recognize that interests are interdependent and that particular interests are dependent on the successful performance of the economy as a whole. Even a man's liberty is not safeguarded solely by the absence of government restraint; as President Johnson said, "The truth is, far from crushing the individual, government at its best liberates him from the enslaving forces of his environment."

Men now view the key problem of government and the economy as the determination of the appropriate combination of economic forces and political action. We now ask: To what extent can economic forces be expected to operate beneficially? And in what ways can government effectively supplement or supplant them?

Finally, we now assume that economic policies will be determined through political processes: contending interests press for advantage within an institutional system in which committee members of Congress and their staff aides, the President and his staff aides, administrative bureaus or commissions, and outside consultants analyze which solutions to problems are both workable and acceptable to the interests to be satisfied.

THE ESTABLISHMENT OF PROGRAMS

Legislation for the initiation of a new government activity is the result of the political processes we have just mentioned. For example, railroad regulation began in this country because users of the railroads—farmers, merchants, and other groups—became indignant over what they felt were exorbitantly high rates and over discrimination in charges among different types of shippers and among different shippers. This indignation led to the establishment of state regulatory commissions, beginning in Illinois in 1871, and to the establishment of the federal Interstate Commerce Commission in 1887. Railroad regulation was thus the result of demands from groups antagonistic to the railroad industry.

Licensing laws represent another source of demands for regulation. Though some licensing laws (for example, in the field of foods and drugs) have resulted from demands of external groups, occupational and industry groups have often demanded these laws for themselves. For instance, lawyers, doctors, teachers, plumbers, and beauticians have obtained licensing for their occupations, and airlines and truckers for service in their industries.

When groups within an industry conflict over whether controls should be established, victory goes to the dominant group. A good example is the establishment of production controls in the oil industry. In 1930 a wildcatter brought in the East Texas oil field, which began to yield oil in unanticipated quantities. The field was occupied by small farmers, city lot holders, and other owners of small tracts. Under the "rule of capture" of Texas law, each owner had the right to capture the oil under his land by drilling wells. Many wells were quickly drilled, and soon a million barrels of oil a day were dumped on a market already reeling from the Depression. The price of crude oil plummeted from over $1 to 10 cents a barrel. Drilling contractors, new refinery companies in the area, many local interests, and independent oil producers (that is, uncontrolled by major companies) were able to make quick financial returns, but the major oil companies and some independent interests found the situation intolerable. The latter interests, aided by the argument that there was a public interest in preventing waste of oil, won the victory in special sessions of the Texas legislature: a system of restricting oil production, called "proration," was established.[7] The victory in Texas was confirmed in Washington by a statute that prohibited shipment in interstate commerce of oil that had been produced in violation of state law.

Legislation arises not only from conflicts among ownership groups but from conflicts between ownership and labor. Both sides have turned to the government for legislation to help their respective positions, and the result is intensive regulation of labor-management relations.

All groups demanding legislation try to show that there is a public need for doing what they demand, and there may be real substance in such claims. Licensing of airline pilots, for example, protects the safety of all air travelers, and prevention of the sale of injurious drugs protects everyone.

[7] See Warner E. Mills, Jr., *Martial Law in East Texas* (University, Ala.: University of Alabama, 1960).

In some cases this need for public action is so evident that the government acts without strong interest-group pressure. An example is the allocation in the 1920's of wavelengths for radio services. The technology of radio communication necessitated the prevention of interference among users, and this need for regulation was to become more urgent as more users and new uses of the electromagnetic spectrum created a shortage of wavelength bands. Similarly, when air-passenger traffic developed, no strong pressure was required to obtain safety legislation in 1938. Yet even when public needs are inherent in a situation, interest groups are influential while programs of government control and service are being established. For example, certain groups were eager to supply radio and air-transportation services for profit. The interests of these groups were influential in determining the scope and types of public legislative policy. Existing airline companies, for example, gained statutory provision for limitation of competition, and communication companies, prohibition of censorship of programs. New government activity is always created in the crucible of politics.

Government programs, however, must do more than merely achieve compromises among interest groups. Legislators, executives, and staff aides must also try to choose technically feasible and economically and socially satisfactory ways of attaining desired objectives. The experiences of the past will often help to reveal methods that can be used to meet a new situation. For example, when the National Labor Relations Act was passed in 1935, the draftsmen built on the procedures of the Federal Trade Commission Act of 1914 and on the 1934 amendments to the Railway Labor Act. Today a considerable body of knowledge of regulatory techniques is available to the legislator—although old models will not always serve. The framers of the Public Utility Holding Company Act of 1935 had to search for new concepts and new techniques. They found that public-utility holding companies could be justified only if they were the means for geographically and economically integrated utility systems, and they devised techniques for attaining this objective.

In searching for new techniques of regulation, politicians must seek the aid of technical experts. One observer has even argued that

> the development of public policy and of the methods of its administration owed less in the long run to the processes of conflict among political parties and social or economic pressure groups than to the more objective processes of research and discussion among professional groups.[8]

Only a rational policy that reflects both political pressures and professional expertise on what is workable can create a solution that is efficient and acceptable to the conflicting interests concerned.

[8] Don K. Price, *Government and Science: Their Dynamic Relation in American Democracy* (New York: New York University Press, 1954), p. v.

THE ADMINISTRATION OF PROGRAMS

As discussed in Chapters 10 and 13, government programs, particularly economic ones, are generally administered by bureaus within departments, independent executive agencies, or independent regulatory commissions.

Agency Operations

Certain objectives have governed the development of administrative operations. First, an effort has been made to ensure that the agencies operate in accordance with standards set forth in legislation. Although they are given wide discretion in applying legal standards, they may be overruled by the courts or subjected to congressional investigation. Second, Congress has usually tried to provide for expert, nonpolitical administration of the agencies. One means is to delegate administrative tasks to commissions composed of members of both parties, serving long, overlapping terms and having substantial independence from the President. However, bureau chiefs usually serve for a much longer period; they have been called the "cream of the experts," and those having regulatory functions have considerable freedom from political pressures from department heads and the President. Finally, procedural requirements, many of which are in the Administrative Procedure Act of 1946, are designed to ensure fairness to affected parties, adequate attainment of statutory objectives, and efficient execution of agency work without unnecessary delays and expense to the government and private parties. There is substantial uniformity in the basic procedures of federal commissions, independent executive agencies, and departments.

Since few agency decisions are reviewed in the courts, agency procedures have special importance. The process by which the Civil Aeronautics Board determines whether to grant a permit to an airline to institute service from one city to another is typical. The application is docketed, grouped with other applications, and the case is then assigned to an examiner by a chief hearing examiner.

The examiner, similar to a trial judge, is substantially independent from agency control. He is appointed from Civil Service Commission lists, his salary is determined by the commission, and he can be removed only after a hearing by the commission.

The examiner will usually call the parties together in a prehearing conference to define the scope of the case and set forth ground rules for the proceedings. In accordance with these rules, written evidence and rebuttals will be submitted by the parties on prescribed dates. Next there will be an open hearing with cross-examination of witnesses on the evidence submitted and with oral arguments by the attorneys. The examiner will then make an *initial decision*, after which the parties may appeal to the board. After the board's decision some parties will probably ask for reconsideration, and the board will probably deny it. Thereafter, any party may appeal to a court of appeals, and thereafter may request review by the Supreme Court.

Another simplified illustration of the work of a regulatory agency is the procedure of the Federal Trade Commission in handling a false-advertising case, such as the Colgate-Palmolive case discussed in Chapter 14. The commission is authorized to issue first a complaint and then a cease-and-desist order if it finds "unfair methods of competition" or "unfair and deceptive acts in commerce." The commission staff handling enforcement cases is divided into three parts: preliminary investigation, prosecution, and hearing. The Administrative Procedure Act requires complete separation of the prosecuting and adjudicating staffs. Certain offices within the commission consider complaints that certain companies have violated the false-advertising prohibition and examine the advertising copy of companies in newspapers and magazines, and on radio and television. A company may learn that its advertising copy is under question and offer to adjust its copy to avoid a complaint from the commission. If a complaint is issued, the companies may, without admitting guilt, sign a *consent decree* to cease and desist. Otherwise the case is docketed for hearing and assigned to an examiner by the chief hearing examiner. The prosecution office within the commission then assigns one or more attorneys for prosecution. The examiner may not consult with either the accused or the commission attorneys without giving to the other notice and the opportunity to participate. After presiding over an open hearing, the examiner will in due time issue an initial decision. Either party may appeal this decision to the commission and then to the courts.

These are examples of judicialized procedures, used when statutes require a decision based on a record made in a hearing. They are required when the proceedings are adjudicatory in nature. Also, rule-making proceedings, such as rate-making, must sometimes follow these procedures. But, where statutes do not require a decision based on a record, the rule-making procedure may be legislative. In these cases the Administrative Procedure Act generally requires only that notice of an agency's intention to make a rule be published and opportunity given to interested persons to present their views. Legislative procedures thus give the agency more flexibility than judicialized procedures.

In still other cases the procedure is administrative—that is, made exclusively by internal administrative discussions. An example is that of the Board of Governors of the Federal Reserve System in making operating decisions on open-market purchases of United States securities. Every three weeks the Board of Governors and the presidents of the Federal Reserve Banks meet in Washington to determine the policy to be followed on open-market purchases. Many kinds of operating decision are made through administrative procedures: for example, decisions to consolidate several airplane applications for airline service, to provide more personnel for a particular task, or to dispose of cases informally by not issuing a complaint or by accepting a party's offer to desist from an offense voluntarily.

The ideal objectives of administrative operations can never be fully attained, of course. In a report to President-elect Kennedy in late 1960, James Landis attacked the "inordinate delays" and costs of administrative proceedings. Second, agency fairness to all parties may be hampered by the failure to develop standards for making decisions, and more adequate standards of decision have been vigorously urged by many professional observers. Third, agencies may be so busy with specific decisions that they have little time to consider emerging or long-standing policy problems. And, finally, expertness may suffer because of the rapid turnover of agency heads or the failure to retain a qualified staff.

The effort to make regulation a nonpolitical process is only partially successful, because politics does not end when a regulatory statute is passed. Some regulatory agencies have the power to grant certificates or licenses that will be worth millions of dollars—for example, a television license in a big city; some agencies can determine rates that business concerns can charge; the Federal Reserve Board and the Federal Home Loan Bank Board can influence interest rates; in fact, all regulatory agencies can take actions that determine how many dollars will go into which pockets. This creates politics at two levels: at that of influence upon decisions in particular cases, and at that of influence on broad policies.

Political Influence in Particular Cases

In 1958 the shocking disclosures of a House subcommittee led to the resignation of two high-ranking public officials. Commissioner Richard A. Mack served on the Federal Communications Commission and cast his vote on which applicant would receive one of the juiciest awards ever given by the commission: the Channel 10 television assignment for Miami, Florida. The testimony before the subcommittee showed that Mack had received substantial sums from companies in which he had invested no money and that the arrangement for this was made by a friend who was expressing interest in the award of Channel 10 to one of the applicants. The other resignation was that of Sherman Adams, assistant to the President of the United States, who had often been referred to as "Assistant President." Adams had intervened "off the record" with the Federal Trade Commission to aid Bernard Goldfine—whose exceedingly close friendship was evidenced by substantial personal gifts to Adams.

The resignation of these two officials concentrated attention on a problem that had previously received insufficient notice. The Mack case exposed a system of off-the-record contacts of senators and other prominent persons with administrative commissioners on cases that were required by law to be decided on the basis of a public record. The Adams case served to emphasize that communications to commissioners from highly placed political officials carried the danger of influence on decisions. Such communications from the President's office were believed to be quite exceptional, but the communications from Congress were known to be a customary part of a congressman's service to his constituents.

In search for a remedy, President Kennedy recommended in 1961 that Congress pass legislation "containing an absolute prohibition against *ex parte* contact in all proceedings between private parties" in which decision was made on the record in a formal hearing. In the absence of congressional legislation he prescribed strict rules to govern the conduct of his own staff and directed each agency to do the same. On matters to be decided on the basis of a record some agencies now require disclosure in the record of all communications received by them or by any staff member. This precaution, however, does not apply to many important types of decisions—such as whether or not to institute a proceeding against an alleged violator of the law. The problem is a difficult one, but fortunately the general consensus about appropriate behavior protects the agencies from the grosser forms of influence, such as those in the Mack and Adams instances.

Political Influence on Broad Policies

The contest over regulatory policy in the natural-gas industry nicely illustrates the continuing impact of politics on regulatory policy. The Natural Gas Act of 1938 provided for regulation by the national government of wholesale sales of gas in interstate commerce; however, the act exempted from regulation "the production and gathering" of gas. Because of the ambiguity of this clause, independent gas producers feared that their sales to pipeline companies might be considered subject to the rate-making powers of the Federal Power Commission (FPC), which administered the act. These producers decided to fight the threatened regulation.

The first round of the battle took place in Congress. Although the FPC tried to allay fears that it would assert jurisdiction, bills to restrict the jurisdiction of the commission over the natural-gas industry were introduced in both houses of Congress. (The bill finally considered was referred to as the Kerr bill, after Senator Kerr of Oklahoma, a gas-producing state.) In 1948 and 1949 the bills passed the House by large majorities but did not emerge from the Senate Committee on Interstate and Foreign Commerce.

In 1949 the second round of the battle was fought over the renomination of Commissioner Leland Olds to the FPC. Olds had argued that the FPC *did* in fact have jurisdiction over the rates of the independent gas producers, and he had opposed the Kerr bill. The gas industry opposed his renomination by charging that Olds in his early manhood had held communist ideas. The battle was fought vigorously in committee and on the floor of the Senate, and Olds's appointment was rejected.

The battle now moved into a third round, Senate consideration of the Kerr bill in 1950. The Federal Power Commission was itself now divided on the issue of whether it had jurisdiction under the act of 1938, and it appeared that if the Kerr bill were *not* passed, the issue would be determined by the new chairman of the commission. The debate was a hard-fought one between senators from gas-producing states and those from consuming states. In the end the bill passed both the Senate and the House, but President Truman vetoed it and thus restored the contest to a draw.

The fourth round was fought inside the commission when it had to determine whether the Phillips Petroleum Company, a large independent gas producer, was subject to the act. The commission held that it was not. Commissioner Draper, who voted with the majority, was subsequently confirmed by the Senate for a new term; Commissioner Buchanan, who voted with the minority for holding the company subject to the act, was not confirmed when his reappointment came up. Round four was another victory for producers.

The fifth round of the battle took place before the Supreme Court, where the Phillips case was appealed. The Court decided by a 5–3 vote that the commission had been wrong—that it did have jurisdiction over the sales of independent gas producers.[9] This decision, a victory for consumers, led to increased effort by legislators representing the gas-producing states.

A sixth round was fought in Congress, which passed a modified bill restricting the commission's jurisdiction. But a startling disclosure tipped the scales back toward the consumers. Senator Case of South Dakota announced that he had been offered a payment of $2,500 to influence his vote on the issue, and President Eisenhower promptly vetoed the bill.

Thus by Supreme Court decision the commission now had the jurisdiction it had previously declined to take, and it faced one of the thorniest problems ever handed to a regulatory agency: By what method should it determine the value of the gas sold by independents to pipelines? The gas industry favored a uniform price for all producers in the gas field, and the commission saw this as a means to escape from the burden of deciding thousands of cases individually. It announced in 1960 that it would proceed on this basis, and in 1965 it set uniform prices for an area in which approximately 11 percent of the nation's natural gas was produced.[10] If the commission is upheld in the courts, the independents will be subject to regulation—but on a looser basis than are monopolistic utilities. Neither side will have won a clear-cut victory.

This example shows that policy issues on which there is deep disagree-

[9] *Phillips Petroleum Co.* v. *Wisconsin*, 347 U.S. 672 (1954).
[10] 35 P.U.R. 3d 199 (1960), Area Rate Proceeding, Docket AR 61-1 *et al.* (1965).

ment among interest groups will spill over from the commissions and courts into the political arena. It shows, second, that appointments to commissions may become political issues and, third, that a dissatisfied or threatened economic interest will shop from one counter to another in government, seeking to obtain the best bargain. Finally, it demonstrates that in the contest of politics the members of the government organs themselves align with various interests. In the natural-gas issue, senators and representatives aligned themselves with producers or consumers according to the composition of their constituencies, while members of the commission were effectively drawn into the conflict because their votes put them on one side or the other.

It must be added, however, that in many cases policy issues are determined within the regulatory agencies without appeal to politics. The government could never carry its burden unless many problems of policy were handled by administrative processes. Commissions and departments themselves become instruments for resolving less sensitive policy conflicts. Thus, for example, the ICC has been quite successful in achieving a balance among interests involved in railroad and motor transportation; so policy issues here do not erupt frequently into the outer realms of politics. But the following question may be asked: When the ICC resolves conflicts, when it achieves a "moving balance" among interests, is it not in effect serving as a political instrument rather than as a judicial agency, as some have implied by calling it the "Supreme Court of the transportation world"?

One other source of political influence on administrative policy-making deserves comment here—the Presidency. Some critics believe that while it is important to maintain safeguards for impartial agency decisions on application of law to particular persons, it is both unrealistic and unwise to try to preserve the independence of regulatory agencies from the Presidency on policy matters. The President cannot help but influence regulatory policy through his appointment of commissioners, designation of chairmen of most commissions, budget recommendations, policy studies, and occasional contacts with commissioners. Since the President must be concerned with the policy decisions of some of the regulatory agencies and with the lack of coordination that may exist among them, it is inconceivable that he would not consider the policy effects of his decisions on appointments and other matters.

The issue was dramatized when in 1965 the Federal Reserve Board, an independent agency, pursued policies designed to raise interest rates, with which President Johnson at least partially disagreed. While the immediate issues of current monetary policy received more attention in the daily newspapers, the long-run issue was also clear: Should the President have a dominant position in the administrative determination of monetary policies and in the coordination of monetary and fiscal decisions of the administrative agencies?

FIVE MAJOR ROLES OF GOVERNMENT

Promoting the Health of the Economy

The most important function of modern economic legislation is the maintenance of the welfare of the economy as a whole to safeguard interdependent interests of men. Although campaigners for public office had long promised "a full dinner pail," "a chicken in every pot," and "two cars in every garage," it was not until the Depression that men became conscious of the large role government might play in the management of the economy. Still, government efforts were regarded as temporary, to be abandoned when recovery was sustained. After the Second World War, however, a serious postwar decline of employment and production was feared, and Congress passed the Employment Act of 1946, which declared that "it is the continuing policy and responsibility of the federal government . . . to promote maximum employment, production, and purchasing power."

A product of many compromises, the act was carefully worded to

Although first published in 1953, this cartoon aptly expresses today's continued conflicts over the effect of foreign trade on the health of our domestic economy.

From *Herblock's Here and Now*,
Simon & Schuster, 1955

emphasize the preservation of "free competitive enterprise"; to make explicit the *sharing* by the federal government, industry, agriculture, labor, and state and local governments of responsibility for attainment of the objectives of the act; and to avoid a commitment to any particular method of attaining its objectives, such as through the expansion of public expenditures. Nevertheless, the act was a charter of responsibility for the national government, and it was understood that fiscal measures would be among those considered.

The President is directed by the act to submit to Congress each year an economic report in which he sets forth a program for carrying out the policy of the act. To assist him Congress provided for a Council of Economic Advisers of three men. To focus congressional attention on policy problems, a Joint Economic Committee was created to study matters relating to the economic report and means of coordinating programs to attain the objectives of the act. One senator has called the Council of Economic Advisers an "economic brain." It represents an effort to supply one of the components of decision-making in a political system—objective study on the ways of accommodating the conflicting and the interdependent interests of men. The other component, of course, is pluralistic politics—the struggle of these interests for government favor.

While the Employment Act reflected the fear of depression, increases in price levels since World War II and concern over the adequacy of our economy's rate of growth have led to new emphases in national-policy objectives. Emphasis is placed on economic growth as the means of ensuring maximum employment, production, and purchasing power and at the same time on preventing serious inflation of prices. The Joint Economic Committee in 1960 offered a revised statement of economic objectives: "a high and stable rate of growth in our national output and productive capacity, and a high degree of stability in the general level of prices." [11]

To carry out the policies of the Employment Act, the government has substantial tools—chiefly fiscal and monetary. The fiscal tools are expenditures, taxing, and borrowing. The government can check a downturn in the economy by increasing expenditures, lowering taxes, and borrowing funds from banks. These same tools can be employed in reverse to check an inflationary trend. (This topic will be discussed more fully in Chapter 22.)

Monetary tools are those influencing the supply of money, and they are exercised chiefly through the Federal Reserve System. An increase in the supply of money without a corresponding increase in the supply of goods will have an inflationary tendency, that is, a tendency to raise price levels. Conversely, a decrease in the supply of money has a deflationary tendency. The monetary supply is determined primarily by the amount of credit created by commercial banks, which is in turn affected by the amount and cost of

[11] U.S. Senate, Joint Economic Committee, *Employment, Growth, and Price Levels*, Senate Report No. 1043 (1961), Eighty-sixth Congress, Second Session, January 26, 1960.

funds available to the banks for loan. The Federal Reserve Board can affect these funds in several ways: (1) by raising or lowering the amount of reserves against demand deposits that must be maintained by commercial banks; (2) by raising or lowering the rediscount rate, that is, the rate that commercial banks are charged by the Federal Reserve Banks for money obtained from them; (3) most frequently, by Federal Reserve Banks' purchases or sales in the open market of government securities, which will increase or decrease the amount of deposits in banks and hence their credit funds.

Another monetary instrument of the government is debt management. The government can add to the credit supply of banks by selling short-term securities to them. A shift to long-term securities or to sales to the general public will have the opposite effect.

Unfortunately, these fiscal and monetary tools are not completely effective. First, given its substantial national-defense needs and welfare commitments, the national government may not find it feasible to diminish its expenditures materially in the face of threatening inflation. Conversely, the government may find it difficult to increase expenditures quickly in the face of a recession. It takes time to vote authorizations for public-works expenditures, to give out contracts, and to get construction under way; and state and local cooperation with the national government may be impaired by

The Need for Economic Planning

Our own democratic society has been strangely inhospitable to all and any new political innovations. Indeed it seems a paradox that a nation born in revolution and proud of its tradition of independent thinking is prone to guard that inheritance by persistent opposition to innovation. We realize how little of forward movement in the handling of our public business has come, at least for a long time now, from acceptance of the logic of any new argument or from persuasion by the fluency of its exponents.

The politician who preaches preventive medicine for the body politic has consistently been rebuked at the polls, and when we have decided (personal experience reminds me) that it is "time for a change," we have meant and believed this is the sense not of moving ahead but simply of passing the deal. The only "planning" we want, and usually get, from government is enough to keep today's crisis from being tomorrow's catastrophe. There is quite a lot of Arkansas Traveler in most of us; and if the roof needs repairing, we are most likely to wait until we have to do it in the rain. So instead of adopting new political ideas consciously and deliberately, we only accept them—usually howling our heads off in protest—when the relentless pressure of events leaves us no alternative.

From Adlai E. Stevenson, *Major Campaign Speeches of Adlai E. Stevenson*, 1952.

debt limitations in state constitutions and city charters. The national government might therefore resort to make-work projects to provide employment, as it did in the New Deal period. Second, there is some question as to how much effect monetary controls have. That is, increasing the interest rate may not prevent industries and persons from borrowing during an inflation; conversely, decreasing the rate may not materially spur investment if there is doubt about the future. Third, it is difficult to coordinate the various government programs and the several agencies responsible for fiscal and monetary controls. For example, the Federal Reserve Board may be interested in curbing credit, while the Treasury may be interested in expanding it so as to obtain a low interest rate on government bonds. Moreover, coordinating national, state, and local expenditures is a well-nigh impossible task. Most important, matters of taxes, expenditures, credit supply, and interest rates are among the most controversial of political issues, because they affect various interests so vitally. Thus, raising interest rates is a damper on inflation and is regarded with favor by those who regard inflation at the time as a serious danger and by those who have money to lend. But those who want to expand their businesses may look with disfavor on the policy, as will those who think the method of control bears too heavily on the poor.

Inflation itself is regarded favorably by many. Some leading economists have expressed the view that a small amount of continuous inflation is favorable to economic growth. And there are enough groups in the population who profit immediately by some inflation to make a strong program to counteract it politically risky. It is easier to obtain popular support for measures against recession than for measures against inflation.

Nevertheless, there is a large measure of agreement that government should exert its powers to check recession or to prevent a high rate of inflation. No political party in power in the future can escape the responsibility of using the government's tool kit to maintain growth and stability in the economy.

Maintaining a Competitive System

The great corporate revolution, which changed the nature of the American economy, started soon after the Civil War. Individualistic Americans demanded legislation to curb the activities of the corporate giants, commonly referred to as "trusts." Antitrust legislation was passed almost simultaneously in many of the states and by Congress, and it still embodies the basic American policy toward business.

The purpose of antitrust legislation is to maintain competition in the economy. Such legislation is a departure from laissez faire, for in order to preserve free competition the government must restrict freedom of contract and combination.

The function of preserving a competitive economy was initially assumed by the federal government in the Sherman Antitrust Act of 1890. This act contained two provisions, both limited to interstate or foreign commerce: Section 1 prohibited "every contract, combination, or conspiracy in restraint of trade," regardless of whether it produced monopoly; Section 2 prohibited monopolizing or attempting to monopolize.

In the Standard Oil case of 1911, Section 1 was interpreted as applying only to unreasonable restraints of trade.[12] Under this interpretation some kinds of restraint, such as price-fixing agreements, are *per se* unreasonable. On the other hand, most types of agreement among competing companies will be held illegal only if there is proof of *undue* restraint on competition.

The "rule of reason" allows the courts flexibility in interpreting the act. Some observers see an advantage in the courts' ability to decide each case in response to the specific circumstances in the industry. Yet this flexibility brings with it uncertainty as to whether particular courses of action will be held illegal.

The Sherman Act can be enforced through suits brought by persons injured or through criminal or civil action brought by the Department of Justice. In practice, however, the department usually combines civil and criminal action and seeks a civil remedy—usually that illegal practices be discontinued or that a combination be dissolved.

Although enforcement of the Sherman Act has vacillated between strong and weak periods, the gradual trend during the twentieth century has been to strengthen its impact by passing additional legislation with more explicit antitrust provisions. Dissatisfaction with early results led the Republican, Democratic, and Progressive parties to propose additional antitrust legislation in 1912, and in 1914 supplementary legislation was enacted. The Federal Trade Commission Act prohibited "unfair methods of competition," and the Clayton Act added several further prohibitions. One of these, Section 7, forbade intercorporate purchases of stock that would substantially lessen competition or tend to create a monopoly. This provision was the basis of the Court ruling in 1957 that Du Pont ownership of 23 percent of the stock of General Motors was illegal because Du Pont's sale of fabrics and finishes to General Motors tended substantially to lessen competition in such sales.[13] The Supreme Court made significant new findings: first, that Section 7 applied to vertical combinations (common control of supplier and purchaser) as well as to horizontal ones (between competitors) and, second, that a stock purchase could become illegal because of its effects even though it was not illegal at the time it was made.

Several subsequent acts have expanded the prohibitions of 1914. The Robinson-Patman Act of 1936 is a detailed statute that tries to protect small retailers against price discriminations that favor large buyers. The

---

[12] *Standard Oil Co. of N.J.* v. *United States*, 221 U.S. 1 (1911).
[13] *United States* v. *E. I. du Pont de Nemours*, 353 U.S. 586 (1957).

Wheeler-Lea Act of 1938 amended the Federal Trade Commission Act to prohibit "unfair methods of competition and unfair and deceptive acts in commerce"—thus extending the protection of the FTC Act to consumers. The new act also strengthened the Federal Trade Commission and imposed special penalties for false advertising of foods, drugs, cosmetics, and mechanical devices (such as those to reduce weight) to change the human figure. The Anti-Merger Act of 1950 very significantly amended Section 7 of the Clayton Act by making the merger of two or more corporations illegal under the same conditions a stock purchase would be—that is, if it tended to lessen competition substantially or to create a monopoly. It had previously been necessary to prove monopoly or intent to monopolize in merger cases. Both the Federal Trade Commission and the Antitrust Division have stopped many large mergers through proceedings to enforce the new provision.

Nonetheless, there have been many limitations on the effectiveness of antitrust policy:

1. The fundamental problem is that support for antitrust policy is weak. Not since President Wilson has any President concentrated attention on antitrust as a major problem of the nation. The Supreme Court has vacillated in its interpretation of the antitrust statutes, though in the past forty years it has given them more force and consistency. There is a lack of legislative consensus on the extent to which antitrust policy should be strengthened, and congressional committees often work at cross-purposes. Moreover, there is no strong general public interest in antitrust policy. Finally, there is a lack of consensus among economists and others as to the extent to which government should intervene to maintain a competitive economy and the means for effecting such action.

2. Antitrust policy has sometimes been undermined by other government policies. Protective tariffs have often set an umbrella on prices, thus protecting monopolistic combinations. By their nature, patents grant monopolies, and the antitrust laws have not always prevented patent pools and restrictions on the use of patents that extended these monopolies even further. Purchases of patents and withholding them from use have been means of protecting existing patent monopolies. Also, statutes have sometimes diluted the antitrust laws by, for instance, authorizing regulatory commissions to approve actions that would otherwise be illegal.

3. There are many gaps and qualifications in the statutes. For example, by retaining ownership of an article and merely consigning it to another, a manufacturer may be able to evade restrictions on his control over the seller. Also while interlocking directorates among competing industrial firms are illegal under stated conditions, interlocking directorates between financial and industrial firms escape this provision.

4. Antitrust is sometimes a weak weapon for meeting new types of situations. When a few concerns supply all or most of the market and

when their capital investments are large, price competition may cease to exist; and yet there may be no evidence of collusion, coercion, or combination. Competition may be active through advertising, product differentiation, or improved service, but companies carefully avoid upsetting the price structure.

5. Enforcement difficulties are great. Small government staffs with limited appropriations struggle against great aggregations of capital with large staffs of attorneys and other experts. Proof of the effects on competition, or of evil intent, or of unreasonable restraint may require months or years of effort. It is often difficult to find an appropriate remedy, particularly when a merger has already taken place and the assets of two companies have been mixed.

Despite the difficulties of gathering proof of collusion in restraint of trade, the government achieved one of its major antitrust victories in the 1961 case of price-fixing in the electrical-equipment industry, a case involving executives of industrial giants like Westinghouse and General Electric and leading to jail sentences for some of those convicted. A few of the men involved, feeling that others were trying to hide behind them, decided to give evidence. Some also hoped to avoid jail by cooperating with the Justice Department. The result was that the department obtained detailed evidence of an extensive price-fixing conspiracy. When making bids on heavy electrical equipment, representatives of more than twenty firms got together to agree on a price and on which company should submit

"Good gracious, you mean to say something's been going on here for fifty years?"

Congress has only occasionally attempted to expose business violations of antitrust policy.

From *Straight Herblock,* Simon & Schuster, 1964

The 1962 Steel Crisis: The Case Against Steel

[The] Simultaneous and identical actions of United States Steel and other leading steel corporations increasing steel prices by some $6 a ton constitute a wholly unjustifiable and irresponsible defiance of the public interest....

If this rise in the cost of steel is imitated by the rest of the industry, instead of rescinded, it would increase the cost of homes, autos, appliances, and most other items for every American family.... It would seriously handicap our efforts to prevent an inflationary spiral from eating up the pensions of our older citizens, and our new gains in purchasing power....

There is no justification for an increase in the steel prices. The recent settlement between the industry and the union, which does not even take place until July 1st, was widely acknowledged to be non-inflationary, and the whole purpose and effect of this Administration's role, which both parties understood, was to achieve an agreement which would make unnecessary any increase in prices.

The Department of Justice and the Federal Trade Commission are examining the significance of this [price increase] in a free, competitive economy. The Department of Defense and other agencies are reviewing its impact on their policies of procurement and I am informed that steps are underway by those members of the Congress who plan appropriate inquiries into how these price decisions are so quickly made and reached, and what legislative safeguards may be needed to protect the public interest.

Price and wage decisions in this country, except for very limited restrictions in the case of monopolies and national emergency strikes, are and ought to be freely and privately made, but the American people have a right to expect in return for that freedom, a higher sense of business responsibility for the welfare of their country than has been shown in the last two days.

From President John F. Kennedy, press conference reported in the New York *Times*, April 1962.

---

the winning low bid on each project. Turns were taken, on a proportional-sharing basis, according to the phases of the moon, with clandestine hotel meetings, secret telephone calls, and all the other appurtenances of television melodrama.[14] After the government had established the facts, hundreds of suits were brought by cities, states, and private parties for the punitive triple damages prescribed by the Clayton Act. Henceforth, every corporation that violates the antitrust laws will shudder at the possibility of customer suits.

Opinions have always differed about what function government should perform in maintaining competition. There has been general agreement

14 For the fascinating details, see John G. Fuller, *The Gentlemen Conspirators* (New York: Grove Press, 1962), or John Herling, *The Great Price Conspiracy* (New York: McKay, 1962).

that government should prevent unfair and coercive competitive tactics. There has also been substantial consensus that collusive arrangements among competitors that materially restrict competition should be prohibited. Some people have argued, however, that such arrangements should be accepted in certain instances, subject to government supervision, and these arrangements have been provided for in regulatory statutes for a number of industries.

The largest difference of opinion has been over the proper response of government to "bigness"—the attainment of size sufficient to permit market leadership or dominance. Some have argued that a few large concerns may be able to control the market or exert dangerous political influence. On the other hand, David E. Lilienthal summarized the views of many in a defense of bigness as the basis of high productivity: "Size," he said, "is our greatest functional asset." [15]

[15] David E. Lilienthal, *Big Business: A New Era* (New York: Harper & Row, 1953), p. 33.

The 1962 Steel Crisis: The Case Against the Government

Last week President Kennedy made a determination that a 3½ percent increase [in the price of steel would] throw the American economy out of line on several fronts. In the next twenty-four hours the President directed or supported a series of Governmental actions that imperiled basic American rights, went far beyond the law, and were more characteristic of a police state than a free government.

We, the members of the Joint Senate-House Republican Leadership, believe that a fundamental issue has been raised: should a President of the United States use the enormous powers of the Federal Government to blackjack any segment of our free society into line with his personal judgment without regard to law?...

Although the President at his press conference made it clear that "price and wage decisions in this country ... are and ought to be freely and privately made," there was nothing in the course of action which he pursued that supported this basic American doctrine.

Indeed, if big government can be used to extra-legally reverse the economic decisions of one industry in a free economy, then it can be used to reverse the decisions of any business, big or small, of labor, of farmers, in fact, of any citizen....

We condone nothing in the actions of the steel companies except their right to make an economic judgment without massive retaliation by the Federal Government.

Temporarily President Kennedy may have won a political victory, but at the cost of doing violence to the fundamental precepts of a free society.

From joint Senate-House Republican leadership, statement in the New York *Times*, April 1962.

Both views are partly correct. Developments in science, technology, and the art of administration have greatly increased man's capacity for efficient conduct of large undertakings. Size has proved to be an asset necessary for production for mass markets and for defense in the nuclear-missile age. Yet questions remain: How large is too large? What are the consequences when units of private power are able to dominate markets? Will these units of power make decisions on price levels and production rates in the context of their own interests?

Many have suggested that government intervention must increase in order to counterbalance the power of private companies over markets. President Kennedy in 1962 used all the powers at his command to get a steel price rescinded, and President Johnson has on several occasions used his influence against price increases on such commodities as aluminum and copper. Bills have been introduced in Congress that would require notice from large corporations before price increases and would require hearings on proposed increases, either on a mandatory basis or at the discretion of the President. Others have proposed utility regulation for industries in which there is a large degree of concentration. But the difficulty of carrying out such measures successfully leads most people to prefer effective antitrust legislation and enforcement.

Fostering Labor-Management Accommodation

Although the government sets minimum standards for the conditions and benefits of employment, employers and employees negotiate terms of settlement above the minimum standards. Great emphasis has been placed in this country on the freedom of private parties to decide for themselves the hours, wages, and other terms of their contracts of employment. Both corporate and union officials treasure this process as a basic freedom.

Yet in no area is the accuracy of Madison's analysis of government as a mediator among "various and interfering interests" more clearly substantiated. Labor organizations desire protection for rights to unionize, bargain collectively, strike, boycott, and picket, while employers desire restrictions on these rights. Employer groups support the use of the injunction in labor disputes; labor groups abhor the instrument. Balancing and regulating the conflicting interests of labor and management has become one of the most difficult and persistent tasks of government.

In addition, however, the government must safeguard the community interest in maintaining peace at the site of labor conflicts, in avoiding interruptions of essential transportation and production, and in settling labor-management disputes in a way that avoids price inflation.

Prior to 1926, policies on labor-management relations were determined and applied almost exclusively by the courts. Since that time these policies have increasingly been formulated in Congress and carried out by administrative agencies. The course of labor-management relations has been significantly shaped by five acts of Congress:

1. *The Railway Labor Act of 1926.* This act ushered in a new period of legislative and administrative control. It stated labor's right to organize without interference from employers, provided for collective labor contracts, and made it the duty of each party to try to reach agreement on a contract. It set up procedures for negotiation and peaceful settlement and established a National Mediation Board to assist the parties in reaching an agreement. In addition, in case of national emergency the President could appoint a fact-finding board to analyze the issues in dispute and make recommendations for settlement.

Until the Second World War the success of this machinery for settlement was widely acclaimed. But the act was inadequate to prevent the serious railroad strikes that broke out in 1946, 1948, and 1950. In all three cases the President—acting under special wartime powers that had not been rescinded—seized the railroads involved. Now that special authority for seizure is no longer delegated to the President the question arises: What shall the government's policy be when the procedures of the Railway Labor Act fail? When a nationwide strike of railroad workers was imminent in 1963, Congress provided for compulsory settlement of the dispute by an *ad hoc* board. But even the board could not solve all issues in dispute, and to avoid a strike President Johnson called the representatives of the roads and the workers to the White House, where, with the aid of government mediators, a settlement was reached. And in 1967, when six shop-craft unions threatened to strike after Railway Labor Act procedures had been exhausted, Congress passed temporary no-strike legislation.

2. *The Norris-LaGuardia (Anti-Injunction) Act of 1932.* The labor injunction, first issued by an American court in 1875, became the chief weapon of the employer for breaking labor strikes. The act of 1932, a major victory for labor, strictly regulated labor-injunction proceedings (requiring hearings, a jury trial in contempt proceedings, and other safeguards), and it narrowly restricted both the causes for issuing injunctions and the actions that could be prohibited. The effect of this act was substantially to take the national courts out of labor disputes; it represented the farthest extension of a "hands-off" policy by government.

The hands-off policy for the federal courts was quickly followed by legislative intervention. In three additional acts, Congress has sought to balance the rights of parties and to protect the interests of the public in labor relations in industry, as it had done earlier for railroads.

3. *The National Labor Relations Act of 1935.* This act was the most notable achievement on behalf of the labor-union movement in our history. Under its protection the number of union members more than quadrupled. It declared the right of employees to self-organization and collective bargaining, and it labeled as "unfair" such practices as interference by an

employer with his employees' choice of union representatives or a refusal on his part to bargain with them. The act set up a National Labor Relations Board to hold elections to determine which organization the employees desired to represent them and to make decisions on alleged violations of the act.

4. *The Taft-Hartley Act of 1947.* Great employer dissatisfaction with the increased strength of organized labor under the 1935 act led to the Taft-Hartley Act, in which the employers regained some of the ground lost to labor. The act recognizes the right of employees *not* to join unions as well as to join them. It prohibits the closed shop, under which a man cannot be hired unless he is already a member of a union. However, the act still allows the union shop—that is, employer-employee contracts providing that a person be required to join a union within a stated number of days of employment. Neither labor nor employers are fully satisfied with this compromise. A 1959 amendment to the act provides that state laws shall apply in types of cases over which the NLRB fails to assert jurisdiction, and many states have "right-to-work" laws, which outlaw the union shop. In 1965 President Johnson recommended the repeal of the provision that allows these state laws to apply to interstate commerce, but Congress did not adopt his recommendation.

There were many other gains for employers in the Taft-Hartley Act. A new category of unfair labor practices was created—those committed by labor organizations. It became an unfair labor practice for a labor union to refuse to bargain in good faith or for labor to use the secondary boycott—that is, to strike or stop work to force their employer to cease doing business with another firm in which there is a labor dispute. Many other protections were given to employers, such as exempting supervisory employees from the protection of the National Labor Relations Act and guaranteeing the employer's right to express his opinions on labor organizations to his employees as long as he does not try to coerce them or promise benefits if they do not join unions. Another section of the act amended the Federal Corrupt Practices Act to prevent labor unions from contributing or expending funds in political campaigns for national office.

Other provisions of the Taft-Hartley Act represented the government's effort to facilitate settlement of labor disputes and to prevent stoppage of commerce without undermining the process of collective bargaining. These provisions were patterned after the Railway Labor Act, except for some procedures during national emergencies. Both parties are required to give notice of their intention to seek modification of a labor contract, both are obligated to bargain, and a new independent agency—the Federal Mediation and Conciliation Service—provides facilities for conciliation, mediation, and voluntary arbitration. In case a dispute imperils the national health or safety, the President can appoint a board of inquiry, and, upon its report, he may direct the Attorney General to seek an injunction against continuance of the strike or lockout for up to eighty days. In the meantime the President reconvenes the board of inquiry, which makes a report at the end of sixty days. Within the remaining twenty days of the injunction period the employees vote on whether to accept the employer's last offer. If the dispute is still not settled the President makes recommendations to Congress for appropriate action.

The growth of national unions during recent years leads to the possibility that whole industries will be tied up by strikes. Given such circumstances, can the national government avoid more intervention in labor disputes than is provided in the Taft-Hartley Act? The government could seize and operate the enterprises involved if an emergency develops, but there are disadvantages in seizure. By continuing the status quo this course of action may unduly favor the employer and remove his incentive to bargain. On the other hand, seizure puts pressure on the government to adjudicate the issues in controversy, which becomes compulsory settlement. Compulsory settlement without seizure has its advocates, but arguments against it have prevailed. It would be difficult, probably impossible, to state clear standards for making a decision so that courts could decide the contests. And the President would be drawn deeper into labor-management politics, increasing the burdens of his office. Moreover, increased government intervention might weaken the freedom and responsibility of the parties that exist in the system of collective bargaining. Finally, decisions adverse to labor might not be accepted by it, and hence strikes might still occur.

President Kennedy tried a gentler form of intervention with the announcement of noninflationary guidelines for settling labor disputes: wage increases were not to exceed the average increase in productivity in the nation. Although President Johnson tried to maintain these guidelines, they broke down in the labor settlements of 1966. In numerous negotiations, labor refused to accept guideline limitations on wage increases, claiming that the huge profits of industry justified larger increases. The President, working toward one government objective—a healthy economy—came into conflict with another objective—freedom of the parties in labor-management negotiations.

5. *The Labor Reform Act of 1959.* This act grew out of a series of investigations of labor racketeering, beginning in 1957 and conducted by the Senate Select Committee on Improper Activities in the Labor or Management Field. The provisions of the act reflect the bitter fight between labor and management over its content. In general, the act does three things:

First, it tightens and extends some of the Taft-Hartley prohibitions against certain labor activities, particularly secondary boycotts and certain kinds of picketing.

Second, the act seeks to establish responsibility in union management. For example, it prescribes the conduct of elections; it requires reporting to the Secretary of Labor on salaries and loans and "conflict of interest" payments to union officers and on other matters; and it defines new categories of federal offenses, such as stealing or misappropriating union funds.

Third, it contains what is called a bill of rights for union members, designed to ensure democracy in the conduct of union affairs and due process before members are disciplined. These guarantees are presumably designed to protect union members; actually they appeal to employer groups because they tend to lessen the power of union leaders.

Promoting and Regulating Industries

Almost every industry is aided directly or indirectly in some way by government. But some are specifically favored through subsidies, loans, insurance, or other forms of direct promotion. The housing industry, for instance, is promoted by means of FHA loans, the chartering of savings-and-loan associations, and the support and regulation of the home-loan market through Federal Home Loan Banks. Also, many industries are subjected to comprehensive regulation. Banks chartered by state and national agencies are regulated by rules and by periodic examination. They are further regulated if they join the Federal Deposit Insurance Corporation or the Federal Reserve System, and all national banks must belong to both. Almost every aspect of railroad management is regulated by state and national agencies. The basic utilities—telephone, power, and gas—are comprehensively regulated by the national government and by most of the state governments. Radio and television communication is regulated by the Federal Communications Commission, chiefly through licensing requirements. Stock and commodity exchanges are regulated by national agencies,

"I just never imagined they wouldn't finally come up with *some* form of government aid."

The public today expects the government to assure the continued operation of any industry important to the nation.

Drawing by Stevenson;
© 1965 The New Yorker Magazine, Inc.

and security issuances by national and state governments. Trucks and buses are subject to safety and load regulations by state governments and also to licensing and rate regulation by the national government on their interstate business and by state governments on intrastate business. Maritime transportation is promoted and regulated by the national government. Finally, the production and marketing of agricultural products are regulated in as complex a system of controls as exists for any industry.

Regulation or promotion for each industry has been the result of dealing *ad hoc* with each problem as it arose. Government policy in regard to the airline industry, for example, illustrates that promotion and regulation are often commingled, that regulation takes diverse forms, and that responses must meet varied—even conflicting—demands. The Civil Aeronautics Act of 1938 declared a policy of promoting civil aviation to meet the needs of the postal system, commerce, and national defense. Congress, in response to industry and community pressures, has promoted airline service by subsidies to airline companies and by granting money, under the Federal Airport Act, to political subdivisions to assist them in building airports. It has responded to the public desire for safe transportation by licensing pilots, planes, and their equipment; by rules governing flying; and by an air-traffic management system controlling takeoff, flying on the airways, and landing. This system of safety regulation and the grants for airport construction are administered by the large Federal Aviation Agency, now in the Department of Transportation.

Congress has also provided for regulation of the economic affairs of the domestic airline industry through a Civil Aeronautics Board. It grants certificates for airline service, passes upon rates, and allots subsidies. To do so, the board must balance varied and conflicting interests. For instance, more and more small cities want airline service, but, at the same time, government subsidies for service must not be increased. Larger cities want more service, but the board must limit the number of trunk lines serving these cities in order to prevent their having to be subsidized.

The board also passes on petitions for airline service between the United States and other countries, but these decisions must be submitted to the President for his approval. Rates for international service and other matters are determined in international agreements negotiated by the Department of State with the cooperation of the board.

Supplying Service Through Government Enterprises

A frequent subject of controversy is whether the government should supply a commodity or service directly instead of regulating and promoting private enterprise. Western nations have made extensive use of government enterprise, and such key industries as transportation and communication are government owned and managed in most countries.

This country has favored regulated private enterprise. Nevertheless, we have a considerable amount of public enterprise at the national level, chiefly in communications, defense enterprises, credit, insurance, and power. The largest public enterprise in the Western world is the United States Post Office, which carries the mail, distributes it through some forty thousand post offices and a system of home delivery, and operates a savings-bank system for small depositors. Atomic energy is a tremendous government monopoly, though much of the operation is carried out by tightly supervised private manufacturers. Military arsenals and Navy construction yards are government undertakings, and during the Second World War the government financed construction of defense plants of various sorts. The government also operates many large-scale insurance enterprises. It insures bank deposits and housing loans, provides insurance for the aged and their survivors and for veterans, and operates a number of other insurance programs.

Government enterprise in the field of credit has been extensive. Beginning in 1916, a system of semipublic credit institutions evolved for short- and long-term loans to agricultural producers. Also, the Commodity Credit Corporation supports farm prices by commodity loans to farmers. Government influence in agricultural credit has been a substantial means of assisting farmers. An agency in the Department of Commerce makes loans to small business, but government activity in business credit has had small impact except in depression and wartime emergencies. The Export-Import Bank is an exception: its primary function is to participate in or guarantee credits extended by United States exporters or financial institutions and to make direct loans to finance United States exports.

The most publicized enterprises of the national government have been the giant river-development projects, to be discussed in Chapter 20. The Boulder Canyon Project, the Tennessee Valley Authority, and the Bonneville Power Administration (for the Columbia River Basin) are among the most notable of these public power undertakings.

Government enterprises are managed in two ways. Many of them—for example, the United States Post Office—are operated as departments or bureaus of departments. Others—such as the Tennessee Valley Authority and the St. Lawrence Seaway Development Corporation—are operated as government corporations. An advantage claimed for government corporations is that they operate with more flexibility in financial matters and are thus freed from complete dependence on annual appropriations: they are usually authorized to borrow money up to stated limits and to reuse the revenues obtained through sales or loan payments. Some have argued that government enterprises should be independent of control by political departments. Others, however, have contended that placing enterprises in departments would allow coordination of their activities with related ones performed by other agencies and give representatives of the people control over their activities, budgets and accounts, and personnel policies.

These opposing views were compromised in the Government Corporation Act of 1945, which accepted the use of the corporate device when authorized by Congress. It provided that the corporations should submit annual budgets to the Bureau of the Budget but that the corporate budget should be a "business-type budget, or plan of operations, with due allowance given to the need for flexibility." The act provided for audits "in accordance with the principles and procedures applicable to commercial corporate transactions." It contemplated the floating of corporate bond issues, as authorized under separate acts, but it gave the Treasury Department control over issuances. Other acts make most government corporations subject to civil-service laws and locate them within a department.

Government enterprises are not always sustained fully by their own revenues. The Post Office operates with a large deficit, and the Rural Electrification Administration subsidizes rural cooperatives by lending them money at 2 percent, a rate lower than that at which the government obtains it. In multipurpose river projects for flood control, power supply, and so on, the government has evolved a complicated basis of allocating costs among the several purposes, and it recoups that portion of costs attributable to power by collecting revenues from the sale of power.

Should the government operate the Post Office at a deficit, thus giving a subsidy for newspaper and magazine circulation and for other interests? Should it subsidize public housing projects for low-income families? Should it subsidize local transportation in order to maintain low rates of charge? Should cities make a profit from their power systems? These questions of policy become political issues. Some people think that government enterprises should stand on their own feet, but others hold that social benefits are of more importance than the financial record of the enterprises.

INTERPRETATION AND PROSPECTS

How can one characterize the substantive interventions of government in the economy in this country? Because solutions have been sought for particular problems on an *ad hoc* basis, there are many inconsistencies in American public policy. Yet there are general patterns: maintenance of free and fair competition, maintenance of collective bargaining in labor-management relations, a minimum base for working standards and compensation, utility-type regulation for monopolies, regulated competition for transportation, aid to sick industries with large employment and importance to the nation, licensing for professions and occupations of various types, and monetary and fiscal controls to ensure growth and stability in the economy.

Many basic government policies aim at supporting private mechanisms. The goal of antitrust policy is to maintain the market as the regulator of price and production; labor policy tries to maintain private bargaining between employers and employees; and monetary and fiscal policy works primarily toward growth and stability in private markets. Other policies, such as minimum labor standards and social-security programs, raise cost levels in industry but still rely on the private entrepreneur to adjust his operations as necessary to cover additional costs. On the other hand, many government programs largely supplant the operation of market forces. This is especially true of production controls in agriculture and oil, price controls in utilities and transportation, quotas and special tariff provisions in international trade regulation, and the sale of a commodity or service by government itself.

Prospects for the future include new problems and more politics. The long-time trend toward concentration both in business and in labor raises questions about the adequacy of traditional policies. Will collective bargaining succeed? Will antitrust alone protect the public from excessive prices? Will efforts to manage the economy through monetary and fiscal controls succeed without some direct control of prices? On the other hand, does experience in the regulation of industries suggest that either price or wage control is likely to succeed? One conclusion appears clear: the extent of success in present policies of collective bargaining, antitrust, and monetary and fiscal control will determine whether deeper penetration of government into the economy will occur in the future.

Another development is the increased importance of comprehensive perspectives and policies in a society of interdependent interests. Surface transportation, for example, has become a complex system interrelating railroads; trucks and buses; ocean, lake, and river vessels; pipelines; and private automobiles regulated by cities, states, and national agencies. The serious need for planning and comprehensive policy development in this area was underscored by the creation of the Department of Transportation in 1967. Even more important, economic growth and stability have innumerable facets and are affected by the action of numerous government agencies. But, in these and other areas of economic policy, the effort to view the whole complex of interests and to develop policies in response to them will be attended with much difficulty, some confusion, and much uncertainty as to results.

SUMMARY

Since the beginning of the Republic, interest groups have sought government intervention to advance their economic welfare. During the nineteenth century, however, the rise of new business interests created by the corporate revolution and supported by the laissez faire ideology restricted government legislation in economic matters—a situation that lasted until the Depression. Today the government is generally accepted as an arena in which economic groups seek promotion of their interests, rival interests are accommodated, and interdependent interests are promoted.

Government legislative programs are invariably established in response to pressure from interest groups who expect benefits from such legislation. Legislation may be the result of demands from outside groups who wish to see a particular industry regulated, the result of demands from within an occupational group for legislative standards, or a prize to the victorious group among several competitors within an industry. Of course, legislation is also initiated partly out of recognition that certain major public needs must be met.

Once legislation has been passed, several safeguards help to ensure that government programs are administered fairly by bureaus, independent executive agencies, and independent regulatory commissions. First, administrative agencies may be overruled by the courts or investigated by Congress. Second, these agencies tend to be bipartisan and to have substantial independence from the President and from political pressures. And, finally, standardized procedures and common patterns of organization largely professionalize the administrative process, standardize the benefits offered under the programs, and protect the agencies from improper influence in particular cases. Nonetheless, the policies of the agencies are continuously influenced by interest groups who desire benefits from these policies.

The government now plays five major economic roles: first, it promotes the health of the economy through such legislation as the Employment Act of 1946 and through various fiscal and monetary tools to counteract inflations and recessions. Second, it helps to maintain a competitive economic system by enforcing a series of antitrust acts beginning with the Sherman Antitrust Act of 1890; however, loopholes in statutes, contradictory government policies, and lack of public interest impair the effectiveness of antitrust legislation. Third, the government fosters labor-management accommodation through a series of congressional statutes that set up administrative controls over labor-management dealings.

These first three roles of the government are designed to shape the economy as a whole into one that is flexible and allows private initiative on investments, prices, wages, and other important matters. If these policies are effective, adjustments of competing interests can be accommodated primarily within the private sector, and the government's task of resolving conflicts will be kept within bounds.

The other two major roles of the government are: first, the promotion of industries through subsidies, loans, insurance, and the like and their regulation through licenses, control of rates, and other means; and, second, the direct supply of service through government enterprises, such as the Post Office or TVA. Both these roles of government have been undertaken on an *ad hoc* basis, only in response to particular problems that have arisen.

The important question of the future is how much responsibility the government will be forced to assume in adjusting and promoting various diverse interests. The answer depends on how effective the loose forms of control embodied in the government's first three roles are and how much special intervention through regulation and government ownership will be demanded by the public.

GOVERNMENT, SCIENCE, AND NATURAL RESOURCES

20

A critical challenge of this generation is the effective management and development of our natural resources and our scientific and technical capacity. The government now plays a major role in meeting this challenge, but the effectiveness of the government's policies is largely shaped by competing interests jockeying for influence. What equilibrium has been worked out between private enterprise and government initiative in our research-and-development policies? Which interest groups exert major influence on these policies, and how? Finally, which forces shape our conservation policies for land use, water, and nonrenewable resources, and what is the distinctive pattern of politics for each natural resource?

The mushroom cloud over Hiroshima, Surveyor II squatting on the moon, giant turbines spinning at Grand Coulee Dam, a black forest of derricks covering a Texas oil field—these illustrate man's increasing mastery over nature. They are also important examples of modern government at work.

Both the manipulation of nature and its conservation have become matters of critical public importance in this generation. As a nation we now recognize that our natural resources are not unlimited and that their effective use and the discovery of substitute materials are essential to our national prosperity and security. We have come to recognize also that our most important national "resource" is our scientific and technical capacity and the opportunity it offers for increased understanding and for control of the physical world to further our national goals.

America has always relied extensively on the free-enterprise system for the development of natural resources: land, water, timber, energy, minerals, and chemicals. Private universities and industrial laboratories are the heart of our scientific research-and-development effort. Yet so important is the management of the country's resource base that the government must inevitably be heavily involved.

This involvement takes three principal forms. First, the government finances and directs extensive research-and-development programs aimed not only at specific goals, such as weapons development and improved health care, but at expanding our existing resource base through exploration, improved methods of use and extraction, research on new materials, and increased scientific manpower. Second, it engages in the direct development, promotion, and management of certain existing resources, most notably land and water, through public agencies such as the Forest Service and the Bureau of Land Management. Third, both the national and state governments undertake to regulate the private development of certain resources, such as oil, natural gas, and timber.[1]

How effectively government performs its three major roles depends on a complex set of political subsystems that shape research-and-development policies and programs of conservation and regulation. Usually these systems consist of the "triple alliances" of government bureaus, private interest groups, and congressional committees, though the extensive involvement of state and even local government in conservation and regulation often adds a fourth dimension to resource politics.

[1] The government also conditions the resource environment indirectly through its economic and monetary policies, through its foreign-relations and national-security programs designed to give us access to the resources of other nations, and as a large purchaser of materials for strategic stockpiling as well as for immediate use.

648

UNDERWRITING INNOVATION: GOVERNMENT SUPPORT FOR SCIENCE AND TECHNOLOGY

The political subsystem that manages our research process is of recent origin, beginning in the Second World War, but the tradition of government support of science and technology is as old as the nation itself.

The establishment of the census, of specific standards for weights and measures, and of provisions for patenting inventions were the first signs of the new nation's respect for science and technology. In the early nineteenth century, the federal government sponsored expeditions to explore the coastal and inland resources of the country and accepted the bequest that made possible the Smithsonian Institution.

The outbreak of the Civil War led to a major expansion in the federal government's relation to science. The military relied extensively on research for weapons and military equipment, most notably for the perfection of ironclad ships. In 1863, with encouragement from the country's most distinguished scientists, Congress established the National Academy of Sciences to provide technical information and assistance to the government. The Morrill Act of 1862 gave grants of land for state agricultural colleges and created research bureaus to investigate farm problems. The elaborate network of agricultural field stations that eventually developed demonstrated the value of systematic research by providing the most productive agriculture the world had ever witnessed.

National emergencies continued to provide the prime impetus for public support of science. During the First World War, the National Advisory Committee for Aeronautics was established; Thomas Edison headed a Naval Consulting Board for science; and President Wilson established the National Research Council as an offshoot of the National Academy of Sciences to work on specific research projects of interest to the government. During the Depression, Franklin Roosevelt established a presidential scientific advisory board. His Administration also produced an important report, *Research—A National Resource*, that explored the potential of science to provide growth in a weak economy.

But it was the Second World War that stimulated a major revolution in the government's attitude toward research. The Office of Scientific Research and Development (headed by Vannevar Bush) was established to coordinate military research and development, and the accomplishments of science in the war—the atomic bomb, the proximity fuse, radar, blood plasma—showed clearly the vast potential of organized research. By the time the war had ended, the research centers the government had established, the new relationships forged between public agencies, industry, and universities, and the research programs under way in military departments had become a unified national enterprise.[2]

Bush laid the groundwork for a permanent alliance between science and government in his report to President Truman in 1945 entitled *Science, The Endless Frontier.* This document made it clear that science was the chief avenue through which new materials, new products, and new resources would become available. In the next two decades, the Atomic Energy Commission and the National Science Foundation were created, and military-research programs were reorganized and expanded. New programs in medical research were instituted by the National Institutes of Health. The National Aeronautics and Space Administration was launched to plan the American space efforts. Nearly every Cabinet department—including the Post Office—has undertaken some kind of research-and-development program.

This basic national commitment to underwrite scientific progress is most dramatically expressed in dollars. While in 1939 the federal budget included some $40 million for research, in 1966 the federal government spent four hundred times that amount—almost $16 *billion*—for research and development. Seventy percent of all research and development carried on in the United States—in universities and private industrial laboratories as well as government installations—is now financed by the federal government.

The new public investment in science and technology has raised a host of policy questions. Should federally supported research be carried on principally within government establishments or in private industrial and university laboratories? How much should the nation spend on research? What scientific fields should be emphasized? Who should decide where and how research activities will be carried on? What guarantees are necessary to ensure that freedom of scientific inquiry will be preserved? How can discoveries and inventions made under public auspices be fed into the private sector?

As policies on these questions have been hammered out, a pattern of politics has emerged. Natural scientists, traditionally aloof from the political arena, have come to be influential in high councils of state; new industries almost entirely dependent on government support have sprung up; and government scientific agencies have developed missions and objectives of their own. An influential political subsystem has emerged from these three groups—so influential, in fact, that President Eisenhower in his farewell address warned that public policy could become "the captive of a scientific-technological elite."

[2] A good historical account of scientists in the Second World War is found in J. P. Baxter, III, *Scientists Against Time* (Boston: Little, Brown, 1946).

Contracts and Grants: A Pattern of Extramural Research

One of the most important issues raised by government entry into science—where research-and-development activities will be lodged—has been resolved in favor of primary reliance on private enterprises and universities. Of the $16 billion authorized for research and development in 1966, over $12½ billion was "extramural"—that is, spent outside government laboratories. In executing research programs, federal agencies have forged working partnerships with business and academic organizations through the use of contracts and grants.

These devices have been used by government for a long time, but they have been substantially modified for use in scientific areas. It is often not possible to advertise for bids in the development of weapons systems or satellites, because the "product" is unknown or hard to specify and because relatively few firms have the skills and resources to engage in this complex work. Hence most research-and-development contracts are negotiated with one of a small number of firms, and the government pays all costs plus a fixed fee. Federal agencies use the contract method also to support entire laboratories rather than specific research projects—as is the case with the Los Alamos Laboratory managed by the University of California or the Lincoln Laboratory of MIT.

The National Science Foundation (NSF), established in 1950, is the federal agency charged with fostering basic research. Annually it awards some $200 million to individual scientists or laboratories to undertake specific research they propose, and it gives general-purpose grants to universities and other research institutions. The National Institutes of Health carry out a similar program in medicine, making grants to researchers, universities, and hospitals to support investigations in certain "target" areas: arthritis, allergy, infectious and metabolic diseases, dentistry, and mental health. The institutes currently support over 22,000 projects annually at 1,600 separate institutions, with appropriations that have grown from $10 million in 1947 to $300 million in 1960 and to $1¼ billion in 1966.

Heavy reliance on extramural research is the distinctive characteristic of publicly organized science in America. It reflects our traditional preference for private enterprise and independent scholarship. It also endows the national research effort with unusual flexibility and capacity for rapid expansion. At the same time, however, the new partnerships raise some knotty problems. The reliance on negotiated contracts with industry tends to reduce price competition and risk-taking, the essentials of the enterprise system. Administered prices and nonmarket controls blur the difference between the public and private sectors. Moreover, with so much work being done "outside," the staffs of government agencies themselves may fail to develop the critical skills essential to direct research-and-development activities.

Finally, the need to assure high technological and managerial competence in defense projects has led to a high concentration of awards to a few large firms. Today, four firms receive 60 percent of all federal research-and-development funds for communications and electrical work. Firms with more than 5,000 employees account for 86 percent of all federal research-and-development contracts. Thus, the government may be encouraging monopolistic tendencies through its scientific programs while the Justice Department seeks to enforce the Sherman antitrust law.

In university-research support, there has been a similar concentration of awards to a relatively few large universities. In 1965, 25 percent of the 1.7 billion federal dollars given to universities and colleges went to ten institutions.[3] The acceptance of government-sponsored research on campuses has raised issues of academic freedom, particularly where classified projects require loyalty and security clearances. And the increase in government funds has brought allegations of university emphasis on science at the expense of the humanities. Nevertheless, both industry and university are becoming increasingly dependent on public support.

What is the decision-making process in extramural research-and-development activities? Who issues priorities in research fields and chooses between alternative grant applications?

In 1952 a presidential commission reported that

> the Government, up from almost nothing since the beginning of the century, is now the great force behind scientific and technical research in this country. . . . Yet this great force is headless. . . . When one looks for a coherent research policy directed toward materials or indeed to anything else equally specific, one does not find it." [4]

By 1966, though no clear-cut overall policy for science had emerged, new decision-making and advisory mechanisms had arisen.

In addition, three interest groups—spokesmen for the scientific community, military leaders and their industrial supporters, and civil servants in the top echelon of the national bureaucracy—have succeeded in achieving powerful spheres of influence in shaping scientific policies. Sometimes they have dramatically confronted one another.

The spokesmen for the scientists are newcomers on the national political scene. Recruited during the Second World War on an emergency basis to turn technological breakthroughs to defense purposes, these scientists emerged with strong convictions about the proper organization of government-sponsored research and the need to ensure that science would not

---

[3] National Science Foundation Publication 66-30, *Federal Support for Academic Science and Other Educational Activities in Universities and Colleges* (1966), p. 25. The concentration has gradually diminished as the funds have increased. In 1965, ninety-eight institutions received at least $5 million.

[4] Report of the President's Materials Policy Commission, Vol. I, p. 144.

become "politicized." In particular, they wanted to ensure that atomic science would be used for international peace.

The "new scientists" first ventured into policy-making by opposing a bill that would have continued the atomic-energy program under military auspices and by lobbying successfully for legislation to create the Atomic Energy Commission as an independent agency under civilian direction. Similar controversies broke out in the establishment of the National Science Foundation and the reorganization of research and development in the military. In 1954 a crisis in science-government relations occurred when a special security-review board created by President Eisenhower denied clearance to the late Robert Oppenheimer, a distinguished physicist, on the ground that his past associations and policy views cast doubt on his reliability. This move, which many scientists regarded as "official McCarthyism," alienated a number of leading scientists from further participation in government programs. Controversies among scientists over appropriate public policies in the development of the hydrogen bomb, nuclear testing, and disarmament further impaired the scientists' political influence in the mid-1950's.

But the Soviet launching of the first Sputnik in 1957 prompted the government to turn again to scientists for counsel, and in that year the post of Special Assistant to the President for Science and Technology was created. The special assistant serves as head of the President's Science Advisory Committee, a group of nongovernment scientists now reestablished at the

"Dear boy, where have you been keeping yourself?"

The scientific success of the Soviet Sputnik in 1957 led to drastic curtailment of loyalty-security tests for American scientists.

From *Herblock's Special for Today,*
Simon & Schuster, 1958

The Military-Industrial Complex: Danger to Democracy

[The] conjunction of an immense military establishment and a large arms industry is new in American experience. The total influence—economic, political, even spiritual—is felt in every city, every State house, every office of the Federal government. We recognize the imperative need for this development. Yet we must not fail to comprehend its grave implications. Our toil, resources and livelihood are all involved; so is the very structure of our society.

In the councils of government, we must guard against the acquisition of unwarranted influence, whether sought or unsought, by the military-industrial complex. The potential for the disastrous rise of misplaced power exists and will persist. We must never let the weight of this combination endanger our liberties or democratic processes. We should take nothing for granted. Only an alert and knowledgeable citizenry can compel the proper meshing of the huge industrial and military machinery of defense with our peaceful methods and goals, so that security and liberty may prosper together.

From President Dwight D. Eisenhower, final address to the Nation, January 1961.

White House level. He is also chairman of the Federal Council for Science and Technology, consisting of the top government scientists, which works to improve coordination among government agencies having substantial research activities. Since 1962 the special assistant has also directed the Office of Science and Technology in the Executive Office of the President, a permanent staff that provides scientific counsel to other executive agencies and to Congress. Assistant secretaries for research and development have been placed in the major departments, and the positions are filled by professional engineers and scientists. Proposals for a Department of Science have been considered seriously.

Within just four years after Sputnik, a new advisory-and-coordinating apparatus with direct access to the President appeared, with strong ties to the scientific community and deep commitments to the value of basic research and to the importance of scientific education and training. In 1963 President Johnson presented Oppenheimer with the Fermi Award for distinguished contributions to atomic research—an event fittingly symbolic of the new rapport between science and government.

Yet the scientists are by no means unchallenged in the making of policy on matters that involve scientific and engineering considerations or in developing a basic approach to research support. Highly placed civil-service "generalists" have worked hard to maintain the preeminence of regular budgetary and administrative procedures in dealing with government science. The generalists often regard the scientists simply as experts who should be kept "on tap but not on top." They opposed the elevation of the Scientific Advisory Committee to presidential level and continue to oppose the establishment of a Department of Science.

Military leaders and the industrial concerns heavily involved in defense work also have great influence in research-and-development policy. In the same speech in which he spoke of the "scientific-technological elite," President Eisenhower warned of the "unwarranted influence" of "the military-industrial complex." As defense expenditures have spiraled and the bulk of research-and-development programs has come under the direction of the Pentagon, the "military lobby" has been viewed with alarm in some quarters. Critics fear not only its vested interest in maintaining defense spending at high levels but also the pressure it may exert on the government to over-emphasize defense-related projects, thus distorting the allocation of scientific manpower. The Defense Department's difficulty in abandoning the B-70 bomber and the Skybolt missile, despite technical consensus that other weapons systems are more effective and reliable, has led some to fear that objective research decisions cannot be made in these areas.

The Military-Industrial Complex: Legitimate Interest Group

[INTERVIEWER]: Mr. President, your predecessor, President Eisenhower, in his farewell message to the people just before he left office, warned of the dangers of a possible military-industrial complex.... Have you felt this threat at all while you're in office?

KENNEDY: Well, it seemed to me there's probably more in that feeling perhaps some months ago than ... today. Of course, every time you cancel a weapons system it affects a good many thousands of people, the interests of a community, the interests of members of Congress, the interests of a state.... We've had a long fight, for example, over the B-70, which we have felt is a weapon that isn't worth the money we'd have to put into it; but it's very difficult to struggle with the Congress. Twice now Congress has appropriated the money for the program and twice we have not spent that money. But I must say that as of today I don't feel that the pressure on me is excessive.

[INTERVIEWER]: Well, I was particularly attracted, sir, by ... a two-page color advertisement this week in one of the national magazines for the project Skybolt missile.... Now did you regard that as pressure on you?

KENNEDY: Well, I think it was an attempt to influence our decision. I see nothing wrong with that.... This Skybolt is very essential to the future of the Douglas Company; there're thousands of jobs that're involved. There're a good many people in the United States who feel that this program would be useful.

From President John F. Kennedy, interviewed on "A Conversation with President Kennedy," produced by ABC, CBS, and NBC, December 1962.

Certain facts about the "military lobby" are clear. First, a large number of retired military officers of high rank are employed by the important defense contractors, raising questions as to their influence in contract procurement. Second, defense companies have engaged in costly advertising campaigns—at government expense—extolling the virtues of their own weapons systems. Third, groups closely associated with the military have great potential political influence. The Association of the United States Army, the Navy League, the Air Force Association, the American Ordnance Association, the Aerospace Industries Association, and the National Security Industrial Association are large groups devoted "to informing and educating" the public. Though they stoutly deny any interest in specific defense projects, the general thrust of their activities seems oriented to the objectives of the services they support.[5]

Political considerations clearly enter into research-and-development decisions. Congressmen seek expenditures in their own districts; small business claims special considerations; reserve and national-guard units protest whenever efforts are made to reduce their size and number on grounds of technological obsolescence. The location of new space- and defense-research centers is a matter of vital political concern. Services, contractors, and Congress provide one of the most dramatic examples of the "triple alliance" at work—one with great consequences for priorities in research and development and the overall research effort.

Over two-thirds of our national research-and-development expenditures are oriented to essentially military missions. These projects produce some spillover into pure research and civilian technology, but by and large they are essentially engineering projects and are directly related to national-defense needs. The Defense Department and its allies determine priorities and decisively influence the total level of government support.

In the realm of basic research, though total government support is much smaller, the scientific community establishes priorities. The advisory panels of the National Science Foundation and the National Institutes of Health are composed of over two thousand scientists drawn from academic circles, and the allocation of funds depends primarily on their judgments.

The Space Program: Something for Everyone

Our national space program, which aims at placing a man on the moon and bringing him back by 1970, is a dramatic example of research politics in which every element of the subsystem is actively engaged. Our space program was given major impetus by the Russian launching of Sputnik I in 1957, which created a violent public and political reaction in this country.

[5] J. Stefan Dupre and Sanford A. Lakoff, *Science and the Nation: Policy and Politics* (Englewood Cliffs, N.J.: Prentice-Hall, 1962), Ch. 2, give an interesting account of the politics of defense research-and-development activities.

The controversy over how to meet the Russian challenge brought the conflicting political interests into sharp relief. The military services wanted the major space activities to remain in the Pentagon, though interservice rivalry led the Air Force ultimately to support a civilian establishment. Several existing federal agencies indicated their suitability for executing a space program. Scientists called for a total reevaluation of the place of the natural sciences in American education; many feared that scientific education and research in general would suffer from overemphasis on a new space program. Congress, alarmed at evidence of Soviet technical superiority, initiated a full-scale inquiry into our defense program.

In the final outcome, all parties gained something. The military was assured control over the space projects deemed essential to its missions. Research budgets for the National Science Foundation and other agencies were rapidly increased, and funds were made available for graduate training in the sciences. An independent civilian agency, the National Aeronautics and Space Administration, was established with a broad program for investigation of outer space. At the insistence of Senator Lyndon Johnson, a National Space Council was set up, consisting of top-level officials in the government and aimed at securing a comprehensive and highly visible space program. Subsequently, appropriations for NASA increased spectacularly, from $700 million the first year to over $5 billion per year after 1963. In a national emergency, science again proved to have irresistible political appeal.

Scientists, public officials, and journalists occasionally voice concern over the size of our space effort, pointing out that we have yet to achieve a balanced and comprehensive total science program. They ask whether devoting the same funds to foreign aid or other scientific-research programs might not more effectively enhance our international position and our

Another Launching

The space program received heavy federal support after Sputnik, but the crisis in Vietnam and in our cities led to cutbacks in space spending in the late 1960's.

Dobbins in the Boston *Herald-Traveler*

national security. But the space program goes ahead, both a testimony to American faith in technology and an indication of the difficulty of developing public policy for our greatest resource, human creativity.

MAINTAINING OUR NATURAL RESOURCES: THE NEW CONSERVATION

Maintaining an adequate resource base is a massive undertaking. By 1965 we were taking from the earth 2½ times more bituminous coal than we had been in 1900; 3 times more copper; 3½ times more iron ore; 4 times more zinc; 26 times more natural gas; and 30 times more crude oil. Under the pressure of an expanding economy, the supply of "exhaustible" resources (ore and oil, for example, take thousands of years to replace) is being reduced at an accelerating rate. Between 1900 and 1950, 40 billion barrels of petroleum were taken from the land. Between 1950 and 1966 our insatiable American appetite required 43 billion more. Even the "renewable" resources, such as timber, agricultural land, and water, are being drawn upon far more rapidly than they are being replaced.[6] Our inventory of saw timber, for example, is being used 40 percent faster than its annual growth rate. Older resource-management policies strove primarily to "lock up" existing supplies; today, however, our policies emphasize acquiring new materials in time to replace dwindling supplies of old ones, achieving cheaper extraction and fuller use of known resources, and making materials work harder and longer, such as by giving scarce resources a "second life" (recycling water or reclaiming scrap metal). Each of these efforts depends ultimately on science and technology.

Advances in science and technology constantly alter the materials available to us and our dependence on old stocks; at the same time they expand the base of usable resources. Sperm whales off Nantucket and buffalo on the Western plains were once vital resources for our ancestors, while the pools of petroleum under Texas, the iron ore of Minnesota, and the phosphate deposits of Florida were of no value. Now the virtual disappearance of the buffalo causes no economic pain, while the supply of petroleum directly affects national security.

More traditional resource-management policies reinforce and supplement the support of research and development. The stock of timber must be replenished through continual reforestation. It is desirable that worn-out

[6] The most comprehensive study of United States national resources of this generation is the five-volume report of the President's Materials Policy Commission published in 1952. In 1963 this was supplemented by the projections included in Hans H. Landsberg, Leonard L. Fischman, and Joseph L. Fisher, *Resources in America's Future.*

Our Machine Civilization: History's First and Last?

We are quickly approaching the point where, if machine civilization should, because of some catastrophe, stop functioning, it will probably never again come into existence. It is not difficult to see why this should be so if we compare the resources and procedures of the past with those of the present. Our ancestors had available large resources of high-grade ores and fuels that could be processed by the most primitive technology—crystals of copper and pieces of coal that lay on the surface of the earth, easily mined iron, and petroleum in generous pools reached by shallow drilling. Now we must dig huge caverns and follow seams ever further underground, drill oil wells thousands of feet deep, many of them under the bed of the ocean, and find ways of extracting elements from the leanest of ores—procedures that are possible only because of our highly complex modern techniques, and practical only to an intricately mechanized culture which could not have been developed without the high-grade [fossil fuel] resources that are so rapidly vanishing. Perhaps there is possible a sort of halfway station, in which retrogression stops short of a complete extinction of civilization, but even this is not pleasant to contemplate.

From Harrison Brown, foreign secretary of the National Academy of Sciences, *The Challenge of Man's Future*, 1956.

farm and grazing lands be reclaimed and that byproducts from oil and mineral extraction be put to use. Control of water pollution and soil erosion is necessary to reduce the pressure on finding new sources. For an increasingly urban population, wildlife havens, forests, lakes, and rivers are important for recreation.

As in the case of research management, the policies involved in managing our land, water, and mineral resources are the product of political subsystems involving private interest groups, congressional committees, and federal departments. The relative influence of the several parties is in turn a product of historical, technical, and political factors.

The Politics of Land Use: The Local Interest Group at Work

The politics of land mangement is organized around one very simple fact: the federal government is the nation's biggest landowner. Except for lands retained by the original thirteen states and by Texas, most of the territory the United States acquired in its continental expansion was once "public domain"—the property of the federal government. By sales to gain revenue, by grants to states, railroads, and other private parties, and by preemption and homestead laws that donated land to settlers, Washington transferred over 1 billion acres to other ownership. Today 765 million acres are still in federal hands. This comprises 48 percent of all the land of the eleven West-

Figure 20–1   The Uses of Federally Owned Land

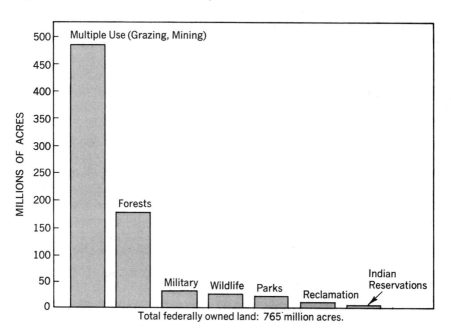

Total federally owned land: 765 million acres.

SOURCE: U.S. General Services Administration; annual report, *Inventory Report on Real Property Owned by the United States Throughout the World, 1965.*

ern states and 98 percent of Alaska. Figure 20–1 shows that more than half this acreage is multiple-use land (primarily open for grazing and mineral development) administered by the Bureau of Land Management in the Department of the Interior. Most of the rest (186 million acres) is set aside for national forests. Reclamation areas, national parks and historic sites, wildlife refuges, Indian reservations, and military uses account collectively for another 94 million federal acres.[7] Figure 20–2 shows that the largest landholder by far among the federal agencies is the Department of the Interior; second, but far behind, is the Department of Agriculture. The fact of government ownership generates a continuing set of political issues: How should government develop these areas? What regulatory policies should it have for private timber and mining operations on its land? Should it continue to function as a landlord at all?

Two great federal agencies, the Department of the Interior and the Department of Agriculture, are responsible for the majority of public-land activities. Around them cluster important private interest groups who make their living from the public lands, as well as private landowners, such as

[7] Current figures are from *Statistical Abstract of the United States* and U.S. Department of the Interior, *Public Land Statistics* (1966).

farmers, whose activities are strongly influenced by the department's activities. These groups, especially in the West, and especially in land managed by the Department of the Interior, tend to dominate policy-making about the public domain.

Established in 1849, the Department of the Interior views itself as the "custodian of natural resources" for the United States. Its concerns range from fish and wildlife conservation to minerals research, but its principal responsibility in the resource field is the management of grazing, mineral, and timber rights on public lands.

The basic law providing for the control and rehabilitation of the topsoil of the "federal range" is the Taylor Grazing Act of 1934. Under this law, the Interior Department's Bureau of Land Management establishes grazing districts in the Western states, calculates their capacity to support livestock, and issues permits to stockmen.

Mining laws dating back a hundred years provide a *location* system for metallic and a few nonmetallic ores, by which private individuals can work and eventually acquire title to land on which they discover mineral deposits,

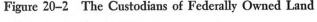

Figure 20–2 The Custodians of Federally Owned Land

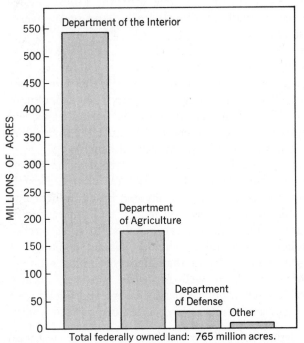

Total federally owned land: 765 million acres.

SOURCE: U.S. General Services Administration; annual report, *Inventory Report on Real Property Owned by the United States Throughout the World*, 1965.

and a *leasing* system for the private extraction of oil, gas, coal, and phosphates. Private timber operations on public land are authorized by competitive bidding and are under supervision designed to assure a sustained yield.

The activities of the Department of Agriculture are complementary to and sometimes competitive with those of the Interior Department. The Forest Service, established in 1905 as part of the Department of Agriculture, manages the timber, mineral, and other resources of 154 national forests. While its activities closely parallel those of the National Park Service in the Interior Department, sharp differences in administrative philosophy and operating techniques exist between the two organizations. Tense confrontations have occurred on such matters as timber operations, mining leases, and sales of public land. Interior's Park Service rangers and their counterparts in the Forest Service have been known to engage in pitched battles with fists and sticks.

The Department of Agriculture also maintains major conservation programs for private land resources. The Soil Conservation Service provides technical assistance to individual farmers in the conservation of their land and water, through a grass-roots organization of three thousand local districts. These districts, directed by boards of local farmers, include over 90 percent of existing American farms. In the same way, the Forest Service provides technical assistance to small woodland owners. And state governments provide similar assistance.

Finally, federal and state governments work together in land use through the land-grant college system. This system, which focuses on the teaching of agriculture, engineering, and home economics, has underwritten the development of many of the nation's state universities and agricultural-experiment stations. Its local extension services, aided by federal funds, and the experiment stations provide close communication among farmers, specialists from both levels of government, and educational centers.

The key institution in the politics of land is the special-purpose local district. This is the instrument through which private interests—the clientele to be served by these districts—exercise a continuing and heavy influence on the programs. They are able to do this because federal and state agencies, by statute and administrative rule, tend to place members of these interest groups in positions of official responsibility on local district committees.[8] By doing so, federal and state agencies ensure the support of interest groups—and thus the support of Congress as well—for their activities, because satisfied customers in soil conservation, timber-management policies, and grazing are likely to be important members of congressional constituencies,

---

[8] For an incisive political analysis of the operations of these local district committees in the Department of Agriculture, see Morton Grodzins, Separate Statement, "Review of the Farm Committee System," United States Department of Agriculture, Study Committee (November 1962) (mimeographed).

"Boy, we could develop that into some fine stumps."

The absence of a strong public consensus on conservation has allowed private groups great freedom to exploit the public domain.

From *Herblock's Here and Now*,
Simon & Schuster, 1955

especially in the West. But the pattern of local districts and committees also makes for tension among national groups intent on a more vigorous conservation practice, professional administrators within the agencies, and the users or direct beneficiaries of the program. In many instances, it appears that the real decision makers in land-management policies are the interest groups involved: the farmers, stockmen, and timbermen.

The influence of the clientele working through the advisory system is the principal factor behind the continued division of federal responsibilities between Interior and Agriculture. For example, in the Bureau of Land Management, the clientele and the congressmen have made league against the bureaucrat, so grazing policy is shaped principally by a small minority of Western stockmen. Representatives of stockmen make up the district, state, and national advisory boards and maintain close contact with congressmen from the range states; and these congressmen serve on the committees and subcommittees overseeing the work of the Bureau of Land Management. The stockmen and congressmen thus converge to keep regulation and supervision at a minimum and to assure that no powerful administrative agency threatens them. "The close collaboration and agreement between stockmen's associations, the advisory boards, certain Western Congressmen and some administrators has at times been an invincible combination.[9]

The clientele-oriented character of land-management politics has con-

[9] Phillip O. Foss, *Politics and Grass: The Administration of Grazing on the Public Domain* (Seattle: University of Washington Press, 1960), provides the most recent political analysis of land politics on the range. The citation is from p. 202.

cerned some students of government for at least a generation, especially those who advocate strengthening the supervisory and executive functions of the President. Since 1937 several proposals have been suggested for introducing uniform policy criteria in the handling of the public domain and the provision of technical assistance to private landowners as well as for consolidating research and information services. All the proposals for reorganization—to establish a Department of Conservation, to establish an Agricultural Resources Conservation Service within the Department of Agriculture, to place the Forest Service in the Department of the Interior, to create a Federal Land Corporation, or to create a Federal Land Review Board—basically aim at consolidating all the major land-management activities under one authority.

To date none of these proposals has been adopted. Understandably, land-interest groups prefer a highly decentralized organization, which assures them of many routes of access to decision makers and a strong voice in policy matters. As for the agencies, they rarely favor the merger of their enterprises with those in other departments; so they have joined forces with clients and congressmen alike to preserve their separate identities.

Water Politics: The Predominance of Federal Executive Agencies

Like the land-management programs, the public activities devoted to assuring the nation of a sufficient water supply are the product of a special political subsystem involving users, federal and state bureaucrats, and legislators, all vying with one another but united in opposing comprehensive executive direction. The water bureaucracies, however, proceed from positions of much greater strength than their counterparts in land management: the sense of agency identity and professionalization is somewhat stronger, their relations with Congress are more harmonious, and the interests with which they deal are more divided. Water has many simultaneous uses in an increasingly urban nation. Hence a number of groups with quite conflicting interests in water development are likely to cluster around a specific project, with no single interest predominating. In such instances it often falls to the public agencies involved to reconcile different objectives in the development of water resources.

Concepts of appropriate water policy have changed radically in the twentieth century. Until thirty years ago the development of water resources proceeded on a project-by-project basis, usually with a single predominant objective. Dams were built and reservoirs created to control floods, supply water for canals, produce public power, or irrigate farm land. With the completion of the Hoover Dam in 1930, however, the concept of the multiple-purpose storage project was born. The act authorizing the Hoover Dam included as its objectives the prevention of floods, the improvement of navigation, the generation of electricity, and the reclamation of land. It firmly established the principle of comparing costs to benefits and using the resulting ratio to measure the desirability of a project.

In succeeding years new standards for sound water policy have emerged. One is the concept of basin-wide development—a system of works, in place of a single project, to coordinate water use for an entire river basin—first applied to the Miami River of Ohio after a devastating flood in 1913, but not instituted elsewhere until the 1930's. Another is the integration of water development with land-use planning, with provision for unified administration.[10]

These concepts, however, are more often acknowledged in principle than adopted in practice. The large multipurpose project is accepted doctrine for all public agencies in the field: almost five hundred such dams have been built in the United States. But the establishment of basin- and region-wide programs relating land and water resources under unified management has been much more difficult.

The lag between concepts and practice is due to the nature of water politics and to the problems involved. Four great federal agencies now share responsibility for water resources; each has different traditions, a different basis of political support, and different policy emphases. Conflicts among these agencies, and among the several congressional committees that oversee their activities, have hampered efforts to adopt integrated planning. In addition, the development of comprehensive basin programs requires resolution of important constitutional questions of federal versus state powers.

The oldest agency concerned with water development is the Army Corps of Engineers. The COE is both a civil and a military engineering and construction agency, responsible since 1879 for flood prevention and since the early 1880's for national internal-improvement programs and for public works for harbors and navigable rivers. Since 1901 local government, civic, and business interests—organized in the National Rivers and Harbors Congress—have worked closely with the corps in identifying and assigning priorities.[11]

Because of the popularity of COE projects with local constituencies, congressmen place special importance on the work of the corps. Each year's rivers-and-harbors appropriation bill is the result of intensive log-rolling among individual members seeking to secure their share from the

---

[10] A full description of these concepts is provided in Roscoe C. Martin, *River Basin Administration and the Delaware* (Syracuse, N.Y.: Syracuse University Press, 1960).
[11] The most comprehensive study of the Corps of Engineers is Arthur Maass, *The Muddy Waters, the Army Engineers and the Nation's Rivers* (Cambridge, Mass.: Harvard University Press, 1951).

pork barrel of suggested projects. The corps works to maintain close legislative relations, often referring to itself as "the engineer consultants to, and contractors for, the Congress of the United States."

The second major water-resources agency is the Bureau of Reclamation in the Department of the Interior. Established in 1902, it is responsible for conservation, development, and utilization of land and water resources in seventeen Western states; hence it focuses on irrigation, power, and other uses besides flood control.

Operating in areas where strong local pressure groups frequently do not exist, the bureau has been more responsive to regional multipurpose approaches than has the COE. It has also been prepared to impose more federal regulations and requirements on power and water users than has the corps and to use different formulas for the calculation of costs and benefits.

A more recent entry into the field is the Department of Agriculture. Since 1936 the department has been authorized to seek means for controlling and using water upstream near its sources. Since 1944 it has been empowered to make upstream installations for watershed protection through small reservoir projects (in contrast to the larger COE and Reclamation Bureau dams).

Finally, the Tennessee Valley Authority, created in 1933, represents the nation's only major experiment in comprehensive regional planning under unified administration. A public corporation possessing considerable financial and organizational autonomy, TVA is concerned with the general development of the entire Tennessee Valley area. Its operations cover seven states and include thirty-one dams and hydroelectric plants and a thousand miles of navigable water. Flood control, navigation improvement, and electric power are TVA's major concerns, but, through a network of agreements with state and local officials, it embraces a number of other programs. It operates the Muscle Shoals fertilizer and munitions plant (established as a First World War government installation) and has developed an active fertilizer research-and-demonstration program to improve regional farm practices. It has a large-scale forestry program and extensive recreational and health programs. It collaborates with state and local agencies in planning and development work. Because the power needs of the valley have exceeded what is available from hydroelectric sources, TVA has built large, coal-fired electric generating plants and is now constructing nuclear-powered plants as well. Supporters of TVA have hailed it as America's best example of modern progressive democracy at work; its detractors have called its programs socialistic.[12]

[12] The classic defense of TVA is David E. Lilienthal, *TVA: Democracy on the March* (New York: Harper & Row, 1944). For an interesting account of the public-power controversy in the 1950's, see Aaron Wildavsky, *Dixon-Yates* (New Haven, Conn.: Yale University Press, 1962).

The existence of these four agencies, each with different policies for water development, has meant continuing conflict over water use, plans, and projects. The Corps of Engineers and the Bureau of Reclamation often compete for the right to plan, design, and construct the same downstream project. Both are critical of the effectiveness of Agriculture's upstream program. All three are suspicious of TVA's program when it is presented as a model for the other major regions of the nation. In addition, because the development of larger interstate rivers poses knotty problems in allocating the available water supply among the states involved, state governments have insisted on the right to be consulted on federal programs and to construct projects of their own.

After years of more-or-less-open warfare, some interagency coordination did emerge. In 1944, under pressure from the Missouri States Committee, the COE and the Bureau of Reclamation concluded a pact for the development of the Missouri Basin. The Pick-Sloan Plan, named after the chief of the Engineers and the commissioner of Reclamation, was a combination of projects and programs previously prepared separately by the two agencies. It included the corps' proposals for flood control and navigational works on the main stem of the river and the bureau's irrigation and power projects upstream. Although later criticized as no real plan at all, but "a division of projects, each agency agreeing to forego the privilege of criticizing projects assigned by agreement to the other," the compact served to bring together seven federal organizations and ten states in continuous working relations to form the Missouri Basin Inter-Agency Committee.[18]

Similar arrangements of voluntary interagency collaboration have been adopted in most other major river basins, but none has resulted in a comprehensive development program. One effort, the Arkansas-White-Red Basins Interagency Committee, involved six federal agencies and eight states in five years of study and planning between 1950 and 1955. The committee was plagued by disagreements, and the final "plan" simply incorporated with little change separate projects already formulated by the participants.

While interagency committees have led to improved interstate and interagency coordination, they have invariably been handicapped by the lack of formal decision-making authority. Not only interagency, but state-federal and interstate conflicts have contributed to this deficiency. The inability of the committees to coordinate budgets has made investigation and study efforts difficult.

An exception to this bleak picture is the Delaware River Basin Compact, a combined multistate-federal compact for the comprehensive development of the Delaware River Basin in which the states and the federal government have delegated a great deal of power to the commission

[18] Martin, *op. cit.*, Ch. 11.

in the river-management area. For example, during the drought in the summer of 1965, the commission was able to supply an additional 300 million gallons of water a day to New York City, despite the fact that the river was low, without getting permission from the various state governments.

The Water Resources Planning Act, enacted in 1965, is the most recent important effort to achieve "comprehensive and coordinated" conservation and development of the nation's water resources. This act provides for the establishment of river-basin commissions and for allotment grants for state planning activities. (The first river-basin commission—for the Pacific Northwest—was created early in 1967.) The act also established the Water Resources Council, composed of the Cabinet Secretaries with related programs and the chairman of the Federal Power Commission.[14] The real achievement of the council so far has been improved budget coordination. It remains to be seen whether the lack of central authority, the necessity for operating on consensus, will once again prove to be a fatal flaw.

So far, proposals for strong, unified *administration* of river-basin development have not been acceptable to Congress. The TVA experiment, although widely praised in planning and conservation circles and politically popular within the valley, has faced stiff opposition from private power companies, from those who view the authority as a forerunner of socialism, and from the other federal agencies. Efforts to combine the national water programs of the major federal agencies have failed. The agencies continue their essentially separate ways, each equipped with strong professional traditions, each supported by different interest groups and different congressional committees, and each persuaded of the superiority of its particular approach. The Delaware River Basin Compact and the Water Resources Council, however, offer hope that this may not always be so.

The Politics of Nonrenewable Resources: The Preeminence of the States

The role of the state governments is more important in the management of nonrenewable resources—especially oil, coal, and gas—than in land and water politics. Though the federal government controls the extraction of minerals found under national public lands, engages in substantial research activities, enforces some interstate regulation, and makes international trade policies, its responsibilities are more limited here than in other areas. The conservation and use of metallic and nonmetallic minerals and energy fuels are determined by the marketplace or by state regulatory policies.

At present, the most important and complex set of regulatory policies deals with the oil industry. Petroleum production involves two economic

---

[14] The original act included the Secretary of the Interior, the Secretary of Agriculture, the Secretary of the Army, and the Secretary of Health, Education, and Welfare. Since then, the Secretary of Transportation has been added.

problems. Existing wells can deliver quantities of oil many times larger than the demand for oil in a given year; this surplus, if not controlled, wastes the commodity and leads to ruinous price competition. On the other hand, total known reserves are considerably smaller than the long-run future demand, so the discovery of new oil pools is essential.

Most of the oil-producing states provide for oil conservation through a system of *proration*, first developed in Oklahoma in 1915. The states assign production quotas to individual wells and regulate the drilling of new wells over known oil pools. The states, with the consent of Congress, cooperate voluntarily through the Interstate Oil Compact Commission. The federal government has made illegal the shipment of oil produced in violation of state orders. More important, by determining the amount of oil that can be imported into the country, Washington in effect controls the total American oil supply.

Critics of the present system argue that the state-dominated, industry-sponsored regulations, while effective in stabilizing prices in periods of lower demand, neither assure the best long-run conservation practices nor protect the consumer in time of prosperity. They argue that the regulations now favor the large producers and do not adequately provide a continuing supply in times of national emergency. The net result, they suggest, is the creation of a "favored" industry rather than sound public policy.

But proposals for a more active federal role and stricter conservation practices have met with little success. On the contrary, in the 1950's the states enlarged their sphere of influence. When technical advances made it possible to drill for oil deposits under the sea, the oil-producing states laid claim to lands three to twelve miles off shore. The Supreme Court ruled that the tidelands were part of the national domain, but Congress enacted legislation giving prerogatives for regulation and royalties chiefly to Texas, California, and Louisiana. Thus the states remain the chosen instruments for the management of oil resources.

Except for federal stockpiling of critical materials and federal and state regulation of working and safety conditions in mines, the conservation of nonrenewable resources other than oil essentially remains the responsibility of the private sector of the economy. The industries continue to prefer to make arrangements at the state level, keeping regulators as close to home as possible.

CONCLUSION: THE ENDLESS FRONTIER

The United States has no comprehensive national plan for scientific exploration or for resource conservation and management. In the past century we have experienced a series of "conservation crises"—all relieved by the arrival of timely innovations. In 1870, when our forest reserves were being rapidly stripped and thousands of acres were left desolate, coal overtook wood as the prime energy source. By the Second World War, when we had almost exhausted our easily available coal reserves, liquid and gaseous fuels took over two-thirds of all energy requirements. While our waste of land through erosion and poor grazing and farming practices has been prodigious, research has so multiplied agricultural productivity that we possess large and continuing farm surpluses. Though occasional water shortages occur in rapidly growing urban areas or in semiarid regions, research in purification and saline-water conversion promises additional water supplies.

Nevertheless, profound transformations in our resource policies have occurred. We have inaugurated broad programs in the better management of renewable resources and the proper extraction of nonrenewable ones.

A New Plateau in Scientific-Technical Knowledge

For the first time in history it is possible to say that the lack of technical knowledge is no longer a major barrier to solving man's material problems.

This does not mean that the physical knowledge is already in hand for all problems of agriculture, energy, exploitation of water and mineral resources, pollution, overpopulation, or any of the other problems that affect man's welfare. It does mean that man now has the tools to seek and find solutions to such problems and has already demonstrated in each category that solutions are possible.

The limitations on the development and application of technological solutions for material problems ... stem [instead] from the cost of the research; the scarcity of scientists and engineers; the cost, relative to other uses for scarce resources, of applying scientific knowledge; the cultural, social, and political barriers to new technology within a society; the political disinterest of the scientific "haves" for the "have-nots"; and the difficulty of making the essential judgments of priority because of the uncertainty of the benefits that will result from each choice.

... [Nonetheless,] a situation in which science and technology can be applied successfully to solve almost any physical problem is a fundamentally new situation with potentially far-reaching implications.... Does this condition carry with it the imperative for the scientifically advanced nations to devote more of their scientific resources to the problems of mankind in other countries? Or, to remove the question from the moral plane, can science and technology more fully and successfully be harnessed to solve the physical problems that contribute to or are the causes of international tension?

From Eugene B. Skolnikoff, former staff assistant to the special assistant to the President for science and technology, *Science, Technology, and American Foreign Policy,* 1967.

We have made great strides in adopting effective land, water, timber, and mineral conservation measures and in assuring an increasingly urban nation of access to nature for recreational purposes.

Yet such is the nature of our political system and our economic base that these programs have rarely achieved their stated goal of the prudent use of existing materials to secure their long-run availability at low cost. In the view of professional conservationists, resource politics still prevents the best applications of our natural wealth, and Americans remain profligate in their attitudes toward the earth and its bounty. The basic reason for our casual approach to resource management, however, is the fact that we continue to live on a frontier. The natural frontier of the West is closed, but Vannevar Bush's "endless frontier of science" appears to offer unlimited abundance.

The management and support of research and development have thus become matters of great importance to the nation. We are turning to science and technology for help not only on the extension of our resources but on problems ranging from urban decay to air pollution, from the prevention of crime to the modification of the weather. In the minds of most Americans, technological ingenuity and scientific creativity remain the ultimate answer to the question of how we propose to support—and perhaps also to save—our civilization.

SUMMARY

This chapter has examined the three major roles of the government in managing this country's resource base: financing and overseeing scientific research-and-development programs; directly managing resources such as land and water; and regulating private development of other resources. These roles are in large part determined by several political subsystems that shape our scientific and conservation policies.

Government support for science and technology, though dating back to the nineteenth century, became a major enterprise only with the Second World War. The equilibrium between the private and public spheres in our scientific research-and-development activities has been based primarily on government financing of research carried out by private industry and universities.

Three major interest groups compete to shape our national research enterprise. First are the scientists, who emerged on the political scene during the Second World War. After being alienated from the government during the McCarthy era, scientists were welcomed back into the fold in 1957, and they are now responsible for a substantial advisory and coordinating apparatus with direct access to the President. Their institutional roots in the government include units such as the President's Science Advisory Committee, the Federal Council for Science and Technology, and the Office of Science and Technology, all helping to make policy for scientific and engineering research.

The second group influencing scientific and engineering research policies consists of highly placed civil servants; they argue that regular administrative and budgetary channels should take precedence over advisory committees composed of scientists in establishing and running scientific programs.

A third source of influence on research-and-development policies is composed of military leaders, private groups closely associated with the military, and business enterprises heavily dependent on government defense contracts. This group has a vested interest in maintaining high levels of defense spending and defense-related research.

Other political considerations affect research-and-development policies, and even ostensibly "technical" decisions—whether to replace one kind of weapons system with another, where to locate new space and defense research centers, and so on—are matters of vital political controversy.

Research programs to develop new technical and natural resources must be supplemented by more traditional conservation of our basic resources: land, water, and nonrenewable resources such as oil. Three types of group are active in the politics of all the basic resources: local interest groups, federal executive agencies, and the states. But, since the relative influence of each group varies with each type of resource, land, water, and nonrenewable resources each present a distinctive pattern of politics.

A key element in the politics of land management is the fact that the federal government is the nation's biggest landowner. Public-land activities are administered principally by two federal agencies—the Bureau of Land Management in the Department of the Interior and the Forest Service in the Department of Agriculture. But in fact the dominant force in land-use politics comes from the private interest groups—Western stockmen, farmers, and timbermen—who are affected by the activities of the federal agencies. These clientele groups ally with congressmen to keep federal regulation and supervision by executive agencies to a minimum.

In water politics, on the other hand, the predominant force is the federal executive agencies—the Army Corps of Engineers, the Bureau of Reclamation in the Department of the Interior, the Department of Agriculture, and the Tennessee Valley Authority. These four agencies have often conflicted with one another, and even today they tend to continue in separate directions, each with a strong *esprit de corps*, each supported by different interest groups and different congressional committees.

In the politics of nonrenewable resources, the state governments are predominant, and they play a major role in maintaining regulatory policies, particularly for oil. The predominance of the states in managing these resources has prevented a more active federal role and has hampered stricter conservation practices. For nonrenewable resources other than oil, conservation remains basically a responsibility of the private sector.

Overriding all these political patterns is the public conviction that American science and technology can solve any material shortage or crisis in resource management. To date, that belief has been upheld.

GOVERNMENT AND WELFARE IN THE AFFLUENT SOCIETY

21

A major change of the twentieth century is that a majority of the American people now expect the government to promote and safeguard their personal welfare. They want public education; health, housing, and consumer protection; minimum benefits as workers; and financial aid in old age, or when unemployed, disabled, or in need of family assistance. People also expect an effort to eliminate poverty. These welfare activities of the government represent a major area of government benefits for the American people. What ideological conflicts do these activities generate? What are the distinctive problems in these areas? How has the politics of welfare affected the level and types of benefits offered under each activity?

The classic pattern of colonial America and the early Republic was one of individual and family self-reliance. An individual was expected to "stand on his own feet," except for periods of dependency—childhood, old age, or physical infirmity—when he relied largely on family aid. Town and county payments to the poor were almost everywhere niggardly; and the eligibility requirements for aid were harsh, as the politically dominant groups felt that generosity would encourage laziness and lack of thrift. There was much debate over whether there should be "indoor" care in almshouses or work colonies to put indigents to profitable social use or "farming out" of indigents to individuals, even by auction.

In the nineteenth century, state institutions were established for care of orphans, the blind, deaf, and mute, and tubercular and mental patients; but funds for these institutions too were usually niggardly. In addition, there were the beginnings of modern legislation to protect workers, and state and local programs for aid to the indigent were expanded.

A great break from the traditional system of personal and family responsibility came with the development of the public-school system in the nineteenth century. A child, however indigent his parents were, could get an education at the expense of those who could pay. Moreover, the American venture in public education was the first move toward welfare services for the benefit of the middle as well as the lower class, which was to become a prominent feature of twentieth-century legislation.

REASONS FOR TWENTIETH-CENTURY LEGISLATION

How can we explain the dramatic growth of welfare legislation for the benefit of the lower and middle classes in the twentieth century? The basic cause is that the nation has moved from self-employment in pioneer, rural conditions to the dependent employment relationships of an industrialized, urbanized society. By 1960, $5 out of every $6 of personal income in this country came from wages and salaries. Today, when employment opportunities contract through recession, automation, or changes in the products of industry, unemployment and an earlier retirement date are the frequent result. Moreover, technical qualifications for employment are constantly changing. These factors have created problems of youth employment, adult retraining, and income maintenance during unemployment or after employment age. Urbanization, which takes people away from the resources of the land and makes them face regular payments for rent, utilities, and food, heightens the dependency of people on regular monetary income. In addition, the increased mobility of the population has impaired reliance on families and destroyed the expectation of aid from neighbors.

As the middle class has become conscious of its own insecurity, its attitude toward the underprivileged has changed. More dependent now on complex and interrelated environmental factors, a majority of the middle class has come to believe that poverty is the result of unfavorable environment rather than shiftlessness. In the late nineteenth century, harsh factory conditions and exploitation of the worker set off a wave of humanitarian sentiment; and, in the early twentieth century, Jane Addams and others attacked slum conditions. The Great Depression of 1929–33, which brought unemployment to 10 million and put 18 million on relief, gave added weight to the view that men were not always responsible for their plight. Even later, when prosperity made this a "land of plenty"— an "affluent society," [1]—it was recognized that as much as one-fifth of our population belonged to what Michael Harrington called "the other America." [2] They have had no place in the system of American opportunity, or have lost their place, and are caught in the grip of poverty from generation to generation. This situation of poverty amidst plenty led to President Johnson's announcement of a "war on poverty," which expanded old welfare programs and established new ones as well.

The public has gradually come to depend on government solutions for problems that cannot be solved individually. Americans learned in the Depression that property accumulation by individuals and private insurance could not adequately protect most people against unemployment, old age, and widowhood; the Social Security Act of 1935 demonstrated how government might provide everyone with at least a minimum of protection against need. New knowledge about mental illness, concern about opportunities for the handicapped, and realization of the role of education and reeducation have motivated searches for solutions to problems that until recently have not been attacked seriously. Problems such as air and water pollution and the dangers of highly potent drugs have increased public awareness that in an industrialized and urbanized society, public solutions are often the only means of protecting individual welfare.

Under Presidents Kennedy and Johnson, the concept of "public welfare" has been broadened to include more than satisfaction of basic material necessities. President Johnson, for example, has spoken of the need to ensure a certain "quality of life" in the Great Society, and public-welfare programs now include highway beautification and grants for the performing arts and for the development of appreciation of the humanities.

[1] David M. Potter, *People of Plenty: Economic Abundance and the American Character* (Chicago: University of Chicago Press, 1954), and John K. Galbraith, *The Affluent Society* (Cambridge, Mass.: Houghton Mifflin, 1958).

[2] Michael Harrington, *The Other America: Poverty in the United States* (New York: Macmillan, 1962).

CONFLICTS OF INTERESTS AND IDEOLOGIES

Despite the increasing trend toward welfare legislation, these programs remain politically controversial because they engender many deep conflicts of interest. First, class differences play a central role in these conflicts. Many people in comfortable economic positions in society are antagonistic to a "welfare state" and to the tax burdens it creates. Those without minimum economic resources, on the other hand, will seek as much government aid as possible.

The balance of power has usually been held by the American middle class, those with incomes today, for example, between $10,000 and $25,000. The Social Security Act of 1935, the largest single advance in welfare legislation, for instance, came about when the middle class, particularly the aged, suddenly became conscious of its economic insecurity and exerted its powerful political influence to support President Roosevelt's welfare proposal. Similarly, the strong appeal of public expenditures for education in this country stems from the fact that public education represents a basic goal of the middle class. The middle class, where affected, has also favored welfare programs based on the insurance principle—where the recipient has an automatic *right* to payments—rather than on a test of means, which many consider an indignity. On the other hand, the middle class is often inattentive to the problems of the very poor, such as provision of new housing for the poor when slum areas are cleared. The movement toward a "welfare state" is further checked by the low level of participation in politics of the lower-income groups.[3]

Second, the rural-urban cleavage is significant in welfare legislation. Urban populations have a greater consciousness of personal insecurity in an industrialized, urbanized society than do rural populations. Welfare programs have traditionally been hampered by the overrepresentation of rural areas in state legislatures and in both chambers of Congress, particularly in the House. The urban gain in representation in the state legislatures and the House of Representatives as a result of *Baker* v. *Carr* and *Wesberry* v. *Sanders*[4] may therefore lead to more social legislation.

Third, the interests and attitudes of functional groups are involved in almost all proposals for welfare legislation. Thus, teachers are interested in more appropriations for education, social workers want more attention paid to problems of dependency, and many doctors want to avoid certain

[3] See Paul Felix Lazarsfeld, Bernard Berelson, and Hazel Gaudet, *The People's Choice* (New York: Duell, Sloan, & Pearce, 1944), p. 145, and E. E. Schattschneider, *The Semisovereign People: A Realist's View of Democracy in America* (New York: Holt, Rinehart & Winston, 1961), Ch. 2.

[4] See p. 385 as well as pp. 841–43 of the national, state, and local edition.

A Conservative Critique of Government Welfare

Let us ... not blunt the noble impulses of mankind by reducing charity to a mechanical operation of the federal government. Let us, by all means, encourage those who are fortunate and able to care for the needs of those who are unfortunate and disabled. But let us do this in a way that is conducive to the spiritual as well as material well being of our citizens—and in a way that will preserve their freedom. Let welfare be a private concern. Let it be promoted by individuals and families, by churches, private hospitals, religious service organizations, community charities and other institutions that have been established for this purpose. If the objection is raised that private institutions lack sufficient funds, let us remember that every penny the federal government does *not* appropriate for welfare is potentially available for private use—and without the overhead charge for processing the money through the federal bureaucracy. Indeed, high taxes, for which government Welfarism is so largely responsible, is the biggest obstacle to fund-raising by private charities.

Finally, if we deem public intervention necessary, let the job be done by local and state authorities that are incapable of accumulating the vast political power that is so inimical to our liberties.

From Senator Barry Goldwater of Arizona, *The Conscience of a Conservative*, 1960.

types of public medical program. Finally, sectional conflicts are sometimes present, as when Southern congressmen have opposed minimum-wage legislation and Northeastern congressmen have favored it.

These differences in interests lead to basic ideological conflicts over the way individual opportunity and security should be provided in the 1960's. Some people still prefer that responsibility for personal needs be placed firmly on the individual and the family, even though this means less opportunity and less security for many. Others believe opportunity and security for all are so important that society should make as complete arrangements for these as possible, even though this results in some decline in personal and family responsibility.

The balances struck between the contending philosophies vary for each area of legislation, reflecting the relative strengths of the forces involved. In education, the needs of the middle class, its belief in the value of education, and recent pressures for equal opportunities for Negroes have led to general acceptance of public responsibility for a system equal for all, irrespective of ability to pay. In housing, on the other hand, middle-class needs have been met by private housing, supported by government loan guarantees and insurance programs, and the tradition of private responsibility has limited public assumption of responsibility for housing

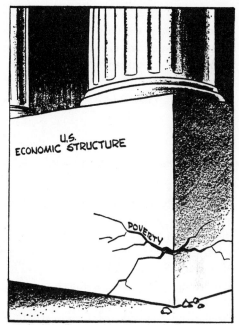

Flaw

Liberals have argued that government initiative in welfare is essential to protect the nation's economic structure.

Palmer in the Springfield, Mo., *Leader and Press*

for the poor. In health, the American Medical Association's opposition to social insurance has materially affected the balances between public and private responsibility. In most fields the government seeks to provide only minimum safeguards, leaving the individual with the responsibility for supplementing them.

A closely related ideological conflict occurs over where responsibility for public welfare should lie. Many people believe that responsibility belongs mainly with the state and local governments—a position consistent with favoring individual responsibility, since the state and local governments cannot provide as extensive a system of welfare protection as the national government can. For this very reason, those who favor increased public responsibility generally believe that public protection should be made uniform and adequate through national, rather than state and local, legislation. Public policy in this regard has also followed a middle path. Since state and local governments were already conducting welfare programs before the national government entered these fields, much national legislation has consisted of grants-in-aid. Cooperation among two or all three levels of government is, therefore, characteristic of much welfare legislation.

A third ideological conflict is over methods of public action. Some people advocate aid to individuals only on the basis of need. Such a policy entails some kind of means test—that is, a test of a person's ability to take care of himself—and a check by an administrative staff on the economic condition of those who solicit aid. Others advocate the use of the insurance principle, under which payments are made automatically to those in defined categories, such as the aged or the unemployed. Both approaches have been used in American legislation, occasionally—as in payments to the aged—in conjunction to solve a given problem. Sometimes, however, this divergence of views is reflected in conflicting recommendations for legislation.

THE EXPANDING NATIONAL ROLE IN WELFARE FUNCTIONS

Prior to the twentieth century the national government was a meager participant in welfare programs. Indeed, the great expansion of national legislation began with the New Deal. By now, however, the federal government has promoted welfare objectives through numerous regulations of commerce as, for example, in food and drug and minimum-wage legislation. Also, the income-tax amendment gave it an enormous source of funds for "the general welfare." Today, welfare activities continuously engage the attention of Congress; their importance in national affairs was emphasized by the creation of the Department of Health, Education, and Welfare in 1951, the Office of Economic Opportunity in 1964, and the Department of Housing and Urban Development in 1965. Still other departments, such as Labor and Agriculture, are engaged in numerous welfare programs. The diversity and complexity of welfare programs today at all three levels of government make their planning, coordination, and direction among the most baffling of national tasks.

The variety of programs carried out by the national, state, and local governments permits only a selective discussion of their general content, political aspects, and characteristic problems.

Education

The national government began supporting education in 1785, when Congress, in arranging for the disposal of Western lands, reserved 640 acres in every township for the endowment of schools. Almost a century later, in a day when higher education was oriented toward law, the ministry, and the classics, Congress stimulated practical and applied education by passing the Morrill Act of 1862, which provided for grants of land to each state for the establishment of colleges "to specialize in agriculture and mechanical arts."

When this land was gone the national government began to give monetary grants to aid education. Before the end of the nineteenth century it initiated monetary aids to the agricultural and mechanical colleges, including grants to aid the extension programs of these colleges. These grants have supported the largest program of adult education in the history of this nation—carried out mainly through county agents and home-demonstration agents. By the Smith-Hughes Act of 1917 Congress initiated grants-in-aid for vocational education in the public schools. More recently, grants-in-aid have been initiated for many special programs. Grants of money and food to support the school-lunch program began in the Depression. Acts passed in 1950 provided for grants for construction, maintenance, and operation of schools in districts where federal activities have resulted in a substantial increase in school population. In the near-panic following the Russians' launching of Sputnik in 1957, Congress—with the National Defense Education Act of 1958—launched a major program of grants to states for the improvement of educational programs in science, mathematics, and foreign languages. High unemployment rates led to the passage in 1961 of an act that provided for grants for training and retraining of unemployed youth and adults—an activity that has been expanded through President Johnson's War on Poverty. Higher education is aided by long-term loans for construction of dormitories and grants for construction of classrooms, libraries, and other academic facilities. The Higher Education Act of 1965 added scholarships and loans for college students and grants for developing institutions, library purchases, and other purposes.

General aid to elementary and secondary education has been a recurring issue in Congress from the Second World War onward, and by 1960 the Republican party was committed to national aid for school construction and the Democratic party to aid for both school construction and teachers' salaries. Repeatedly, however, general aid foundered on three issues. First, many legislators opposed it on general principle, fearing increased expenditures and national control of education. And chances for a coalition in favor of aid to education were further reduced by conflict on two other issues: aid to parochial schools and withholding aid from segregated schools. Among the lobbies in favor of general aid were the National Education Association, the AFL-CIO, the American Association of American Women, Americans for Democratic Action, the National Congress of Parents and Teachers, the Farmers' Union, the American Veterans Committee, and the American Association of School Administrators; opposed to aid were the United States Chamber of Commerce, the Southern States Industrial Council, the National Association of Manufacturers, the National Conference of State Taxpayers Association, and the Daughters of the American Revolution. Not surprisingly, Protestant organizations opposed aid to parochial schools; Catholic organizations favored it. Because the 1960 general-aid-to-education bill included a rider prohibiting aid to segregated schools, Southern Democrats allied with Republicans who opposed the bill on general principles, and it was defeated. A coalition of Catholics,

Republicans, and Southern Democrats defeated the aid-to-education bill of 1961.

Success came to proponents of aid with the Elementary-Secondary Education Act of 1965. The religious issue was skirted by a new approach, which emphasized aid to children rather than to schools. Aid would be given to school districts on the basis of number of children from low-income families in the area and to private-school children through the loan of federally financed textbooks and joint public-private services such as shared-time teaching and educational television. This approach won back the support of Northern Democrats from Catholic districts who had opposed the 1961 bill. Southern and conservative Republican opposition was insufficient to kill the bill; in fact, strong presidential leadership won the support of over 40 percent of the Southern Democrats.

Administration of the act has given rise to new problems of coordination between national and state educational agencies. Moreover, the national "guidelines" for progress toward school integration issuing from the Department of Health, Education, and Welfare and the Justice Department—combined with the provisions of the Civil Rights Act of 1964 barring national assistance to districts practicing discrimination—continue to breed controversy in Southern areas.

Workers' Welfare

Maintenance of an economy that provides employment opportunities at satisfactory wages and an educational system that trains all workers for employment are the most basic welfare programs for workers. These general policies are supplemented, however, by four special programs.

Safety and health

The oldest of these programs protects the safety and health of workers. Legislation for these purposes was a natural result of the Industrial Revolution in the nineteenth century. But revelations of horrible working conditions in the first decade of the twentieth century led to more vigorous measures. Ultimately, many states adopted comprehensive safety codes and authorized administrative agencies to issue regulations under the codes and to inspect premises to ensure compliance.

Early safety legislation is now supplemented by public efforts toward the vocational rehabilitation of those handicapped by disease, congenital defect, or accident. Congress enacted the Vocational Rehabilitation Act in 1920 and expanded the program in the Barden–La Follette Act of 1943. The program is administered by the Office of Vocational Rehabilitation in the Department of Health, Education, and Welfare. The office makes grants to the states, which usually administer their programs through an office of vocational rehabilitation in the state department of education. These offices provide many services, including physical examination to determine work capacity; medical, surgical, psychiatric, and hospital treatment; artificial limbs and hearing aids; job training; maintenance during training; occupational tools; and placement aid and adjustment aid after employment.

Child labor

Child-labor legislation is designed to protect the health and safety of children and to protect adult employment from competition. The states were the first to pass such legislation, giving attention primarily to hazardous and unhealthy work in places such as mines or tenement factories. National legislation was stalemated for several decades by Supreme Court decisions declaring such statutes unconstitutional.[5] However, changing constitutional attitudes led the Supreme Court to uphold national prohibitions on child labor in the Fair Labor Standards Act of 1938.[6]

Perhaps more effective than direct legislation prohibiting child labor have been two other kinds of public program that reduce the pressure for child employment. The first is the state compulsory-school-attendance laws. Although these laws have often allowed exceptions where children were needed to help support their families, they have expressed society's expectancy that children be in school, and they have been rigidly enforced. Second, the pressure for children to work is reduced by the aid-to-dependent-children program and the social-security program's distribution of survivors' benefits—both discussed later in the chapter—which provide assistance to needy families.

Length of the workweek

Legislation limiting the hours in the workweek was originally designed to protect the health of the worker; the laws were passed when a week of sixty or more hours was quite common and "keeping idle hands from mischief" was the moral defense of a "total" workday. Early legislation was limited to women or to men in particularly hazardous occupations; later, the states passed laws limiting the hours of all workers. During the first quarter of this century, the forty-eight-hour week became standard in industry. Then, when the Great Depression threw one-fourth to one-third of the working population out of jobs, a movement developed for a shorter workweek in order to spread employment around. The result was a provision for a forty-hour week in the Fair Labor Standards Act of 1938, with time-and-a-half wages required for overtime work.

---

[5] *Hammer* v. *Dagenhart*, 247 U.S. 251 (1918), and *Bailey* v. *Drexel Furniture Co.*, 259 U.S. 20 (1922).
[6] *United States* v. *Darby*, 312 U.S. 100 (1941).

Many labor contracts now provide for less than forty hours of work per week. In August 1961, officials of the AFL-CIO called for a thirty-five-hour week, and this objective is now a major item in labor's legislative program.

Minimum wages

Statutes providing minimum wage levels were first passed by states in the early part of this century. These statutes applied only to women, and their asserted justification was the protection of health and morals. In 1923, however, the Supreme Court held that a statute of Congress setting minimum wages for women in the District of Columbia was unconstitutional;[7] the Court held, in effect, that no government in this country could compel payment of minimum wages. In the Depression, however, the ideas developed that those who cut wages below a minimum level were unfair competitors and that it was in the public interest to maintain the purchasing power of the lower-income groups. Thus in 1933 the National Recovery Administration included minimum-wage provisions in codes of fair competition approved by it. These provisions applied to male and female employees and thus set a new pattern for minimum-wage legislation. But the provisions expired when the NRA program was held unconstitutional in 1935.

In the meantime, however, states again enacted minimum-wage laws for women, and the Supreme Court—in one of its reversals of position—upheld such a statute in 1937.[8] Congress then included minimum-wage provisions for both men and women in the Fair Labor Standards Act of 1938.

Conflicts over policy

The Fair Labor Standards Act of 1938 was actually quite limited in its coverage, since it applied only to certain of the workers engaged in commerce or the production of goods for commerce. From 1959 to 1966 there was a continuing battle in Congress over extension of the act's coverage, primarily over whether to include retail and service employees under minimum-wage and maximum-hour provisions. President Kennedy in 1961 recommended inclusion of about 4,300,000 additional workers. A conservative coalition in the House prevented complete victory, but the President and Senate had substantial success with the 1961 bill, and certain retail and service groups were included under its coverage. President Johnson's recommendations led to inclusion of still more workers in amendments of 1966. Included now under wage-hour provisions are concerns substantially involved in interstate commerce and such establishments as retail stores and filling stations that have over a certain volume of sales, restaurants and hotels, and laundries. Agricultural processors, large farms, and many other

[7] *Adkins* v. *Children's Hospital*, 261 U.S. 525 (1923).
[8] *West Coast Hotel Co.* v. *Parrish*, 300 U.S. 379 (1937).

types of previously exempted firms are also now included under all or some of the provisions of the act. But there are still special provisions with respect to many employments. For example, child labor is prohibited in hazardous farm occupations, but exemptions are granted for family employment and hand-harvest laborers; and the time-and-a-half overtime-pay requirement is relaxed or removed for seasonal or irregular employment, for companies that sign contracts limiting hours over a six-month or full-year period, and for a variety of occupations such as food service, automobile repair, and agriculture.

The second issue in amending the Fair Labor Standards Act has been the level of minimum wages. The latest amendments set a rising scale, reaching $1.60 in February 1968 for businesses included under the act since 1961, and the same figure by 1971 for newly covered concerns, except for agriculture, where the rate will reach $1.30 in 1969.

Conflicts over both coverage and wage levels are expected to continue in Congress in the future. Should existing exemptions be trimmed further? Should the level of minimum wages be raised? These questions will create sectional cleavages—representatives from older areas of industrialization with union wage scales tending to favor such legislation and those from newly industrialized areas with a low unionization rate tending to oppose it. Representatives from Southern states—reflecting employer interest in preserving low wage rates in textile, tobacco, and other industries—may continue to be the strongest opponents of increases in minimum wages. Since small retailers are now exempted, they may be expected to oppose (and large retailers and unions to favor) amendments to extend the act to them. Such differences in interest will be accompanied by differences of opinion on the economic effects of minimum-wage legislation and by strong ideological differences. Some persons argue that minimum-wage standards increase unemployment, others that they increase purchasing power and thus stimulate employment. Some stress the social arguments rather than the economic— that it is undesirable to have substandard wages and that the existence of such wages leads to the need for supplementary income for families through public aid. It may be noted that a minimum wage of $1.60 with continuous employment provides the worker with $3,328 per year, which is only slightly above the $3,000 per year considered by the Council of Economic Advisers to be the poverty level.

Social Insurance

In the twentieth century the national and state governments have given increasing attention to some of the tragic hazards of life, such as the death of the wage earner, sudden unemployment, old age, blindness, sickness, and injury in the course of employment. On June 8, 1934, President Roosevelt said in a message to Congress that the American people wanted "some safeguard against misfortunes which cannot be wholly eliminated in this man-made world of ours." The recommendations of his Committee on Economic Security formed the basis for the Social Security Act of 1935. This act, more than any other statute passed by Congress, has altered the relations of people to government. Two of the most important programs in this omnibus legislation are social insurance for the unemployed and for retired persons.

Unemployment compensation

Unemployment compensation was a product of the Depression, which made people acutely aware of technological and cyclical unemployment. Moreover, the experience of England led to the belief that, in addition to helping the unemployed, insurance payments could be a built-in stabilizer for the economy—counteracting a depression by sustaining purchasing power.

Wisconsin broke the ice by establishing an unemployment-insurance program in 1932. But the states were reluctant to inhibit the growth of industry in their states by burdening them with the costs of insurance unless other states competing for the same industries did the same. The Social Security Act provided an answer: it imposed on employers a national tax of 3 percent of their payroll. However, in any state that adopted an approved unemployment-compensation plan, employers had to pay only one-tenth of this tax. Needless to say, all states promptly legislated for unemployment insurance. The states now administer programs approved by the Department of Labor. With the funds it collects from the tax on employers (now .35 of 1 percent of the payroll) the national government grants money to the states for administration of their unemployment-insurance plans. The states also collect taxes for their programs, and they have all adopted merit-rating programs, under which the amount of state tax paid by the employer is dependent upon his own record in avoiding unemployment among his employees.

The general pattern of unemployment insurance is to pay the unemployed person a percentage of his wages for a certain number of weeks or until he again becomes employed. Most states provide a waiting period, perhaps a week, before payments begin. To be eligible a person must be able to work and must be available for work; workers discharged for misconduct, leaving work without cause, or refusing to accept suitable employment are not eligible. Also, state laws usually prohibit or restrict payment of benefits to those participating in a strike.

There are a number of problems with the present provisions for unemployment insurance. First, many employed persons are not covered. The national statute requires only that employers of four or more persons make payments, although many states have decreased this figure, and about one-third have reduced it to one employee. The national law allows other exclusions, and the states have commonly used this authority to exclude agricultural labor, domestic service, employment for state and local governments, and employment for nonprofit organizations. Second, payments are often not large enough to provide the unemployed worker with a reasonable amount of purchasing power. A maximum of $35 to $40 per week is typical among the states. This is a great help to low-paid employees but not to the person who has been making $150 or more per week. Legislatures have raised levels of payment, but in many states these increases have not equaled cost-of-living increases. Third, periods of unemployment may be more prolonged than the periods allowed for benefits. In 1961–62, when a considerable number of unemployed persons had exhausted their insurance, Congress provided national funds for extension of payments. Fourth, there are abuses of the system. Some persons try to avoid obtaining employment in order to remain on the rolls for unemployment compensation. But states try to prevent such malingering by restricting payments to a percentage of one's past wage and by maintaining close cooperation between the placement officers of the state employment services and the payment officers for unemployment insurance.

There is relatively little political attention given to unemployment insurance now, but the levels and periods of benefits would almost certainly gain increased attention should a major depression occur.

Old Age, Survivors, and Disability Insurance

From the debate over social security in 1935 until today, income for the aged has remained a perennial political issue. Aged persons characteristically are unemployable, have inadequate savings, are in frequent need of medical care, and have no dependable family support. Moreover, the aged (who constitute about 9 percent of our population), their families, and those who expect to join their ranks in the near future are a strong influence on politics. Under every President since Roosevelt, benefits to the aged have been increased through amendments to the 1935 social-insurance legislation.

Social-security legislation now provides some income to almost everyone who reaches sixty-five. The law requires most business firms to participate, and, in addition, self-employed persons, charitable organizations, and state and local governments may join the program if they choose. The amount of payment received by a retiree depends on his wage record and whether he has dependents: the minimum monthly payment for a person with no dependents who retires at age sixty-five or above is $44; the maximum is $168. Payments are made automatically (that is, not based on need) to all who have participated in the program for a minimum number of quarters of years. The benefits are financed through equal contributions from employers and employees, with the employer deducting the employee's contribution from his wage payment. Social security is administered exclusively by the national government through a division of the Department of Health, Education, and Welfare.

A modified form of life insurance, called survivors' benefits, and a system of disability insurance have been added to the system. When a person covered by the plan dies at any age or is permanently disabled, benefit payments are made for his children under stated ages and for his aged dependents. Health insurance (discussed later in this chapter) was added in 1966.

The social-security system is not identical with private insurance. First, amendments to the Social Security Act have brought many of the present aged population into the system to whom benefits will be paid without substantial funds having been accumulated by taxes on their wages. Second, the amount of benefits to which a worker is entitled, though based on income, is not exactly equal to the taxes paid on his wages. For example, a retired person whose average monthly income had been $250 would receive $101.70 per month, while a worker whose average income had been $550 would receive only $168. Third, a worker's retirement payments may be reduced or denied if he receives more than a certain amount in income from employment he engages in after reaching retirement age.

The American system is a compromise system. It is not like the pre-1961 British flat-rate system, under which everybody's contribution and benefits were substantially the same; such a system must lead to low benefits for everyone because of the inability of low-paid workers to pay for adequate benefits. Nor is it like private insurance, in which variable benefits are adjusted neatly to variable contributions; such a system would lead to low benefits for those most in need of benefits. The American system builds the system of social payment based on need into the schedule of benefits. Fundamentally the American system is designed to guarantee to most of the population a minimum level of protection, and thereby to reduce the need for payments under public-assistance programs based on tests of financial means.

Workmen's compensation

Workmen's compensation is the only form of social insurance that is in no way subsidized by the national government. The states continue to provide workmen's compensation through legislation, a practice begun by New York in 1910—the first social-insurance legislation in this country.[9]

Under common law a worker who was injured on his job could sue his employer for the injury, but the employer could avoid payment through several defenses: that the worker was negligent, that fellow workers con-

[9] For the history of workmen's compensation, see Walter F. Dodd, *Administration of Workmen's Compensation* (New York: Oxford University Press, 1936).

tributed to the accident (the "fellow-servant" doctrine), or that the worker assumed the risks of hazardous occupation by accepting his employment. Investigations showed that the system produced a host of harmful effects to workers and society: lengthy court contests led to delays in payments to workers; major portions of the recovery money were eaten up by attorneys' fees; and the injured person or his survivors received inadequate compensation, if they could collect at all. At the beginning of the twentieth century, legislation was passed modifying the common law. The states, however, adopted a new system that became known as "workmen's compensation." It (1) removed the employer's common-law defenses, except for special contributing causes such as drunkenness of the injured employee, (2) limited the employer's liability to amounts stated in the statute, (3) provided administrative tribunals to hear cases, and (4) provided for insurance of the employer's liability. This system gave the laborer more security through simplified and faster procedures and through removal of the employer's defenses; it simultaneously limited the employer's liability and provided for employer insurance against suits.

These statutes have been amended to provide payments to employees who contract diseases as the result of employment and to reduce the types of employment exempted from coverage—the most common remaining exemptions are farm employment, domestic employment, and establishments with only a few workers.

Does the worker fare adequately under these statutes? In automobile-injury cases today the plaintiff is sometimes awarded as much as $50,000 to $200,000, while the payments provided under state workmen's-compensation statutes have often not kept pace with inflation and higher living standards.[10] The amount and duration of payments to injured workers will be on the agenda for consideration in state legislatures in the future.

Public Assistance

In public-assistance programs, direct monetary grants are made to individuals on the basis of need. Beginning with the Social Security Act, national grants-in-aid have been made to the states for assistance to special categories of needy persons. These grants are administered by the Department of Health, Education, and Welfare and by a department of welfare in each state. Each state is required by national law to have a merit system for the selection of welfare-department employees, and in the main the system is administered by professional social workers, who evaluate the need of applicants for assistance.

Initially the largest of the programs was the one for the needy aged. As

[10] For a thorough analysis of present-day workmen's-compensation laws, see Herman Miles Somers and Anne Ramsay Somers, *Workmen's Compensation: Prevention, Insurance, and Rehabilitation of Occupational Disability* (New York: Wiley, 1954).

was anticipated, however, the broadening of social-security coverage has brought a decline in the percentage of the aged receiving public assistance. On the other hand, for about 30 percent of the recipients, assistance payments supplement inadequate social-security payments. The average monthly assistance payment per recipient in 1966 was about $77, with considerable variation among the states.

In terms of number of persons assisted, aid to families with dependent children (AFDC) is now the largest of the programs. Payments are made to the family where the father is dead, incapacitated, estranged from the family, or unemployed. About 4 percent of the nation's children are now partially supported under this program. No welfare program stirs up more pointedly conflicting ideological views and difficulties in administration. Some people argue that the public should be liberal in its financial assistance because the needs of the children are paramount; others argue that too much assistance to children only reduces the parents' sense of responsibility. Welfare workers must make continuous checks to determine whether fathers are making contributions to support, whether widows are trying to find employment, and what the minimum family needs for help are. The most serious aspect of the problem is that the cycle of poverty and dependency often continues from generation to generation. Actually, public payments for dependent children have been low in comparison with those for the aged, blind, and disabled. This tendency may be due both to the lack of political influence of poor families and to the need to compromise between the desire to provide sustenance and opportunity for children and the fear of encouraging parental irresponsibility.

Two smaller programs are now well established. Federal grants are given to the states for aid to the dependent blind and to those who are permanently and totally disabled. And there is a medical program, to be discussed below. All public-assistance programs, however, alleviate the *effects* of poverty rather than erasing its causes. They can be reduced in magnitude only if the War on Poverty, discussed later, is successful.

Health

People's health has become a major concern of government. In no other area of government activity is there a more extensive system of cooperative relationships among the local, state, and national governments. The customary agency of administration in local and state governments is the health department; in the national government it is the Public Health Service of the Department of Health, Education, and Welfare. Other national agencies with significant health functions are the Veterans Administration, the Food and Drug Administration, and the Bureau of Public Assistance.

There are four main categories of public-health activity:

1. *The maintenance of a physical environment conducive to good health.*

Long-established functions—such as quarantine, sewage disposal, water sanitation, and inspection of eating places—are constantly being supplemented by new ones—such as the avoidance of air pollution and protection against radiation effects from nuclear fission.

2. *Hospital service.* State and local governments have provided most of the mental and tuberculosis hospitals and also have maintained general hospitals through which much charity care is provided. The national government operates veterans' hospitals and a number of special-purpose hospitals, such as those for care of lepers and narcotics addicts. To overcome a serious hospital shortage throughout the nation, Congress in 1946 passed the Hospital Survey and Construction (Hill-Burton) Act, making available through the states funds for construction of public and private hospitals and other health facilities—now including such things as nurses' residences and rehabilitation centers. In fourteen years nearly six thousand hospital projects were assisted at a total cost of about $5 billion, about one-third of which came from the national government.[11]

3. *Research.* The national government, with expenditures of over $1 billion annually, is now sponsoring about 40 percent of the medical research in the country. This program is conducted through a number of national institutes, which are the research arm of the Public Health Service and which operate their own laboratories and make grants for research to universities, hospitals, and other institutions.

4. *The payment of medical costs.* It is this category of public-health activity that has generated fierce controversy at the national level for at least two decades. As medical care has improved, its costs have increased, and the ever present danger of hospitalization, with expenses of perhaps $50 per day and accompanying physician's costs, is among the most frightening threats to poor and middle-class families. In general, there are four possible ways to meet this threat. One is by private insurance, as is now provided by Blue Cross and Blue Shield and other insurance organizations. The costs of adequate programs are high for lower-income groups, and there have been proposals for public subsidization of the programs.

Another method is direct supply of medical care through government institutions. This is the method for supplying medical care to armed-services personnel and their families and to veterans who have service-connected disabilities or who state that they are unable to pay for medical care. The service is rendered mainly through government hospitals. In addition, free care is given in state mental and tuberculosis hospitals and to millions of charity patients in other state and local hospitals. This method is pure government care, "socialized medicine" in a true sense.

The third method is for government to make medical-assistance payments to those unable to pay for medical care. These benefits would be paid

[11] U.S. Department of Health, Education, and Welfare, *Annual Report* (1961), p. 153.

"Someone's at the door, Grandma!"

The Case Against Medicare

Knox in the Nashville *Banner*

either to the needy or directly to hospitals, nursing homes, or medical personnel for their care. Payments by this method would be based on need, as determined by state and local personnel. The fourth method is social insurance, which would provide payments for medical expenses as a right for persons covered by the insurance.

Presidential attempts to implement this last approach have led to major political battles in Congress since 1948, when a compulsory health-insurance program for the entire country was recommended to the legislature by President Truman. This proposal aroused the vigorous opposition of the American Medical Association, which employed the public-relations firm of Whittaker and Baxter and spent $4,678,000 in three and a half years on a "national education campaign." [12] In contrast, President Eisenhower proposed reinsurance for private health-insurance organizations on some large risks. Neither proposal got out of committee in Congress. President Kennedy revived the idea of government insurance for medical expenses but confined his proposal to the aged who were entitled to Old Age, Survivors, and Disability Insurance benefits. The American Medical Association fought this program as vigorously as it had fought President Truman's broader one. In 1961 it created the American Medical Political Action Committee to marshal attacks on what had now come to be called "Medicare."

[12] See Stanley Kelley, Jr., *Professional Public Relations and Political Power* (Baltimore: Johns Hopkins Press, 1956), Ch. 3, for a description of the American Medical Association's campaign.

The Case for Medicare

Edmund MacIntosh was depending on the theory that hard-boiled eggs and opened cans of Spam need no refrigeration. And he was sick.

He had also depended on the theory that if you work hard, live frugally, and mind your own business, you'll get by without help. And now he was seventy-four years old and needed help.

Mr. MacIntosh depended on hard-boiled eggs because his hotel room has no refrigerator and he can't afford to eat out. He is trying to live on his $50-a-month Social Security check. Room rent is $38.50 a month, which provides a room with clean linen every two weeks and clean towels every day. The remainder goes for food and chewing tobacco.... He boils his eggs at once and eats them morning and evening. He stretches a can of Spam for three days or so. It has cost him violent nausea to discover that hard-boiled eggs and opened Spam need refrigeration in warm weather....

"What I need most is a doctor. But I don't know no doctor I can call. I need something for my eyes.... If I shut my right eye I can't see that doorknob over there. My hearing's going, too ... I keep having these dizzy spells. I keep getting sick to my stomach. There's not a thing on my stomach right now. I guess what I want more than anything else is a doctor. Some good medicine...."

"Maybe if I just had some good company I guess that would be all right, too. I ain't had a letter in twelve months. And that was from the bank about my account."

From Ben Bagdikian, *In the Midst of Plenty*, 1964.

Medicare for the aged passed, as an amendment to the Social Security Act, in 1965. In general, it provides for automatic insurance of costs for hospital and related post-hospital services (within certain limitations, such as no more than 90 days payment for hospitalization for any illness, and certain deductions, including the first $40 of hospital expense) and voluntary insurance for physician's expenses. Aged persons may be included in the latter program by payment of $3 per month, and the program pays 80 percent of the doctor bills with $50 deductible.

The initiation of this program gave rise to several problems. Only hospitals meeting quality standards can be included in the program; these are certified with the cooperation of state health departments. Some hospitals in the South have chosen to remain outside the program, rather than agree to accept clients without racial discrimination. In scattered actions medical associations threatened to continue their opposition by boycotting the system, but these threats quickly subsided. Hospitals and physicians now complain of reports that must be signed certifying services rendered to the aged.

The enduring problem, however, is a broader one and was only accentuated by Medicare—the shortage of medical facilities of almost every type to provide care both for the aged and others.

For needy persons who are not covered or are not adequately covered by Medicare, the national government has adopted the public-assistance payment. Limited programs of this type were supplemented in 1965 by a comprehensive program called "Medicaid," which will supplant all other medical-assistance programs by 1970. Grants-in-aid will be given to the states to enable them to pay costs for hospital care, skilled nursing-home care, physicians' services, and laboratory and X-ray services. To obtain the national grants, state plans must include under this program all recipients of aid under other national-state assistance programs, and by 1975 the state must include all medically needy persons. It is estimated that one-fifth of the population will be covered by this grants-in-aid program.

In sum, the national government helps defray costs of medical care through assistance payments to the poor, direct supply of medical care to armed-services personnel and veterans, and social insurance for the aged. The civilian, nonveteran middle class is left with responsibility to provide for its own medical expenses, mainly through private insurance. At present the politics of medical care centers in the state legislatures, where consideration is being given to assistance programs, and in Congress, where bills have been introduced for extension of Medicare to disabled persons. In the long run, it may be expected that extension of coverage under the assistance and social-insurance programs will be a political issue, as it was for earlier programs of the same types.

Housing and Urban Development

Housing has become a matter of increasing government concern over the past few decades. At the same time, and particularly in the last five years, there has been a growing realization of the close relationship between housing and the sound growth of the nation's cities and suburbs.

Local governments have long maintained some standards with respect to housing through their building codes and their sanitation and safety regulations. But the Depression marked the shift of leadership in housing activity, as in so many areas, to the national government.

From that time on, the national government has encouraged the flow of private capital into housing construction. An early means of doing this was the creation in 1932 of the Federal Home Loan Bank system, which provides a credit reservoir for the nation's savings and loan industry. Another means of stimulating private investment in housing is through insurance of savings accounts up to $15,000 in federal savings and loan associations and approved state-chartered associations. This is done by the Federal Savings and Loan Insurance Corporation, which makes insurance assessments on member institutions.

The most important federal means of facilitating both housing construction and home ownership is the insurance of home mortgages. This is done through the Federal Housing Administration, which insures approved loans at one half of 1 percent of the unpaid principal. To support liquidity and price levels of mortgages, the Federal National Mortgage Association (nicknamed "Fannie Mae") buys and sells FHA mortgages. Both FHA and FNMA are now part of the Department of Housing and Urban Development.

The effect of these banking and insurance measures is to maintain a flow of low-interest, long-term loans for private housing. No other industries except agriculture and commercial banking have been so extensively supported by government. As a result of the arrangements for public and private collaboration, almost two-thirds of the nonfarm homes of the country were owner-occupied in 1967 as compared with about one-third in the 1890's.

Housing for low-income families was another national commitment first undertaken during the Depression. It began when the federal government, in an effort to provide employment, constructed more than fifty housing projects. These were subsequently transferred to local governments, but in 1937 Congress provided for construction of public housing by state and local governments with the help of a capital grant or an annual subsidy from the national government. Thirty years later, more than 610,000 units of low-rent subsidized housing were available in fifty states.

An outgrowth of federal assistance for low-income housing was assistance to communities for slum clearance and urban redevelopment. This program was established by Title I of the Housing Act of 1949 and substantially expanded in the Housing Act of 1954. Under these acts national grants may be made to defray two-thirds of the costs of urban-renewal projects. The usual procedure is for a city to develop a plan for an area, acquire the properties, demolish the structures that cannot be rehabilitated, and either use the land for a city housing project or sell it to private developers.

Urban renewal is now an established and growing program. Seventeen years after the first legislation, 1,812 projects had been approved in 846 participating cities. Yet progress in the program is slow;[13] it takes years to make plans, buy property, and arrange for the relocation of residents. Both the slowness of the program and its impact have been criticized. Completed private projects have often been luxury apartments for upper-income groups, and new slum areas have been created by simply shifting low-income families from one deteriorating residential area to another.[14] Renewal authorities and the federal government have responded to these

[13] U.S. Department of Housing and Urban Development, *Second Annual Report* (1967). Only 289 projects had been completed by the end of 1966.
[14] On the problems and needs, see Catherine Bauer Wurster, "Framework for an Urban Society," in President's Commission on National Goals, *Goals for America* (1960), pp. 225–47.

criticisms with an increased emphasis on careful relocation, code enforcement, rehabilitation rather than clearance, community renewal, and provision of low-income housing in renewal areas. It is still too early to know whether these efforts will produce substantial changes.

To these major roles in mortgage insurance, public housing, and urban renewal, the federal government added a series of new efforts in the mid-60's to secure the ambitious goal of the 1949 Housing Act: "a decent home and a suitable living environment for every American family." In 1965 the nation's growing urban constituency was afforded Cabinet status with the establishment of a Department of Housing and Urban Development. This department was given the job of coordinating existing housing programs and of relating these to the problems of explosive metropolitan growth and central-city decay.

That same year, Congress authorized "rent supplements," a new approach to low-income housing through federal subsidy of the gap between the economic rent and that which a resident family can afford. Other new programs offer assistance to communities to acquire "open spaces" in anticipation of continued growth, to build or retool rapid-transit systems, to provide neighborhood centers, and to pay for heavy initial investments in water and sewer facilities. Mortgage insurance has been made available for developers who build "new towns."

The most ambitious and far-reaching federal urban effort of recent years has been the proposal to establish "demonstration cities" (now more modestly referred to as "model neighborhoods"). Under this program, the federal government is substantially underwriting on an experimental basis local efforts to "turn the tide" in large deteriorating neighborhoods through the concentrated use of all existing federal aids and broad-gauge and experimental local efforts. If the program is successful, it seems certain to generate a great many changes in the government's housing, education, health, and employment activities as well as in the traditional patterns of federal-local relationships. Reasonably large sums of money will be required, however, if "model neighborhoods" are to be born on a substantial basis, and a national consensus on such an investment is still uncertain. In any event, the federal government is now committed to an active role in the future development of America's urban areas.

Consumer Protection

Although all persons are consumers, we have no strong organization in our society for the promotion of consumer interests. The Consumers Union conducts an educational program through its monthly bulletin, and many women's organizations and professional home economists support consumer interests. But most people are more aroused by government programs that affect their earnings or taxes than by those that affect their spending.

Consequently, the interests of consumers are often neglected or over-whelmed by opposition from powerful producer interests.

Great advances in legislation for consumer protection have often come only after revelation of grave threats to the public. Upton Sinclair's blistering exposé in *The Jungle* of conditions in the Chicago stockyards led to passage of the Meat Inspection Act in 1906; deaths from the improper use of sulfanilamide led to amendments of the Food and Drug Act in 1938; the births of deformed babies when mothers-to-be used thalidomide led to further amendments of the act in 1962; and Ralph Nader's book on automobile hazards led to passage of the automobile-safety act in 1966.[15] Journalistic exposure or a popular book is apparently a prerequisite for a major enactment for consumer protection.

After an act is passed the superior access of producers to regulatory agencies administering the act may weaken its effectiveness. For thirty-three years the Food and Drug Act was administered in the Department of Agriculture, where dedicated specialists struggled to give protection to the public under a weak statute, with inadequate appropriations, and against vigorous pressure from agricultural processors who could sometimes get support from the politically appointed top administrators of the department.[16] Producer interests are constantly and vigorously represented in the complicated flow of activity in regulatory agencies, and they keep a watchful eye, frequently with the aid of congressional committees, on trends in regulatory decisions. The member of an agency such as the Federal Communications Commission or the Civil Aeronautics Board who raises issues of public service that challenge producer interests may find himself in a political vacuum because of the lack of organized consumer support.

Nevertheless, consumer interests obtain considerable protection through government statutes. Sometimes these laws are passed because the interests of consumers coincide with those of some producer groups with strength. Though the laws may be of only limited effectiveness, they do elicit some voluntary compliance and are supported in some measure by administrative action. The laws usually establish centers of administration in which men struggle for the maintenance of the legal standards and for their improvement through further legislation. Also, those government agencies that are large purchasers keep a watchful eye on costs and quality and in this way protect all consumers. Similarly, cities often initiate action before state and national utility commissions for protection of consumer interests.

It has sometimes been suggested that additional representation in government be provided for consumer interests through consumer advisory councils, consumer representatives in regulatory agencies, or a consumers'

[15] *Unsafe at Any Speed: The Designed-In Dangers of the American Automobile* (New York: Grossman, 1965).

[16] See E. Pendleton Herring, *Public Administration and the Public Interest* (New York: McGraw-Hill, 1936), Ch. 15.

department in the executive branch. Consumer advisory councils have been used, and they may be of real value; but it is doubtful whether they can accomplish much with the regulatory agencies, whose programs are oriented to producer interests. The idea of appointing a consumers' counsel to initiate cases and represent consumer interests before regulatory agencies has much appeal, but the appointment of such officials would diminish the sense of responsibility of the agencies themselves to protect consumer interests.[17] This last argument is also advanced to oppose a consumers' department, for it is important that the departments and agencies of government regard *themselves* as having a responsibility to consumers. There would be a problem, moreover, as to which agencies should be transferred to such a department and a question as to whether a real gain would be made by such transfers.

Nonetheless, official efforts to organize the consumer interests are increasing. President Kennedy sent to Congress the first special message ever devoted solely to consumer protection, and President Johnson has added a Special Assistant for Consumer Affairs to the White House staff.

The largest government program for consumer protection safeguards the public from unhealthy foods and drugs. The Meat Inspection Act of 1906 provided for government inspection of meat shipped in interstate commerce. The Food and Drug Act of 1906 prohibited interstate commerce in adulterated or misbranded foods and drugs. The act is administered by the Food and Drug Administration, now in the Department of Health, Education, and Welfare. In 1938 Congress expanded the act's coverage to include cosmetics (excluding soap) and therapeutic devices and increased the penalties for violation. False advertising, however, falls under the jurisdiction of the Federal Trade Commission. An amendment to the Federal Trade Commission Act in 1938 makes a manufacturer who falsely advertises a drug, food, cosmetic, or body device subject to a cease-and-desist order, a court injunction, and criminal penalties.

In 1958 a Senate subcommittee chaired by Senator Estes Kefauver began an investigation of drug-marketing, and Senator Kefauver, with the aid of a handful of senators, labored doggedly for passage of amendments to add effective safeguards against untested drugs. This effort appeared to be stymied until it was discovered that thalidomide, a sedative given to pregnant mothers, was alleged to have caused 3,500 to 5,000 deformed babies in Western Europe. It had not been marketed in this country only because an employee of the Food and Drug Administration—a physician, Dr. Frances O. Kelsey—had repeatedly called for more information about the drug and had temporarily prevented its certification. The thalidomide

---

[17] For disappointing results from a consumers' counsel in an agency established to promote producer interests, see Kathryn Arnow, *The Consumers' Counsel and the National Bituminous Coal Commission*, rev. ed. (University, Ala.: University of Alabama Press, 1950).

"You better untie me before there's a 'next time.' "

The thalidomide drug scandal in 1962 led the public to demand increased powers for the Food and Drug Administration.

Yardley in the Baltimore *Sun*

revelations led to enactment in 1962 of many of the Kefauver proposals. The amendments provided among other new safeguards that new drugs could not be certified without the Food and Drug Administration's evaluation of their effectiveness and safety.

Except for foods and drugs, however, purchasers of goods must still be governed by and large by the doctrine of "Let the buyer beware." Notable exceptions are the prohibitions against false and deceptive advertising in the Federal Trade Commission Act, requirements for the labeling of a few products such as wool and furs, and requirement of safety installations on automobiles. In addition, Congress has recently passed a bill for regulating the packaging and labeling of products to prevent deception of consumers. Cigarette packages must carry a statement that cigarette smoking may be hazardous to health, but proposals that advertising carry the same warning have not been enacted.

The War on Poverty

The newest welfare program is the War on Poverty, based on an act of Congress in 1964. President Johnson declared an "unconditional war on poverty," and Sargent Shriver, head of the Office of Economic Opportunity created by the act, has said, "We have the knowledge to set 1976 as the

War on Poverty: The Strategy

In the 1960's, we have begun to devise a total strategy against poverty. We have recognized that public housing, minimum wages and welfare services could not, standing alone, change the bleak environment of deprivation for millions of poor families.

A successful strategy requires a breakthrough on many fronts: education, health, jobs and job training, housing, public assistance, transportation, recreation, clean air, and adequate water supplies. The basic conditions of life for the poor must, and can, be changed.

We must deal with a wide range of physical and human needs. On the human side alone, the strategy must respond to a variety of problems.

Some of the poor—the aged and the hopelessly disabled—are unable to make their own way in this world because of conditions beyond their control. For them, social security, veterans pensions and public assistance can assure a life at minimum levels of human decency and dignity.

Others in our society are working at very low wages or are unemployed. But they are capable of helping themselves if given an opportunity to do so. To launch them on the road to a self-sufficient life, special education, training, and employment opportunities will be necessary.

We have made substantial gains [toward these goals]. But we have also come to see how profound are the problems that confront us, how deeply ingrained are the customs and practices that must be changed, how stubbornly the heritage of poverty persists from generation to generation.

From President Lyndon B. Johnson, message to Congress on the War on Poverty, March 1967.

target date for ending poverty in this land." Yet no domestic program of government has been involved in more complexities or more political controversy.

The antipoverty war involves many agencies of government in a wide range of programs. The 1964 act provided new functions for the Departments of Labor, Agriculture, Commerce, and HEW and it was expected that old functions of agencies would be coordinated with new ones. It assigned the task of coordination to the head of the OEO, which also administers the Job Corps, VISTA (a domestic peace corps), and community-action programs. The last of these is a major innovation in government. It asks public and private welfare agencies in a community jointly to develop and administer programs for such activities as Head Start (preschool preparation for children of disadvantaged families), legal services for the poor, and services to migrant workers, Indians, and the aged.

The Antipoverty Act calls for "maximum feasible participation" of

Poverty War

One problem of the War on Poverty has been the fighting among government agencies and interest groups over "battle strategy."

© 1966, The Chicago *Sun Times*. Reproduced by permission of Wil-Jo Assoc., Inc., and Bill Mauldin.

the poor in the program. But this participation, regarded by OEO officials as crucial for elevating the status of the poor, is both difficult to achieve and potentially explosive in its results. Sometimes the poor are underrepresented in these programs. One commentator complained that Chicago's antipoverty planning board consisted of "men who drive Cadillacs, eat three-inch steaks, and sip champagne at their luncheon meetings." At the other extreme, sometimes the participation of the poor upsets the political equilibrium of local governments. For example, the mayor of Syracuse complained that OEO funds had been used to agitate occupants of public housing to demand better treatment from the city government. Mayors have demanded that all community-action funds be distributed through agencies approved by local government officials. OEO administrators find it difficult to maintain an acceptable representation of the poor without upsetting power balances in the community.

Conflicts have also developed over administrative control of programs. First, congressmen and city officials have each complained that the other has captured the bounty of the new programs. Second, under the original Antipoverty Act, governors were given the right of veto over such activities as Job Corps and community-action programs in their states. But this power aroused sufficient antagonism from rival political interests within the states to produce a congressional amendment giving the head of the OEO the power to override gubernatorial vetoes. A group of Republicans have in turn called for the abolition of the OEO and the transfer of its functions to old-line agencies; this proposal has been opposed by the United States Conference of Mayors. The underlying problem for the government in all these controversies is that of balancing local initiative in planning and administering local funds with sufficient national controls to ensure that national policies are followed and that funds are used legally and efficiently.

Labor leaders keep a watchful eye on wages paid in work-training programs. One said, "If we're not consulted on a program, we'll knock its damned head off." Leaders of minority groups have sometimes complained of discrimination; on the other hand, Shriver has asserted that the record of his agency on this score has been as good as that of any other in government.

Some elements of the War on Poverty have such wide appeal that their continuance seems assured in spite of controversy. Among these are the various forms of youth training and the Head Start program, an innovation in the American educational system that may be expanded to include all children. Moreover, the War on Poverty is only a central feature of the many-faceted activities in education, housing, civil rights, and rehabilitation designed to alleviate the condition of the poor and to provide them with an entry into the American opportunity system. There is, however, reason to suspect that the dimensions and costs of eradicating poverty have not been fully assessed and that politicians find little political appeal in programs that tax the middle and upper classes to provide opportunities for the poor. Congress made heavy cuts in the President's recommendations for funds for OEO for fiscal year 1967—particularly for the community-action program—and the President proposed only a modest increase in funds for 1968. Many feel that the Vietnam war and the lack of political organization among the poor have brought the program to at least a temporary standstill—and that continued riots in the streets may be the only force that will expand or even sustain the War on Poverty. A proposal for a fuller attack on poverty by guaranteeing a minimum income to every family has gained no substantial political support.

SUMMARY

The role of the government in welfare activities has vastly increased during the twentieth century as a result of three factors: the nation's shift from a pioneer, rural society to an industrialized, urban one; increasingly tolerant attitudes of the middle class toward underprivileged groups; and the gradual public acceptance of government programs to solve welfare problems.

Even today, however, welfare programs generate strong ideological controversy. Those opposed to them argue that responsibility belongs with individuals, or with state and local governments, and that benefits should be granted on the basis of need. Proponents of welfare, on the other hand, argue that minimum opportunity and security should be provided as an automatic right of all Americans and that the national government should play a strong role. The outcome of this conflict is that initiatives in welfare now come primarily from Washington, although cooperation among the three levels of government is characteristic of many welfare programs.

What are the basic features of today's welfare programs? In education the national government offers grants-in-aid to help underwrite adult education courses, vocational training, programs in science, mathematics, and foreign languages, and the training and retraining of unemployed youths and adults. Higher education is aided by loans or grants for classrooms, libraries, and dormitories and through scholarships and loans for students. In addition, a bill providing general aid to elementary and secondary education—a highly controversial issue because of the questions of whether to give aid to parochial and segregated schools—passed Congress in 1965.

To safeguard the welfare of American workers, the government relies on legislation (1) protecting the safety and health of workers, (2) prohibiting child labor, (3) setting maximum hours of labor per week, and (4) requiring payment of minimum wages. Successive amendments to this legislation have given rise to political controversy over the scope of its coverage and the level of the minimum wage to be set.

To protect Americans from some of the hazards of life, government offers several kinds of social insurance: (1) unemployment compensation, (2) disability insurance and social-security benefits for the aged as well as for survivors, and (3) workmen's compensation for those injured on the job, supported solely by state and local governments. In addition, national grants-in-aid help to support state public-assistance programs for families with dependent children, for the aged, and for the blind or disabled. A major welfare activity of the national government is the protection of public health. The government helps to maintain a safe physical environment, underwrites some hospital service and construction, and sponsors medical research. The federal government's attempt to underwrite payment of medical care, however, has generated substantial political controversy over the last twenty years. But recently bills providing Medicare for the aged and Medicaid for the poor were passed by Congress.

With the growing importance of urban and suburban centers in recent years, housing and urban development have become matters of increasing concern to the national government, as symbolized by the establishment of a Cabinet-level Department of Housing and Urban Development in 1965. First, the government encourages the investment of private capital in housing construction, primarily through low-interest, long-term loans to homeowners. Second, the government undertakes construction of public housing for low-income families as well as financial aid to local communities for slum clearance and urban redevelopment. Third, the government has recently authorized "rent supplements" and experimentation in the development of "model neighborhoods."

Although political organizations to protect consumer interests in our society are weak, these interests still receive considerable protection from the government, primarily through administrative agencies that seek to maintain minimum product standards. The largest government program of this type is that protecting consumers from unhealthy food and drugs.

The War on Poverty, introduced in 1964, has been partially effective and has gained widespread support for such programs as youth training and Head Start. But the poverty program has met with significant political problems, such as the difficulty of securing participation of the poor in programs and the conflicts that have developed, for example, over administrative control of the Job Corps, VISTA, and community-action programs.

In sum, the United States is not a true "welfare state"; primary responsibility for personal welfare still rests on the family and the individual. Personal welfare is sought through a mixture of private, quasi-public, and public activities.

Much welfare legislation—such as that for education, social insurance, and consumer protection—provides benefits for all, particularly the middle class. Other legislation—such as for minimum labor standards, assistance payments, and antipoverty programs—gives special benefits to the poor. In general, political support is strong for programs benefiting the middle class, but weak for programs designed to help the very poor. The major question of the future is whether we will develop the political support necessary to eliminate poverty in an economy of abundance. This is the basic test of how responsive government is to the needs of all the people.

AMERICA
AND THE
WORLD
Defense and
Foreign
Policy

22

In its development from a weak and isolated new nation to a twentieth-century superpower, the United States historically pursued three main goals of defense and foreign policy: survival of our nation, extension of our national borders to their "natural limits," and the promotion of American commerce around the globe. How have our policies toward Europe differed from those toward countries in our own hemisphere? How did we implement our policy of "containment" toward Russia after World War II? What new challenges are presented by the "multipolar era" of today? Finally, how has the United States dealt with the problems of defense and foreign policy that confront every world power?

In a single generation we have witnessed a revolution in the priorities of government. Although our relations with other countries have always been important to us, it is only in the mid-twentieth century that the problems of foreign affairs and defense have cast a shadow over all else. They dominate the headlines, preempt the attention of statesmen, consume two-thirds of our annual national budget, and significantly affect the course of domestic politics. The United States Government must today respond to a host of problems presented by communists and by the rise of the newly independent "nonwhite" nations. On the nature of these responses depends our physical survival and the freedom of our society.

In international politics our nation since its establishment has passed through two periods and into a third. In the first—from 1789 to 1914—we moved from a position of weakness to one of strength. Like the fledgling nations of Africa and Asia in the twentieth century, we began with a problem of survival in a world dominated by strong powers, and we sought to avoid involvement in the struggles among these powers. At the same time, the nation was offered opportunities for expansion, economic growth, and development of its world position that ultimately made it one of the strong nations of the world.

In the second period—from 1914 through the Second World War—the United States—with Great Britain, Germany, France, Italy, Russia, and Japan—was established firmly as one of the great powers in a multipower complex. Yet we were a reluctant member of this complex and clung initially to the policies that had preserved us in the past, even in the midst of new conditions that made these ineffective. Finally, however, we accepted the role of a great power in world politics.

After the Second World War the United States moved into a third period when it assumed the role of a superpower—a role that has forced us into the maelstrom of international politics at every turn of events. As a superpower, we have faced rapidly changing conditions that have carried us through a *bipolar* phase, in which the United States and Russia were leaders of rival power blocs, and into a *multipolar* phase, in which the power centers of international politics are more diffused. As a superpower in a multipolar world, we now face challenges of even greater complexity than we did in a bipolar world. We are confronted with problems of adjusting the continuing aspects of our foreign and defense policies and with profound questions about our attitudes and our ability to carry the burdens of world leadership.

PRELUDE TO POWER:
DEFENSE AND FOREIGN POLICY BEFORE 1914

A balanced view of America's diplomacy from 1789 to 1914 must include both the policies that reflected our readiness to grasp opportunities and take risks for growth and survival and the policies that restricted the involvement of a weak nation in the conflicts of other nations.

The Expansion of Our Borders

The most important aspects of our foreign policy were those related to opportunities to expand our borders. The United States claimed Western lands, fought Indian wars, purchased the Louisiana Territory and Florida, disputed northeastern boundaries, annexed Texas, fought the Mexican War, negotiated the Gadsden Purchase, and competed for the Oregon Territory with the slogan "Fifty-four forty or fight." We gained Alaska by a diplo-

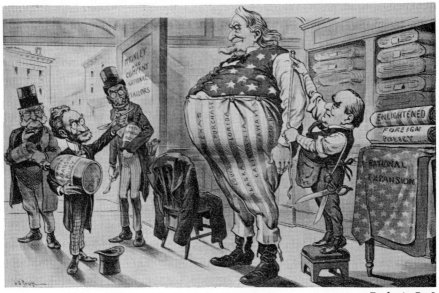

Pughe in *Puck*

Declined with Thanks

The Anti's: "Here, take a dose of this anti-fat and get thin again!"
Uncle Sam: "No, Sonny! I never did take any of that stuff, and I'm too old to begin!"

Our acquisition of overseas territory in the Spanish-American War produced sharp public debate between expansionists and anti-imperialists. Here President McKinley measures Uncle Sam for a new suit of "expansion" cloth while anti-imperialists offer him medicine to "reduce."

matic deal, Hawaii by a treaty of annexation, and the Philippines and Puerto Rico by a war with Spain. Expansionism was viewed by some as the "Manifest Destiny" of the nation, but "destiny" was assisted by a combination of diplomacy, migration of people, and force. Military policy became a function of the drive to acquire and hold new real estate.

In the Northwest Ordinance of 1784 Congress had announced the principle that territories should ultimately be admitted to the Union as states. This principle has been followed for all continental territory, including Alaska, and has been extended to Hawaii. Independence was given to Cuba and, much later, to the Philippines. Commonwealth status was eventually accorded to Puerto Rico. Some feared that acquisition of noncontiguous territory with different racial groups and a low level of economic development would lead to American colonialism, and to a certain extent these fears were justified. The United States had to put down a revolt to hold the Philippines, and we kept them as a colony for almost half a century. Hawaii and Puerto Rico were maintained as unincorporated territories for what, in retrospect, seem embarrassingly long times. On the whole, however, the American record was good, and the development of Cuba and Puerto Rico suggests a rethinking of the relative merits of independence as opposed to other solutions for the problems of underdeveloped areas.

The American Policy Toward Europe

To understand the policies that restricted the involvement of a weak nation in the conflicts of Europe, it is necessary to note the difference between neutrality and isolation. *Neutrality* is a deliberate policy followed by a state when it finds itself in a particular international situation. *Isolation* is simply the condition or circumstance of not being involved.

In the early years of our nation, our government chose a policy of neutrality in the power struggles of Europe precisely because the new United States was *not* isolated from the politics of the Continent. The course enjoined by President George Washington in his Neutrality Proclamation ("pursue a conduct friendly and impartial towards the belligerents") was a calculated plan to preserve American independence at a time when the Old World powers were still active in the Americas.

Isolation, of course, was something devoutly desired by statesmen of our formative period. Jefferson wished the United States "to stand with respect to Europe precisely on the footing of China." Within three decades isolation was actually achieved. Europe's overseas influence progressively declined, and the Monroe Doctrine, enunciated in 1823, represented a simple announcement of the fact that the Continental powers were no longer decisive in the New World.

The Monroe Doctrine stated an American policy for Europe: "in wars of European powers in matters relating to themselves we have never taken any part, nor does it comport with our policy so to do. We would be concerned only when our rights are invaded or seriously menaced." These aloof sentiments were encouraged by a set of fortuitous circumstances: our oceans separated us from powerful nations; the British Navy maintained the freedom of the seas desired by America; and a Pax Britannica prevailed over the world. Not until the rise to power of a newly unified Germany was this Pax Britannica threatened, and by that time American interests elsewhere in the world were already expanding. In 1898 the United States was launched into the Spanish-American War, and in 1900 we declared an Open Door policy for China.

The American Policy Toward Latin America

Our Latin American policy, however, was distinctly different. It reflected readiness to take the risks of confrontation with Old World powers. Again the United States' position was stated in the Monroe Doctrine. Though the rights of European powers with respect to existing colonies were recognized, the doctrine stated the United States would consider any attempt of the European powers "to extend their system to any portion of this hemisphere as dangerous to our peace and safety." A serious challenge was presented to the policy in 1861 when Napoleon III sent armies into Mexico, but the threat dissolved when American troops were moved to the Rio Grande in 1865. At the turn of the century, Presidents Cleveland and Roosevelt stiffened the doctrine by demanding in 1895 that Great Britain arbitrate a boundary dispute with Venezuela and in 1902 that Germany and other powers arbitrate monetary claims against Venezuela. Both demands were successful, and the threatened interventions of European powers in a Latin American country were avoided.

At the same time, however, the United States was intervening in Latin America almost at will. In 1902 it exploited a revolutionary situation in order to obtain the Panama Canal Zone. In 1904 President Roosevelt declared that "chronic wrongdoing" might, in Latin America, "require intervention by some civilized nation, and in the Western Hemisphere, the adherence of the United States to the Monroe Doctrine may force the United States however reluctantly, in flagrant cases of such wrongdoing or impotence, to the exercise of an international police power." Giant American concerns like the United Fruit Company came almost to own some Latin American countries (hence, they were derisively called "Banana Republics"), and Americans came to manifest a proprietary feeling toward the territories and peoples to the south. "Speak softly," said the first Roosevelt, "but carry a big stick"; and an American-named receiver administered the financial affairs of the Dominican Republic under protection of the United States Navy. In 1915 the United States landed Marines in Haiti and assumed financial supervision and administrative control over Haitian affairs; to protect United States citizens and property Marines were kept in Nicaragua from 1911 to 1925. Such exercise of power led to Latin American charges of American imperialism and fostered a smoldering resentment of the "Yankee," which has burst into flame in our own time. Meanwhile a third element in American policy was developing: the Pan-American movement, which aimed at strengthening economic, social, and political relations among Latin American countries. The first Pan-American conference was held as early as 1889, and at the fourth such conference in 1910 the Pan American Union was established, with headquarters in Washington. After the First World War, building on the heritage of the Pan-American movement, the United States sought to alter its interventionist posture toward Latin America and embarked on a "Good Neighbor" policy. This policy was formally initiated in the Hoover Administration and carried forward enthusiastically by President Roosevelt and his first Secretary of State, Cordell Hull. At the Montevideo Conference of 1933 the United States and the Latin American countries pledged nonintervention in one another's affairs, and in Buenos Aires in 1936 they agreed on the principle of consultation among all American countries if the security of the hemisphere were threatened.

American Economic Relations

In its economic relations with other nations, American policy reflected conflicting domestic interests. On the one hand, we were a nation of exporters, particularly of grain and cotton. In the twentieth century, we were to become a nation of investors as well, notably in Latin America. Supporting trade and investment required bold promotive policies like freedom of the seas, the opening of trade with Japan, the Open Door policy in China, and intervention in Latin America. On the other hand, manufacturing and agrarian interests demanded protection of the home market for American industry, which called for restrictive trade policies. The fluctuation of our tariff rate in the first century and a half of our nation reflected the continuing seesaw between interests that wanted strong restrictive policies and those that wanted stronger promotive policies and low tariff rates. The nation moved from a moderately protective position in the beginning to greater protectionism from 1812 to 1833, then into a period of declining protectionism until the middle of the nineteenth century, and then into a forty-year period of peace on the tariff issue. The end of the century, however, brought a revival of the contest, with higher protectionism after the Wilson Act of 1894, lower after the Underwood Act of 1913, higher again after the Fordney-McCumber and Smoot-Hawley Acts of 1922 and 1930, respectively, and lower after the Reciprocal Trade Act of 1934.

Principles of International Conduct

During the first century and a half of our independence, the American nation became committed to certain broad principles of international conduct. To protect our interests we asserted the rights of neutrals in war and the concomitant principle of freedom of the seas. Similarly, we struggled against exclusive rights for any nation and for equal rights for the United States in areas newly opened to commerce. Although we annexed certain developing Western lands and intervened repeatedly in Latin America, we supported the principle of nonintervention in the internal affairs of nations and the right of self-determination of peoples. We advocated submitting disputes to arbitration, supported international law, and flirted with the idea of outlawing war. The nation thought that peace and order were normal conditions of international relations, that morality could govern in the affairs of nations, that military power was an evil to be avoided, and that America's duty to itself and the world was merely to demonstrate the viability of domestic institutions built on freedom and democracy.

A WORLD POWER: TRANSITION IN POLICY

The shots at Sarajevo signaled the collapse of an intricately balanced world order and rang up the curtain on what the French political scientist Raymond Aron has called "the century of total war." For the United States the condition of isolation was over, and total involvement lay ahead, but one would never have guessed it from the detachment with which most Americans viewed the eruption across the Atlantic. Had a public-opinion sample been taken, it would certainly have shown dominant pro-Allied sentiment in this country, but the overriding desire was to stay out. "I didn't raise my boy to be a soldier," sang American mothers, and President Wilson spoke of a people "too proud to fight."

When the President was forced by events to commit America to the struggle, he justified the move on millennial moral grounds—it was to be a "war to end all wars." America would lead the squabbling powers of Europe to a lasting peace based on a rejection of the old diplomacy and statecraft. "Open covenants, openly arrived at" would ensure the rights of all peoples to self-determination. The First World War was oversold to the nation, and as a result it was followed by proportionately bitter disillusionment. Peace, many believed, was something concomitant with military victory. They did not understand that the continued application of American power was needed to stabilize the international environment. A wave of disillusionment helped to sweep the United States away from the League of Nations and send Wilson to his death. America hoped for isolation once more.

But the world had changed since the war, and the old international system from which America had benefited for so long could not be "put back together." The scientific revolution, which had made the Great War so devastating, was accelerating, not slowing down. The Italian strategist Douhet was developing a theory of how to fight a war from the air, and American Army Colonel Billy Mitchell was busy proving air power's effectiveness by simulated attacks on capital ships in the Navy's mothball fleet. The country managed to ignore all this, however, and the standard historical interpretation of the 1920's and 1930's as an inward-looking period is certainly correct. The nation was preoccupied with domestic crises, and responses to crises abroad were limited to treaties renouncing force (the Kellogg-Briand Pact of 1927) and then to Neutrality Acts (in 1935, 1936, and 1937). But while neutrality had been a rational and successful policy for the new and weak America, it was neither rational nor successful for the economically mature America of the late thirties. The United States was a great power; it had proved this in 1917. And the threat of expansionist regimes in both Europe and the Far East demanded that the United States act like one again. All this was quite apparent to Franklin Roosevelt as his attention shifted from domestic to foreign concerns after 1937.

In a speech in October of 1937, the President used a forceful metaphor to advocate active American collaboration with European democracies against Germany, Italy, and Japan:

> It seems unfortunately true that the epidemic of world lawlessness is spreading. When an epidemic of physical disease starts to spread, the community approves and joins in a quarantine of the patients in order to protect the health of the community against the spread of the disease.

The public and press reaction to this "Quarantine Speech" was so negative, however, that Roosevelt was forced to proceed with great caution in preparing America, morally and physically, to engage Germany and Japan. Even the fall of France to Hitler's blitzkrieg in the spring of 1940 did not bring domestic opinion around to accepting the necessity of involvement. Roosevelt felt impelled to declare in a campaign speech in Boston in October of 1940, "I shall say it again and again and again. Your boys are not going to be sent into any foreign wars." Great Britain was to be shored up by "all aid short of war." Congress did accept the nation's first peacetime draft in 1940; and after three months of agonizing politicking, the Lend-Lease program was approved early in 1941. Under this arrangement a steady stream of sustaining war materiel was pumped into England and the USSR.

The shock of Pearl Harbor, however, changed everything overnight. As in 1917, after we declared war we developed an absolute commitment to a moral crusade and put naive faith in military victory—which became the single all-demanding goal. Thus the one test of any proposal, any program, any initiative became, "Will it bring unconditional surrender any faster?" This policy of putting purely military goals above all other considerations (called by H. Bradford Westerfield the policy of "total war and limited diplomacy") improved morale, but it often resulted in gross misuse of the options available to our leaders.

Nowhere was this clearer than in our relations with the Soviet Union. On many occasions the United States gave way to Stalin in diplomatic negotiations for fear that otherwise Russia would reduce its war effort. Perhaps most important, we failed to occupy as much of defeated Germany as possible, and the consequences of this failure haunt us today in the shape of communist East Germany. As one analyst has put it:

> The original decision not to [push on as far to the East in Europe as possible in order to increase our bargaining power with the Russians] was made with tragically little scrutiny on the part of top officials either in Britain or the United States. In Washington, the policymakers were even influenced by a positive desire to minimize American occupation responsibilities in Germany so that more troops could be moved to the Far East.[1]

Nonetheless, the concentration on victory at the price of larger political considerations did not altogether preclude official thinking about America's role in keeping the future peace. Roosevelt and his advisers were determined that Wilson's fate would not be theirs—this time there would be no American withdrawal from responsibility. From the beginning the United States took a leading part in creating the United Nations. We emerged from the struggle with a commitment to the continuing job of keeping the new peace. But the country wanted the troops home and the rationing system abolished at a stroke—an old story. While Americans were resigned to the fact that they could not put their burden down as they had attempted to do after 1918, they did feel that it ought to become much lighter with the fall of Hitler and the Mikado. The reverse, however, proved true.

SUPERPOWER POLITICS: FOREIGN POLICY SINCE 1945

In 1945 the people of the United States did not realize the extent of the burden that had in fact been thrust upon them. Before the Second World War they had reluctantly accepted their position as one nation in a world of strong states. After the war, however, Britain, France, and Italy were facing severe economic and political problems, Germany and Japan were prostrate, Russia was consolidating her gains in Eastern Europe, China was in civil war, and desperate human needs existed around the globe. The United States was by comparison a superpower—stronger than any other power in the West since Rome had dominated it. As a superpower the

[1] H. Bradford Westerfield, *The Instruments of America's Foreign Policy* (New York: Crowell, 1963), p. 91.

United States thus faced a concentration of responsibilities that no power in the prewar period had had to grapple with.

The immediate problems were those of relief and rebuilding of the war-stricken areas. But new forces were being shaped that would increase the difficulties of the United States in her new role. A revolution with two dimensions was under way in the underdeveloped areas of the world. One aspect was political: the movement for national independence. The nationalism that had stirred the European continent through the nineteenth century and the early part of the twentieth and had animated the struggle for independence in Latin America in the nineteenth had now burst into Africa and Asia. The postwar period has been one of liquidation of Western colonialism and the rise of new nations. Peoples who only yesterday had been dependent colonials have been admitted to the family of nations. The second dimension of the revolution was social and economic. The peoples in the underdeveloped areas of the world, after exposure to Western affluence and technology, wanted a new life. They desired to move their countries swiftly into the twentieth century. Most of these peoples were interested in avoiding alignment in the struggle of big powers, for they were concerned primarily with their own survival and economic development.

Finally, there was the Soviet Union and what was soon to become known as the Cold War. In early 1946, speaking at Westminster College in Fulton, Missouri, Winston Churchill denounced the Soviet Union as an expansionist state and declared to the American people:

> From Stettin in the Baltic to Trieste in the Adriatic, an iron curtain has descended across the Continent. Behind that line lie all the capitals of the ancient states of Central and Eastern Europe. Warsaw, Berlin, Prague, Vienna, Budapest, Belgrade, Bucharest, and Sofia, all the famous cities and the populations around them lie in the Soviet sphere and all are subject in one form or another, not only to Soviet influence but to a very high and increasing control from Moscow.

During the war years American leaders had hoped that after the victory the Soviet Union would conduct herself as a responsible member of the community of nations, and the very structure of the United Nations rested on the assumption of "great-power unity." It was considered imperative that the two nations get along. Presidential adviser Harry Hopkins had said after the Big Three conference at Yalta:

> We really believed in our hearts that this was the dawn of the new day. . . . The Russians had proved that they could be reasonable and farseeing, and there wasn't any doubt in the minds of the President or any of us that we could live with them and get along with them peacefully for as far into the future as any of us could imagine.[2]

---

[2] Robert E. Sherwood, *Roosevelt and Hopkins: An Intimate History* (New York: Harper & Row, 1948), p. 870.

These hopes died hard, and it took many months for the men who made American foreign policy to accept the difficult reality of Russian aggression and intransigence.

The psychological problem of facing the Soviet threat was compounded by a practical problem: the military capacity of the United States to meet a new threat had been seriously impaired by our swift demobilization in 1945—so rapidly did it proceed that by the end of 1946 the great war machine was decimated. In the words of W. W. Rostow:

> By 1947 the Navy and Air Force were cut to about one-seventh of wartime peak strength, the Army to one-sixteenth. Over-all total military personnel were reduced by mid-1947 to 13 per cent of the mid-1945 peak. But figures alone do not adequately convey the impact of demobilization. Due to the discharge of key trained men, a lack of volunteers, and the need to maintain overhead establishments and noncombat units, the number of combat divisions at readiness was pitifully low. The Air Force reported in December 1946 only two and in June 1947 only 11 groups at combat effectiveness, out of the 52 groups provided as peacetime establishment. The Navy, perhaps less drastically affected than the other two services, was nevertheless stretched thin by a more rapid demobilization of personnel than of base units, which resulted in nominally active units being immobilized for lack of crews.[3]

We did, of course, enjoy a monopoly of the new atomic weapons, but our stockpile was very small, and their use would have exposed all of Western Europe to Soviet occupation, which we lacked the ground forces to prevent.

The Era of Bipolarity: The Policy of Containment

Alexis de Tocqueville, writing about America and Russia in the 1830's, remarked that "each of them seems marked out . . . to sway the destinies of half the globe." On March 17, 1948, one month after the communists seized control of Czechoslovakia, President Truman in a message to Congress identified the Soviet Union as the one nation blocking peace. And from the Truman message until the Cuban confrontation of 1962, De Tocqueville's prediction of more than a century before seemed to have become a reality. Polarity—the confrontation of two superpowers representing conflicting ideologies—was the hallmark of international politics.

In the years following the Truman statement, the United States evolved a policy toward the communist world called *containment*. An influential ideologist of containment was the career diplomat George Kennan, who, under the nom de plume of "Mr. X," published an article in the July 1947 issue of the influential periodical *Foreign Affairs*, entitled "The Sources of Soviet Conduct." Kennan wrote that "the main element in any United States policy toward the Soviet Union must be that of a long-term, patient but firm and vigilant containment of Russian expansive tendencies."

[3] W. W. Rostow, *The United States in the World Arena* (New York: Harper & Row, 1960), p. 172.

As a policy, containment was given substance by the action of our government in certain crises involving the Soviet Union and ourselves. The first of these was the decision to aid Greece and Turkey, accompanied by the announcement of the Truman Doctrine. On the afternoon of February 21, 1947, a representative of the British Embassy delivered at the Department of State two notes that reviewed the dire economic and military positions of Greece and Turkey and indicated that Britain was unable to continue to support them despite the threat of their falling under Russian control. At this moment Great Britain "handed the job of world leadership, with all its burdens and all its glory, to the United States."[4] Addressing Congress on March 12, President Truman said, "I believe that we must assist free peoples to work out their own destiny in their own way." Congress responded, and the United States gave Greece and Turkey economic and financial aid, thus removing the immediate threat that the Russians might dominate the Mediterranean and through it the Middle East and Southern Europe.

A second decision was foretold in a speech by Secretary of State Marshall at Harvard's commencement exercises on June 5, 1947. He told of the imminent economic collapse of Western Europe unless aid came promptly and declared, "It is logical that the United States should do whatever it is able to assist in the return of normal economic health in the world, without which there can be no political stabilization or assured peace." The Marshall Plan, under which the United States offered multibillion-dollar economic aid to the nations of Western Europe, grew out of this statement. The announced enemies were "hunger, poverty, desperation, and chaos," and assistance by other nations was invited. Russia adamantly refused to participate. The massive aid given by the United States at this time restored the economies of Western Europe and in so doing removed the threat of communist takeover in that part of the world.

The first major confrontation with the communists came on June 24, 1948, when the Soviet Union, after preliminary obstructions to Western commerce with Berlin, stopped all rail and road traffic between Western Europe and the western sector of Berlin. The United States broke this blockade with the Berlin airlift—the flying of food and other necessities into Berlin. On June 11 the Senate had passed the Vandenberg Resolution, which called for American military support to regional alliances under Article 51 of the United Nations Charter; and on April 4, 1949, the treaty for the North Atlantic Treaty Organization (NATO) was signed. This was the first peacetime military alliance entered into by the United States since the eighteenth century, and its significance as a counter to Soviet expansion can hardly be overstressed. The member states agreed that an attack on one would be an attack on all and further agreed "to unite their

---

[4] Joseph M. Jones, *The Fifteen Weeks* (New York: Viking, 1955), p. 7.

efforts for collective defense and for the preservation of peace and security." To buttress this commitment a complex organization was established, including, among other things, a joint command system. The United States committed troops and bombs to this alliance, establishing a "forward" defense line at the Elbe River.

In 1949 our foreign-aid program was broadened to include military, economic, and technical assistance. A Mutual Defense Assistance Act in 1949 authorized the President to furnish "military assistance" to parties to the North Atlantic Alliance. Earlier in the year President Truman had stressed a so-called Point Four Program (point four in his inaugural address) in which he called for technical aid to underdeveloped areas.

A test of containment came suddenly in Korea on June 24, 1950. The last American fighting forces had been withdrawn from that divided country almost a year before, and the Republic of Korea must have looked to the communist leaders like a plum ripe for plucking. Truman was faced with an awesome decision, which he had to make alone and at once—there was no time to ask Congress for a decision, no time to let a popular consensus take shape, not even time to wait for United Nations action. As Republic of Korea forces reeled before the initial thrust of the invasion, the President of the United States committed our armed forces to the struggle. We fought this "nasty little war," along with our UN allies, until the truce was signed at Panmunjom on July 27, 1953. The struggle cost 23,300 American lives, and our UN allies lost 14,000. Critics of the Truman Administration argued that simply repulsing an invasion was too small a victory for so much blood. The debate still continues as to whether the fighting should have been carried into China (after the latter's intervention in the conflict), in order to unify Korea. There were, however, three gains from the war:

First, the United States demonstrated that in the face of overt communist aggression, it was willing to put its troops on the line. Second, the Korean War rearmed America. To meet pressure of the war, Congress appropriated the money to create a realistic defense establishment. The armed forces grew from 1.5 to 3.5 million men, and the annual defense budget grew from $12 billion to $41 billion.

Third, America demonstrated to itself that it was capable of fighting a limited war. Such pragmatic considerations as matching limited objectives with the limited applications of force took precedence over the calls for a crusade, for absolute victory. "The subordination of the military point of view to the political," the nineteenth-century strategist Karl von Clausewitz had stated, "is . . . the only thing that is rationally possible." Americans were learning this lesson.

Another test came suddenly on October 14, 1962—a test of "nerve and will." Rolls of film taken by American planes revealed the beginnings of Soviet medium-range missile bases in Cuba. Russia was invading the

Western Hemisphere in daring contravention of American policy since President Monroe; moreover, it was about to establish a missile base about 100 miles from our coastline. Such action threatened not only American security but also the balance existing between the two superpowers, which had excluded Russia from military power in the United States' peculiar sphere of influence–the Western Hemisphere.

In several days of secret, tortuous deliberations, President Kennedy and his advisers sought the appropriate response. (For discussion of this decision-making process, see pages 765–67.) The alternatives ranged from doing nothing to invading Cuba or conducting an air strike on her. The first alternative was rejected because of its military implications and its adverse effects on the global political balance, and there seemed little hope of prompt results by purely diplomatic approaches. Invasion or a "surgical" air strike was rejected because either one would alienate Latin Americans and present a direct military challenge to the Soviet Union.

Missiles in Cuba: Threat to the Status Quo

Within the past week, unmistakable evidence has established the fact that a series of offensive missile sites is now in preparation on [the island of Cuba].

The purpose of these bases can be none other than to provide a nuclear strike capability against the Western Hemisphere....

This urgent transformation of Cuba into an important strategic base—by the presence of these large, long-range and clearly offensive weapons of sudden mass destruction—constitutes an explicit threat to the peace and security of all the Americas, in flagrant and deliberate defiance of the Rio pact of 1947, the traditions of this nation and hemisphere, the joint resolution of the 87th Congress, the Charter of the United Nations, and my own public warnings to the Soviets on Sept. 4 and 13....

This secret, swift and extraordinary build-up of Communist missiles—in an area well-known to have a special and historical relationship to the United States and the nations of the Western Hemisphere, in violation of Soviet assurances, and in defiance of American and hemispheric policy—this sudden, clandestine decision to station strategic weapons for the first time outside of Soviet soil—is a deliberately provocative and unjustified change in the status quo which cannot be accepted by this country, if our courage and our commitments are ever to be trusted again by either friend or foe....

Our unswerving objective, therefore, must be to prevent the use of these missiles against this or any other country, and to secure their withdrawal or elimination from the Western Hemisphere.

From President John F. Kennedy, message to the Nation, October 1962.

An intermediate approach was finally chosen: a blockade—called a "quarantine" by the President—against incoming vessels that could be carrying the nuclear weaponry. Dramatically, the President spoke to the American people and told them of the decision. He informed the UN and our allies and obtained the approval of the Organization of American States. Premier Khrushchev harshly rejected the quarantine as "piracy." Eighteen Soviet dry-cargo ships, soon joined by six submarines, were moving across the Atlantic toward Cuba, and American naval vessels waited to stop them for inspection. People throughout the world watched this critical confrontation anxiously, fearing nuclear interchange between the two nations.

The threat eased, however, when the Soviet ships turned back to their home ports. But a new crisis arose: an American U-2 was shot down, and the American demand that Russian missile sites in Cuba be dismantled was met by the counterdemand that United States missiles be removed from Turkey—indicating greater Soviet interest in extending its own sphere of influence in the East than in establishing a new one in the West. Fear of a Soviet move on Berlin, Turkey, or some other area mounted. The President was being urged by some advisers to take stronger action in Cuba immediately. The two nations were moving to military readiness. Then, suddenly, on a bright Sunday morning, a message came from Khrushchev accepting Kennedy's demand that Russian weapons systems in Cuba be dismantled under UN supervision.

The world had passed its first nuclear crisis, and some lessons about pursuit of foreign-policy objectives had been demonstrated. The President had looked cautiously for the response that was sufficient but would not aggravate—avoiding all pressures to be bellicose or to overact; while firm, he had looked for the point of concession in the letters that came to him from Khrushchev; carefully he had left his opponent a way out. This confrontation demonstrated the value of the firm but limited response and also the value of direct communications; the heads of the two states, who had earlier measured each other's will in a conference in Vienna, exchanged about a dozen letters during the Cuban crisis.

The Era of Multipolarity: Complex Challenges to a Superpower

Since the early 1960's the world has moved into a new phase of multipolar politics. The Cold War between two superpowers is not ended, but the control of each over "the destinies of half the globe" has been weakened. On the communist side, China has detonated the bomb and is soon to be a nuclear power. Moreover, it has stretched its web of influence into the unsettled politics of the underdeveloped nations. Its long boundary with the Soviet Union makes the latter conscious of the need to preserve its own national interests, irrespective of ideological affinities. A contest over doctrine and policy has developed between China, in the early phases of revolution and with unrealized goals, and the Soviet Union, now having consolidated its internal power and having become a nation with benefits to preserve and expand for its people. The will to foster revolutions in other countries is strong in China, weaker in Russia, and their national interests conflict. In Europe the nationalism that led Yugoslavia to break with the Soviet Union in 1948 and to follow an independent course now breathes more strongly in the satellite nations on the fringes of the Soviet Union as they struggle to build their own economies through independent policies that include trade with the West.

On the Western side, de Gaulle has asserted French independence of American leadership and is as openly critical of the United States as China is of the Soviets. He seeks a "new Europe" in which French leadership will prevail and American influence will be excluded. To this end, he is building an independent nuclear force and in 1966 called for the withdrawal of NATO headquarters and installations from France. He courts friendly relations with the Soviet Union and tries to draw West Germany and Great Britain away from American influence. West Germany, however, bordering the Russian "sphere of influence" and eager for reunification with East Germany, still looks for support from the United States. It supports the NATO alliance, in which American strength in Europe is preserved, and fears the withdrawal of American troops from within its borders. Great Britain, too weak to build its defenses independently, still links itself with the United States but is tempted to accept French conditions for entrance into the European Economic Community. In its war in Vietnam the United States gets no support from its European allies, and they pursue their independent policies on trade with China. As for the underdeveloped countries of the world, they maintain a neutralist position with respect to the struggle of world powers. In sum, all around the globe, the struggle for national unity, independence, and strength overshadows the issues of the Cold War and weakens the willingness to follow the leadership of either of the giants. Capitalist, communist, and neutralist states resemble one another in being nationalist first.

With multipolarity have come more complex challenges for the United States. The Korean and Cuban crises represented direct and uncomplicated threats to existing power balances. But later American intervention in Santo Domingo and Vietnam illustrates the growing complexity of leadership in a world with many conflicting national interests and many simmering cauldrons.

Santo Domingo

In Santo Domingo one of a series of revolutions erupted on April 24, 1966. Four days later President Johnson sent some four hundred Marines to Santo Domingo, announcing to the American people that this was necessary to protect American lives—to prevent a "blood bath in the streets." A few days later he declared that communists had influenced the revolution and explained, in what some have called the Johnson Doctrine: "The American nations cannot, must not, and will not permit the establishment of another Communist government in the Western Hemisphere." He enlarged the Marine force on the island to about 22,000, supported by American ships and sailors offshore. The Marines evacuated nearly 3,000 Americans and a lesser number of foreigners, stood guard over the armed groups that faced each other across the streets, stayed until an election had been held and an effective government established, and then were withdrawn.

Debate over the justification for these actions has been spirited and will be continued by historians. Critics have charged first that Johnson's action represented a revival of "big stick" diplomacy that was contrary to the Good Neighbor policy and the spirit of the Alliance for Progress. Second, critics argued that the intervention violated the charter of the Organization of American States, in which the United States and other nations in the hemisphere had renounced any right of intervention in the affairs of any other state and had bound themselves to collective action in meeting threats to peace and security. Immediately after his initial dispatch of troops, President Johnson sought the support of the Organization of American States, and within a few weeks it had approved the intervention 14–5, resolved to send an Inter-American peace-keeping force to Santo Domingo, and dispatched a five-man peace mission to the island. Third, critics charged that the President's allegation of communist influence was erroneous or exaggerated, that Marines assisted rightist forces in Santo Domingo, that the President had been guilty of "overkill" (using more force than was necessary), and that the United States was trying to act as a world policeman.

This episode suggests two hazards—one for all governments, the other for democratic governments in particular—in responding to sudden changes in situations. First, a decision may be forced on the administration before the relevant facts, and the weights to be given to them, are conclusive—presidents and prime ministers cannot enjoy the luxury of time afforded the research scholar. Under these circumstances the government may respond incorrectly: it may lose an opportunity for action, or it may over-react to a situation. Second, the obscurity of the facts in such a situation may well confuse the public, particularly when—as in the Santo Domingo incident—critics of the administration charge that the government has not told the people the correct story. Thus, the public is left without a sound basis for evaluating the action of its public officials. The people cannot know during the period of crisis whether the quick response was correct, and by the time the data is complete other events will have their attention.

The role of the United States as "policeman" reveals the contradictions within American policy and the sacrifice of some objectives in order to attain others. Santo Domingo is in an area so important to United States security that it will be kept within an American "sphere of influence." As

Walter Lippmann said: "spheres of influence are fundamental in the very nature of international society. They are as much a fact of life as are birth and death. Great powers will resist the invasion of their spheres of influence." [5] But a country's assertion of power to protect its spheres of influence irritates neighbors, particularly those with ambitions of their own. Since the Second World War, the United States has taken bold steps to buttress its Good Neighbor policy: it supported the Organization of American States through which the nations of the Western Hemisphere could take joint action for regional security; and the Kennedy Administration launched the Alliance for Progress, an enlarged program of economic aid for Latin American countries adopting programs of economic and social reform. But the effect of our efforts toward good will and of our economic aid is undercut by Latin American resentment of American "interventionalism," which is now motivated by our resolve to avoid more communist states in this hemisphere.

Vietnam

While quick reaction to sudden confrontation has marked American responses in many situations, in Vietnam our involvement grew gradually from small beginnings to massive dimensions. Moreover, in contrast to Korea, where direct aggression took place across national boundaries, Vietnam has been the victim of a new kind of invasion: infiltration, terrorism, and political subversion, which have developed into an internal war.

American economic aid to Vietnam was initiated in 1951, five years after the conflict there began and two years after the communists gained power in China. After the French withdrew from Vietnam in 1954, the United States took over the training of the South Vietnamese Army, and, in the years that followed, American involvement in strengthening the Saigon government increased. The appointment of Ngo Dinh Diem as premier in 1954 and his elevation to the Presidency in 1955 initially offered promise for strong government in Saigon. But in various ways the situation in South Vietnam deteriorated. The elections leading to the unification of North and South Vietnam, called for by agreements in Geneva in 1954, were bypassed in 1956. Diem simply announced—with tacit concurrence of the United States—that since the communists would not permit free electioneering in North Vietnam he would not permit free elections in South Vietnam. In 1957 guerrilla warfare expanded in South Vietnam; in 1958 trained cadres of troops began infiltrating South Vietnam from North Vietnam over the network of Ho Chi Minh trails; and in 1959 the Communist party of North Vietnam advocated the "liberation" of the south and the unification of Vietnam. In the meantime, China's leader Mao had taken a hard line

[5] New York *Herald Tribune*, May 4, 1965.

toward the West, announcing that the "East wind prevails over the West wind."

As time passed American involvement continued to expand. In 1961, after the American–South Vietnamese position had further deteriorated, President Kennedy increased American aid, and the positions of the great powers were affirmed—China accused the United States of aggression, Russia charged that we had created "a serious danger to peace," and President Kennedy declared that the United States would do all it could to save South Vietnam from communism. In 1964, events demonstrating the weakness of Saigon led to further American involvement. Diem's harsh repression of Buddhist protest led to his ouster and assassination. Internal divisions within South Vietnam threatened the viability of the Saigon government, and pacification efforts in the villages were failing. United States ships were attacked in the Gulf of Tonkin, and Congress, with only two dissents in the Senate and none in the House, approved a resolution giving the President authority to resist aggression in Southeast Asia. In 1965, in order to reduce the flow of supplies and men from North Vietnam into South Vietnam, President Johnson launched continuous bombings of North Vietnam; also, American ground forces, heretofore serving as advisers, became openly engaged in the conflict.

By this time the justifications for American involvement had been repeatedly stated by American officials. One was given by President Johnson in a speech at Johns Hopkins University: "We are there because we have a promise to keep." The government in Saigon and the people of the world understood that the United States had committed itself; its honor and the credibility of its other commitments were now at stake.

But why had the pledge been given? The direct answer of American officials has been that we are engaged in a struggle against aggression. They argue that this struggle is morally justified because it is protecting the right of the people of South Vietnam to self-determination. For President Johnson the struggle is also essential to prevent the same type of cumulative aggressions that led to the Second World War. Howard K. Smith, news commentator, has said, "We are in a hurry to establish that principle [that borders should not be changed by violent means] . . . before China is a nuclear power. . . . That is why we are resisting in Vietnam." The Administration has coupled this fight against aggression with the fight against communism: it fears aggressive Chinese expansionism under the banner of communism. Two theories suggest how this expansion might take place: the "domino theory," according to which neighboring countries would crumble before Communist China if the United States withdrew or capitulated in South Vietnam, and the "checkers theory," according to which communist nations could jump to whatever position offered opportunities if aggression were not stopped now.

All these justifications, and others, have been attacked in perhaps the

"Well, what is it—a hawk or a dove?"

The public debate over escalation versus deescalation of the Vietnam war in the late 1960's polarized the American population into competing camps.

Gaberg in the *Saturday Review*

most open discussion ever allowed in a country engaged in a war. Moreover, issues of tactics as well as of principle have split the nation into three groups: the "doves," who want to deescalate the war or get out; the "hawks" who want to escalate American military action to whatever extent is necessary to provide the traditional quick and all-out American victory; and those who in general support the middle course pursued by the President.

Behind these conflicts are profound political questions: What is the size of the American commitment to world leadership? Is it a truly global commitment? The encirclement of the Soviet Union by postwar alliances and our responses in Greece, Berlin, and Korea were affirmative answers to this question. Must the Cold War, once fought so single-mindedly and persistently against the Soviets, now be fought against China? Are there limitations to what is possible and what is desirable? Should China be granted a "sphere of influence" in the Asian world, just as we asserted one for ourselves in Cuba and Santo Domingo and recognized one for Russia in Hungary? What would be involved in such a decision? Acceptance of expansion by aggression, of unimpeded Chinese expansion through South Asia and the Far East, of withdrawal of the West from the East? Can West and East be separated in the world of tomorrow?

And then there are issues of tactics: What military battlegrounds must the United States accept? Can limited wars be fought and limited responses be made if these appear to be in the national interest? Can diplomacy regain allies for American positions in the postpolarization stage?

Complicating these problems are the difficulties facing the United States in the conduct of the Cold War. First, the communists have certain advantages in psychological warfare. Their doctrine is dramatic and simple: capitalism and imperialism are responsible for the troubles of the world; communism offers a means of salvation, and its victory is inevitable. Western liberalism is a more complex body of ideas, and hence more difficult to present in street-corner oratory. Second, the enemy is supremely flexible and follows the communist doctrine that "action programs" should change as conditions change. Direct assault may be suspended, but infiltration and propaganda continue. Any means that ultimately advance the cause of communism are moral. Third, the necessary conditions for growth of Western political and economic institutions do not exist in many underdeveloped countries. Democracy has proved viable in countries with a large middle class, high literacy, and experience in local self-government. Capitalism has thrived in countries with surplus private savings; and "welfare capitalism," with few exceptions, has flourished in countries with democratic institutions. The process of development on the Western model is very slow—as witnessed by the experience of India. The communists, by contrast, offer glib promises of quick progress. Fourth, it is often difficult for the United States to respond to communist efforts to subvert a noncommunist government. Are we justified in intervening in the domestic political life of a "target" nation such as Cuba or Laos? Finally, the Cold War tests American wisdom and will. The United States must now make flexible responses to a complex world situation. In a nonpolarized world the alignment of interests will vary somewhat from issue to issue. Friends will thus be less dependable, although we will no doubt continue our broad system of alliances with nations that have been our friends since the Second World War. Conversely, opportunities may be presented for reconciliation of differences and increased trade with Russia and its satellites. But correct choices of policy and tactics are difficult in a nonpolarized situation, and the choices will not always bring complete success. Americans, accustomed to quick and decisive victory, find the costs, the strains, and the frustrations of the Cold War difficult to understand. Many Americans, indeed, are beginning to take a neo-isolationist position: they suggest that we restrict our commitments abroad in order to conserve our resources for the improvement of conditions in American cities. This position conflicts with the opinion of those who believe that America is rich enough to afford both world leadership and domestic improvement. Given these conflicts, it is difficult for the government to maintain a rational and consistent policy. The American people may well be tested for the patience, perseverance, and unity required for wise world leadership.

CONTINUING PROBLEMS OF DEFENSE AND FOREIGN POLICY

The vastly increased American involvement in world affairs since 1945 has meant that our decision makers not only must face specific crises as they occur around the globe but must cope with many continuing problems and issues in defense and foreign policy. This section examines some of these central issues.

Preparedness for the "Flexible Response"

When America began to rearm during 1950 and 1951, it created a military establishment with one purpose—to contain the expansion of the communist bloc. But now that the Soviet Union possesses thermonuclear weapons and the capacity to deliver them, American military policy has developed two objectives: first, ensuring that the Soviet Union never finds that it is in its national interest to launch a nuclear attack against the United States; second, preventing the expansion of communism by aggression. To do these separate jobs a balance of nuclear and conventional forces is obviously necessary; the "great debates" over defense in the late fifties and early sixties revolved around the proper nature of this balance and how much the country could afford to pay for it.

In 1953 a new national administration took power, committed to reducing the expenditures of the federal government. Although the American monopoly of nuclear striking power was fast becoming a thing of the past, the Administration decided that principal reliance could be placed on atomic weapons for halting communist aggression. Ground troops are expensive to keep—putting the money into the Strategic Air Command would, it was suggested, give "more bang for the buck." If the Soviet leaders started trouble anywhere in the world, we would simply order them to desist or be subjected to "massive retaliation." But as Soviet strategic power grew, the credibility of massive retaliation became less persuasive. It was obvious that the United States would not use nuclear weapons against Moscow to punish a limited Soviet thrust (like closing the autobahn to Berlin) when the Soviet Union was in a position to level American cities in return. An overnuclearized American military establishment was in danger of becoming muscle-bound.

Thus, in the later years of the Eisenhower Administration and the first years of the Kennedy Administration, there was a reexamination of our ability to wage war with conventional arms. It was the aim of the "Kennedy men" to prepare the United States for response to diverse situations with an *appropriate* application of force for each. Thus the President would have a range of options in dealing with an aggressive act, rather than being limited to launching a nuclear attack or backing down. Since this buildup of conventional forces took place in addition to the perfecting of our nuclear arsenal, its cost was considerable. The Kennedy defense budgets ran approximately $10 billion per year over the amount the Eisenhower Administration had spent in its last year.

In recent years we have had to broaden our responses even further to deal with "unconventional war." Such warfare is conducted by guerrillas, and its goal is to win—through terror, propaganda, or favors—the support of communities. This kind of warfare was fought by underground movements in Poland, Italy, and other occupied nations during the Second World War; it has been employed by communists, successfully in China, Cuba, and other places and unsuccessfully in Malaya and the Philippines; it is now being fought in Vietnam. In such warfare, the enemy avoids direct combat; he must be sought out individually or in small groups in jungles and villages. Moreover, Starfire jets and homing Sidewinder rockets are of little help in raising living standards in an Asian village or in persuading peasants that the established government is interested in their welfare. A guerrilla war is won by effective political action at the grassroots, or not at all. The American military officer is now busy learning a new role as leader of a civic-action team.

Arms Control and Disarmament

Disarmament has been under public discussion and the subject of innumerable conferences since 1946. In 1961 the United States Arms Control and Disarmament Agency was created to deal with the problem. Two kinds of pressure create interest in this issue. First is the increasing cost of armament, which strains the economy and diverts the resources of the nation from social welfare to military programs. Second is the concern that a nuclear war might be started deliberately or by accident. The danger will grow as France, China, and other nations expand or develop nuclear capacity. Yet the problems of disarmament are so difficult and national interests are so deeply involved that agreement, even among the few powers now having nuclear weapons, has been difficult to achieve.

It has been said that "Much East-West 'negotiation' [on arms control] has been in fact diplomatic shadow-boxing, thoroughly overladen with propaganda." [6] But there have also been periods of renewed hope, and the seriousness of the problem and the public interest in it have kept the discussions alive. In 1946 the United States suggested the Baruch Plan, specifying United Nations ownership, management, and/or licensing of all atomic materials and facilities. The Soviet response to this was negative. In recent years the United States position has called for limited measures of *arms control* (as opposed to complete disarmament), coupled with insistence on effective inspection. We have held that there can be no limitation of nuclear stockpiles or cessation of production unless a system of inspection and control is agreed to beforehand. The Soviet Union, on the other hand, has advocated broad programs of general and complete disarmament (extending to both conventional and nuclear armaments) but has been unwilling to

[6] Louis Henkin, ed., *Arms Control: Issues for the Public* (Englewood Cliffs, N.J.: Prentice-Hall, 1961), p. 19.

agree in advance to inspection and control of the demilitarizing process. This difference in positions has brought most conferences to a stalemate.

A step toward ending the arms race was taken in a treaty signed by the United States, the Soviet Union, and a number of other nations—not including Communist China and France—in 1963. The treaty provides for cessation of above-ground testing of nuclear weapons, with the reservation that a nation may resume testing after notifying the other parties to the treaty. The immediate effect of this limited test ban was to stop the pollution of the atmosphere and the resulting dangers of genetic damage to the world's population. A further step was taken in a treaty signed by sixty nations in 1967, banning the orbiting of nuclear weapons in outer space, the testing of weapons on the moon, and the assertion of territorial claims to the moon's surface.

Foreign Aid

Assistance from strong to weak nations is a feature of twentieth-century international relations. Not only the United States but Russia, China, and some Western European nations now give aid to less developed nations. Foreign aid is an instrument of foreign policy—of strengthening allies, winning friends, or preventing nations from moving into a rival sphere of power. It can also reflect a genuine interest in helping other peoples to attain higher living standards and to achieve viable economic and political systems.

The American aid program since the Second World War has gone through several phases. The Marshall Plan provided aid to rebuild previously developed economies that had been damaged by war. After 1949 there was an increased emphasis on military aid. Then President Kennedy stressed the objective of stimulating economic development through institutional and programatic innovations such as the Alliance for Progress, capital loans, and the Peace Corps. President Johnson has offered a multibillion-dollar aid program to Southeast Asia and has called for aid in population control.

Our aid effort is continually under criticism and subject to congressional scrutiny. The President has great difficulty each year in preventing drastic cuts in appropriations for the program. Part of the reason is that attacks focus attention on real problems in the administration of aid. Waste occurs, and often the money does not reach the people of a nation but is drained off by corrupt local bureaucracies and politicians. The problem is to avoid this drain without interfering too much with the affairs of the receiving countries. Second, there has been violent criticism of aid to communist countries like Poland and Yugoslavia, given in order to help these countries toward independence from Soviet influence. Third, many critics are restive about aid to neutral countries that often criticize the United States, but it is neither possible nor desirable to purchase full agreement with United

States policies by allocations of money. Criticism about aid to underdeveloped countries is increased by the meager results often produced by our aid, for it is difficult to achieve economic development in countries with a large population growth, few capital resources, entrenched aristocracies, and no viable political institutions; yet the alternative to making an effort may be communist takeover.

The United Nations

One of the continuing problems of United States foreign policy is participation in the United Nations. The United States was a chief sponsor of the United Nations and has given it support since its charter was signed in 1945. The objective in creating the UN was collective security for the peoples of the world, and it was hoped that unity among the great powers, operating through the UN, would preserve the peace as the ill-fated League of Nations had not.

The United Nations, like the League of Nations, is not a world government or a superstate; it is a voluntary association of sovereign states, and it depends for its funds and military manpower on these members. It is the diplomatic representatives of member states rather than representatives of peoples who participate in UN deliberations and cast the votes.

The UN charter provides for two main organs: the General Assembly, representing all member states equally and giving each only one vote, and the Security Council, composed of eleven members, five of which—the United States, the Soviet Union, the United Kingdom, France, and Nationalist China—are permanent members and six of which are elected by the General Assembly for two-year terms. In the General Assembly, passage of the most important matters requires a two-thirds vote, others a majority vote. In the Security Council, procedural matters are decided by vote of seven members, substantive matters by vote of seven members subject to the veto of any permanent member of the Council.

The General Assembly is an organ of discussion and of loose supervision over the many parts of the United Nations system. The charter has delegated the most important functions, however, to the Security Council. It may investigate disputes or situations leading to international friction and make recommendations to the parties on pacific settlement; it may call on member states to interrupt economic relations, communications, or diplomatic relations with offenders; it may decide to use armed force and call on member states to supply the necessary contingents of men.

Although it has suffered many reverses, the United Nations has shown a flexibility in its operations somewhat comparable to that of the United States under its Constitution. Several major developments have occurred. First, the Council has deteriorated. The development of the East-West conflict after the Second World War destroyed the high hopes that some had for security in the world based on a concert of great powers. Instead of unanimity in the Council there has been a succession of vetoes—the Soviet Union has used the veto over one hundred times. As a result, the Council cannot function as an organ of peace and security on matters in dispute between the major powers.

Second, the Assembly has grown in influence. Article 14 of the charter gives it authority to "recommend measures for the peaceful adjustment of any situation," and the Assembly has done more than the charter provision specifically authorized it to do. When South Korea was invaded in 1950 it decided that when the Security Council was deadlocked or failed to act the Assembly could call on states for collective measures; it created a United Nations Emergency Force with contingents from ten states during the Suez dispute in 1956; and it supported the Secretary General in measures to restore peace in the Congo in 1961 and in Cyprus in 1964. Yet its weakness, too, has been revealed. The refusal of France and the Soviet Union to contribute money for the Congo peace mission, thereby threatening the solvency of the UN, showed that the support of the big powers is essential. During the Israeli-Arab war in June 1967 the conflict among the great powers and other powers as well permitted only a compromise resolution calling for withdrawal of Israeli troops; resolution of the issues in the conflict, upon which withdrawal of troops would depend, was impossible in an arena of such divided interests.

Third, the influence of small nations in the UN has increased, partly because their ranks have been expanded by the newly independent nations of Asia and Africa and partly because the Assembly has grown in influence, while the Security Council, bailiwick of the major powers, has declined. The Assembly has thus become a forum for the airing of the grievances and the hopes of the underdeveloped nations.

Fourth, the three Secretaries General have demonstrated the possibilities for strong leadership at the top, and this leadership accounted in no small part for the effectiveness of the United Nations in a number of situations where peace was threatened.

Fifth, the auxiliary and affiliated units of the United Nations have had a vigorous life. The Economic and Social Council has made studies and recommendations, operated relief and rehabilitation programs, and spawned a number of its own subsidiaries. The International Bank for Reconstruction and Development has made loans to members, and the United Nations has conducted a program of technical assistance. The United Nations Educational, Scientific, and Cultural Organization (UNESCO) has promoted cooperation among scholars and cultural groups and given new impulse to many educational developments throughout the world.

In sum, the effectiveness of the United Nations must be evaluated from a perspective different from that of its founders. The United Nations has *not* fulfilled their expectations as an organ of collective security: it has been unable to deal effectively with the issues separating East and West; and China, the most likely threat to collective security in the future, is not even a member. On the other hand, the United Nations has served some useful functions: it is a forum in which the interests of the world's nations —weak as well as strong—are expressed. Its auxiliary and affiliated units have won widespread acceptance of their activities. And, finally, it has restored peace in many local conflicts that might otherwise have led to worldwide engagement.

The future holds large questions for the United States with respect to its relation to the United Nations. Given the new influence of small nations in the UN, that body's decisions may be expected to go against the United States more often than in the past—the progressive increase in the number of votes favoring admission of Communist China is an index of the decline of our influence. In the UN, as in other diplomatic arenas, the multipolar conflict of powers may be expected to produce fluidity in their combinations as different issues are presented. Defeats for American positions will lead to new demands from groups within this country for us to restrict our participation. In any case, our policy makers will be faced with difficult decisions as to what problems should and what problems should not be "taken to the United Nations."

Foreign Trade

Foreign trade is, on the one hand, an instrument of foreign policy by which friends are won or kept, enemies are penalized, and the substantive aims of America are achieved. It is, on the other hand, an instrument for promoting internal economic prosperity. Thus, any trade policy must accommodate both foreign and domestic considerations. In the postwar period the President, whether Democrat or Republican, has been more sensitive than Congress to the international effects of trade policy, while Congress has been more sensitive to its effects upon sectional domestic interests. Until 1951 the congressional division on trade policy was substantially a party division, with the Democrats favoring a liberal (low-tariff) trade policy and the Republicans opposing it. From 1951 onward, however, there has been substantial defection from the party position by Southern Democrats from textile-manufacturing areas, followed by other Democrats distressed over oil and coal imports. Similarly, the traditional Republican unity in favoring protectionist tariffs has been broken by Midwestern and Eastern defectors who believe that farm interests and mass-production industries would be assisted by expansion of export markets. In the fifties these sectional interests formed bipartisan coalitions for and against liberalized trade policy.[7]

[7] See Joseph R. Wilkinson, *Politics and Trade Policy* (Washington: Public Affairs Press, 1960).

"If you like it, spread the word around."

Recent administrations have supported trade with Communist satellite countries as a way of breaching the wall of Eastern Europe.

The postwar trade policy of the United States has passed through three phases.[8] Following the war the United States adopted a liberal trade policy in order to assist in the restoration of Western Europe, the development of Japanese industry, and the economic growth of the underdeveloped nations. During this period the United States participated in framing a charter for an International Trade Organization, but the President dropped the proposal after its unfavorable reception by Congress. In place of this, a more limited instrument called the General Agreement on Tariffs and Trade was drafted, which serves as a forum for negotiation among the nations of the world on tariff reductions. The United States has participated in GATT since it was established, though it has never been endorsed by Congress.

During the second phase of our trade policy, we gradually moved toward a position of preventing competitive threats to American industry. Congress put restrictions on presidential reductions of tariffs below "peril points" and enacted an escape clause through which reductions, once effected, could be withdrawn. Congress expanded "buy American" legislation, which required government agencies to give preference to domestic suppliers. Quota restrictions were imposed on imports of oil, textiles, and some agricultural products receiving price support at home.

[8] For summary see William Siebold, Jr., "Trade Policies Since World War II," *Current History,* Vol. XLII (June 1962), pp. 356–61.

"Yeah—but I might hit the jackpot."

Critics of our foreign-trade policy, however, believe that Uncle Sam gets only "lumps" in the trade.

Hesse in the St. Louis *Globe-Democrat*

A third phase began with the Trade Expansion Act passed by Congress in 1962. From 1934 until the passage of this act, the President had authority to negotiate tariff reductions under the Trade Agreements Act of 1934, which was renewed and amended periodically. The 1962 act, however, gave the President larger tariff-cutting authority than he had ever been granted before. He was also authorized to give "trade-adjustment assistance" to industry and labor injured by tariff reductions: loans, loan guarantees, technical assistance, and special tax reductions could be made for industry, and retraining and relocation allowances and other benefits could be given to labor. Thus, the 1962 act provided a new means for assuring "no serious injury" to domestic interests, while maintaining a liberal international trade policy.

In addition, the Trade Expansion Act granted special authority for eliminating tariffs on categories of goods where the United States and the European Common Market countries [9] accounted for 80 percent of free-world trade. The significance of this provision was, of course, diminished by Britain's exclusion from the Common Market. But hope remains high that the new trade policy can serve the United States' international interests without damaging its domestic economy.

[9] By the 1957 Treaty of Rome, France, West Germany, Italy, and the Benelux countries agreed to an arrangement for merging their national economies (over a period of time) into a single European economy. The United States economy will be increasingly taxed to compete with this new Europe. Only if we reduce tariffs on Europe's goods will we retain access to Europe's markets.

MYTHS AND FOREIGN POLICY:
UNDERLYING AMERICAN ATTITUDES

In a healthy democratic system leaders should sometimes move ahead of popular opinion—but never too far ahead. This simple ground rule produces a problem in foreign-policy making. When the town mayor proposes a new sewer system, his constituents have some basis in their own experience for evaluating what he has to say. Most of these citizens, however, have no such capacity for evaluating the progress of the war in South Vietnam. But they do have opinions on the subject, and these opinions are largely a function of certain basic assumptions about the nature of the external world and the potential of United States power, combined with the sketchy information provided by news media. These broadly shared attitudes—public opinion—place significant limits on the range of policy choices open to those in power. We have already noted, for instance, how President Franklin Roosevelt was forced to draw back from a commitment to oppose the dictators in 1937 by the icy reception accorded his Quarantine Speech. He had challenged the public assumption that the balances of power in Europe and Asia were none of America's business.

Of course all democrats agree that leaders reflect their constituents' beliefs to some extent. At the same time, however, democrats recognize the responsibility of leaders to inform the public on policies deemed desirable by them. A central problem of carrying on foreign relations is that of creating understanding of the issues and consensus on responses among those "opinion leaders"—public officials, news commentators, newspaper editors, and scholars—who can lead the nation in intelligent discourse.

The problem is only partially one of conveying facts on strange and remote situations. National leaders must also get people to correlate their attitudes and expectations with the realities of world affairs. In many ways history has left the American people ill prepared for the Cold War struggle and worldwide involvement. Certain "myths" or prejudices—Walter Lippmann called them "stereotypes"—survive from the past and limit the effectiveness of national leaders in reaching viable positions on foreign-affairs issues. Let us examine a few of these.

Simplicity and Conspiracy

It is difficult to grasp the complexities of a single foreign-policy situation, and it is impossible to comprehend them for all situations that call for American attention. One American tendency is to oversimplify these situations by assuming that the United States has much greater control over world events and processes than in fact it does. If things go badly for the United States, critics charge that stupid leaders are making silly mistakes or that wicked leaders are sabotaging our country's interests. World history is seen as something "made in U.S.A.," and if it comes out badly someone is just not doing his job. "Who lost China?" thundered critics of the State Department in 1949 and 1950. Their question rested on the assumption that the State Department *had* China.

A closely related oversimplification is the assumption that the natural condition of the world is one of harmony and peace; conflicts or revolutionary ferment are seen not as clashes of incompatible national interests but as the work of conspirators—Wall Street, the British, Harvard, international Jewry, or Mao Tse-tung. Thus, complicated patterns of events, involving agonizing choices among competing evils, are reduced to the level of a Western movie—the only problem is to find the bandits who are poisoning the waterhole.

Fulbright's Thesis: We Must Abandon Foreign Policy Myths

We are a people used to looking at the world, and indeed at ourselves, in moralistic rather than empirical terms. We are predisposed to regard any conflict as a clash between good and evil rather than as simply a clash between conflicting interests. We are inclined to confuse freedom and democracy, which we regard as moral principles, with the way in which they are practiced in America—with capitalism, federalism, and the two-party system, which are not moral principles but simply the preferred and accepted practices of the American people....

It has become one of the "self-evident truths" of the postwar era that just as the President resides in Washington and the Pope in Rome, the Devil resides immutably in Moscow. We have come to regard the Kremlin as the permanent seat of his power and we have grown almost comfortable with a menace which, though unspeakably evil, has had the redeeming virtues of constancy, predictability, and familiarity....

I believe that we must try to overcome this excessive moralism, which binds us to old myths and blinds us to new realities and, worse still, leads us to regard new and unfamiliar ideas with fear and mistrust.

We must dare to think about "unthinkable" things. We must learn to explore all of the options and possibilities that confront us in a complex and rapidly changing world. We must learn to welcome rather than fear the voices of dissent and not to recoil in horror whenever some heretic suggests that Castro may survive or that Khrushchev isn't as bad a fellow as Stalin was.

From Senator J. William Fulbright of Arkansas, "Old Myths and New Realities," speech to the United States Senate, March 1964.

Rebuttal to Fulbright: We Cannot Abandon Our Myths

Senator Fulbright deplores what he terms "excessive moralism." Yet if the U.S. abandons moral principles in world policy and turns toward the so-called "practical" side, with its materialistic motivation, and, in effect, admits that it cannot exercise its influence in the world for the good of downtrodden nations just because success is not immediately attainable, then the hopes of many peoples—that some day they may depend on the moral support of this country as they try to liberate themselves from dictatorship—will be wrecked on the seas of despair.

Senator Fulbright's speech undoubtedly will be widely discussed, for it represents a point of view of many persons inside and outside our government who believe, as Chamberlain did in 1938, that a little bit of appeasement can never be harmful or bring on war. History, however, tells a different story.

From David Lawrence, syndicated column in the New York *Herald Tribune*, March 1964.

The Demand for Solutions

As a people, we have tended to assume that with sufficient application of American initiative and resources anything could be "fixed" in a very short period of time. The results of the Marshall Plan were very satisfying because they were speedy and tangible, but few of the problems to which the United States must respond in the sixties and seventies are so tractable. Vietnam is particularly frustrating because immediate solutions are not available. In many areas (such as aid to developing countries), expensive programs, running over many years, produce unspectacular (although important) results. This means that programs must often be oversold to the American people in order to achieve their adoption by Congress—with the inevitable accompanying disillusionment. The Alliance for Progress, for instance, was presented to Congress amid such optimistic predictions that one reporter remarked that it seemed as though all of Latin America would look like Miami Beach by 1965. The backlash of disappointment over the slow progress of the Alliance program was partly responsible for the foreign-aid "revolt" that saw presidential appropriation requests cut almost in half in late 1963.

Victory, Not Compromise

Americans have been accustomed to victory. We have never lost a war, and we had our way with the Indians and the neighbors on our frontiers. Since our founding we have believed that the New World was superior to the Old and that it was right for America to prevail. Hence, it is difficult for Americans to accept something less than complete victory. Many were disillusioned over Korea because there was no victory over the Chinese. Similarly, many Americans find the Cuban situation frustrating because American interests do not prevail. It has been hard to accept the idea that the Latin American countries, our allies in Europe, and even the Russians had stakes in Cuba—all of which forestalled complete American victory. The realization that politics is the adjustment of conflicts is essential in the poker game of international affairs. In a multipolar world many players sit around the table, and we must come to terms with the views not only of our allies, such as Great Britain and Germany, but with our Cold War antagonists, with nations such as France whose friendships are in a state of flux, and with neutrals around the globe.

Rebuttal to Fulbright: We Already Have Abandoned Our Myths

It is easy to recognize the cogency of much that [Senator Fulbright] says, harder to understand exactly whom he is trying to say it to, and even harder to understand exactly what he wants this country to do in certain areas.

None of these arguments is news to the "intellectual community"; large books making these and other points have been coming out for at least three years. It is not news to the Administration, which has been saying many of these things at least since the Kennedy speech at American University [in July 1963]. It may be news to a few extreme right-wing leaders and their pockets of followers around the country, but the generality of citizens has not been in a rigid, frozen state of mind for a long time.

The majority of Americans have calmly accepted restraint and flexibility in our foreign policy, and restrained and flexible it has surely been in most respects, ever since the Korean war when we did accept very limited victory for the first time since the War of 1812. We did not hit Russia when we had overwhelming nuclear superiority. We did not "unleash" Chiang Kai-shek. We did not act recklessly in Berlin, over the blockade or the wall. Not for years have we talked about "liberating" the satellite countries. We do not on the whole treat countries like Poland and Yugoslavia as simple Communist units, without independence.

We no longer object to neutralism. We are not forcing ourselves and our defense strategies upon "Europe"; we have, in fact, been endlessly patient with the deep disagreements between the European capitals. We did not invade Cuba. We have allowed the Russians to take their own time about getting troops out of there, and it is manifestly untrue that we are "so transfixed" by Cuba that we are neglecting the rest of Latin America, as Senator Humphrey claims we are.

We did sign the atomic test ban treaty with Russia. We did agree to send wheat to Russia and we are most sincerely trying to negotiate some measure of disarmament with Russia.

From Eric Sevareid, syndicated column in the Rockland County *Citizen*, April 1964.

Idealism and Realism

Historically, Americans have believed that moral principles should govern international policies and have proudly proclaimed that our nation was one that had stood for right and justice. We have abhorred the doctrines that "might makes right" and that "the end justifies the means." We fought one war to "make the world safe for democracy" and another to crush fascist dictatorship, and we have since proclaimed the cause of freedom against communist dictatorship. We have favored self-determination of peoples, protection of the rights of weak nations, maintenance of international law, and a world of peace and good will.

Americans have generally either refused to recognize, or have been apologetic about, actions that were at variance with the goal of peaceful pursuit of righteous aims, such as gunboat diplomacy, our "big stick" policy (especially when American economic interests were at stake), and our callousness toward Indians. Of greater significance than these intermittent episodes, however, is the abhorrence of power in the American tradition. Our moralism has made the use of power suspect—we have gone to war not merely as a way of obtaining some politically desirable end, but rather as a means of ending the need to use military power.

The realization, therefore, that the use of power is an essential instrument of national diplomacy comes as a shock to many Americans. Our national leaders have had to justify to the American public the maintenance of a costly military apparatus and to explain that American soldiers were being sent to Korea and Vietnam not to end the use of force or abolish dictatorships—as in the First and Second World Wars—but to support American diplomatic aims abroad. This latter goal receives much less public understanding and support because of the strain on the American conscience resulting from the conflict between the way nations do act and our views of how nations *should* act. On the one hand, Americans continue to treasure the idea that conditions which have characterized social advance—law, machinery for adjustment of differences among men, trade and communication, and freedom and peace—can come to prevail in world affairs. On the other hand, they realize that the contest among national states is an unending struggle for power. The combination of idealism (without utopianism) with realism that accepts the necessity of power without making it an end is no easy challenge for Americans to meet.

SUMMARY

During the life of our Republic, American foreign policy has passed through two stages and is now in a third. Throughout the first stage (1789–1914) our primary goal—like that of other new nations—was to ensure our national survival. But the American definition of "survival" has been distinctive in encompassing both protection of the American way of life at home and promotion of world conditions that would preserve American strength and American ideals abroad. During this first period, our policy of assiduous neutrality in regard to European power struggles contrasted sharply with our repeated intervention in the affairs of Latin American countries. The Monroe Doctrine expressed our unwillingness to permit European intervention in the Western Hemisphere. In this early stage we aggressively expanded our national borders and boldly promoted American economic interests abroad, but we continued to believe that morality could govern international affairs, that peace and stability were the normal international conditions, and that we could avoid arming our country militarily.

During the second stage of our development (1914–45), we were a reluctant world power. We were too large and powerful to remain aloof from the First or Second World Wars, but we yearned for neutrality and regarded our military involvement as temporary moral crusades to "end all wars."

The end of the Second World War brought the third stage of our foreign policy: superpower politics. From 1945 to the early 1960's, world politics passed through the era of "bipolarity" as the United States and Russia became the leaders of two great alliance systems. During this period the United States adopted a policy of "containment" toward the expansionist communist world. To implement our policy, we helped to underwrite the economic rebuilding of Western Europe through the Marshall Plan, established an elaborate system of alliances, and offered technological aid to underdeveloped countries through the Point Four Program. In addition, we took action in response to communist political and military provocations during the Berlin blockade of 1948, the Korean War, and the Cuban missile crisis of 1962.

During the early 1960's international politics passed from bipolarism to "multipolarism," bringing new problems and challenges to the United States. In both East and West, the monolithic alliances of the postwar era have been frayed by the rising strength of Soviet and American allies. China, France, Yugoslavia, Poland, and Germany alike are all tending to reflect their new economic and military prowess by pursuing national rather than coalition interests. Similarly, the underdeveloped countries of Africa, Asia, and Latin America are anxious to remain neutral in the struggle between Russia and the United States in order to further their own political and economic survival. The new complexities of the multipolar era are demonstrated by the web of issues raised by our intervention in Santo Domingo and Vietnam in the late 1960's.

The United States has met the more complex challenges of the multipolar era by devising broader and more flexible responses to the continuing problems of defense and foreign policy that confront all world powers.

First, the difficulties of reaching agreement with the Soviet Union on arms control and disarmament have led to heavy emphasis on military preparedness in this country. Our military establishment has shifted in emphasis from "massive retaliation" during the early 1950's to the "flexible response" of the 1960's. Second, despite sharp criticism from opponents, both Democratic and Republican administrations have employed foreign aid and foreign trade as instruments for implementing our military and political goals abroad. And, finally, the United States has been an active supporter of the United Nations in the postwar era, although the new importance of the neutralist Afro-Asian and Latin American countries in the General Assembly raises new questions about which questions the United States should take to the United Nations.

The new problems of today's multipolar world have forced Americans to reexamine the traditional "myths" of our foreign policy—that all nations opposing American goals are "evil"; that quick solutions are available for every world problem; and that moral principles will govern international politics. The diversity of national interests in today's world is gradually making the American people aware of the obstacles to quick, clearcut victory; the value of the carefully measured, limited response; the complexity and obstinacy of international problems; and the need to balance idealism with the use of power.

THE MAKING OF DEFENSE AND FOREIGN POLICY

23

As Chapter 22 has suggested, today's multipolar era presents complex challenges for American foreign-policy makers. Who participates in making American defense and foreign policy today, and how? This chapter examines the distinctive characteristics of American institutions and processes for foreign-policy making. What actors and agencies provide the President with the information and advice he needs to be a "mainspring" of our foreign-policy system? What special problems does the Secretary of Defense face in coordinating his department's activities? How significant a role does Congress play in foreign-policy making? And, finally, how does the process of policy-making vary with the type of decision being made?

The making of defense and foreign policy in the United States today is probably as complex a task as ever confronted man. A Russian move in Berlin, an Egyptian action in Suez, or a revolution in Cuba calls for immediate new analyses and extensive revision of United States positions. Moreover, American policy must consider the reactions of enemies, neutrals, and allies. A move in Cuba must be weighed in relation to Latin American reactions, and a decision on intervention in Southeast Asia must take into account our alliances, our ability to succeed, and our reserve capacity for other situations. There are also difficulties in coordinating the actions of agencies within our own government. Robert A. Lovett, one-time Secretary of Defense, has referred to the participation of agencies with disparate interests in foreign-policy making as "the foul-up factor."

> This is really a method of requiring power to be shared—even though responsibility may not be—and of introducing rival claimants from another department with a different mission into the policy-making or decision-taking process.
> This is the "foul-up factor" in our methods . . . .[1]

If one scans the pages of the *U.S. Government Organization Manual* or examines organizational charts showing the formal relationship of one agency to another, he will not see how conflicts among participants develop. The charts seem to make clear who is responsible to whom and how power and responsibility are located within the system. The reality of power, however, is infinitely more complex. For example, the Joint Chiefs of Staff enjoy a particularly ambiguous position—they are the "principal" planning staff for both the President and the Secretary of Defense. Although organizationally the chain of command for military operations extends from the President to the Secretary of Defense to the Joint Chiefs, a strong chairman of the Joint Chiefs can in practice be a formidable competitor for any civilian Secretary. It is necessary to know not only the formal position of the bureaucracies involved in defense and foreign policy but also the actual interrelationships in the process of decision.

THE PRESIDENT AND HIS PERSONAL ESTABLISHMENT

At the vortex of the policy-making process is the President, the "mainspring" of the system, who must propose, coordinate, and decide. He must also keep himself from becoming a captive of the bureaucracies that are designed to help him. Both the Constitution and his nationwide electorate place this staggering responsibility on him—"Advisers," as President Ken-

[1] Robert A. Lovett, Statement Before the Senate Subcommittee on National Policy Machinery, February 23, 1960.

nedy once said, "can always go on to other advice, but the President must act." Within the White House Office staff (examined in Chapter 10) the President has a tiny but significant "personal establishment" that extends his power and influence over the making of foreign policy. These few men provide him with intelligence he might not otherwise get or might get only in diluted form. For example, position papers from the executive departments sometimes gloss over differences of opinion within these departments that it is very much in the President's interest to know about.

The key man among these personal aides in recent years has been the special assistant to the President for national-security affairs. This position has existed officially only since 1953, but Presidents in the past had co-opted into their official family trusted persons who served as personal advisers on matters of defense and foreign affairs. Woodrow Wilson made such use of Colonel Edward House, and Franklin Roosevelt did the same with Harry Hopkins. Presidents still use persons not on the White House payroll as personal agents in the policy-making process. Attorney General Robert Kennedy was often used this way by his brother—notably in the review of Central Intelligence Agency operations that took place after the abortive Bay of Pigs landings in Cuba in the spring of 1961. President Johnson has frequently called in such trusted advisers as Abe Fortas, now a Supreme Court justice, and former Secretary of State Dean Acheson. The main duties of the security assistant under Eisenhower, Kennedy, and Johnson have been to keep the President informed on topics he must discuss easily and to see that the options for decision are kept open for the President.

The importance of the security assistant's functions is illustrated by the five days of concentrated consideration of policy on the multilateral nuclear defense force (MLF) for the NATO allies in preparation for the visit of Prime Minister Harold Wilson of Great Britain in the spring of 1965. President Johnson called for discussions with a group of advisers composed of the Vice-President, the Secretary and Under Secretary of State, the Secretary of Defense, the ambassador to Great Britain, Dean Acheson, and McGeorge Bundy, the security assistant. Since the last year of the Eisenhower Administration we had given the impression that the United States favored MLF, and the main trend of advice initially given by Johnson's group was that we should give Wilson a firm commitment to support MLF or a similar force. But the President probed further with searching questions, for the attitudes in European capitals were difficult to appraise, and the President was doubtful of his ability to sell MLF to the Senate. When the President asked what his predecessor's opinion had been, Bundy produced a study he had made for President Kennedy and followed this with a fresh appraisal of the problem for Johnson. Bundy's appraisal and his participation in discussions helped to keep open choices for the President, whose decision was ultimately contrary to advice he initially received. A competent observer has concluded: "It was a classic exercise in the adroit use of White House staff as a diviner of Presidential inclinations, a protector of Presidential interests, a widener of Presidential choices, and a gadfly in the governmental processes when the President was confronted by a spirited, consecrated, nearly united bureaucracy." [2]

The security assistant offers the President certain unique assets. He has no departmental constituency that might impair his absolute loyalty to the "boss," and he has immediate access to intelligence estimates, country surveys, and other things the President may want to know about on fifteen minutes' notice. Since different Presidents have different styles of operation and organize and utilize their personal staffs in different ways, it is difficult to predict how the job of security assistant will develop. It is clear, however, that this position serves very important functions for the President.

THE DEPARTMENT OF STATE

The Secretary of the Department of State, generally considered the government post second only to the President in importance, is the senior adviser to the President on foreign affairs. Past Presidents have sometimes ignored Secretaries of State, but in our day the Secretary is becoming more and more essential to the President. In postwar years the position has been held by men like George C. Marshall, Dean Acheson, and John Foster Dulles, who have left their imprints on American policy. Acheson has described the intimate working relations of the Secretary with the President. He saw "the President on business almost every day, and rarely less than four times a week," and sent a constant stream of communications to the President.[3]

Behind the Secretary is the department with its Washington headquarters and its field stations. The Washington office is organized in part along geographical lines and in part along functional ones. The primary organization is geographical, with separate bureaus for each major area of the world. This pattern dates from 1833. Within the geographical bureaus are the "country desks," a term that originated when there was a single man keeping track of each foreign country. The secondary organization is functional, with separate offices for such major functions as economic affairs, cultural relations, and intelligence. The functional organization has grown rapidly in recent years as multilateral diplomacy has tended to replace bilateral diplomacy and as problems are increasingly approached on a worldwide or regional basis. There is inevitably some struggle and often deep conflict between those dealing with geographical areas and those

---

[2] Philip Geyelin, *Lyndon B. Johnson and His World* (New York: Praeger, 1966), p. 162.
[3] "The President and the Secretary of State," in Don K. Price, ed., *The Secretary of State* (Englewood Cliffs, N.J.: Prentice-Hall, 1960), pp. 45–46.

"What's our firm, unswerving Asia policy this week?"

Though first published during the Eisenhower Administration, this cartoon still accurately reflects the problems of formulating administration policy for areas in which American public attitudes are sharply divided.

From *Herblock's Here and Now,*
Simon & Schuster, 1955

dealing with functional problems that are global in scope. Both points of view are useful in foreign-policy making.

At the top of the department are policy and managerial aides for the Secretary. Included is a Policy Planning Council, created in 1947 as a flexible body for long-range study and planning. It assists the Secretary in evaluating the adequacy of current policy and weighs the advisability of new initiatives. Another top-level unit, headed by the Executive Secretary, coordinates the flow of paper to the Secretary and assures the implementation of his decisions throughout the department. There is also an Under Secretary of State, serving as full deputy to the Secretary, as well as an Under Secretary for economic affairs. Though the department is always "reorganized" when new Secretaries come to office, these basic arrangements remain.

In the field are the consular representatives, who look after the property, business, and personal interests of Americans, and the diplomatic representatives, who conduct our political relations with other governments. A diplomatic mission is headed by an ambassador or minister serving in the capital city óf a nation recognized by the United States. Other departments and agencies of our government also operate abroad, with as many as fifteen in a single capital. The ambassador faces the problem of coordinating and supervising practically all the representatives of the United States in "his" country. A 1963 Senate staff study observes that:

> Although all members of the country team . . . respect [the ambassa-dor's] precedence as chief of mission . . . their dependence on him and their desire to be coordinated by him differ greatly. As a general rule, their readi-ness to accept his right of decision varies with the degree to which they are involved in operational matters, such as the conduct of aid programs, and have their own reporting lines to Washington.
>
> The political counselors and other old-line members of the diplomatic staff are most dependent on the ambassador and have the greatest interest in supporting him. They have no lines of reporting except through the ambassador—and informal letters to colleagues in Washington. At the other end of the spectrum is the MAAG [military assistance advisory group]. Its work is highly operational, it has its own lines to the Pentagon, and it tends to take a restricted view of the ambassador's right to interpose himself between it and the Pentagon on budgetary, programing, and operational decisions. The other groups fall somewhere between these positions. CIA is closer to the MAAG model, while USIS falls closer to the diplomatic model and AID somewhere in the middle.[4]

In addition to its ambassadors to foreign nations, United States repre-sentation now includes ambassadors or similar officials at a number of im-portant posts, such as the United Nations and NATO.

The State Department has its own special personnel problems. In Wash-ington the permanent home staff is part of the classified civil service. Abroad, the United States has been represented by Foreign Service officers, who, under the Rogers Act of 1924, form a separate corps. Though tra-ditionally drawn from an Ivy League élite base and trained as generalists, the Foreign Service was recently broadened by the addition of specialists in propaganda, economics, labor, and cultural affairs. In addition, as a re-sult of a report to Secretary Dulles by Henry Wriston, then president of Brown University, there has been a substantial integration of the home serv-ice with the Foreign Service Corps. The latter now totals about four thou-sand persons, including many who held important positions in the Depart-ment of State; there is also provision for people to alternate between the home and Foreign services.

Another personnel problem has been the appointment of mission heads abroad. There has been an increasing trend toward promotion of Foreign Service officers to the post of ambassador or minister, and about two-thirds of these positions are now held by career officers. But some of the most im-portant posts go to political appointees—for two main reasons: first, the posts carry honor and prestige and are valuable political capital, and, second, they are too expensive for any but extremely wealthy persons to hold. Al-though some political appointees have been among the nation's ablest, many

4 U.S. Senate, Committee on Government Operations, Subcommittee on National Security Staffing and Operations, *Administration of National Security* (1963), pp. 10–11.

believe that the "treatment of embassies as political patronage is an unalloyed evil." [5] Congress, critics suggest, should increase the expense allowances for our large embassies so that the President could choose first-rate men without regard to whether prospective appointees owned personal fortunes or had made substantial campaign contributions.

As principal agent for the President, the State Department today is engaged in a range of activities that would have been unthinkable a few decades ago, and this expansion of functions has led to increased responsibility for subordinate officials. Secretary Rusk, testifying before a Senate committee, put it this way:

> You see, today, sir, because of the pace of business, relatively junior officers in the Department of State are sending out telegrams on matters which before World War II might well have gone to the Secretary himself. Our business could not be handled in any other way. We have to give broad policy guidance, but we also have to let our junior colleagues act because not to act itself is a decision.[6]

THE UNITED STATES INFORMATION AGENCY

The mission of the USIA is to make American policies understood sympathetically abroad through such means as broadcasting (Voice of America), motion pictures, and the distribution of American publications. The agency's program is geared to persuading people that their interests and objectives in the world are harmonious with the policy of the United States. The USIA grew out of several smaller organizations that had experimented with the techniques of "psychological warfare"; their efforts had come to little, however, because of their tendency to put out "sell America" material without reference to what our government was actually doing in the target country. The USIA, notably under the directorship of Edward R. Murrow from 1961 to 1963, has attempted to avoid this mistake.

The USIA, organizationally independent of the State Department, carries on its operations through several hundred field offices around the world. Since the agency is charged with the responsibility of interpreting United States moves for overseas audiences, it has an obvious interest in participating in decisions affecting our foreign relations. In addition, the agency has developed a reputation for expertise in "public relations," and Presidents have often felt that USIA advice should be sought before our government

---

[5] Henry M. Wriston, "The Secretary and the Management of the Department," in Price, *op. cit.*, p. 95.

[6] U.S. Senate, Committee on Government Operations, Subcommittee on National Policy Machinery, *Organizing for National Security* (1961).

undertakes any initiative. Thus, during the Cuban missile crisis of October 1962, President Kennedy sought the counsel of Edward R. Murrow as to what United States actions would receive popular support in what countries. After his accession to the Presidency, Lyndon Johnson asked the incumbent USIA director to attend meetings of the National Security Council.

THE AGENCY FOR INTERNATIONAL DEVELOPMENT

Since the Second World War, American foreign aid has been administered through a succession of organizations. Economic aid is now handled by the Agency for International Development (AID), located within the Department of State. AID has a difficult institutional life. It has no great domestic constituency to support it, and its activities (spending taxpayers' dollars abroad) are always attractive targets for congressional sharpshooting. AID operates programs of development loans, grants, and investment guarantees—including the Alliance for Progress program—and it carries on research into the problems of economic growth and development. In addition, AID exercises control over the famous Contingency Fund, which allows the United States to respond to rapidly developing situations with offers of assistance. Despite the annual agonies of the appropriation battle, economic assistance has become a principal instrument of American foreign policy.

THE UNITED STATES ARMS CONTROL AND DISARMAMENT AGENCY

In 1961 a specialized agency of government was set up to deal with the very complicated and intractable problems of controlling the proliferation of weapons. Although United States policy has been directed primarily toward achieving some measure of arms control, the new organization was also mandated to examine the possibilities of eventual disarmament. The director of the Disarmament Agency serves as "principal adviser" to both the President and the Secretary of State. The agency is charged with carrying on research to solve problems of arms control, with preparing position papers for consideration by the National Security Council, and with actually conducting disarmament and arms-control negotiations. Its director leads the American delegation in disarmament discussions at Geneva. The agency's counsel will be sought on security policy when such policy is affected by arms control and disarmament negotiations.

THE DEPARTMENT OF DEFENSE

From 1798, when the small United States Navy "won its independence" from the War Department, until the mid-twentieth century, the American military establishment was split between the Departments of War and Navy. The hostility between the Army and Navy, which continues even today, is deeply rooted in a century and a half of separation and elaborate justifications for it.

Early twentieth-century attempts to coordinate the Army and Navy were thoroughly ineffectual. Not until 1947 did new pressures force greater integration of the services. The greatest pressure at first was the desire of the Army Air Corps for a separate status, which apparently could most easily be achieved in a single new military department. Also, there was a particular need for more effective machinery for resolving the intense interservice competition that developed in 1945 and 1946 as each establishment sought to stake out claims to particular missions and to sponsor particular programs. After extensive studies of the problem, President Truman sent to Capitol Hill proposals for consolidation upon which Congress eventually acted, despite opposition from many high officials who doubted the wisdom of a single defense department.

Unification came in stages. The National Security Act of 1947 created a third department, that of the Air Force. Each department was to be independently administered by its own Secretary. Created also was a Secretary of Defense, whose most significant power was to "supervise and coordinate" the budget estimates of the three departments. In 1949 the "military establishment" was elevated to the status of an executive department, and the Defense Secretary's staff was expanded. Provisions were made for strong financial controls over the services by the Department of Defense through the establishment of a comptroller, who has become one of the most powerful budget officers in government. President Eisenhower in 1953 further strengthened the department by creating new aides with responsibilities in such fields as manpower and personnel, supply and logistics. Then by act of Congress in 1958 the Secretary of Defense was given direct authority over unified commands (such as the North American Air Defense Command) and authority to provide centralized direction of research and development through a director of research and engineering. He also gained the power to transfer weapons systems from one service to another. These powers have provided the basis for centralized direction of our defense apparatus.

The job of running this department, however, has remained difficult. Several Defense Secretaries have had great difficulty in making their views

Army: "Golly! And you were supposed to be efficient. Perhaps, some day, they'll discover that I'm not an irresistible horde."

Rivalry among the military services has been a chronic problem since the United States became a world power. This 1915 cartoon shows the Army's jealousy at naval appropriations during World War I.

Dart in *Life,* 1915

prevail over those of the service Secretaries and uniformed leaders. There is still a kind of "legalized insubordination" authorized by the National Security Act—which gives service Secretaries the right to take problems directly to the President in certain circumstances. The rivalries of course remain. The services are backed by established national associations, such as the Air Force Association and the Navy League, and by the industrial concerns producing their weapons. They have also carefully developed their liaison with Congress, and a service can marshal considerable support when one of its projects is threatened. When these multiple centers of power converge to influence congressional action, they can limit the strength of the Secretary of Defense and the President himself. As old strategic questions are settled, new ones emerge, and interservice rivalry has continued over such issues as "who would build the missiles, who would operate them, and how much would be spent on one missile system against another." [7]

Additional factors have increased the pressure on the Secretary of Defense. One is the need for a civilian intermediary between the Joint Chiefs of Staff and the President so as to relieve the load of strategic planning that has rested on the President since the creation of the Joint Chiefs during the war. Thus the Defense Secretary has gradually come to be a sort of second in command to the President. As weaponry has changed, it has been

[7] Samuel P. Huntington, "Interservice Competition and the Political Roles of the Armed Services," *American Political Science Review*, Vol. LV (March 1961), p. 50.

"Not in the corridors, dammit!"

This cartoon portrays the continued rivalry of the military services even after their consolidation into the Defense Department.

From *Herblock's Special for Today*,
Simon & Schuster, 1958

necessary to reorganize the services, with many resulting tensions.[8] Finally, as coordination of the military with the Department of State, the Bureau of the Budget, and other agencies became a dominant requirement in the making of national policy, the need for a single office representing the defense establishment in these relations increased. Necessity has thrust more and more duties upon the Defense Secretaries, who have tended in recent years to exercise them strongly, but the legacy of separation remains.

The structure of military forces maintained and administered from the Pentagon is as impressive in totality as it is secret in detail. Before the outbreak of the Korean War, the defense budgets had been running about $12 billion per year. The National Security Council had approved a plan for sweeping rearmament (stressing the importance of conventional capabilities); but, until the communist world attacked South Korea, there had been little incentive for Congress to appropriate the necessary funds. As Table 23–1 shows, the Korean War brought a dramatic increase in defense spending, and since that time, except for the severe cutback of ground forces in the mid-fifties, post-Korean development has been toward a more versatile, harder-hitting, larger, and much more expensive defense apparatus.

The instruments of violence controlled from the Pentagon today can be grouped under four broad headings: [9]

[8] See Gene M. Lyons, "The New Civil-Military Relations," *ibid.*, pp. 53–63.
[9] These categories are suggested by Roswell L. Gilpatric, "Our Defense Needs," *Foreign Affairs*, Vol. XLII (April 1964), p. 366.

Table 23–1 Defense Budgets as a Percentage of the American Gross
National Product, Selected Years

Calendar year	Gross national product (billions of dollars)	National defense spending (billions of dollars)	Percentage
1945	213.6	75.9	35.5
1948	257.6	10.7	4.2
1949	256.5	13.3	5.2
1950	284.8	14.1	5.0
1951	328.4	33.6	10.2
1952	345.5	45.9	13.3
1955	398.0	38.6	9.7
1960	503.7	44.9	8.9
1965	681.2	50.1	7.4
1966	739.5	60.0	8.1

SOURCE: *Economic Report of the President,* Transmitted to the Congress, January 1967, Together with the Annual Report of the Council of Economic Advisers, Appendix B-1, p. 213.

1. *Strategic retaliatory forces.* These forces are capable of destroying an attacking nation. They consist of intercontinental ballistic missiles in hardened (protected) sites, certain older unprotected missiles, the seagoing Polaris system (intermediate-range missiles fired from beneath the surface), and a number of manned bombers.

2. *Continental air- and missile-defense forces.* These forces consist of an integrated system of early-warning radar (one network for manned bombers and another for missiles), interceptor aircraft, and interceptor missiles. At present, the interceptor missiles are effective only against aircraft, but new systems, designed to destroy incoming missiles, are under development.

3. *Strategic reconnaissance forces.* U-2 aircraft and SAMOS "spy" satellites provide the Defense Department and the President with "hard" photographic intelligence of Soviet and East European capabilities. More sophisticated systems based on sound and infrared light are projected for the future.

4. *General-purpose forces.* Eighteen Army and four Marine divisions, supported by aircraft of the Tactical Air Command Navy carrier aircraft, and the two Marine air wings, are the heart of our conventional war forces. Their employment around the globe depends on the sea-lift capacity of

the Navy and on the Air Force's Military Airlift Command. Increasing emphasis is being placed on grouping these forces in functional commands (tailored to do a certain job) that can be moved rapidly by air to anywhere trouble breaks out.

The Joint Chiefs of Staff

The Joint Chiefs of Staff in its present form is another creation of the National Security Act of 1947. The staff is composed of a chairman (drawn from the Army, Navy, or Air Force), the chief of staff of the Army, the chief of staff of the Air Force, and the chief of naval operations. The commandant of the Marine Corps also attends and sits as a co-equal to other members of the Joint Staff when matters directly affecting the Marine Corps are considered. The chairman, appointed by the President with the advice and consent of the Senate, automatically becomes the ranking officer of the military establishment. During the first decade of the staff's existence under the National Security Act, the position rotated among the three services. In 1962, however, President Kennedy ended the tradition by appointing Army General Maxwell Taylor to succeed Army General Lyman Lemnitzer, and in 1964 Taylor was succeeded by yet another Army general, Earle G. Wheeler.

The Chiefs, who report to the Secretary of Defense, have two functions: planning for all possible military contingencies and exercising operational control over certain joint and specified commands (such as the joint STRIKE command—an air, sea, ground command prepared at a moment's notice to tailor a force to fit a particular situation). In carrying out their planning mission the Chiefs are assisted by a joint staff of officers drawn from all services. Various sections of the Joint Staff examine problems of operations, logistics, personnel, and intelligence. In addition, specialized groups apply themselves to long-range forecasting of the military situation and to "programing" our requirements for years to come.

There has been heated debate over the proper role of the JCS, and its growing influence has been resented by some senior service officers, who seem to feel, alternately, that the Joint Chiefs are doing too much or that they do too much talking and too little acting. This latter criticism has found expression in the often quoted quip of a senior naval officer that "the Congress *debates*, the Supreme Court *deliberates*, but for some reason or other the Joint Chiefs of Staff just bicker." [10] It is important to remember that the Chiefs have operational control not over all the armed forces but only over certain commands and that each of the services has a planning apparatus of its own. The JCS play an important part in making defense

[10] Quoted in Samuel P. Huntington, *The Common Defense* (New York: Columbia University Press, 1961), p. 170.

policy, but they by no means make it alone; the individual services through their Secretaries can still exert influence on the Secretary of Defense and, through him, on the President.

THE EXECUTIVE OFFICE OF THE PRESIDENT

The Executive Office (see Chapter 10) is a collection of disparate agencies, some working very closely with the President and others enjoying no closer relationship with him than do other bureaucratic agencies. Several of them play major roles in making defense and foreign policy.

The National Security Council

How do we achieve the marriage between foreign policy and military policy necessary to make them effective? If our structure of policy is not aligned with our structure of forces, the nation cannot act effectively in the world; yet throughout most of our history no mechanism other than the President himself existed for effecting such coordination. Then in 1947 Congress created the National Security Council, to be composed of the President as chairman, the Vice-President, the Secretary of State, the Secretary of Defense, and the director of the Office of Emergency Planning, assisted by a council staff (see pages 331–32). The council was designed as a mechanism for what Samuel P. Huntington has called the "great equation"—matching foreign policy and military policy with each other and with the resources the nation can afford.

Different Presidents have used the council in different ways. Truman feared a possible usurpation of his own powers by the NSC. He considered it his council, with no authority in its own right, but he found it valuable as an advisory body.

Eisenhower, on the other hand, regarded the NSC as an institution in its own right. His first assistant for national-security affairs, Robert Cutler, worked hard to institutionalize the council—to turn it into an organ that would present unified recommendations to the President and then monitor the implementation of the President's decisions.

Kennedy and Johnson continued to use the council but with less dependence on its formal mechanisms. For example, they have met informally at frequent intervals with the Secretary of State, the Secretary of Defense, and other officials concerned with national security. When a policy decision was to be made they have tailored the composition of their advisory group to the problem at hand, augmenting the membership of the council as seemed necessary to get the information that was needed and advice in which they would have confidence. (See the discussions on pages 743–44 and 765–67 of the deliberations on MLF and the Cuban missile crisis.) The council staff has participated in the preparation for meetings, has kept records of the proceedings, and has followed the execution of decisions.

The Central Intelligence Agency

Because so little is known about the Central Intelligence Agency, much nonsense is said about it. A few contemporary writers seem to have singled it out as the "invisible government"—a sinister élite that "really" manages America's defense policy. Certainly the existence of a secret and expensive operation of this sort (the agency's appropriations are estimated at around $2 billion per year) poses a problem for an "open society," but let us examine the CIA's role in perspective.

Before the Second World War the United States, incredible as it may seem, possessed almost no machinery for covert intelligence-gathering. The prevailing view was expressed in a statement attributed to Hoover's Secretary of State, Henry L. Stimson, upon his discovery that a small office had been established within his department for the purpose of breaking codes. "Gentlemen," said the Secretary, "do not read each other's mail." During the war an apparatus was set up for gathering intelligence by espionage and for carrying out clandestine operations, often paramilitary,

"Keep the faith, babies."

The discovery that the CIA had paid private groups to conduct anti-Communist activities at home and abroad led to a public debate in the late 1960's over the independence of the private sector from the government.

© 1967, The Chicago *Sun Times*. Reproduced by permission of Wil-Jo Assoc., Inc., and Bill Mauldin.

in foreign countries. This Office of Strategic Services (OSS) was dismantled after 1945; but it was soon apparent that if the United States was to contain the Soviet Union, it would need detailed knowledge on which to act. The Security Act of 1947 provided for the establishment of the CIA, and the agency developed three main functions: the collection of raw intelligence or information; the study and interpretation of this material; and the conduct of clandestine political operations overseas. The CIA, for example, assisted in 1954 in the overthrow of the communist-oriented Arbenz regime in Guatemala and coordinated the training and arming of Cuban exiles in the United States for the Bay of Pigs fiasco.

Almost no one would challenge the appropriateness of gathering intelligence in the modern age, even if this must be done by covert means. There is even general agreement that the process by which this is accomplished must be kept secret from the American people. But there is widespread doubt about the desirability of the CIA's helping to subvert or prop up foreign governments. In addition, the revelation in 1967 that the CIA had been financing overseas activities of student organizations, labor unions, news outlets, and other private organizations led to sharp public criticism, condemnation by top public officials, and widespread suspicion that this was neither necessary for protection of national interests nor consonant with the traditional independence of such organizations from political influence.

The CIA, of course, is not the only intelligence-gathering unit of the government. It pools its information with that drawn from such agencies as the State Department's Bureau of Intelligence and Research, the National Security Agency (which makes and breaks codes), and the Defense Intelligence Agency (which draws on the intelligence-gathering agencies of the uniformed services). The director of the CIA serves as chairman of the United States Intelligence Board (composed of the heads of intelligence-collecting organizations), which seeks to integrate efforts within this intelligence community. The products of all these efforts are submitted to the National Security Council and the President.

The priorities and command decisions of American intelligence-gathering and clandestine operations are made by a special group consisting of the President, the Secretary of Defense, the Secretary of State, and the director of the CIA. Presidents Kennedy and Johnson set up special committees to be watchdogs of the CIA, but there is still skepticism outside the Administration as to the adequacy of supervision. Proposals have been made that a joint committee of Congress (similar to the Joint Committee on Atomic Energy) be created with access to the information gathered by intelligence agencies, so that it would be able to criticize decisions and review requests for appropriations. The special presidential team, headed by General Maxwell Taylor and including Attorney General Robert Kennedy, that surveyed CIA activities in connection with the Bay of Pigs fiasco rejected this suggestion as impractical. They argued that the information necessary for effective operation of such a committee could not safely be dispersed beyond the President and a few of his closest advisers.

The Bureau of the Budget

In a very real sense, the budget *is* the policy of the United States on any given issue—expressed in the ultimate vocabulary of dollars and cents. Through the Bureau of the Budget come the budget requests of State, Defense, USIA, AID, and CIA. The bureau includes an International Division and a Military Division. Its influence in deciding what can safely be spent ensures it a role in the shaping of security policy.[11]

The Office of Emergency Planning

What is the domestic capacity of the United States for dealing with crises? The Office of Emergency Planning is responsible for this area. It stockpiles materials (e.g. copper) that may be needed for national defense and welfare in an emergency. It develops, in cooperation with other agencies, plans for mobilizing economic resources and for stabilizing the economy in emergencies, through such tools as manpower utilization; allocation of scarce materials; and price, rent, and rationing controls. It also assists the states in planning and coordinating operations with respect to natural disasters. The director of the OEP is a statutory member of the NSC, and, as adviser to the President on what the country has in readiness and what we can do in an emergency, he can affect decisions on foreign policy and defense.

CONGRESS

As was discussed in Chapter 9, the President supplies the initiative and direction for defense and foreign policy, but Congress still exercises real power and influence.

In national defense, Congress has determined several aspects of the defense establishment's organization since the Second World War: for example, it has created the Department of the Air Force and the Department of Defense, and it has outlined the positions of the Joint Chiefs and

---

[11] For more detailed discussions of how the bureau exercises its influence, see pp. 328–30, and Ch. 24.

The Contribution of Congress to Foreign Policy

The primacy of the Executive Branch in foreign affairs in no way lessens the moral and legal responsibility of the Congress to work for national policies which come to grips responsibly and realistically with urgent demands of the world crisis. In this connection the Senate's activities go far beyond scrutinizing treaties and Presidential appointments. Former Secretary of State Dean Acheson has correctly observed that in one "aspect of foreign affairs Congress is all-powerful. This is in the establishing and maintaining of those fundamental policies, with their supporting programs of action, which require legal authority, men and money...." Parliamentary bodies cannot govern, and our Congress is no exception. But with its power of the purse, and through the right to investigate, to criticize and to advocate, the Congress does exert a significant influence on the quality and direction of United States foreign policy....

The foreign policy committees of Congress must have the resources to enable them to question, review, modify or reject the policies of the Executive Branch. The information, intelligence and insight available to the Executive Branch are vast and continue to expand. This is a natural development in an era of total diplomacy. But in contrast, says Myron M. Cowen ..., there is "a concurrent scarcity of vigorous and continuing *countervailing expertise*" in Congress. Such independent expertise is absolutely necessary if the House and Senate are to fulfill their Constitutional responsibility of surveillance and initiative.... Adequate staffing alone will enable Congress to escape from uninformed acquiescence on the one hand and irresponsible obstruction on the other.

From Senator Hubert H. Humphrey of Minnesota, "The Senate in Foreign Policy," *Foreign Affairs*, July 1959.

the powers to be exercised by the Secretary of Defense. Congress has increasingly become an overseer of the administration of the Pentagon—requiring even that certain decisions be cleared with the Armed Services Committees of Congress. Questions strictly about military strategy rarely come before Congress, but the legislature does consider questions of the structure of forces to implement strategy. Rarely do the lawmakers make any major cuts in the defense budget (no senator or congressman wants the responsibility for denying the military a weapon or resource that might "save American lives"), but Congress has great concern about whether the Air Force or another service is liberally treated, which company will build a plane, and where military bases will be located. Since 1950 Congress has voted just about what was asked for defense and has exercised its power by making microadjustments in the ways defense monies were spent.[12]

Congressional involvement is much greater in the making of foreign

[12] See Huntington, *The Common Defense, op. cit.*, pp. 123–66.

"For political reasons, we should spare Hanoi, Haiphong, and the Senate Foreign Relations Committee."

Robinson in the Indianapolis *News*

Relations between the Johnson Administration and the Senate Foreign Relations Committee became unusually strained during the Vietnam war.

policy. It has in recent years usually reduced the appropriation for foreign aid requested by the President, and it has, either by specific restrictions or by manifest attitudes, limited the President's use of foreign aid to particular countries. Its legislation has determined the foreign-trade policy of the nation, and it has further affected our relations with other countries through enactments on such matters as immigration and naturalization. In addition, Congress offers continuous discussion, investigation, criticism, and suggestion on foreign policy.

Since Congress conducts much of its business in committees, certain groups (the Foreign Affairs and Foreign Relations committees of the House and Senate, respectively, the Armed Services committees, the Military Appropriations subcommittees, and the Joint Committee on Atomic Energy) are particularly crucial for an administration's program. The chairmen of important committees—such men as Senator Fulbright (Democrat from Arkansas), chairman of the Senate Foreign Relations Committee; Senator Russell (Democrat from Georgia), chairman of the Senate Armed Services Committee; and Representative Mahon (Democrat from Texas), chairman of the House Appropriations Committee—and the ranking minority members, along with the majority and minority leaders of the houses, must be informed, courted, and often coaxed by the President if he is to pursue the policies he desires.

Some persons have desired to strengthen the checks and balances in foreign-policy making. This purpose was reflected, for example, in the Bricker Amendment, which failed by one vote to obtain a two-thirds majority in the Senate. This amendment proposed that Congress have power "to regulate all executive and other agreements with any foreign power or international organization." On the other hand, many have been concerned over the constitutional provision that gives a minority (one-third plus one) of the Senate the power to block treaties and over the threats to unity and strength implicit in the sharing of powers by Congress and the President. It may be noted, however, that flexible interpretation of the Constitution has allowed Congress to delegate powers to the President—on trade, foreign aid, and other matters—that have strengthened the President, while at the same time Congress has retained checks on the President by giving authorizations for only short periods and by retaining its powers of appropriation, investigation, and discussion. The bridge between a President seeking to provide a vigorous foreign policy and a Congress reflecting the divisions of a pluralistic society and suspicious of executive power can only be maintained through the executive's making as much information available to Congress as will be useful to it and not hazardous to national security, through the willingness of both sides to seek accommodation, and through the ability of the President to persuade Congress that his policies are correct.

OTHER PARTICIPANTS IN FOREIGN-POLICY MAKING

While defense and foreign policy is made primarily by the agents described so far, the sources of influence on policy are much broader. Almost every department or agency of the government becomes involved from time to time in foreign policy. For example, the Council of Economic Advisers and the Secretary of the Treasury advise the President on the impact of appropriation requests on the economy; the National Aeronautics and Space Administration and the Office of Science and Technology give him advice on scientific developments affecting military potential and diplomatic policy; and the Departments of Commerce and Agriculture participate with the Department of State in the negotiation of international trade agreements.

It hardly needs saying that the group basis of American politics (described in Chapter 4) carries over into the realm of foreign policy. Industrial groups with government defense contracts, communities with defense installations, Jews supporting the state of Israel, managerial and labor interests demanding protective tariffs against Japanese cotton goods—all these and a multitude of others are participants in the process of foreign-policy making.

It should be equally clear that the party politics described in earlier chapters extends constantly to foreign-policy issues. In the difficult period after World War II when Cold War policies were being developed, the President and the congressional majority represented different parties, but bipartisan cooperation developed between President Truman and Republican Senator Vandenberg, chairman of the powerful Senate Foreign Relations Committee. In later years the President has consulted with the opposition leaders in Congress and sought their support. While constrained not to damage American interests, party leaders are, however, ready to take advantage of foreign-policy issues in elections. Eisenhower capitalized on discontent over the war in Korea in 1952, Kennedy and Nixon debated issues of national strength and prestige in 1960, and the conduct of the war in Vietnam, an issue in the 1966 elections, will almost certainly continue to be a major campaign issue until the war is settled. Finally, issues of foreign policy are kept alive through discussion in all the communications media, in scholarly journals, and sometimes through popular demonstrations as well.

These varied participants complicate the process of foreign-policy making. They carry all the advantages and disadvantages of a democratic polity into the foreign-policy area: on the one hand, they protect disparate interests and help guard against precipitate decisions, but, on the other hand, the national interest is sometimes compromised in the face of strong domestic pressures; this country frequently displays a lack of unity before the nations of the world; and those who are responsible for decisions always face the added burden of seeking assent from the public.

"But we're getting some dandy pictures of what's on the moon."

A perennial complaint of the press is that both executive agencies and congressional committees invoke secrecy to prevent the public from learning about foreign and defense policy.

© 1967 Herblock in the Washington *Post*

STUDIES IN THE PROCESS OF POLICY-MAKING

One newspaperman who covers the State Department recently remarked:

> Foreign policy is not really made at all, only managed, on an *ad hoc* basis at best. It is buffeted by the colliding visions, gripes, talents, fights, fears, errors, powers, and pressures of hundreds of people and dozens of institutions, of politicians and scholars, businessmen and newspapermen, foreign and domestic.[13]

In Chapter 22 we saw historical patterns in American decisions that were clearly "policies." But the operating officials who must act and react day in and day out cannot function in terms of grand designs alone. We say that the American foreign policy toward the communist world is "containment"; yet to the man on the spot the important question is, "What, in the light of the consensus on 'containment,' should I recommend on two problems about which I must brief my Secretary at four-thirty this afternoon?" "Policy" is something that grows usually out of a multiplicity of past decisions and comes to influence future decisions.

The process of policy-making varies according to the kind of decision being made. Let us examine the American response to four specific issues— each illustrating a general category of foreign- and defense-policy issues. In each case we will focus on two questions. First, who participates in decision-making? And, second, what are the conditions in which the decision is taken? Openly or in secret? Tentatively or irreversibly?

The Traditional Diplomatic Issue

In 1903 the United States Government signed a treaty with the Republic of Panama fixing the conditions under which the new Panama Canal was to operate. The treaty accorded the United States the right to run the canal and to exercise control over the Canal Zone—the narrow strips of land along each side of the passageway. In 1903 Panamanian leaders felt they were fortunate in obtaining such an arrangement; by 1964 they had changed their minds. By the early sixties the Panamanians had come to resent bitterly the existence of an American enclave within their national territory. In 1962 Panamanian President Roberto Chiari asked President Kennedy to consider revision of the treaty to give Panama greater control of the waterway. Kennedy responded favorably to the overture, but officials of the State Department cautioned against hasty action, and nothing significant was accomplished. Throughout 1962 and 1963 the government

[13] Max Frankel, New York *Times*, June 29, 1964.

of Panama continued to warn the United States that popular feeling in its country was running high on the issue of the canal.

On January 9, 1964, rioting broke out when American high-school students within the Canal Zone hauled down the Panamanian flag that flew in front of their school and ran up the Stars and Stripes. Panamanian crowds crossed into the Canal Zone, and the American military commander, viewing the problem as one of protecting a strategic defense installation, met the crowds with combat troops and tear gas. Within forty-eight hours Panama broke off diplomatic relations with the United States, and our "Panamanian policy" was a shambles.

The United States ambassadorship to Panama was vacant when the rioting broke out, but President Johnson quickly appointed Edwin Martin, former Assistant Secretary of State for Latin American affairs, to act as chief United States negotiator in attempting to effect the restoration of relations. President Johnson himself talked by telephone with President Chiari. The Organization of American States, with the blessings of the State Department, set up a peace committee through which Martin could discuss with Panama's foreign minister, Galileo Solis, the differences that separated the United States and Panama. Panama demanded that the United States agree to a revision of the 1903 treaty as a precondition for resuming normal relations. The United States was willing to entertain the question of treaty revision but was unwilling to agree in advance, and under pressure, to renegotiate the pact. Washington (that is, the President, Secretary of State Rusk, and newly appointed Assistant Secretary for Latin America Thomas Mann) felt that to do so would set a bad precedent and expose the Administration to the Republican charge that it had knuckled under to international blackmail. Some verbal formula had to be found that would allow both governments to save face in the eyes of their own people and open the way for discussions of the substantive problem of the canal.

There followed intense, and often seemingly petty, diplomatic-semantic wrangles over whether the United States was agreeing to "discussions" or "*negociaciónes formales.*" Several times talks broke up with exchanges of recriminations. The Johnson Administration sought to make maximum use of the machinery of the OAS, and, when Panama invoked the Rio Treaty of 1947 (which provided for an OAS determination of whether aggression had taken place), the United States went along with the move. Through the patient application of traditional diplomatic bargaining skills and intervention of the OAS, an established agency for international adjustment, a cooling-off period was agreed to. During this period Panamanian national elections were held, and President Chiari's party maintained itself in power. After this victory, a face-saving phraseology was quickly worked out, and the first steps toward a new treaty were taken.

In responding to a traditional diplomatic issue of this sort, the principal decision makers were the President, the Secretary of State, whose primacy as adviser to the President goes almost unquestioned in such matters, and the geographic section of the State Department directly concerned. Since the whole effort was conducted rather openly (the press was kept almost up to the minute on the course of the talks), immediate congressional and popular reactions had to be taken into account before each decision or proposal was made. None of the decisions taken during the crisis was really final—all were subject to reversal.

The Issue of Cold War Politics

On August 13, 1961, East Germany walled itself off from West Berlin. By fall, the Soviet Union had stepped up its harassment of American transportation (ground and air) moving into West Berlin. Washington felt that this action represented a serious attempt by the Soviet Union to alter the status of West Berlin and to abrogate the rights of the other Allies (Britain, France, and the United States) guaranteed by four-power accords drawn up in 1945 for governing the city. The United States had tolerated the construction of the wall, and it now seemed that the Soviets sought to exploit the momentum of events in order to gain their long-standing objective of moving the "imperialists" back behind the Elbe. The Soviet Union possessed a superiority of conventional forces in Berlin, and for American leaders the central problem was one of convincing the Soviets of our firm intention to defend Berlin with any increment of force required.

The American response to Soviet probing took weeks to decide upon and months to execute. On an issue of Cold War strategy, the State Department and the President do not work out decisions alone—the Defense Department, the Joint Chiefs of Staff, and the CIA all had a part in shaping the American response in Berlin. President Kennedy made little use of the machinery of the NSC in the "Berlin buildup of 1961"; instead he brought the principal participants to his office individually or in small groups to hear their reports and recommendations. The first Administration counter-measure was to dispatch to Berlin retired Army General Lucius Clay—who, as military governor during the Berlin blockade of 1948–49, had become a symbol of American determination to preserve the freedom of West Berlin. Clay, as the President's personal representative, insisted on the maintenance of Allied rights in the city to the extent of sending military police patrols into the Soviet sector with United States tanks positioned to ensure that the patrol car was not held up at the Soviet checkpoint. In addition, President Kennedy announced a buildup of the United States Army (adding two new divisions) and called thousands of reservists to active duty.

Since part of the American strategy was to keep the Soviet Union guessing as to exactly what its next move would be (while making it clear that there would be some move if the Soviets did not desist), a veil of secrecy was thrown around the decision-making process. Only selected pieces of information were released, and only some United States actions were announced publicly. Congressional and public reactions could not be discounted no matter which course the Administration took; and, no matter how secret its deliberations were kept, the confrontation on the streets of Berlin was quite visible. Nonetheless, the policy-making process is much more "closed" when the issue is specifically one of Cold War politics than when it is not. The Administration realized full well that a disaster in Berlin would bring eventual punishment at the polls, but secrecy gave it room to make decisions without weighing immediate public and congressional reactions quite as heavily as would be necessary in a traditional diplomatic issue.

Finally, the decisions taken in respect to Berlin had a degree of finality about them missing from the conventional diplomatic situation. In the latter case, tentative agreements can be retracted at the next session of the talks or rejected by the Senate; but when the United States makes it clear to another nation with nuclear weapons that we will shoot at its military personnel if they take certain actions, the credibility of our foreign policy is at stake, and the price of backing down is far greater.

The Crisis Issue

Another type of Cold War situation is the crisis in which our leaders are called upon to commit this country, within a matter of days or hours, to use nuclear weapons against the Soviet Union if certain Soviet behavior is not halted or undertaken. It is difficult to generalize about decision-making in such situations, since, fortunately, there are few cases to work from. The Cuban missile crisis of October 1962 is the classic case of nuclear decision-making, and its lessons are of preeminent importance.

Intelligence was the key to "Cuba II." It was both the trigger of the confrontation and the instrument that finally allowed the United States to handle the affair with something less than an invasion of Cuba. Before the beginning of the Soviet buildup in Cuba in the summer of 1962, U-2's flown by civilian CIA pilots had carried out photo missions over the island. The introduction of surface-to-air missiles into Cuba prompted our switch to Air Force planes and pilots. It was one of these planes, making the first reconnaissance over the western half of Cuba since early September, that photographed mobile medium-range missiles near San Cristobal on the morning of October 14.

This "hard intelligence" was relayed to Washington and, after analysis, passed to McGeorge Bundy. Bundy informed the President at eight o'clock on the morning of October 16. Kennedy at once summoned to the White House a group of selected advisers, who, with certain additions, came to be known during the next two weeks as the Executive Committee of the

Decision-Making in the Cuban Crisis

[Interviewer]: How does a President go about making a decision? Like Cuba, for example.

Kennedy: The [Cuba decision] was hammered out ... over a period of five or six days. During that period the fifteen people, more or less, who were directly consulted frequently changed their view because whatever action we took had so many disadvantages to it, and each action that we took raised the prospect that it might escalate the Soviet Union into a nuclear war. Finally, however, I think a general consensus developed, and it certainly seemed after all alternatives were examined that the course of action that we finally adopted was the right one.... If we had had to act on Wednesday, in the first twenty-four hours, I don't think we would have chosen as prudently as we finally did—the quarantine against the use of offensive weapons. In addition, that [strategy] had much more power than we first thought it did, because I think the Soviet Union was very reluctant to have us stop ships which carried with them a good deal of their highly secret and sensitive materials....

There was some disagreement with the course we finally adopted, but [it] had the advantage of permitting other steps if this one were unsuccessful. In other words, we were starting, in a sense, at a minimum place. [If necessary] we could have gradually stepped it up until we had gone into much more massive action.

From President John F. Kennedy, interviewed on "A Conversation with President Kennedy," produced by ABC, CBS, and NBC, December 1962.

National Security Council (Excom). This *ad hoc* team consisted of McGeorge Bundy, Attorney General Robert Kennedy, Vice-President Lyndon Johnson, Secretary of State Dean Rusk, Secretary of Defense Robert McNamara, his deputy Roswell Gilpatric, General Maxwell Taylor, Major General Marshall Carter (who was deputy director of the CIA—Director John McCone was out of town), presidential adviser Theodore Sorensen, Secretary of the Treasury Douglas Dillon, Under Secretary of State George Ball, and Assistant Secretary of State for Latin America Edwin Martin. Adlai Stevenson, American ambassador to the UN, and McCone joined the group later that day, and former Secretary of State Dean Acheson and former Secretary of Defense Robert Lovett were co-opted later in the week.

No decisions were reached quickly; various courses of action were debated. By Friday, October 19, a "rolling" consensus was achieved on a blockade, coupled with the promise of further action if the missiles were not removed. It was not until Monday evening, however, that the public or the leaders of Congress were informed of what was occurring. The President, during his televised address to the nation, committed the United

States to stopping Soviet ships on the high seas and escalating the crisis to any level the Soviet Union felt it could afford. The decision-making process had been completely closed and the decision was in a real sense final. There was always the possibility of not actually stopping the Soviet ships, but Kennedy was very close to the kind of decision that is truly irreversible. We had announced to the Soviet Union exactly what we intended to do; to back down from such a posture would have been disastrous, because it would have given the Soviet Union good reason to believe that it could behave as it wished anywhere in the world without United States force being used against it.

Of the three issues and responses examined so far, the Panamanian example reflects the most open decision-making process and the least expensive in terms of immediate stakes. The Cuban missile crisis represents a closed arena of choice and almost absolute stakes. The Berlin confrontation of 1961 falls in between.

The Issue of Resource Allocation

Decisions as to how much we will spend on which military programs are a crucial aspect of national policy. The primary decision makers in resource allocation are the President, the Secretary of Defense, the Joint Chiefs, the Bureau of the Budget, and the Secretary of State. (The Department of State has a great deal to say about what military forces are required to support our foreign policy.) In addition, the individual services (as potential competitors) become involved in policy-making, as does the intelligence community (in defining what opposing forces we must be prepared to counter in which areas of the world). Defense contractors also intrude into the policy process. For example, in the two weeks in the summer of 1963 before President Kennedy announced the scrapping of the Skybolt missile system (which had consistently failed to perform under test conditions), North American Aviation—prime contractor for the system—ran full-page advertisements in national magazines touting the effectiveness of "their" weapon.

Congress is also involved in struggles over defense programs, and each service can count on certain partisans among representatives and senators at appropriations time. In spite of this, little real public scrutiny or participation with respect to issues of resource allocation is possible. The facts needed to evaluate competing options are so highly classified and so complex that only a small circle of people in the executive branch, Congress, and the defense industry are "literate" in such matters.

In late 1963 and early 1964, an issue of resource allocation developed with the Army and Air Force on one side and the Navy on the other. The issue was the relative emphasis (in dollars and cents) to be given to seapower and airlift capacities. In the fall of 1963, the Army and Air Force had conducted a dramatic joint exercise (Big Lift), in which the personnel of an entire Army division were airlifted to Europe in the course of three days. The military implications of the effort were painfully obvious to both the Navy and our European allies. By using air transport to deploy troops directly from the continental United States, it would be possible to bring home certain forces garrisoned abroad (with a favorable effect on the nagging balance-of-payments problem) and to cut down on our Navy fleets and task forces, with their organic complements of Marines, which had thus far provided our only capacity to apply power swiftly around the world. As a result of Big Lift's success, Army leaders argued that military forces should henceforth be organized in functional, tailored commands to be deployed by air at the onset of trouble. In December 1963, the Army won an important victory for functionalism and airlift capacity when responsibility for defense of the Middle East, the Indian subcontinent, and Africa south of the Sahara was shifted from naval commanders to the head of the United States STRIKE command in Florida. The process by which the United States is shifting its emphasis from sealift to airlift capacity is invisible to the public and difficult to comprehend. This shift exemplifies the fact that although certain issues of resource allocation can be transformed into public questions (as in the debates over an anti-ballistic-missile system), the great majority of these very significant decisions will be hammered out in "restricted areas" of the security bureaucracy.

CONCLUSION: CAN AMERICAN DEMOCRACY SURVIVE IN A MULTIPOLAR WORLD?

Will the instruments and processes we have developed to protect ourselves in the last twenty years alter our democratic political system and libertarian political ethics to the extent that we lose the very thing we seek to preserve? Two major problems of the new "security politics" bear careful watching: first, the need for secrecy for security reasons may prevent public understanding and discussion of the issues. Second, the advent of continuous readiness and the enormous increase in the size of the military defense system give a new dimension to the traditional problem of civilian control over the military. Our major response to these problems has been to rely on publicity to air conflicts requiring public opinion and on structural arrangements for civilian control over the military.

Decision processes such as those on Berlin and Cuba (and those on Santo Domingo discussed in Chapter 22) cause grave concern to those who believe that public discussion is a necessary protection against unwise decisions. In such crises, safeguards lie only in the adequacy of intelligence and the quality of the deliberations in the executive chambers. On the other hand, where past decisions are revocable or future decisions open —as in the Vietnam war—criticism and defense of policy and the search for desirable courses of action have been preserved in Congress, the press, and other forums in which public opinion is expressed and policy influenced.

The traditional civilian control over the military can be exerted through a multitude of structural centers. Congress, the President, the Secretary of Defense and the Secretaries of the three services, the Bureau of the Budget and the comptrollers (budget officers) in the military departments, the Atomic Energy Commission and the National Aeronautics and Space Administration, the Federal Aviation Agency, and the National Security Council are but some of these centers. The military is dependent upon science and money—and thus ultimately upon civilian aid and control. It is hedged in by the large corps of professional civilian employees in the defense establishment and by the scientists, budget makers, and policy makers outside. On the other hand, military officers or ex-military officers are often appointed to top civilian positions. Moreover, military personnel serve on coordinating committees and are assigned to service in other agencies. All these arrangements result in reciprocal influences of military and civilian bureaucracies at successive levels up the administrative hierarchy. Policy must be made with the participation of the new civilian science and budgeting bureaucracies, the new military leadership interested in weapons technology and foreign and economic policies, and a political leadership whose task is to reconcile, limit, and set priorities.

In case of an open conflict between military and civilian authorities the power to decide belongs to the President. This was forcefully demonstrated in the Truman-MacArthur conflict. The continuing need, however, is for military power to be kept in its proper place: an essential instrument coordinated with and subservient to the foreign policy of the nation.

SUMMARY

Making defense and foreign policy is a highly complex task in today's multi-polar era, and the primary responsibility for its coordination and development rests with the President.

He is assisted within the executive branch by a number of actors and institutions that play a significant continuing role in foreign-policy making. In addition, agencies not primarily concerned with foreign policy may become involved from time to time in decisions affecting their domains.

Within the executive branch the President is assisted by an inner circle of personal advisers—particularly his special assistant for national-security affairs. This aide, with loyalty solely to the President and immediate access to intelligence estimates, is pivotal in ensuring that the President gets to explore all options in making decisions.

The President is also assisted by his "senior adviser on foreign affairs"—the Secretary of State, who has close communication with the President and carries out a wide range of foreign-policy responsibilities. An important task of the Secretary is the coordination of the Department of State. The Washington office is organized primarily along geographic lines, but its functional offices are becoming increasingly important as multilateral diplomacy replaces bilateral diplomacy. The Secretary also supervises the work of the Policy Planning Council, his other policy aides, and our embassies abroad.

Also participating in foreign-policy making are the United States Information Agency, the "public relations" agency for the United States abroad; the Agency for International Development, which administers our economic-aid programs; and the United States Arms Control and Disarmament Agency, which carries out research and conducts negotiations at Geneva.

Another important adviser to the President is the Secretary of Defense, who is second in command to the President on military strategy. The Secretary's task of coordinating his department's activities is made difficult, however, by several factors: the deeply rooted rivalry among the Army, Navy, and Air Force; the alliances of each service with powerful interest groups and congressmen; and the formidable competition a civilian Secretary may face from the chairman of the Joint Chiefs of Staff.

Several agencies in the Executive Office of the President play major roles in defense- and foreign-policy making. Among them, the National Security Council, designed to coordinate our military and foreign policy, is used as an advisory body in varying degrees by each President. The Central Intelligence Agency gathers and interprets intelligence and conducts undercover political operations abroad. Critics of the CIA have advocated congressional supervision of the agency, but Presidents have argued that the need for secrecy makes this suggestion impractical.

Congress makes an important contribution to the formulation and execution of our defense and foreign policy in several ways: its legislative powers have helped to shape our defense establishment and its power of the purse allows it to influence the specific allocation of defense monies, to restrict or reduce foreign aid, and to shape our foreign-trade policy. Despite the vastly increased foreign-policy initiatives of the President during the twentieth century, Congress retains effective checks on our policies through its practice of making short-term appropriations and its powers of investigation and public debate. And it is Congress that often expresses the preferences of the indirect participants in foreign policy—the political parties, interest groups, the news media, and the public itself.

While it is possible to describe in general the major institutions and actors in making foreign policy, it is important to remember that the specific process of foreign-policy making varies with the type of decision at hand. Issues range from traditional diplomatic ones, in which the principal decision makers are generally the President and the Secretary of State, to the crisis issues, in which the participants vary with the specific situation and may consist of a large *ad hoc* team of advisers selected by the President. In the traditional diplomatic issue, negotiations are likely to be conducted openly, and the reactions of Congress and the public may well affect the course of decision-making. Moreover, since the immediate stakes tend to be relatively low, decisions are subject to reversal. In the crisis issue, by contrast, immediate stakes are very high, decision-making tends to be closed, and the choices are final.

The need for secrecy in some crisis decisions—coupled with their irreversibility—has raised the question of whether our system provides adequate controls over our political decision makers and over our military establishment. We have traditionally relied on structural arrangements to keep the military subordinate to civilian policy makers and on congressional and public debate to evaluate decision-making. It is too soon to know whether these safeguards are adequate for a nation with a huge military establishment in "continuous readiness" and whose political decision makers are forced to cope with complex crises around the world.

GOVERNMENT
AND
MONEY

24

All government functions providing benefits to individuals and groups must ultimately be calculated in terms of dollars, and decisions must be made on how best to allocate benefits and costs among various groups in the population. The instrument for allocating benefits is the budget. What conflicts have arisen over its proper role? Who are the primary institutional actors in the politics of budgeting? And what are some of the problems of appropriating funds? The last part of the chapter discusses taxation, the primary source of revenues to pay for government functions. What ideological conflicts does taxation generate, and what are the political problems of raising revenues?

On a typical day, the average American may take his children to a public school on a public street past a public hospital and a public housing project and feel the jar of an Air Force jet breaking the sound barrier overhead. The water he drinks, the cream in his coffee, the vitamins he has just taken, even the air he breathes have all been matters of public regulation. The policeman at the intersection, the fire house on the corner, the public park, and the city coliseum he is passing are all evidence that government's activity on his behalf stretches from his security to his recreation.

These functions of government must be translated into dollars. Decisions must be made on how much will be spent, how the money will be obtained, and how the flow of funds will be regulated through accounting procedures.

THE PATTERN OF PUBLIC EXPENDITURES

Some basic facts about public expenditures are essential for background to this chapter. Government statisticians now accumulate figures on the gross national product (GNP)—that is, all goods and services produced in the nation—and on government purchases of goods and services.[1] These figures show, first, that the percentage of the nation's productive output being used for public programs has increased greatly in the last thirty-five years. Table 24-1 on page 714 shows that in 1929 government purchases represented less than 10 percent of the output of society. During the Depression a new plateau of about 15 percent was reached. In the Second

---

[1] Inaccurate conclusions are often drawn from statistics on public finance because their meaning is not understood:

1. There is an important distinction between total expenditures and the expenditures that take goods and services from the economy. Total expenditures include *transfer payments*, such as pension payments out of public funds and net interest payments. These payments transfer money from those who pay taxes to those who receive payments, but they do not extract from the economy any portion of its output for public uses. If we deduct these payments from total expenditures, we are left with government purchases of goods and services. These purchases represent the value of that portion of the nation's currently produced output bought directly by government. This figure obviously provides a more accurate estimate of the cost to society of the public sector of the economy than does the total-expenditure figure.

2. Monetary figures may be given on a gross or a net basis. The Bureau of the Census accumulates data on a gross basis, including all receipts and expenditures of special funds and enterprises; the Bureau of the Budget reports data on a net basis, including in the budget only the net surplus or deficit for a special fund or enterprise such as the Post Office.

3. Expenditures may be overstated by double inclusions: for example, a grant of money from the federal government to a state government, which then expends the funds, may be counted as an expenditure of both governments. A more accurate statement would count expenditures only for the first government disbursing the funds.

Table 24–1   Government Purchases in Selected Years, 1929–63

Year	Percentage of total economy	Year	Percentage of total economy
1929	8.16	1949	15.61
1930	9.98	1954	20.78
1934	15.26	1961	20.82
1939	14.79	1966	20.70
1944	46.26		

SOURCE: Percentages are derived from figures in *Economic Report of the President,* Transmitted to the Congress, January, 1967, Together with the Annual Report of the Council of Economic Advisers (Washington, 1967), Appendix B-1, p. 213.

World War and the Korean War the percentage temporarily climbed much higher, but then there was a leveling off at a new plateau of about 21 percent.

Statistics also show that the purchases of goods and services by the national government have now become larger than those of state and local governments combined, primarily because of an increase in military purchases. In 1929 state and local governments spent $7.2 billion purchasing goods and services, while the national government spent only $1.3 billion. In 1966, however, national purchases ($77 billion) actually topped combined state and local purchases ($76.2 billion).

Nevertheless, the expenditures of government have been increasing at all three levels. Figure 24–1 shows that over a fifty-year span, from 1913 to 1965, local expenditures became about twenty-five times greater, while state and national expenditures both became over a hundred times greater. It also reveals the startling fact that, in spite of national-defense expenditures, state expenditures grew at a slightly *greater* rate than national expenditures from 1950 to 1965.

Figure 24–2 on page 776 shows the allocation of the national government's dollar as estimated for the 1968 budget. The bulk of the expenditures goes to a few major functions: national defense, 44 percent; trust funds except for the poor (but including social security), 20 percent; and aid to the poor, 14 percent.

Decisions on the expenditure of public funds are crucial determinants of the role of government, the quantity and quality of its services, the allocation of its benefits, and the health of the economy. Decisions on the means of raising the money for these expenditures determine the distribution of costs among various groups in the population. Thus the processes of

Figure 24–1   Expenditures of National, State, and Local Governments for Selected Years from 1913 to 1965 (in billions of dollars)

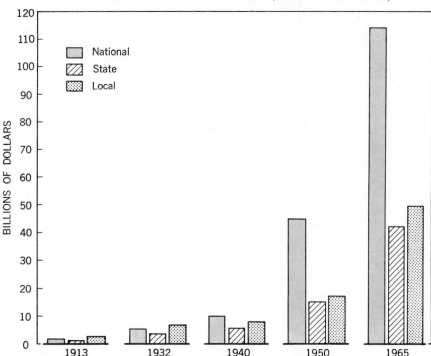

SOURCE: Figures for 1913–50 are derived from U.S. Bureau of the Census, "Historical Summary of Governmental Finances in the United States," *1957 Census of Governments* (1959), Vol. XIV, No. 3, pp. 16–17 (national-government data), pp. 20–21 (state-government data), and pp. 22–23 (local-government data). Data for 1965 are derived from U.S. Bureau of the Census, *Governmental Finances in the United States, 1964–5* p. 22. Intergovernmental revenues not deducted from expenditure figures. Figures not adjusted for changes in the value of the dollar.

decision-making and the problems of public finance are among the most important in public affairs today. This chapter will deal with the national government only; Part VI (in the national, state, and local edition) discusses the revenues and expenditures of state and local governments.

BUDGETING: ITS ROLE AND ITS FEATURES

The budget—a single document containing plans for expenditures of the government as a whole for a definite period—is the central instrument of government finance. Its importance is reflected in the fact that in nearly

Figure 24–2   Allocation of the Government Dollar, 1968 Budget Estimate

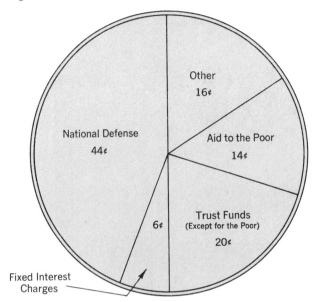

SOURCE: U.S. Bureau of the Budget, *The Budget in Brief* (fiscal year, 1968), p. 18.

all governments the chief executive is responsible for preparation of the budget; the budget office is either a staff unit in his office or part of a department of finance responsible to him.

The budget is a relative newcomer to government. In the United States the movement for budgeting originated in the cities, following revelations of municipal corruption at the turn of the century. The movement spread quickly to the states, most of which set up budget systems of some sort between 1910 and 1920. Meanwhile, in the national government the diminishing surpluses of customs revenues over expenditures led to greater interest in economical use of funds. A report released in 1912 by President Taft's Commission on Economy and Efficiency eventually led to passage of the Budget and Accounting Act of 1921, which made the President responsible for the preparation of a budget and its submission to Congress and created the Bureau of the Budget to assist him.[2]

What Is the Role of the Budget?

Three aspects of budgeting are significant at the national level. First, the budget is an instrument of financial management. It is a means of looking at both revenues and expenditures to determine how much money will be

[2] On these developments, see Jesse Burkhead, *Government Budgeting* (New York: Wiley, 1956), Ch. 1.

spent for an ensuing fiscal period. The budget is customarily accompanied by reports on revenues and expenditures, estimated or actual, for the current year and one or two past years. It provides an overall view of the financial operations of the government and offers an opportunity to trim the fat from agency appropriation requests. This planning, reporting, and trimming is a major part of the business side of government.

Second, the budget is a means of appraising government programs and determining their scope and objectives. Most agencies develop their plans and make their choices among competing pressures for expansion when they frame their budgets. In the process of "screening, filtering, and revising" agency budgets,[3] the President and Congress are able to exercise continuous influence on the policies of agencies and on the scope of their activities. In these processes mountains of data are submitted by agencies and blue-penciled by reviewers at successive stages, but the decisions reflect the preferences of decision makers as to who will get what the government has to give. This system obviously entails more than mere business management; it is a political process of allocating money to preferred uses.

Third, the federal budget is an instrument of economic planning. There is an element of economic planning in any decision of government to use its kit of available tools to affect the course of the economy, and the budget is the chief tool in this kit. Expenditures can be raised or taxes cut to stimulate the economy; expenditures can be cut or taxes raised to dampen inflationary tendencies. Only the national government, however, can play this game with any degree of effectiveness,[4] for the resources of the states and localities are limited, and their constitutions or charters usually restrict their debt-creating and taxing authority.

The national government first used fiscal—that is, expenditure and taxing —policy to strengthen the economy during the depression of the 1930's. In the same decade the English economist John Maynard Keynes advocated the use of fiscal policy to compensate for the slackening in investment and expenditure in the private sector. To do this effectively, data on the aggregate level of production of goods and services in the economy were needed; such information was developed in the 1940's with the national-income accounts. Other statistical measures, such as the annual rate of economic growth, have also been perfected. In budgeting, consideration can now be given to measures of growth and stability in the economy as a whole and to the relationship of government fiscal policy to these ends. Thus the practical need for recovery measures during the Depression led to the formulation of an economic theory, and the specific application of the theory was in turn made possible by statistical data.

[3] Verne B. Lewis, "Budgetary Administration in the Department of Agriculture," in John M. Gaus and Leon O. Wolcott, *Public Administration and the United States Department of Agriculture* (Chicago: Public Administration Service, 1940), p. 405.
[4] For limitations on this effectiveness, see pp. 629–30.

Liederman in the Long Island *Press*

War Orphan

President Johnson emphasized Great Society programs early in his Administration, but as Vietnam war costs rose in the late 1960's, domestic spending had to be cut back sharply.

Fiscal policies give rise to some of the deepest conflicts in public opinion. Many people still regard the national budget as a matter of internal housekeeping—an instrument of sound finance and of decision on competing program claims. They believe it should be balanced except for occasional emergencies. Others look at the national budget as an instrument for promoting economic growth and stability. They argue that the budget should be unbalanced to produce a surplus when there is threat of inflationary instability and unbalanced to show a deficit when there is a threat of recession or a slowdown in economic growth.

The tax reduction enacted by Congress in 1964 illustrates both views of budgeting. It will go down in history books as our first purposeful increase of an expected deficit in order to stimulate employment and economic growth; but at the same time President Johnson felt it politically essential to call for an economy drive on government expenditures to assuage the balanced-budget advocates. The President is the nation's Chief Budgeter; but the chairmen of the Senate Finance Committee and the House Ways and Means Committee are coordinate policy makers for taxation, and Chairman Harry F. Byrd of the Senate committee required economy as the price for tax reduction. The issue of budget-balancing thus involves estimates not only of expenditures but of projected revenues for the government. One's desire for a balanced budget may conflict with one's eagerness to reap the personal benefit of a reduced tax burden.

The two opposing concepts of what the budget is for are reflected in appointments to the Bureau of the Budget. President Eisenhower emphasized the concept of the budget as a device for achieving economy and efficiency through appointments of men with business management and accounting backgrounds to the directorship of the bureau. Presidents Kennedy and Johnson, on the other hand, appointed men trained as economists, emphasizing the economic role of the budget.

How Is the Budgetary Process Distinctive?

Budgeting is the only government process in which an effort is made to encompass all government functions in one set of decisions. In no other process are the competing claims of national defense, education, public works, agricultural stabilization, urban development, and other functions weighed in a single chain of decisions. Consequently, in the historical development of budgeting, emphasis has been placed on the need to get a comprehensive view of government operations. Only in this way, it has been believed, could intelligent decisions be made on priorities among competing claims and expenditures be kept in balance with general objectives—whether budget-balancing or stimulation or restraint of the economy. On the other hand, it is now recognized that it is not feasible to reconsider all government operations every year. In preparing and approving the budget, therefore, executives and legislators normally accept established programs and activities without question—thus providing continuity and stability to government operations. But they take a close look at new activities. As Congressman Rooney of New York observed, "This may be only $250, but this is the camel's nose. These things never get out of the budget. They manage to stay and grow." [5] For old programs the issue is whether increases or decreases in funds should be made and in what amounts. Normally, budgetary policy is incremental—like a tree, it grows by adding branches and twigs.[6] Moreover, decisions must be made separately on numerous fragmented parts of the budget. A significant feature of the budgetary process is the ever present conflict between the search for a comprehensive view of the budget and the realities of incremental, fragmented decision.

Although interest-group influences are exerted during the budgeting process, this influence is generally less apparent and its scope more limited than it is in the process of passing congressional legislation. First, demands for funds are pressed primarily by government agencies rather than by interest groups; second, House-committee hearings are not open to the

---

[5] Quoted in Aaron Wildavsky, *The Politics of the Budgetary Process* (Boston: Little, Brown, 1964), p. 112.

[6] On incremental decision-making, see Charles E. Lindblom, "Policy Analysis," *American Economic Review*, Vol. XLVIII (June 1958), pp. 298–312. On the concept of the "decision tree," see Herbert A. Simon, *Administrative Behavior*, 2nd ed. (New York: Macmillan, 1957), pp. xxvii–xxxiii.

public; and, third, the procedures and roles of the key institutional actors in the executive and legislative branches are firmly established. For these reasons the politics of budgeting takes place mainly among these institutional actors. Our discussion of the budgetary process will therefore concentrate on the internal politics of budgeting and on the roles of the chief actors in government in helping to meet the enormous task of rolling out a budget each year.

THE BUDGETARY PROCESS IN THE NATIONAL GOVERNMENT

The budgetary process in the national government consists of four parts: the preparation of the budget, an executive responsibility; the appropriation of funds, a legislative responsibility; the execution of the budget, an executive process; and the final accounting of expenditures, done by an auditor who is an agent of the legislature and is independent of executive authority.

The Preparation of the Budget

The fiscal year of the United States Government runs from July 1 to June 30 and is named for the later year. Thus, fiscal 1969 ends June 30, 1969. The planning for that budget cycle begins in the spring of 1967. Hence a budget cycle includes a prolonged period of planning and expenditure and overlaps with other budget cycles. Agencies in the spring of 1968 are executing the 1968 budget, arguing in Congress for the 1969 budget, and planning the 1970 budget.

Executive planning of the budget takes place in three stages. The first work on a 1970 budget begins about March 1968, when the bureaus and the department budget offices begin work on estimates of their needs. At the same time, the Bureau of the Budget engages in conversations with the Treasury Department and the Council of Economic Advisers on anticipated national income and tax yields, with major spending agencies on their probable requirements, and with the President on his response to these forecasts of revenue and statements of need.

Then, around June, the bureau will initiate the second stage by transmitting to the major spending agencies a policy letter that sets forth guidelines and probably defines tentative limits on agency spending. There will also be a "call for estimates," with deadlines and specific instructions on budget forms and other technical matters. From June through September the agencies conduct department reviews and internal hearings and adjust their figures before sending their budgets to the Bureau of the Budget.

The third stage—that of top-level consideration of the estimates—begins usually in September. During September and October the bureau conducts hearings at which each agency argues its case. The recommendations of the various government bureau chiefs and further pleas by the agencies are then evaluated by committees composed of the top officials of the Bureau of the Budget and led by the bureau director. In the meantime, conferences are held with the President for his decision on crucial issues, including the amount to be recommended for each agency, and for his instructions on the preparation of his budget message. In January the President submits his budget message and budget to Congress.

This process engages actors throughout the executive branch. The preparation of detailed estimates begins at the operating level—a bureau in the Department of Commerce or a regional office in the Department of Health, Education, and Welfare. At this level men are primarily concerned with ensuring that funds are adequate for effective programs. Because their emphasis is on ways to improve the services of their agencies, they almost always ask for increased appropriations. To combat this tendency, the downward flow of instructions from above almost always calls for economy: "Hold the line," "Ask for increases only where the need is imperative," or "Achieve a reduction."

The estimates of need prepared at the operating level travel upward through budget offices at bureau, departmental, and presidential levels, and at each stage estimates from a variety of services must compete with one another. Budget officials, whose ears are attuned to the executives they serve, reduce the requests of the various services in order to make them palatable at still later stages of the process. These officials operate on the assumptions that operators ask for too much and that their own basic function is to trim the fat and get the totals down to the limits set by their instructions. Thus the higher the claims of each service move, the more they are trimmed by the pressure for economy.

At the pinnacle the President strives for a comprehensive view of policy needs—he looks at the condition of the economy, the major defense needs, his domestic-policy objectives, and the economic and political implications of the budget's total. His resulting policy objectives are communicated to the Bureau of the Budget and the departments. At the lower levels budget makers then construct their case for incremental increases, seeking their fair share of whatever is available. At the department level and in the Bureau of the Budget primary attention will be given to the requests for increases, and these will be considered within the framework of the policies announced by the President. In the bureau an adjustment is achieved between the synoptic view of the President and the incrementalism of the claimants. To perform this task the bureau parcels out various parts of the budget to different specialists and coordinates their judgments through intercommunication and reviews by higher officials.

The form in which the executive branch prepares the budget is important to the meaningful consideration of estimates. Most government budgets were originally built around objects of expenditure, such as salaries, travel costs, and capital expenditures. Today, however, budget-planning centers on the functions and activities for, which funds are required. Following World War II the new terms *performance budgeting* and *program budgeting* came into use. A performance budget states the costs in terms of units of activity, such as the number of miles of highway to be constructed or the number of public housing units to be built. These performance estimates, based on past costs, can be aggregated into a program budget, which summarizes the estimated expenditures in terms of results to be accomplished. Although more difficult to construct than one that merely classifies expenditures by objects, this type of budget gives the President and Congress a better picture of what government will do with its money.

A still newer development in budgeting is called PPBS or PPB (*Planning, Programing, Budgeting System*). It assumes that long-range plans can be developed, programed over a period of time, and converted into budget estimates for each year. PPB enlarges the objectives of program budgeting in three ways: it groups programs according to broad objectives, which may even extend across agency lines (e.g., elimination of poverty in rural areas); it develops a multiyear program and financial plan for making annual budget decisions; and it allows quantitative analysis of the costs and effectiveness of alternative courses of action. In sum, PPBS seeks long-range, interagency program planning through the use of computer technology and thus is an ambitious effort toward synoptic budgeting. The techniques of PPB were developed in the Department of Defense, and in 1965 President Johnson directed the other departments and agencies to introduce these techniques. It is too early to know how successful this latest effort to accumulate data in meaningful form will be; but many people doubt whether the methods used to budget for military hardware—an area involving largely quantitative judgments—can be used effectively in civilian-oriented programs to measure costs and benefits and to guide choices among alternative activities. For quantitative measures of costs and benefits for Job Corps students do not measure the quality of their instruction, and figures alone do not determine whether to expand public housing and welfare benefits. These major decisions are ultimately influenced by value judgments and political considerations.

The Appropriation of Funds

Congress legalizes the spending of money through a two-part process. First, it must pass legislation *authorizing* the expenditure. Such legislation goes to the program committees, such as the Armed Services Committees and the Agriculture Committees, and then to the House and Senate as a whole for a vote. Some authorizations are open ended and place no limits on the total amount of money to be expended, although they almost always contain some restrictions on such items as salaries and the number of supergrade positions. On the other hand, authorization may be quite explicit: limitations may be placed on the total amount to be spent, the duration of the authorization, and the specific activities to be supported. The authorizations may be extended or amended in subsequent sessions of Congress, and battles over the terms of these authorizations may occur concurrently with the next stage.

Second, Congress must pass a legislative *appropriation* of money to pay for expenditures authorized in the laws. Budget estimates for these expenditures go to the House and Senate Appropriations Committees for consideration. Each house has one appropriations committee, which operates through many subcommittees. House action on appropriation bills always precedes Senate action, and the House subcommittees tend to consider budget estimates more thoroughly.

All authorizations are in fact ultimately dependent on the appropriations recommended by the House and Senate subcommittees and voted on by the houses. The appropriations often fall short of the amounts of authorizations. Program committees are often quite responsive to interests seeking benefits and sympathetic to the development of government functions committed to their jurisdiction; appropriations committees, on the other hand, must be more concerned with compromising all authorizations into a feasible budget. The State Department official who sought to rely on an authorization when he was in an appropriations hearing was reminded by Representative Rooney "never [to] lose sight of the fact that the Appropriations Committees are the saucers that cool the legislative tea. Just because you have an authorization does not mean a thing to us. . . ." [7]

Their great power of the purse gives both the House and Senate appropriations subcommittees, along with the program committees, great power over agencies and bureaus, thus contributing to the joint executive-legislative supervision of the administrative apparatus. Subcommittee members not only supervise the budgets of executive bureaus and agencies but often take an interest in their methods of administration and even their policies. Particularly strategic is the position of the subcommittee chairman, whose sympathy or antagonism will mean much to an agency.

The House subcommittees are among the hardest-working units of Congress,[8] and a member of the Appropriations Committee may hold no

[7] Quoted in Wildavsky, *op. cit.*, p. 100.

[8] On congressional consideration, see Arthur W. Macmahon, "Congressional Oversight of Administration: The Power of the Purse," *Political Science Quarterly*, Vol. LVIII (June and September 1943), pp. 161–90, 380–414; Richard F. Fenno, Jr., "The House Appropriation Committee as a Political System: The Problem of Integration," *American Political Science Review*, Vol. LVI (June 1962), pp. 310–24; Fenno, *The Power of the Purse: Appropriation Politics in Congress* (Boston: Little, Brown, 1966).

A House Appropriations Subcommittee in Action: Uncovering Administrative Weakness

Representative Rooney: I find a gentleman here, an FSO–6. He got an A in Chinese and you assigned him to London.

[State Department official]: Yes, sir. That officer will have opportunities in London—not as many as he would have in Hong Kong, for example—

Representative Rooney: What will he do? Spend his time in Chinatown?

[State Department official]: No, sir. There will be opportunities in dealing with officers in the British Foreign Office who are concerned with Far Eastern affairs....

Representative Rooney: So instead of speaking English to one another, they will sit in the London office and talk Chinese?

[State Department official]: Yes, sir.

Representative Rooney: Is that not fantastic?

[State Department official]: No, sir. They are anxious to keep up their practice....

Representative Rooney: They go out to Chinese restaurants and have chop suey together?

[State Department official]: Yes, sir.

Representative Rooney: And that is all at the expense of the American taxpayer?

From Representative John J. Rooney of Brooklyn and an anonymous State Department official, quoted in Aaron Wildavsky, *The Politics of the Budgetary Process*, 1964.

other committee assignment. Months of hearings are held on appropriation requests, followed by executive sessions of the subcommittees. The subcommittees, assisted by the committee staff, specialize in their respective parts of the budget and determine the committee's position on most budget items.

Despite the specialization of the subcommittees, the Appropriations Committee is a smoothly operating political subsystem, integrated through the socialization of members to its habits and norms, and their realization that the chairman of the committee can—primarily through subcommittee assignments—determine their influence within the committee. Committee members stress teamwork, bargaining, and compromise, normally with a minimum of partisanship.[9]

The norm that provides consensus in the subcommittees and the committee is that they are watchdogs of the Treasury. One member declared, "No subcommittee of which I have been a member has ever reported out a bill without a cut in the budget." One investigator found that the House

[9] For a full discussion, see Fenno, *The Power of the Purse*, especially Ch. 5.

Appropriations Committee, in considering thirty-seven bureau budgets from 1947 to 1959, reduced estimates 77.2 percent of the time.[10] Nonetheless, some committee members do identify completely with agency programs and back them staunchly. "To me forestry has become a religion," said one member.

The Senate Appropriations Committee serves primarily as a court of appeals for agencies whose budgets have been cut in the House. The most common type of case on the docket of the Senate committee is "a plea for the restoration of money cut by the House." [11] An observer has remarked that a Senate Appropriations Committee member "is likely to conceive of his proper role as the responsible legislator who sees to it that the irrepressible lower House does not do too much damage either to constituency interests or to national interests.[12] The Senate's expectations of the committee are "tilted more toward program support than toward economy," [13] and the committee's composition accentuates this inclination. Senate rules allow a senator to serve on two committees; hence every member of the Senate Appropriations Committee is a member of a program committee as well. The Senate committee is an interlocking directorate, containing over one-fourth of the members of the Senate and including leaders of both parties and many ranking members of program committees. Moreover, in the Senate, in contrast to the House, the senators choose subcommittees according to their program interests. Thus the Senate committee is a favorable appeals court for agencies pushing for program interests.[14]

Technically, subcommittee recommendations must be approved by the Appropriations Committee as a whole and then by the House or Senate. But in practice the respect of each member—and particularly of each subcommittee chairman—for the special domains of the other subcommittee members and chairmen gives much finality to subcommittee recommendations at the committee stage. A similar spirit of reciprocity among committee chairmen in both the House and the Senate makes substantial amendment on the floor of either house unlikely. Since the House and Senate rarely pass identical appropriation bills, the two versions almost always go to a conference committee, where a compromise is achieved. After both houses approve the bill, it is sent to the President for his signature.

The problems of appropriating funds

Limitations on control of expenditures There are several limitations on the ability of the President and Congress to control the flow of expenditures

[10] Wildavsky, *op. cit.,* pp. 47–48.
[11] Fenno, *The Power of the Purse,* p. 535.
[12] Wildavsky, *op. cit.,* p. 51.
[13] Fenno, *The Power of the Purse,* p. 504.
[14] *Ibid.,* Ch. 10.

into the economy at any given time. First, many expenditure items are continued from previous years unless a drastic overhaul of programs is made. And, second, as Figure 24-3 shows, appropriations may authorize contracts in stated amounts within the fiscal year, but the money may not be completely spent until later years when the contracts are completed. In military and space programs this accumulation of obligations from prior years diminishes the government's opportunity to reduce the rate of flow of expenditures promptly; similarly, the time lag between the planning for expenditures and the actual spending reduces the opportunity to increase the flow of expenditures quickly.

The figures in the chart, however, reflect only partially those policy commitments that have not been fully embodied in appropriation acts. For example, a major step in Defense Department budgeting since 1961 has been the practice of projecting the costs of each weapons system for five years ahead. A currently small appropriation grant may commit the government to a program that will be much more expensive half a decade later. The manned-space programs provide an even more dramatic illustration. President Kennedy's 1962 decision to press forward with the man-to-the-moon program, involving $20 billion over eight or nine years, will circumscribe the budgeters very substantially for at least a decade.

A final limit on government control of annual expenditures is the fact

Figure 24-3   The Relation of Appropriations to Expenditures, 1968 Budget Estimate

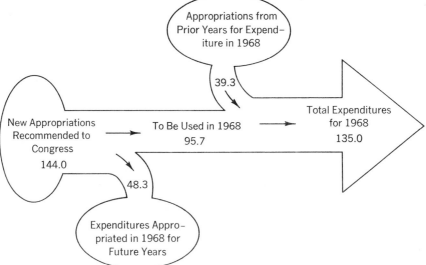

SOURCE: Data from U.S. Bureau of the Budget, *The Budget in Brief* (fiscal year, 1968), p. 53.

that the process of planning must begin so early that many changes in conditions affecting needs for funds cannot be anticipated. One result is that supplementary appropriation acts must sometimes be passed; a more serious effect is that public programs may be strait-jacketed by lags in the appropriation process.

The need for annual appropriations   The system of annual appropriations, once regarded as an important protection of the citizen's liberty, has several disadvantages in today's highly complex technological society. First, annual appropriations hinder long-range planning. The Defense Department, for example, spends a good deal of time breaking down estimates year by year —time that might be more efficiently used for long-range projections; similarly, the Department of State is limited in making arrangements with foreign countries by its inability to commit funds for longer than a year.

A Critique of Long-Term Budgeting

[A] question which frequently arises is whether or not we would profit from budgeting for longer periods of time—say for 5 years. Here I believe we should distinguish carefully between planning and budgeting. There is no question but that *planning* for years ahead is desirable. However, *budgeting*, in the sense of seeking appropriations for such periods of time, could create several types of serious problems.

The net effect of a multiyear budget for any period for any program is to give that program an absolute priority over all other programs which do not enjoy such an automatic availability of funds. In other words, in the preparation of each year's budget, it would be necessary to allocate to such a program whatever amount had previously been appropriated in advance, regardless of the requirements of other programs. Assuming that funds are not unlimited, and since the controllable portion of the annual budget is relatively small, this could effectively destroy budgetary management.

... A 5-year program budget could deny to one or even two succeeding Congresses any control over that program through the appropriations process.

One of the most serious objections to any 5-year budget lies in the fact that it is almost impossible to project requirements so far ahead.... The 5-year projection may turn out to represent more than is actually required, so that adherence to the plan would represent a waste of funds. If the projection turns out to represent less than is required the result is to place completely undesirable restraints on the program.

From Budget Director Maurice H. Stans, testifying before the Subcommittee on National Policy Machinery, Senate Committee on Government Operations, July 1961.

Finally, Congress does not always pass the appropriation bills before the beginning of the fiscal year. This delay necessitates special authorizations for short periods, forcing agencies to delay forward planning and commitments pending passage of the annual appropriation bills. One commentator has suggested that since all appropriations are not actually reviewed each year anyway, a thorough analysis of appropriations for those activities that do not change much from year to year should be made only once every four or five years.[15]

The difficulties of coordination   Consideration of the budget in fragments is inevitable because of the size, diversity, and complexity of government programs. Moreover, quality analysis of these fragments can be achieved only through expert consideration of numerous details. Budgeting has become a highly professionalized aspect of management, and the Bureau of the Budget attracts men who want careers in management and are challenged by the opportunity to work in a center having government-wide responsibilities. Members of the House Appropriations Committee remain for extended periods, becoming experts in their subcommittee work. They are assisted by the largest committee staff in Congress. Yet the task is tremendous, and the difficulties of obtaining a grasp of even the incremental points in budget estimates appear insuperable. Some argue, however, that more attention should be given to the total budget and to the overall allocation of money to each major program and activity. This is the traditional contention that the view of the forest is lost by too close an examination of the trees. In the Bureau of the Budget, intercommunication and review procedures, along with presidential directives, preserve a balance between incremental and synoptic procedures—that is, between budgeting for the separate activities and budgeting within a total sum in accordance with general policies. But in Congress the separateness of subcommittees and the degree of finality of their recommendations has led to concern among those interested in coordination and limitation of the budget total.

Congressional efforts to overcome the decentralization and specialization of the subcommittee system by focusing attention on budget aggregates have been unsuccessful. For example, the Legislative Reorganization Act of 1946 provided for a joint committee on the legislative budget to set a ceiling on total appropriations. But the effort to arbitrate and reduce the proposals coming from the separate subcommittees was ineffective, and the system was abandoned after 1949. In 1950 the House Appropriations Committee reported out an omnibus appropriation, later passed by both houses, that contained in one bill all the year's appropriations. This procedure has not been followed since, for mere aggregation in one bill serves no useful purpose.

[15] Wildavsky, *op. cit.*, p. 150.

Recently, observers have suggested that the reality of "specialized, incremental, fragmented, sequential, non-programmatic" budgeting be taken as given, "excepting what the President can manage through the Budget Bureau." It is argued that the participants in the subcommittees have an implicit understanding of what the fair share of each program is and that informal coordination is achieved by tacit agreements and an awareness of what other participants are likely to do.[16] This reflects the view that synoptic planning is really not possible nor essential at the congressional stage—that a congressman's skill lies in the incremental adjustment of conflicting preferences, that the socialization of members in the House Appropriations Committee is so complete that much informal coordination is achieved through mutual acceptance of the goal of budget reduction, and that additional coordination is achieved through the controls exerted by the committee and subcommittee chairmen. It seems clear that incremental practices are so firmly established in Congress that the influence of synoptic procedures will come only from the Presidency and from forms of budgetary *preparation* (like PPBS) that emphasize comprehensive planning.

The lack of an executive item veto A final problem in appropriations is the lack of an effective executive check upon appropriation bills. Congressional committees may pad bills with funds for pet projects of congressmen on behalf of their constituents; they may include details of administration that impair executive responsibility; and they may even attach legislative riders having little or no connection with the appropriation of money. But the President lacks the power to veto single items in an appropriation bill, and he is usually unable to veto the entire bill because this would leave agencies without funds. Some have argued that a presidential *item veto* would provide a check against excessive expenditures and prevent congressional encroachment on administration. But opponents of the item veto argue that it would encourage Congress to add still more special projects and thus pass the buck to the President. The decisive consideration has been that members of Congress oppose the item veto because it would remove useful leverage against the President and shift decision-making power from the Capitol to the White House.

The Execution and Auditing of the Budget

Execution of the budget consists of the expenditure of allocated funds and the controls exercised over the process. A central problem is the amount of flexibility allowed an agency in this execution. The *line-item* appropriation specifies each item of expenditure separately; the *lump-sum* appropriation, on the other hand, allocates funds to the agency either in a single sum

---

[16] Aaron Wildavsky, *Congress: The First Branch of Government* (Washington, D.C.: American Enterprise Institute, 1965).

or in large categories of expenditure. A line-item appropriation encourages legislative meddling in administrative detail and inhibits flexibility in expenditures over the fiscal year. On the other hand, Congress often wishes to determine the scope of specific activities and habitually specifies allocations for local projects dear to the hearts of individual congressmen. Congress therefore combines specific designation of funds for many projects with lump-sum appropriations for some categories of expenditure, along with specific limitations on expenditures for stated purposes such as travel, publications, and administrative expense.

There are several ways of establishing centralized executive control over budget execution: the primary method used in the United States is the apportionment of funds. The Bureau of the Budget requires each agency to divide its annual appropriation into quarterly segments, so that maximum limits are placed on the amount to be expended for each period. This ensures that the money appropriated will last through the fiscal period, except for unusual contingencies that justify a request for a supplementary appropriation.

Our national government has an elaborate system of checks on the disposal of funds. Money is appropriated to administering agencies, which are subject to legal and administrative requirements. Accounts must meet the requirements of the Joint Accounting Program developed cooperatively by the Comptroller General (the government auditor), the Treasury, and the Bureau of the Budget. Within each agency, maximum expenditures are allotted to each component unit. Funds are set aside for the account of the agency on the books of the Treasury, and when an appropriate official in an agency certifies the legality of the expenditure to the chief disbursing officer of the Treasury, checks are written by the Treasury and debited to the agency accounts.

An audit of accounts is made by the Comptroller General, head of the General Accounting Office, who is considered the agent of Congress. He is appointed by the President with the advice and consent of the Senate for a fifteen-year term and is removable only by a resolution of the houses of Congress.

SOURCES OF GOVERNMENT REVENUES

Almost all the revenues of the national government come from taxes, although the Post Office, public power projects, and other government activities are financed wholly or partly by the sale of goods and services to the public. Taxes arouse deep emotions, conflicting opinions, and much politics. Some people accept taxes fatalistically, recognizing that part of the expenditure is for sheer survival and perhaps believing, as Justice Holmes did, that when one pays taxes he "buys civilization." On the other hand, many people regard taxes as an onerous and even unjust personal deprivation or as an encumbrance on the private economy. They believe that government should limit its services and control waste in order to reduce or prevent further advances in taxes.

There are also profound conflicts over the apportionment of taxes among the different groups in the population. According to their effect on population groups there are three types of taxes: *proportional* taxes, where the tax rate remains constant at all levels; *progressive* taxes, where the rate rises as the base on which the tax is levied increases; and *regressive* taxes, where the rate decreases as the base increases. Some people believe strongly in the principle of taxation according to ability to pay. They stress the fact that high taxes on low-income earners merely reduce their purchasing power, thus restricting production for a mass market and growth of the economy. Others believe that costs should be distributed in accordance with benefits received. They point out that high taxes on high incomes reduce the investment necessary for an expanding economy. These philosophical positions usually reflect concrete differences of interest between the rich and the poor. Thus, every tax bill brings some conflict in Congress between those who want to get the money from those with substantial incomes and those who want to avoid this by "broadening the tax base."

The decision makers in government therefore find that getting the money is a necessary but thankless and difficult endeavor. One consideration influencing their decisions is fairness. Sometimes this leads to agreement on taxation according to benefits received, as when the costs of an irrigation project are apportioned among the users; at other times, it is difficult to evaluate what is fair because so many considerations are involved. A second consideration is the adequacy of government revenues. The government must be supported, and one test of a good tax is whether it will produce the needed money without producing intolerable burdens on particular groups. A third factor is whether the tax can be efficiently administered. How high are the costs of collection, and how serious are the opportunities for evasion or unequal treatment? Finally, the effect of a tax on the national economy may be taken into account. Does the tax contain enough flexibility to be less onerous in hard times and to raise more money in prosperous times, thus offsetting recessions and inflations?

In the twentieth century, national decision makers have often resorted to deficit financing, because taxes are unpopular or because they consider the effect of taxes on the economy so crucial that it should take precedence over the test of adequacy, which is dominant at other levels of government. The result is an increasing national debt.

A Conservative View of Taxation: Threat
to Individual Freedom

We have been led to look upon taxation as merely a problem of public financing: How much money does the government need? We have been led to discount, and often to forget altogether, the bearing of taxation on the problem of individual freedom. We have been persuaded that the government has an unlimited claim on the wealth of the people, and that the only pertinent question is what portion of its claim it should exercise....

The "nature of things," I submit, is quite different. Government does *not* have an unlimited claim on the earnings of individuals. One of the foremost precepts of the natural law is man's right to the possession and use of his property. And a man's earnings are his property as much as his land and the house in which he lives. Indeed, in the industrial age, earnings are probably the most prevalent form of property.... How can a man be truly free if he is denied the means to exercise freedom? How can he be free if the fruits of his labor are not his to dispose of, but are treated, instead, as part of a common pool of public wealth? Property and freedom are inseparable: to the extent government takes the one in the form of taxes, it intrudes on the other.

From Senator Barry Goldwater of Arizona, *The Conscience of a Conservative*, 1960.

The national debt was less than $17 billion in 1929 but was above $336 billion before the end of 1967. The burden of such a debt on the people and the economy may be reduced by inflation or by increased production, both of which are reflected in the gross national product. In fact, the ratio of the government's debt to the GNP declined sharply from 118 percent in 1947 to 49 percent in 1965. Obviously, deficit financing can be a significant source of revenue if the GNP expands rapidly. On the other hand, deficit financing arouses the antagonism of those who fear inflation and those who regard a balanced budget as the basis for a sound economy.

The Problems of Raising Revenues

The tax sources of the national government have been limited by constitutional provisions. First, the government cannot tax exports. Second, an indirect tax—that is, a duty, impost, or excise—must be geographically uniform for a given article. However, the Supreme Court has held [17] that it is constitutional to allow reduced federal estate-tax rates in states that also

[17] *Florida* v. *Mellon*, 273 U.S. 12 (1927).

Split-Level Living

From *Straight Herblock*, Simon & Schuster, 1964

Liberals often argue that the health of our economy is undermined when private spending is emphasized at the expense of public services supported by taxation.

levy such taxes. Third, direct taxes must be apportioned among the states according to their population. Land taxes, for example, have been held to be direct taxes. But a land tax apportioned according to population would be absurd; hence this tax is eliminated as a source of national revenue. The Supreme Court in 1895 held that an income-tax law that included levies on income from property was also a direct tax,[18] thus eliminating this tax source until the passage of the Sixteenth Amendment. Fourth, there is a judicial rule that the national government cannot tax state functions in such a way as to impair state sovereignty, but the precise line of limitation is a technical one. Finally, in 1936 the Supreme Court declared that a tax must be for national rather than local welfare,[19] but in fact no tax since then has been held unconstitutional on this ground.

The Constitution opened the way for the levying of customs duties, which until the adoption of the Sixteenth Amendment in 1913 were the chief source of national revenue. The adoption of the Sixteenth Amendment

[18] *Pollock* v. *Farmers' Loan & Trust Co.,* 157 U.S. 429 (1895).
[19] *United States* v. *Butler,* 297 U.S. 1 (1936).

Figure 24–4   Revenue Sources of the Government Dollar, 1968 Budget Estimate

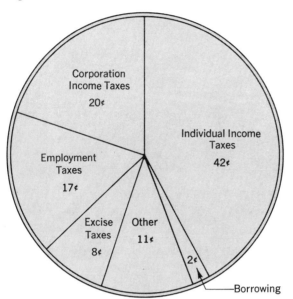

SOURCE: U.S. Bureau of the Budget, *The Budget in Brief* (fiscal year, 1968), p. 18.

was a watershed in national financing, for the income tax is now the largest revenue producer. Figure 24–4 shows the sources of the budget dollar as estimated for 1968.

But the potential revenues from the Sixteenth Amendment are reduced by a mass of special provisions designed to ease the burden of income-tax laws for many special interests. Such provisions include a lower rate of taxation on capital gains, deductions for business expenses, depletion allowances on income from the production of oil and other natural resources, deferred tax payments on retirement annuities (usually resulting in lower rates), investment credits, and accelerated depreciation allowances.

As these special provisions suggest, the politics of tax exemption is one of the most active arenas of the governmental process. All the major interests participate in it, seeking new exemptions or the protection of old ones. These interests justify the exemptions or reductions in rate on various grounds—stimulation of investment, fairness, alleviation of hardship, or social benefit (e.g., encouragement of private contributions for charity or of saving for old age). Success has gone in largest measure to those interests—business and investor groups, oil lobbies—that have had the most favorable access to Congress. Once exemptions have been established, they have persisted against attack. Thus, when the Internal Revenue Service proposed recently to tighten the rules on deductible business expenses, companies and their association representatives, individuals who made frequent business

"Fortunately, nobody's worrying about holding us!"

Sanders in the Milwaukee *Journal*

A persistent complaint of liberal critics during the late 1960's was that Congress would neither increase taxes nor raise revenues by plugging tax loopholes for special interests.

trips, transportation companies, hotels, restaurants, night clubs, and others were roused for successful defense of their tax-protected interests.

Because some types of income are taxed at lower rates than others and some are not taxed at all, one may have a very substantial income and yet pay little or no tax. The author of a recent book on the tax system tells us that in 1959 seventeen Americans had incomes of $1 million or more, yet they had to pay no federal income tax. One man earned $20 million but owed no tax.[20]

The yield of the income tax is also affected by the economy itself. As recession sets in, the tax yield declines; as recovery ensues, the yield grows. The tax is therefore a built-in stabilizer of the economy, for the economy is less weighted with taxes when recovery is needed and most weighted when inflation is threatened. This effect may be accentuated by positive decisions of government, as when taxes were reduced in 1964 to stimulate economic growth.

But the utility of the tax system as a tool of economic stabilization is diminished by its rigidity. It is usually many months after a tax change is needed that its effects are finally felt in the economy. For the need must first be assessed, recommended by the President, and passed by Congress, and each is a time-consuming process. In 1961 the Commission on Money and Credit, a high-level voluntary study group, advocated granting discretionary authority to the President to vary the basic rate within a 5-point range for limited periods of time to increase the flexibility of the income-tax

[20] Philip M. Stern, *The Great Treasury Raid* (New York: Random House, 1964), p. 4.

system. President Kennedy included this proposal in his 1962 Economic Report but did not push it when Congress showed antagonism. There is nothing congressmen are more jealous about than their prerogatives in taxation. They are, of course, conscious of the sensitivity of their constituents on taxation, and they have been trained to believe that control of taxation by representative bodies is one of the foundations of representative government. They know also that control of taxation affects other issues in which they have profound interests, such as the scope of government functions, the level of government expenditures, and the means and timing of government intervention in the economy.

We can see, then, that taxation is a highly political issue. Those who want extensive action programs by government will be more inclined to accept a higher level of taxation than those who would like to see government activities (and therefore expenditures) reduced. And of course we would all like to keep our cake while eating it—to reduce taxes but maintain expenditure on all worthy programs. Politics unites the two sides of the coin: expenditures and taxation.

SUMMARY

The most significant facts about government expenditures are that the percentage of the nation's gross national product that is used for public programs has more than doubled since 1930, and the purchases of goods and services by the national government are now larger than those of the state and local governments combined.

The budget is the primary instrument for planning how these expenditures will be allocated among individuals and programs. A basic conflict over the role of the budget occurs between those who feel that the budget should be used primarily as a means for financial management—and should thus be balanced except for occasional emergencies—and those who feel that it should be used to promote economic growth and stability—and thus unbalanced when necessary to offset threats of inflation or recession.

Budgeting is the only government process that weighs the competing claims of all government programs—from defense-planning to urban development—in a single hierarchy of decision-making. The first stage, preparation of the budget, is an executive responsibility. The basic job of the Budget Bureau is to achieve a compromise between the incremental, piecemeal requests of the competing claimants for various government programs on one hand and the President's comprehensive view of overall policy needs and objectives on the other.

At the second stage, congressional appropriation of funds, great power is exerted by the program committees, who pass legislation *authorizing* expenditures, and by the House and Senate subcommittees who recommend the actual legislative *appropriation* of money. Ultimate authority is in fact wielded by the House and Senate appropriations subcommittees, since authorizations are dependent on appropriations, which are often less than the authorized amounts.

There are several continuing problems of appropriating funds: (1) the President and Congress have only limited ability to control the flow of expenditures into the economy at a given time; (2) the tradition of annual appropriations hinders long-range government planning; (3) the decentralization and specialization of the subcommittee system in Congress hamper efforts to appraise the budget as a whole; and (4) the President's lack of an item veto often forces him to accept unwanted riders tacked onto appropriations bills.

The two final stages of the budget process are the execution and auditing of the budget. Centralized presidential control over budget execution is achieved primarily by the system of apportioning funds for limited periods. There is an elaborate procedure for checking on the disposal of funds, with final auditing of accounts by the Comptroller General, who acts as an agent of Congress.

The primary source of government revenues is taxation, and, not surprisingly, taxes generate deep ideological and political controversies. Some people favor taxation according to ability to pay, in order to ensure the purchasing power necessary for a mass market and a growing economy. Others favor taxation according to benefits received, because when the rich are taxed, the investments needed for an expanding economy are reduced.

The government chooses its methods of taxation by weighing several considerations: Is the tax fair? Does it produce the necessary revenues without putting intolerable strains on any group? Can it be efficiently administered? And what will be the effect on the economy? In addition, there are some basic problems in obtaining revenues. First, tax legislation is the objective of intensive political activity by interest groups. The result is that the government's potential revenues from the income tax are substantially lowered by special legislative provisions that in effect reduce income-tax payments for many special interests.

Second, the rigidity of the tax system makes it only somewhat effective as a tool of economic stabilization. Partly because of these problems, the government has often resorted to deficit financing, and the result is an increasing national debt.

Decisions on the allocations of benefits and costs affect the population so profoundly that they are heavily influenced at every turn by politics. But the structure and procedures of the decision-making processes repeatedly absorb and mediate the conflicts of interests among competing claimants and between claimants and the taxpayer.

(Acknowledgments continued from p. iv.)

COMMENTARY—For excerpt from Richard N. Goodwin, "The Shape of American Politics," reprinted from *Commentary*, by permission; copyright © 1967 by the American Jewish Committee.

DOUBLEDAY & COMPANY, INC.—For excerpts from Ray C. Bliss, "The Role of the State Chairman," and John F. Kennedy, "Why Go Into Politics?" in James M. Cannon, ed., *Politics U.S.A.*, copyright © 1960 by James M. Cannon. Also for excerpt from Richard M. Nixon, *Six Crises*; copyright © 1962 by Richard M. Nixon; reprinted by permission of Doubleday & Company, Inc.

HARCOURT, BRACE & WORLD, INC.—For excerpts abridged and adapted from Edward N. Costikyan, *Behind Closed Doors*, copyright © 1966, by Edward N. Costikyan. Reprinted by permission of Harcourt, Brace & World, Inc.

HARPER & ROW, PUBLISHERS, INC.—For excerpts from Theodore C. Sorensen, *Kennedy*, pp. 162–63 and 197–98. Copyright © 1965 by Theodore C. Sorensen. Reprinted by permission of Harper & Row, Publishers.

HARVARD UNIVERSITY PRESS—For excerpts reprinted by permission of the publishers from Robert H. Jackson, *The Supreme Court in the American System of Government*, Cambridge, Mass.: Harvard University Press, Copyright, 1955, by William Eldred Jackson and G. Bowdoin Craighill, Jr., Executors. Also for excerpt reprinted by permission of the publishers from letter by Theodore Roosevelt to George Otto Trevelyan, June 19, 1908, in Elting E. Morison, ed., *The Letters of Theodore Roosevelt*, Vol. VI, Cambridge, Mass.: Harvard University Press, Copyright, 1952.

HODDER AND STOUGHTON LIMITED—For excerpts from Theodore C. Sorensen, *Kennedy*, reprinted by permission.

BERTHA KLAUSNER INTERNATIONAL LITERARY AGENCY, INC.—For excerpt from Adam Clayton Powell, Jr., "The Duties and Responsibilities of a Congressman to the United States," reprinted by permission. First published in *Esquire Magazine*, September 1963.

DAVID LAWRENCE ASSOCIATES—For excerpt from David Lawrence, syndicated column in New York *Herald Tribune*, March 1964. Copyright, 1964, New York Herald Tribune, Inc.

LITTLE, BROWN AND COMPANY—For map from Herbert Jacob and Kenneth N. Vines, eds., *Politics in the American States: A Comparative Analysis*. Copyright © 1965, by Little, Brown and Company (Inc.). Reprinted by permission of the publisher.

HAROLD MATSON COMPANY, INC.—For syndicated column by Eric Sevareid in Rockland County *Citizen*; copyright © 1964, by Eric Sevareid. Reprinted by permission of Harold Matson Company, Inc.

THE NEW YORK TIMES COMPANY—For excerpt from Dean Acheson, "Thoughts About Thought in High Places," *The New York Times Magazine*, © 1959 by The New York Times Company; reprinted by permission. For excerpt from Arthur J. Goldberg, "Equal Justice for the Poor, Too," *The New York Times Magazine*, © 1964 by The New York Times Company; reprinted by permission. For excerpt from John F. Kennedy, press conference, *The New York Times*, © 1962 by The New York Times Company; reprinted by permission. For excerpt from joint Senate-House Republican leadership, statement in *The New York Times*, © 1962 by The New York Times Company; reprinted by permission. For excerpts from Harry S Truman, speech at Truman Birthday Dinner, *The New York Times*, © 1954 by The New York Times Company; reprinted by permission.

RANDOM HOUSE, INC.—For excerpt from Charles Silberman, *Crisis in Black and White*, © Copyright, 1964, by Random House, Inc.; reprinted by permission of Random House, Inc.

PAUL R. REYNOLDS, INC.—For excerpt from Will Stanton, "The View from the Fence or How to Tell a Democrat from a Republican," *Ladies' Home Journal*. Copyright © 1962 by Curtis Publishing Company, Inc. Reprinted by permission of Paul R. Reynolds, Inc., 599 Fifth Avenue, New York, New York 10017.

CHARLES SCRIBNER'S SONS—For excerpt from Theodore Roosevelt, letter of July 1902, from Henry Cabot Lodge, *Selections from the Correspondence of Theodore Roosevelt and Henry Cabot Lodge, 1894–1918*. Reprinted by permission of Charles Scribner's Sons.

VICTOR PUBLISHING COMPANY, INC.—For excerpts from Barry Goldwater, *The Conscience of a Conservative* (Victor Publishing Company, Inc., Shepherdsville, Kentucky), copyright © 1960.

THE WORLD PUBLISHING COMPANY—For excerpts reprinted by permission of The World Publishing Company from Harry Golden, *Only in America*. Copyright © 1958, 1957, 1956, 1955, 1954, 1953, 1951, 1949, 1948, 1944 by Harry Golden.

THE CONSTITUTION OF THE UNITED STATES OF AMERICA

We the people of the United States, in order to form a more perfect Union, establish justice, insure domestic tranquility, provide for the common defence, promote the general welfare, and secure the blessings of liberty to ourselves and our posterity, do ordain and establish this Constitution for the United States of America.

ARTICLE I

Section 1. All legislative powers herein granted shall be vested in a Congress of the United States, which shall consist of a Senate and House of Representatives.

Section 2. 1. The House of Representatives shall be composed of members chosen every second year by the people of all the several States, and the electors in each State shall have the qualifications requisite for electors of the most numerous branch of the State Legislature.

2. No person shall be a representative who shall not have attained to the age of twenty-five years, and been seven years a citizen of the United States, and who shall not, when elected, be an inhabitant of that State in which he shall be chosen.

3. Representatives and direct taxes [1] shall be apportioned among the several States which may be included within this Union, according to their respective numbers, which shall be determined by adding to the whole number of free persons, including those bound to service for a term of years, and excluding Indians not taxed, three-fifths of all other persons.[2] The actual enumeration shall be made within three years after the first meeting of the Congress of the United States, and within every subsequent term of ten years, in such manner as they shall by law direct. The number of representatives shall not exceed one for every thirty thousand, but each State shall have at least one representative; and until such enumeration shall be made, the State of New Hampshire shall be entitled to choose three, Massachusetts eight, Rhode Island and Providence Plantations one, Connecticut five, New York six, New Jersey four, Pennsylvania eight, Delaware one, Maryland six, Virginia ten, North Carolina five, South Carolina five, and Georgia three

4. When vacancies happen in the representation from any State, the executive authority thereof shall issue writs of election to fill such vacancies.

5. The House of Representatives shall choose their speaker and other officers; and shall have the sole power of impeachment.

Section 3. 1. The Senate of the United States shall be composed of two senators from each State, chosen by the legislature thereof,[3] for six years; and each senator shall have one vote.

2. Immediately after they shall be assembled in consequence of the first election, they shall be divided as equally as may be into three classes. The seats of the senators of the first class shall be vacated at the expiration of the second year, of the second class at the expiration of the fourth year, and of the third class at the expiration of the sixth year, so that one-third may be chosen every second year; and if vacancies happen by resignation, or otherwise, during the recess of the legislature of any State, the executive thereof may make temporary appointments until the next meeting of the legislature, which shall then fill such vacancies.[4]

3. No person shall be a senator who shall not have attained to the age of thirty years, and been nine years a citizen of the United States, and who shall not, when elected, be an inhabitant of that State for which he shall be chosen.

4. The Vice President of the United States shall be President of the Senate, but shall have no vote, unless they be equally divided.

5. The Senate shall choose their other officers and also a president pro tempore, in the absence of the Vice President, or when he shall exercise the office of President of the United States.

6. The Senate shall have the sole power to try all impeachments. When sitting for that

[1] See the 16th Amendment.
[2] See the 14th Amendment.

[3] See the 17th Amendment.
[4] See the 17th Amendment.

purpose, they shall be on oath or affirmation. When the President of the United States is tried, the Chief Justice shall preside: and no person shall be convicted without the concurrence of two-thirds of the members present.

7. Judgment in cases of impeachment shall not extend further than to removal from office, and disqualifications to hold and enjoy any office of honor, trust or profit under the United States: but the party convicted shall nevertheless be liable and subject to indictment, trial, judgment and punishment, according to law.

Section 4. 1. The times, places, and manner of holding elections for senators and representatives, shall be prescribed in each State by the legislature thereof; but the Congress may at any time by law make or alter such regulations, except as to the places of choosing senators.

2. The Congress shall assemble at least once in every year, and such meeting shall be on the first Monday in December, unless they shall by law appoint a different day.

Section 5. 1. Each House shall be the judge of the elections, returns and qualifications of its own members, and a majority of each shall constitute a quorum to do business; but a smaller number may adjourn from day to day, and may be authorized to compel the attendance of absent members, in such manner, and under such penalties as each House may provide.

2. Each House may determine the rules of its proceedings, punish its members for disorderly behaviour, and, with the concurrence of two-thirds, expel a member.

3. Each House shall keep a journal of its proceedings, and from time to time publish the same, excepting such parts as may in their judgment require secrecy; and the yeas and nays of the members of either House on any question shall, at the desire of one-fifth of those present, be entered on the journal.

4. Neither House, during the session of Congress, shall, without the consent of the other, adjourn for more than three days, nor to any other place than that in which the two Houses shall be sitting.

Section 6. 1. The senators and representatives shall receive a compensation for their services, to be ascertained by law, and paid out of the Treasury of the United States. They shall in all cases, except treason, felony, and breach of the peace, be privileged from arrest during their attendance at the session of their respective Houses, and in going to and returning from the same; and for any speech or debate in either House, they shall not be questioned in any other place.

2. No senator or representative shall, during the time for which he was elected, be appointed to any civil office under the authority of the United States, which shall have been created, or the emoluments whereof shall have been increased, during such time; and no person holding any office under the United States shall be a member of either House during his continuance in office.

Section 7. 1. All bills for raising revenue shall originate in the House of Representatives; but the Senate may propose or concur with amendments as on other bills.

2. Every bill which shall have passed the House of Representatives and the Senate, shall, before it becomes a law, be presented to the President of the United States; if he approves he shall sign it, but if not he shall return it, with his objections, to that House in which it shall have originated, who shall enter the objections at large on their journal, and proceed to reconsider it. If after such reconsideration two-thirds of that House shall agree to pass the bill, it shall be sent, together with the objections, to the other House, by which it shall likewise be reconsidered, and if approved by two-thirds of that House, it shall become a law. But in all such cases the votes of both Houses shall be determined by yeas and nays, and the names of the persons voting for and against the bill shall be entered on the journal of each House respectively. If any bill shall not be returned by the President within ten days (Sundays excepted) after it shall have been presented to him, the same shall be a law, in like manner as if he had signed it, unless the Congress by their adjournment prevent its return, in which case it shall not be a law.

3. Every order, resolution, or vote to which the concurrence of the Senate and the House of Representatives may be necessary (except on a question of adjournment) shall be presented to the President of the United States; and before the same shall take effect, shall be approved by him, or being disapproved by him, shall be repassed by two-thirds of the Senate and House of Representatives, according to the rules and limitations prescribed in the case of a bill.

Section 8. The Congress shall have the power

1. To lay and collect taxes, duties, imposts, and excises, to pay the debts and provide for the common defence and general welfare of the United States; but all duties, imposts, and excises shall be uniform throughout the United States;

2. To borrow money on the credit of the United States;

3. To regulate commerce with foreign nations, and among the several States, and with the Indian tribes;

4. To establish an uniform rule of naturalization, and uniform laws on the subject of bankruptcies throughout the United States;

5. To coin money, regulate the value thereof, and of foreign coin, and fix the standard of weights and measures;

6. To provide for the punishment of counterfeiting the securities and current coin of the United States;

7. To establish post offices and post roads;

8. To promote the progress of science and useful arts, by securing for limited times to authors and inventors the exclusive right to their respective writings and discoveries;

9. To constitute tribunals inferior to the Supreme Court;

10. To define and punish piracies and felonies committed on the high seas, and offences against the law of nations;

11. To declare war, grant letters of marque and reprisal, and make rules concerning captures on land and water;

12. To raise and support armies, but no appropriation of money to that use shall be for a longer term than two years;

13. To provide and maintain a navy;

14. To make rules for the government and regulation of the land and naval forces;

15. To provide for calling forth the militia to execute the laws of the Union, suppress insurrections and repel invasions;

16. To provide for organizing, arming, and disciplining the militia, and for governing such part of them as may be employed in the service of the United States, reserving to the States respectively, the appointment of the officers, and the authority of training the militia according to the discipline prescribed by Congress;

17. To exercise exclusive legislation in all cases whatsoever, over such district (not exceeding ten miles square) as may, by cession of particular States, and the acceptance of Congress, become the seat of the government of the United States, and to exercise like authority over all places purchased by the consent of the legislature of the State in which the same shall be, for the erection of forts, magazines, arsenals, dockyards, and other needful buildings; and

18. To make all laws which shall be necessary and proper for carrying into execution the foregoing powers, and all other powers vested by this Constitution in the government of the United States, or in any department or officer thereof.

Section 9. 1. The migration or importation of such persons as any of the States now existing shall think proper to admit, shall not be pro-

hibited by the Congress prior to the year one thousand eight hundred and eight, but a tax or duty may be imposed on such importation, not exceeding ten dollars for each person.

2. The privilege of the writ of habeas corpus shall not be suspended, unless when in cases of rebellion or invasion the public safety may require it.

3. No bill of attainder or ex post facto law shall be passed.

4. No capitation, or other direct, tax shall be laid, unless in proportion to the census or enumeration herein before directed to be taken.[5]

5. No tax or duty shall be laid on articles exported from any State.

6. No preference shall be given by any regulation of commerce or revenue to the ports of one State over those of another: nor shall vessels bound to, or from, one State be obliged to enter, clear, or pay duties in another.

7. No money shall be drawn from the treasury, but in consequence of appropriations made by law; and a regular statement and account of the receipts and expenditures of all public money shall be published from time to time.

8. No title of nobility shall be granted by the United States: and no person holding any office of profit or trust under them, shall, without the consent of the Congress, accept of any present, emolument, office, or title, of any kind whatever, from any king, prince, or foreign State.

Section 10. 1. No State shall enter into any treaty, alliance, or confederation; grant letters of marque and reprisal; coin money; emit bills of credit; make any thing but gold and silver coin a tender in payment of debts; pass any bill of attainder, ex post facto law, or law impairing the obligation of contracts, or grant any title of nobility.

2. No State shall, without the consent of the Congress, lay any imposts or duties on imports or exports, except what may be absolutely necessary for executing its inspection laws: and the net produce of all duties and imposts laid by any State on imports or exports, shall be for the use of the treasury of the United States; and all such laws shall be subject to the revision and control of the Congress.

3. No State shall, without the consent of the Congress, lay any duty of tonnage, keep troops, or ships of war in time of peace, enter into any agreement or compact with another State, or with a foreign power, or engage in war, unless actually invaded, or in such imminent danger as will not admit of delay.

[5] See the 16th Amendment.

ARTICLE II

Section 1. 1. The executive power shall be vested in a President of the United States of America. He shall hold his office during the term of four years, and, together with the Vice President, chosen for the same term, be elected, as follows:

2. Each State shall appoint, in such manner as the legislature thereof may direct, a number of electors, equal to the whole number of senators and representatives to which the State may be entitled in the Congress: but no senator or representative, or person holding an office of trust or profit under the United States, shall be appointed an elector.

The electors shall meet in their respective States, and vote by ballot for two persons, of whom one at least shall not be an inhabitant of the same State with themselves. And they shall make a list of all the persons voted for, and of the number of votes for each; which list they shall sign and certify, and transmit sealed to the seat of the government of the United States, directed to the president of the Senate. The president of the Senate shall, in the presence of the Senate and House of Representatives, open all the certificates, and the votes shall then be counted. The person having the greatest number of votes shall be the President, if such number be a majority of the whole number of electors appointed; and if there be more than one who have such majority, and have an equal number of votes, then the House of Representatives shall immediately choose by ballot one of them for President; and if no person have a majority, then from the five highest on the list the said House shall in like manner choose the President. But in choosing the President, the votes shall be taken by States, the representation from each State having one vote; a quorum for this purpose shall consist of a member or members from two-thirds of the States, and a majority of all the States shall be necessary to a choice. In every case, after the choice of the President, the person having the greatest number of votes of the electors shall be the Vice President. But if there should remain two or more who have equal votes, the Senate shall choose from them by ballot the Vice President.[6]

3. The Congress may determine the time of choosing the electors, and the day on which they shall give their votes; which day shall be the same throughout the United States.

4. No person except a natural born citizen, or a citizen of the United States, at the time of the adoption of this Constitution, shall be eligible to the office of President; neither shall any person be eligible to that office who shall not have attained to the age of thirty-five years, and been fourteen years a resident within the United States.

5. In case of the removal of the President from office, or of his death, resignation, or inability to discharge the powers and duties of the said office, the same shall devolve on the Vice President, and the Congress may by law provide for the case of removal, death, resignation or inability, both of the President and Vice President, declaring what officer shall then act as President, and such officer shall act accordingly, until the disability be removed, or a President shall be elected.

6. The President shall, at stated times, receive for his services a compensation, which shall neither be increased nor diminished during the period for which he shall have been elected, and he shall not receive within that period any other emolument from the United States, or any of them.

7. Before he enter on the execution of his office, he shall take the following oath or affirmation:—"I do solemnly swear (or affirm) that I will faithfully execute the office of President of the United States, and will to the best of my ability, preserve, protect and defend the Constitution of the United States."

Section 2. 1. The President shall be commander in chief of the army and navy of the United States, and of the militia of the several States, when called into the actual service of the United States; he may require the opinion, in writing, of the principal officer in each of the executive departments, upon any subject relating to the duties of their respective offices, and he shall have power to grant reprieves and pardons for offenses against the United States, except in cases of impeachment.

2. He shall have power, by and with the advice and consent of the Senate, to make treaties, provided two-thirds of the senators present concur; and he shall nominate, and by and with the advice and consent of the Senate, shall appoint ambassadors, other public ministers and consuls, judges of the Supreme Court, and all other officers of the United States, whose appointments are not herein otherwise provided for, and which shall be established by law: but the Congress may by law vest the appointment of such inferior officers, as they think proper, in the President alone, in the courts of law, or in the heads of departments.

3. The President shall have power to fill up all vacancies that may happen during the recess

[6] Superseded by the 12th Amendment.

of the Senate, by granting commissions which shall expire at the end of their next session.

Section 3. He shall from time to time give to the Congress information of the state of the Union, and recommend to their consideration such measures as he shall judge necessary and expedient; he may, on extraordinary occasions, convene both Houses, or either of them, and in case of disagreement between them with respect to the time of adjournment, he may adjourn them to such time as he shall think proper; he shall receive ambassadors and other public ministers; he shall take care that the laws be faithfully executed, and shall commission all the officers of the United States.

Section 4. The President, Vice President, and all civil officers of the United States, shall be removed from office on impeachment for, and conviction of, treason, bribery, or other high crimes and misdemeanors.

ARTICLE III

Section 1. The judicial power of the United States shall be vested in one Supreme Court, and in such inferior courts as the Congress may from time to time ordain and establish. The judges, both of the supreme and inferior courts, shall hold their offices during good behaviour, and shall, at stated times, receive for their services, a compensation, which shall not be diminished during their continuance in office.

Section 2. 1. The judicial power shall extend to all cases, in law and equity, arising under this Constitution, the laws of the United States, and treaties made, or which shall be made, under their authority;—to all cases affecting ambassadors, other public ministers and consuls;—to all cases of admiralty and maritime jurisdiction;—to controversies to which the United States shall be a party;—to controversies between two or more States;—between a State and citizens of another State; [7]—between citizens of different States—between citizens of the same State claiming lands under grants of different States, and between a State, or the citizens thereof, and foreign States, citizens or subjects.

2. In all cases affecting ambassadors, other public ministers and consuls, and those in which a State shall be party, the Supreme Court shall have original jurisdiction. In all the other cases before mentioned, the Supreme Court shall have appellate jurisdiction, both as to law and fact, with such exceptions, and under such regulations as the Congress shall make.

3. The trial of all crimes, except in cases of impeachment, shall be by jury; and such trial shall be held in the State where the said crimes shall have been committed; but when not committed within any State, the trial shall be at such place or places as the Congress may by law have directed.

Section 3. 1. Treason against the United States shall consist only in levying war against them, or in adhering to their enemies, giving them aid and comfort. No person shall be convicted of treason unless on the testimony of two witnesses to the same overt act, or on confession in open court.

2. The Congress shall have power to declare the punishment of treason, but no attainder of treason shall work corruption of blood, or forfeiture except during the life of the person attainted.

ARTICLE IV

Section 1. Full faith and credit shall be given in each State to the public acts, records, and judicial proceedings of every other State. And the Congress may by general laws prescribe the manner in which such acts, records and proceedings shall be proved, and the effect thereof.[8]

Section 2. 1. The citizens of each State shall be entitled to all privileges and immunities of citizens in the several States.

2. A person charged in any State with treason, felony, or other crime, who shall flee from justice, and be found in another State, shall on demand of the executive authority of the State from which he fled, be delivered up to be removed to the State having jurisdiction of the crime.

3. No person held to service or labour in one State under the laws thereof, escaping into another, shall, in consequence of any law or regulation therein, be discharged from such service or labour, but shall be delivered up on claim of the party to whom such service or labour may be due.[9]

Section 3. 1. New States may be admitted by the Congress into this Union; but no new State shall be formed or erected within the jurisdiction of any other State; nor any State be formed by the junction of two or more States, or parts of States, without the consent of the legislatures of the States concerned as well as of the Congress.

2. The Congress shall have power to dispose of and make all needful rules and regulations respecting the territory or other property belonging to the United States; and nothing in this

---

[7] See the 11th Amendment.

[8] See the 14th Amendment, Section 1.
[9] See the 13th Amendment.

Constitution shall be so construed as to prejudice any claims of the United States, or of any particular State.

Section 4. The United States shall guarantee to every State in this Union a republican form of government, and shall protect each of them against invasion; and on application of the legislature, or of the executive (when the legislature cannot be convened) against domestic violence.

ARTICLE V

The Congress, whenever two-thirds of both Houses shall deem it necessary, shall propose amendments to this Constitution, or, on the application of the legislatures of two-thirds of the several States, shall call a convention for proposing amendments, which, in either case, shall be valid to all intents and purposes, as part of this Constitution, when ratified by the legislatures of three-fourths of the several States, or by conventions in three-fourths thereof, as the one or the other mode of ratification may be proposed by the Congress; provided that no amendment which may be made prior to the year one thousand eight hundred and eight shall in any manner affect the first and fourth clauses in the ninth section of the first article; and that no State, without its consent, shall be deprived of its equal suffrage in the Senate.

ARTICLE VI

1. All debts contracted and engagements entered into, before the adoption of this Constitution, shall be as valid against the United States under this Constitution, as under the Confederation.[10]

2. This Constitution, and the laws of the United States which shall be made in pursuance thereof; and all treaties made, or which shall be made, under the authority of the United States, shall be the supreme law of the land; and the judges in every State shall be bound thereby, any thing in the Constitution or laws of any State to the contrary notwithstanding.

3. The senators and representatives before mentioned, and the members of the several State legislatures, and all executive and judicial officers, both of the United States and of the several States, shall be bound by oath or affirmation to support this Constitution; but no religious test shall ever be required as a qualification to any office or public trust under the United States.

ARTICLE VII

The ratification of the conventions of nine States shall be sufficient for the establishment of

[10] See the 14th Amendment, Section 4.

this Constitution between the States so ratifying the same.

Done in Convention by the unanimous consent of the States present the seventeenth day of September in the year of our Lord one thousand seven hundred and eighty seven, and of the independence of the United States of America the twelfth. In witness whereof we have hereunto subscribed our names.

Articles in addition to, and amendment of, the Constitution of the United States of America, proposed by Congress and ratified by the legislatures of the several States, pursuant to the fifth article of the original Constitution.

AMENDMENTS

[FIRST TEN AMENDMENTS PASSED BY CONGRESS SEPTEMBER 25, 1789. RATIFIED BY THREE-FOURTHS OF THE STATES DECEMBER 15, 1791.]

AMENDMENT I

Congress shall make no law respecting an establishment of religion, or prohibiting the free exercise thereof; or abridging the freedom of speech, or of the press; or the right of the people peaceably to assemble, and to petition the government for a redress of grievances.

AMENDMENT II

A well regulated militia, being necessary to the security of a free State, the right of the people to keep and bear arms, shall not be infringed.

AMENDMENT III

No soldier shall, in time of peace, be quartered in any house, without the consent of the owner, nor in time of war, but in a manner to be prescribed by law.

AMENDMENT IV

The right of the people to be secure in their persons, houses, papers, and effects, against unreasonable searches and seizures, shall not be violated, and no warrants shall issue, but upon probable cause, supported by oath or affirmation, and particularly describing the place to be searched, and the persons or things to be seized.

AMENDMENT V

No person shall be held to answer for a capital or otherwise infamous crime, unless on a presentment or indictment of a grand jury, except in cases arising in the land or naval forces, or in the militia, when in actual service in time of war or public danger; nor shall any person be subject for the same offence to be twice put in jeopardy of life or limb; nor shall be compelled in any criminal case to be a witness against himself, nor be deprived of life, liberty, or property, without due process of law; nor shall private property be taken for public use, without just compensation.

AMENDMENT VI

In all criminal prosecutions, the accused shall enjoy the right to a speedy and public trial, by an impartial jury of the State and district wherein the crime shall have been committed, which district shall have been previously ascertained by law, and to be informed of the nature and cause of the accusation; to be confronted with the witnesses against him; to have compulsory process for obtaining witnesses in his favor, and to have the assistance of counsel for his defence.

AMENDMENT VII

In suits at common law, where the value in controversy shall exceed twenty dollars, the right of trial by jury shall be preserved, and no fact tried by a jury shall be otherwise reexamined in any court of the United States, than according to the rules of the common law.

AMENDMENT VIII

Excessive bail shall not be required, nor excessive fines imposed, nor cruel and unusual punishments inflicted.

AMENDMENT IX

The enumeration in the Constitution of certain rights shall not be construed to deny or disparage others retained by the people.

AMENDMENT X

The powers not delegated to the United States by the Constitution, nor prohibited by it to the States, are reserved to the States respectively, or to the people.

AMENDMENT XI

[PASSED BY CONGRESS MARCH 5, 1794. RATIFIED JANUARY 8, 1798.]

The judicial power of the United States shall not be construed to extend to any suit in law or equity, commenced or prosecuted against one of the United States by citizens of another State, or by citizens or subjects of any foreign State.

AMENDMENT XII

[PASSED BY CONGRESS DECEMBER 9, 1803. RATIFIED SEPTEMBER 25, 1804.]

The electors shall meet in their respective States, and vote by ballot for President and Vice President, one of whom, at least, shall not be an inhabitant of the same State with themselves; they shall name in their ballots the person voted for as President, and in distinct ballots, the person voted for as Vice President, and they shall make distinct lists of all persons voted for as President and of all persons voted for as Vice President, and of the number of votes for each, which lists they shall sign and certify, and transmit sealed to the seat of the government of the United States, directed to the president of the Senate;—The president of the Senate shall, in the presence of the Senate and House of Representatives, open all the certificates and the votes shall then be counted;—The person having the greatest number of votes for President shall be the President, if such number be a majority of the whole number of electors appointed; and if no person have such majority, then from the persons having the highest numbers not exceeding three on the list of those voted for as President, the House of Representatives shall choose immediately, by ballot, the President. But in choosing the President, the votes shall be taken by States, the representation from each State having one vote; a quorum for this purpose shall consist of a member or members from two-thirds of the States, and a majority of all the States shall be necessary to a choice. And if the House of Representatives shall not choose a President, whenever the right of choice shall devolve upon them, before the fourth day of March next following, then the Vice President shall act as President, as in the case of the death or other constitutional disability of the President. The person having the greatest number of votes as Vice President shall be the Vice President, if such number be a majority of the whole number of electors appointed, and if no person have a majority, then from the two highest numbers on the list, the Senate shall choose the Vice President; a quorum for the purpose shall consist of two-thirds of the whole number of Senators, and a majority of the whole number shall be necessary to a choice. But no person constitutionally ineligible to the office of President shall be eligible to that of Vice President of the United States.

AMENDMENT XIII

[PASSED BY CONGRESS FEBRUARY 1, 1865. RATIFIED DECEMBER 18, 1865.]

Section 1. Neither slavery nor involuntary servitude, except as a punishment for crime whereof the party shall have been duly convicted, shall exist within the United States, or any place subject to their jurisdiction.

Section 2. Congress shall have power to enforce this article by appropriate legislation.

AMENDMENT XIV

[PASSED BY CONGRESS JUNE 16, 1866. RATIFIED JULY 28, 1868.]

Section 1. All persons born or naturalized in the United States, and subject to the jurisdiction thereof, are citizens of the United States and of the State wherein they reside. No State shall make or enforce any law which shall abridge the privileges or immunities of citizens of the United States; nor shall any State deprive any person of life, liberty, or property, without due process of law; nor deny to any person within its jurisdiction the equal protection of the laws.

Section 2. Representatives shall be apportioned among the several States according to their respective numbers, counting the whole number of persons in each State, excluding Indians not taxed. But when the right to vote at any election for the choice of electors for President and Vice President of the United States, representatives in Congress, the executive and judicial officers of a State, or the members of the legislature thereof, is denied to any of the male inhabitants of such State, being twenty-one years of age, and citizens of the United States, or in any way abridged, except for participating in rebellion, or other crime, the basis of representation therein shall be reduced in the proportion which the number of such male citizens shall bear to the whole number of male citizens twenty-one years of age in such State.

Section 3. No person shall be a senator or representative in Congress, or elector of President and Vice President, or hold any office, civil or military, under the United States, or under any State, who having previously taken an oath, as a member of Congress, or as an officer of the United States, or as a member of any State legislature, or as an executive or judicial officer of any State, to support the Constitution of the United States, shall have engaged in insurrection or rebellion against the same, or given aid or comfort to the enemies thereof. But Congress may by a vote of two-thirds of each House, remove such disability.

Section 4. The validity of the public debt of the United States, authorized by law, including debts incurred for payment of pensions and bounties for services in suppressing insurrection or rebellion, shall not be questioned. But neither the United States nor any State shall assume or pay any debt or obligation incurred in aid of insurrection or rebellion against the United States, or any claim for the loss or emancipation of any slave; but all such debts, obligations, and claims shall be held illegal and void.

Section 5. The Congress shall have power to enforce, by appropriate legislation, the provisions of this article.

AMENDMENT XV

[PASSED BY CONGRESS FEBRUARY 27, 1869. RATIFIED MARCH 30, 1870.]

Section 1. The right of citizens of the United States to vote shall not be denied or abridged by the United States or by any State on account of race, color, or previous condition of servitude.

Section 2. The Congress shall have power to enforce this article by appropriate legislation.

AMENDMENT XVI

[PASSED BY CONGRESS JULY 12, 1909. RATIFIED FEBRUARY 25, 1913.]

The Congress shall have power to lay and collect taxes on incomes, from whatever source derived, without apportionment among the several States, and without regard to any census or enumeration.

AMENDMENT XVII

[PASSED BY CONGRESS MAY 16, 1912. RATIFIED MAY 31, 1913.]

The Senate of the United States shall be composed of two senators from each State, elected by the people thereof, for six years; and each senator shall have one vote. The electors in each State shall have the qualifications requisite for electors of the most numerous branch of the State legislature.

When vacancies happen in the representation of any State in the Senate, the executive authority of such State shall issue writs of election to fill such vacancies: provided, that the legislature of any State may empower the executive thereof to make temporary appointments until the people fill the vacancies by election as the legislature may direct.

This amendment shall not be so construed as to affect the election or term of any senator chosen before it becomes valid as part of the Constitution.

AMENDMENT XVIII [11]

[PASSED BY CONGRESS DECEMBER 17, 1917. RATIFIED JANUARY 29, 1919.]

After one year from the ratification of this article, the manufacture, sale, or transportation of intoxicating liquors within, the importation

[11] Repealed by the 21st Amendment.

thereof into, or the exportation thereof from the United States and all territory subject to the jurisdiction thereof for beverage purposes is hereby prohibited.

The Congress and the several States shall have concurrent power to enforce this article by appropriate legislation.

This article shall be inoperative unless it shall have been ratified as an amendment to the Constitution by the legislatures of the several States, as provided in the Constitution, within seven years from the date of the submission hereof to the States by Congress.

AMENDMENT XIX

[PASSED BY CONGRESS JUNE 5, 1919. RATIFIED AUGUST 26, 1920.]

The right of citizens of the United States to vote shall not be denied or abridged by the United States or by any State on account of sex.

Congress shall have power to enforce this article by appropriate legislation.

AMENDMENT XX

[PASSED BY CONGRESS MARCH 3, 1932. RATIFIED JANUARY 23, 1933.]

Section 1. The terms of the President and Vice President shall end at noon on the 20th day of January, and the terms of senators and representatives at noon on the 3rd day of January, of the years in which such terms would have ended if this article had not been ratified; and the terms of their successors shall then begin.

Section 2. The Congress shall assemble at least once in every year, and such meeting shall begin at noon on the 3rd day of January, unless they shall by law appoint a different day.

Section 3. If, at the time fixed for the beginning of the term of the President, the President elect shall have died, the Vice President elect shall become President. If a President shall not have been chosen before the time fixed for the beginning of his term, or if the President elect shall have failed to qualify, then the Vice President elect shall act as President until a President shall have qualified; and the Congress may by law provide for the case wherein neither a President elect nor a Vice President elect shall have qualified, declaring who shall then act as President, or the manner in which one who is to act shall be selected, and such person shall act accordingly until a President or Vice President shall have qualified.

Section 4. The Congress may by law provide for the case of the death of any of the persons from whom the House of Representatives may choose a President whenever the right of choice shall have devolved upon them, and for the case of the death of any of the persons from whom the Senate may choose a Vice President whenever the right of choice shall have devolved upon them.

Section 5. Sections 1 and 2 shall take effect on the 15th day of October following the ratification of this article.

Section 6. This article shall be inoperative unless it shall have been ratified as an amendment to the Constitution by the legislatures of three-fourths of the several States within seven years from the date of its submission.

AMENDMENT XXI

[PASSED BY CONGRESS FEBRUARY 20, 1933. RATIFIED DECEMBER 5, 1933.]

Section 1. The Eighteenth Article of amendment to the Constitution of the United States is hereby repealed.

Section 2. The transportation or importation into any State, Territory, or possession of the United States for delivery or use therein of intoxicating liquors, in violation of the laws thereof, is hereby prohibited.

Section 3. This article shall be inoperative unless it shall have been ratified as an amendment to the Constitution by conventions in the several States, as provided in the Constitution, within seven years from the date of the submission thereof to the States by the Congress.

AMENDMENT XXII

[PASSED BY CONGRESS MARCH 12, 1947. RATIFIED MARCH 1, 1951.]

No person shall be elected to the office of the President more than twice, and no person who has held the office of President, or acted as President, for more than two years of a term to which some other person was elected President shall be elected to the office of the President more than once.

But this article shall not apply to any person holding the office of President when this article was proposed by the Congress, and shall not prevent any person who may be holding the office of President, or acting as President, during the term within which this article becomes operative from holding the office of President or acting as President during the remainder of such term.

This article shall be inoperative unless it shall have been ratified as an amendment to the Constitution by the legislatures of three-fourths of the several States within seven years from the date of its submission to the States by the Congress.

AMENDMENT XXIII

[PASSED BY CONGRESS JUNE 16, 1960. RATIFIED MARCH 29, 1961.]

Section 1. The District constituting the seat of Government of the United States shall appoint in such manner as the Congress may direct:

A number of electors of President and Vice President equal to the whole number of senators and representatives in Congress to which the District would be entitled if it were a State, but in no event more than the least populous State; they shall be in addition to those appointed by the States, but they shall be considered, for the purposes of the election of President and Vice President, to be electors appointed by a State; and they shall meet in the District and perform such duties as provided by the twelfth article of amendment.

Section 2. The Congress shall have power to enforce this article by appropriate legislation.

AMENDMENT XXIV

[PASSED BY CONGRESS AUGUST 27, 1962. RATIFIED JANUARY 23, 1964.]

Section 1. The right of citizens of the United States to vote in any primary or other election for President or Vice President, for electors for President or Vice President, or for senator or representative in Congress shall not be denied or abridged by the United States or any State by reason of failure to pay any poll tax or other tax.

Section 2. The Congress shall have the power to enforce this article by appropriate legislation.

AMENDMENT XXV

[PASSED BY CONGRESS JULY 6, 1965. RATIFIED FEBRUARY 11, 1967.]

Section 1. In case of the removal of the President from office or of his death or resignation, the Vice President shall become President.

Section 2. Whenever there is a vacancy in the office of the Vice President, the President shall nominate a Vice President who shall take office upon confirmation by a majority vote of both Houses of Congress.

Section 3. Whenever the President transmits to the President pro tempore of the Senate and the Speaker of the House of Representatives his written declaration that he is unable to discharge the powers and duties of his office, and until he transmits to them a written declaration to the contrary, such powers and duties shall be discharged by the Vice President as Acting President.

Section 4. Whenever the Vice President and a majority of either the principal officers of the executive department or of such other body as Congress may by law provide, transmit to the President pro tempore of the Senate and the Speaker of the House of Representatives their written declaration that the President is unable to discharge the powers and duties of his office, the Vice President shall immediately assume the powers and duties of the office as Acting President.

Thereafter, when the President transmits to the President pro tempore of the Senate and the Speaker of the House of Representatives his written declaration that no inability exists, he shall resume the powers and duties of his office unless the Vice President and a majority of either the principal officers of the executive department or of such other body as Congress may by law provide, transmit within four days to the President pro tempore of the Senate and the Speaker of the House of Representatives their written declaration that the President is unable to discharge the powers and duties of his office. Thereupon Congress shall decide the issue, assembling within forty-eight hours for that purpose if not in session. If the Congress, within twenty-one days after receipt of the latter written declaration, or, if Congress is not in session, within twenty-one days after Congress is required to assemble, determines by two-thirds vote of both Houses that the President is unable to discharge the powers and duties of his office, the Vice President shall continue to discharge the same as Acting President; otherwise, the President shall resume the powers and duties of his office.

SELECTED BIBLIOGRAPHY

I. Democracy and the American Way

POLITICAL SYSTEMS

David Easton, ed., *Varieties of Political Theory*, Prentice-Hall Contemporary Political Theory Series (Englewood Cliffs, N.J.: Prentice-Hall, 1966). The most recent formulation of a distinguished modern American political theorist.

Eugene J. Meehan *et al.*, *The Dynamics of Modern Government* (New York: McGraw-Hill, 1966). A study of political institutions and problems in democratic and authoritarian governments.

Ithiel Pool *et al.*, *Contemporary Political Science* (New York: McGraw-Hill, 1967). A penetrating analysis of frontier problems of modern political systems.

Austin Ranney, *The Governing of Men: An Introduction to Political Science*, rev. ed. (New York: Holt, Rinehart and Winston, 1966). A new edition bringing up to date the concepts of the discipline.

H. V. Wiseman, *Political Systems: Some Sociological Approaches* (New York: Praeger, 1966). An important sociological interpretation of political systems.

GENERAL OVERVIEWS OF THE AMERICAN SYSTEM

James Bryce, *The American Commonwealth* (New York: Macmillan, 1888). A classic roadmap of American government during the late nineteenth century by a distinguished British scholar and statesman.

James MacGregor Burns, *Presidential Government: The Crucible of Leadership* (Boston: Houghton Mifflin, 1966). A study of presidential power and leadership in the late fifties and early sixties.

Harold J. Laski, *The American Democracy* (New York: Viking Press, 1948). An analysis of the American system from a Marxist viewpoint.

Max Lerner, *America as a Civilization* (New York: Simon and Schuster, 1957). An ambitious effort to reduce all the variety of the American experience to print.

Arnold M. Rose, *The Power Structure* (New York: Oxford Univ. Press, 1967). A sociologist's analysis of the structure of political power in America.

Alexis de Tocqueville, *Democracy in America*, trans. by Henry Reeve, Henry Steele Commager, ed. (New York: Oxford Univ. Press, 1947). A classic analysis of the distinctive political, social, and cultural characteristics of the United States as seen by a nineteenth-century Frenchman.

SOCIAL BASIS

Gabriel A. Almond and James S. Coleman, *The Politics of the Developing Areas* (Princeton, N.J.: Princeton Univ. Press, 1960). One of the most influential books on political systems analysis from a social point of view.

—— and Sidney Verba, *The Civic Culture* (Princeton, N.J.: Princeton Univ. Press, 1963). A cross-national study of those attitudes which support democratic political processes, treating the United States, Great Britain, Mexico, Italy, and the Federal Republic of Germany.

Raymond A. Bauer, ed., *Social Indicators* (Cambridge, Mass.: M.I.T. Press, 1966). A major effort to isolate social indicators that measure social values in ways parallel to indicators of economic values.

Hadley Cantril, *The Human Dimension: Experiences in Policy Research* (New Brunswick, N.J.: Rutgers Univ. Press, 1967). A presentation of underlying psychological factors that influence political behavior, recruitment, and action.

James S. Coleman, ed., *Education and Political Development* (Princeton, N.J.: Princeton Univ. Press 1965). Studies in political development as related to educational patterns and policies.

David Potter, *People of Plenty* (Chicago: Univ. of Chicago Press, 1954). A historian argues that American attitudes and expectations are, in large part, a function of material plenty.

Lucian W. Pye, *Aspects of Political Development* (Boston: Little, Brown, 1966). An analytical study of economic development, revising previously published material.

Robert A. Solo, *Economic Organizations and Social Systems* (Indianapolis, Ind.: Bobbs-Merrill, 1967). An exploration of alternative means open to a society for allocation of resources.

AMERICAN POLITICAL IDEAS

Daniel Boorstin, *The Genius of American Politics* (Chicago: Univ. of Chicago Press, 1953). A statement of the uniqueness of American democracy.

Richard E. Flathman, *The Public Interest: An Essay Concerning the Normative Discourse of Politics* (New York: Wiley, 1966). An analysis of the concept of "public interest" for its significance for political ideas.

Louis Hartz, *The Liberal Tradition in America* (New York: Harcourt, Brace & World, 1955). An argument for the centrality of Lockean ideas in American reflections on politics.

Richard Hofstadter, *The American Political Tradition* (New York: Knopf, 1951). A lucid exposition of the thought of eleven Americans from Jefferson to F. D. R.

Charles E. Merriam, *American Political Ideas* (New York: Macmillan, 1920). This small volume is still the best primer on American political thought.

Vernon L. Parrington, *Main Currents in American Thought* (New York: Harcourt, Brace & World, 1927–30). The classic Jeffersonian rendering of American political ideas.

DEMOCRACY

Robert A. Dahl, *Political Oppositions in Western Democracies* (New Haven, Conn.: Yale Univ. Press, 1966). A comparison of patterns of political opposition between the United States and Western Europe.

————, *A Preface to Democratic Theory* (Chicago: Univ. of Chicago Press, 1956). A discussion of the possibility that problems of democratic theory can be quantified and manipulated mathematically.

Anthony Downs, *An Economic Theory of Democracy* (New York: Harper & Row, 1957). An attempted definition of democracy in terms of an economic "market" model.

J. Roland Pennock, *Liberal Democracy: Its Merits and Prospects* (New York: Holt, Rinehart and Winston, 1950). A philosophic consideration of the strengths and limitations of democracy.

David Spitz, *Patterns of Anti-Democratic Thought* (New York: Macmillan, 1949). An attempt to clarify the idea of democracy by considering its opposites.

Robert P. Wolff, Barrington Moore, Jr., and Herbert Marcuse, *A Critique of Pure Tolerance* (Boston: Beacon Press, 1965). A challenge to prevailing notions of pluralist democracy.

F. J. Wright, *An Introduction to the Study of Democratic Government* (London: Barrie, 1967). A comparative history of Great Britain, France, and the United States relating the form of democracy to constitutional development.

CONSTITUTIONALISM

Carl J. Friedrich, *Constitutional Government and Democracy* (Boston: Ginn, 1946). A comparative study of constitutional systems.

Charles H. McIlwain, *Constitutionalism, Ancient and Modern* (Ithaca, N.Y.: Cornell Univ. Press, 1947). A standard text.

Franz Neumann, *The Democratic and the Authoritarian State* (New York: Free Press, 1957). Essays dealing with the theme of constitutionalism.

Louis H. Pollak, ed., *The Constitution and the Supreme Court: A Documentary History*, 2 vols. (Cleveland: World, 1966). With an introduction by George F. Scheer, a documented analysis of the way in which the Supreme Court implements and protects the Constitution.

Arthur E. Sutherland, *Constitutionalism in America: The Origin and Evolution of Its Fundamental Laws* (New York: Blaisdell, 1965). Informative essays on constitutionalism from 1628 to the present, seen through the perspective of Supreme Court decisions.

Francis D. Wormuth, *The Origins of Modern Constitutionalism* (New York: Harper & Row, 1949). A search for the genesis of constitutional ideas.

FRAMING THE CONSTITUTION

Charles A. Beard, *An Economic Interpretation of the Constitution of the United States* (New York: Macmillan, 1913). An argument that the most influential members of the Constitutional Convention acted on the basis of economically interested motives.

Robert E. Brown, *Charles Beard and the Constitution* (Princeton, N.J.: Princeton Univ. Press, 1956). Brown takes Beard to task for cavalier use of sources and over-hasty generalization in his "economic interpretation" of the Constitution.

Jonathan Elliot, *The Debates in the Several State Conventions on the Adoption of the Federal Constitution* (Philadelphia: Lippincott, 1836–59). A standard reference work.

Max Farrand, *The Framing of the Constitution* (New Haven, Conn.: Yale Univ. Press, 1926). The classic study.

————, ed., *The Records of the Federal Convention* (New Haven, Conn.: Yale Univ. Press, 1911, 1937). Primary source material.

Alexander Hamilton, James Madison, and John Jay, *The Federalist*, B. F. Wright, ed. (Cambridge, Mass.: Harvard Univ. Press, 1961). These essays, originally published in various New York newspapers, represented an effort by the authors to persuade the citizenry of that city and state that the new governmental instrument was worthy of support. Required reading for all who would approach the subject.

Merrill Jensen, *The New Nation* (New York: Knopf, 1950). A good treatment of the period between the Revolution and the Constitutional Convention of 1787.

Samuel J. Konefsky, *John Marshall and Alexander Hamilton* (New York: Macmillan, 1964). A comparative study of the ideas of Marshall and Hamilton and their contribution to the Constitution.

Forrest McDonald, *We the People: The Economic Origins of the Constitution* (Chicago: Univ. of Chicago Press, 1958). A refutation of Charles Beard's conclusions on the economic motivation of the Constitution.

Clinton Rossiter, *1787: The Grand Convention* (New York: Macmillan, 1966). A survey of the Constitution from the Convention to ratification and of the early years of the Republic, with interesting biographical insights into the Framers.

FEDERALISM

Daniel J. Elazar, *American Federalism: A View from the States* (New York: Crowell-Collier, 1966). An up-to-date survey of the problems of federalism in America, with emphasis on the directions of change.

Morton Grodzins, *The American System: A New View of Government in the United States* (Chicago: Rand McNally, 1966). A scholarly analysis of the features and results of American federalism.

Arthur Maass, ed., *Area and Power* (New York: Free Press, 1959). Studies of the operational problems of divided power.

Arthur W. MacMahon, ed., *Federalism: Mature and Emergent* (New York: Doubleday, 1955). Essays considering American federalism from varying perspectives—law, administration, political parties, and others.

Alpheus T. Mason, *The States-Rights Debate: Antifederalism and the Constitution* (Englewood Cliffs, N.J.: Prentice-Hall, 1964). A study of the roots of American federalism from the late colonial period to the adoption of the Bill of Rights.

William H. Riker, *Federalism: Origin, Operation, and Significance* (Boston: Little, Brown, 1964). A recent theoretical and critical analysis of the origins and consequences of federal systems.

K. C. Wheare, *Federal Government* (London: Oxford Univ. Press, 1951). A standard comparative study of federalism.

Aaron Wildavsky, *American Federalism in Perspective* (Boston: Little, Brown, 1967). An introduction to the study of federalism, with readings on conceptual analysis, general theory, comparative examples, and historical experience.

II. The Political Process

INTEREST GROUPS

Arthur F. Bentley, *The Process of Government*, rev. ed. (Bloomington, Ind.: Principia Press, 1949). The classic statement of the group theory of politics.

Bernard Berelson, Paul Lazarsfeld, and William McPhee, *Voting* (Chicago: Univ. of Chicago Press, 1954). This study represents an intermediate stage in the development of theories of voting behavior.

Douglass Cater, *Power in Washington* (New York: Random House, 1964). A journalist's examination of how power is organized and exercised in official Washington.

Abraham Holtzman, *Interest Groups and Lobbying* (New York: Macmillan, 1966). An integrated, comprehensive analysis of interest-group theory and structure and their relationship to legislators, the executive, the judiciary, and the grassroots.

Harry R. Mahood, ed., *Pressure Groups in American Politics* (New York: Scribner's, 1967). Collected writings exploring the role of formally organized pressure groups in public-policy formation, stressing a group theory of politics.

Lester W. Milbrath, *The Washington Lobbyists* (Chicago: Rand McNally, 1963). A competent full-length portrait of the lobbyist as a political actor and his role in the political system.

Arnold M. Rose, *The Power Structure* (New York: Oxford Univ. Press, 1967). A sociologist's explanation of elite groups and their relationship to the democratic process.

David B. Truman, *The Governmental Process* (New York: Knopf, 1951). A very important effort to apply modified group theory to the American political experience.

Harmon Zeigler, *Interest Groups in American Society* (Englewood Cliffs, N.J.: Prentice-Hall, 1964). A study of interest-group theory, the political culture and institutional context in which the groups move, and the place of organized groups in the legislative, administrative, and judicial processes.

PARTY FUNCTIONS

Samuel J. Eldersveld, *Political Parties: A Behavioral Analysis* (Chicago: Rand McNally, 1964). A book distinguished by its sophisticated linking of theory and empirical analysis.

Fred I. Greenstein, *The American Party System and the American People* (Englewood Cliffs, N.J.: Prentice-Hall, 1964). An interpretive summary of the operation of American parties.

V. O. Key, Jr., *Politics, Parties, and Pressure Groups*, 5th ed. (New York: Crowell-Collier, 1964). An excellent text by a distinguished scholar.

Frank J. Sorauf, *Political Parties in the American System* (Boston: Little, Brown, 1964). A good, readable overview of the American party system.

PARTY HISTORY AND DEVELOPMENT

Wilfred E. Binkley, *American Political Parties: Their Natural History*, 4th ed. (New York: Knopf, 1964). An excellent historical treatment of party development.

William N. Chambers, *Political Parties in a New Nation: The American Experience, 1776–1809* (New York: Oxford Univ. Press, 1963). A very useful study of the evolution of informal alignments into self-conscious parties.

Richard P. McCormick, *The Second American Party System: Party Formation in the Jacksonian Era* (Chapel Hill, N.C.: Univ. of North Carolina Press, 1966). A summary of the development of the second American parties, setting forth their distinctive features.

Malcolm C. Moos, *The Republicans* (New York: Random House, 1956). A history.

PARTY ORGANIZATION

Edward C. Banfield and James Q. Wilson, *City Politics* (Cambridge, Mass.: Harvard Univ. Press and M.I.T. Press, 1963). A study of city government in America as a political process in which the resolution of conflict is paramount.

Edward Costikyan, *Behind Closed Doors: Politics in the Public Interest* (New York: Harcourt, Brace & World, 1966). An exceptional insight into the political process through political memoirs of recent New York City political leaders.

Samuel J. Eldersveld, *Political Parties: A Behavioral Analysis* (Chicago: Rand McNally, 1964). An empirical study of local party organization, characteristics, perceptions, attitudes, and communication in Michigan.

John H. Fenton, *Midwest Politics* (New York: Harcourt, Brace & World, 1966). A good treatment of the historical development of party politics in six Midwestern states.

Alexander Heard, *The Costs of Democracy* (Chapel Hill, N.C.: Univ. of North Carolina Press, 1960). The standard work on party finance.

E. Pendleton Herring, *The Politics of Democracy: American Parties in Action* (New York: Norton, 1965). A classic analysis of the American party system, with a new preface by the author.

Herbert Jacob and Kenneth N. Vines, eds., *Politics in the American System* (Boston: Little, Brown, 1965). A collection of essays examining individual party systems at the state level.

Frank Kent, *The Great Game of Politics* (Garden City, N.Y.: Doubleday, 1923). A journalist's classic exposition of the facts of life of urban politics.

V. O. Key, Jr., *American State Politics* (New York: Knopf, 1956). An important study of the weaknesses of state party organizations.

Duane Lockard, *New England State Politics* (Princeton, N.J.: Princeton Univ. Press, 1959). Six excellent case studies.

Wallace S. Sayre and Herbert Kaufman, *Governing New York City* (New York: Russell Sage Foundation, 1960). An excellent treatment of party organization and its impact on the nation's largest city.

Allan P. Sindler, *Political Parties in the United States* (New York: St. Martin's Press, 1966). An analytical and evaluative treatment of the American party system.

Frank J. Sorauf, *Political Parties in the American System* (Boston: Little, Brown, 1964). A succinct survey of the American party system and an analysis of its role, function, and the political motivation of its membership, with some comparative references to parties abroad.

VOTING BEHAVIOR

Gabriel A. Almond and Sidney Verba, *The Civic Culture* (Princeton, N.J.: Princeton Univ. Press, 1963). A comparative study of five Western political cultures, the process of participation, and the relationship between the individual adult and the governmental authority in each system.

Eugene Burdick and A. J. Brodbeck, eds., *American Voting Behavior* (New York: Free Press, 1956). A collection of essays on the components of voter choice.

James MacGregor Burns, *The Deadlock of Democracy* (Englewood Cliffs, N.J.: Prentice-

Hall, 1962). A statement of the disutility of present party alignments.

Angus Campbell *et al.*, *The American Voter* (New York: Wiley, 1960). An important, major study of voting behavior.

———, *Elections and the Political Order* (New York: Wiley, 1966). A thorough examination of the nature of the vote and the function of elections in the political system that carries forward the analysis of *The American Voter* into the 1960's.

Governmental Affairs Institute, *America at the Polls: A Handbook of American Presidential Elections, 1920–1964*, comp. and ed. by Richard M. Scammon (Pittsburgh, Pa.: Univ. of Pittsburgh Press, 1966). A very useful compilation of voting statistics.

Fred I. Greenstein, *Children and Politics* (New Haven, Conn.: Yale Univ. Press, 1965). A basic study of the formation of political attitudes in young children.

M. Kent Jennings and Harmon Zeigler, eds., *The Electoral Process* (Englewood Cliffs, N.J.: Prentice-Hall, 1966). Readings on the electoral process from individual voter to local political activity to the machinery of national campaigns.

V. O. Key, Jr., *Public Opinion and American Democracy* (New York: Knopf, 1961). A study of the role of public opinion in the American political process.

———, *The Responsible Electorate* (Cambridge, Mass.: Belknap Press of Harvard Univ. Press, 1966). An analysis of the degree of rationality in presidential voting behavior from 1936 to 1960.

Robert E. Lane, *Political Life: Why and How People Get Involved in Politics* (New York: Free Press, 1959). One of the first comprehensive views of popular participation in American democracy.

Paul Lazarsfeld, Bernard Berelson, and Hazel Gaudet, *The People's Choice* (New York: Columbia Univ. Press, 1948). The first major scientific study of voting behavior.

Seymour M. Lipset, *Political Man: The Social Bases of Politics* (New York: Doubleday, 1959). A political sociologist's analysis of the social bases of voting and group participation.

——— and Stein Rokkan, eds., *Party Systems and Voter Alignments* (New York: Free Press, 1967). A comprehensive report on cross-national behavioral research on voting patterns and the social basis of party support.

Samuel Lubell, *The Future of American Politics*, 2nd ed. (Garden City, N.Y.: Doubleday, 1956). A lively treatment of the changing alignments within the electorate, keyed to an explanation of Truman's 1948 upset victory.

Donald R. Matthews and James W. Prothro, *Negroes and the New Southern Politics* (New York: Harcourt, Brace & World, 1966). A study of the way in which Negro leaders and new voters handle the changing political scene in the South.

Lester W. Milbrath, *Political Participation:*

How and Why Do People Get Involved in Politics? (Chicago: Rand McNally, 1965). An empirical analysis of the motivations of political activity.

Austin Ranney and Willmoore Kendall, *Democracy and the American Party System* (New York: Harcourt, Brace & World, 1956). A standard text.

E. E. Schattschneider, *Party Government* (New York: Holt, Rinehart and Winston, 1942). An argument for a restructuring of American parties along the more disciplined lines of the British model.

CHOOSING THE PRESIDENT

Paul T. David, Ralph M. Goldman, and Richard C. Bain, *The Politics of National Party Conventions* (Washington, D.C.: Brookings Institution, 1960). This standard work considers conventions from historical and functional points of view.

————, Malcolm Moos, and Ralph M. Goldman, eds., *Presidential Nominating Politics* (Baltimore: Johns Hopkins Press, 1954). A compilation of case studies by a task force of political scientists.

Eugene H. Roseboom. *A History of Presidential Elections* (New York: Macmillan, 1957). A useful narrative.

Theodore H. White, *The Making of the President, 1960* (New York: Atheneum, 1961). A vivid journalistic account of the 1960 presidential battle.

————, *The Making of the President, 1964* (New York: Atheneum, 1965). A journalist surveys the 1964 campaigns for nomination and election.

III. The President, Congress, and the Executive Branch

THE PRESIDENT—TASKS AND RESOURCES

Edward S. Corwin, *The President: Office and Power*, 4th ed. (New York: New York Univ. Press, 1957). A standard catalog of tasks, powers, and precedents.

Louis W. Koenig, *The Invisible Presidency* (New York: Holt, Rinehart and Winston, 1960). A study of presidential alter egos.

Richard E. Neustadt, *Presidential Power* (New York: Wiley, 1960). A remarkable study of the dilemmas of the modern President who is compelled to rule rather than simply reign.

Clinton Rossiter, *The American Presidency* (New York: Harcourt, Brace & World, 1956). A discussion of the various presidential roles in a historical context.

————, *The Chief Executive* (New York: Harcourt, Brace & World, 1964). This study focuses on the obstacles in the path of an activist President.

THE PRESIDENT IN ACTION

John M. Blum, *The Republican Roosevelt* (Cambridge, Mass.: Harvard Univ. Press, 1954). A lively study of the presidential style of Theodore Roosevelt.

————, *Woodrow Wilson and the Politics of Morality* (Boston: Little, Brown, 1956). A consideration of the collisions between ideal and political reality in the Presidency of Woodrow Wilson.

James MacGregor Burns, *Roosevelt: The Lion and the Fox* (New York: Harcourt, Brace & World, 1956). A sensitive exploration of the F.D.R. technique of governing.

Rowland Evans and Robert Novak, *Lyndon B. Johnson: The Exercise of Power* (New York: New American Library, 1966). A good treatment of President Johnson's congressional career and his transition to presidential politics.

Roger Hilsman, *To Move a Nation* (Garden City, N.Y.: Doubleday, 1967). An excellent treatment of the President's role in foreign-policy making.

Arthur M. Schlesinger, *A Thousand Days* (Boston: Houghton Mifflin, 1965). A treatment of the Kennedy years by a White House aide who was principally concerned with foreign policy.

Theodore C. Sorensen, *Kennedy* (New York: Harper & Row, 1965). The memoirs of Kennedy's special counsel and close friend.

THE PRESIDENT AND HIS INSTITUTIONAL ENVIRONMENT

Wilfred E. Binkley, *President and Congress* (New York: Knopf, 1947). A useful history of the various conceptions of what the Presidency should be.

Elmer E. Cornwell, Jr., *Presidential Leadership of Public Opinion* (Bloomington, Ind.: Indiana Univ. Press, 1965). A study of the ways in which the President deals with communications media.

Richard F. Fenno, Jr., *The President's Cabinet* (Cambridge, Mass.: Harvard Univ. Press, 1959). The standard study of the Cabinet.

Joseph P. Harris, *The Advice and Consent of the Senate* (Berkeley, Calif.: Univ. of California Press, 1953). An account of the confirmation and rejection of presidential appointments.

Clinton Rossiter, *The Supreme Court and the Commander in Chief* (Ithaca, N.Y.: Cornell Univ. Press, 1951). Details of the development of the dimension of the Presidency.

Glendon A. Schubert, Jr., *The Presidency in the Courts* (Minneapolis, Minn.: Univ. of Minnesota Press, 1957). An examination of the ways in which the Chief Executive has used and been used by the judiciary.

THE LEGISLATIVE PROCESS

Stephen K. Bailey, *Congress Makes a Law* (New York: Columbia Univ. Press, 1950). A case study of the passage of the Employment Act of 1946 and an excellent picture of interest-group behavior.

Richard F. Fenno, Jr., *The Power of the Purse* (Boston: Little, Brown, 1966). An excellent examination of the appropriation process on Capitol Hill.

George B. Galloway, *The Legislative Process in Congress* (New York: Crowell-Collier, 1953). A standard text.

Ernest Griffith, *Congress: Its Contemporary Role*, 3rd ed. (New York: New York Univ. Press, 1961). An analysis by a sympathetic observer with long experience.

Joseph P. Harris, *Congressional Control of Administration* (Washington, D.C.: Brookings Institution, 1964). An exploration of the ways in which Congress oversees the operations of the executive bureaucracy.

Malcolm E. Jewell, ed., *The Politics of Reapportionment* (New York: Atherton Press, 1962). Essays on the issues involved in reapportionment.

Donald R. Matthews, *U.S. Senators and Their World* (Chapel Hill, N.C.: Univ. of North Carolina Press, 1960). A study of the Senate and its folkways.

David R. Mayhew, *Party Loyalty Among Congressmen* (Cambridge, Mass.: Harvard Univ. Press, 1966). A study of the relationship of congressional constituencies to the cohesion of congressional parties.

Lester W. Milbrath, *The Washington Lobbyists* (Chicago: Rand McNally, 1963). A quantitative study of the behavior of those who attempt to influence Congress.

Robert L. Peabody and Nelson W. Polsby, eds., *New Perspectives on the House of Representatives* (Chicago: Rand McNally, 1963). An anthology of some of the best recent writing on the subject.

Lindsay Rogers, *The American Senate* (New York: Knopf, 1926). Still a useful introduction to the subject.

David B. Truman, *The Congressional Party* (New York: Wiley, 1959). An effort to determine, through analysis of roll-call votes, the structure and leadership roles of the parties in Congress.

———, ed., *The Congress and America's Future* (Englewood Cliffs, N.J.: Prentice-Hall, 1965). Essays on congressional reorganization prepared for the American Assembly.

John C. Wahlke and Heinz Eulau, eds., *Legislative Behavior: A Reader in Theory and Research* (New York: Free Press, 1959). Varied studies of the legislative process.

Woodrow Wilson, *Congressional Government: A Study in American Politics* (Boston: Houghton Mifflin, 1885). A classic study of the power in the congressional committee leadership in the late nineteenth century.

THE BUREAUCRACY

Paul H. Appleby, *Big Democracy* (New York: Knopf, 1945). Reflections on giant bureaucracies as a permanent feature of post–World War II American life.

Marver H. Bernstein, *The Job of the Federal Executive* (Washington, D.C.: Brookings Institution, 1958). A description of the world of top-level administrators and the problem of recruiting talent for these posts.

Peter M. Blau, *Bureaucracy in Modern Society* (New York: Random House, 1956). A brief, general discussion of the problem of bureaucracy.

Anthony Downs, *Inside Bureaucracy* (Boston: Little, Brown, 1967). An attempt to build a model of the behavior of a governmental bureau.

Emmette S. Redford, *Ideal and Practice in Public Administration* (University, Ala.: Univ. of Alabama Press, 1958). A consideration of the values and the environment of the administrator.

Herbert A. Simon, *Administrative Behavior*, 2nd ed. (New York: Macmillan, 1957). A classic analysis of the process of bureaucracy.

Aaron Wildavsky, *The Politics of the Budgetary Process* (Boston: Little, Brown, 1964). The budget is treated as the focus of struggles over policy.

Peter Woll, *American Bureaucracy* (New York: Norton, 1963). An attempt to describe the impact of bureaucratic growth on the constitutional dispersion of power.

IV. Liberty, Justice, and Law

THE AMERICAN LEGAL SYSTEM

Henry J. Abraham, *Courts and Judges* (New York: Oxford Univ. Press, 1959). An introduction to the functions of operations of the judicial process.

Benjamin N. Cardozo, *The Nature of the Judicial Process* (New Haven, Conn.: Yale Univ. Press, 1921). An argument for the centrality of social utility in the job of judging.

Jerome Frank, *Courts on Trial* (Princeton, N.J.: Princeton Univ. Press, 1950). A study which emphasizes that the judge's choice is inevitably between competing social values.

Oliver Wendell Holmes, *The Common Law* (Boston: Little, Brown, 1881). A classic study of the growth of law in response to the needs of society.

Willard Hurst, *The Growth of American Law* (Boston: Little, Brown, 1950). A useful history.

Herbert Jacob, *Justice in America: Courts, Lawyers, and the Judicial Process* (Boston: Little, Brown, 1965). A realistic and politically oriented discussion of the American court system and the milieu of judicial decision-making.

Jack W. Peltason, *Federal Courts in the Political Process* (New York: Random House, 1955). An examination of the power exercised by the lower federal courts.

Report of the President's Commission on Law Enforcement and Justice, *The Challenge of Crime in a Free Society* (Washington, D.C.: Government Printing Office, 1967). A comprehensive survey of our legal system, the process of criminal justice, and the dilemmas of law-enforcement and civil-liberties guarantees in contemporary American society.

Victor G. Rosenblum, *Law as a Political Instrument* (Garden City, N.Y.: Doubleday, 1955). An analysis of courts as policy-makers.

Glendon A. Schubert, Jr., ed., *Judicial Behavior: A Reader in Theory and Research* (Chicago: Rand McNally, 1964). A collection of papers and studies presenting behavioral approaches to the study of what courts and judges do.

Alan F. Westin, *The Anatomy of a Constitutional Law Case* (New York: Macmillan, 1958). An exploration of the process of constitutional adjudication.

JUDICIAL REVIEW

Charles A. Beard, *The Supreme Court and the Constitution* (New York: Macmillan, 1912). An argument that a majority of the founding fathers favored some sort of judicial negative over acts of Congress.

Alexander M. Bickel, *The Least Dangerous Branch* (Indianapolis, Ind.: Bobbs-Merrill, 1962). A critical study of the work of the Court over the past decade.

James E. Clayton, *The Making of Justice* (New York: Dutton, 1964). A case study of the work of the Court during a single term (1962–63).

Edward S. Corwin, *Constitutional Revolution, Ltd.* (Claremont, Calif.: Claremont Colleges, 1941). A leading scholar's reaction to the new approaches taken by the Court after 1937.

———, *Court over Constitution* (Princeton, N.J.: Princeton Univ. Press, 1938). A contradiction of Beard's argument for a judicial negative over acts of Congress.

Felix Frankfurter and James M. Landis, *The Business of the Supreme Court* (New York: Macmillan, 1927). A minor classic on the development of the Court's jurisdiction and its control over its docket.

Paul A. Freund, *On Understanding the Supreme Court* (Boston: Little, Brown, 1949). An excellent guide to the Court's ways of working, with special reference to consideration of the Constitution.

John A. Garraty, ed., *Quarrels That Have Shaped the Constitution* (New York: Harper & Row, 1964). Famous United States Supreme Court cases since *Marbury* v. *Madison* reconsidered by leading historians and social scientists.

Charles G. Haines, *The American Doctrine of Judicial Supremacy*, 2nd rev. ed. (New York: Russell & Russell, 1959). A survey of the Court's "formative period" and of the development of the doctrine of judicial review.

Charles Evans Hughes, *The Supreme Court of the United States* (New York: Columbia Univ. Press, 1928). An insight by a distinguished lawyer who had already sat upon the Court as an associate justice and was to return as its Chief.

Leonard W. Levy, ed., *Judicial Review and the Supreme Court* (New York: Harper & Row, 1967). Selected essays on the history, development, and contemporary applications of the theory of judicial review.

Robert G. McCloskey, *The American Supreme Court* (Chicago: Univ. of Chicago Press, 1960). An excellent short history of the Court.

Walter F. Murphy, *Elements of Judicial Strategy* (Chicago: Univ. of Chicago Press, 1964). An inquiry into the role and role perception of Supreme Court justices.

C. Herman Pritchett, *The Roosevelt Court: A Study in Judicial Politics and Values, 1937–1947* (New York: Macmillan, 1948). An effort to discover the patterns of alignment among the justices with regard to various issues coming before the Court.

Glendon A. Schubert, *The Judicial Mind: Attitudes and Ideals of Supreme Court Justices, 1946–1963* (Evanston, Ill.: Northwestern Univ. Press, 1965). A study of the ideologies of eighteen justices and an analysis of the decisions of merit over the last two decades.

Charles Warren, *The Supreme Court in the United States History* (Boston: Little, Brown, 1922). Dated, but still the standard history of the Court's development.

LAWYERS, JUDGES, AND SUPREME COURT JUSTICES

Albert J. Beveridge, *The Life of John Marshall* (Boston: Houghton Mifflin, 1916–19).

Alexander M. Bickel, ed., *The Unpublished Opinions of Mr. Justice Brandeis* (Cambridge, Mass.: Belknap Press of Harvard Univ. Press, 1957).

A. Dunham and P. B. Kurland, eds., *Mr. Justice* (Chicago: Univ. of Chicago Press, 1956). Brief studies of nine justices, dealing with both their work on the Court and their pre-Court experience.

Heinz Eulau and John D. Sprague, *Lawyers in Politics: A Study in Professional Convergence* (Indianapolis, Ind.: Bobbs-Merrill, 1964). An empirical and theoretical analysis of the roles of lawyers and bar groups in the political process.

Joel B. Grossman, *Lawyers and Judges: The ABA and the Politics of Judicial Selection* (New York: Wiley, 1965). The effect upon judicial decision-making of the conception of the judicial role held by the judges.

Willard L. King, *Melville Weston Fuller* (New York: Macmillan, 1950).

Samuel J. Konefsky, *Chief Justice Stone and the Supreme Court* (New York: Macmillan, 1945).

Alpheus T. Mason, *Harlan Fiske Stone: Pillar of the Law* (New York: Viking Press, 1956).

———, *William Howard Taft, Chief Justice* (New York: Scribner's, 1965).

Wallace Mendelson, *Justices Black and Frankfurter: Conflict in the Court*, 2nd ed. (Chicago: Univ. of Chicago Press, 1966).

Donald G. Morgan, *Justice William Johnson, The First Dissenter* (Columbia, S.C.: Univ. of South Carolina Press, 1954).

Joel F. Paschal, *Mr. Justice Sutherland: A Man Against the State* (Princeton, N.J.: Princeton Univ. Press, 1951).

Merlo J. Pusey, *Charles Evans Hughes* (New York: Macmillan, 1951).

Stephen Strickland, ed., *Hugo Black and the Supreme Court* (Indianapolis, Ind.: Bobbs-Merrill, 1967).

Carl B. Swisher, *Stephen J. Field* (Washington, D.C.: Brookings Institution, 1930).

Benjamin R. Twiss, *Lawyers and the Constitution: How Laissez-Faire Came to the Supreme Court* (Princeton, N.J.: Princeton Univ. Press, 1942). A fascinating study of the way in which the bar of the Supreme Court helped shape the opinions of the courts in the field of business regulation during the latter decades of the nineteenth century.

CIVIL LIBERTIES

Ralph S. Brown, Jr., *Loyalty and Security* (New Haven, Conn.: Yale Univ. Press, 1958). A study of the problem of ensuring that the interests of the government are protected while affording maximum "due process" to the individual employee.

Zechariah Chafee, Jr., *Free Speech in the United States* (Cambridge, Mass.: Harvard Univ. Press, 1941). A widely read history.

Morris L. Ernst and Alan V. Schwartz, *Censorship: The Search for Obscenity* (New York: Macmillan, 1964). A survey of material documenting the search for meaningful standards by Congress, the courts, and the community since the Puritans.

Osmond K. Fraenkel, *The Supreme Court and Civil Liberties: How the Court Has Protected Minority Rights* (New York: Oceana, 1963). A survey of Court decisions to protect civil liberties guarantees.

Ronald Goldfarb, *Ransom: A Critique of the American Bail System* (New York: Harper & Row, 1965). An influential study of the shortcomings of the American bail system.

Morton Grodzins, *The Loyal and the Disloyal* (Chicago: Univ. of Chicago Press, 1956). An analysis of what sorts of people, sociologically and psychologically, commit disloyal acts.

Milton R. Konvitz, *Expanding Liberties, Freedom's Gains in Postwar America* (New York: Viking Press, 1966). The implications for civil liberty posed by American social change since the mid-1930's.

Jacob W. Landynsky, *Search and Seizure and the Supreme Court: A Study in Constitutional Interpretation* (Baltimore: Johns Hopkins Univ. Press, 1966). A balanced historical and analytical account of the Court's interpretation of the Fourth Amendment.

Anthony Lewis, *Gideon's Trumpet* (New York: Random House, 1964). A journalist's in-depth account of a major court case in the Supreme Court.

Leo Pfeffer, *Church, State, and Freedom*, rev. ed. (Boston: Beacon Press, 1966). A strict separationist viewpoint detailing existing areas of contention in the contemporary church-state controversy.

Edward A. Shils, *The Torment of Secrecy* (New York: Free Press, 1956). A study of the social-psychological costs of closed politics.

George W. Spicer, *The Supreme Court and Fundamental Freedoms* (New York: Appleton-Century-Crofts, 1967). A brief analysis of the role of the Supreme Court as guardian of fundamental constitutional liberties.

Murray S. Stedman, Jr., *Religion and Politics in America* (New York: Harcourt, Brace & World, 1964). A study of the relations between religious forces and the government in recent times.

Samuel A. Stouffer, *Communism, Conformity, and Civil Liberties* (Boston: Heath, 1952). An examination of, among other things, which groups within the community react to anticommunist excesses.

Arnold S. Trebach, *The Rationing of Justice* (New Brunswick, N.J.: Rutgers Univ. Press, 1964). An important empirical study of law and legal guarantees in practice.

Alan F. Westin, *Privacy and Freedom* (New York: Atheneum, 1967). An account of the impact of new technological developments on privacy, with suggestions for public responses in the 1970's.

CIVIL RIGHTS

A. P. Blaustein and C. C. Ferguson, Jr., *Desegregation and the Law* (New Brunswick, N.J.: Rutgers Univ. Press, 1957). A useful introduction to the legal dimension of the civil-rights revolution up to 1956.

William Brink and Louis Harris, *Black and White* (New York: Simon and Schuster, 1967). A report of a nationwide survey of opinion on racial attitudes in the United States in 1967.

Kenneth B. Clark, *Dark Ghetto: Dilemmas of Social Power* (New York: Harper & Row, 1965). A comprehensive study of the total phenomena of the ghetto in Harlem by a Negro social psychologist.

Robert Conot, *Rivers of Blood, Years of Darkness* (New York: Bantam, 1967). The story of the Watts riot based on interviews, reports, and personal observations.

Eli Ginzberg *et al.*, *The Middle-Class Negro in the White Man's World* (New York: Columbia Univ. Press, 1967). Case study investigations into the career plans and expectations of middle-class Negro youth.

Harry Kalven, Jr., *The Negro and the First Amendment* (Columbus, Ohio: Ohio State Univ. Press, 1965). A study of the impact of the civil-rights movement on judicial doctrine interpreting the First Amendment.

Martin Luther King, Jr., *Where Do We Go from Here?* (New York: Harper & Row, 1967). A plea by the civil-rights leader for real progress in the important areas of the racial conflict.

Anthony Lewis, *Portrait of a Decade: The Second American Revolution* (New York: Random House, 1964). A vivid first-hand account of the civil-rights struggle from 1954 to 1964, as seen by Lewis and other New York *Times* correspondents.

Malcolm X, *The Autobiography of Malcolm X* (New York: Grove Press, 1965). An illuminating account of the life of the Black Muslim leader and the philosophy of black supremacy and separatism.

Loren Miller, *The Petitioners: The Story of the Supreme Court of the United States and the Negro* (New York: Pantheon, 1966). A review of Court struggles to secure Negro civil rights.

Gunnar Myrdal, *An American Dilemma* (New York: Harper & Row, 1944). A landmark study that became a potent weapon in the civil-rights struggle.

Fred Powledge, *Black Power, White Resistance: Notes on the New Civil War* (Cleveland: World, 1967). An explanation of the theory of "black power."

Charles Silberman, *Crisis in Black and White* (New York: Random House, 1964). A study of the deteriorating relationship between Negroes and whites in the United States and of the need for immediate efforts to help the Negro overcome his accumulated disadvantages.

Alan F. Westin, ed., *Freedom Now!* (New York: Basic Books, 1964). A collection of essays and articles treating various aspects of the civil-rights struggle. Particular attention is paid to the debate over the means by which Negroes should seek to advance their cause.

Whitney M. Young, *To Be Equal* (New York: McGraw-Hill, 1964). The civil-rights revolution and its ideology by a Negro moderate.

V. Government in Action

GOVERNMENT AND THE ECONOMY

Irving Bernstein, Harold L. Enarson, and R. W. Fleming, eds., *Emergency Disputes and National Policy* (New York: Harper & Row, 1955). A review of American experience in the settlement of labor disputes and the development of alternative policies.

Marver H. Bernstein, *Regulating Business by Independent Commission* (Princeton, N.J.: Princeton Univ. Press, 1955). A reasoned analysis of the problems and prospects of these instruments.

Edwin A. Bock, ed., *Government Regulation of Business: A Casebook* (Englewood Cliffs, N.J.: Prentice-Hall, 1965). Seven case studies of regulation.

Robert A. Dahl and Charles E. Lindblom, *Politics, Economics, and Welfare* (New York: Harper & Row, 1953). A study of the American style in decision-making and value allocation.

Merle Fainsod, Lincoln Gordon, and Joseph C. Palamountain, Jr., *Government and the American Economy* (New York: Norton, 1959). An excellent text.

E. Pendleton Herring, *Public Administration and the Public Interest* (New York: McGraw-Hill, 1936). An old but very useful analysis of the politics of regulation.

James M. Landis, *The Administrative Process* (New Haven, Conn.: Yale Univ. Press, 1938). An enthusiastic account by a talented participant of the possibilities of administrative regulation of economic activity.

Earl Latham, *The Group Basis of Politics: A Study in Basing-Point Legislation* (Ithaca, N.Y.: Cornell Univ. Press, 1952). A study of the impact of group pressures on Congress' consideration of legislation.

Michael D. Reagan, *The Managed Economy* (New York: Oxford Univ. Press, 1963). An analysis of the challenge to democratic government in the development of corporate power.

Emmette S. Redford, *Administration of National Economic Control* (New York: Macmillan, 1952). A detailed study of the difficulties and possibilities of ministering to an unplanned economy.

——, *American Government and the Economy* (New York: Macmillan, 1965). A comprehensive text.

SCIENCE, TECHNOLOGY, AND NATURAL RESOURCES

Marion Clawson, *Man and Land in the United States* (Lincoln, Neb.: Univ. of Nebraska Press, 1964). The director of the Land Use and Management Program, Resources for the Future, considers the subject in all aspects—agriculture, grazing, forestry, recreation, and urban use.

F. Fraser Darling, ed., *Future Environments of North America* (Garden City, N.Y.: Natural History Press, 1966). The report of a conference of ecologists, regional planners, economists, and conservationists, held in 1965 under the auspices of The Conservation Foundation.

George R. Hall, *Strategy and Organization in Public-Land Policy* (Santa Monica, Calif.: RAND Corporation, 1966). An appraisal of current public-land management policies and suggestions for their improvement.

Herman J. Kahn and Anthony J. Wiener, *The Year 2000: A Framework for Speculation on the Next 33 Years* (New York: Macmillan, 1967). A group study by members of the Hudson Institute, sponsored by The American Academy of Arts and Sciences.

Richard L. Meier, *Science and Economic Development: New Patterns of Living*, 2nd ed. (Cambridge, Mass.: M.I.T. Press, 1966). An exploration of the possible uses of modern scientific knowledge for developmental planning.

Michigan University, Architectural Research Laboratory, *Series 1: Environmental Abstracts; Series 2: Environmental Evaluations; Series 3: Environmental Analysis* (Ann Arbor, Mich.: Univ. of Michigan Press, 1965). A collection of technical papers exploring the scientific aspects of environmental design and its effect on human behavior and learning.

National Academy of Sciences, Committee on Natural Resources, *Natural Resources: A Summary Report to the President of the United States* (Washington, D.C.: National Academy Research Council, 1962). A discussion, salient findings, and recommendations in the area of renewable resources.

Don K. Price, *Government and Science* (New York: New York Univ. Press, 1954). An authoritative survey of the growing involvement of the federal government in scientific research.

Leo Francis Schnore and Henry Fagin, eds., *Urban Research and Policy Planning* (Beverly

Hills, Calif.: Sage Publications, 1967). A report on urban research since World War II and the resulting changes in public-planning policies, including the use of modern technology.

Eugene B. Skolnikoff, *Science, Technology, and American Foreign Policy* (Cambridge, Mass.: M.I.T. Press, 1967). An authoritative analysis of the degree to which technological progress has influenced the framing and exercise of American foreign policy.

Charles P. Snow, *Science and Government* (Cambridge, Mass.: Harvard Univ. Press, 1961). A provocative treatise on political power and the participation of national scientists.

Stephan B. Sweeney and James C. Charlesworth, eds., *Governing Urban Society: New Scientific Approaches* (Philadelphia: American Academy of Political and Social Sciences, 1967). An exploration of ways of applying new science and technology to urban government.

U.S. Forest Service, *The American Outdoors: Management for Beauty and Use* (Washington, D.C.: Government Printing Office, 1965). A study of the application of aesthetic and productive concepts to land management.

U.S. National Commission on Technology, Automation, and Economic Progress, *Technology and the American Economy*, 7 vols. (Washington, D.C.: Government Printing Office, 1966). An assessment of the effects and probable future uses of recent scientific and technological discoveries.

U.S. President's Science Advisory Committee, *Science, Government, and Information: The Responsibilities of the Technical Community and the Government in the Transfer of Information* (Washington, D.C.: Government Printing Office, 1963). A landmark report dealing with the mounting problem of how best to facilitate the dissemination of scientific information.

Jerome B. Wiesner, *Where Science and Politics Meet* (New York: McGraw-Hill, 1965). A valuable contribution to the understanding of contemporary relationships between science and technology and public affairs.

GOVERNMENT AND WELFARE

Oscar E. Anderson, Jr., *The Health of a Nation: Harvey W. Wiley and the Fight for Pure Food* (Chicago: Univ. of Chicago Press, 1958). A study of the difficulties attendant upon performance in this most basic area.

E. M. Burns, *Social Security in Public Policy* (New York: McGraw-Hill, 1956). A general survey of performance and problems.

Michael Harrington, *The Other America* (New York: Macmillan, 1962). A vivid account of the problems of the poor.

Ben B. Seligman, ed., *Poverty as a Public Issue* (New York: Free Press, 1965). Essays on the extent, aspects, and politics of poverty.

Herman M. and Anne R. Somers, *Workmen's Compensation* (New York: Wiley, 1954). A penetrating analysis of experience with the nation's oldest social-insurance legislation.

DEFENSE AND FOREIGN POLICY

Gabriel A. Almond, *The American People and Foreign Policy* (New York: Harcourt, Brace & World, 1956). A valuable study of the domestic politics of foreign policy.

Cecil V. Crabb, *American Foreign Policy in the Nuclear Age*, 2nd ed. (New York: Harper & Row, 1965). A useful text.

Paul Y. Hammond, *Organizing for Defense* (Princeton, N.J.: Princeton Univ. Press, 1961). An anatomy of the military establishment.

Roger Hilsman, *To Move a Nation: The Politics of Foreign Policy in the Administration of John F. Kennedy* (Garden City, N.Y.: Doubleday, 1967). A scholar and participant in the Department of State surveys and interprets foreign policy through eventful years.

Samuel P. Huntington, *The Common Defense* (New York: Columbia Univ. Press, 1961). A valuable survey of defense policy after World War II.

George Kennan, *American Diplomacy 1900–1950* (Chicago: Univ. of Chicago Press, 1951). A minor classic by an exceptionally able scholar-diplomat.

Sherman Kent, *Strategic Intelligence for American World Policy* (Princeton, N.J.: Princeton Univ. Press, 1966). An able analysis by a now high-ranking CIA official.

Henry A. Kissinger, *Nuclear Weapons and Foreign Policy* (Garden City, N.Y.: Doubleday, 1957). An influential suggestion of alterations in our foreign-policy thinking necessitated by the new weapons technology.

———, *Problems of National Strategy* (New York: Praeger, 1965). A useful book of readings.

Dexter Perkins, *Foreign Policy and the American Spirit* (Ithaca, N.Y.: Cornell Univ. Press, 1957). A study of the ideological matrix of American foreign policy.

Burton M. Sapin, *The Making of United States Foreign Policy* (Washington, D.C.: Brookings Institution, 1966). A scholarly, up-to-date account of this subject.

——— and Richard C. Snyder, *The Role of the Military in American Foreign Policy* (Garden City, N.Y.: Doubleday, 1954). A brief but useful account of the post–World War II role of the American military.

Richard P. Stebbins, *The United States in World Affairs* (New York: Harper & Row, 1967). A comprehensive annual report prepared for the Council on Foreign Relations.

GOVERNMENT AND MONEY

Jesse Burkhead, *Government Budgeting* (New York: Wiley, 1956). A thorough analysis of all aspects of budgeting.

Richard F. Fenno, Jr., *The Power of the Purse: Appropriations Politics in Congress* (Boston: Little, Brown, 1966). A scholarly, comprehensive analysis of committee activity on appropriations.

Robert L. Heilbroner and Peter L. Bernstein, *A Primer on Government Spending* (New York: Random House, 1963). A neatly written effort to part the clouds of myth and misunderstanding that shadow much discussion of government borrowing and spending.

Harvey C. Mansfield, *The Comptroller General* (New Haven, Conn.: Yale Univ. Press, 1939). A comprehensive analysis of financial control and accountability in the national government.

Frederick C. Mosher, *Program Budgeting* (Chicago: Public Administration Service, 1954). An analysis of theory and practice with particular reference to the United States Department of the Army.

Paul J. Strayer, *Fiscal Policy and Politics* (New York: Harper & Row, 1958). An introduction to and discussion of government's financial options.

Aaron Wildavsky, *The Politics of the Budgetary Process* (Boston: Little, Brown, 1964). A lively and imaginative discussion of the budgetary process.

AUTHOR INDEX FOR BOXED QUOTATIONS

INDEX